T0358198

Land Rights, Ethno-Nationality, and Sovereignty in History

The complex relationships between ethno-nationality, rights to land, and territorial sovereignty have long fed disputes over territorial control and landed rights between different nations, different ethnicities, and different religions. These disputes raise a number of interesting issues related to the nature of land regimes and to their economic and political implications.

The studies drawn together in this volume explore these and related issues for a broad variety of countries and times, and illuminate the diverse causes of ethno-national land disputes, and the different forms of adjustment and accommodation to the power differences between the contesting groups. This is done within a generalized framework outlined by the editors in their analytical overview, which offers contours for comparative examinations of such disputes, past and present. Some of the issues discussed include:

- the structure and functioning of land markets in which the participation of "others" (ethno-nationally, religiously, or otherwise identified) has been restricted or barred altogether;
- the political and economic underpinning of such constraints;
- the implications of ethno-nationally restricted land markets for the allocation and utilization of resources, income distribution, and economic performance in the societies concerned.

Providing conceptual and factual analyses of a comparative nature and a wealth of empirical material (both historical and contemporary), this book will appeal to economic historians, economists, political scientists, sociologists, anthropologists, and all scholars interested in issues concerning ethno-nationality and land rights in historical perspective.

Stanley L. Engerman is John H. Munro Professor of Economics and Professor of History at the University of Rochester, New York, USA.

Jacob Metzer is Alexander Brody Professor of Economic History at the Hebrew University of Jerusalem.

Routledge explorations in economic history

1 **Economic Ideas and Government Policy**
Contributions to the contemporary economic history
Sir Alec Cairncross

2 **The Organization of Labour Markets**
Modernity, culture and governance in Germany, Sweden, Britain and Japan
Bo Stråth

3 **Currency Convertibility**
The gold standard and beyond
Edited by Jorge Braga de Macedo, Barry Eichengreen and Jaime Reis

4 **Britain's Place in the World**
A historical enquiry into import controls 1945–1960
Alan S. Milward and George Brennan

5 **France and the International Economy**
From Vichy to the Treaty of Rome
Frances M. B. Lynch

6 **Monetary Standards and Exchange Rates**
M. C. Marcuzzo, L. Officer and A. Rosselli

7 **Production Efficiency in Domesday England, 1086**
John McDonald

8 **Free Trade and its Reception 1815–1960**
Freedom and trade: Volume I
Edited by Andrew Marrison

9 **Conceiving Companies**
Joint-stock politics in Victorian England
Timothy L. Alborn

10 **The British Industrial Decline Reconsidered**
Edited by Jean-Pierre Dormois and Michael Dintenfass

11 **The Conservatives and Industrial Efficiency, 1951–1964**
Thirteen wasted years?
Nick Tiratsoo and Jim Tomlinson

12 **Pacific Centuries**
Pacific and Pacific Rim economic history since the 16th century
Edited by Dennis O. Flynn, Lionel Frost and A. J. H. Latham

13 **The Premodern Chinese Economy**
Structural equilibrium and capitalist sterility
Gang Deng

14 **The Role of Banks in Monitoring Firms**
The case of the crédit mobilier
Elisabeth Paulet

15 **Management of the National Debt in the United Kingdom, 1900–1932**
Jeremy Wormell

16 **An Economic History of Sweden**
Lars Magnusson

17 **Freedom and Growth**
The rise of states and markets in Europe, 1300–1750
S. R. Epstein

18 **The Mediterranean Response to Globalization Before 1950**
Sevket Pamuk and Jeffrey G. Williamson

19 **Production and Consumption in English Households 1600–1750**
Mark Overton, Jane Whittle, Darron Dean and Andrew Haan

20 **Governance, The State, Regulation and Industrial Relations**
Ian Clark

21 **Early Modern Capitalism**
Economic and social change in Europe 1400–1800
Edited by Maarten Prak

22 **An Economic History of London, 1800–1914**
Michael Ball and David Sunderland

23 **The Origins of National Financial Systems**
Alexander Gerschenkron reconsidered
Edited by Douglas J. Forsyth and Daniel Verdier

24 **The Russian Revolutionary Economy, 1890–1940**
Ideas, debates and alternatives
Vincent Barnett

25 **Land Rights, Ethno-Nationality, and Sovereignty in History**
Edited by Stanley L. Engerman and Jacob Metzer

Land Rights, Ethno-Nationality, and Sovereignty in History

Edited by
Stanley L. Engerman and
Jacob Metzer

Routledge
Taylor & Francis Group

LONDON AND NEW YORK

First published 2004
by Routledge
2 Park Square, Milton Park, Abingdon, Oxon, OX14 4RN

Simultaneously published in the USA and Canada
by Routledge
605 Third Avenue, New York, NY 10017

Routledge is an imprint of the Taylor & Francis Group, an informa business

© 2004 editorial material and selection, Stanley L. Engerman
and Jacob Metzer; individual chapters the contributors

Typeset in Bembo by
Florence Production Ltd, Stoodleigh, Devon

British Library Cataloguing in Publication Data
A catalogue record for this book is available from the British Library

Library of Congress Cataloging in Publication Data
A catalog record for this book has been requested

ISBN 13: 978–0–415–77119–1 (pbk)
ISBN 13: 978–0–415–32126–6 (hbk)

Contents

List of illustrations   viii
List of contributors   xi

Introduction   1
STANLEY L. ENGERMAN AND JACOB METZER

PART I
Setting the stage   5

  1 **Some considerations of ethno-nationality (and other
     distinctions), property rights in land, and territorial
     sovereignty**   7
     JACOB METZER AND STANLEY L. ENGERMAN

PART II
**Nations, land regime, and territorial sovereignty
in old and new states**   29

  2 **Were there alternatives to disaster? The removal of
     Indians from the southeastern United States in
     the 1830s**   31
     LEONARD A. CARLSON

  3 **Ethno-nationality and property rights in land in
     Prussian Poland, 1886–1918: buying the land from
     under the Poles' feet?**   56
     SCOTT M. EDDIE

  4 **Jewish land – Israel lands: ethno-nationality and land
     regime in Zionism and in Israel, 1897–1967**   87
     JACOB METZER

5 Markets and meanings: nationalism, land, and
   property in Lithuania   111
   RAWI ABDELAL

PART III
**Religion, ethno-nationality, and economics in
land struggles**   129

6 Irish agriculture after the Land War   131
   CORMAC Ó GRÁDA

7 Land disputes and ethno-politics: northwestern
   Anatolia, 1877–1912   153
   YÜCEL TERZIBAŞOĞLU

PART IV
**Indigenous peoples, colonial settlers, and migrating
laborers: ethnic rivalries and rights to land, past
and present**   181

8 Explaining divergence in property rights: Fiji and
   Hawai'i in the nineteenth century   183
   SUMNER J. LA CROIX

9 Equals in Markets? Land property rights and ethnicity
   in Fiji and Sri Lanka   210
   V. NITHI NITHIYANANDAM AND RUKMANI GOUNDER

10 Indigenous accumulation and the question of land:
   the Kimberley region of Western Australia in the
   second half of the twentieth century   236
   TONY SMITH

11 Sub-Saharan Africa: land rights and ethno-national
   consciousness in historically land-abundant
   economies   276
   GARETH AUSTIN

12 Ethnic competition and claims to land in South Africa:
   the Kat River valley, Eastern Cape   294
   ROBERT ROSS

PART V
**Natural resources and the livelihood of native
populations: economy and environment in tradition
and modernity**   **317**

13 **Survival through generosity: property rights and
   hunting practices of Native Americans in the
   subarctic region**   319
   ANN M. CARLOS AND FRANK D. LEWIS

14 **Owners, intruders, and intermediaries: the claim for
   lands within the Mbyá-Guaraní community (Valley
   of Cuñapirú, Misiones, Argentina)**   347
   MARÍA ROSA MARTÍNEZ, MARTA ALICIA CRIVOS, AND
   LAURA TEVES

15 **Establishing territorial sovereignty in Finland:
   the environmental consequences of ethno-nationalization
   of resource management in Inari**   358
   JUKKA NYYSSÖNEN

Index   389

Illustrations

Cartoons

6.1	The new Danish invasion of Ireland	139
6.2	Another Danish invasion	140

Figures

3.1	Estate purchases by the Settlement Commission	59
3.2	Estate purchases by the Settlement Commission (in percentage of the total area purchased annually)	60
3.3	Settlement Commission purchases of estates, by *Regierungsbezirk*	61
3.4	Share of all land purchased by the Settlement Commission by the end of 1913 and share of all land owned by Germans, by riding	62
3.5	Purchases of peasant farms by the Settlement Commission	71
3.6	Purchases of all peasant farms by the Settlement Commission (in percentage of the total area purchased annually)	72
3.7	"Consolidating" German land ownership: number and total area of properties "consolidated" by the Settlement Commission	75
3.8	"Consolidating" German land ownership: average size of "consolidated" properties	75
6.1	Monthly supply to Cork Butter Market, 1875 and 1885	146
6.2	Milk supply to creameries, 1934–1998	146
6.3	Mean daytime temperature in Dublin and Copenhagen	148
6.4	Irish and New Zealand milk supplies, 1998	148
13.1	Simulated beaver populations: York Factory and Fort Albany, 1700–1763	322
13.2	Fur prices at Fort Albany and York Factory	323
13.3	Fur prices and the share of producer goods in Native expenditure: York Factory, 1716–1770	331

13.4   Native population and large game   338
13.5   Native population and game: adjustments to shocks   339
13.6   Animal and human populations: $P_0 = 4,000$; $e = 0.005$ 341
13.7   Animal and human populations: $P_0 = 2,500$; $e = 0.005$ 341
13.8   Animal and human populations: $P_0 = 4,000$; $e = 0.004$ 342
13.9   Animal and human populations: $P_0 = 2,500$; $e = 0.004$ 342
15.1   The amount of timber logged in the District of Inari, in
       cubic meters, 1946–1999   370
15.2   The number of reindeer in Inari 1954–1995   376

Maps

2.1   Indian land cessions until 1809   45
2.2   Indian land cessions until 1819   47
2.3   Indian land cessions until 1829   48
2.4   Emigration routes in the removal of the southern Indians   49
3.1   Central Europe, 1910   57
7.1   Anatolia, 1913   155
10.1   The Kimberley, Northwestern Australia   237
12.1   The Kat River Settlement in the Eastern Cape   295
13.1   Hudson's Bay Company hinterlands   321
14.1   Province of Misiones, Argentina, and the area belonging
       to UNLP   348
15.1   The rural District of Inari   362

Tables

3.1   Population by mother tongue, 1890   57
3.2   Price determination regressions for private purchases   66
3.3   Predicted prices of Settlement Commission purchases from
       coefficients of Equation 1 (in Table 3.2)   68
3.4   Results of pooled regressions, dependent variable: deflated
       actual price paid   70
3.5   Price determination regressions for peasant farm purchases   73
3.A1   Definitions of dummy variables used in peasant farm
       regressions   81
6.1   Total factor productivity change, 1850s–1910s   133
6.2   Output and productivity in 1912 and 1925–1926   134
6.3   Non-Catholic farmers as a percentage of the total, 1926   143
8.1   Population of Hawai'i, 1778–1865   186
8.2   Government revenue and land sale revenue, Hawai'i,
       1846–1857   192
8.3   Native population of Fiji, 1844–1921   195
8.4   Revenue from cotton production in Fiji, 1863–1870   197

10.1   Lease numbers and business number changes between 1963
       and 1983   249
10.2   Kimberley division: agricultural and pastoral Aboriginal
       employment   251
13.1   Goods received at York Factory, 1716–1770
       (made beaver)   328–330

Contributors

Rawi Abdelal is Associate Professor in the Graduate School of Business Administration, Harvard University, Cambridge, Massachusetts, US.

Gareth Austin is Lecturer in the Department of Economic History, London School of Economics and Political Science, London, UK.

Ann M. Carlos is Professor in the Department of Economics, University of Colorado, Boulder, Colorado, US.

Leonard A. Carlson is Associate Professor in the Department of Economics, Emory University, Atlanta, Georgia, US.

Marta Alicia Crivos is Professor at Facultad de Ciencias Naturales y Museo, Universidad Nacional de La Plata, La Plata, Argentina.

Scott M. Eddie is Professor Emeritus in the Department of Economics, University of Toronto, Toronto, Canada.

Stanley L. Engerman is Professor in the Departments of Economics and History, University of Rochester, Rochester, New York, US.

Rukmani Gounder is Associate Professor in the Department of Applied and International Economics, Massey University, Palmerston North, New Zealand.

Sumner J. La Croix is Professor in the Department of Economics, University of Hawai'i, Honolulu, Hawai'i, USA, and Senior Fellow, East–West Center, Honolulu, Hawai'i, US.

Frank D. Lewis is Professor in the Department of Economics, Queen's University, Kingston, Canada.

María Rosa Martínez is Professor at Facultad de Ciencias Naturales y Museo, Universidad Nacional de La Plata, La Plata, Argentina.

Jacob Metzer is Professor in the Department of Economics, The Hebrew University of Jerusalem, Jerusalem, Israel.

V. Nithi Nithiyanandam is Senior Lecturer in the Department of Commerce, Massey University, Albany Campus, Auckland, New Zealand.

Jukka Nyyssönen is Research Fellow in the Department of History, University of Tromsø, Tromsø, Norway.

Cormac Ó Gráda is Professor in the Department of Economics, University College Dublin, Dublin, Ireland.

Robert Ross is Professor in the Department of African Studies, Leiden University, Leiden, Netherlands.

Tony Smith is post-doctoral researcher in the School of Economics and Finance, University of Western Sydney, Sydney, Australia, and Senior Project Officer at the Gumala Aboriginal Corporation, Tom Price, Australia.

Yücel Terzibaşoğlu is Instructor in the History Department, Bogaziçi University, Istanbul, Turkey.

Laura Teves is Ph.D. Candidate at Facultad de Ciencias Naturales y Museo, Universidad Nacional de La Plata, La Plata, Argentina.

Introduction

Stanley L. Engerman and Jacob Metzer

Land as geographical place, primary factor of production, and source of wealth has been a major component of the economic, political, and social aspects of human life, carrying with it also significant religious and cultural weight. These multifaceted attributes have made the rights to land – whether kept in collective memory, actually utilized, or sought to be realized – an instrumental factor in the formation of territorially linked collective identities and ethno-national consciousness.

The close association in history between ethno-nationality and territory involves, quite naturally, the complex and often disputed relationships between individual and group rights in land and territorial sovereignty. Indeed, disputes involving territorial control and rights to land between different nations, different ethnicities, and different religions, have characterized human societies from ancient days to the contemporary world. These disputes raise a number of interesting questions concerning the link between (exercised or struggled for) territorial control and various exclusionary land policies. Among them: the structure and functioning of land markets in which the participation of "others" (ethno-nationally, religiously, or otherwise, identified) has been restricted or barred altogether; the political and economic underpinning of such constraints; and the implications of ethno-nationally restricted and segregated land markets for the allocation and utilization of resources, income distribution, and economic performance in the societies concerned.

While individual cases have been amply studied, there have been few attempts to bring together a large number of different examples to provide a basis for comparative analysis of these and related questions over time and across space. In this volume on *Land Rights, Ethno-Nationality, and Sovereignty in History*, we have drawn together studies dealing with a broad variety of countries, regions, and times, to indicate the widespread and diverse nature of the issues concerned, and the varying approaches and measures used to address them.

Ten of the chapters in this volume were first presented at a session on "Ethno-Nationality, Property Rights in Land and Territorial Sovereignty in Historical Perspective," at the XIII International Economic History

Congress, held in Buenos Aires, Argentina, July 22–26, 2002. Our interest in the topic motivated us to organize this session, and we were gratified by the quality of the papers and the scholarly interest in the subject. After the Congress we planned to make the papers into a book, and, to provide for broader coverage, we commissioned five additional contributions (Chapters 4, 5, 6, 7, and 11). The volume includes fourteen area-specific studies and an analytical and historical overview by the editors.

Ethno-national problems of land rights can arise in several different manners, and with rather different power relations among the parties. Perhaps most frequent is the arrival of new peoples (typically as colonial settlers or as non-settling colonial rulers) into already settled areas, with the ability to enforce controls, either by military actions or by economic design, upon those already resident. Or, as in the cases of Fiji, British Guiana, and Trinidad, among British areas, the in-migration of indentured labor of different ethnicities may lead to changes in the ethnic composition of population in the countries of destination, not altogether favorably received by their indigenous ethno-nationals. Examples of these patterns and their legacies that are discussed in this volume include: North American Indians (Leonard A. Carlson, Ann M. Carlos and Frank D. Lewis), Fiji and Hawai'i (Sumner J. La Croix), Sri Lanka vis-à-vis Fiji (V. Nithi Nithiyanandam and Rukmani Gounder), Argentina (María Rosa Martínez, Marta Alicia Crivos, and Laura Teves), Australia (Tony Smith), South Africa (Robert Ross), and Sub-Saharan Africa more generally (Gareth Austin). In these cases the outcomes were often the control of land by the invading power, either for their own farming use or for use in conjunction with coerced labor of the resident, native population. In other instances tension arises from attempts to purchase, or otherwise acquire, land in order to increase settlements and spatial control by one group relative to another in ethno-nationally divided territories, as in the cases of the Polish provinces in Imperial Germany (Scott M. Eddie) and of Palestine (Jacob Metzer). Other examples of difficulties and conflicts occur with sudden changes in political controls, which gave rise to nationalist feelings to exclude other ethno-nationals, as with post-Soviet Lithuania (Rawi Abdelal), or from severe losses to the previous major power, opening up the need of a reassignment of land rights, and dislocating ethnically and religiously identified peoples, as in the case of Anatolia in the late Ottoman period (Yücel Terzibaşoğlu). It may also be variations in technology and environmental factors which influence economic requirements of competing ethnic groups, as in northern Finland (Jukka Nyyssönen), or else variations in political influences which alter the internal political regime and landholding rights, as in Ireland (Cormac Ó Gráda).

While dealing with many similar and even identical problems, the area-specific contributions are sufficiently distinct by their main concerns to enable their grouping into four thematic parts (Part II to Part V of the book). Part II concentrates on questions of group land rights, territorial sovereignty, and land regimes in the context of state versus nation(s); Part III focuses on the intertwined issues of religion, ethno-nationality, and economics in land disputes; in Part IV, questions of ethnicity and land rights of indigenous peoples and other groups in colonial and post-colonial settings are examined; and Part V dwells on some economic and environmental aspects of the livelihood of native populations in pre-modern colonial times and in the contemporary world.

As is vividly demonstrated by the varied, although far from exhaustive, set of examples illuminated in this volume, there have clearly been diverse causes of ethno-national land disputes, and many different forms of adjustment and accommodation to the power differences between the contesting groups. To try to understand the reasons for these differing patterns and outcomes, comparisons among specific cases are most useful, and we hope that the contributions assembled here will help to promote them.

Part I

Setting the stage

1 Some considerations of ethno-nationality (and other distinctions), property rights in land, and territorial sovereignty

Jacob Metzer and Stanley L. Engerman

Ethno-nationality and other group distinctions have been major determinants and basic manifestations of human territoriality, affecting the formation, modi operandi, and consequences of land regimes in history and their relationship to the concept of territorial sovereignty. In this chapter we explore some of the issues stemming from these associations, providing a generalized framework for, as well as relating to, the area-specific chapters which follow. Drawing mainly on the experience of the European world and its global extensions, the first section of the chapter offers some conceptual and historical observations on the property–sovereignty nexus and on the exclusionary restrictions, variously imposed, on land rights. And in the second section, a number of economic and political economy considerations of ethno-nationality and rights to land are taken up.

Property, sovereignty, and "others"

In his well-known essay on "Property and Sovereignty," which was originally written in 1927, Morris Cohen, the renowned American jurist, advances the proposition that property is sovereignty (Cohen 1978). Although acknowledging the contemporary (legal) dichotomy between the concepts of property (in private law) and sovereignty (in public law) – to be distinguished from the feudal inseparability of land ownership and local political sovereignty – Cohen argues that property rights, being an exclusionary relation between owners and other individuals regarding (material) things, are an interpersonal power relation. Therefore, and contrary to the Roman-inherited distinction between property (*dominium*) and sovereignty (*imperium*), property rights should be perceived, according to Cohen, as embodying both dominion over things and *imperium* over human beings, i.e. they should be regarded as manifestations of sovereignty. We may either accept or reject this sweeping notion of sovereignty and its derived generalizations, but in either case, the indiscriminate identification of property with sovereignty needs to be qualified before progress can be made in examining the relationships between property rights in land and territorial sovereignty.

A more nuanced approach to the sovereignty–property link is provided by the British economist Ralph George Hawtrey. In the book he published in 1930 on the *Economic Aspects of Sovereignty*, he accepts the notion that the modern concept of sovereignty has evolved from the post-feudal separation between sovereignty and property, but stresses, nonetheless, that sovereignty "carries with it important economic rights which are closely related to the rights of property" (Hawtrey 1930: 18). Among those he mentions are, on the one hand, the power of the state to encroach on (private) property rights by means of taxation, requisition, and regulation, and on the other hand, the various state-granted rights and concessions to control tracts of land, natural resources, and developmental projects.

The recognition of such governmental prerogatives as expressions of sovereignty is consistent with the well-accepted view that the various rights in land are best classified for the post-Westphalia European world by an hierarchical order, with the state's territorial sovereignty placed at the top (see for example Goertz and Diehl 1991 and Burch 1998). The political philosopher Allen Buchanan elaborates further on the matter. In his well-known treatise on the morality of secession (Buchanan 1991), he suggests the following illuminating distinction (which we quote at some length) between land ownership and territorial sovereignty in modern states:

> At least under modern conditions, the relationship between the state and its territory is *not* the same as that between a person and the land which is her private property. It may be true that in earlier periods of history a ruler or ruling family was thought to own the territory of the state, to possess it as a piece of private property. But modern states, whether socialist or capitalistic, are not conceived of in this way. This is perhaps clearest in states where private citizens own land; they, not the state, are the property holders. But even where there is virtually no private property in land, the official rationale, at least, is that the state holds and administers the land and the resources it contains, and defends the borders *for the people*, that is, the citizens collectively. Thus the relationship between the state and "its" territory is that between an agent and the principal that authorizes the agent to perform certain functions on the principal's behalf.
>
> . . . "Territorial sovereignty", therefore, signifies not a property right ascribed directly to the state but, rather, a complex relationship among the state (the agent), the territory, and the people (the principal) . . . to talk about the state's territory in the territorial sovereignty sense . . . it is to say that the state is authorized to exercise certain limited forms of control over the citizen's private property (e.g. the power of eminent domain), and to control the borders surrounding it.
>
> (Buchanan 1991: 108–109)

The notion of inter-temporal *agency relationships* between people and state is certainly useful in identifying (modern) territorial sovereignty and conceptually differentiating it from – either private or public – land ownership. But it needs to be supplemented by the input of history for unveiling the mechanisms by which individual and/or collective property rights in land and their exclusionary attributes have been linked to the identity of the relevant *people* (the *principal* in Buchanan's terminology) and to the formation and preservation of the territorial sovereignty of their (*agent*) states.

Concentrating on Europe and on its global extension, the basic pattern inside Europe was the movement along the "rough" historical path, which took the continent's polities and society from the feudal realm (characterized by a multitude of local and regional sovereigns with overlapping rights and obligations), through the unsettled era of changing periodic equilibria between multi-national empires and single centralized states, to the contemporary arena of territorially well-defined sovereign states that are commonly identified, and mostly dominated, by their respective ethno-national majorities. A corollary to this dynamic has been the functional separation of land ownership from territorial sovereignty and the evolving marketability of land (with the former Communist countries following suit, at least partly, in the last decade).

In some of the (mainly west) European states, land markets have turned into relatively unrestricted economic arenas where citizens, non-citizen residents, and foreigners alike have been able to transact in landed property, while in others, various restrictions have been imposed on non-citizens (variously defined). Take, for instance, Switzerland. As late as the mid nineteenth century, non-cantonal citizens could be discriminated against in the cantonal land markets and the cantonal citizens had the right to "redeem" their property. Even after the elimination of these restrictions by the Swiss confederate constitution of 1874, the "right of free settlement" within the Confederation was granted only to Swiss citizens (see Hannum 1996). Likewise, in the Finnish, autonomous, Aland Islands, only holders of the islands' regional citizenship are allowed to own land freely; all others need to have a land owning permission from the Provincial Executive Council. Moreover, any land transferred to a person without a domiciliary right can be "redeemed" by any legal entity holding such right at an agreed upon, or court determined, price (Hannum 1996). Similar restrictions, barring non-citizens from owning land, have been instituted in 1991 in the (post-Soviet) Baltic states (see Smith 1994 and Rawi Abdelal's discussion in Chapter 5), and several states of the United States have maintained restrictions on the rights of real property ownership by non-resident aliens, and in a few cases, by resident aliens as well (Shapiro 1993).

Historically, the roots of the "citizens only" constraints on land markets can be traced, at least in part, to the notion, prevalent in the early phases of modern political representative regimes, that full participation in the body politic (such as the right to vote) requires ownership of landed property.

Accordingly, land ownership turns to be an identifier of the relevant "people" – the *principal*, à la Buchanan – for whom the state functions as *agent*. Indeed several nations, including Britain and Australia, long maintained a system of plural voting, where individuals were enabled to vote in as many electoral districts as they held land of sufficient value.

While the ownership of land as a prerequisite for enfranchisement has long been abandoned in modern democratic states, the above examples demonstrate that by making the "entrance" to the land market an exclusionary prerogative of citizenship, the separation of property rights in land from sovereignty has, in a number of modern states, not been pushed to the logical conclusion of eliminating all such restrictions. On a conceptual level this may reflect some kind of an accommodation between nationalism, whose basic attitude towards land as a place – a homeland belonging to the nationals – made its thinking often blur the distinction between sovereignty and ownership, and liberalism, in which land is perceived as alienable property to be freely traded in the market place.[1]

On a more practical level, it may be suggested that at least some states have not regarded their ultimate controlling power over the entire land area and natural resources within their borders (such as the requisition power of eminent domain, zoning, and taxation) as sufficient guardians of their territorial sovereignty, and possibly of their ethno-national integrity and hegemony. A vivid illustration of these considerations is provided by the ban on non-citizens' land ownership in Lithuania's post-Soviet constitution, and, as examined by Rawi Abdelal in Chapter 5, by the process that has recently led to the constitutional amendment relaxing it. The particularities of Israel's land regimes, which are outlined by Jacob Metzer in Chapter 4, are another illuminating case in point.

Administrative barriers to entry, however, have not been the only mechanism linking the land market to the goal of maintaining and cementing territorial sovereignty. Another mechanism was the participation of the state as an active player in the land market. A prominent case of such involvement, which Scott Eddie elaborates on in Chapter 3, was the attempt to "Germanize" the eastern (Polish) territories of Imperial Germany. Activating a specially designed "Royal Prussian Settlement Commission," the German government was engaged in the late nineteenth and early twentieth centuries in a concerted effort to purchase large tracts of farm land owned by Poles, to subdivide them, and to subsidize their acquisition and settlement by German, preferably self-employed, farmers. The newly established farms were to be of small and medium size to avoid the need of hiring Polish laborers. Furthermore, the settled German farmers, while allowed to sell their property, were prohibited from reselling it to Poles.

The implementation of this scheme, although hardly a success story from the German point of view, provided some kind of a role model for the Zionist land acquisition and colonization strategy in early twentieth-century Palestine – another well-known attempt to use the land market for the promotion of ethno-national territorial interests (see Chapter 4). In the Zionist case, too, the goal was to purchase land owned by non-nationals (mostly Arabs) and subsidize the agricultural settlement of immigrating (Jewish) nationals on it. But unlike the German case, the Zionist "blue-print," as crystallized in the Mandate period, called for the collective retention of the purchased land by the Zionist body politic.

The distinct feature of the Zionist experience – ethno-national collective action in a non-state situation – exemplifies another facet of the ownership–sovereignty nexus; the acquisition and use of property rights in land as a vehicle for strengthening (future) claims to territorial sovereignty, and – given the power of guiding and controlling the economic activity on collectively owned land, even if to a limited extent – also as some kind of a substitute for such sovereignty. Note, however, that the principle of inalienable national land has remained the cornerstone of the land regime in the State of Israel as well. Following the aftermath of the 1948 war, more than 93 percent of the state's land area (within the pre-1967 borders) were turned into public domain, enabling Israel to pursue policies which promoted Jewish-national interests in the spatial arena. These policies and their underlying land regime should be seen as an additional manifestation of the complex and versatile state-shaped relationship between property rights in land and territorial sovereignty, particularly in ethno-nationally split citizenries (see Chapter 4).

In the Zionist–Israeli experience as well as in the German story, the exclusionary attributes of property rights in land, apart from differentiating the own citizenry, or the otherwise-identified membership of the body politic in question, from the rest of humanity, were specifically aimed at certain, well-defined, groups. "Targeted" exclusion of this kind, as history informs us, has been exercised in numerous instances where individuals or groups, identified by their subordinate class, religion, or ethno-nationality (or by some combination of the three) have been discriminated against in the land market of their encompassing polities.

An early prominent example of "targeted" exclusion involving both ethno-nationality and religion is that of Ireland, which, following the twelfth-century conquest and settlement by the English, may be viewed as the first "overseas" English settlers' colony. The creation of the Irish kingdom under Henry VIII in 1541 launched a long period of land confis-cation and subsequent disqualification of Roman Catholics from equal rights to land. Consequently, most of the island's land turned into English-owned territory by the beginning of the eighteenth century, with the Irish peas-ants in the South becoming tenants of English landlords, and with English and Scottish settling immigrants partly displacing the indigenous inhabitants in the North (Christopher 1997). The national cum religious strife resulting from these exclusionary policies, and from some of the myths surrounding them, has set the stage for the Irish Land War of the late nineteenth century, and, as Cormac Ó Gráda demonstrates in Chapter 6, has provided polemic weapons that have been extensively used in the political and economic disputes of its aftermath.

The early Anglo-Irish history may be seen as a prelude to the developments in the outer-Europe scene. It is this scene in which European settlers' colonialism and its subsequent new states wrote an important chapter in the evolving story of rights to land and territorial sovereignty.

European colonial settlement, from its inception in sixteenth-century America, through its continuation in Australia and Asia, and up to its last phase in twentieth-century Africa, devised various mechanisms for consolidating the settler colonies (and the states that originated from them) and for handling the unavoidable confrontations between settlers, intending to occupy and extend the colonized land under their control, and the indigenous people living on it. Typical of such confrontations was the seizure of substantial tracts of land by the colonial governments and by their subsequent independent states for the private and/or public use of the settling (non-indigenous) population. This activity was usually coupled with the exclusion of the indigenous people from the settlers' land markets, while assigning them to "protected" reserves of land, whose total area would amount to just a miniscule fraction of their pre-colonial holdings. These mechanisms, particularly as they evolved in the Anglophone colonial and post-colonial scene of America and Australia (and to some extent in Latin America, in the British colonies in Africa and in the French-controlled Maghreb, as well) bring to the fore some fundamental issues concerning the meanings of rights in land and the origins and nature of territorial sovereignty (see Albertini 1982; McAlister 1984; Tully 1994; Christopher 1997).

In Australia, the legal status of the aboriginal population was based for about 200 years (until 1992) on the notion that the Australian continent-state originated from the British occupation of a *terra nullius*. The indigenous peoples were regarded not to have reached, at the time of the colonial occupation and inland expansion, the political and stable sedentary stage of organization and economic life to be recognized as actual landowners and sovereigns. Thus, none of the deep-rooted aborigines' perceptions of belonging and attachment to their land of hunting, gathering, or habitation, nor their traditionally enshrined communal landed rights, allocated largely on a functional basis, had been accepted by the colonial and post-colonial regimes as valid substitutes for common-law, spatially based, titles or as legitimate justifications for granting them.[2] Consequently, the Australian legislature and courts, guided by the *terra nullius* legal concept, had consistently rejected all claims for property rights in land or for territorially linked autonomy, which the aborigines were making on the basis of their pre-colonial holdings and territorial presence.

It was only in the 1970s, after the aborigine population was finally given voting rights in 1962, that things started to change with some revisionist legislative acts. In Chapter 10, Tony Smith documents and analyzes some of the new policies and their economic underpinnings, examining them from the microcosmic perspective of the Western Australian Kimberley region. These developments culminated in the celebrated Mabo judgment of the High Court in 1992, which eliminated the *terra nullius* legal grounds for rejecting the aborigines' land rights, and accepted their traditional customary laws as a legitimate basis for reclaiming them. Note, however, that although accepting the validity of the aborigines' prior rights to land, the Mabo decision rejected any claims for sovereignty, or self-government, based on the pre-colonial state of affairs (Reynolds 1996; Christopher 1997; Levy 2000).

The dividing line between pre-colonial times and the colonial era, which was long maintained by the *terra nullius* principle, marks Australia in the pre-Mabo period (and other settler colonies that followed the principle of the *terra nullius* directive) as a reference case for keeping the concept of land ownership at a "safe distance" from the traditional (pre-colonial) notion of land holdings by indigenous peoples, let alone from making those holdings an acceptable basis for recognizing property rights in land in the "modern" sense. Moreover, the sharp line that the Mabo decision of 1992 drew between the recognition of the aborigines' pre-colonial rights to land and the outright rejection of the idea that sovereignty of any kind did exist in the pre-colonial times, leaves Australia as an illuminating example in which a complete property–sovereignty dichotomy, in so far as the native population is concerned, is maintained in a "post-settler colony" state.

Unlike the Australian dichotomy, the North American story reveals a much more complex property–sovereignty relationship.[3] In the early days of settlement in Virginia, entrepreneurs were offered royal charters to exploit and occupy the land "not actually possessed by any Christian Prince, nor inhabited by Christian People" (Robinson 1957: 2, cited by Christopher 1997: 9). The nature of these charters implies that the English Crown did not recognize at the time the sovereign rights of the indigenes but claimed a general title to the area by the prevailing right of discovery and annexation.

Things, however, started to change pretty rapidly. In 1646 a treaty was signed between Necotowance, the chief of the Powhatan Indian tribe, and William Berkeley, the governor of Virginia, ending the third Anglo-Indian War. The treaty provided for mutual recognition of land rights and for the transfer of Indian land to the colony. Since then the treaty concept became the legal foundation of the relationships between the colonies (and later the US federal government) and the indigenes. It established those relationships on a contractual basis, which typically institutionalized the induced, and mostly enforced, surrender of most of the Indian land, in return for some (usually quite modest) compensation and for the official recognition of the Indians' permanent rights to governmentally designated tracts of land (on the reservations). Similar policies were followed by the Canadian government in the nineteenth and twentieth centuries.

But inferior as the standing of the Indian tribes was in the formulation and realization of their bilateral treaties with the colonies and subsequently with the US government, the treaties laid the ground for the special, though quite ambiguous, status of the Indian tribes as a distinct polity – *Indian Nations* (or in Canada, *First Nations*) – in terms of property rights in land and territorial sovereignty. In his famous judgments in the *Cherokee Nation v. The State of Georgia*, 1831, Chief Justice Marshall stated that "the Indians are acknowledged to have an unquestionable, and, heretofore, unquestioned right to the lands they occupy, until that right shall be extinguished by a voluntary cession to our government" (cited by Singer 1991: 15). In *Worceser v. Georgia*, 1832, Marshall elaborated further, affirming that the "Indian nations had always been considered as distinct, independent political communities, retaining their original natural rights, as the undisputed possessors of the soil, from time immemorial . . ." (cited in Deloria and Lytle 1984: 17). Note, however, that these natural rights, which did not allow for the sale of Indian land to private (non-Indian) parties, were inferior to "common law"-type property rights.

Recognizing the "natural rights" of the Indians to the land they occupied, and linking their communal independence to these rights, Marshall was provided with the legal justification for his characterization of the Cherokees as a *domestic dependent* [on the federal government] *nation* and for his decision that the State of Georgia had no sovereign power inside the territory of the Cherokee Nation within its borders. The judgments of the Supreme Court, however, did not prevent the final removal of the Cherokees from the State of Georgia – a move that Leonard Carlson discusses in Chapter 2, while elaborating on the issues of sovereignty and property between the state of Georgia, the Indian nation, and the federal government. Nonetheless, these judgments became the basis for the prevailing constitutional notion of *Indian domestic sovereignty* and for the exclusion of state governments from Indian affairs, which have since been dealt with at the federal level only.

The (domestic) sovereignty of the Indian nations inside the United States, being derived from their recognized rights to land, was defined in spatial terms and confined to the territories of their reservations.[4] However, this rather peculiar type of sovereignty, although acknowledged in the various US–Indian treaties, has been quite limited and subject to the regulatory power of the US legislature, even in matters concerning the social life and the provision of separate education to the Indian community. Moreover, the sovereignty of the tribal governments would typically not apply to the non-Indian residents on the reservations, and would generally not carry with it the power to zone, or otherwise regulate, property located within the reservations' boundaries, which is fee-owned by non-members of the tribe.[5]

The Supreme Court has justified these exclusions on the ground that since non-tribal property owners were not members of the Indian self-ruling polity, and were therefore barred from participating in its political process, the property they owned inside the reservation was to be rightly immune from the regulatory jurisdiction of the tribal government. Note, however, that within the US federal system, such limitations have been saved only for the domestic sovereignty of the Indian Nations, and have not been imposed on states, counties, or local governments. Having said that, it should be borne in mind, though, that indigenous (recognized or claimed) land rights, in the US and elsewhere, have typically involved a collective component, either in the regulatory sense and/or in terms of property rights held by the indigenous collectivity. While the link between collective land rights and some kind of self-government has been widely recognized, the difficulties of determining the nature and extent of (sovereignty-like) jurisdictions in the context of collective rights to land, and the built-in tension between such rights and the liberal notion of land as alienable property, may have partially prompted the US Supreme Court to limit the Indians' regulatory rights within their reservations.[6]

The qualifications, limiting the jurisdiction of tribal governments to tribe-members and to the land they own on the reservations (by fee or by common title), draw a clear line between the commonly perceived notion of territorial sovereignty and Indian domestic sovereignty. The former notion implies regulatory control of the government in place (be it of an independent state, a component polity in a federal structure, an autonomous entity within a larger state, or a local government) over the *entire* territory under its jurisdiction, irrespective of the landowners' citizenship, place of residency, or any other characteristics by which they may be identified. The latter concept, on the other hand, limits the spatial extent of sovereignty to the land collectively owned by the body politic in question and/or privately by its members. Sovereignty of this kind overlaps essentially the holding of property rights in land, and as such comes quite close to Cohen's assertion that property is sovereignty.

The American approach to (non-Indians') individual property rights in land versus (Indian) domestic sovereignty is an example of the superior position that land ownership may hold in the hierarchy of legal and constitutional (group) rights within a given body politic. Another example of such a ranking is provided by the case of Fiji. The right to (collectively) own (inalienable) land has been granted in colonial as well as in independent Fiji to ethnic Fijians only, making it inaccessible to about half of the country's citizenry – those migrating from India and their descendants. Besides the economic interests underlying the ethnic-specific restrictions imposed on Fiji's land market, they illustrate the use of property rights in land as a means to reserve for a certain (in this case the indigenous) people an exclusive identification with the land of their country-state, of which the rest of the citizenry is denied. These particularities are taken up, among other issues, in the analysis that Sumner La Croix offers in Chapter 8, comparing the emergence of Fiji's restrictive land regime with the free market for land evolving in Hawai'i, and in the study by

V. Nithi Nithiyanandam and Rukmani Gounder, who confront in Chapter 9 the Fijian ethnically divisive rights to land with the contested rights in the ethno-politically split island of Sri Lanka.

Making the ethnicity of citizens a determinant of property rights in land draws attention to the complexity involved in the mutual accommodation of the two, often irreconcilable, attributes of sovereignty: territory and people. The experience of the late nineteenth century and particularly that of the twentieth century is a rich source of observations on the matter.[7] Prominent building blocks of this experience include, in its early phase, the conflicts (particularly in the Balkans) leading to World War I, the break-up of the multi-national empires during the war, and the attempts to apply the Wilsonian principle of self-determination to their separate ethno-national components. In the later phase, we should notice the post-World War II creation (primarily in Africa) of new post-colonial states on the basis of the colonially drawn borders. This was done, however, with little regard for the territoriality of tribal ethnicities, which by themselves may have been, at least partly, induced by the colonial regimes. Likewise the recent geopolitical changes in Central and Eastern Europe, following the demise of the Soviet Empire and the other Communist regimes on the continent, provide additional evidence on the issues at hand. In all these instances the tension between territory and people and its implications for the rights-to-land question is amply revealed.

A number of examples, highlighting these issues, are discussed in several of the following chapters. In Chapter 7, Yücel Terzibaşoğlu analyzes the land disputes in northwestern Anatolia that were prompted by the changing borders and the relocation of people in the aftermath of the 1877–1878 Ottoman–Russian war. In these disputes, which could be viewed as an harbinger of the post-World War I transfer of population between Turkey and Greece, ethno-national and religious rhetoric was widely used.[8] Another case, which is elaborated on by Gareth Austin in Chapter 11, concerns the dynamics leading to the formation of exclusionary land rights, ethno-national consciousness, and tribal struggles in Sub-Saharan Africa (V. Nithi Nithiyanandam and Rukmani Gounder deal with similar questions in their Fiji–Sri Lanka comparison of Chapter 9). The special case of South Africa, moving from colonialism, through apartheid to the post-apartheid "New South Africa," is treated by Robert Ross in Chapter 12. Ross looks at the South African story by analyzing the complex past and the present state of affairs involving the aftermath of colonialism, ethnic identities, and claims to land in the Kat River valley of the Eastern Cape. Finally Rawi Abdelal (as mentioned above) examines in Chapter 5 the question of land owner-ship and citizenship in post-Soviet Lithuania.

These observations complete our examination of some of the general questions, providing an anchor for the discussion in the next section, which concentrates on the economic underpinnings and implications of the restric-tions imposed on the use and ownership of land by *others*.

Some economic (and political economy) aspects of ethno-nationality and land rights

The first part of the economic discussion reviews a number of possible approaches to the analysis of the driving forces in ethno-national land disputes and group-specific practices in the land market. And the second part dwells on some of their economic consequences and effects.

Considering motivations, the relatively easy ones to identify are those that relate to struggles for power and territorial control stimulated by material gains, whether zero or positive sum. The dynamics of European settlers' colonialism is an obvious case in point. The material incentives, which prompted the typical Europe-originated settlers and their governments to dispossess indigenous people in the newly colonized areas of the world, are self-evident. The settlers' (growing) demand for land provided the stimulus, and their superior power the means to impose their will. The desire to acquire land has further benefits than land ownership. By owning land it was possible to remove the rights of other possible occupants, forcing them off the land and, by limiting this alternative, driving them into the wage labor force to work for the proprietors of the land.

These patterns were undoubtedly aided by custom-based systems of land rights in tribal societies, which, by being mostly devised in functional terms and thus often not including any notion of ownership, had reduced the cost of dispossession. Although the colonizers' perception may have varied from complete rejection to qualified acceptance of the natives' pre-colonial landed rights, these variations may have affected the technique but rarely the end result of displacement and dispossession.

The ethnic and cultural distinction of the indigenous people, distinguishing them from the European settlers and civilization, marked them – collectively, even if not individually – as *others*. In some cases it was desired to use the indigenous peoples as a controlled labor force, but in other cases, particularly if there were alternative sources of labor, there was no need or desire to have them as a central part of the labor force, and what was wanted was out-migration to otherwise unsettled regions of the nation (see for example Carlson in Chapter 2). This may have added another (psychic) cost-reducing element, further inducing discrimination against natives (see the discussion of xenophobia, below). In this respect the *otherness* of the aborigines should have had similar effects to that of Africans in reducing the non-pecuniary cost (and possibly the pecuniary cost as well) of enslavement and of maintaining slavery in Africa and in the Americas.[9]

Note, however, that although the economic motivations underlying the (mis)treatment of aborigines' land rights were of a rather common nature, the dynamics of dispossession may have reflected, in a number of instances, conflicting political (economy) interests. A particularly vivid illustration of the role that such interests played is provided in Carlson's account (Chapter 2) of the Indians' removal from the southeastern United States.

The interplay between economic and political interests is observed also in other spheres of history (and in the contemporary world) where rights to land of well-defined groups or classes have been involved. For example, the rich literature on the political economy of serfdom offers some good, even if not always consistent, explanations (that need not be outlined here) for the economic cum political rationale of curtailing the landed rights, as well as restricting the mobility, of peasants in various European "old regimes" (Engerman 1996, 1999; see also Ó Gráda in Chapter 6). Another case in point is the all-out resistance of the English gentry to the broader marketability of land (i.e. to its loss of exclusivity), prior to the enactment of the Law of Property Act in 1925. As Cohen pointed out in his above-mentioned article:

> Once land becomes fully marketable it can no longer be counted on to remain in the hands of the landed aristocratic families; and this means the passing of their political power and the end of their control over the destinies of the British Empire.
>
> (Cohen 1978: 157)

Likewise, the different policies concerning the rights of foreigners to purchase and own land that were adopted in the mid-nineteenth-century Hawaiian kingdom and in colonial and independent Fiji, are an additional source of enlightening information on the matter (La Croix, Chapter 8).

Returning to the economic motivations for the curtailment of property rights in land, the issue becomes more complicated when attention is shifted to instances of land market restrictions (and other exclusions) as expressions of ethno-nationalism (sometimes coupled also with religious identity) and/or of nation and state building programs, where no material gains are easily detected (see particularly Chapters 3 to 5). This leads the discussion to the broader question of ethno-nationalism as a (possibly) rational pursuit and to the way it has been treated in the economic literature.

The theoretical economic literature on nations, nationalism, and states consists largely of two, interrelated, lines of inquiry. One line conceptualizes the nation as a well-defined (administratively and spatially) body politic, which facilitates, by the homogeneity of culture, language, and communication, the realization of coordination and network externalities, and of gains from low transaction costs in exchange and from the smoothness of labor specialization within its borders. Viewing the state as an administratively unified entity generating material benefits, research in this mode has typically concentrated on the determinants of the optimal size and number of single states. In particular, the trade-off between the efficiency gains of large jurisdictions and the cost of heterogeneity of large and diverse populations and of the loss of control on political decisions has been conceptually explored.[10] Applying similar reasoning to the analysis of investment in intra-ethnic networks and trust formation, studies along the same line have dwelt upon ethnic rent-seeking and materially driven conflicts within ethnically divided polities, as well as upon the economic incentives of ethnic minorities to secede from such polities and form their own sovereign jurisdictions (Buchanan 1991; Wintrobe 1995).

The second line of inquiry has been mainly concerned with problems of collective action, associated with the public good characteristics of many attributes and benefits of ethnicity and nationalism. The rational choice literature, in particular, has struggled with the question of how to conceptualize the willingness of individuals to invest in, and to make sacrifices for, the causes of ethno-nationality. Besides pointing to the collective (governmental) power of coercion as a means to facilitate communal as well as individual investment, studies in the rational choice tradition have endeavored to solve the free-rider puzzle by suggesting that at least part of the attributes of ethno-nationality should be perceived as private goods, benefiting individually the members of the polities concerned.[11]

This has been conceptually done by referring to possible mechanisms that could turn collective rights into individual gains. These gains could be either of a material kind (for instance, preferred jobs or property rights in land), or of a non-material type, derived from such characteristics of ethno-nationality as the sense of belonging and togetherness, cultural and social affinity, and/or the position of power and prestige vis-à-vis *others*. It is these issues that are closely related to the subject matter of our concern, and we turn now to several studies in which they are explored.

Ugo Pagano (1995) elaborated on the non-material attributes of ethno-nationalism, arguing that "utility maximization should not only take into account the utility of what *we have* (and the activities we carry out) but also the utility we get from what (we think) *we are*" both individually and as group members (Pagano 1995: 190). Following Nozick (1989), Pagano defined the latter type as "symbolic utility." It is the desire to capture the benefits from this type of utility which should induce individuals to act in the public sphere (for example, by seemingly irrationally taking the "pain" of voting, or deciding to redistribute wealth within the national society to care for its needy members). Individuals would do so in order to define their group identity and thereby nurture their sense of belonging, or, in other circumstances, consume the "positional goods" of nationalism such as power and prestige.[12] Pagano summarizes these arguments as follows:

> Symbolic utility and positional goods can offer a way to make the generosities and the atrocities of nationalism compatible with rational choice types of explanations. Individuals may wish to define themselves as members of powerful nations and may wish to consume pride and superiority with respect to other national and ethnic groups. Unfortunately, if many national groups share these wishes, then an

overinvestment in nationalism takes place. This overinvestment by possibly rational agents may perhaps help to explain some of the most regrettable aspects of our age.

(Pagano 1995: 196)

The conceptual aspects of investment (and overinvestment) in nationalism have been examined along similar lines also by Albert and Margot Breton (Breton and Breton 1995). In their paper, which builds on Albert Breton's pioneering study of the economics of nationalism (Breton 1964), they propose the following characterization of nationalism as a basis for their analysis:

> Though we recognize that nationalism is multidimensional, we submit that one permanent and essential dimension of the phenomenon is national, ethnic and/or racial ownership of property – for example, of territory (land), factories, refineries, infrastructures, government machinery, bureaucracies, and movie studios – and of the flows which derive from these assets.

(Breton and Breton 1995: 100)

This viewpoint, although somewhat extreme, enabled Breton and Breton to develop an insightful analysis of the "investment" made in excluding non-nationals from various economic arenas within the national jurisdiction, of which the ownership of property and the market for preferred white-collar jobs are especially noticeable. These investments tend to restrict the free mobility of resources, distort their allocation, and consequently reduce the level of material production within the national territory. While the loss of output could, in principle, be viewed as the cost of the non-material, public good-type, benefits of nationalism, these benefits, claim Breton and Breton, are not sufficient to explain the investment in nationalism (note the free rider problem). For a satisfactory explanation one needs to resort to the redistributional aspects (in terms of material income) of that investment, which are related to the fact that it is typically the middle-class elite that over time gains materially from the national ownership of assets, primarily by securing "good jobs" and incomes for itself.

Breton and Breton point out that investments in the exclusionary attributes of nationalism are mostly undertaken by "governments through purchases (nationalizations), confiscations, harassments, prohibitions, and conventional commercial policies" (Breton and Breton 1995: 107). Since the costs involved in these activities are borne by the general tax-paying public, the material benefits of nationalism are essentially a transfer from the rest of the nation to its middle-class elite. That being the case, investment in nationalism should be facilitated, either by the dominant political position of the rent-seeking (and capturing) elite, and/or by its ability to persuade the rest of the nation to substitute the non-tangible gains of nationalism (in terms of the positional goods and symbolic utility, discussed above) for material income.

An instrumental element smoothing such efforts of persuasion, and thus reducing the cost to the elite of its nationalistic rent-seeking activity is, according to Breton and Breton, the allocation of resources to investment in what they call cultural nationalism (composed of various means aimed at cultivating ethno-national pride and loyalty). Particularly illuminating for the questions related to the exclusion of *others* is the role that Breton and Breton attribute to xenophobia in their formulation. They interpret xeno-phobia as consisting (in its mild forms) of activities "aimed at excluding, physically or symbolically, 'relevant' foreigners from the lives, activities, and institutions of nationals or ethnics, at downgrading, often humorously (ethnic jokes), their way of life, their speech, their eating habits, their leisure activities, and so on . . ." (Breton and Breton 1995: 110–111). Viewed thus they suggest that:

> Xenophobia, . . . is therefore best conceived as a barrier that protects the national or ethnic masses from information originating in "foreign" groups that would allow them – the masses – to discover that what we have called belonging and identity can have very little or nothing at all to do with national or ethnic background, folklore, distinctiveness, and feeling of special collective destiny.
>
> (Breton and Breton 1995: 111)

Xenophobia, according to this view, increases the effectiveness of invest-ments in cultural nationalism, whether on the basis of ethnicity or race, thereby raising their rates of return and, by association, the rates of return on investments in political (exclusionary) nationalism as well. In other words, nurturing xenophobia may be perceived, at least in part, as a delib-erate (rational) activity undertaken by ethno-national elites to reduce the psychic costs of excluding foreigners (and/or other non-nationals) from owning "national" assets, and to increase the utility that nationals derive from "consuming" the non-material – public good-type – attributes, of such exclusionary practices. These ends are sought even when the shares of the minority groups in the population or as property owners appear to be very small. The shares of Indians in the population of the United States and Canada are only about 1 percent, and their share of total wealth is consid-erably below that. The same low shares are also seen for aborigines in Australia. Likewise, xenophobia may be a reaction to what may be regarded by nationals as "excess" foreign ownership of such assets. Breton and Breton mention as an example the signs of xenophobia that could be observed in the US in connection with the increasing proportion of "national" assets owned by Japanese interests.

The rational choice approach to nationalism (particularly of the Pagano and Breton and Breton versions), which was outlined here, clarifies the nature of the costs and benefits involved in investments in exclusionary national ownership of assets (and in investments in ethno-nationalism in general), and provides, undoubtedly, a useful organizing theme for their analysis. But having said that, it should be kept in mind that this approach runs, by its very nature, the risk of tautology and, moreover, that it does not invalidate competing interpretations, some of which may even defy, à la Connor (1994), the notion of rationality in ethno-nationalism altogether.

Given the a priori and the empirical difficulties of identifying the motivational underpinning of nationalistic collective action and of discriminating between competing explanations, a somewhat different, and more modest, approach to the issues at hand has also been put forward in the economic literature. Reference is here to the mode of analysis epitomized by the "taste for nationalism" notion described by Harry Johnson (1965), transforming Gary Becker's (1957) concept of the "taste for discrimination" into the scene of economic nationalism.

This approach, while not abandoning the self-interest basis for the analysis of economic nationalism, takes the discriminatory distinctions and attitudes of ethno-nationalism to be taste-driven and, therefore, exogenously given. Consequently, it shifts the focus of attention, from attempting to explain ethno-nationalism in terms of rational choice, to examining the economic manifestations of the policies set in motion by the "taste for nationalism," and to analyzing their effects. Concentrating on the latter, this approach serves as some kind of a "bridge" between the questions of economic motivation and incentives to that of economic attributes and outcome, which are addressed next.

Considering the relevant "taste" factors, we should include in the context of our discussion such characteristics as religious animosity, xenophobia, and the ideological (even at times mystical) associations between land and their ethno-national and/or religious collective identity that various societies have been nurturing (see O'Brien 1988). We should also add to this list "projects" of nation and state building, which (as discussed in the previous section) have induced nationally motivated land policies, aimed at establishing and securing the territorial sovereignty and integrity of the jurisdictions concerned and at cementing their ethno-national identification (see Chapters 2 to 5).

The collective actions driven by these tastes, as well as other policies restricting the rights to land of particular groups, have all affected the operation of the markets for land. Some of these markets may have been otherwise well-functioning, and others, limited, to begin with, by all kinds of different constraints. Assuming that the attributes of the policies in questions could be separated, conceptually and empirically, from all other market conditions, we should in principle be able to get a handle on some of their possible allocative and distributional effects.

Regarding the allocation of resources, questions of "common pool," resource depletion, and environmental concerns come naturally to mind in the context of the coexistence of traditional (typically common) rights to use certain tracts of land – which have long been saved for indigenous societies – with modern systems of public and/or private property rights. Such questions, among others, are addressed in the fifth part of this book. Ann Carlos and Frank Lewis analyze in Chapter 13 the hunting practices of North American natives subject to their particular communal hunting rights, and their implications for wild life depletion in the eighteenth-century Hudson Bay area. María Rosa Martínez, Maria Alicia Crivos, and Laura Teves, in their ethnographic study of Chapter 14, look into the meanings and implications of land rights as reflected in the attitudes of the Mbyá-Guaraní ethnic group in the Misiones region of modern Argentina. And Jukka Nyyssönen addresses in Chapter 15 the complex economic and environmental issues of resource management between the indigenous Sami and the "colonizing" Finns in northern Finland.[13]

A different issue of allocation is related to the efficiency implications of the administered, probably non-equilibrium, land prices, which were characteristic of some of the exclusionary land regimes. Such prices could be found in any of the systems in which ethno-nationals were institutionally encouraged by various subsidization schemes to settle, and thereby establish permanent presence, in certain areas. Examples should include the American (and Canadian) homesteading policies, the above-mentioned attempts to "Germanize" Polish Prussia, and the Zionist-led settlements efforts in Mandatory Palestine (Chapters 3 and 4). To the extent that these, and similar schemes, have caused a misallocation of resources, they have certainly reduced efficiency, and as such negatively affected economic growth. Note, though, that such efficiency losses, assuming they are measurable, may be interpreted as the social (shadow) price paid for the realization of the ethno-national goals concerned, and, at least in part, also as a means to economize on the cost of policing and enforcing property rights and territorial integrity.

Resource misallocation of a more general kind that we should be concerned with could arise from the impediment to factor mobility caused by exclusionary land policies. Consider, for example, the separated land markets by ethno-nationality in settler and in other divided economies. Their existence has certainly hindered the equalization of factor returns by restricting the mobility of labor and capital when such was called for by differences in relative factor endowments and productivity across markets and industries.[14] Likewise, foreigners' limited investment opportunities in national economies where they were prevented from owning land, should have had negative effects on capital inflows to these economies, whether in accompanying labor migration or otherwise (see the treatment of these issues in the context of Fiji and Hawai'i by Sumner La Croix in Chapter 8).

Misallocation and efficiency losses may result also from the application of group-specific collective rights to land, commonly demanded and often granted to indigenous peoples. Apart from the above-mentioned "common pool" problems, such rights generally, and when coupled with various restrictions on the alienability of land particularly, limit the range of economic options available to individual group members. Depending on the exact nature of the collective rights to land, these restrictions could range from various constraints on the individuals' ability to freely use (within the collectivity's spatial jurisdiction) their own landed property as fungible assets, to extreme situations, in which individual group members may lack independent rights of any kind to the collectively held (non-alienable) land. At times inhibiting economic mobility, these constraints may curtail efficiency and growth, let alone the realization of potential income increasing opportunities by the indigenous people themselves (see Buchanan 1993; Kymlicka 1995: ch. 3; Levy 2000: ch. 7).

On the distributional front, the major questions center on the allocation of rents generated by acts of dispossession or by barriers to enter the markets for land, and on the income transfers they entailed (an illuminating discussion dwelling on these questions in the Irish case is provided by Cormac Ó Gráda in Chapter 6). In zero sum game situations, where landholders were dispossessed of their holdings or underpaid for the land they relinquished (as was typically, although not exclusively, the case in settler societies), the direction of the wealth and income redistribution was obviously quite clear. However, in ethno-nationally divided jurisdictions, in which unidirectional transfers of land, induced by nation-building motives, were the outcome of free market transactions (see the discussion in the first section), a "national" premium may have been added to the price of land paid by ethno-nationals, enabling non-national land sellers (and owners) to capture the extra rent involved. Such a rent may have been captured, for example, in Mandatory Palestine by non-Jewish sellers of land to Jewish buyers (see Metzer's discussion in Chapter 4), but, as Scott Eddie demonstrates in Chapter 3, no similar rents were found in the case of Prussia's Poland.

Note, though, that in ethno-nationally divided countries, where the right to own land has been saved exclusively for nationals, while non-nationals (citizens and foreigners alike) could only lease it, the former have had an additional advantage – being able to use their landed property as collateral in the credit market. This advantage of accessibility can also be interpreted as some kind of a rent, which ethno-nationals enjoy at the expense of the non-national residents (and citizens) of their countries.

In instances where only foreigners have been prevented from owning assets within the state, the distributional effects would be similar in nature to those generated by the imposition of an import-preventing tariff. Namely, a transfer from the domestic tax-paying public in general or from the consumers (in the tariff example) to the segments of society who benefit from the exclusion (the domestic producers, in the case of tariff).

This mechanism does not rule out losses to foreigners whose property may have been confiscated or nationalized without due compensation, but it still leaves the major part of the resources facilitating the rents, due to foreigner-exclusion policies, to be "mobilized" via an internal inter-sectoral transfer within the national community.

This concludes our review of some (but by no means all) of the economic aspects of land-related ethno-national policies, but the real-world story of such policies is far from being concluded. Its latest chapter, which started to unfold in the last three to four decades, is still in the making. It is about the political attempts being made in various corners of the globe to, at least partly, undo, rectify, and to some extent possibly compensate for, past wrongdoing.[15] Several contributors to this volume (Tony Smith, on Australia in Chapter 10, Robert Ross, on South Africa in Chapter 12, and Jukka Nyyssönen, on Finland in Chapter 15) address various aspects of these attempts, but more will surely be revealed and discussed in the future. The future should also provide an answer to the "big" question. Will the dynamics of free movement of people, capital, know-how, and ideas leave the ethno-nationally-driven restrictions as part of past history only, or will the forceful "taste for ethno-nationalism" prevail?

Notes

1 This observation has been articulated by Levy in his insightful discussion of "Blood and Soil, Place or Property: Liberalism, Land, and Ethnicity" (Levy 2000: ch. 7).

2 For the distinction between functional and spatial property regimes and for the transition from the former to the latter, see Banner (2002).

3 Levy (2000: ch. 6) provides an interesting account of the differences between the Australian and the North American "models" of indigenous rights, based on the different compositions of the three modes – customary law, Common Law, and self-government – that Australia, the United States, and Canada have used for incorporating indigenous laws into their respective legal systems.

4 The following remarks draw on Singer's (1991) excellent discussion of the legal aspects of Indian sovereignty and property rights in land and of the changes over time in the courts' interpretation of the two concepts and of their mutual accommodation.

5 The US Indians were not recognized as full citizens until 1924, although the issue of individual rights versus tribal membership was not resolved until the second half of the twentieth century. Also important as a result of land claims regarding treaty rights have been the rights of Indian tribes to set their own laws, including non-collection of taxes on alcohol and tobacco, and the ability to open and operate gambling casinos.

6 For an elaborate conceptual analysis of collective rights (of indigenous people) versus individual rights in the western world and their legal, political, and economic implications, see Buchanan (1993). For further discussions and different approaches to the matter see Tully (1994), Kymlicka (1995: ch. 3), and Levy (2000: chs 6 and 7).

7 For a useful collection of case studies addressing the people and territory issues, see Coakley (2003).

8 The historical account that Terzibaşoğlu provides in Chapter 7 contains also an analysis of the transformation, which took place in the Ottoman Empire during

the second half of the nineteenth century, from the traditional land regime, partly based on customary, functionally determined, collective rights, to a modern regime of spatially-based land ownership. The analysis focuses on the implications of this regime change for the settlement of nomadic tribes, and it sheds additional light on the issue of individual versus collective rights that was discussed above in the context of indigenous land rights.

 9 For comparative discussions of slavery, serfdom, and other forms of coerced labor, see Engerman (1996, 1999).

10 For an informative presentation of this approach, see for example Bolton and Roland (1997) and Alesina and Spolaore (2003).

11 The studies put together by Breton *et al.* (1995) in their edited volume on *Nationalism and Rationality* provide an excellent presentation of the rational choice approach to nationalism and ethnicity.

12 Pagano's "self-interest" interpretation of ethno-nationalism may largely be viewed as part of the recent endeavor in economic thinking to incorporate the personal sense of group identity and belonging in the analysis of individual economic behavior. See for instance Akerlof and Kranton (2000), Bodenhorn and Ruebeck (2003), and the studies they cite.

13 See also Kymlicka (1995: ch. 5) for a general discussion of these issues.

14 See for example Mosley (1983) for a discussion of such problems in Kenya and Rhodesia, and Metzer (1998) for dealing with them in the context of Mandatory Palestine.

15 Note, though, in this respect that Kymlicka (1995: ch. 6) points out, rather convincingly, that the argument in support of indigenes' land claims, which is based on the premise that all citizens should be treated equally, is essentially cast in terms of the indigenes' current needs and not their past losses. Thus, their claims to land should be justified on grounds of distributive justice and not on the basis of compensatory justice.

Bibliography

Akerlof, G.A. and Kranton, R.E. (2000) "Economics and Identity," *Quarterly Journal of Economics*, 115: 715–753.

Albertini, R.V. (1982) *European Colonial Rule 1880–1940: The Impact on the West on India, Southeast Asia and Africa*, Oxford: Clio.

Alesina, A. and Spolaore, E. (2003) *The Size of Nations*, Cambridge, MA and London: The MIT Press.

Banner, S. (2002) "Transitions between Property Regimes," *Journal of Legal Studies*, 32: S359-S371.

Becker, G.S. (1957; 2nd edn 1971) *The Economics of Discrimination*, Chicago, IL: University of Chicago Press.

Bodenhorn, H. and Ruebeck, C.S. (2003) "The Economics of Identity and the Endogeneity of Race," NBER Working Paper Series 9962.

Bolton, P. and Ronald, G. (1997) "The Breakup of Nations: A Political Economy Analysis," *Quarterly Journal of Economics*, 112: 1057–1090.

Breton, A. (1964) "The Economics of Nationalism," *Journal of Political Economy*, 72: 376–386.

——— and Breton, M. (1995) "Nationalism Revisited," in Breton *et al.*

———, Gianluigi, G., Salmon, P. and Wintrobe, R. (eds) (1995) *Nationalism and Rationality*, Cambridge and New York: Cambridge University Press.

Buchanan, A. (1991) *Session: The Morality of Political Divorce from Fort Sumter to Lithuania and Quebec*, Boulder, CO: Westview Press.

—— (1993) "The Role of Collective Rights in the Theory of Indigenous Peoples' Rights," *Transnational Law and Contemporary Problems*, 3: 89–108.

Burch, K. (1998) *"Property" and the Making of the International System*, Boulder, CO, & London: L. Rienner Publishers.

Christopher, A.J. (1997) "Spatial Aspects of Indigenous Lands and Land Claims in the Anglophone World," Department of Land Economy, University of Cambridge, Discussion Paper 84.

Coakley, J. (ed.) (2003) *The Territorial Management of Ethnic Conflict* (revised and expanded edn), London: Frank Cass.

Cohen, M. (1978) [originally published in 1927] "Property and Sovereignty," in C.B. MacPherson (ed.) *Property: Main Stream and Critical Positions*, Toronto: University of Toronto Press.

Connor, W. (1994) *Ethnonationalism: The Quest for Understanding*, Princeton, NJ: Princeton University Press.

Deloria, V. Jr and Lytle, C.M. (1984) *The Nations Within: The Past and Future of American Indian Sovereignty*, New York: Pantheon Books.

Engerman, S.L. (1996) "Slavery, Serfdom and other Forms of Coerced Labor: Similarities and Differences," in M.L. Bush (ed.) *Serfdom and Slavery: Studies in Legal Bondage*, London and New York: Longman.

—— (1999) "Introduction," in S.L. Engerman (ed.) *Terms of Labor: Slavery, Serfdom, and Free Labor*, Stanford, CA: Stanford University Press.

Goertz, G. and Diehl, P.F. (1991) *Territorial Changes and International Conflict*, London: Harper Collins.

Hannum, H. (1996) *Autonomy, Sovereignty and Self Determination: The Accommodation of Conflicting Rights* (revised edn), Philadelphia, PA: University of Pennsylvania Press.

Hawtrey, R.G. (1930) *Economic Aspects of Sovereignty*, London: Longmans, Green.

Johnson, H. (1965) "A Theoretical Model of Economic Nationalism in New and Developed States," *Political Science Quarterly*, 80: 165–185.

Kymlicka, W. (1995) *Multicultural Citizenship: A Liberal Theory of Minority Rights*, Oxford: Oxford University Press.

Levy, J.T. (2000) *The Multiculturalism of Fear*, New York and Oxford: Oxford University Press.

McAlister, L.N. (1984) *Spain and Portugal in the New World, 1492–1700*, Minneapolis, MN: University of Minnesota Press.

Metzer, J. (1998) *The Divided Economy of Mandatory Palestine*, Cambridge: Cambridge University Press.

Mosley, P. (1983) *The Settler Economies: Studies in the Economic History of Kenya and Southern Rhodesia, 1900–1963*, Cambridge: Cambridge University Press.

Nozick, R. (1989) *The Examined Life: Philosophical Meditations*, New York: Touchstone Books.

O'Brien, C.C. (1988) *God Land*, Cambridge, MA: Harvard University Press.

Pagano, U. (1995) "Can Economics Explain Nationalism?," in Breton *et al.*

Reynolds, H. (1996) *Aboriginal Sovereignty: Reflections on Race, State and Nation*, St Leonards, NSW: Allen & Unwin.

Robinson, W.S. (1957) *Mother Earth – Land Grants in Virginia 1607–1699*, Williamsburg, VA: Virginia 350th Anniversary Celebration Corporation.

Shapiro, M. (1993) "The Dormant Commerce Clause: A Limit on Alien Land Laws," *Brooklyn Journal of International Law*, 20: 217–253.

Singer, W.J. (1991) "Sovereignty and Property," *Northwestern University Law Review*, 86: 1–56.

Smith, G. (ed.) (1994) *The Baltic States: The National Self-Determination of Estonia, Latvia and Lithuania*, London: Macmillan.

Tully, J. (1994) "Aboriginal Property and Western Theory: Recovering a Middle Ground," *Social Philosophy and Policy*, 11: 153–180.

Wintrobe R. (1995) "Some Economics of Ethnic Capital Formation and Conflict," in Breton *et al.*

Part II

Nations, land regime, and territorial sovereignty in old and new states

2 Were there alternatives to disaster?

The removal of Indians from the southeastern United States in the 1830s*

Leonard A. Carlson

Introduction

In 1837 roughly 18,000 members of the Cherokee Nation in North Carolina and Georgia traveled to new lands in Oklahoma in what is know as the "trail of tears." In one week in the spring of 1837, soldiers forcibly rounded up members of the tribe and took them to forts to prepare for the trip west. From these forts the army planned to move the Cherokees to land in Oklahoma granted to the tribe by the Treaty of New Echota, which had been signed by a minority faction in the tribe in 1835. The first wave of emigrants left in the summer of 1837 under armed guard. The heat and hardships faced by that group were so intense that the rest of the tribe agreed to leave without further coercion if they could wait until the cooler fall, which was agreed to. By the time it was done, a large number of people had died (sometimes estimated as 4,000 out of 18,000). Neither Indian nor white leaders expected such a disaster. Historians have assigned the blame to many parties, including Andrew Jackson and the leadership of the Cherokee.

Removal of the Cherokee is clearly a dark chapter in American history and the actual removal could have been handled far more humanely than it was, but was it the best of a bad set of alternatives? At first glance the alternative seems obvious. Simply let the Cherokee and other tribes stay on the land they already occupied in Georgia and other states. The peculiar nature of Indian political rights in the United States and the nature of politics at the time would have made that more difficult than it might seem at first.

Francis Paul Prucha, the leading historian of Indian policy, concludes that removal was the best available choice. In addition to removal, Prucha lists: (1) annihilation, (2) maintenance of Indians in place, and (3) immediate assimilation (Prucha 1969: 234–236). These were probably the alternatives that were imagined by policy makers in the 1830s. Prucha concludes that Andrew Jackson's policies were a sincere attempt to make the best of a bad situation.

Robert Remini, the leading biographer of Jackson, is critical of Jackson's role in the trail of tears, but points out that Jackson did not see the hardships coming. This does not exonerate Jackson in his view, but Remini agrees with Prucha that it was not possible in 1830 to protect the Cherokee nation in Georgia (Remini 2002).

To understand why allowing the Cherokee to stay was so difficult requires a careful look at the nature of tribal property rights in the nineteenth century and a consideration of the politics of land and slavery as well.

The Indian Removal Act of 1830

A key event in the years before the trail of tears was the passage of the Indian Removal Act of 1830. On May 26, 1830, the US House of Representatives passed the Indian Removal Bill, officially titled "An act to provide for an exchange of lands with Indians residing in any of the States or Territories, and removal West of the river Mississippi." The vote in the House was a dramatic showdown between Andrew Jackson's supporters who favored removal and Jackson's opponents who supported allowing tribes such as the Cherokee and other southeastern tribes to remain on their lands in Georgia, Alabama, Mississippi, North Carolina, Tennessee, and Florida. The bill was important to Jackson, and his opponents hoped to hand him a major defeat. The bill authorized the President to negotiate with tribes to trade their land in the east for land west of the Mississippi River and appropriated $500,000 for this purpose. After fierce debate, the Indian Removal Act narrowly passed in the House of Representatives by a vote of 102 to 97 (United States Congress 1830a: 730). The bill passed the Senate earlier on a vote of 28 to 18 (United States Congress 1830b: 382–1135).

The debate over the Removal Bill is described by Remini (2001: 268) as a "verbal brawl." The debates in Congress concerned several issues. In general proponents of removal made three main points: (1) that it was humanitarian action needed to protect Indian from vices learned from civilization; (2) that land needed to be opened up to farmers and that farmers had a God-given right to land; Indians who were willing to give up "the hunt" and agree to hold title under state law could remain; and (3) that the federal government had promised to remove Indians from Georgia and the state did not recognize the right of the Cherokee to establish a self-governing republic within the bounds of the state of Georgia.

The first argument of humanitarian gesture, that, left in the east, Indians would simply learn vices from whites, was expressed during the Senate debate by Wilson Lumpkin of Georgia who described removal as "their [the Cherokee] only hope of salvation." And he assured the house that "No man entertains kinder feelings toward the Indians than Andrew Jackson" (quoted in Remini 1981: 260). The case for the humanitarian argument was not without empirical evidence. Tribes in the east that had not moved west had in many cases not done well.

The humanitarian argument for removal had been made by people such as Lewis Cass, the leading scholar of Indian languages of his day. According to Anthony Wallace:

> Thus, in his [Cass's] view "they" (i.e., the men) were ill adapted to sedentary civilized life and languished in indolence and vice when unable any longer to hunt and fight. The only solution was to remove Indians to the forests and plains west of the Mississippi, where they could either choose to return to their former way of life in the untrammeled hunter state or to gradually embrace civilization.
>
> (Wallace 1993: 48)

Wallace is critical of the factual basis of Cass's views, which ignored the tradition of farming by women among eastern Indians. He also notes that:

> To some extent Cass was correct in his characterization of the Eastern Indians. Many of the smaller communities, particularly in the North, were slums in the wilderness, occupied by demoralized hunters unable to hunt, warriors unable to fight, riddled by disease, many addicted to alcohol; men, women, and children alike were all too often victims of mutual mayhem and murder; and their chiefs were notoriously open to bribery by whites seeking to buy land or other privileges. . . . But . . . Cass' theory of degeneracy of the hunter state seriously misrepresented the actual condition of some Native American communities east of the Mississippi River. . . . And he should have known . . . not only of the impressive recent progress of the Five Civilized Tribes of the Southeast but also their traditional practice of communal agriculture and large, well-planned towns.
>
> (Wallace 1993: 47–48)

Indeed, congressional debaters sometimes referred to Indians as hunters who could be allowed to remain if they gave up the hunt. The charge was also made that most Indians wished to move west, but were prevented from doing so by chiefs who stood to gain from keeping the tribe living where they were.

The discussion was framed in terms of extending the laws of Georgia into the Cherokee nation. Under the trade and intercourse laws, only federal authority operated in Indian country, but they were not so clear about land within a state's borders. As of 1830, Georgia had not passed laws for the Cherokee nation. A constitutional argument for the rights of the state of Georgia to extend its laws over the Cherokee was made, for example, by Robert Adams of Mississippi who "insisted that everyone living within the boundaries of a particular state is subject to the laws of that state. Otherwise chaos reigns. Or has a new set of rights been discovered? In addition to federal and state rights we will now have 'Indian rights.' What folly!" (quoted in Remini 1981: 260). In the congressional debates the rights of Georgia are mentioned many times.

The proponents of removal also made less altruistic states rights' arguments. John Forsyth of Georgia denounced a speech in favor of allowing the Cherokee to remain by saying:

> The Indians in New York, New England, Virginia etc etc are to be left to the tender mercies of those States, while the arm of the General Government is to be extended to protect the Choctaws, Chickasaws, Creeks and especially the Cherokees from the anticipated oppressions of Mississippi, Alabama and Georgia. What the north and east have already gotten away with is not to be denied the south.
>
> (quoted in Remini 1981: 260)

The man who most shaped the anti-removal argument was Charles Everts, a prominent protestant thinker in the northeast with ties to protestant missionaries among the Cherokee. In Congress, the opposition to the Removal Act was led by Charles Frelinghuysen from New Jersey, a leader of the anti-Jackson National Republicans. Frelinghuysen argued that federal government was obliged to protect Indian rights against the claims of all, including the states (Remini 1981: 261). He also argued that Jackson had not properly consulted with Congress and was improperly asserting his authority. As part of a long speech he also asked:

> how can we ever dispute the sovereign right of the Cherokees to remain east of the Mississippi, when it is in relation to that very location that we promised our patronage, aid, and good neighborhood? Sir, is this high-handed encroachment of Georgia to be the commentary on the pledge given.
>
> (reprinted in Prucha 1990a: 51)

Others in Congress seconded his arguments, emphasizing the promises made to Indian tribes. Congressman Evans, for example, stated that:

> in all our relations with them, to respect their rights of soil and jurisdiction – to treat them as free and sovereign communities. We have uniformly acknowledged the binding force of our engagements with them, and we have promised that we would be faithful and true in performance of all our stipulations. . . . Hold out as many inducements as you please, to persuade the Indian tribes to exchange their country for another beyond the Mississippi, but at the same time assure

them that until they freely and voluntarily consent to remove, they shall be protected in the possession of the rights . . . we have solemnly guaranteed them in existing treaties.

(United States Congress 1830b: 1037–1038)

Some also were concerned about the potential cost of the removal, suggesting it might run to millions.

Carlson and Roberts (2003) analyze the statistical factors that led to the passage of the Removal Bill. They find that three factors are statistically significant in explaining a Congressman's vote on removal. These variables are party (Democrats supported removal), the percentage of slaves in a Congressman's district (the greater the percentage of slaves to total population, the more likely a Congressman would support removal) and how he voted on the preemption law three days later. Those who favored extending preemption rights to squatters also favored removal, suggesting an alliance between the South and the northwest.

The bill's passage gave the full weight of the federal government to the movement for removal. But to understand the vote it is necessary to understand the legal status of tribes in the United States and the history of federal land distribution policies.

The evolution of federal policy towards Indians

The question of how states and later the federal government would treat Indian tribes was in flux following the American Revolution. Many tribes had sided with the British in the American Revolution and some states treated western tribes as defeated enemies who had thereby forfeited their claims to land. This led to warfare along the frontier as settlers pushed into lands occupied by Indians. This policy proved costly and unworkable and led to a return to the British practice of negotiating treaties with tribes to cede their claims to western lands. According to Perdue and Green, Henry Knox, the first Secretary of War and the man in charge of Washington's Indian policy:

> was convinced that the encroachment of settlers and others onto their [Indian] lands was the primary cause of war on the frontier and that the only way to bring peace to the frontier was to exert legislative controls over aggressive United States citizens. Furthermore, Knox thought that the federal government had a moral obligation to preserve and protect Native Americans from the extinction he believed was otherwise inevitable when "uncivilized" people came into contact with "civilized" ones. Knox also fully concurred with the general American view that as the population of the United States grew, Indians must surrender their lands to accommodate the increased numbers. These views added up to

a policy aptly described by one historian as "expansion with honor," the central premise of which was that United States Indian policy should make expansion possible without detriment to the Indians.

(Perdue and Green 1995: 10)

A key part of this policy was enacted into law with the passage of the first Trade and Intercourse Act in 1790. The Act gave the federal government control over trade with Indians by licensing traders and established the principle of special laws for Indian country. In particular, the Act sought to control the trade in guns and alcohol, which were dangerous mixtures on the frontier. The federal government also set up trading posts to try and manage trade with Indians. Not surprisingly, much trade occurred outside federal control.

Conflict continued for decades, but after the 1790s it was clearly established that Indian tribes would cede land by concluding treaties with the federal government and approved by the Senate. The attempt to have expansion with honor was often not successful, of course. Conflicts between settlers and tribes continued for decades.

Further east, Indians in western New York either fled to Canada or remained on lands recognized by the state of New York and made a switch to more settled agriculture. Other small bands of Indians also remained in the northeast and southeast.

In the Old Northwest, many tribes moved further west to avoid settlers who drove away wild game that was an important part of the subsistence of these tribes along with farming. Encouraged by the British, these tribes also resisted the encroachment of settlers into western lands. The battle for what would become the state of Ohio was settled by the victory of General "Mad Anthony" Wayne at the Battle of Fallen Timbers in 1794. A second attempt at organized resistance ended with the defeat of an alliance of tribes organized by the Shawnee Chief Tecumseh (who was away for the battle) at the hands of William Henry Harrison at the Battle of Tippecanoe in 1811. With the end of the War of 1812, tribes north of the Ohio River generally abandoned armed resistance and moved to reservations west of the Mississippi or to reservations in Michigan or Wisconsin where population densities were low enough to allow tribes to continue a mixture of settled agriculture and hunting.[1]

Tribes south of the Ohio River – the Creek, Cherokee, Seminole, Choctaw, and Chickasaw (the so-called "Five Civilized Tribes") – had moved further toward adopting settled agriculture as the mainstay of their subsistence. Unlike the northern tribes, the southern tribes were matrilineal, which meant that the children of white traders and Indian women were fully recognized as members of the tribe. Children of these unions played an influential role in tribal society and became a bridge between the two cultures. Some of these mixed bloods became planters and slaveholders on the American model.

One of these tribes, the Creeks, maintained a stable confederation of towns balanced between the competing European powers throughout much of the eighteenth century. The defeat of the French in 1763 left them without an important potential ally and the confederation weakened. Some towns allied themselves with the British in the War of 1812 and were defeated in 1814. A real possibility of war remained as long as Spain controlled Florida, which it did until 1819 (Prucha 1984). After 1814, the Creeks were badly divided over how to deal with the American expansion. In 1825, for example, Chief William McIntosh of the Creeks signed the Treaty of Indian Springs which ceded a large tract of Creek land to the federal government without permission of the tribal council, who then ordered his execution (Prucha 1984: 220–221). After the American Revolution it was the Cherokee Indians who most effectively challenged the movement of settlers from the state of Georgia on to their lands.

During the American Revolution the Cherokee in western North Carolina and Georgia had initially sided with the colonists, but they soon grew tired of the undisciplined behavior of the colonists and switched sides to support the British government. Colonial forces reacted fiercely and the tribe was forced to sign the treaty of Fort Hopewell, ceding lands in the east. Fighting continued after the revolution, with some bands resisting until 1791. During the war, colonial troops destroyed 50 Cherokee towns and the associated fields. Many Cherokee died in the famine that followed. After that defeat, the Cherokee nation went through a period of peaceful relations with the new United States and developed new forms of governance.

Along with deciding how to treat Indian tribes, the new government had to find a way to administer land in the west and reconcile the claims of the original states. A notable success for the government established under the Articles of Confederation was the resolution of these issues. Of the original 13 colonies, 7 had claims, often overlapping, to land in the west. The six landlocked states were concerned that if these western lands were settled the states with western lands would grow large and populous and dominate the new nation. The solution was for the states to cede their western lands to the federal government. Beginning with New York in 1780 and followed by Virginia in 1784, all of the original states eventually ceded their claims to western lands. According to Robbins:

> These cessions [New York and Virginia's] made possible the first legal union of the thirteen states and conveyed to the government of these states the title to a body of land known as the public domain. Between 1784 and 1802 the remaining five states also ceded their western lands.
> (Robbins 1962: 5)

These cessions were followed by two of the most important pieces of legislation passed under the Articles of Confederation: the Land Law of 1785 and the Northwest Ordinance of 1787. These two laws set the terms for the sale of land in the new territories and for the method by which new states were to be admitted into the union. Land was to be surveyed in a large grid and individual parcels were to be sold in fee simple to private citizens, without feudal obligations to the government. Some land was reserved for public purposes, such as schools and courthouses. Laws for the governance of the new territories were established by the Northwest Ordinance, which authorized the creation of territorial governments and established the rules whereby new states could enter the union in equality with the existing states. Under the Northwest Ordinance, slavery was outlawed north of the Ohio River and, by omission, permitted south of the Ohio.

Once it was decided how public land in the west was to be surveyed and sold, there remained the question of the price and terms under which land would be offered for sale. In the early years the Federalists supported a policy of selling land at relatively high prices and in relatively large units to generate revenue for the new government, encourage manufacturing, and protect the interests of eastern landowners. Democrats tended to favor lower prices and smaller parcels to encourage the purchase of land by relatively poor settlers.

At first, the sale of public land was one of the few sources of federal revenue and so the terms were dictated by the need to raise revenue (Atack and Passell 1994: 253). The minimum price for land was $1.00 per acre under the Land Law of 1785 with a minimum purchase of 640 acres. The price was raised to $2.00 per acre in 1796. Thereafter terms of sale were made easier, with smaller minimum purchases, lower prices for land, and sometimes credit purchases. (Atack *et al.* 2000: 292–296) Selling land at auction was only one way that land was transferred to private ownership. Some land was granted to military veterans, as was done for veterans of the war with Mexico in the 1840s. In the 1860s the federal government would grant land for railroad construction into undeveloped areas and states had made similar grants earlier.

According to Atack *et al.*, however:

> Such idealism aside, the debate over the transfer of public land into private hands was dominated by self-interested rent-seekers. The property-less stood to gain a saleable asset from Jefferson's policy, while cheap land was a threat to all existing property owners, limiting, if not actually diminishing their property's value. Keeping land prices high benefited existing landowners; setting them low benefited the poor, especially if credit were available, and increased the opportunities for profitable speculation.
>
> (Atack *et al.* 2000: 288)

After 1790 the general trend was for land policy to favor the Jeffersonian position. A continuing problem was what to do about squatters – people who settled on public land that they did not own – before it was surveyed and offered for sale. These people were often relatively poor, but influential on the frontier.

Looking at the history of land policy within the historical tradition inspired by Turner, Robbins wrote:

> The fact is that much of the history of the national land system centers around the struggle between squatterism and speculation, between the poor man and the man of wealth. Ever since the early colonial days the danger of frontier revolt had menaced established society. The opening of vacant lands to the westward always stimulated a frontier spirit – a peculiar democratic leveling influence, likely to be arrogant, dangerous, and even uncontrollable. The frontiersman wanted free access to the soil, but the forces of established order, on the other hand, contended that free land would destroy the economic and political values upon which the government was founded.
>
> (Robbins 1962: 9; emphasis added)

Squatters created many problems for federal authorities. At times military force was used to evict squatters from federal lands. These efforts were unpopular on the frontier and often ineffective. When land was eventually offered for sale at auction, residents would try to ensure that squatters could buy the land that they had settled. Armed groups at the auctions would sometimes try to intimidate outsiders to prevent them from buying land. Over time the claims of squatters came to be recognized by special legislation (Kanazawa 1996: 231). The success of these efforts encouraged still more anticipatory settlement by frontiersmen.

Granting property rights on a first-come first-served basis encourages wasteful early settlement.[2] Thus, from the point of view of economic efficiency, land policy moved from policies that were more efficient (and less aggressive towards Indians) to a more wasteful system of encouraging settlers to move west "too soon."[3]

There are conflicting views in the literature about the evolution of land policy. One view, emphasized by Robbins and echoed by many scholars today, stresses the distributional issues and sees the battle between those who favored the poor and the west versus the east, manufacturers, and the wealthy. In this view the preemption law and, later, the Homestead Act were victories for the poor man and his allies. Atack and his co-authors argue that behind the rhetoric was a struggle between competing economic interests over rents.

Even with low land prices, the total cost of setting up a farm in the west required a reasonable amount of wealth for a working family.[4] Allen (1991) recently defended the Homestead Act as an efficient policy that encouraged settlement and thereby secured property rights against the incursion of Indian tribes. Kanazawa, however, argues that the passage of the preemption act reflected the effectiveness of a special interest group and enforcement costs rather than a quest for efficiency.[5] According to Kanazawa:

> The ascendancy of preemption may be understood as a process whereby squatter rights were legitimized and integrated into federal land disposal policies. Early congresses made every effort to suppress squatters' rights, even passing a law in 1807 calling for the use of military force to remove squatters from public lands. Over time, however, Congress took an increasingly lenient stance toward squatters, granting preemption rights selectively in individual cases before passing the first general preemption law in 1830. Squatting activity probably influenced this policy evolution in two distinct ways. First, squatters exerted political pressure on Congress for preemption through numerous memorials and petitions, and through western Congressmen who represented their interests in Congress. The story is, however, more than simply the emergence of a new interest group with effective political power. Squatters also disrupted the operation of the local land auctions, thus reducing auction revenues and making adoption of preemption less unacceptable to its (mostly eastern) opponents in Congress. They thus altered the terms of the political debate in their favor, enabling them to gain valuable policy concessions.
>
> (Kanazawa 1996: 228)

In stressing the role of squatters in shaping policy by their willingness to disrupt local land auctions, Kanazawa is agreeing with earlier historians such as Robbins.

After 1830, preemption was renewed annually until it became a permanent part of land law with the passage of the General Preemption Bill of 1840. There was a big increase in land purchases during the first half of the 1830s and the primary issue was that the federal government would require that land be purchased with specie.

After 1840, the movement towards easier land policies focused on a Homestead Act – which would allow settlers to acquire 160 acres of unclaimed public land without charge if they maintained residency for a period of 5 years. This became a source of sectional conflict, with southern Congressmen solidly against passage of a Homestead Act. It was not until the Civil War, when the South was not represented in Congress, that the Homestead Act of 1862 was passed.

States rights, federalism, and slavery

The issue of Indian removal arose against the background of a battle over the rights of states relative to the federal government. The constitutional issue of the powers of the states relative to the federal government was tied closely to the desire of southern states to protect their property in slaves.

The state of Georgia had threatened before to directly challenge the federal government. In 1825, for example, Governor George Michael Troup had threatened to use force to remove the Creek Indians from middle Georgia. This was followed by the signing of the Treaty of Indian Spring by Chief William McIntosh, without the consent of the tribal council. The tribal council sentenced Chief McIntosh to death for signing the treaty without authorization and he was later killed (Coleman 1978: 34).

In the 1830s, at the time that the Cherokee appealed to the Supreme Court, the State of South Carolina passed its nullification ordinance which "nullified" the federal tariff of 1828 within its borders. On this issue Jackson sided with the pro-central government position and denied the right of South Carolina to do this. Faced with this threat to federal authority, northern support for the Cherokee eroded. According to Prucha (1969), northern supporters of the Indians supported the President in the confrontation with South Carolina.

Cooper and Terrill, viewing the debate from the perspective of historians of the South, point out that:

> In pushing the Indians out of the old Southwest, Andrew Jackson had wielded the power of the federal government to do just what those states wanted. Now millions of acres of land in Georgia, Alabama, and Mississippi were opened to white settlers and they poured in. No white person in the South forgot who had made those lands available to whites. Thus the distress occasioned among many southerners by Jackson's stance on nullification and withdrawal was tempered by his acquisition of Indian land.
>
> (Cooper and Terrill 2002: 158)

Carlson and Roberts (2003) find that Congressmen who supported preemption were more likely to support removal, even when party and section are controlled for. Those in the north and northwest who favored the claims of squatters and others frontiersmen to claim land on the frontier were more likely to support removing Indians from the southeast, even though most of the potential settlers who would move into that region were from the South. The motives of southerners were very much tied to slavery. The fact that Indians were being moved from land that would support slave agriculture gave all southerners, even those in eastern states, reasons to support removal. The potential rise in the value of slaves would be more than offset by a possible downward pressure on the price of land in the eastern states. These results also help explain the shift in the political stance of southern Congressmen toward land policies after 1840. Southern Congressmen in the 1850s were virtually all opposed to making it easier to acquire land more cheaply. Indeed, according to Roger Ransom:

Settlement of western lands had always been a major bone of contention for slave and free-labor farms. The manner in which the federal government distributed land to people could have a major impact on the nature of farming in a region. Northerners wanted to encourage the settlement of farms, which would depend primarily on family labor by offering cheap land in small parcels. Southerners feared that such a policy would make it more difficult to keep areas open for settlement by slaveholders who wanted to establish large plantations. This all came to a head with the "Homestead Act" of 1860 that would provide 160 acres of free land for anyone who wanted to settle and farm the land. Northern and western Congressmen strongly favored the bill in the House of Representatives but the measure received only a single vote from slave states' representatives. The bill passed, but President Buchanan vetoed it.

(Ransom 2001)

Indeed, the Homestead Act was not passed until 1862, when the South was not represented in Congress. Yet in the 1820s, southern Congressmen strongly favored cheap land policies and played a major role in the passage of the Preemption Act of 1830. More broadly, the South and West seemed to have been good candidates to be political allies against the manufacturing oriented northeast. Both regions, for example, favored lower tariffs. But after 1840, the South and West split on the issue of a liberal land policy.

On the removal vote in the Senate, all southern senators, including those who were anti-Jackson, voted for removal except one senator from Maryland, a border state (United States Congress 1830b). In the Senate, all northern Jackson supporters voted for removal and all opponents against.

In the House, the vote was more divided, but in the South, 65 Congressmen voted for removal and only 21 against. All Congressmen from Alabama, Mississippi, Georgia and South Carolina voted for removal. There was support for removal among non-Democrats who were not allies of Jackson. A total of 12 of 24 non-Democratic Congressmen in the South supported removal. (The vote is in United States Congress 1830a.)

The vote on removal was a showdown between the pro-Jackson and anti-Jackson representatives, but even without Jackson it may not have been possible for the Cherokee to stay in Georgia. The vote on removal was intertwined with the key issues of the day: state's rights, slavery, and land policy (Carlson and Roberts 2003).

The Cherokee and the State of Georgia

The Treaty of Hopewell in 1791 had not ended conflict on the southern frontier as both Washington and Knox had hoped. According to Perdue and Green:

The failure of the Treaty of Hopewell to end the encroachment of settlers and the resulting warfare between them and the Cherokees was, to Knox, "disgraceful." But the thousands of settlers who had entered the Cherokee Nation in violation of the treaty could hardly be removed. Instead, Knox and Washington believed that the United States should negotiate a new treaty with the Cherokees, buy the land the settlers illegally occupied, survey a new boundary, strictly prohibit any further encroachment, and take the first steps toward "civilizing" the Cherokees.

(Perdue and Green 1995: 11)

The goal of Knox and Washington to keep settlers out of Cherokee lands ultimately proved impossible. The goal of "civilizing" the Cherokee, however, was more successful because many members of the tribe chose to learn more American ways. The Cherokees responded to defeat in the American Revolution and the subsequent pressure to cede their territory by making significant changes in their society. Missionaries from New England were invited to set up schools to teach basic literacy in return for allowing these sects to preach the Christian gospel. The relationship created allies for the Cherokee among the missionary groups in New England as well as education. In a number of cases, Scottish traders among the Indians married Indian women and arranged for their children to receive a European education. These mixed-blood individuals were often the ones who established large plantations to grow cotton using slave labor on the American model. These individuals often played an important role in tribal affairs.

Sequoyah, a full-blooded Cherokee, brought about another major change when he invented a phonetic syllabary for the Cherokee language that allowed many Cherokee to become literate in their own language. A tribal newspaper, the *Cherokee Phoenix*, was published in both English and Cherokee, beginning in the late 1820s.

The Cherokee and other southeastern tribes made impressive changes but results were hardly uniformly positive. According to Wallace:

> But away from the agencies and the schools, and off the main roads lined with cotton plantations and comfortable inns, lived thousands of Native Americans who did not share in this prosperity and who were all too likely to turn to alcohol to dull the pain of poverty and loss. In the South, it would appear something like an Indian class system existed, perhaps a relic from pre-Colombian times, when differences in rank and privilege were the norm. . . .
>
> Most tribes were split into at least two factions, a pro-assimilation "progressive" faction and an anti-assimilation "conservative" faction. They debated fiercely and sometimes came to blows over acceptance or rejection of various white practices, from the Christian religion to English education to metal tools.

(Wallace 1993: 61)

The Cherokee made a transition from a division of labor where women grew crops and men hunted, to a system where men were more actively involved in farming. One result of this increased effort in farming was that more food could be produced on the remaining Cherokee lands. According to detailed calculations preformed by David Wishart (1995), at the time of the 1835 Census, the Cherokee generated a food surplus sufficient for the tribe to be self-supporting. This supports the view that the Cherokee were not the primitive hunters pictured by the defenders of removal.

The conflict between the State and the Cherokee

Georgia plays a special role in the removal of the Cherokee and Creek and other Indians from Georgia and the southeast. Importantly, Georgia was the only one of the original states where Indian tribes controlled most of the state's territory when the US achieved independence from Britain. This can be seen in Map 2.1. In 1789, white settlement in Georgia was limited to a band along the coast and the border with South Carolina, but the territorial claims of Georgia reached as far as the Mississippi River. As discussed earlier, all of the original states ceded their western claims to the federal government, but the last state to do so was Georgia, which only did so in 1802. Lands within the original states were not ceded to the federal government so federally owned public lands did not exist in its borders. This meant that any land ceded by Indian tribes in Georgia would be owned by the state, not the federal government.

Under the terms of the 1802 agreement with the State of Georgia, the federal government agreed to move Indians from the new boundaries of the state as soon as it could reach agreements with the tribes. As interpreted by Georgia politicians, this agreement required the federal government to eventually move all Indians out of Georgia. Indeed, throughout the years after 1790, there was a steady expansion of Georgians into land formerly controlled by Indians. Thus the demands of Georgia to open land in its state to white settlement was directly at odds with the expanding agriculture of the Cherokee.

A unique aspect of the conflict between Georgia and the Indians in that state was Georgia's system for selling its public lands. This developed after the notorious Yazoo Land case. In 1790, the Georgia legislature sold land along the Yazoo River in what was to become the State of Mississippi to a private land company for a fraction of its value, in return for outrageous bribes in the form of stock in the company. The next year, the people of Georgia elected a new group of legislators who tried to revoke the contract, but the Supreme Court ruled in 1795 that the contract was binding.

Distrust of the legislature contributed to Georgia's unique way of disposing of public lands. Unlike federal land, public land in Georgia acquired from Indian tribes after 1805 was distributed via a land lottery. Winners usually had the right to claim 202.5-acre plots.[6] Fees were just

Map 2.1 Indian land cessions until 1809
Source: Prucha (1990b: 22).

enough to pay the state for the costs of the lottery. Male citizens over 21,
widows, and orphans who had not already acquired public land from the
state could participate in the land lottery. Veterans, heads of households,
and others got extra chances. Winners had one year to claim land (Weiman
1991: 839). Land won through the lottery was often quickly sold in a
secondary market, allowing large planters to acquire the best cotton lands
quickly (Weiman 1991). While Alabama and Mississippi were also states

with substantial Indian populations, Georgia was exceptionally aggressive in pursuing the removal of Indians from its territory.

The movement to removal

After 1802, residents of Georgia waited impatiently for the opening of more Indian land for the expanding cotton economy. As shown in Maps 2.1–2.3, there was a steady cession of Indian land in the Old Southwest, but large tracts of Indian land remained in the hands of the Creek, Cherokee, Choctaw, Chickasaw, and Seminole, the so-called "Five Civilized Tribes." This was still the case after the Treaty of Fort Jackson in 1814, in which the chiefs of the lower Creek towns signed an agreement ceding much of the territory of both the Upper Creek in Alabama and their own territory in Georgia. The Cherokee had allied themselves with the United States in the War of 1812 with Great Britain and did not lose additional territory.

Even after the treaty of Fort Jackson, Andrew Jackson was able to persuade the Chickasaw, the Creek, and the Cherokee to cede additional vast tracts in Alabama, Mississippi, and Georgia. After 1820, agitation for moving more Indians out of the South became less intense in Alabama and Mississippi, but remained high in Georgia (Schoenleber 1986: 390–401).

President John Quincy Adams narrowly defeated Andrew Jackson (who had a plurality of the vote) in the election of 1824. He was sympathetic to southern claims to open Indian land to settlement but was reluctant to break treaties with Indian tribes. Jackson ran against Adams again in 1828 and won. Jackson represented the western wing of the Democratic Party and brought a more aggressive style to national politics and tended to favor the westerners, the poor, and the newly wealthy over older established interests in the east. This set the stage for a direct conflict between the impatient Georgia settlers and the increasingly politically sophisticated Cherokee.

From the Removal Act to removal

After the passage of the Indian Removal Act, the State of Georgia voted to extend its laws over the Cherokee nation. In doing this it outlawed the Cherokee national government, required a loyalty oath for white citizens living in the Cherokee nation, and created the Georgia guard to enforce state law in the Cherokee Nation (Perdue and Green 1995: 177). The state also authorized a land lottery to make Cherokee lands available to white settlers. The tribe challenged the state's actions in the Supreme Court, which struggled with the unique legal status of the tribe. In *Cherokee Nation v. Georgia* (1831) Chief Justice Marshall, writing for the majority of the court, expressed deep sympathy for the Cherokee, but found that the court did not have standing since the Cherokee were not a foreign nation, but a "Domestic Dependent Nation." A year later the case of Samuel Worchester, a missionary among the Cherokee, reached the Supreme Court. Worchester had been arrested by Georgia for entering Cherokee lands without a license. In that case the court reversed itself and found that all laws dealing with the Cherokee were unconstitutional and of no effect. According to Remini:

> Jackson is reported to have said on hearing the decision, "Well, John Marshall has made his decision: *now let him enforce it!*" Actually Jackson said no such thing. It certainly sounds like him, but he did not say it because there was nothing for him to enforce. The court had rendered its judgment, directed an action by the state's superior court, and then

Map 2.2 Indian land cessions until 1819

Source: Prucha (1990b: 23).

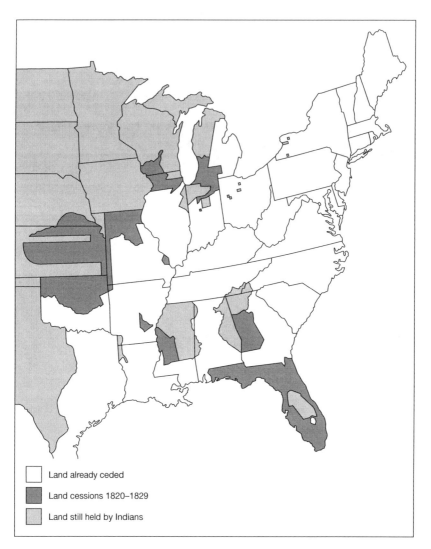

Map 2.3 Indian land cessions until 1829
Source: Prucha (1990b: 25).

adjourned. It would not reconvene until January 1833. Neither Georgia
nor the state's superior court responded to the order. . . . Rather, he
said that "the decision of the Supreme Court has fell still born, and
they find that it cannot coerce Georgia to yield to its mandate."

(Remini 2002: 24–25)

Even thought the Cherokee won the case, support was dwindling due
to the nullification crisis with South Carolina. Those who supported

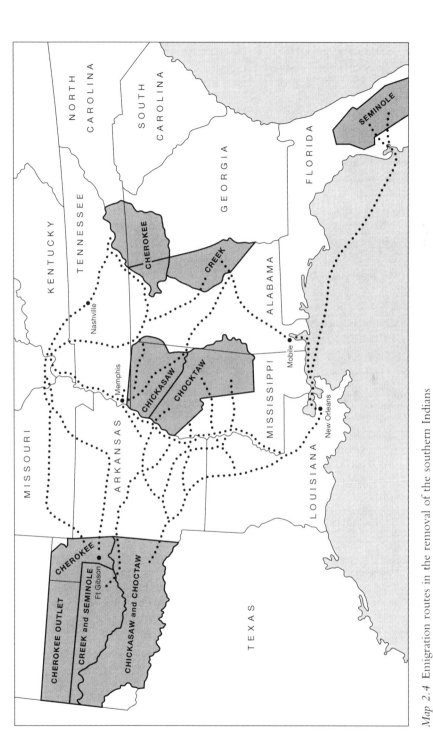

Map 2.4 Emigration routes in the removal of the southern Indians

Source: Prucha (1990b: 117).

the Cherokee also supported Jackson and the federal government versus South Carolina. The Governor of Georgia offered Samuel Worchester a pardon and he left the state.

Georgia went ahead with its land lottery in 1832, assigning land in the Cherokee nation to Georgia settlers. After Worchester, some among the Cherokee began to realize that they would not be supported in their efforts to stay in Georgia. A faction led by Major Ridge, Speaker of the Cherokee National Council, his son John Ridge, and son-in-law Elias Boudinot, editor of the tribe's newspaper, the *Cherokee Phoenix*, began to argue that removal was inevitable and that they should agree to move. The majority of the tribe, following Principal Chief John Ross, did not agree. The Treaty Party representing a minority of the tribe signed the treaty agreeing to removal. John Ross of the Treaty Party was later assassinated in the bitterness that continued when the tribe reached Oklahoma.

In the end all the Cherokee in Georgia were forced west (see Map 2.4) and John Ross was criticized by some for not leading his people to accept the inevitable. A thousand or so Cherokee remained in a remote part of North Carolina. They were protected by an earlier treaty, which gave them land under state jurisdiction, and a deal they made with General Scott who granted them the right to stay in return for the tribe's cooperation in a murder case.

Alternatives to removal?

Was there an alternative to removal for the Cherokee and the other Indians moved from the southeast? Simply allowing the Cherokee nation to function under its constitution of 1828 would have created massive enforcement problems. This is the view that Remini and Prucha hold. Georgia's 1832 land lottery gave settlers a legal claim to land in the Cherokee nation. But even without that incentive, settlers undoubtedly would have continued to move into unoccupied Indian land. Troops commanded by Andrew Jackson had had to remove illegal settlers from Creek lands in the 1820s. After 1830, squatters moved on to land that tribes had ceded in Alabama and Mississippi, but which was supposed to remain exclusively in Indian hands until the Indians moved. Settlers fully expected that their claims would be legitimized, as had other squatters on Indian or federal land. Had federal troops tried to remove settlers from Cherokee lands in the 1830s there would have been a confrontation between federal and state authority and no one wanted that at the time.

It would have taken a very strong central government to prevent this settlement. The British had tried to prevent such settlement in colonial times and failed. This was made extremely difficult in the 1830s by the twin issues of slavery and state's rights. State's rights in the 1830s were closely tied to the concerns of white southerners who wished to protect slavery from federal intervention as slaveholders became an increasingly small minority in the United States. Indian removal was an issue for state's rights and slavery since Georgia was asserting its claims as an original state. The land covered by the Indian Removal Act was all in states where slavery was legal.

As a tribe, the Cherokee were not opposed to slavery. Wealthy members of the tribe owned slaves on the typical southern model. Indeed after removal to Oklahoma an influential segment of Indian society backed the South in the Civil War (1861–1865). The complaint against the Cherokee was that they were denying white southerners access to cotton land and preventing the spread of slavery fast enough.

One alternative that was considered at the time was to grant Indians regular state title to the land that they occupied. Indeed, granting title to land to Indians in "allotments" was part of the removal treaties concluded with Indians in Alabama and Mississippi. In practice it did not work. Federal officials issued allotments to individuals, giving them title to the farms they had built or to elicit cooperation by key leaders. In fact most of this land was quickly sold and the owners moved on (see Young 1961). Only in North Carolina (Cherokee) and Mississippi (Choctaw) did small bands of Indian farmers remain behind. Staying in place would make Indians a small minority in the states in which they lived and many understandably were concerned about how well their rights would be protected from the majority.

If the Cherokee and the other tribes had remained in Georgia, large tracts of land could have remained idle. There were only about 22,000 or so Cherokee in Georgia, occupying the northwest corner of the state (Thornton 1991: 78). In a market economy such lands would be transferred to higher valued uses through sale or lease. But non-Indians couldn't buy land in the Cherokee nation. White men sometimes acquired land by marrying Indian women, or settling illegally. Looking ahead in history, the same problems arose in the Indian nations in Oklahoma in the latter part of the nineteenth century as that land became more densely populated. Some Indian families claimed large territories that they in turn leased to whites. In the "Indian Territory" there was also a problem of lawlessness since non-Indians would move into the Indian nation to escape state authorities.

The institutional problem was the uncertain status of Indian tribes in the Anglo-American legal system. A virtue of that system is the fact that property rights are relatively secure from the state and this gives individuals protection from confiscation by government authorities without due process and just compensation. But the system is based on the assumption that all land was originally owned by the sovereign. But it was not clear how to recognize Indian rights in that legal system. What might have been done? Beginning in the 1850s federal policy began to recognize Indian reserves (reservations) – land set aside for tribes. The reservation system that evolved much later in the nineteenth and twentieth centuries solves the problem by making crimes on the reservation federal crimes with federal law enforcement working with tribal law enforcement to keep order on the reservation for both Indians and non-Indians. An institutional failure here was the fact that in US law towards Indians, as it evolved in the eighteenth and nineteenth centuries, there was no way to blend tribal control with the power of the state. Thus Prucha (1969) sees the prospect of simply having allowed the southern Indians to hold their land under state jurisdiction as "immediate assimilation." Such immediate assimilation presented practical problems of how Indians would adjust to a market economy. This could have easily led to the kind of "outdoor slums" that Wallace describes. Insofar as Indians wanted to preserve their heritage and work in their common interests, there was no clear model. The prevailing wisdom of the time was either separate Indians from whites or have the Indians move west to give them more time to adjust to the spread of settlement. This was based in part on the incorrect assumption that there was more land in the west of the Mississippi River than anyone would want for a long time. When this proved false, policy gradually shifted to the establishment of the reservations on more limited areas.

Taking the later reservation system as a model, allowing the Cherokee to remain in Georgia would have required the creation of a kind of reservation with federal marshals to enforce criminal law on Indians and whites. Such federal authority would have been hard to create in the South with the belief in state's rights and a belief that this right was needed to protect slavery. Another difficult problem for a reservation system would have been whether or not to allow whites to buy land in Indian country. In the 1890s the Five Tribes in Oklahoma again lost their sovereignty with the dissolution of the tribal governments and the division of tribal property among registered members of the tribe. Land was held under state title. The system allowed for the rapid sale of massive amounts of land to white settlers and some Indians were defrauded out of their land. As in New York State, Indians and whites blended and over time a more limited form of tribal rights emerged.

If there had been less pressure from the citizens of the State of Georgia, and less pressure from slaveholders throughout the South to open new lands to settlement, it is conceivable that, with time, institutions that allowed more autonomy could have evolved; for example, tribal government similar to that of the Mohawk and Seneca Indians in New York or the Cherokee Nation in Oklahoma today. These are federally recognized tribes, which control limited tribal areas, but most of their members live on lands within state jurisdiction. Getting to this solution would not have been easy. The Cherokee in North Carolina and the Choctaw in Mississippi experienced hard times during the nineteenth and early twentieth centuries. The Choctaw Tribe in Mississippi today have thriving tribal enterprises that range from manufacturing to gambling casinos.

In the end, however, given the institutions that existed in 1830, I agree with Prucha and Remini that there was no way that the federal government could have protected the rights of the Cherokee against the pressures of the State of Georgia and squatters willing to defy federal authority and move on to unoccupied lands. It would have taken a very strong federal government, much stronger than existed in the years before 1860, to enforce the boundaries of the Indian nations. And a strong federal government was a challenge to state authority that implied that in the future the federal government could threaten the rights of citizens in the states to own slaves.

Notes

* This chapter was first presented at the International Economic History Association Congress, Buenos Aires, 2002. Thanks to Claudio Saunt, Richard Sutch, and Susan Carter for comments. Jerry Thursby provided valuable organizational insights and John Juricek provided very helpful comments on the nature of how the English treated the land rights of Indian tribes and the nature of southeastern Indian institutions. As usual, they are not responsible for any remaining errors.

1 The "Black Hawk War" of 1831–1832 was an exception to this generalization, although Prucha argues that this brief conflict could have been avoided if the government had more effectively dealt with "squatters" on Indian lands and treated the Sac and Fox Indians more honorably (1984: 256).
2 Homesteading, the practice of granting land to actual settlers for free after a period of years of occupancy, in particular has been criticized as wasteful (see Anderson and Hill 1990).
3 For a discussion of these issues see Atack and Passell 1994: 260–270.
4 It has been estimated that it was ideal to have roughly $1,000 in cash in order to start a 40-acre farm, a considerable sum in those days. Atack and Passell argue that only the top one fourth of farmers had this much wealth. Even establishing a tenant farm was out of the reach of roughly one third of the population. See Atack and Passell (1994: 278–279) and Atack *et al.* (2000).
5 The Homestead Act was passed long after preemption and primarily affected settlement west of the Mississippi River, so Kanazawa and Allen are addressing different times and places to some degree.
6 Not all plots were of the same size. In early allotments there were cases of 490-acre plots in 1805 and 1820 and 250-acre plots in some counties in 1820. In 1832, there was a special lottery of 40-acre parcels in gold country in addition to a regular lottery. Fragments were auctioned off at the state capital. See the Georgia Secretary of State web site, http://www.sos.state.ga.us/archives/rs/lotteries.htm #intro (accessed April 6, 2003).

Bibliography

Allen, D.W. (1991) "Homesteading and Property Rights. Or, 'How the West was Really Won'," *Journal of Law and Economics*, 34: 1–23.
Anderson, T.L. and Hill, P.J. (1990) "The Race for Property Rights," *Journal of Law and Economics*, 33: 177–197.
Anderson, W.L. (ed.) (1991) *Cherokee Removal: Before and After*, Athens, GA: University of Georgia Press.
Atack, J. and Passell, P. (1994) *A New Economic View of American History*, New York: W.W. Norton & Co.

——, Bateman, F., and Parker, W. (2000) "Northern Agriculture and the Westward Movement," in S. Engerman and Robert Gallman (eds) *The Cambridge Economic History of the United States, Volume II*, New York and Cambridge: Cambridge University Press.

Barrington, L. (1999) "Native Americans and Economic History," in L. Barrington (ed.) *The Other Side of the Frontier*, Boulder, CO: Westview Press.

Carlson, L.A. (1985) "What Was it Worth? Economic and Historical Aspects of Determining Awards in Indian Land Claims Cases," in I. Sutton (ed.) *Irredeemable America: The Indians Estate and Land Claims*, Albuquerque, NM: University of New Mexico Press.

—— and Roberts, M. (2003) "Indian Lands, 'Squatterism,' and Sectional Alliances: Economic Interests and the Passage of the Indian Removal Act of 1830," Working paper, Emory University.

Coleman, K. (1978) *Georgia History in Outline*, revised edition, Athens, GA: University of Georgia Press.

Cooper, W. and Terrill, T. (2002) *The American South: A History, Vol. I*, New York: McGraw Hill.

Hagan, W.T. (1979) *American Indians*, revised edition, Chicago, IL: University of Chicago Press.

Juricek, J.T. (ed.) (1989) *Georgia Treaties, 1733–1763*, Washington, DC: University Press of America. [Vol. 11 of *Early American Indian Documents: Treaties and Laws, 1607–1789*, A.T. Vaughn, general editor.]

Kanazawa, M.T. (1996) "Possession is Nine Points of the Law: The Political Economy of Early Public Land Disposal," *Explorations in Economic History*, 33: 227–249.

Martis, K.C. (1982) *The Historical Atlas of the United States 1789–1983*. London: Collier Macmillan Publishers.

Parsons, S., Beach, W.W., and Hermann, D. (1978) *United States Congressional Districts 1788–1841*, Westport, CT: Greenwood Press.

Perdue, T. and Green, M.D. (eds) (1995) *The Cherokee Removal*, Boston, MA: Bedford Books.

Prucha, F.P. (1969) "Andrew Jackson's Indian Policy: A Reassessment," *Journal of American History*, 26: 527–539.

—— (1984) *The Great Father, Vol. I*, Lincoln, NE: University of Nebraska Press.

—— (ed.) (1990a) *Documents of American Indian Policy*, second edition, expanded, Lincoln, NE: University of Nebraska Press.

—— (1990b) *Atlas of American Indian Affairs*, Lincoln, NE: University of Nebraska Press.

Ransom, R.L. (2001) "The Economics of the Civil War," *EH.Net Encyclopedia*, edited by R. Whaples, August 25, 2001. Available at http://www.eh.net/encyclopedia/contents/ransom.civil.war.us.php.

Remini, R.V. (1981) *Andrew Jackson: Volume Two, The Course of American Freedom, 1822–1832*, Baltimore, MD: The Johns Hopkins University Press.

—— (2001) *Andrew Jackson and His Indian Wars*. New York: Viking Books.

—— (2002), "Jackson Versus the Cherokee Nation," *Chicago History*, 30: 22–35.

Robbins, R.M. (1962) [originally published, 1942] *Our Landed Heritage: The Public Domain, 1776–1936*. Lincoln, NE: University of Nebraska Press.

Roberts, M.A. (1997) "Terms of Surrender: An Econometric Analysis of the Congressional Vote on Removal," Honors thesis, Emory University, Atlanta, GA.

Schoenleber, C.H. (1986) "The Rise of the New West," Dissertation, University of Wisconsin, Madison, WI.

Statz, R.N. (1991) "Rhetoric Versus Reality: The Indian Policy of Andrew Jackson," in W.L. Anderson (ed.) *Cherokee Removal: Before and After*, Athens, GA: University of Georgia Press.

Thornton, R. (1991) "The Demography of the Trail of Tears Period: A New Estimate of Cherokee Population Losses," in W. Anderson (ed.) *Cherokee Removal: Before and After*, Athens, GA: University of Georgia Press.

United States Census Office (1821) *Census for 1820*, Washington, DC: GPO.

United States Congress (1830a) *Journal of the House of Representatives of the United States 21st Congress, First Session*, Washington, DC: GPO.

United States Congress (1830b) *Register of Debates in Congress*, Vol. 6, Washington, DC: Gales and Seaton Publishers.

Wallace, A.F.C. (1993) *The Long Bitter Trail: Andrew Jackson and the Indians*, New York: Hill & Wang.

Walton, G. and Rockoff, H. (1998) *History of the American Economy*, eighth edition, Fort Worth, TX: Dryden Press, Harcourt Brace & Co.

Weiman, D. (1991) "Peopling the Land by Lottery? The Market in Public Lands and the Regional Differentiation of Territory on the Georgia Frontier," *Journal of Economic History*, 51: 835–860.

Wilder, L.I. (1953) [first published 1935] *Little House on the Prairie*, New York: Scholastic Press.

Wishart, D.M. (1995) "Evidence of Surplus Production in the Cherokee Nation Prior to Removal," *Journal of Economic History*, 55: 120–138.

Young, M. (1961) *Redskins, Ruffleshirts, and Rednecks: Indian Allotments in Alabama and Mississippi, 1830–1860*, Norman, OK: University of Oklahoma Press.

3 Ethno-nationality and property rights in land in Prussian Poland, 1886–1918

Buying the land from under the Poles' feet?*

Scott M. Eddie

Introduction

A full seventy years after the 1815 Congress of Vienna had sanctioned the earlier partition of Poland among Prussia, Russia, and Austria, Prussia was still having difficulty digesting her Polish provinces. The "Polish Question" had, by 1885, become one of the German Reich's most pressing problems (Grześ 1979: 202).[1] Where earlier the Prussian government had attempted to Prussianize the Poles through language, schooling, and religious restrictions, the seemingly relentless increase in the sheer numbers of Poles led the government, in 1886, to a direct anti-Polish demographic policy. The centerpiece of this policy was an attempt to change the population proportions in favor of ethnic Germans by settling German farmers on the land in the "Polish Provinces." The "Royal Prussian Settlement Commission in the Provinces of West Prussia and Poznania" (*Königlich preußische Ansiedlungskommission in den Provinzen West Preussen und Posen*),[2] established by the law of April 26, 1886 "concerning the promotion of German settlement in the provinces of West Prussia and Poznania", was to buy up large landed properties from Poles, subdivide these properties into smaller farms, and settle German peasants on the parcels. In this way "the proven Germanizing power of the German peasantry" (National Liberal Party deputy Enecerus, as quoted in Galos 1969: 49) could be brought to bear on the demographic problem: the advantage of large numbers and the influence of increasing share in the population were thus to begin to turn to favor the German side over the Poles.

Table 3.1, showing the ethnic distribution of population in Prussia's four eastern provinces, illustrates why the focus of settlement fell on Poznania (primarily) and West Prussia (definitely secondarily, see Figures 3.3 and 3.4 on pp. 61–62).

Buying land from Poles was not the *object* of the exercise, but merely the *instrument* by which the Prussian government sought to change the demographic balance in favor of Germans. The Prussians did not regard Polish

Map 3.1 Central Europe, 1910
Source: Magocsi (2002: 118).

land ownership per se as a threat to their hegemony; indeed, both Polish and German farmers could take advantage of later policies to establish the *Rentengut* (annuity property) form of ownership in the eastern provinces (see the section on "consolidating" German landownership, below). But because many large estates were owned by Polish nobles, purchasing these

Table 3.1 Population by mother tongue, 1890

Province	German*	Polish**	Other	German* %	Polish** %	Other %
East Prussia	1,525,920	316,190	116,553	77.9	16.1	6.0
West Prussia	949,117	483,957	607	66.2	33.8	0.0
Poznania	702,357	1,048,576	709	40.1	59.9	0.0
Silesia	3,153,888	999,885	70,685	74.7	23.7	1.7

Source: *Statistisches Handbuch des Preußischen Staates*, vol. 2 (Berlin, 1898): 99, 118–119. The year 1890 chosen because of more accurate definition of mother tongue than in previous censuses (Buzek 1909: 538).

Notes:
* includes individuals who have two mother tongues.
** includes small numbers speaking Masurian, Kassubian, and Wendish.

estates and parceling them out to Germans in family-size farms could achieve two of Bismarck's goals at once: to disestablish the group that he regarded as the principal agitators for Polish nationalism, and to move significant numbers of ethnic Germans into the Polish territories (Kouschil 2002: 5). Moreover, establishing German family farms that could be operated with no outside labor would also help prevent the employment of Polish labor in the settlements (AK 1907: 47), strengthening the desired demographic impact.

The process, in its extreme form, would have worked as the Polish MP von Brodnicki complained that it did:

> The main thing is not that the Polish owner, with his family, abandons the manor house. What happens to the hundreds of Polish farm workers, who up to this time have lived peaceably on their native soil in the Polish districts? As soon as the estates are bought, the parcel-lization carried out, and the settlement takes place, they are summarily driven out without mercy, because they are Poles and because the law has given itself the task of settling only Germans, and displacing and rooting out the Poles. Thus thousands upon thousands have become unemployed and homeless since the establishment of this law.
>
> (PSA, I Rep 87B, Nr 9600, sheet 141)

Others saw the outcome differently. Hans Delbrück, who favored forcibly expropriating Polish lands and resettling their former owners in West Germany (Grześ 1979: 207), contended that the land purchases of the Settlement Commission (hereafter SC) actually enhanced the Polish position in land ownership: debt-ridden Polish landlords sold their neglected and poorly cultivated estates to the SC at high prices, paid off their debts, and then bought better land with the net proceeds, often in the same district and often from Germans, where they of course employed Polish labor to operate their newly acquired property (Delbrück 1894). Moreover, there were Polish settlement societies and settlement banks competing directly or indirectly with the SC in the same districts, thus introducing a "battle for the land" (*Kampf um den Boden*), about which more later.

Each of these views is strongly colored by ethnic nationalism. While it is both difficult and beyond the scope of this chapter to try to determine the ultimate demographic effect of the SC's settlement activities (which, in total, brought in about 22,000 families, some 150,000 persons in all, to the 2 provinces) (Grześ et al. 1976: 268), the SC did try to follow the fate of 170 Polish landlords who had sold it a total of 175 properties. It managed to find out what happened to 154 of them:

22 bought other properties, only 1 out of province
3 leased land in either Poznania or West Prussia
15 settled on their other properties in Poznania or West Prussia

18 changed occupation
61 "have beeñ without occupation"
33 emigrated
2 were legal persons.

(AK 1907: 40)

While these data say nothing of the fate of the former Polish laborers on these estates, they do imply that Brodnicki presented a more accurate view than did Delbrück: only 24 of the 154 Polish landlords (15.6 percent) – the 21 who bought, and the 3 who leased, property in Poznania or West Prussia – could have exhibited Delbrückian behavior; all the rest clearly did not.

But the question is really moot: exactly at the time that Brodnicki was making his argument, a Polish boycott of land sales to the SC reduced the opportunity to buy Polish estates to near zero; the SC reported that it could purchase Polish estates "only rarely and only through a middleman" after about 1902 (AK 1907: 24). In fact, as Figures 3.1 and 3.2 show clearly, the increase in land purchases which began with the major budget increase of 1898 coincided exactly with a strong drop-off in the share of total land purchased from Poles.

The SC, headquartered in the city of Posen (Poznań), began its opera- tion with a total budget of 100 million marks. First augmented in 1898, and more frequently thereafter, the resources available to the SC during its active lifetime (1886–1918) amounted to about 955 million marks (Grześ *et al.* 1976: 268). Purchases of land took about half of this total, so admin- istration, parcellization, building of infrastructure, etc. accounted for the

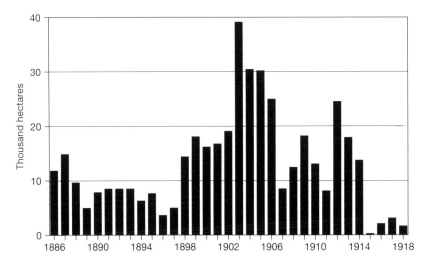

Figure 3.1 Estate purchases by the Settlement Commission
Source: Reports of the Settlement Commission.

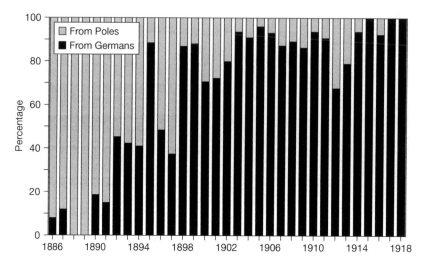

Figure 3.2 Estate purchases by the Settlement Commission (in percentage of the total area purchased annually)

Source: Reports of the Settlement Commission.

rest. The SC bought 828 "estates"[3] with a total area of 430,450 hectares (1 hectare is equal approximately to 2.5 acres), at an overall cost of 443 million marks. It also purchased 631 "peasant farms" totaling 30,434 hectares for 44.5 million marks. Of the 828 estates, the SC bought 214 (115,525 ha.) from Poles for 96.4 million marks and 614 (314,926 ha.) from Germans for 346.7 million marks. For the 631 peasant farms, the figures were 274 (11,152 ha.) for 16.6 million marks and 357 (19,282 ha.) for 27.9 million marks, from Poles and Germans, respectively (Eddie and Kouschil 2002: 4).

With regard to the timing of these purchases, as we have noted above, "by the time the SC received its first major budget infusion in 1898, its purchases from Poles had dropped off significantly" (Eddie and Kouschil 2002: 8). The SC's greatest activity in the land market occurred from 1898 through 1906. Purchases peaked in 1903 at nearly 40,000 hectares (Eddie and Kouschil 2002: 8).

The SC entered the land market in the same ways that other buyers did. It both received and solicited offers of sales from intermediaries; many owners contacted it directly about the potential purchase of their properties, and it occasionally attended auctions of property (such as foreclosure sales). Besides its budget, it had other restrictions on its activities, imposed from above or, as in the case of its refusal to bid against German buyers at foreclosure sales, self-imposed. To go beyond certain pricing guidelines, expressed in terms of purchase price per mark of land tax assessment or per hectare of land area, the SC had to obtain ministerial approval. Otherwise, its own local executive committee discussed and either approved or rejected each individual purchase (PSA, I Rep 87B). Besides financial limitations, the most important restriction on the SC's purchases was the requirement to obtain ministerial permission to purchase land from a German *in each individual case* (PSA, I Rep 87B and I Rep 90a). After 1896, however – when the supply of properties available for purchase from Poles had begun to shrink noticeably – the council of ministers gave blanket permission for such purchases.

Although the SC had a much freer hand after 1896 in the purchase of individual properties, it still had to adopt an overall strategy because its budget was not unlimited. It decided, as a general policy, to concentrate on those ridings where its purchases had the promise of creating (or maintaining) a German population majority, or at least a strong minority of Germans. It thus tried to avoid buying in areas where the German majority was already very strong, as well as in areas where the German minority was so small that there was no hope of bringing it to significant size. It did, however, violate these general rules in specific cases: e.g., the SC would make a "defensive purchase" of German property, even in a heavily German area, if it were threatened with purchase by a Pole, especially if the German school or church system might thereby be put in danger (AK 1907: 23). Figures 3.3 and 3.4 show the results of the strategy up to the outbreak of World War I.

Figure 3.3 shows clearly that the SC concentrated its activities in the province of Poznania, where both the German share in land ownership and

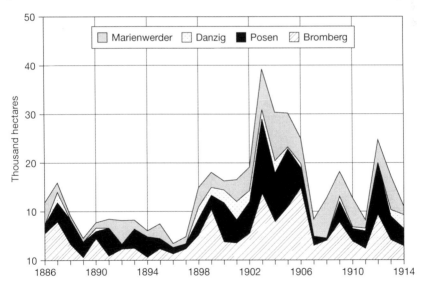

Figure 3.3 Settlement Commission purchases of estates, by *Regierungsbezirk.*
Source: Reports of the Settlement Commission.

Note:
Marienweder and Danzig in West Prussia; Posen and Bromberg in Poznania.

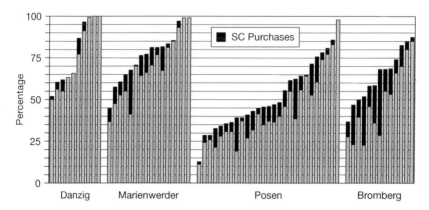

Figure 3.4 Share of all land purchased by Settlement Commission by the end of
1913 and share of all land owned by Germans, by riding.

Source: PSA I Rep 151 IC, Finanz-Ministerium, Nr. 12506.

Note:
Ridings in each RB arranged in ascending order of German land ownership in May 1914.

the German share in total population were much smaller than in West
Prussia. Germans made up about two-thirds of the population of West
Prussia, but only about 40 percent of the population of Poznania in 1890
(see Table 3.1 on p. 57). Their share in land ownership in 1914 was 76
percent and 59 percent, respectively (calculated from data appearing in PSA,
I Rep 87B, Nr 9624, sheets 57–60).

Figure 3.4 shows details of the purchase policy by riding. In all cases it
exaggerates the effect of the SC on the ethnic distribution of land ownership, since only purchases from Poles would *change* this distribution, while
purchases from Germans would not. But since the goal was population, not
land ownership per se, purchase from a German might still have (indeed
was likely to have) displaced Polish farm laborers in favor of German settlers.

By and large the picture from Figure 3.4 is consistent with the overall
strategy outlined above: we find the SC's purchases heavily concentrated in
Poznania, in absolute measure in the *Regierungsbezirk* ("Administrative
District," hereafter RB) of Posen, but relatively much more strongly in the
RB of Bromberg, where its purchases of "estates" amounted, cumulatively,
to some 14.5 percent of all the land.[4] In other areas where the German land
ownership share was three-quarters or more, the SC hardly bought any
land at all.

Did the SC pay "too much" for the land it bought?

A recurring theme in the literature on the activities of the SC is that competition between it and Polish settlement societies and banks – the "battle

for the land" – drove land prices up beyond all reason in the areas in which
the SC operated.[5] Even the SC itself believed that it had had this effect (AK
1907: 37). Because this appeared self-evident, the literature never really
confronts the other question of whether, in the absence of a general price-
raising effect, the SC could nevertheless have overpaid for the properties
that it bought. This could have occurred, for example, if political considerations (or corruption) drove the SC to offer unreasonably high prices
for particular individual properties, while keeping out of the competition
for the others offered on the market.

A basic familiarity with the land market in Prussia, and some simple economic reasoning, would argue strongly against the thesis that the "battle for
the land" drove land prices in general to economically unreasonable heights.
Consider the following:

1   Through the end of 1913, the SC had bought up about 5.4 percent of
    the land in West Prussia and 10.4 percent in Poznania.[6] Converted to
    an annual rate of purchase over 28 years, this amount appears too small
    to have had a major demand-led effect on the overall price level for
    agricultural land.
2   Over time, taking this much land out of the market could have raised
    prices through a supply restriction. But the ultimate supply-restricting
    effect, while not zero, must have been much smaller than the demand
    enhancement, since the German settlers could in fact resell their land
    – just not to a Pole.
3   It would be difficult to contend that all private buyers, or even the
    majority, could be permanently seized by irrationality, paying prices far
    beyond those which would earn them the going rate of return on their
    capital. The market for agricultural land in one region cannot operate
    in isolation from that in adjoining regions in the same country, even
    though differences in prices of land of comparable type and quality may
    exist from region to region (e.g., because of differences in proximity to
    major markets or transportation facilities). Buyers have the opportunity
    to look in other areas for purchases if they find the prices in one area
    too high. If the competition between the SC and the Polish settlement
    agencies had driven the prices of land in the region where they oper-
    ated out of all relation to the value of the land for use in production
    or consumption, then private buyers, motivated by economic consid-
    erations, would have disappeared from the market there. That they did
    not, and that they even outbid the SC for some properties it was inter-
    ested in, is prima facie evidence that this competition did not drive up
    the general level of land prices beyond all reason.

If we accept the preceding argument, the SC still could have paid "too much"
for some or all of the individual properties that it purchased without driving
up the general price level beyond what existing economic forces would

have produced. There are data available which allow us, for at least one area where the SC was active, to test the paid-too-much thesis statistically.

In 1893, as part of Finance Minister Miquel's tax reform package, Prussia enacted a wealth tax, which fell on land as well as other assets. For purposes of assessing this tax, the Finance Ministry charged the district cadastral offices with the duty of collecting data on all land transactions (see the Appendix on pp. 80–82 for details of these data).

Only a few of what had been copious records[7] of such transactions have survived. I have been able to find these price records for only one riding (*Kreis*) where the SC operated. This was the riding of Wirsitz (Wyrzysk) in the Administrative District of Bromberg (Bydgoszcz) in the province of Poznania. During the years 1901 through 1913, the SC bought 25 large properties in the riding of Wirsitz, totaling 15,687 hectares, or 13.5 percent of the territory of the riding. In only three of the 28 ridings in RB Posen, and in four of the 14 ridings in RB Bromberg did the SC purchase a higher share of the land. In terms of total land purchased (including peasant properties), the SC purchases in the riding of Wirsitz were just about at the average for the RB Bromberg (15.0 percent versus 14.5 percent, respectively). The choice of Wirsitz therefore ranks, fortunately for the purposes to which we wish to put the data, among the ridings where the SC was most active. If the SC's activities in the land market drove up land prices, it should have driven them up in *Kreis* Wirsitz.

The data on private land purchases in the riding of Wirsitz are missing for the years 1901 through 1903, and for 1912 and 1913, but we do have the full details for 157 privately purchased properties of 5 hectares or larger[8] in size for the years 1903 through 1911. In this same interval the SC purchased 19 properties, totaling 11,556 hectares. I have chosen to compare these purchases in two ways:

1   To compare actual price paid by the SC for a given property to the price it might have commanded in the private market (the price predicted from regression coefficients for the determinants of land prices in private sales).
2   To pool the two groups of properties in a single regression, using a dummy variable to identify SC purchases, and look at the coefficients estimated for variables using the dummy, assessing their sign and significance. The first method will use the net, or corrected, price and a simpler form of the regression; the second will use the actual price paid and include more explanatory variables. Details follow.

The cadastral officials had not only to record the actual price paid for each property sold in their district, they also were to calculate, when appropriate, a "net price" (*Reinpreis*), by adjusting for such things as discount (or premium) paid by a relative, missing or particularly good inventory, the existence of a *Gasthaus* or other enterprise on the property, and so forth.

The net price was supposed to be the normal price that the property, with standard inventory, would have commanded on the local market as an agricultural enterprise in a typical arm's-length sale. This net price, deflated to constant 1913 marks using the Jacobs-Richter wholesale price index (Jacobs and Richter 1935), became the dependent variable in the first regressions. The better the cadastral officials did in their calculations, the more variance they should have removed from the determination of price. As we shall see in Table 3.2 on p. 66, they appear to have done very well indeed.

Ideally, the independent variables should have been the amounts of different types of land in each property, adjusted for quality (see Appendix for discussion). Limitations of the data on purchases by the SC – it recorded the area of plow land, garden, meadow, etc., but not their individual tax assessments, only the *total* taxable net yield for the property as a whole – have required the use of areas, rather than tax assessments, for the individual land types, but this does not materially affect the power of the regressions, as we will see. Especially within a small geographical area like a single riding, the variations in quality are not likely to be so great as they would be over a larger area, and that appears to have been the case here.

Because prices of different agricultural products will change at different rates, the relative prices of the various land types may change as the relative prices of the products produced by those land types change. In turn, land prices in general may not follow the overall price index exactly. Therefore the price paid for a farm in, say, 1900, when deflated to marks of general 1913 purchasing power, may be very different from the price at which that farm would have sold in 1913. For this reason, an additional set of independent variables, each of which represents a trend factor applied to each of the basic independent variables, has been added to the equation. This trend variable was simply the product of (*year of purchase* – *1913*) and the value of the variable for the given observation. The value of this composite variable in every case was negative, except in 1913, when it was uniformly zero. Thus a positive coefficient would indicate a trend toward increasing value over time for this type of land, and negative coefficient a trend toward decreasing value.

The foregoing considerations produced an estimating equation of the following general form (*Equation 1*):

$$DeflatedNetPrice = f(PlowArea, PlowAreaTrend, GardenArea,$$
$$GardenAreaTrend, \ldots, FarmYardArea,$$
$$FarmYardAreaTrend)$$

An additional variable, the building tax value, is available in the Finance Ministry forms, but not for the properties purchased by the SC. In Table 3.2, regressions with and without this variable are presented as a check on how important building value might be in price determination.

Preliminary regressions using all land types as independent variables showed several variables – water, moor, unproductive land, and farmyard – to be statistically insignificant in all regressions; these were therefore dropped from the final estimating equation used. Moreover, there was a saving in degrees of freedom with no loss of explanatory power by combining some of the remaining land types: plow land and garden were added into a single variable,[9] as were pasture and woodland. These combinations therefore also grouped different types of land according to intensity of cultivation. Finally, regressions were run both with and without a constant term. Suppressing the constant has virtually no effect on the power of the estimating equation, as theory tells us it should not have: a positive significant constant term would amount to a payment for nothing, or a uniform bonus to landowners for selling a property of any size to the SC. I therefore used the regression without a constant term. The results are shown in Table 3.2.

We see from these data that using area, rather than tax value, still provides remarkably strong explanatory power for our analysis of the determination of land prices. Much of the "tight fit" of the equation may be due to the cadastral officials' accuracy in removing anomalies from the prices paid, but this is, of course, no disadvantage for this particular calculation.

While the coefficient for building tax value was statistically significant in the regressions for Table 3.2, we can see from the numbers that it did not add much to the explanatory power of the equation, i.e., it was lacking in "oomph," to use Professor McCloskey's distinction. This is fortunate for our purposes, since the tax value of buildings was not reported for properties purchased by the SC. Please note two considerations in this regard:

Table 3.2 Price determination regressions for private purchases

Dependent variable: DeflatedNetPrice	Regressions with the building tax value		Regressions without the building tax value	
Independent variable	Coefficient	Std error	Coefficient	Std error
Plow + Garden hectares	941	80.5	1,028	76.1
Plow + Garden trend	0.58	13.8	6.43	13.5
Meadow hectares	3,739	401	4,421	357
Meadow trend	389	68.3	480	64.9
Wood + Pasture hectares	1,383	378	1,660	381
Wood + Pasture trend	47.6	74.2	79.3	76.0
BldgTaxValue marks	53.2	17.2	–	–
BldgTaxValue trend	6.13	2.19	–	–
Standard error of estimate		6,327		6,561
Mean of dependent variable		29,240		29,240
R^2	0.987		0.986	
Number of observations	157		157	
Degrees of freedom	149		151	

(1) as a normal rule, the larger the property, the smaller the share of buildings in its total value; and (2) the properties purchased by the SC were considerably larger, on average, than the rest of the properties in the sample. Leaving building value out of the estimating equation tends to inflate the coefficients of the different land types, both in theory and in practice (see comparative values in Table 3.2), which would bias upward the predicted values for SC purchases calculated from these coefficients. Therefore, if the predicted prices of properties purchased by the SC are not lower than the actual prices paid by the SC, the conclusion that the SC did not overpay would be all the stronger.

The coefficients estimated from the regressions in Table 3.2, when applied to the values of the corresponding variables for the properties purchased by the SC, yield the results presented in Table 3.3.

Let us first consider the totals from the table. Overall, it appears that the SC did not appreciably overpay for the properties it purchased in the riding of Wirsitz. This confirms the result of a cruder calculation with almost the same set of properties from an earlier paper (Eddie and Kouschil 2002: 22). We also see that, for individual properties, there is a wide variance between the actual and predicted prices. Can we observe any pattern in these variations?

There is some positive correlation (0.326) between the share of plow land, garden, and meadow in a given property and the size of the percentage difference between actual and predicted prices, so the SC appears to have been somewhat willing to pay extra for properties that had high shares of arable land. A somewhat weaker positive correlation with the year of purchase of the property (0.215) is also apparent, implying some small tendency to pay a bigger premium in later years. Larger properties appear to have been somewhat less desirable than smaller ones, with size of property and premium paid showing a negative correlation of −0.443.

None of these correlations is strikingly high, however, indicating that there were other factors entering into the price differences that we have not easily captured in the regressions or the correlations. And, of course, none of this explains anything about the "bargains": why in some cases did the SC seem to enjoy a substantial discount from what a property should have been worth in the market? Perhaps it was "other factors," perhaps it was because the SC typically bought a kind of property that did not often enter onto the market, and therefore the coefficients estimated from another set of properties do not fit these very well.

It is likely that the only way to answer these questions definitively would be to examine the archival record of each individual purchase. Since that is beyond the scope of the present chapter, suffice it here to note that the bargains just about exactly offset the overpayments, so no general tendency to overpay can be observed. Our second method of examining the question of whether the SC overpaid for its purchases, using regressions with pooled

Table 3.3 Predicted prices of Settlement Commission purchases from coefficients of Equation 1 (in Table 3.2)

Year	Name of property	Size (ha.)	Nominal price	Deflated price		Actual − Predicted	
				Actual	Predicted	Difference	% Difference
1903	Klaske	140	165,000	132,000	123,766	8,234	6.7
1903	Wirsitz Nr 209	166	200,000	160,000	133,575	26,425	19.8
1904	Seehof	421	360,000	291,600	317,412	-25,812	-8.1
1905	Wiele	901	577,500	496,650	688,100	-191,450	-27.8
1905	Seedorf	551	460,000	395,600	485,953	-90,353	-18.6
1905	Marienthal	177	180,000	154,800	156,942	-2,142	-1.4
1905	Schönrode	151	175,000	150,500	147,160	3,340	2.3
1906	Herrschaft Lindenwald	2,142	2,200,000	2,002,000	2,230,791	-228,791	-10.3
1906	Erlau Nr 1	523	975,000	887,250	515,647	371,603	72.1
1906	Victorsau	583	605,000	550,550	542,242	8,308	1.5
1906	Wolfshagen Bd. I, Bl. 1 and Kaiserdorf Bd. I, Bl. 8	322	470,000	427,700	316,646	111,054	35.1
1906	Nakel	213	530,000	482,300	212,370	269,930	127.1
1906	Kunau Nr 35 and 46	143	160,000	145,600	107,262	38,338	35.7
1907	Gross Elsingen	896	1,190,000	1,130,500	927,718	202,782	21.9
1908	Grabowo and Kaiserswalde	2,313	1,895,000	1,686,550	2,566,416	-879,866	-34.3
1908	Rittershof	187	340,000	302,600	240,163	62,437	26.0
1909	Poburke	853	1,417,500	1,289,925	925,382	364,543	39.4
1909	Wertheim 1	243	470,000	427,700	238,386	189,314	79.4
1910	Julienfelde	631	811,757	746,816	718,422	28,394	4.0
Total		11,556	13,181,757	11,860,641	11,594,353	266,288	2.3

data and dummy variables to identify which properties were purchased by the SC, may offer some additional illumination or confirmation. We turn to that now.

Because we have no "net price" determination for properties purchased by the SC, and because of the considerable variance in prices predicted by using net price in the estimating equation, when we pool the data for our next test we will need to use the deflated *actual* price paid for the property as the dependent variable.

Using the actual price paid requires the inclusion of several more variables that can affect the price, but whose effects were removed when the cadastral officials estimated the "net price" – what the property should have sold for, absent any skewing of the price because of discount to a relative or some other factor.

Two important issues arise simply because the properties purchased by the SC were much larger than the average property in the sample: one is that large properties often had a non-agricultural establishment on their land – a *Gasthaus*, a mill, a brickworks, a brewery or distillery, etc.; the other is the case of market segmentation by size which I have considered in an earlier paper (Eddie and Kouschil 2002: 22). These and other binary characteristics (present or absent) can most easily be handled by constructing the appropriate dummy variables. Please refer to the Appendix for details about the construction of these variables.

Of particular interest to the question of whether the SC overpaid for properties it bought would be the coefficients of the "SC Buys" variables: a positive, significant sign on the "SC Buys" variable would indicate the size of the premium paid, and the sign of the coefficient for the associated trend variable (if significant) would indicate whether that overpayment was increasing or decreasing over time. The results of the estimation are found in Table 3.4.

Not only does the equation fit the data very well, nearly all of the coefficients are highly significant. We should note in particular, however, the *insignificant* coefficient for the "SC Buys" variable. This implies that, on balance, the SC paid *about the same as* the average buyer of landed properties for those it bought (i.e., the "premium" it paid was not significantly different from zero), at least in the riding of Wirsitz. The negative coefficient for the *trend* in this variable indicates that, over time, the "premium" paid by the SC was becoming smaller – or, in this case, less significant. These results, therefore, lend no support whatever to the contention that the SC overpaid for what it bought.

A key to understanding this point may lie behind the coefficient for "Non-agricultural Enterprise." The substantial size of this coefficient, amounting to nearly 18 percent of the mean deflated price paid by the SC for the 19 properties here considered, shows that industrial establishments could represent a very sizable share of the value of some large properties.

Table 3.4 Results of pooled regressions, dependent variable: deflated actual price paid

Variable	Coefficient	Std error	T-value[1]
Plow + Garden hectares	1,625	419	3.88****
Plow + Garden trend	34.6	63.6	0.54
Meadow hectares	2,071	1,281	1.62
Meadow trend	246	202	1.22
Wood + Pasture hectares	−2,672	400	−6.68****
Wood + Pasture trend	−494	61.3	−8.06****
Relative Buys (Thaler)	−156	80.7	−1.94*
Relative Buys trend	−20.1	18.5	−1.09
Over 100	357	331	1.08
Over 100 trend	162	51.5	3.14***
Non-agricultural Enterprise (number)	111,116	27,254	4.08****
Non-agricultural Enterprise trend	13,630	4,291	3.18****
SC Buys (Thaler)	9.14	62.0	0.15
SC Buys trend	−28.1	10.7	−2.62***
Standard error of estimate (marks)		31,510	
Mean deflated price paid (marks)	92,035		
R^2	0.986		
Number of observations	176		
Degrees of freedom	162		

Notes:
* = significant at 5 percent level or better.
** = significant at 2.5 percent level or better.
*** = significant at 1 percent level or better.
**** = significant at 0.1 percent level or better.

To my knowledge, this point has never been mentioned in any of the discussions of the prices paid by the SC. Uniformly the critics have pointed either to the cost per hectare or the cost per mark of tax assessment *of the land alone* as being "inflated." Given that the SC purchased large properties to subdivide for settlement, and that the larger properties often had one or more industrial establishments on site, it is then no wonder that the cost of the property per hectare of agricultural land or per mark of land tax assessment might be higher than the average for the land market as a whole.

In summary, the data for the riding of Wirsitz support neither the general nor the particular version of the thesis of overpaying for land. There was no general tendency for the SC to pay "too much" for the properties it bought: it apparently overpaid for some, and got bargains on others. These cases effectively cancel each other out. If the data from Wirsitz are representative of the data from other ridings which are no longer available – and I argue above that that appears to be the case – then the claim that the SC paid too much for the land it bought, or that it drove up prices for everybody, has been seriously weakened.

The Settlement Commission in the market for peasant properties

The SC's original mandate did not include purchasing peasant properties at all, and the settlers' own preference for moving into a community rather than onto isolated farmsteads (AK 1907: 25) reinforced its preference for subdividing larger estates. As a result, the SC only occasionally purchased a peasant property, usually only from a Pole and only if that property abutted an SC property. After 1901, however, the SC entered more actively into the market for peasant farms, with an increasing push to strengthen or create a German majority in ethnically mixed areas. It also began to engage in defensive purchases, to prevent a property from falling into the hands of a Pole or to forestall "the settlement of the first Pole" in a given area (Buzek 1909: 321).

Figures 3.5 and 3.6 show the amount and distribution of the SC's purchases of peasant farms. Purchase of peasant farms was heavily concentrated in the years 1902 through 1910, with a sharp drop-off after that. The years of peak activity were also years in which the SC bought the majority of these peasant properties from Germans. Such properties appear often to have been purchased for a special purpose: to "round off" a settlement, to provide a site for school or other public buildings, to provide a pub, as a site for workers' settlement, etc. For 560 of the 594 properties purchased between 1886 and 1913[10] there exist data with notes regarding these special characteristics (PSA, I Rep 87B, Nr 9550).

Dummy variables were assigned for the characteristics noted in the archival records (see Appendix, Table 3.A1 for details), taking the value of

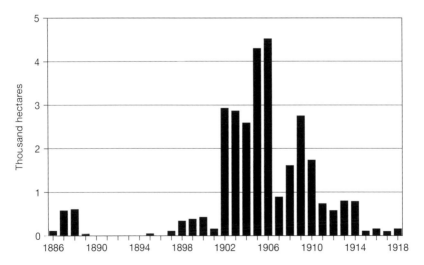

Figure 3.5 Purchases of peasant farms by the Settlement Commission
Source: Reports of the Settlement Commission.

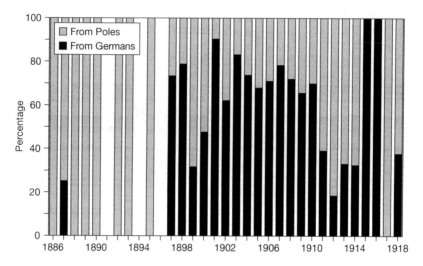

Figure 3.6 Purchases of all peasant farms by the Settlement Commission
(in percentage of the total area purchased annually)

Source: Reports of the Settlement Commission.

1 if the characteristic was noted for the given property, 0 otherwise. If the dummy implied that more (or less) would be paid *per hectare* for properties of different sizes, it was multiplied by the size of the peasant property in hectares when used as an independent variable in the regressions.

Because not all property records contained data about the various land types (plow land, meadow, etc.), the principal independent variables had to be total area of the property (AREA), and a trend applied to that area (ATREND, calculated as in the previous section on estate purchases). In addition, I added a relative quality index (QINDEX), which was the net tax yield per hectare of the property in question divided by the average net tax yield per hectare for the 560 properties, multiplied by the area of the property in hectares. The results of this regression are shown in Table 3.5. ("Unit" refers to the measurement unit of each independent variable.)

As with the estate purchases, so with the purchases of peasant properties: they exhibit considerably more variance than did the purchases of landed properties by private individuals, at least those in the riding of Wirsitz, most likely because these SC purchases were scattered over two provinces, not concentrated in a single riding. In consequence, our regression explains only about 70 percent of the variance in the (deflated) price paid for peasant farms by the SC, but the conclusions we can draw from this regression[11] are nevertheless interesting:

1   Quality seemed to matter. The QINDEX coefficient is both positive and highly significant, and in addition to that, so is the premium for

Table 3.5 Price determination regressions for peasant farm purchases

Variable	Unit	Coefficient	Std error	T-value	Signif. 5%?
AREA	Hectares	751	74.1	10.1	yes
ATREND	Hectares	42.7	4.72	9.05	yes
QINDEX	Hectares	215	28.6	7.52	yes
POLISH	Hectares	−44	43.3	−1.02	no
OVER100	Hectares	−231	55.1	−4.19	yes
UNDER5	Hectares	−560	2,313	−0.242	no
QUALITY	Hectares	394	82.9	4.76	yes
BUILDING	Number	16,199	7,260	2.23	yes
ROUNDING	Hectares	249	111	2.24	yes
SCHOOL	Number	−389	20,315	−0.019	no
ROAD	Hectares	−9,795	58,078	−0.169	no
BUILDSITE	Hectares	1,361	194	7.00	yes
TAVERN	Number	11,046	10,803	1.02	no
INDUSTRY	Number	38,723	10,195	3.8	yes
CITY	Hectares	922	155	5.96	yes
NEARCITY	Hectares	−126	160	−0.787	no
FROMSTATE	Hectares	22.6	17.9	1.27	no
POLITICAL	Hectares	181	245	0.741	no
CHURCH	Hectares	475	1,556	0.305	no
Intercept	Marks	4,293	3,078	1.40	no
R^2		0.709			

    QUALITY, the dummy for a special quality such as good location, extraordinary inventory, etc.

2   The SC seemed indifferent between buying peasant farms from Poles or from Germans. This suggests that the characteristics of the peasant farm itself were much more important to the SC than who owned it.

3   Large properties did not command a premium; quite the opposite: the SC did not want to create settlement parcels so large that they would have to use outside (read: Polish) labor, and there may have been some difficulty with subdividing the peasant farms. Very small properties (under 5 hectares) did not command a premium nor sell at a discount to the SC.

4   Sites suitable for building appear to have been especially important, since the premium per hectare that they commanded (1,361 marks/ha.) was the largest of all, nearly half again as much as the premium for a city property (922 marks/ha.).

5   Political and church interests did not lead the SC to pay any extra for a peasant property, nor did the presence of a tavern or nearness to a city. On the other hand, the SC did pay extra for something concrete such as a brickworks (large positive, significant coefficient for INDUSTRY).

Overall, these results imply that, in the purchase of peasant properties, it was primarily the economic characteristics and the suitability for the specific purposes of the SC that principally determined what the SC was willing to pay for a peasant farm – no sign of irrationality in this market either.

"Consolidating" German landownership

In its settlements, the SC made extensive use of the particular German ownership form of the *Rentengut* ("annuity property"), in which a purchaser acquires ownership through a series of annual payments, which may even be perpetual. Until the contract is fully paid, the seller retains a direct owner-ship interest. Because its residual ownership interest gave it the right to veto any sale to a Pole, the SC could ensure that its settlement farms would remain in German hands.

The SC was the obvious choice of institution to administer a new pro-gram promulgated in 1900. The government, worried over increasing sales of German farms to Poles, wanted to promote "consolidation" (*Befestigung*) of German land ownership. The program was essentially a credit subsidy scheme: farmers burdened by debt and in danger of losing their prop-erty would sell to the SC; the SC would pay off the debt, then resell the property – in most cases back to the original owner – as a *Rentengut*.[12] The new payments, although they might be for a longer term, were always lower than before, and at a lower rate of interest. Although the SC admin-istered the plan, it was primarily financed by two newly created German banks: the *Bauernbank* (Peasants' Bank) in West Prussia and the *Deutsche Mittelstandskasse* (German Middle Class Fund) in Poznania (Jakóbczyk 1976: 174–176).

"Consolidation" did not really get underway until it received significant budget funds – 125 million marks[13] – in 1908, as is clear from Figure 3.7. It quickly picked up speed, however, so that in 1911, 1912, and 1913 the government "consolidated" some 20,000 hectares of German property per year, more than the *total* average annual land purchases of the SC in those same years (17,000 hectares of "estates" and 700 hectares of "peasant farms"). Figure 3.8 brings home the point that this was quite remarkable: the mean size of farm "consolidated" fell to less than 15 hectares by 1913; in all, the SC "consolidated" 3,931 farms in those 3 years, an average of over 1,300 per year. This clearly required a very substantial commitment of adminis-trative resources.

The increasing activity in the peasant land market, both purchases and "consolidating" of peasant holdings, likely represents an increasing recog-nition by the Prussian government that its settlement policy was not achieving its goal. The great offensive push of 1902–1906, when both estate purchases and the purchase of peasant properties peaked, apparently did not significantly alter the situation, and preceded a more defensive posture in the years just before the Great War. The amount of resources, which the

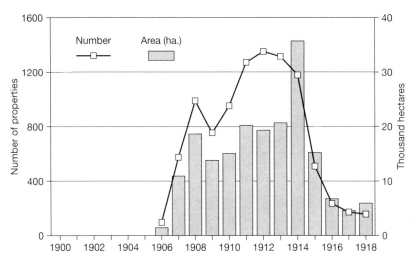

Figure 3.7 "Consolidating" German land ownership: number and total area of properties "consolidated" by the Settlement Commission

Source: Reports of the Settlement Commission.

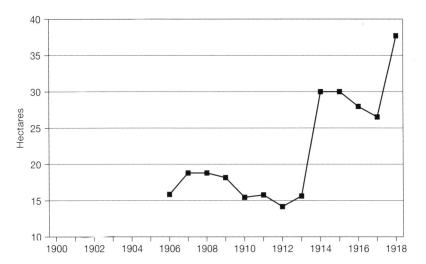

Figure 3.8 "Consolidating" German land ownership: average size of "consolidated" properties

Source: Reports of the Settlement Commission.

SC devoted to the program of "consolidating" German landownership, which characterized this defensive stance, must have been a considerable share of the total resources available to it.

Other anti-Polish measures in the land market

To supplement and reinforce the efforts of the SC, the Prussian government introduced three major measures to impede the activities of the Polish settlement societies and to make it more difficult for Poles to acquire land:[14]

1   A law of July 8, 1896 effectively introduced entail for settlers' land acquired from the SC: the land could be sold freely only to the settler's next of kin; SC approval was required for any other sale.
2   A law of August 10, 1904 abolished the legal difference between "colony" and "settlement" (essentially between multiple and single settlements), so that thereafter *any* new settlement required a building permit, even if it were only for renovation of an existing building to make it habitable. Local officials routinely denied these permits to Poles (Jakóbczyk 1976: 140). Moreover, §13 of the law made it explicit that a permit could be denied if granting it would "contradict the aims" of the Settlement Act of June 26, 1886 (Wajda 1964: 44–47).
3   The most controversial measure, however, was the law of March 20, 1908 giving the SC the right to expropriate up to 70,000 hectares of land from Poles (Kaczmarczyk 1945: 221). This unleashed a storm of protest, both domestic and international (Eddie and Kouschil 2002: 23–24). Because of the protest and because of internal divisions within the Prussian government, the SC availed itself of this provision only once (in 1912) to expropriate four properties, a total of 1,656 hectares. Was it perhaps pangs of conscience that led the SC to pay a higher average price per hectare for the expropriated properties than it did for the others that it purchased that year? (Eddie 1993: 109).

Striking a balance

World War I doomed the Settlement Commission. Although it officially existed until 1924, officials in the newly reconstituted Poland had taken over its headquarters and most of its property in 1919 (Falk 1927: 39–41). Only 3.9 percent (18,200 ha.) of all the land purchased by the SC remained within the new German borders. The Poles refused to recognize the ownership rights of most of the German settlers, about half of whom fled (or were driven out of) Poland (Falk 1927: 61). Thus all the expense and effort of settlement ended ignominiously, from the German point of view.

We have seen in the foregoing that the SC went to great effort and expense to fulfill its mandate. Although as time passed it had increasing difficulty in buying from Polish owners, the SC apparently tried to remain as true to its original mandate as budget and other conditions allowed: it concentrated its purchases in areas where it thought it could make a difference, and it took on additional tasks to further the goal of strengthening the German element in the population of the districts of its jurisdiction, including the very large program of "consolidating" German ownership of existing peasant farms. Its operations were neither so large nor so wildly unconstrained that they had any appreciable effect in the land market. The analysis here presented substantially confirms the contemporary view of the only three systematic studies of the land market that I could find, which argued that the observed general rise in prices of agricultural land in the area of operation of the SC were primarily the result of the following:

1   Intensification of agricultural production, especially the introduction of new rotations (which reduced the share of fallow land) and artificial fertilizers.
2   General improvements in technology and transport, especially a doubling of the length of the railway net after 1880.
3   Drainage and other forms of land quality improvement, especially through investments by *private* landowners.
4   Substantial improvement in the availability of credit for land purchase.
5   Rising agricultural prices after the low point of the mid 1890s, along with (near the end of the period) the tariff of 1902, which led to a substantial increase in grain prices in the German domestic market (Chłapowski 1913: 282–285; Chrzanowski 1914: 47–48, 66–90).[15]

To this list one must also add population growth: an increase in the labor/land ratio will increase the price of land, *ceteris paribus*. Recall that it was the Prussian government's fear of the Poles' substantially higher birth rates, compared to ethnic Germans, which prompted the settlement policy in the first place. If the data were available, it would be instructive to compare the trends in land prices in East Prussia, which was losing population, to those of West Prussia and Poznania.

Improvement in the cultivation of rye – the principal crop of both provinces – probably went further in Poznania than anywhere else in Prussia, so that not long after the turn of the twentieth century "rye cultivation [there] was the most intensively practiced in the entire Prussian Monarchy" (Krische 1907: 177). Yields in Poznania reached or even surpassed those of the western provinces, and the area devoted to cultivation of grains and potatoes, the crops with greatest yield growth, increased faster in Poznania than in Prussia as a whole (Chrzanowski 1914: 61–64). Normally, an increase in yields will result in a more-than-proportionate increase in net income from the land,[16] and therefore in the market price of that land, *ceteris paribus*. The province of Poznania benefited from a double increase in average yields: both a shift of cultivation toward crops with higher yield growth, and faster-than-average growth in the yield of its principal crop. It is no wonder, then, that land prices (at least in the province of Poznania, where the SC was most active) rose relative to land prices elsewhere – but for reasons that had nothing to do with the SC's activities, and were anything but "non-economic."[17] Note also that an increase in the supply of credit available for land purchase is further strong evidence that the land market was *not* characterized by prices that had risen beyond all economic reality.

The data on land purchases by the SC have shown that it was too small a player in the land market to have had any detectable price-raising effect. Moreover, the most careful study of price that I have seen points out that the resources of the Polish settlement societies were but a trivial fraction of those of the SC (Chrzanowski 1914: 91–105). So, even though the Poles may have used their money more effectively in settlement activities, their impact on the market had to have been even smaller than the negligible effect of the SC. In addition, the continuing presence of independent buyers, undeterred by the allegedly unreasonably high prices, even in those ridings in which the SC was active, argues strongly against the supposed effect of the "battle for land." Good substitutes for land in Poznania and West Prussia, in the form of agricultural lands in other provinces, were available to these potential buyers, yet they did not disappear from the market in the two provinces in question. For all the foregoing reasons, the thesis of uneconomically high land prices, where and because the SC bought land, seems to me to be completely unsustainable.

Let us take one other final point: Max Sering's notion that the SC worked "well, but expensively" (as quoted in Schultz-Klinken 1973: 205) seems to mean, on the basis of evidence presented here, that the expensive part was the parcellization and the administration (including administration of the "consolidation" program), not the purchase of land per se. The SC did not appear to have let politics distort its judgment on land purchases generally, even if it may have gone overboard on some individual purchases.

We saw above that the Great War and the subsequent border changes involved in the reconstitution of Poland as an independent state effectively nullified almost all of the SC's efforts. The focus of the present chapter was not broad enough to allow the drawing of overall conclusions about the achievements of the SC before the outbreak of the War. In this final section, therefore, I turn to two standard interpretations of the general effect of the SC's activities – one contemporary, one current.

First, the contemporary view, from Ludwig Bernhard in 1920:

> Only in 15 ridings of the provinces of Poznania and West Prussia have the Germans gained land from 1896 to 1914. In 49 ridings, on the other hand, despite all the exertions of the Prussian Settlement Commission, despite the exceptional laws against Polish settlement, the Germans have been driven back. . . .

The belief that the State could decide the battle for land through its financial power has been revealed as mistaken. The monetary might of the State treasury was outbid by the credit audacity of private speculators and surpassed more and more each year. The Prussian Fiscus became an object of speculation. The result was the demoralization of the eastern land market and finally the complete isolation of the Settlement Commission.

On the other hand the battle for land brought to the Poles a social and economic reorganization, forced them into a reordering of their unhealthy land distribution, compelled them into reforms that the old Szlachta [translator's note: Polish nobility] would never have tolerated in peacetime, and developed on the new land a polity that appeared to the Poles as the embodiment of Slavic culture.

(Bernhard 1920: 569, 572)[18]

Contrast this with Thomas Nipperdey's view from 1992:

The "battle for the land," which in any case the Prussian government had introduced as a political measure, and which the Polish banks, cooperatives, and settlement societies took up, indeed did essentially alter the agrarian system in Poznania: Of the cultivable land 16.2 per cent was newly settled by the Prussian state and 16.8 per cent was newly distributed privately; the share of properties larger than 100 hectares declined from 58.5 per cent in 1882 to 46 per cent in 1907;[19] the Settlement Commission had – with an expenditure of a billion gold marks – created almost 22,000 new farms, plus nearly 5000 Rentengüter (that was another, not nationalistically motivated program). Polish as well as German estates passed into peasant possession and the peasant holdings of the Germans increased more strongly than that of the Poles. In 1913 the land was almost exactly half German, half Polish.

But the population proportions were only slightly changed from 1871 through 1890 to 1910 (Poles: 61–63.3–64.7 per cent, Germans: 35.1–33.9–34 per cent, Jews: 3.9–2.5–1.3 per cent); only between 1900 and 1910 did the German rural population increase more than the Polish (11.5 to 6.5 per cent in Poznania). That was also a result of settlement, but it barely made up for the "losses" of previous decades. The influx as a result of the settlement policy (about 81,000) and the Polish emigration which set in after 1890 did not offset the much higher Polish birth-rate. . . .

The settlement policy stabilized the situation for a while, but in the long run it could not. Overall: Neither language nor school policy, nor land and settlement policy had Germanized and integrated, or repressed, the Poles; these did not halt the process of their nationalization, but rather abetted it.

(Nipperdey 1992: 275–276)

While the two interpretations do differ at important points, they are clearly in agreement on the major issue: the Settlement Act was not, and could not be, the solution to the "Polish Question" for the Prussian government. Even as a concept it had a fatal flaw: the government did not have, and never would have, the means to buy its way to a major change in the demographic balance, and trying to buy the land out from under the feet of the Poles was worse than fruitless. The activities of the Settlement Commission for West Prussia and Poznania increased the cleavage and exacerbated the tension between the two ethnic groups. Moreover, they led to strongly repressive measures against the German settlers when "payback time" arrived after the end of World War I.

Appendix: details of data used in the regressions

Price data from wealth tax records: the cadastral officials had to fill out a printed form which required descriptive details of the property, including the area and taxable value of its different categories of land (plow land, garden, meadow, pasture, etc.) and the taxable value of buildings, as well as information on standing crops and timber; the condition of inventory of buildings, equipment, and animals; whether there was a tavern, brickworks, or other non-agricultural enterprise located on the property, etc. The form also contained information on whether the sale was between relatives or at a forced auction, and the cadastral officials adjusted the actual price paid, if appropriate, to take account of deviations from "normal" conditions.[20]

Variables in the price-determination regressions: the principal independent variables in these regressions should ideally have been the amounts of land of each type contained in a given property, each land type adjusted for quality. That adjustment was contained in the "net yield for land tax" (*Grundsteuerreinertrag*), which had been estimated by local assessors for each parcel of land. This figure, a uniform percentage of which would be taken in land tax, was to represent the net income that that parcel, operated under normal management and with local prices for produce, would have provided in a normal year at the time of assessment in 1860–1864. In practice this meant classifying the parcel according to type (e.g., plow land, garden, woodland), and within each type, into one of eight quality grades. A local "cadastral key" – a cross-tabulation of the appropriate net yield values for one *Morgen*[21] of each type and grade of land – when multiplied by the number of *Morgen* in the parcel, produced the taxable net yield for that parcel. This process assured both local uniformity and regional diversity to take account of different fertility, growing conditions, access to markets, etc., and thus can be taken as an excellent measure of the combination of area and quality of any piece of land. I have used these net yield data in a previous work, and have shown how well they work in a hedonic regression explaining the net price paid (Eddie 1997: 195–216).

Dummy variables constructed for the regressions: because there is no information on the value or size of any of the industrial establishments on the properties, we will simply have to note their presence or absence. Although the SC did not usually record in the notes whether there was such an establishment on a property it purchased, we can turn to the data of the *Handbooks of Landownership in the German Empire*[22] to see whether a given estate also was home to some sort of industrial establishment. Of the 19 properties listed in Table 3.3, the relevant volume of the *Handbook* listed 12. Of these 12, 6 had 1 or more industrial establishments. A dummy variable to indicate the presence of some sort of non–agricultural enterprise on a property was set to 0 if there was no such enterprise, otherwise it was set equal to the number of such enterprises on the property. Of the 157 non-SC properties only 7 had 1 such enterprise each; 2 of the SC purchases had 3 (e.g., brickworks, distillery, dairy plant) and another had 2. Thus for the 6 SC properties for which an industrial enterprise could be found, for 3 the value of the dummy was 1, for 1 it was 2, and for 2 others, 3. For the other 13 SC properties, the value of this dummy was set to 0.

Similarly, if the property had been sold between relatives (e.g., father to son-in-law), a "Relative Buys" dummy took the value of 1, otherwise 0.

Table 3.A1 Definitions of dummy variables used in peasant farm regressions

Dummy variable	Definition	Multiplied by area for the regression
POLISH	Purchased from a Pole	yes
OVER100	Property was larger than 100 hectares	yes
UNDER5	Property was smaller than 5 hectares	yes
QUALITY	Notation made of particularly high quality, including especially favorable location	yes
BUILDING	Contained especially good buildings	no
ROUNDING	Purchased to round off a settlement	yes
SCHOOL	Existing school site	no
ROAD	Purchased as a site for road(s)	yes
BUILDSITE	Purchased as a building site (for school, industry, etc.)	yes
TAVERN	Noted as "tavern ground"	no
INDUSTRY	Contained an industrial establishment (brickworks, etc.)	no
CITY	Property within a city	yes
NEARCITY	Property near a city (i.e., located in a riding surrounding or bordering a city)	yes
FROMSTATE	Purchased from the state	yes
POLITICAL	Property was of "political interest" (only one case of this)	yes
CHURCH	Purchased for "church interests"	yes

If the property was larger than 100 hectares, the traditional cut-off point between large and middling size property, an "Over 100" dummy took the value of 1, otherwise 0. Finally, an "SC Buys" dummy variable was set = 1 for the 19 properties purchased by the SC, 0 otherwise.

Because the properties were of different sizes, it was necessary to multiply the value of the dummy times a size variable in order to produce a proper variable to include in the regression. The "Over 100" dummy was multiplied by the total number of hectares in the property, while the "Relative Buys" and "SC Buys" dummy variables were each multiplied by the total tax assessment, which is a very good proxy for the total value of the property (Eddie 1993: 101–140) before being entered into the equation. Each of these variables in turn was matched to a trend variable constructed in exactly the same way as it was for each of the other variables in the equation.

The definitions of dummy variables for the regression for purchases of "peasant properties" are presented in Table 3.A1. In all cases, a value of "1" indicates presence, and "0" absence, of the defined characteristic.

Notes

* The author would like to thank Paul Brykczynski, Grzegorz Hajdrych, Barbara Radoń, Lucy Rzhi Li, Kim Pagel, and Joanna Sobala for research assistance. I am grateful also for the cooperation and assistance of the directors and staff of the following archives: Geheimes Staatsarchiv Preußischer Kulturbesitz, Berlin-Dahlem; Archiwum Państwowe w Bydgoszczy (State Archive in Bydgoszcz); Archiwum Państwowe w Poznaniu, Oddzial w Gnie Ynie (State Archive in Poznan, Branch in Gniezno). The author owes a special debt of gratitude to Dr Christa Kouschil for ideas, advice, and information which materially improved this chapter. Financial assistance has been provided by the University of Toronto, the Social Sciences and Humanities Research Council of Canada, and the U of T/DAAD Joint Initiative in German and European Studies. All translations of German texts are my own.

1 In the Russian Empire the "Polish Question" consisted primarily in the nationalist aspirations of the Polish nobility, whose serfs were often not Polish, but rather Ukrainian or Russian. The Peasant Emancipation in 1861 punished these Polish landlords by keeping compensation for their lost serfs and privileges lower than that awarded landlords in other regions of Russia. The multi-national Habsburg Empire, on the other hand, was content to let its Polish provinces enjoy a degree of local autonomy. Indeed, support of the "Polish Club" in the Austrian *Reichsrat* (Parliament) became essential to the German-Austrians in their dealings with the more fractious Czechs and Magyars in the latter half of the nineteenth century. Thus the perceived demographic threat, which was at the heart of the "Polish Question" in Prussia, simply did not exist in either Russia or Austria.

2 Although some Polish sources translate this literally as "Settlement Commission" (*Komisja Osadnicza*), the majority seem to prefer the more politically charged "Colonization Commission" (*Komisja Kolonizacyjna*). The problem of translation may also stem from the abolition of the legal difference between "settlement" and "colony" in Prussian law in 1904 (see the section on other anti-Polish measures in the land market).

3 The SC distinguished between "estates" (*Güter*) and "peasant farms" (*Bauern-wirtschaften*) in its purchases, and we will adopt the same distinction here: normally,

a *Gut* would be purchased for parcellization, while a *Bauernwirtschaft* was purchased to "round out" a settlement scheme, to provide a site for a school, etc. Some of the larger peasant farms were, however, bigger in total area than some of the smaller estates.

4 Between 1886 and 1913, the SC purchased 7.7 percent of the land in the *Regierungsbezirk* Posen, 6.6 percent in Marienwerder, and only 2.7 percent in Danzig (AK 1913: Anlage II).

5 See for example Balzer (1990: 62), or Tonnies (1923: 7). For a contrary view, see Swart (1941: 593).

6 Calculated from figures quoted in AK 1913, Anlage II.

7 The Prussian Statistical Bureau published a volume of analysis of land prices based on over two million observations gathered about transactions between 1895 and 1912 (PSL 1917).

8 I limit the sample to this size range because 5 hectares represented a standard (in the German literature) minimum size for a parcel of land to be considered a "farm" rather than something like a garden plot.

9 Since garden was not always reported separately, but sometimes included in the amount of plow land, this addition actually made the data more consistent.

10 In all areas, not just in the riding of Wirsitz.

11 To avoid clutter, only the regression with a constant term is presented. As before, the constant is not statistically significant, and the regressions with the constant suppressed are virtually identical except for the constant term.

12 In the standard, typical contract, the SC retained one mark of ownership interest when it (re)sold the property as a *Rentengut*.

13 They received an additional 100 million in 1913, but could not use all of it because of the outbreak of war (Jakóbczyk 1976: 179–180).

14 For a more complete treatment, see Eddie and Kouschil (2002: 16–17).

15 Chrzanowski's book (1914) was written explicitly as a sequel to Sarrazin (1897).

16 Chłapowski (1913: 283–285) estimates that marketed surplus probably doubled in 20 years and calculates that, with the increases in yields and prices, a land price increase of 100 percent was "nothing extraordinary."

17 In fact, Sarrazin (1897: 866) argues that there were, in general, no unnatural price tendencies at all in the market in the province of Poznania, and Chrzanowski (1914: 99) finds it unjustified to blame the SC for a rise in land prices caused by other economic factors.

18 Bernhard had access to unpublished records of the Prussian Statistical Bureau on the ethnic distribution of land ownership. These are no longer available; his data in the first quoted paragraph therefore cannot be verified.

19 Note that Nipperdey's claim about the decreasing share of large properties cannot be taken at face value: given the years that he compares, he is obviously using the data from the German agricultural censuses of 1882 and 1907, which did not count *properties*, but rather *operating units*. One property may be divided into several operating units, or several properties may be combined into one operating unit. At the time, the former was more likely for large properties, as owners often farmed a part themselves and leased out the rest. Moreover, a reduction in the average size of operating units could well be the result of the intensification of cultivation noted earlier. Hence the reduction in the total area of large operating units can tell us (and Nipperdey) nothing whatever about what happened to the share of large properties in total land used for agriculture. In fact, the share of *properties* over 100 hectares in size did decline, but by considerably less than Nipperdey claims: from 58.8 percent of the total area of the province of Poznania in 1884 to 51.8 percent in 1910 (calculated from data in Ellerholz 1884 and 1910).

20 We shall see later, in the regressions, how well these adjustments appear to have been made.
21 A Prussian *Morgen* was just slightly larger than 0.25 hectare.
22 *Handbuch des Grundbesitzes im Deutschen Reiche*, a series of volumes from Paul Parey Verlag in Berlin. Each volume covered a single province and purported to include all properties of 100 hectares or larger; new editions appeared (normally) every 5 to 10 years.

Bibliography

AK (Ansiedlungskommission) (1907) *20 Jahre deutscher Kulturarbeit* (Denkschrift, Haus der Abgeordneten, 20. Legislaturperiode, III. Session 1907, Posen).
——— (1913) Denkschrift für das Jahr 1913, in Sammlung der Drucksachen des Preußischen Hauses der Abgeordneten (Anlagen zum stenographischen Bericht) 1. Wahlperiode, 1. Tagung 1921: Drucksache 900.
Balzer, B. (1990) *Die preußische Polenpolitik 1894–1908 und die Haltung der deutschen konservativen und liberalen Parteien (unter besonderer Berücksichtigung der Provinz Posen)*, Frankfurt am Main, Bern, New York, Paris: Peter Lang.
Bernhard, L. (1920) *Die Polenfrage: Der Nationalitätenkampf der Polen in Preußen*, 3rd edition, Munich and Leipzig: Duncker & Humblot.
Buzek, J. (1909) *Historia polityki narodowosciowej rzadu pruskiego wobec Polakow. Od traktatow wiedenskich do ustaw z r. 1908* [History of Nationalistic Politics of the Prussian Government Towards the Poles. From the Treaties of Vienna to the Special Acts from Year 1908], Wiedza i Zycie, Wydawnictwo Zwiazku Naukowo-Literackiego we Lwowie, Seryl IV, Tom III [Knowledge and Life, Publishers of the Scientific-Literary Association in Lwow, Series IV, Vol. III], Lwow: Naklad Ksiegarni H. Altenberga [H. Altenberg Booksellers].
Chłapowski, S. von (1913) "Der wirtschaftliche Wert der bäuerlichen Kolonisation im Osten," *Preussische Jahrbücher*, 51: 264–329.
Chrzanowski, B. von (1914) *Die Preisbewegung landwirtschaftlicher Güter in der Provinz Posen in den Jahren 1895–1912 und die Begründung der Preissteigerungen*, Posen: Praca.
Delbrück, H. (1894) *Die Polenfrage*, Berlin: Verlag von Hermann Walther.
Eddie, S.M. (1993) "The Distribution of Landed Properties by Value and Area: A Methodological Essay based on Prussian Data, 1886–1913," *Journal of Income Distribution*, 3: 101–140.
——— (1997) "The Price of Land in Eastern Prussia: Data from Capital Gains Tax Records, 1891–1907," *Historical Social Research/Historische Sozialforschung*, 22: 195–216.
——— and Kouschil, C. (2002) *The Ethnopolitics of Land Ownership in Prussian Poland, 1886–1918: The Land Purchases of the Ansiedlungskommission*, Trondheim Studies on East European Cultures and Societies, No. 9, May, Trondheim, Norway: NTN.
Ellerholz, P. (ed.) (1884) *Handbuch des Grundbesitzes im Deutschen Reiche*, Berlin: Paul Parey.
——— (ed.) (1910) *Handbuch des Grundbesitzes im Deutschen Reiche*, Berlin: Paul Parey.
Falk, C. (1927) *Die Ansiedlungskommission für Westpreußen und Posen: In und nach dem Kriege, Ergebnis und Abschluß ihrer Tätigkeit*, Ph.D. dissertation, Friedrich-Wilhelms-Universität zu Berlin.

Galos, A. (1969) "Utworzenie Komisji Kolonizacyjnej a sprawa wewnetrznej kolonizacji w Niemczech" [The Creation of the Colonization Commission and the Question of Internal Colonization in Germany], *Zeszyty Naukowe Uniwerystetu Jagiellońskiego, Prace Historyczne*, 26: 37–55.

Grześ, B. (1979) "Teoretyczno-propagandowe aspekty dyskryminacji Polakow w Poznańskiem na przelomie XIX i XX wieku" [Theoretical-propaganda Aspects of Discrimination against the Poles in Turn of the Century Poznania], in L. Trzeciakowski, and S. Kubiak, (eds) *Rola Wielkopolski w dziejach narodu Polskiego* [The Role of Greater Poland (Poznania) in the History of the Polish Nation], Poznań: Wydawnictwo Naukowe Uniwersytetu im. Adama Mickiewicza w Poznańiu.

——, Kozłowski, J., Kramski, A. (1976) *Niemcy w Poznańskiem wobec polityki germanizacyjnej 1815–1920* [The Germans in Poznania and the Politics of Germanization 1815–1920], Studium Niemcoznawcze Instytutu Zachodniego [German Department of the Western Institute], No. 29, Poznań: Instytut Zachodni [Western Institute].

Jacobs, A. and Richter, H. (1935) *Die Grosshandelspreise in Deutschland von 1792 bis 1934*, Sonderhefte des Instituts für Konjunkturforschung, No. 37, Berlin: Hanseatische Verlagsanstalt Hamburg.

Jakóbczyk, W. (1976) *Pruska Komisja Osadnicza, 1886–1919* [The Prussian Settlement Commission, 1886–1919], Poznań: Wydawnictwo Poznańskie [Poznań Publishers].

Kaczmarczyk, Z. (1945) *Kolonizacja niemiecka na wschod od Odry* [German Colonization East of the Oder], Poznań: Wydawnictwo Instytutu Zachodniego [The Western Institute Publishers].

Kouschil, C. (2002) "Die Ansiedlungskommission. Zur Rolle Bismarcks bei ihrer Entstehung und Installation," unpublished typescript, March/April.

Krische, P. (1907) *Die Provinz Posen, ihre Geschichte und Kultur unter besonderer Berücksichtigung ihrer Landwirtschaft*, Stasfurt: R. Weicke.

Magocsi, P.R. (2002) *Historical Atlas of Central Europe*, revised and expanded edition, Toronto: University of Toronto Press.

Nipperdey, T. (1992) *Deutsche Geschichte, 1866–1918*, Vol. 2, Munich: C.H. Beck.

PSA (Prussian State Archive) I Rep 87B (Ministry of Agriculture, Domains and Forests).

—— I Rep 90a (Cabinet).

—— I Rep 151 IC, Finanz-Ministerium, Nr. 12506.

PSL (Preußisches Statistisches Landesamt) (1917) "Kaufpreise ländlicher Grundstücke in Preußen im Durchschnitt aus den Jahren 1895 bis 1912," *Zeitschrift des Preußischen Statistischen Landesamtes*, Ergänzungsheft 44, Berlin: Preußisches Statistisches Landesamt.

Sarrazin, H. (1897) "Die Entwicklung der Preise des Grund und Bodens in der Provinz Posen," *Landwirtschaftliche Jahrbücher*, Berlin: Parey.

Schultz-Klinken, K.-R. (1973) "Preußische und deutsche Ostsiedlungspolitik von 1886 bis 1945; ihre Zielvorstellungen, Entwicklungsphasen und Ergebnisse," *Zeitschrift für Agrargeschichte und Agrarsoziologie*, 21: 198–215.

Swart, F. (1941) "Die Preußische Ansiedlungskommission," *Schmollers Jahrbuch für Gesetzgebung, Verwaltung und Volkswirtschaft im Deutschen Reiche*, 65: 585–612.

Tonnies, F. (1923) *Innere Kolonisation in Preussen insbesondere in den ehemaligen Provinzen Posen und Westpreussen*, Berlin: Franz Vahlen.

Wajda, K. (1964) "Działanie pruskiej ustawy o osadach z 1904 roku na Pomorzu Gdańskim i w Wielkopolsce w latach 1904–1913" [The Functioning of the Settlement Amendment of 1904 in West Prussia and Poznania in the Years 1904–1914], *Zapiski Historyczne* [Historical Review], 29: 43–65.

4 Jewish land – Israel lands

Ethno-nationality and land regime in Zionism and in Israel, 1897–1967*

Jacob Metzer

The late nineteenth century saw the inception of nationally motivated Jewish immigration and settlement in Palestine, and the establishment of the World Zionist Organization (WZO), aiming at the formation of a Jewish, territorially identified, national entity in Palestine – the ancient Land of Israel.[1] From a very modest beginning in the late Ottoman period, the Zionist project of nation building advanced rapidly in the three, post-World War I, decades of British rule. The British government – ruling Palestine by a League of Nations Mandate that called for the formation of a Jewish National Home in Palestine while maintaining the rights of the country's non-Jewish inhabitants – enabled a fast-growing Jewish population of immigrating settlers to evolve into a largely autonomous ethno-national community, voluntarily self-ruled by the governing bodies of the WZO and by its elected institutions.

The Jewish community, although increasing about tenfold over the Mandatory era, remained nevertheless a minority in the country, reaching only 32 percent of Palestine's population by the end of the Mandate (650,000 out of a total of about 2 million in early 1948), with the rest (1.35 million) consisting of the Arab majority. The national aspirations of the mostly indigenous Palestinian Arabs were, not surprisingly, diametrically opposed to those of the Jews and crystallized in part as a response to the successful (and from the Arab view point threatening) Zionist build-up.

The sharp ethno-national divide and the continuing (often violent) conflict between Arabs and Jews led gradually to the idea of dividing the area of Mandatory Palestine into two states. Partition was first suggested in 1937 by a British Royal Commission that was appointed to seek a solution to the conflict following the outbreak of the Arab revolt in 1936. The notion of partition was abandoned by the British government in 1939 as impractical, only to be revived later by a UN Special Committee on Palestine (UNSCOP) that the General Assembly appointed in 1947. With the moral burden of the holocaust and the pressing need to find its displaced survivors a refuge, and with the highly explosive state of affairs in Palestine calling for an urgent solution, the UN General Assembly resolved on November 29, 1947 to partition Palestine into two, Arab and Jewish, states, as recommended by UNSCOP. In doing so it paved the way for the termination of the British Mandate in May 1948.

The Arab–Jewish armed conflict, launched by the Palestinian Arabs aiming to annul the Partition Resolution, escalated into an all-out war between the newly created (on May 14, 1948) State of Israel and the Arab states invading it. By the end of the war, in early 1949, Israel was in control of about 76 percent of the area of former Mandatory Palestine (compared to 56 percent allotted to the Jewish State in the Partition Resolution). The massive, largely involuntary, exodus of Arabs during the war, and the enormous inflow of Jewish immigrants, left the State of Israel by the end of 1952 with a population of 1.6 million, of whom 1.4 million (89 percent) were Jews and only 179,000 (11 percent) Arabs (Ben-Porath 1966). The next territorial turnabout took place in the 1967 war, in which Israel captured the entire area of former Mandatory Palestine (in addition to the Golan heights and the Sinai peninsula), and fully controlled it for the following three decades. The rest is still history in the making.

In this complex process of nation building and state formation and maturing in an ethno-nationally divided and contested territory, land did naturally play, and continues to play, a pivotal and highly sensitive role.[2] Furthermore, the Zionist-Israeli story, both in its planning aspects (at the Zionist "drawing board" of nation building) and in its realization, constitutes an exemplary case in which major issues concerning the interplay between property rights in land and territorial sovereignty in an ethnonational divide can be readily explored.

Drawing on primary sources and on the research literature, I shall dwell in this chapter on some of these issues, concentrating largely on the Jewish National Fund (JNF) – the main Zionist organ for the acquisition, reclamation, and collective possession of Jewish land in Mandatory Palestine and Israel. The formation of the JNF, its changing functions in the transition from the Jewish National Home to statehood and its incorporation into the institutional setting of Israel's land regime, provide us – as will be demonstrated in the rest of the chapter – with a rich source for the examination of the issues concerned.

The chapter is divided into three sections. The first section deals with the pre-state phase. In the second section, the discussion turns on the first long decade of statehood (1948–1961), during which the existing land regime of Israel and its institutional framework were established by law and in practice. And in the concluding section, a postscript is offered, highlighting recent legal developments that may lead to future changes in the ethno-national attributes of this regime.

Note that the examination of the land regime in Israel is confined here to the state within the pre-1967 borders. Questions concerning land and Jewish settlement in the West Bank and the Gaza strip are undoubtedly highly significant, but dealing with them requires different terms of reference and a separate discussion, which are outside the scope of this chapter.

Jewish land prior to the Jewish State

The question of land acquisition for Jewish settlement in Palestine and the nature of property rights in land were put on the agenda of modern Jewish nationalism from the very early days of Zionist thinking and planning. The First Zionist Congress, convening in 1897, took notice of these issues, which at the time were highly academic, and in response to a proposal put forward by the Rabbi and mathematician Herman Schapira of Heidelberg, resolved to examine the idea of a Fund for Zionist purposes and to devise a plan for its establishment (Boehm and Pollak 1939: part I).

Schapira's proposal called for the creation of a general fund, to be financed by donations from Jews all over the world, whose prime task would be to acquire land in Palestine and retain it in perpetuity. The fund would then lease, according to the proposal, plots of its inalienable land to settling Jews for periods not exceeding 49 years. In the spirit of these guidelines, the Jewish National Fund (JNF) was created by the Fifth Zionist Congress in 1901 as an organ designed to acquire and allocate land for Jewish settlement in Palestine, and started to operate in 1902. The exact terms of reference for the operation of the JNF were formulated in the Sixth Zionist Congress of 1903, and it was incorporated in London in 1907 under the Companies Act as an "Association Limited by Guarantee without Capital Divided into Shares" (Boehm and Pollak 1939: part I; Orni 1981; Shilony 1998: ch. 3).

In the years leading to World War I, the land-acquiring activities of the JNF were quite limited in scope, bringing its total land holding in Palestine to no more than 16,000 dunams[3] (constituting about 4 percent of all Jewish land possessions in the country) in 1914. A somewhat more active role in land acquisition and settlement was played, though, by the WZO's Palestine Bureau and the Palestine Land Development Company (PLDC) that was itself partly owned by the JNF. Both institutions were established in 1908, under the leadership of the Zionist activist Arthur Ruppin, to facilitate, plan, and coordinate, in cooperation with the JNF, the practical work of Zionism in Palestine (Metzer 1998: ch. 4; Katz 2001: ch. 1).

This work, interestingly enough, was largely inspired by the experience of the German colonization efforts in Posen, which are thoroughly documented and analyzed by Scott Eddie in Chapter 3 of this volume. At the core of the German efforts, as Eddie demonstrates, lay the attempts by the government-appointed German Settlement Commission to purchase Polish estates and farms, subdivide them, and sell them to labor-self-sufficient German peasants, in order to alter the ethno-national mix of the largely Polish-populated areas of the Ostmark.

The German colonization project, in which market transactions in land had been used to promote ethno-national territorial interests, served the Zionist practitioners an appropriate model to follow in their settlement activity. A good number of the persons involved were, like Ruppin, of

German origin and some even closely familiar with the German endeavor
(Reichman and Hasson 1984; Shilony 1990, 1998: chs 1–2; Penslar 1991).
There was one difference though: in Palestine, some kind of a division of
roles developed between the PLDC, which was mandated to acquire land
and sell it to the JNF as well as to private Jewish settlers and entrepreneurs,
and the JNF itself, which kept its acquired lands inalienable.[4]

By the end of World War I, Zionist expectations for the imminent
launching of the Jewish nation-building project (the creation of a Jewish
National Home, to use the wording of the Balfour Declaration of 1917,
and of the League of Nations Mandate) in Palestine under British rule were
running high. These heightened expectations were in turn accompanied in
Zionist deliberating and decision-making circles by a sense of urgency
regarding the formulation of a "blueprint" for the practical work lying
ahead (see Metzer 1977, 1979). Note also, that the WZO was recognized
by the League of Nations and by the British Mandate as the official Jewish
public body (Jewish Agency), which according to the Mandate was to be
formed "for the purpose of advising and cooperating with the Administration of Palestine in such economic, social, and other matters as may
affect the establishment of the Jewish national home and the interests of the
Jewish population in Palestine" (Article 4 of the Mandate, quoted in Metzer
1998: 4).

Naturally, issues regarding (Jewish) land acquisition and tenure under
Palestine's new regime occupied a prominent position on the "check list"
for action, and required the Zionist Organization to reiterate in explicit
terms its stand on these matters. The challenge was taken up at the organization's London Conference of July 1920. In this conference, the pressing
issues concerning land were deliberated (among other practical matters of
immigration and settlement) and concluded in six basic resolutions,
expressing the Zionist consensual approach to land acquisition and retention and shaping the organization's actual land policies for years to come.
Because of their importance these resolutions are reprinted here in their full
original (English) text and are elaborated on thereafter:

1   The fundamental principle of Zionist land policy is that all land on
    which colonization takes place should eventually become the
    common property of the Jewish people. The Executive is called
    upon to do all in its power to carry this principle into effect.
2   The organ for carrying out Jewish land policy in town and country
    is the Jewish National Fund. The objects of this body are: To use
    the voluntary contributions received from the Jewish people as a
    means for making the land of Palestine the common property of the
    Jewish people; to give out the land exclusively on hereditary lease
    hold and on hereditary building-right; to assist the settlement on their
    own farms of Jewish agricultural workers; to see that the ground is
    worked, and to combat speculation; to safeguard Jewish labour.

3   The credit resources of the Zionist organization are to be placed, in the first instance, at the service of such settlers as undertake to comply with the principles of the Jewish National Fund.

4   In order to give the Jewish National Fund a dominating position in the real estate market, adequate means must always be placed at its disposal. In order to enlarge its sphere of operations, the Jewish National Fund shall raise loans, of which the interest and sinking-fund are to be paid off through its leasehold rentals. The Jewish National Fund shall be entitled, even in disregard of the obligation it has hitherto been under of setting aside certain sums for reserve, to invest the whole of its funds without any restrictions in Palestine. The carrying through of the land policy of the Jewish National Fund must be assisted by credit institutes for agricultural and urban property.

5   The transaction of land purchases in Palestine shall be centralized in the hands of an officially recognized institution under the control of the Zionist Organization.

6   In order to bring large portions of the land of Palestine into Jewish possession as rapidly as possible, the Jewish National Fund shall devise means by which, along side of the capital of the Jewish National Fund itself, private capital can also be utilized for the purchase of land under conditions which will assure the eventual transference of land so bought into the national possession.

(Reports 1921: part III, section B, subsection a)

The opening resolution is a clear and unequivocal statement of the principle of Jewish land inalienability. By declaring that *all* Jewish lands in Palestine should be collectively owned, the resolution went beyond previous declarations of intent and specific decisions that referred only to the perpetual ownership of the land acquired by the JNF, and expressed a wide Zionist consensus regarding the nature of the land regime aimed for, that overrode virtually all the factional differences in the movement concerning the desired economic structure of the Jewish community in Palestine and its public–private mix.

The idea of common property rights in land as an ethno-national directive reflected the notion that land ownership by the Jewish national collective – and not just by individual Jews – was necessary in order to secure the formation of a Jewish territorial body politic in Palestine. It was to serve at once as a precondition for future sovereignty and as a substitute for it under the British rule. Ideologically this notion harks back to the biblical land and jubilees laws, prohibiting the sale of land in perpetuity, "for the land is mine" (Leviticus, 25:23), while replacing, in Zionist modern thinking, God and the divine right to the land of Israel by the collective entity of the "Jewish People," who ought to *redeem* the land (Metzer 1977, 1978).

Applying this notion to the scene of contemporary Palestine obviously implied an asymmetric approach to the land market. On the one hand Zionism sought to exploit a relatively free market (under Ottoman and British rules, alike), in order to purchase and gain collective ownership of non-Jewish land, and on the other hand, it aimed to prevent the resale of land to non-Jews by "nationalizing" it, thereby causing the transactions "across ethno-national lines" in Palestine's land market to be uni-directional.[5] But note that it is precisely these transactions that constituted the essence of the *redemption* of the Land of Israel, which has been a prime ideological tenet in Zionism.

Note also that the phrase "Jewish people" refers in Zionist terminology to all the Jews in the world, not just to the Jewish community of Palestine. Hence, it was world Jewry as a whole that would hold the common title to the Jewish purchased and perpetually possessed land in Palestine. This inference is readily deduced from the second resolution cited above, characterizing the JNF as a fund to be financed by contributions made voluntarily by the Jewish people. The idea of Jewish contributions big and small being a source of funding and a basis for the common, all-inclusive, ownership of land, goes back to Schapira's original plan of 1897 where he proposed that "Single and periodic contributions shall be collected from Jews all over the world, without any distinction between rich and poor – so far as the laws of the various countries permit – for a great common Jewish Fund" (quoted in Boehm and Pollak 1939: 20).

The second land resolution of the London Conference made the JNF responsible for carrying out the Jewish (i.e. Zionist) land policy both in "town and country," and stipulated the goals to be achieved by allocating national land on a hereditary leasehold basis. These goals, which emphasized the provision of land for agricultural settlement, included: assuring continuous cultivation, preventing speculation, and securing Jewish labor.[6]

Assuring continuous cultivation and preventing speculation were believed necessary to guarantee the stability of the Jewish agricultural settlement, which was considered in Zionism to be the backbone of Jewish, territory-wise, national revival. Such stability could be hindered in a regime of private land ownership, since landowning farmers, according to Zionist accepted wisdom, would be tempted to sell their property for profit (presumably for non-farm uses), if and when land prices rose fast enough. Moreover, private economic agents might buy land for speculative purposes and leave it unsettled and uncultivated altogether. Securing continuous cultivation by the lessees of publicly owned farmlands should prevent such eventualities.[7] In addition, since full physical utilization of arable land was believed in common Zionist thinking to be tantamount to its efficient use, land nationalization was preferred to private ownership also on – Zionist-perceived (albeit erroneously) – efficiency grounds.

It should be pointed out, though, that the widely held Zionist objection to speculative profits from land, was motivated by considerations of equity as well. Partly influenced by physiocratic ideas in their modern dress of Henry George's single (land) tax, the consensual approach in Zionism was to object to private capital gains from land, although not to similar gains from other assets. In linkage with the Zionist concern about speculative gains, thought was given to the need to prevent landholders from profiting from a possible increase in the value of their land (by selling or renting it at prices that would reflect the heightened value), if and when generated by exogenous factors that raised the demand for it. Such factors could include economic advance at large, newly constructed transport networks, and other exogenous, location-rent-producing, developments. The proposed scheme of national land ownership, granting the lessees only the income to be derived from their own work, including full economic compensation for their own capital investment on the land, should have indeed prevented, according to Zionist thinking, such undeserved profits from being realized.[8]

As for the employment clause of the second resolution, it reflected the prevailing Zionist approach on two related points: (a) that securing Jewish employment on Jewish farms should generate the necessary labor demand to accommodate the prospected inflow of Jewish immigrants; and (b) that it should provide a safeguard against turning the Jewish settlement endeavor into a colonialist-type enterprise, employing "cheap" Arab labor and thereby threatening its Jewishness, and delegitimizing its nature as a respected undertaking of nation building. Allotting nationally owned land to settlers in relatively small plots that could not be consolidated would minimize such "colonialist" risks, according to this line of thought, since it would prevent Jewish landholders from acquiring the necessary market power to drive farm labor wages below the "Jewish threshold."[9] Furthermore, while the compliance of settlers on national land with the national – Jewish labor – guidelines would be secured by the lease contracts, the Zionist Organization would use its means of financial assistance, as implied by the third resolution, to guarantee compliance by all Jewish settlers seeking such assistance.

In the fourth and fifth resolutions notice was implicitly taken of the possibility that the nationally motivated high Jewish demand for land could drive the supply price of non-Jewish land over and above its value as a factor of production. The centralization of land purchases by the JNF, which was supposed to dominate the real-estate market, was aimed at creating a countervailing monopsonistic force in Palestine's land market that was supposed to minimize, or at least reduce, the extent of the problem.

The last resolution brought things from the sphere of high-spirited ideas and principles down to practical considerations. Its main premise was to present a workable solution, reached by the London Conference, for accommodating both the widely accepted notion that in the long run all of Palestine's Jewish land should be nationalized, and the need to cope with the financial constraints, limiting the ability of the JNF to meet the urgent needs of acquiring as much land as possible in the shortest of time.

In reality, though, the JNF acquired about two-thirds of all the non-Jewish land (mostly Arab owned) which was purchased by Jews during the Mandate period. The fund increased its holdings from 22,000 dunams in 1920, to 926,000 dunams in 1947, constituting about half of all Jewish land possessions, 1.85 million dunams, in the latter year (see Katz 2001: appendix 5). The JNF allotted most of its land by leasehold to cooperative settlements (*kibbutzim* and *moshavim*) affiliated with the Zionist labor movement – the leading political and social power in the Jewish community of Palestine and in the WZO from the mid 1930s onwards. Note, however, that impressive as the land accumulation by the JNF may have been, all the Jewish-possessed land in the country constituted by the end of the Mandate no more than 7 percent of the entire area of Palestine (or about 11 percent of its non-desert area).

But notwithstanding the small extent of Jewish land acquisitions relative to the size of Palestine, the Zionist ethno-national agenda driving them was well understood by all the parties concerned. The non-trivial number of Arab tenants that were dispossessed by the sale of their landlords' property to the Jews only added to the politically loaded ramifications of these land transactions, to which both the Palestinian Arabs and the government were challenged to respond.[10]

The Palestinian national movements reacted both internally and externally. They exerted pressure on Arab landowners to refrain from selling their property to the Jews, and demanded that the government put a halt on such sales altogether and protect Arab tenants tilling the land from possible dispossession. The government on its part acted on the two interrelated matters by attempting various regulatory constraints on inter-communal land transactions and by issuing periodic "protection of cultivators ordinances," culminating in the highly restrictive land-transfer regulations of 1940. In addition, it devised and operated in the 1930s a tenants' compensation scheme, but it was rather poorly designed and ill executed (Porath 1974, 1977; Stein 1984; Metzer 1998: ch. 4).

In the land market itself, however, Arab landowners continued to offer land for sale regardless of all those restrictive moves, and the volume of actual transactions at the prevailing supply prices seem to have been largely determined by the resources available on the Jewish demand side (Stein 1984). Note, though, that this observation does not rule out the possibility that the prevailing market prices at which Jewish demand did not exhaust the Arab supply of land, were higher, due to the above mentioned restrictions, than the minimum (threshold) prices at which land would be offered in an unrestricted and politically neutral market. The fact that the index of land prices rose faster than any other price index in Palestine between the late 1920s and the mid 1940s only supports this conjecture (Metzer 1998: ch. 4). Nonetheless, even if such a price wedge did exist and caused the volume of inter-communal land transactions to be smaller than it otherwise would be, it certainly did not stop those transactions and, given the existing evidence, did probably have only little effect on their extent (Metzer 1998: ch. 4; Katz 2001).

It can thus be concluded that although land acquisition in the open market was a pivotal factor in consolidating a viable Jewish national entity in Palestine, providing a territorial basis for its future sovereignty, the ethnonational struggle over the country's territory was carried on during the Mandate period mainly in the political and military arena, and not in the land market itself, which remained for the most part relatively free.

Israel's land regime between state and (Jewish) nation: the formative years, 1948–1961

The creation of the State of Israel in May 1948 raised afresh the question of what should the functions of collective land possession be, if at all required, once statehood and sovereignty had been established. This question was closely linked to, and became essentially part of, two other interrelated problems that needed to be tackled in Israel's early phase of state building.

The first problem was urgent: how to handle the sizable areas of land left behind by the massive exodus of their Arab holders during the 1948 war. Because of ambiguities of land registrations and titles inherited from the Mandate period, the size of these areas has never been precisely determined, but none of the existing estimates quotes numbers smaller than 4.2 million dunams, with some reaching even as high a quotation as 5.8 million dunams (see Kark 1995). Frank Lewis, in a recent attempt to assess the value of the agricultural property of the 1948 Arab refugees, reached an estimate, which seems to be most reasonable, of about 4.8 million dunams for the size of their abandoned rural land area (Lewis 1996).

These vast chunks of land constituted between 20 and 25 percent of Israel's area within the lines of the 1949 armistice agreements, and more than 40 percent of the state's total non-desert area. The need to decide on these lands was particularly pressing in view of the decision, taken by the Israeli government early on, not to allow the Arab refugees, who left the area during the war, to return to their abandoned homes and lands within the state's borders (the armistice lines). It was further aggravated by the pressure of the demand for cultivable land and food production that was generated by the mass Jewish immigration of 1949–1952 (Golan 1995, 2001; Kark 1995; Kleiman 1997).

The other problem was of a more structural nature and had to do with the institutional aspects of the transition from Mandate to statehood. Specifically, what role should the WZO–Jewish Agency and the JNF play in the State of Israel? Did these institutions, leading the Jewish community in Palestine to statehood, become superfluous with the sovereign State of Israel coming into being? If not, what purpose were these "exterritorial" Zionist/Jewish institutions supposed to serve in the newly born state?

In considering these problems it should be borne in mind that, while being self-perceived as a Jewish State, Israel was committed, as stated in its Declaration of Independence, to complete social and political equality of all its citizens (Jews and non-Jews alike), regardless of religion, race, and gender.

In the rest of this section I shall discuss the ways and means that were used by the State of Israel to deal with these complex issues. In doing so I shall dwell on the insight they provide into the nexus between property rights in land and territorial sovereignty, and elaborate on the ethno-national context of the institutional and functional aspects of the state's land regime in the making.

By the end of 1948, the government of Israel controlled directly 17.8 million dunams, constituting 87.1 percent of the state's total area of 20.4 million dunams (these were composed of about 10.9 million dunams of desert, at least 4.2 million dunams of abandoned Arab land held in custodianship, and 2.7 million dunams of lands that were registered in the name of the (Mandatory) government, and other unregistered and concession lands). Another 940,000 dunams (4.6 percent of the total) were possessed by the JNF, and the remaining 1.7 million dunams, amounting only to 8.3 percent of the entire area of the state, were privately owned by Israeli Arabs (52 percent) and Jews (48 percent).[11]

In January 1949, the government sold about 1.1 million dunams of abandoned Arab rural lands to the JNF, and an additional chunk of 1.3 million dunams, in October 1950, thereby increasing the landed property of the JNF more than two and a half fold, and granting the fund ownership of more than half of all the abandoned lands (see Granott 1956: ch. IV). Concurrently, a series of legislative steps was undertaken by government initiative, providing a legal basis for these and other moves and laying the foundations for Israel's land regime and policies.

Two pieces of legislation that were passed by the Israeli parliament (Knesset) in 1950 were particularly significant in this context. The first was the *Absentees' Property Law* of March 1950, vesting all the absentee's property in the Custodian for Absentees' Property to be appointed by the Minister of Finance. The law provided for a rather broad definition of absentees, including not just Arab refugees and residents of the belligerent Arab states, but also persons who may have been present in Israel when their property was legally classified as *Absentees' Property*, and who became thus identified as *present absentees*. The *Absentees' Property Law* did not give the absentees the right to return to their land, let alone regain possession of their property, but allowed for future compensation for their losses.

The law did enable, however, the transfer of the absentees' property from the Custodian to a statutory Development Authority, which was to be established under a separate law (to be discussed next). And, indeed, in September 1953 all the remaining property that was held by the Custodian of

Absentees' Property at the time (after the above mentioned sales to the JNF) was transferred by the Custodian to the Development Authority which started to function on January 1 of that year (Kretzmer 1990: ch. 4).

The *Development Authority (Transfer of Property) Law* of July 1950 was the second significant piece of legislation. It stipulated a legal mechanism for the transfer of property in general, and of absentees' property in particular, to and by the statutory Development Authority that the government was authorized to create. The notable feature of this law was the proviso disallowing the Development Authority to sell, or otherwise transfer, land (except for a maximum of 100,000 dunams of urban property) except to four public entities: the State, the JNF, a governmentally approved institution for settling landless Arabs, or municipalities. Moreover, the JNF was granted in this law the right of first refusal insofar as any urban land was offered for sale by the Development Authority (Kretzmer 1990: ch. 4; Katz 2002: ch. 3).

Note that an institution for settling landless Arabs was never created and municipalities would under no circumstances acquire more than limited tracts of land within their jurisdiction. Hence, abandoned Arab rural lands could be sold only to the state or to the JNF and, as indicated above, the latter did already acquire the greater part of those lands from the Custodian even before the Development Authority began its operations.

The practical and legislative acts I have just described demonstrate that by its dealing with the complexities involving the Arab abandoned lands, the State of Israel established the role of the JNF as an essential partner in pursuing its land policies. This partnership was even further cemented in the additional legislative and administrative developments of the decade, culminating in the *Lands of Israel* legislation of 1960, and in the signing of the covenant between the state and the JNF in 1961.

In November 1952 the *World Zionist Organization–Jewish Agency Status Law* was enacted, granting the Jewish National Institutions, including the JNF, a formal status as non-state institutions, statutorily responsible for handling Jewish immigration, absorption, and settlement in Israel. Being non-state organs, the Jewish National Institutions would have been free to openly pursue various Jewish-specific tasks within the State of Israel, and would have the advantage of being able to raise tax-deductible donations, in the United States and in other countries, to finance these tasks (Kretzmer, 1990: ch. 6). Likewise, in dealing with organizational matters of migration, the National Institutions, not being official bodies of the destination country, should have found it easier to function in certain countries of origin.

A year later, in November 1953, a separate *Jewish National Fund Law* was passed in the Knesset, authorizing the Minister of Justice to approve the memorandum and articles of association of the JNF as a new company (alongside, and essentially identical to, the "old" London incorporated JNF) to be incorporated in Israel and register all the JNF property in the state in its name.

The memorandum, approved in 1954, reinstated the Jewish-specific goal of the JNF, stating that its object is:

> purchasing, acquiring by lease or exchange, receiving by lease or in any other way, lands, forests, rights of possession or easements and all other such rights, as well as immovable property of any sort, in the designated area (which includes the State of Israel and any area controlled by the Government of Israel) for the purpose of settling Jews on the said lands and property.
>
> (quoted in English in Kretzmer 1990: 62)

Note, though, that unlike the memorandum of the "old" company, that of the Israeli-incorporated JNF did not explicitly state that land is to be leased to Jews or Jewish corporate bodies (Katz 2002: appendix 1). Nonetheless, the object of *settling Jews*, as stated in the memorandum of the "Israeli" JNF, was taken to imply that lands owned by the JNF may not be leased, at least on a long run basis, to non-Jews (Kretzmer 1990: ch. 4).

In July 1960, after lengthy preparations and deliberations, the Knesset enacted the major legislative package that finally shaped the legal status of the lands owned by the state (directly, or through the statutory Development Authority) and by the JNF, and established the institutional framework for administrating them (note that these lands constituted 92 percent of the entire area of Israel). The *Basic Law: Israel Lands* declared the JNF lands, the state lands, and the lands owned by the Development Authority as Israel Lands and determined their status as a perpetual public domain, not to be sold, donated, or otherwise transferred, except for certain kinds of lands and transactions to be specified by law. The *Israel Lands Law* specified precisely those exceptions (notable among them was the provision facilitating the transfer of lands to "present absentees" in compensation for their lands, which were declared absentees' property). The third piece of the said legislation, the *Israel Lands Authority Law*, provided for the establishment of the Israel Lands Administration (ILA), a governmental body, which since that year has managed under one institutional and administrative roof all the Israel Lands (Kretzmer 1990: ch. 4; Katz 2002: ch. 5).

Following this legislation, a formal – truly power sharing – covenant between the state of Israel and the JNF was signed in November 1961. It outlined the structure of the ILA and the terms of reference for its unified management (including leasing) of all the Israel Lands. Besides stating that the ILA director was to be nominated by the government in consultation with the JNF, it stipulated that the government was to have only a majority of one in the membership of the Israel Lands Council, the governing body of the ILA. The remaining council members were to be nominated by the JNF. Likewise, in reciprocity to the management of its lands by a governmental organ, the JNF would be responsible, according to the covenant, for the reclamation, development, and forestation of the Israel Lands. For this task it would create and run a Land Development Administration and would hold a majority of one in its Council.

Furthermore, following the affirmation that all the Israel Lands will be administered according to the "lease only" principle of the above Basic Law, the covenant stipulated that the ILA will administer the JNF-owned lands (about 19 percent of all the Israel Lands) also in accord with the Memorandum and Articles of Association of the JNF. In addition, the covenant restated the status of the JNF as an institution of the WZO, to be supported by the government of Israel in its informational activities in Israel and abroad (Katz 2002: appendix 15).

Thus, by the end of this decade-long process it was amply revealed that the Jewish National Institutions in general, and the JNF in particular, were far from becoming redundant either in the transition from the Jewish National Home to statehood or in Israel. The JNF played a major role in the formation and management of the ILA, and its cornerstone principle of collective land ownership was fully adopted by the state.

Moreover, public ownership of most of the land within the state's borders, which the government widened even further by expropriations and specific legislation, affecting mainly the Arab population, provided it with powerful means to pursue its national objectives in the spatial arena.[12] These included the dispersion of (Jewish) population, partly for security reasons, in frontier zones and also in internal regions (like the Galilee) that were heavily populated by Arabs, and the settlement of Jewish immigrants, mostly on Arab abandoned lands, the larger part of which had become, as indicated above, JNF property already in 1950.

It is in this context that the distinction between state lands, to which no overt discrimination on an ethno-national basis could be legally applied, and JNF lands, that would be leased on a long-run basis solely to Jews, was highly significant. This, and similar distinctions between the state and the Jewish National Institutions enabled Israel to legalistically accommodate some of the incompatibilities between (Jewish) *nation* and *state* and rationalized the retention of those institutions as useful promoters of Jewish nation building even under statehood.

Although the "end result" of Israel's land regime and the role of the JNF has already been "revealed," it would be useful, nevertheless, to dwell on some of the (Jewish) positions that were expressed in the deliberative process leading to it. In examining these positions, as will be done next, we should be able to appreciate not just the various attitudes involved, but also their meaning in a more general context of property rights in land and territorial sovereignty in new, ethno-nationally divided, states.[13]

In the Knesset debate on the *World Zionist Organization–Jewish Agency (Status) Law* in November 1952, Eliezer Livne MK (Member of the Knesset), a dissenting member of the Mapai ruling party, made the following remarks:

What was the main function of the Zionist Organization and the Zionist movement until establishment of the state? Its function was to organize the Jews in the Diaspora so as to build up the land. What did the Zionist movement engage in during the time of Mandate? Settlement, absorption and education of immigrants – here in the land [of Israel]. Why did it engage in all of these? Because it was "a state on the way". . . . In other words, the Zionist Organization served as a substitute for the state; the offices established in Jerusalem, the activities that the Zionist Organization carried out through the Jewish Agency were the activities of a surrogate state. And here there has been a change. A state now exists. Why should the state not do all these things? This function of the Zionist movement has come to an end.

(quoted in English in Kretzmer 1990: 91–92)

These remarks are an unequivocal statement, advocating the termination of all the state-like activities of the Jewish National Institutions (of which the JNF was obviously an integral part), which should be undertaken by the sovereign State of Israel. Statehood thus made the National Institutions, according to Livne's position, largely redundant, and they should therefore be left only with the work in the Diaspora, promoting Jewish education and immigration and raising funds for Jewish and Israeli causes.

Interestingly, David Ben-Gurion, the renowned founding father and first Prime Minister of Israel, expressed quite similar views on the JNF, and its celebrated principle of collective land holding, in the Cabinet discussion of the draft proposal of the *Transfer of Property Law* in November 1949. The draft proposal, contrary to the finally approved version, included a clause enabling the Development Authority to sell its lands without any strings attached. Ben-Gurion, consistent with his general embracing of etatism, defended this clause (but remained in a minority of one when it was voted on in the Cabinet), essentially on the ground that the sovereignty of the state was absolute and all-inclusive, and did not require public land ownership in order to be realized.

Likewise, the legitimacy and soundness of the role assigned to the JNF by the state, particularly in the *Basic Law* of 1960, was questioned and quite strongly objected to in the Knesset debates by representatives of the far left as well as those of the center-right parties. Moshe Sneh, a veteran Zionist activist but at the time an MK representing the Israeli Communist party, argued that the JNF should practically be dissolved and its lands be transferred to full state ownership, similar to other governmental functions, such as in the areas of education and security, that were taken over by the state upon its creation from the National Institutions. Being a socialist, he advocated full land nationalization, but his argument, like those made by Livne and Ben Gurion, was largely based on the notion of complete state sovereignty. In this context he questioned the justification for the special position that the JNF continued to hold in the public-land arena, which was incompatible, in his view, with the state's territorial sovereignty, since the Fund, being an organ of the WZO, was an international and not an Israeli institution.

Sneh based his call for the nationalization (i.e. state ownership) of the JNF lands also on his strong objection to the embodiment in a basic constitutional law of a provision – related to the JNF lands – which would allow, in defiance of Israel's Declaration of Independence, for ethno-national discrimination in the leasing of public land. On this point he was joined by no less a devout Zionist than Shlomo Zalman Abramov MK of the center right – free market oriented – General Zionists Party, as well as by Menachem Begin, the leader of the right-wing national Herut Party (who became in 1977 the Prime Minister of Israel, following the merger of the two parties into the Likud Party).

Abramov stated in most unequivocal terms that the accommodation by the state of an institutional body (the JNF) that practices discrimination on an ethno-national basis contradicts the wording and intent of the Declaration of Independence. In other words, both Sneh, from the left side of the political spectrum, and Abramov, from its center right found unacceptable an arrangement that would allow Israel to pursue Jewish-specific goals by excluding Arabs from the JNF lands that it was supposed to manage, while formally holding to the principle of equal rights for all its citizens.

Moreover, in objecting to the status of the JNF, Abramov, like Sneh, took notice of the problematic incorporation in the law of an "ex-state" body that is free to change its statues and bylaws without the state's consent. In the same spirit, he asked what right did the State of Israel have to impose legal restrictions (as the *Basic Law: Lands of Israel*, actually did) on possible future changes in the status of lands that were owned by the Jewish people at large (to whom the JNF belongs) and were not state property.

But being an advocate of private enterprise and perceiving the concept of territorial sovereignty to be independent of land ownership, Abramov, unlike Sneh, rejected the whole idea of land nationalization, questioning the supposed "sanctity" of the land as an asset and its implied inalienability. He viewed land to be no different than any other productive capital asset and saw no reason why the state should not be free to sell any parts of the public domain, as it saw fit. A similar view on the land nationalization question was expressed by Yohanan Bader MK of the right-wing Herut Party. He argued that the land inalienability principle of the JNF was primarily prompted by the risk that Jewish land might be sold to non-Jews. But, he claimed, the very establishment of the state eliminated the risky consequences (from a Jewish national point of view) of such sales. Put differently, territorial sovereignty rendered the ethno-national identity of landowners within the state immaterial.

Note, though, that both Abramov and Bader represented constituencies that on the whole benefited little from the JNF leasehold arrangements. The rural constituency of the Zionist non-socialist parties, primarily the General

Zionist Party, consisted mainly of private farmers in non-cooperative villages (*Moshavot*), owning their own land, or leasing it from private land-owning companies.

While the Abramov–Bader view was compatible with the classic liberal perception of land as alienable *property*, a diametrically opposed view, very much in tune with the typical conceptualization of land in nationalist thinking, as *place* – a homeland belonging to the nation, was held by Yoseph Weitz, a key figure in the Zionist land apparatus.[14] Weitz headed the JNF's Land Department since 1932 and was nominated in 1960 to be the first Director of the ILA. In 1949 he remarked that "Certain circles within the Hebrew public . . . are of the opinion that since the State of Israel was created, the entire country belongs to it anyway . . . and thus – the land problem became resolved by itself. The land was redeemed. . . ." But, he was quick to add, since all the citizens of the state hold the same rights to government (state) land, "the Jewish government is not free to use it so as to benefit one party only, but everything it does with this land, it is obliged to do in such a way that will benefit the Jews and the Arabs alike." This observation and the fact that most of the arable lands within the borders of the UN-designated Jewish State were owned by Arabs, led Weitz to conclude "that it is necessary to see to it that most of the land belongs to the Jews . . . and therefore land redemption must be continued" as had been done before the UN adopted the partition resolution (Weitz 1950: 143–145).

In these remarks, which may have partly reflected inertia of attitudes and deeds from the pre-state era, Weitz rightly observed that the state's capacity to pursue Jewish-specific goals by resorting to ethno-national distinction in the allocation and utilization of state lands was limited, if at all possible. Hence acquisition by the JNF of non-Jewish land – referring primarily to the lands abandoned by the Arab refugees during the 1948 war – should be continued even under statehood. Such purchases and the resulting JNF land ownership should facilitate, according to Weitz, the realization of, spatially related, Jewish national goals within the sovereign state of Israel, and, at the same time, provide a financial basis for the eventual compensation of the Arab refugees for their lost land (Weitz 1950: 145–157).

With the sale of most of the Arab-abandoned rural lands to the JNF in 1949–1950 (as discussed earlier) land acquisition à la Weitz (although not expropriation) had been largely exhausted, and the idea of land redemption, which the Israeli Jewish public and its parliamentary majority continued by and large to embrace, retained mainly its inalienability and reclamation components. And, indeed, most of the opinions that were expressed in the press and in the parliamentary deliberations in support of the land legislative initiatives and policies drew on the ideology underpinning the inalienability of (Jewish) land. Members of the Zionist-religious parties highlighted primarily its national–religious legacy, while members of the secular parties, particularly of the Zionist labor movement, praised in addition its egalitarian aspects, and resorted to what we may possibly characterize as ideological "path dependence."

For example, Levi Eshkol, the Minister of the Treasury, presented in the Knesset the land legislative package of 1959–1960 as a triumph of the founding idea of the JNF in the spirit of the nation forefathers' vision. Likewise, David Bar-Rav-Hai, a Mapai MK, in defending the inalienability of the public domain in the Knesset, asserted in 1960 that "state land owner-ship is one of the principles that we were educated on. And I do not accept the claim that what was right in the pre-state era is not right now."[15] In the same fashion, Yisrael Guri, the chair of the Knesset Finance Committee, when bringing the *Israel Lands Law* to a final vote, introduced it as a real-ization of one of the sacred values of Zionism and the nation that was embodied in the idea of the JNF.

While the ideological zeal with which the parties of labor Zionism (secular and religious alike) supported the land inalienability principle was unrelenting, it should be noticed that it might have been, at least partly, fed by the interests of the cooperative agricultural settlements (*Kibbutzim* and *Moshavim*), who were possibly the most influential constituencies of those parties at the time. The cooperative settlements, constituting the majority of the Jewish rural settlements in the country, were virtually all built on JNF or state land and have long cherished the extremely generous terms and security of their long run leaseholds.

A digression on equity considerations in the handling of Israel Lands

Notice that the compatibility of the interests of the agricultural cooperative settlements with the equity goals of national land ownership – as crystal-lized already in the Zionist deliberations of the late 1910s and early 1920s (see pp. 90–93) and restated by the proponents of the *Lands of Israel* legis-lation – has been put recently to a serious test. The issue at hand involves a major dispute that arose in the 1990s, and remains still unresolved, concerning the criteria for, and the size of, the compensation that co-operative settlements should be entitled to for their agricultural land (leased from the ILA for farming only), if and when appropriated by the ILA for (non-agricultural) development.

Drawing support from revisionist decisions that the ILA Council had taken on the matter in the first half of the 1990s, the cooperative settle-ments and their organizations held the position that the compensation in question should be based on the value of the land in its "new," non-agricultural use. In other words, beyond payments to properly compensate the settlements for their investments on the land, loss of income, and early termination of their leases, the compensation should also include a substan-tial fraction of the land's, exogenously determined, location rent (see also Yiftachel and Kedar 2000).

This viewpoint was vigorously challenged by the *Mizrahi* (Oriental) *Democratic Rainbow* (MDR), a voluntary association concerned with issues of social equality primarily in relation to the status of oriental Jews in Israel. In its fierce objection to the compensation scheme based on the non-agricultural value of the land, and in the petition it submitted to the High Court of Justice (HCJ) to that effect in January 2000, the MDR reiterated essentially the old, equity-oriented, Zionist rationale for land nationalization (MDR 2003). As was shown in the first section of this chapter, land nationalization in Zionist thinking was supposed, among other things, to prevent landholders in leasehold from capturing, unjustifiably, exogenously generated capital gains to their land. It is the *people* at large, commonly owning the land, that should be entitled to these gains – to be realized once the land becomes available for non-farm uses – and not the individuals or the cooperative settlements to whom it was leased exclusively for farming.

In practice, this rationale underlay also the ground-setting Decision no. 1 of the ILA Council in 1965, guiding its policy until the turnabout of the 1990s (ILA 2003). The HCJ, in a ruling on the above petition, which was issued on November 29, 2002, concurred with the MDR and ordered the ILA to formulate a new equitable compensation scheme. The matter is still pending while an additional petition, filed by the MDR in July 2003, is awaiting a follow-up decision by the HCJ (MDR 2003).

Conclusion

To summarize the points raised in the land legislation debates, the opponents of the legislation (or of parts of it) seem to have had the upper hand as far as the soundness of their arguments is concerned. Nonetheless, the government–JNF alliance, backed by the proponents of the laws, had prevailed. This implied, essentially, that the State of Israel, in granting a special status to the JNF, and to the Jewish National Institutions generally, did willingly accept the constraints imposed on its own territorial sovereignty in order to pursue its Jewish-specific goals in the land allocation arena.

Postscript: the Katzir ruling, a court decision looking to the future

With the passing of the *Lands of Israel* legislation and the establishment of the Israel Lands Administration (ILA), the land regime of the state (within its pre-1967 borders) was put firmly in place and our story could be concluded at that. Recently, however, a landmark decision by the Supreme Court (sitting in its capacity as the High Court of Justice) may have produced the first significant amendment affecting the ethno-national implications of the regime, thereby possibly opening a new chapter in the story of land rights and the relation between citizenship and nationality in Israel.[16]

The decision, which is now widely recognized as the *Katzir Ruling*, was issued in March 2000 on a petition submitted to the HCJ in 1995 by an Israeli Arab married couple, Adel and Iman Ka'adan, with the encourage- ment and legal backing of the Association for Civil Rights in Israel. The petitioners sought to build their home in Katzir, a communal settlement in the Eron River region of northern Israel. The settlement was established back in 1982 by the Jewish Agency on state lands that were allotted to it by the ILA in leasehold, for the purpose of subleasing and settling on those lands the members of the Katzir Cooperative Society.

Since the Cooperative Society in question (as is customary for settlement societies of this kind) accepts only people to whom Israel's *Defense Service Law* applies, i.e. it does not accept Arabs as members, the petitioners were denied membership and were refused permission to acquire land, build a home, and settle in Katzir. The petitioners claimed that this refusal consti- tuted discrimination on the basis of religion or nationality, which was prohibited by law with regard to the allocation and use of state land.

Their complaint was directed primarily against the ILA, arguing that by allocating land to institutional bodies (such as the Jewish Agency and the Katzir Cooperative Society) that apply criteria of discrimination and inequality to the use of the land, the ILA violated its obligation to operate as a trustee for all the state's citizens and to treat them equally. It is inter- esting to note, in this respect, that insofar as the management of the JNF urban lands is concerned, the ILA attempted, successfully, to avoid legal confrontations in the past. In several instances where Arabs applied for a leasehold on JNF urban land, those lands were transferred to the Development Authority (a move allowed by the *Israel Lands Law*), which, not being bound by the Memorandum and Articles of Association of the JNF, would then lease them to the Arab applicants (Kretzmer 1990: ch. 4).

To the Ka'adan petition, however, the ILA responded by stating that it had acted according to the 1952 *World Zionist Organization Jewish Agency (Status) Law* and the 1979 Covenant between the government of Israel and the Jewish Agency, and the action was therefore lawful.[17] The Jewish Agency added that its goal of settling Jews on Israel Lands all over the state, and particularly in regions (like that of the Eron River) where Jewish pres- ence is sparse, was a legitimate goal incorporated in, and recognized by, the above law and covenant.

The Court, being fully aware of the, potentially, far-reaching implica- tions of the case, tried to avoid ruling on it and attempted to get the parties to resolve the issue by out-of-court conciliation. But when these attempts failed to produce an agreed solution, judicial ruling became inevitable.

The ruling stated as a baseline that the equality principle, which prohibits the state from using religion or nationality as distinguishing devices in treating its citizens, applies also to the allocation of state lands. Moreover, the ruling emphasized that:

the State engages in impermissible discrimination even if it is also willing to allocate State land for the purpose of establishing an exclusively Arab settlement, as long as it permits a group of Jews without distinguishing characteristics to establish an exclusively Jewish settlement on State land.[18]

This part of the ruling, concerning the direct allocation of state lands to their final users, was hardly "revolutionary," but it provided the legal and ethical foundation for its, unquestionably, novel part, which reads as follows:

Where one may not discriminate directly, one may not discriminate indirectly. If the State, through its own actions, may not discriminate on the basis of religion or nationality, it may not facilitate such discrimination by a third party. It does not change matters that the third party is the Jewish Agency. Even if the Jewish Agency may distinguish between Jews and non-Jews, it may not do so in the allocation of State land.

While on matters of principle the ruling was unequivocal, the Court was more reserved when it came to consider the specific relief requested by the petitioners, which involved changes of a retroactive nature in a 14-year-old setting. Taking all the relevant considerations into account, and explicitly recognizing that its ruling marks the first step on a difficult and sensitive path, the HCJ came up with the following definitive judgment:

A. We hold that the State of Israel was not permitted, by law, to allocate State land to the Jewish Agency for the purpose of establishing the communal settlement of Katzir on the basis of discrimination between Jews and non-Jews.

B. The State of Israel must consider the petitioners' request to acquire land for themselves in the settlement of Katzir for the purpose of building their home. The State must make this consideration based on the principle of equality, and considering various relevant factors – including those factors affecting the Jewish Agency and the current residents of Katzir. The State of Israel must also consider the numerous legal issues. Based on these considerations, the State of Israel must determine with deliberate speed whether to allow the petitioners to make a home within the communal settlement of Katzir.

Although confined to State lands only, the *Katzir Ruling*, by shaking the foundations of the "division of labor" between the State of Israel and the Jewish National Institutions in the area of land policy, may have opened the door for questioning the legitimacy of a wider range of "Jewish-specific" attributes of Israel's land regime. And in doing so it may have paved the way for moving this regime closer to ethno-national blindness.

Notes

* I would like to thank Nachum Gross and Hagit Lavsky for their helpful comments and suggestions.

1 The original name of the World Zionist Organization was the Zionist Organization. The "World" part was added to the name at a later date, but for simplicity I am using throughout the chapter the current full name.
2 There is a substantial body of literature on the ethno-national aspects of the land question in pre-state Zionism and Israel. A selected, but far from exhaustive, list should include the following items: Granott (1952, 1956); Metzer (1977, 1978, 1998); Reichman (1979); Kimmerling (1983); Stein (1984); Shafir (1989); Kretzmer (1990); Golan (1995, 2001); Kark (1995); Yiftachel (1998); Kedar (1998, 2001); Katz (2001, 2002).
3 One metric dunam equals in size approximately one quarter of an acre; one square kilometer contains exactly one thousand dunams.
4 Two qualifications should be made on this point, though. One is that the JNF leasehold scheme was not much different from the *Rentengut* ("annuity property") system that the Prussian Settlement Commission extensively used (see Chapter 3). The second qualification relates to the JNF-owned *Himanuta* Company which was established by the fund in 1938 in order to conduct unrestricted transactions in the land market (including selling landed property), effectively on behalf of the JNF, and continues to operate to this date (see Katz 2001: ch. 2).
5 It should be emphasized, though, that the Zionist principle of retaining Jewish land in Jewish hands was in general adhered to by private Jewish landowners as well, thus questioning in this regard the necessity of nationalizing the land (see Metzer 2003).
6 The emphasis on agricultural settlement was clearly noticeable in the actual purchases of the JNF, which consisted mostly of arable rural land, with urban land constituting only a negligible share of the fund's total acquisitions during the Mandate period. For a detailed discussion of the concentration on the acquisition of rural land by the JNF and of the rationale underlying it, see Lavsky (1999).
7 Continuous cultivation was to serve also as a safeguard against the possibility, albeit remote, of the sovereign repossessing uncultivated farmland. The Ottoman Land Code of 1858 (which was amended in 1912 and remained in force in Mandatory Palestine and in Israel until 1969, when it was replaced by the newly enacted *Israeli Land Law*) provided for the option of such state repossession of formally state-owned agricultural land (*miri*-type) in cases where the individual title holder to the land left it uncultivated for three consecutive years (see Granott 1952: ch. V).
8 For further elaboration on the Zionist arguments for land nationalization see Metzer (1977). See also Shilony (1998: ch. 1) for a discussion of land nationalization and agrarianism in European social and economic thinking of the nineteenth and early twentieth centuries, which may have influenced Zionist ideas on the matter.
9 These considerations (Metzer 1977, 1998: ch. 4) resemble quite closely the design of the German colonization in Posen (see the discussion above and Chapter 3 in this volume).
10 I attempted elsewhere a conjectural estimate of the dispossessed Arab tenants and arrived at an upper bound of 16,000 tenant male workers, making for at most 9 percent of the Arab male labor force in the mid period (Metzer 1998: ch. 4).
11 The numbers were adjusted to the end of 1948 from Kark (1995: table 21.1), which provides the distribution of land by types of ownership for the end of 1949.

12 See Kretzmer (1990) and Kedar (1998, 2001) for comprehensive documentation
    and highly illuminating analysis of the expropriation policies (exercised in the first
    three decades of statehood) and of the various legislative acts that the State of
    Israel resorted to in order to expand the area of state lands, mostly at the expense
    of Arab landed property. Land expropriation was a source of resentment and
    bitterness within the Israeli Arab community, culminating on March 30, 1976 in
    a general strike, during which six Arabs were killed in clashes with the police.
    Expropriation had all but stopped afterwards, and March 30 became a day of
    ethno-national protest and commemoration for the Arab community in Israel to
    be known since as *the land day* (see Kretzmer 1990: ch. 4).
13 The following discussion of the parliamentary debates draws on the detailed docu-
    mentation contained in Katz (2002: chs 3 and 5). Rich material on the issues at
    hand is found also in Oren-Nordheim (1999).
14 For an illuminating discussion of land in liberal and national thinking, see Levy
    (2000: ch. 7).
15 Quoted in Hebrew in Katz (2002: 70).
16 The following discussion draws on the High Court of Justice ruling (HCJ 2000)
    and on the case summary in English as communicated by the Court's
    Spokeswoman on March 8, 2000, and printed on the website of the Israel Ministry
    of Foreign Affairs (MFA 2003).
17 The *World Zionist Organization–Jewish Agency (Status) Law, 1952* stipulated that the
    details of the status of these two bodies, which were not separated at the time,
    and the modes of cooperation between them and the government of Israel will
    be spelled out in a covenant to be signed between them and the government. Such
    a covenant was indeed signed in 1954. Following the expansion of the Jewish
    Agency's ranks in 1971, the original law of 1952 was amended, and in 1979 two
    separate covenants, one between the government and the WZO and the other
    between the government and the Jewish Agency, were signed, replacing the 1954
    covenant. The covenants of 1979 specified the respective functions of the WZO
    and the Jewish Agency. They included, among others, agricultural settlement,
    purchase and development of land, and participation in the funding and extension
    of development projects in Israel (see Kretzmer 1990: ch. 6).
18 This and the following quotations in this section are all taken from the English
    case summary in MFA 2003.

Bibliography

Ben-Porath, Y. (1966) *The Arab Labor Force in Israel*, Jerusalem: Maurice Falk Institute
    for Economic Research in Israel.
Boehm, A. and Pollak, A. (1939) *The Jewish National Fund (Keren Kayemeth Leisrael):
    Its History, Function and Activity*, Jerusalem: Head Office of the Jewish National
    Fund.
Golan, A. (1995) "The Transfer to Jewish Control of Abandoned Arab Lands during
    the War of Independence," in S.I. Troen and N. Lucas (eds) *Israel: The First Decade
    of Independence*, Albany: State University of New York Press.
—— (2001) *Wartime Spatial Change: Former Arab Territories within the State of Israel
    1948–1950*, Sede Boker: Ha-Mercaz Le-Moreshet Ben Gurion; Be'er Sheva': Ben
    Gurion University Press (in Hebrew).
Granott, A. (1952) *The Land System in Palestine*, London: Eyre & Spottiswoode.
—— (1956) *Agrarian Reform and the Record of Israel*, London: Eyre & Spottiswoode.
HCJ (2000) High Court of Justice, "HCJ 6698/95, Ka'adan v the ILA and others,
    March 8th 2000," Jerusalem: The Supreme Court (in Hebrew).

ILA (2003) "Council of the Israel Lands Administration," online, available at http://www.mmi.gov.il (accessed August 6, 2003) (in Hebrew).

Kark, R. (1995) "Planning, Housing, and Land Policy 1948–1952: The Formation of Concepts and Governmental Frameworks," in S.I. Troen and N. Lucas (eds) *Israel: The First Decade of Independence*, Albany: State University of New York Press.

Katz, Y. (2001) *The Battle for the Land: The Jewish National Fund (K.K.L.) before the Establishment of the State of Israel*, Jerusalem: The Hebrew University Magnes Press (in Hebrew).

—— (2002) *"The land shall not be sold in perpetuity": The Legacy and Principles of Keren Kayemeth Leisrael (Jewish National Fund) in the Israel Legislation*, Jerusalem: The Research Institute for the History of JNF and the Chair for the Study of JNF History, Bar-Ilan University (in Hebrew).

Kedar, A. (1998) "Majority Time, Minority Time, Land, Nation, and the Law of Adverse Possession in Israel," *Tel Aviv University Law Review*, 21: 665–746 (in Hebrew).

—— (2001) "The Legal Transformation of Ethnic Geography: Israeli Law and the Palestinian Landholder 1948–1967," *New York University Journal of International Law and Politics*, 33: 923–1000.

Kimmerling, B. (1983) *Zionism and Territory: The Socio-Territorial Dimensions of Zionist Politics*, Berkeley, CA: Institute of International Studies, University of California.

Kleiman, E. (1997) "The Waning of Israeli *Etatisme*," *Israel Studies*, 2: 146–171.

Kretzmer, D. (1990) *The Legal Status of the Arabs in Israel*, Boulder, CO: Westview Press.

Lavsky, H. (1999) "Theory and Praxis: The Agrarian Policy of the Jewish National Fund during the Mandatory Period," in Y. Ben-Artzi, I. Bartal, and E. Reiner (eds) *Studies in Geography and History in Honour of Yehoshua Ben-Arieh*, Jerusalem: The Hebrew University Magnes Press and The Israel Exploration Society (in Hebrew).

Levy, J.T. (2000) *The Multiculturalism of Fear*, New York and Oxford: Oxford University Press.

Lewis, F.D. (1996) "Agricultural Property and the 1948 Palestinian Refugees: Assessing the Loss," *Explorations in Economic History*, 33: 169–194.

MDR (2003) "Misrahi Democratic Rainbow," online, available at http://www.hakeshet.org (accessed August 6, 2003) (in Hebrew).

Metzer, J. (1977) "The Concept of National Capital in Zionist Thought 1918–1921," *Asian and African Studies*, 11: 305–336.

—— (1978) "Economic Structure and National Goals – Jewish National Home in Interwar Palestine," *Journal of Economic History*, 38: 101–119.

—— (1979) *National Capital for a National Home 1919–1921*, Jerusalem: Yad Izhak Ben-Zvi Publications (in Hebrew).

—— (1998) *The Divided Economy of Mandatory Palestine*, Cambridge: Cambridge University Press.

—— (2003) "From the Jewish National Home to the State of Israel: Some Economic Aspects of Nation and State Building," in A. Teichova and H. Matis (eds) *Economic Change and the Building of the Nation State in History*, Cambridge: Cambridge University Press.

MFA (2003) "Ministry of Foreign Affairs," online, available at http://www.mfa.gov.il (accessed August 6, 2003).

Oren-Nordheim, M. (1999) "The Crystallization of Settlement Land Policy in the State of Israel from its Establishment and During the First Years of the Israel Lands

Administration (1948–1965)," unpublished Ph.D. dissertation, The Hebrew University of Jerusalem (in Hebrew).

Orni, E. (1981) *Land in Israel, History, Policy Administration, Development*, Jerusalem: Jewish National Fund.

Penslar, D. (1991) *Zionism and Technocracy: The Engineering of Jewish Settlement in Palestine, 1870–1918*, Bloomington and Indianapolis, IN: Indiana University Press.

Porath, Y. (1974) *The Emergence of the Palestinian-Arab National Movement 1918–1929*, London: Frank Cass.

—— (1977) *From Rise to Rebellion: The Palestinian-Arab National Movement 1929–1939*, London: Frank Cass.

Reichman, S. (1979) *From Foothold to Settled Territory: The Jewish Settlement, 1918–1948*, Jerusalem: Yad Izhak Ben-Zvi Publications (in Hebrew).

—— and Hasson, S. (1984) "A Cross-cultural Diffusion of Colonization: From Posen to Palestine," *Annals of American Geographers*, 74: 57–70.

Reports (1921) *Reports of the Executive of the Zionist Organisation to the XII Zionist Congress*, Part III: Organisation Report, London: National Labour Press.

Shafir, G. (1989) *Land, Labor and the Origins of the Israeli–Palestinian Conflict 1882–1914*, Cambridge: Cambridge University Press.

Shilony, Z. (1990) "German Antecedents of Rural Settlement in Palestine up to World War I," in R. Kark (ed.) *The Land that Became Israel: Studies in Historical Geography*, New Haven, CT: Yale University Press; Jerusalem: The Hebrew University Magnes Press.

—— (1998) *Ideology and Settlement: The Jewish National Fund, 1897–1914*, Jerusalem: The Hebrew University Magnes Press.

Stein, K.W. (1984) *The Land Question in Palestine, 1917–1939*, Chapel Hill, NC: University of North Carolina Press.

Weitz, Y. (1950) *The Struggle for the Land*, Tel Aviv: Tversky (in Hebrew).

Yiftachel, O. (1998) "The Internal Frontier: Territorial Control and Ethnic Relations in Israel," in O. Yiftachel and A. Meir (eds) *Ethnic Frontiers and Peripheries: Landscapes of Development and Inequality in Israel*, Boulder, CO: Westview Press.

—— and Kedar, A. (2000) "Landed Power: The Making of the Israeli Land Regime," *Theory and Criticism*, 16: 67–100 (in Hebrew).

5   Markets and meanings

Nationalism, land, and property in Lithuania*

Rawi Abdelal

Land is one of the most important intersections of social purpose and economic choice. Nationalist movements have invariably ascribed important meanings to patterns of land ownership, as well as the uses to which land is put. As Colin Williams and Anthony Smith observe, "Whatever else it may be, nationalism is always a struggle for control of land; whatever else the nation may be, it is nothing if not a mode of constructing social space" (Williams and Smith 1983: 502; see also Smith 2000; Penrose 2002). Markets for land are indeed full of social meanings. Governments therefore often regulate ownership in land in order to serve purposes. Those purposes are determined by various collective identities within a society. A society's national identity, in particular, has historically been the source of such social purpose.

In this chapter I explore the relationship between land markets and national meanings in Lithuania after the fall of the Soviet Union in 1991. Lithuania is a small country of approximately three and a half million citizens nestled between the other post-Soviet states of Belarus, Latvia, and Russia, in addition to Poland to the southeast. Lithuania's location on the Baltic Sea has led observers regularly to refer to it as 1, along with Estonia and Latvia, of the 3 Baltic states of the former Soviet Union. Although these 3 Baltic states differ a great deal, they share a political bond: of the 15 post-Soviet states, only these 3 unambiguously rejected membership in the Commonwealth of Independent States (CIS) and, instead, embraced the European Union (EU) and North Atlantic Treaty Organization (NATO).

The Lithuanian government, thus, rejected the East and turned toward the West in its foreign economic policies. Motivated by widely shared interpretations of social purpose – interpretations originally proposed by *Sajudis*, the nationalist movement – the Lithuanian government was among the first post-Soviet states to introduce an independent currency and exit the monetary union inherited from the Soviets. Lithuania refused to join a customs union or free trade agreement with Russia and other CIS states, and sought instead to reorient its commerce toward the EU. Political priorities dominated the country's trading and monetary arrangements.

These priorities were reproduced in the market for land, and debates about foreign ownership of Lithuanian land mirrored broader societal debates about the content of Lithuanian national identity.

In this chapter I first outline the relationship between nationalism and political economy in post-Soviet Lithuania. Then I describe the importance of the idea of Lithuanian society's European-ness to its national identity. Next I trace the changes in the Lithuanian government's policies toward land markets, linking those changes to public and parliamentary debates over the meaning of foreign land ownership. Finally, I highlight the implications of the Lithuanian case for understanding the purposive and directional characteristics of nationalisms.

Nationalism and political economy in Lithuania

Lithuanian nationalism has powerfully influenced the country's politics and economics. To be more precise, Lithuanian society's consensus about the content of its national identity endowed foreign economic policy with specific social purposes, including the nation's "return to Europe." This consensus lengthened the time horizons of Lithuanian society and government, for although the country's political–economic reorientation entailed obvious and acknowledged material sacrifice in the short run, it was believed that future generations of Lithuanians would benefit from the deprivation of the present.

At first there was an agenda to be set. Lithuanian nationalists took up this task, and offered the rest of society their proposal for the content of Lithuanian national identity. In the middle of the 1980s, a number of Lithuanian intellectuals in the Academy of Sciences created the *Lietuvos Persitvarkymo Sajudis*, or Lithuanian Movement for Restructuring (perestroika), which, at first, merely sought to promote political change and independence from the Communist Party of Lithuania (CPL). The Movement, or *Sajudis*, as it came to be known, held its founding congress in October 1988. At that time it proclaimed its support of perestroika and proposed greater Lithuanian autonomy within the Soviet federation and more economic self-management. In November *Sajudis* elected Vytautas Landsbergis, a music professor, as its president and adopted increasingly radical goals regarding Lithuania's place in the Soviet Union. *Sajudis* was transformed from a movement for perestroika into a nationalist front demanding independent statehood in the space of little more than a year (see Vardys 1995; Muiznieks 1995).

The CPL's reaction to *Sajudis* during its rise to prominence varied over time. Originally, the CPL sought to contain *Sajudis* influence, but eventually embraced *Sajudis* support of a new model of Soviet federalism put forward by Estonian nationalists. The Party lacked *Sajudis* resolve, at least early on. Under pressure from the Communist Party of the Soviet Union (CPSU), the CPL backed down from the Estonian federal model.

However, Algirdas Brazauskas, a young party leader, pushed the Party to change more quickly with the times. Brazauskas' popularity and political savvy led to his appointment on October 20, 1988 as First Secretary of the CPL, the Party's highest post. Brazauskas was clearly in touch with Lithuanian sentiment regarding the opportunity for change presented by perestroika. Two days after his appointment, Brazauskas addressed the founding congress of *Sajudis*, his first major public audience as First Secretary. Attempting to connect with Lithuania's increasingly influential nationalists, he told *Sajudis*, "on matters of principle, we think alike" (Vardys 1989: 65). A second speech he gave to the congress revealed his commitment to change, as he spoke of the "revival of Lithuanian national consciousness" (Senn 1990: 222).

When First Secretary Brazauskas called the twentieth congress of the CPL in December 1989, he proposed a dramatic break with the past. It was at this congress that the CPL announced its independence from the CPSU. Lithuania's Communists thus sent a clear message to the Lithuanian public and to Moscow, where Soviet authorities condemned the move. Subsequently, the CPL cooperated more intensively with *Sajudis* during the drive toward independence. Indeed, the memberships of *Sajudis* and the Communist Party of Lithuania increasingly overlapped: approximately half of the Initiative Group that began *Sajudis* were Party members. And when the Party elected its new Central Committee in 1989, over half of its members were of self-described "*Sajudis* orientation" (Senn 1990: 222). Later, in 1990, the CPL recast itself as a social democratic party, "in the west European tradition," and renamed itself the Lithuanian Democratic Labor Party (*Lietuvos Demokratine Darbo Partija*, or LDDP).[1]

Events moved quickly during 1990. Gorbachev visited Lithuania in January to campaign against secession from the Union. However, in the February 1990 elections to the Lithuanian Supreme Council, independence-minded *Sajudis* candidates won more than 70 percent of the seats. A month later, in March, the Supreme Council voted 124–0 to declare independence from the Soviet Union. Landsbergis of *Sajudis* was elected Chairman of the Council, a parliamentary post that also made him the newly declared state's first president.

Although other nationalist political parties emerged after independence, *Sajudis* remained the most prominent and influential proponent of a vision for the future of the nation and set of purposes for the state. In 1993, *Sajudis*, which had, in fact, only been a movement rather than an official party, reorganized itself as a political party called Homeland Union, which remained the dominant nationalist party throughout the decade.

Homeland Union's leaders, and most of Lithuania's other nationalists, organized their policy proposals around three main ideas. First, they argued that Lithuania's inter-war state had been lost to Soviet influence, which they associated with Russia, and that after the Cold War Lithuania's newly regained statehood was threatened most by Russia. A strong state was therefore to be an important defense of the sovereignty of the Lithuanian nation (Matulionis 1994; see also Clark 2000). Second, Lithuania's nationalists argued that economic dependence on Russia was the state's primary security threat (Abdelal 1998a). Third, they argued that the state should therefore "reorient" its politics and economy from East to West (Abdelal 1998b; see also Lofgren 1997; Clark 2000). That is, Lithuania should cultivate close economic relationships with "European" states and reduce its economic dependence on Russia. And while the Lithuanian government should become part of the EU, NATO, and other western institutions, it should reject under all circumstances multilateral, institutionalized economic and political relationships with post-Soviet states as a group, especially the CIS.

Thus, *Sajudis*, and later Homeland Union, essentially put forward specific proposals for the content of Lithuanian national identity. These ideas and policy proposals became popular between 1988 and 1991, when Lithuania was on its way to independent statehood. Almost all Lithuanians accepted the arguments of these nationalists. There were no influential organized groups that contested them. Lithuanians largely agreed on what it meant to be Lithuanian, what the government should do in its relations with other governments, and what were the purposes of the state. As Soviet authority collapsed, the popularity of these ideas was reflected in the popularity of the *Sajudis* itself, which virtually swept the 1989 elections to the Congress of People's Deputies and 1990 elections to the parliament.

The coherence and consensus of Lithuanian national identity was even more clearly illustrated when *Sajudis* lost parliamentary and presidential elections to former Communists several years later. In October 1992, a little over a year after the Soviet authorities recognized Lithuanian independence, Lithuania was the first country in eastern Europe or the former Soviet Union to return its former Communists to power in an election. Lithuanians gave the LDDP a parliamentary majority in 1992 and elected the former First Secretary Brazauskas in the 1993 presidential election.[2] For five decisive years in the middle of the decade, Lithuania was ruled by essentially the same party that had controlled the republic during the Soviet era, and many of its leaders were the same people, the old nomenklatura.

Lithuania's former Communists were unlike many former Communists throughout the region. Brazauskas had cooperated with *Sajudis*, and had broken with the CPSU even before formal independence had arrived. Most Lithuanians trusted the commitment of the LDDP and Brazauskas to an independent Lithuanian state (see Senn 1995; Clark 1995; Clark et al. 1999). After Brazauskas was elected President, he explained that Lithuanians knew they could trust the former Communists, because "in the former Communist Party maybe three percent were communists and the rest were just members" (Tammerk 1993). In other words, everyone knew that they never really meant it (see Senn 1992; Christophe 1997). The intellectual Algirdas Julius Greimas expressed it thus in 1954: "Even a Communist Lithuanian is a real Lithuanian, if he is concerned with the well-being of society" (Rindzeviciute 2003: 81).

Indeed, Lithuania's former Communists had become nationalists, in the sense that they used the symbol of the nation in the same ways that *Sajudis* and Homeland Union did, and to legitimate the same foreign policy goals. Lithuanians elected a nationalist, pro-European LDDP in 1992, which had foreign policy goals that were essentially identical to those of the original nationalists (see Lithuanian Democratic Labor Party 1992; Tuskenis 1992a, 1992b; Lucas 1992a, 1992b, 1992c; Ashbourne 1999). Thus, Lithuania's former Communists proclaimed the nationalists' main goals as their own as well. As an LDDP leader explained, in Lithuania "the Communists are more nationalist than the nationalists," because they are better at achieving the same goals (Abdelal 1998b).

Furthermore, all five of Lithuania's major political parties shared the same foreign policy objectives (see Homeland Union 1996; Lithuanian Democratic Labor Party 1996; Lithuanian Christian Democratic Party 1996; Lithuanian Center Union 1996; Lithuanian Social Democratic Party 1996). That is, all five – Homeland Union, the Lithuanian Christian Democratic Party, the LDDP, the Center Union, and the Lithuanian Social Democratic Party – legitimated these goals of reorientation with the symbol of the nation. These 5 accounted for over 90 percent of parliamentary seats throughout the decade. When the Lithuanian parliament ratified the Europe Agreement in June 1996, only 1 MP voted against Lithuania's membership.

In sum, Lithuanians, especially the Lithuanian political elites elected during the 1990s, agreed on the meaning of their national identity and on the fundamental purposes of their statehood. In the late 1980s *Sajudis* emerged as a nationalist movement that proposed pro-European and anti-Soviet content for their society's identity, and they were successful. Most significantly, Lithuania's former Communists, the other major political force in the country, agreed, and adopted the foreign policy goals and national symbolism of *Sajudis*. The prevailing construction of Lithuanian national identity was both clear and consensual.

This clarity resulted in a post-Soviet foreign economic policy for Lithuania that was coherent, purposive, and single-minded. Lithuanian national identity framed the society's political and economic debates. Economic reintegration with the East was not a legitimate option. Lithuanians believed that reorienting their economy toward Europe was the best path to wealth, even if only in the long run. The widely shared content of national identity gave both government and society the political will to endure the economic sacrifice of reorienting toward Europe, sacrifice that was understood to be quite significant, as oil and gas prices rose and eastern markets were lost. Most Lithuanians acknowledged that some economic sacrifice was worth this national purpose. As Michael Wyzan argues, "economic belt-tightening was associated with regaining political independence. People felt that they were sacrificing their living standards for a worthy cause" (Wyzan 1997: 14; see also Jeziowski 1992). In the long run, a European state and economy for the Lithuanian nation would pay off, Lithuanians argued. The central theme of Lithuania's economic policies was the victory of the long view over the short (see Girnius 1997; Abdelal 1998a, 1998b).

The past is another continent: from Eurasia to Europe

Lithuanians' interpretation of Europe was central to their interpretation of their nation during the 1990s (see Rindzeviciute 2003). The most important meaning Lithuanians attached to Europe was its cultural, religious, and historical separateness from Russia and from the post-Soviet space, or "Eurasia." Almost everyone agreed that Lithuania, having regained independence, would "return to Europe," with the EU as Europe's most concrete symbol and EU membership the ultimate recognition of being a European state. For many Lithuanians, the tasks of orienting their state toward Europe and away from Russia were equivalent. In an interview with historian Timothy Garton Ash, a member of the Lithuanian parliament, the Seimas, articulated this definition: "Europe is . . . not-Russia!" (see Ash 1994; Jurgatiene and Wæver 1996; Bunce 1997; Nekrasas 1998).

Trade with the EU was to be welcomed, while trade with Russia was a threat to state security and political autonomy. The government sought to join Europe's monetary union, but refused membership in the ruble zone. "Integration" into the EU, NATO, and other institutions of the western, "trans-Atlantic Community" was the government's most important strategic goal. But the government rejected all post-Soviet institutions, the CIS included, and any efforts toward the "reintegration" of the Eurasian economic space. Indeed, Lithuania's potential participation in post-Soviet regional institutions was pronounced unconstitutional. In June 1992 the Lithuanian parliament adopted the Constitutional Act on Nonalignment of the Republic of Lithuania to Post-Soviet Eastern Alliances, which specified that the state would "never and in no way join any new political, military, economic or any other state alliances or commonwealths formed on the basis of the former USSR" (Supreme Council 1992).

The government's attempt to reorient the Lithuanian economy exacerbated the country's economic crisis associated with economic transition. Russia offered subsidies and favorable trade agreements to reintegrationist states like Belarus, thus easing the costs of Soviet economic dissolution. In contrast, it charged world prices for energy and raw materials exports to Lithuania. Russia also withheld most-favored-nation trade status as punishment for Lithuania's rejection of the CIS and unwillingness to compromise on issues important to the Russian government, like military transit across Lithuania to the Kaliningrad region of Russia.[3]

Lithuania's cultivation of European economic ties began immediately upon the achievement of statehood. In 1992, Lithuania and the European Union signed an Agreement on Trade and Commercial Cooperation, which came into force in 1993. Then in June 1993 in Copenhagen EU leaders confirmed their intention to enter into Europe (Association) Agreements with the three post-Soviet Baltic republics. In July 1994 Lithuania and the EU concluded a free trade agreement, which came into effect in January 1995. Then in June 1995 the Lithuanian–EU free trade accord was incorporated into an agreement that Lithuania would become an Associate Member of the EU. Lithuania's pro-EU economic orientation was well institutionalized by the end of the decade, and the structure of Lithuania's trade had changed significantly. For example, between 1991 and 1996, EU markets increased their share of Lithuanian exports from 2 to 33 percent, while the share of CIS markets dropped from 86 to 45 percent. Similarly, imports from the CIS, which had accounted for 80 percent of Lithuania's total in 1992, added up to only 29 percent in 1997.

Markets for land

On the way to the Europe, however, Lithuanians discovered that their land must accompany them. In addition to the complicated application and evaluation process, including translating and codifying the 80,000 pages of *acquis* legislation, it was discovered that Lithuanians would be obliged to amend their new constitution. At issue was Article 47, which forbade non-citizens from owning land. Article 47 would thereby conflict with the European single market.

From the perspective of this volume, Lithuania represents a fascinating case of an ethno-nationally restricted land market, with obvious implications for the allocation of resources, income distribution, and growth. For Lithuanians, land had traditionally played a large role in nationalist thought, reflecting the society's rural and agricultural past. Compared to Estonia and Latvia, their Baltic neighbors, Lithuania is much more agricultural – in 1990, as the Soviet Union was collapsing, one third of Lithuania's GDP was derived from agriculture, while the comparable figure for both Latvia and Estonia was one fifth (World Bank 1992).

Non-agricultural land

Lithuanian politicians dealt first with the land about which society was less sensitive: non-agricultural land. It was the farmers who most opposed the selling of land to foreigners. Perhaps even more importantly, it was the farmers who filled the national imagination, epitomizing the independent Lithuanian. Thus, land in the cities, and particularly for commercial purposes, was seen as an easier problem to solve.

Nevertheless, Lithuanians expressed a variety of concerns about even this first step. The most significant connection was drawn between the independence of the country and indigenous ownership of the land (Raugalas 1994). In the spring of 1995 a conference, organized under the auspices of the UN, was devoted to the issue, partly an attempt by some members of the government to publicize how problematic the land issue truly was for the country's international relations. Among the arguments in favor of liberalization were the improvement in the climate for foreign investment, as well as the resultant influx of foreign capital that would energize the stagnant land market. More philosophically, liberals insisted that if the government were serious about enabling property rights then landholders would be allowed to sell to whomever they wished. Some Lithuanians were unconvinced, however, and highlighted the "danger to national security" from the land purchases of "Russian colonists and the Russian security services" (Račas 1995a).

In December 1995 the issue became more pressing, as the government submitted its application for membership to the European Union. The same day Lithuania applied for EU membership, members of parliament agreed in principle to amend the constitution to allow foreign ownership of land (Račas 1995b). Not only would the restriction on the land market keep the country out of Europe, it also, many politicians argued, hindered economic development (Prunskienė 1995; see also Baltic News Service 1995). Still, there was no shortage of evocative dissent. Some Lithuanians objected to the marketization of sacred assets, for example:

> The land of the nation is not only the place where the foreign company can build a gas station or camping ground. It is the substance where our lives and fates merge, where the bones of our ancestors are buried, where their experience and wisdom lies; by not departing from them, by keeping our connection with them we have managed to become not nomads, but to become a durable state.
>
> (Jasukaitytė 1996)

Members of parliament carefully, and in much consultation with all represented political parties, drafted a constitutional amendment and a set of supporting laws (Gečas 1996). The consensus eventually achieved on amending the constitution was such that every single political party represented in the Seimas had agreed in principle and taken part in the drafting, with the exception of the party of Nationalists, whose four members opposed EU membership altogether (Baltic News Service 1996a, 1996b).

The parliamentary debates about the 1996 amendment revealed a great deal about the motivation of the legal change. The few skeptical members of parliament echoed concerns that had been expressed in the media. A.P. Tauras worried, "There were attempts to colonize us during the tsarist times; there were attempts to colonize us very subtly during the Stalinist occupation; and now will we not be colonized by the power of money?" (Seimas 1996a).

Those Seimas members who justified the amendment emphasized the motivation to adhere to European norms, as well as to satisfy the EU's criteria for accession. Egidijus Jarašiūnas explained, "The main goal of the amendment is to create the legal grounds to ratify the European Agreement, to implement the integration of Lithuania into European and Western structures" (Seimas 1996a). Kazys Bobelis emphasized that Lithuania should avoid being left behind by neighbors who were prepared to meet the EU's accession criteria unhesitatingly:

> We are going to the West, trying to ensure our economic, social, and cultural security. Reflecting this approach, we have to adjust to the standards and the requirements of the Western states. If all states are doing this and all are adjusting, then we cannot stay alone, isolated, and fall into the Russian sphere of influence and control again.
>
> (Seimas 1996b)

Vytautas Pleckaitis argued that the amendment was part of the package of policies that would ensure the future prosperity of the nation:

> The constitutional amendment is important not only because it gives investors the possibility of owning the land needed for a particular investment, it is important because it builds the groundwork for our society to integrate more quickly into the family of European nations, bringing closer European standards of living that would assure many Lithuanians an affluent life.
>
> (Seimas 1996c)

Finally, Andrius Kubilius suggested that Lithuania's very modernity was at stake arguing, "This amendment is the necessary condition for Lithuania to become a modern state. The center of Europe cannot remain a province of Europe" (Seimas 1996b).

Thus, after several years of internal debate and negotiations with the EU, the Seimas gave land ownership a pro-European and anti-Russian direction. The Seimas voted to amend the constitution to allow citizens of other countries to own non-agricultural land for business purposes. Under the amendment not all foreign citizens could own land in Lithuania. Only members or associate members of the EU, NATO, and OECD can, because they are, according to the Seimas, "foreign subjects meeting the criteria of European and trans-Atlantic integration" (Seimas 1996d: I-1392). In contrast, Russians, and citizens of other CIS countries, cannot own land in Lithuania (see Laskevich 1996; Reuters 1996; Burbulis 1996).

Agricultural land

Ultimately, Lithuania also had to address the issue that so incensed its farming community: the sale of agricultural land to foreigners. By 2002 Lithuanian representatives had closed the EU negotiations on the *acquis* chapter dealing with land markets and capital movements. Having liberalized the market for non-agricultural land in 1996 – at least for Europeans and other members of the presumed trans-Atlantic community – all that remained was to open the market for agricultural land to European ownership as well. There was far less consensus with the Seimas on agricultural land, however (ELTA 2000a).

The most outspoken and influential critics of the proposal to liberalize the agricultural land market were the farmers (ELTA 2000b). Lithuanian farmers regularly accused Lithuanian politicians of betraying the homeland, and portrayed the government as a lackey of the EU, criticizing it for "bowing on its knees" before the West (Gudavičius 2001; see also Lenčiauskas 2001). Lithuanian farmers expressed their concerns through the powerful Chamber of Agriculture, which regularly warned that liberalizing the land market would be "a direct road to the selling out of Lithuania" (Baltic News Service 2002a). Whereas the debate on non-agricultural land had been tense, the interchange on agricultural land was downright acrimonious. Some Lithuanian nationalists' fears were expressed in subtly, and even often explicitly, anti-semitic terms (see Bieliauskas 2001).

The farmers also appealed to two economic arguments. First, Lithuanian farmers insisted that the relative inexpensiveness of Lithuanian land would allow foreigners to expand their holdings much more quickly than locals. Thus, the benefits of the activation of the land market would accrue primarily not to current holders of land, but to foreign speculators. Lithuanian farmers therefore demanded a transition period. Second, because agricultural land had been collectivized during the Soviet period, and was still in the process of being privatized, farmers expressed concern that until pre-Soviet claims to land had been sorted through it would be premature to allow foreigners to hold title. Kazys Maksvytis, general director of the National Land Service, argued, "Right now only 30 percent of farmers in Lithuania own their own land. Farmers here need time to adjust to the new rules before foreign interests with more capital join the market" (Paulikus 2003).

Government representatives attempted to allay these concerns. The Seimas chairman, Arturas Paulauskas, announced his worry that the farmers' organizations threatened the entire process of EU integration with their insistence on maintaining a restricted land market or insisting upon a transition period (Baltic News Service 2002b; ELTA 2002a). Opponents of the transition period appealed to the rationality and reasonableness of liberalizing the land market, particularly to EU, NATO, and OECD citizens. Reflecting on the fact that foreigners currently rented only 22,000 hectares of land in Lithuania – 0.6 percent of all agricultural land, and 1.5 percent of all rented land – Lithuania's chief EU negotiator called the decision a "political compromise to comfort the farmers" (Baltic News Service 2002f). Lithuania's Free Market Institute insisted that continued restrictions on the sale of land to foreigners would hinder the country's integration into the EU, slow the development of the economy, and delay much-needed agricultural reforms (Baltic News Service 2002g).

In the spring and summer of 2002 the Seimas considered how to proceed. The primary concern raised was the effect of the amendment on farmers. As Ramunas Karbauskis put it, "If we speak about the sale of land to foreigners, it is necessary to say that it is not the question of how much the land will cost in one or two years. It is the question of whether there will be at least one Lithuanian farmer" (Seimas 2002b). A few liberal MPs questioned why the land market should be opened only to those from the West. Julius Veselka queried:

> I want to get a logical answer why, according to the prepared constitutional law, a Lithuanian can sell one hectare of land to George for 500 litas, but not to Ivan who will offer for the same hectare of land one million litas; the Lithuanian will not be able to sell his land to Ivan.
>
> (Seimas 2002a)

In March MPs voted 119–4 in favor of a constitutional amendment liberalizing the land market (Seimas 2002a; Gudavičius 2002). According to the constitution, however, the Seimas must consider amendments twice, with at least three months elapsing in between votes. In the summer supporters of the amendment planned the next vote (ELTA 2002b).

By then the farmers had mobilized against the amendment. In the summer of 2002 associations of farmers, and most prominently the Chamber of Agriculture, threatened massive public protests if the Seimas were to vote on the proposed constitutional amendment without acceding to their demand for a transition period (Baltic News Service 2002d, 2002e; ELTA 2002c).

By July the government relented, and announced that indeed Lithuania would seek a transition period (Baltic News Service 2002f; see also Seimas 2002c). Apparently the contest came down to a bargain between Seimas speaker Arturas Paulauskas and the agricultural community: in exchange for calling off their strike, Paulauskas promised farmers that Lithuania would reopen the closed *acquis* chapter and request a 7–10-year transition period (ELTA 2002d). In November 2002, the EU agreed to a transition period, to commence when Lithuanian enters the EU in May 2004. When the Seimas finally voted again on the constitutional amendment, the vote was 116–4 in favor (Baltic News Service 2003a).

The Seimas then also adopted a series of laws – so-called "safety catches" – designed to limit land speculation and ensure the survival of Lithuanian farmers (Baltic News Service 2003b). Among the more interesting safeguards were: limits on the maximum area of land that could be owned in absentia; the provision that state-owned farming land could be sold only where once-nationalized land has been restored; the right of first priority in land purchases for neighboring landholders; and demanding criteria for agricultural landownership – two years' farming experience and a Lithuanian or European agricultural diploma or five years' farming experience and a successful exam (ELTA 2003b; see Seimas 2003b). Of course, the most important safeguard limited agricultural land ownership to "only those foreign entities which meet the European and Trans-Atlantic integration criteria of Lithuania" (ELTA 2003a). The transition period was set at seven years (ELTA 2003c). The outcome, in sum, is a land market that is still very much restricted (see Valatka 2003a, 2003b).

Conclusions

Once it became clear that Lithuanians would have to amend their constitution in order to meet the EU's accession criteria, they began to debate the meaning of property in land. Two fears dominated Lithuanian political thought: first, that Lithuanians' defining "other," Russians, would continue to subjugate the economy long after political control of the Soviets had disintegrated; and second, that the Lithuanian farmer, who epitomized the independent Lithuanian, would be eclipsed by foreign agriculture and its greater access to capital. The solution Lithuanians found to their constitutional dilemma managed to allay both fears.

Part of the solution was straightforward: because Lithuanians understood themselves to be "European," while Russians are not, and the EU demands only a single European market (rather than a universally liberal market), it was possible simply to allow property in land just to a subset of foreigners. As it was explained by Vytautas Landsbergis: "We made the principled decision because we want to be in the EU. Otherwise, we are shut out, and we stay with Mr. Lukashenko," the authoritarian Belarusian leader who has embraced economic reintegration with Russia (Seimas 2003a). So, Lithuanians allowed Europeans to own their land. But simply allowing the Europeans in would have satisfied the EU. Interestingly, Lithuanians expressed a broader set of political priorities in their decision. Rather than just European integration, "transatlantic" integration informed their choice to allow citizens and firms of NATO and OECD countries to own land as well.

In this chapter I took the content of national identity as exogenously given and explored the political–economic consequences of the prevailing definition and interpretation of purposes of Lithuanian nationhood. The Lithuanian case reveals several general lessons about the relationship between nationalism and political economy. Nationalism has four primary effects on governments' foreign economic policies: it endows economic policy with fundamental social purpose, related to protecting and cultivating the nation; it engenders the economic sacrifice necessary to achieve societal goals; it lengthens the time horizons of a national community; and, most significantly, it specifies a direction for policy, away from a nation's "other" and, often, toward another cultural space.

Notes

* The research for this chapter was supported by the Division of Research, Harvard Business School. I am grateful for the excellent research assistance of Dovile Jakniunaite, who collected and translated the materials published in Lithuanian. Donna Isaac assisted with countless details.

1 A few Soviet loyalists retained the CPL name for their organization until the party was banned in August 1991.
2 The 1992 constitution created the presidency.
3 Kaliningrad, which borders Poland and Lithuania and is on the Baltic Sea, is separated from the rest of the territory of the Russian state by Latvia and Lithuania.

Bibliography

Abdelal, R. (1998a) Interviews Homeland Union, Vilnius, July.
—— (1998b) Interviews LDDP, Vilnius, August.
—— (2001) *National Purpose in the World Economy: Post-Soviet States in Comparative Perspective*, Ithaca, NY: Cornell University Press.
Ash, T.G. (1994) "Journey to the Post-Communist East," *New York Review of Books*, June 23.
Ashbourne, A. (1999) *Lithuania: The Rebirth of a Nation, 1991–1994*, Lanham, MD: Lexington.
Baltic News Service (1995) "Major Lithuanian Parliamentary Political Forces Agree on Amendment of Article 47 of Constitution and Constitutional Law," *Baltic News Service*, December 8.
—— (1996a) "On Thursday, Seimas is going to Begin Amending Article 47 of the Constitution," *Baltic News Service*, January 31.
—— (1996b) "The Majority of the Seimas Factions are for the Land Sale to Foreigners," *Baltic News Service*, April 19.
—— (1996c) "Lithuanian Lawmakers Pass Constitutional Amendment on Land Purchase," *Baltic News Service*, June 20.
—— (2002a) "The Farmers Are Threatening Unrest if the Seimas Does Not Negotiate About the Liberalization of the Land Market," *Baltic News Service*, January 18.
—— (2002b) "The Chairman of the Seimas Prompts Farmers Not to Destroy the Integration of Lithuania into the EU with Radical Proposals," *Baltic News Service*, February 6.
—— (2002c) "Seimas has Adopted the Constitutional Amendment on the Sale of Land," *Baltic News Service*, March 7.
—— (2002d) "Farmers are Threatening the Multi-Day Meeting by the House of Parliament," *Baltic News Service*, June 26.
—— (2002c) "After the Concessions the Farmers Cancel the Protest Actions," *Baltic News Service*, July 2.

—— (2002f) "Lithuania Will Seek a Transition Period, Decided the Government," *Baltic News Service*, July 10.

—— (2002g) "The Experts Are Saying that Restrictions on the Sale of Land to Foreigners Will Stop Integration into the EU," *Baltic News Service*, July 11.

—— (2003a) "Seimas Adopted the Constitutional Amendment on the Liberalization of the Land Market," *Baltic News Service*, January 23.

—— (2003b) "Seimas Adopts Laws Regulating Agricultural Land Sale," *Baltic News Service*, January 28.

Bieliauskas, J. (2001) "Apginkime Lietuvą apsiginkime patys" [Let's Defend Lithuania, Let's Defend Ouselves], *Lietuvos aidas*, February 13.

Bunce, V. (1997) "The Visegrad Group: Regional Cooperation and European Integration in Post-Communist Europe," in P. J. Katzenstein (ed.) *Mitteleuropa: Between Europe and Germany*, Providence, RI: Berghahn.

Burbulis, V. (1996) "Lithuania Permits Land Purchase By Foreigners Not From CIS," *ITAR-TASS*, June 20.

Christophe, B. (1997) *Staat versus Identität: Zur Konstruktion von 'Nation' und 'nationalen Interesse' in den litauischen Transformationdiskursen 1987 bis 1995*, Köln: Verlag Wissenschaft und Politik.

Clark, T.D. (1995) "The Lithuanian Political Party System: A Case Study of Democratic Consolidation," *East European Politics and Societies*, 9: 41–62.

—— (2000) "Nationalism in Independent Lithuania," unpublished manuscript, Creighton University.

——, Holscher, S.J. and Hyland, L. (1999) "The LDLP Faction in the Lithuanian Seimas, 1992–1996," *Nationalities Papers*, 27: 227–246.

ELTA (2000a) "Farmer Party Fiercely Opposed to Land Sell-Off to Foreigners," *ELTA*, January 27.

—— (2000b) "Political Parties View Sales of Farming Land to Foreigners as Premature," *ELTA*, September 19.

—— (2002a) "Speaker Paulauskas to Dispel Farmer Phobia About Land Sale to Foreigners," *ELTA*, January 14.

—— (2002b) "Seimas to Hold Extraordinary Session on Land-Related Constitutional Change," *ELTA*, June 21.

—— (2002c) "Lithuanian Farmers to Go On a 10-Day Strike Over Land Sale to Foreigners," *ELTA*, June 26.

—— (2002d) "Seimas Speaker Convinced Farmers to Quit Protest Over Land," *ELTA*, July 2.

—— (2003a) "Seimas Adopts a Safeguard law on Acquisition of Farming Land," *ELTA*, January 28.

—— (2003b) "Seimas to Adopt Safeguard Laws on Farming Land Sale," *ELTA*, January 27.

—— (2003c) "Foreigners Will Be Allowed to Buy Farming Land in Lithuania after 7-year Transitional Period," *ELTA*, March 20.

Gečas, K. (1996) "Pakeliui į Europą Seimo naariai bijo išduoti Tevynę" [On the Way to Europe Seimas Members are Afraid to Betray the Homeland], *Lietuvos rytas*, February 22.

Girnius, S. (1997) "Back in Europe, to Stay," *Transitions*, 3: 7–10.

Gudavičius, S. (2001) "Aistros dėl žemės pardavimo užsieniečiams: žemdibiai kaltina politikus Lietuvos išdavimu" [Flames About the Land Sale to Foreigners: Farmers Accuse Politicians of Betraying Lithuania], *Kauno diena*, November 13.

—— (2002) "Žengtas pirmas žingsnis" [The First Step was Taken], *Kauno diena*, March 8.

Homeland Union (1996) *Lithuania's Success*, Vilnius: Homeland Union.

Jasukaitytė, V. (1996) "Ar atversime pilies vartus?" [Will We Open the Gates of the Castle?], *Lietuvos rytas*, April 10.

Jeziowski, A. (1992) "Hardest Winter Ever for Lithuania, Premier Predicts," *Baltic Independent*, October 23.

Jurgatiene, J. and Wæver, O. (1996) "Lithuania," in H. Mouritzen, O. Wæver, and H. Wiberg (eds), *European Integration and National Adaptations*, Commack, NY: Nova Science.

Laskevich, N. (1996) "Inostrantsy smogut pokupat' zemliu v Litve, no tol'ko ne rossiiane" [Foreigners Will Be Able to Buy Land in Lithuania, But Just Not Russians], *Izvestiia*, June 25.

Lenčiauskas, J. (2001) "Žemdirbiai nelaukia užsieniečių [Farmers Are Not Looking Forward to Foreigners], *Kauno diena*, December 13.

Lithuanian Center Union (1996) *The New Lithuania*, Vilnius: Lithuanian Center Union.

Lithuanian Christian Democratic Party (1996) *To Serve for Lithuania*, Vilnius: Lithuanian Christian Democratic Party.

Lithuanian Democratic Labor Party (1992) "Platform of the Lithuanian Democratic Labor Party for the Parliamentary Elections," *Tiesa*, October 7; *FBIS-USR*, November 20: 92–149.

—— (1996) *With Work, Concord, and Morality into the Twenty-First Century*, Vilnius: LDDP.

Lithuanian Social Democratic Party (1996) *Labor, Truth, and Justice*, Vilnius: Lithuanian Social Democratic Party.

Lofgren, J. (1997) "A Different Kind of Union," *Transition*, 4: 47–52.

Lucas, E. (1992a) "*Sajudis* Last Stand Ends in Defeat," *Baltic Independent*, November 20.

—— (1992b) "LDDP Coasts to Easy Victory," *Baltic Independent*, November 20.

—— (1992c) "Brazauskas Takes Power," *Baltic Independent*, November 27.

Matulionis, A. (1994) "Nationalism and the Process of State-Building in Lithuania," *Sisyphus*, 8: 121–124.

Muiznieks, N.R. (1995) "The Influence of the Baltic Popular Movements on the Process of Soviet Distintegration," *Europe-Asia Studies*, 47: 3–25.

Nekrasas, E. (1998) "Is Lithuania a Northern or Central European Country?," *Lithuanian Foreign Policy Review*, 1: 19–45.

Paulikus, S. (2003) "Land Privatization Amendment Passed," *Baltic Times*, January 30.

Penrose, J. (2002) "Nations, States, and Homelands Territory and Territoriality in Nationalist Thought," *Nations and Nationalism*, 8: 227–297.

Prunskienė, K. (1995) "Konstitucijos 47-ojo straipsnio patisa – Seimui neįveikiama kliūtis" [Constitutional Amendment of Article 47 is the Hindrance for the Seimas that is Impossible to Overcome], *Diena*, October 9.

Račas, A. (1995a) "Žemės pardavimas užsieniečiams" [Land Sale to Foreigners], *Lietuvos rytas*, April 28.

—— (1995b) "Du Lietuvos žingsniai suvienytos Europos kryptimi: Vakar Seime susitarta dėl narystės Europos Sajungoje ir žemės pardavimo užsieniečiams" (Two Steps for Lithuania Toward the European Union: Yesterday in the Seimas there was Agreement on Membership in the European Union and the Sale of Land to Foreigners), *Lietuvos rytas*, December 8.

Raugalas, E. (1994) "Biznis žemė" (Land Business), *Valstiečų laikraštis*, October 22.

Reuters (1996) "Lithuania Passes Foreigner-friendly Land Law," *Reuters European Business Report*, June 20.

Rindzeviciute, E. (2003) "'Nation' and 'Europe'," *Journal of Baltic Studies*, 34: 74–91.

Seimas of the Republic of Lithuania (1996a) Sitting 70: 512, February 1.

—— (1996b) Spring Session 7: 533, March 19.

—— (1996c) Fall Session 82: 524, February 21.

—— (1996d) "Constitutional Law on the Subjects, Procedure, Terms, and Conditions and Restrictions of the Acquisition into Ownership of Land Plots Provided for in Article 47, Paragraph 2 of the Constitution of the Republic of Lithuania," I-1392, June 20.

—— (2002a) Extraordinary Session, Sitting 5: 195, March 7.

—— (2002b) Spring Session, Sitting 59: 255, June 24.

—— (2002c) "On the Expediency and Time Limits of the Transitional Period for Acquisition of Agricultural and Forest Land in Lithuania by Foreign Nationals," Ix: 1003, July 1.

—— (2003a) Fall Session, Sitting 56: 332, January 23.

—— (2003b) "Provisional Law on the Acquisition of Agricultural Land," Ix: 1314, January 28.

Senn, A.E. (1990) *Lithuania Awakening*, Berkeley, CA: University of California Press.

—— (1992) "The Political Culture of Independent Lithuania: A Review Essay," *Journal of Baltic Studies*, 23: 307–316.

—— (1995) "Post-Soviet Political Leadership in Lithuania," in T. J. Cohon and R. C. Tucker (eds) *Patterns of Post-Soviet Leadership*, Boulder, CO: Westview.

Smith, A.D. (2000) "The 'Sacred' Dimensions of Nationalism," *Millennium*, 29: 791–814.

Supreme Council of the Republic of Lithuania (1992) "Constitutional Act on Nonalignment of the Republic of Lithuania to Post-Soviet Eastern Alliances," I-2622, June 8.

Tammerk, T. (1993) "Brazauskas Storms Into Office," *Baltic Independent*, February 19–25.

Tuskenis, E. (1992a) "Brazauskas Returns," *Baltic Independent*, October 30.

—— (1992b) "*Sajudis* Faces Clouded Future," *Baltic Independent*, November 6.

Valatka, R. (2003a) "Žemės rinkai – raudonas saugiklis" (To the Land Market – the Red Safety Catch), *Lietuvos rytas*, February 3.

—— (2003b) "Naujas įstatymas visiškai sustingdė žemės rinką" (The New Law has Totally Frozen the Land Market), *Lietuvos rytas*, April 26.

Vardys, V.S. (1989) "Lithuanian National Politics," *Problems of Communism*, 39: 53–76.

—— (1995) "Sajudis: National Revolution in Lithuania," in J. A. Trapans (ed.) *Toward Independence: The Baltic Popular Movements*, Boulder, CO: Westview.

Vardys, V.S. and Sedaitis, J.B. (1997) *Lithuania: The Rebel Nation*, Boulder, CO: Westview.

Williams, C. and Smith, A.D. (1983) "The National Construction of Social Space," *Progress in Human Geography*, 7: 502–518.

World Bank (1992) *Statistical Handbook: States of the Former Soviet Union*, Washington, DC: World Bank.

Wyzan, M. (1997) "Economies Show Solid Performance, Despite Many Obstacles," *Transition*, 3: 11–14.

Part III

Religion, ethno-nationality, and economics in land struggles

6 Irish agriculture after the Land War*

Cormac Ó Gráda

Irish agriculture's shift from a system of landlord-and-tenant to peasant proprietorship was the product of an on-again, off-again Land War that lasted from 1879 to 1903. Broadly speaking, the landlord–tenant cleavage complemented the division between pro-British Unionism and Irish Nationalism. Moreover, again broadly speaking, the demise of the landlords entailed a return of the land to people who saw themselves as descendants of those who had lost their lands in the bloody Tudor, Jacobean, Cromwellian, and Williamite confiscations of the sixteenth and seventeenth centuries. The myth of vicarious dispossession distorted the historical record since, as far as the native masses were concerned, the confiscations for the most part had meant new landlords rather than dispossession. By the early eighteenth century the bulk of Irish land had passed from Gaelic or Old English (as the Catholic descendants of earlier conquerors are known) to New English or Scottish land owners. The myth also ignored the fact that a sizeable minority of tenants were the descendants of planters and immigrants who had arrived at the time of the confiscations. Though the Land War was really a struggle about who should capture the Ricardian rents, both sides emphasized the implications for farm productivity. Those implications have been much debated, then and since. The research of recent decades suggests that while farmers' rhetoric exaggerated the likely gains, landlords exaggerated the likely losses.

In this chapter we look at four aspects of the relationship between land tenure, nationality, and agricultural performance. The first section offers a brief overview of the debate about productivity change. The second assesses the impact of the Irish tenurial revolution on the market in land. The third section reviews the claim that in their quest for peasant proprietorship farmers sacrificed the efficiency improvements to be gained from agricultural cooperation, while the fourth is about the related issue of winter dairying.

Productivity change

Since the 1960s several studies have sought to infer the impact of tenurial change from estimates of agricultural output before and after the change.

Estimating Irish agricultural productivity in the past is not so easy, however. Even Ireland's precocious agricultural statistics (which date from 1847) shed little or no light on milk yields, carcass weights, animal mortality, product quality, fertilizer inputs, seed ratios, and the like. These are all necessary building blocks in calculating output. Yet evaluations of tenure have turned largely on movements in output and productivity (Crotty 1966; Solow 1971; Ó Gráda 1993; Turner 1996; Solar 1998).

The "revisionist" literature on Irish land tenure dates from Raymond Crotty's wayward but brilliant *Irish Agricultural Production* (1966). Before Crotty there was a broad consensus that what anti-landlord leader Michael Davitt dubbed the "fall of feudalism" made both ethical and economic sense. Crotty, on the contrary, believed the old tenurial system to have been more productive than what replaced it. This was because its rent-maximizing landlords forced their tenants to be efficient. In their wake, there was no longer an active market for holdings forcing incompetent farmers to cede their holdings to those better qualified. Crotty invoked the apparent failure of agricultural output to expand under owner-occupancy as evidence of the reduced pressure on farmers to produce. With the demise of the landlords, the lack of a market in holdings left an ever-higher proportion of the land in the hands of under-performers. But Crotty was no pro-landlord apologist: a follower of Henry George and Michael Davitt, he believed that land nationalization would generate the same outcome in terms of efficiency as landlordism.

Crotty's comparisons of output and productivity before and after the Land War were evocative but hardly rigorous. His findings bear comparison with Barbara Solow's analysis of landlord behavior in the post-famine era, which was published in 1971, but the product of research completed some years earlier. Like Crotty's, Solow's conclusion was strikingly "revisionist," in that it also suggested that the Land War was bad for Irish agriculture. However, Solow's landlords were much less likely to evict than Crotty's, and more moderate in their rent demands. The Land War, by concentrating farmers' attention on extracting more of the Ricardian rent from landlords, rather than on managerial choices that would increase output and productivity, damaged Irish agriculture at a crucial juncture. In this view Irish farmers were too preoccupied with night raids and boycotts to be interested in the centrifugal separator or the latest chemical fertilizers. But Solow also invoked output data to argue that the Land War and peasant proprietorship were bad for Irish agriculture, buttressing her case with brand new estimates of net output in 1876, 1881, and 1886.[1]

In this chapter I rely instead on Michael Turner's recent estimates of agricultural output and productivity between the Great Famine and the Great War. It seems unlikely that these will be bettered in the near future, even bearing in mind the cautions registered by Peter Solar (1998). Table 6.1 reproduces the most relevant of Turner's numbers. While the lower

Table 6.1 Total factor productivity change, 1850s–1910s (percentage per annum)

	[1]	*[2]*	*[3]*
1850s–1870s	0.58	0.54	0.55
1870s–1890s	0.42	0.43	0.42
1890s–1910s	0.81	0.83	0.79

Source: Turner (1996: 138).

Notes:
[1] using starting decades for factor shares.
[2] using finishing decades for factor shares.
[3] using fixed factor shares.

growth in the middle period could be interpreted as implying that the Land War exacted a cost in terms of productivity, the most striking aspect of Turner's numbers is the acceleration in productivity growth in the final period. While Turner's estimated annual growth rate of 0.8 percent in the 2 decades or so preceding World War I is less than rates achieved in the US, Japan, or Denmark in these decades, it is very impressive by comparison with that of the neighboring island (Turner 2000: 318–19). Only a radical revision of Turner's numbers would overturn their implication that, at the very least, the shift to owner-occupancy did not hurt Irish agricultural productivity.

The Unionist/landlord versus Catholic/tenant cleavage mentioned above does not fit much of the northern province of Ulster. In political terms Ulster Unionism was almost exclusively non-Catholic, but it transcended class differences in the countryside, as indeed did the Orange Order. One by-product of radical nationalists exploiting the land question was the equivocal attitude of Unionist farmers in Ulster towards the struggle for land reform.

The majority of Northern Ireland farmers were descendants of settlers from Scotland and northern England in the seventeenth and early eighteenth centuries, and it has long been argued that the resulting landlord–tenant nexus in Ulster differed from that prevailing in the rest of Ireland. Ulster farmers benefited from "Ulster custom", a variant of tenant right whereby a departing tenant could cash in the value of any unexhausted improvements carried out by him. This custom gave the Ulster tenant the reassurance that eviction would not rob him of the fruits of his investments. Another difference between North and South is that during the Land War Ulster tenants tended to opt for negotiation rather than confrontation. Comparing productivity levels and rates of change in Northern and Southern Ireland is therefore also apposite.

William Gladstone's land reforms of the 1870s and 1880s in effect sought to spread the benefits of "Ulster custom" to the rest of the island. But the signs of any resultant improvements are elusive. There was no disproportionate jump in farming stocks and yields outside Ulster in the wake of the legislation. On the eve of World War I outbuildings were no more numerous in Ulster than in the other three provinces. Inter-provincial comparisons suggest that, as far as farming is concerned, the Ulster versus the Rest contrast has been overdone. On the one hand, Ulster custom was much more widespread than implied. On the other, the need for such an institutional remedy was mitigated by the reality that, both before and after the Gladstonian reforms, most farms were passed on from father to son (Ó Gráda 1993: 156–159).

Estimates of agricultural output in the two Irelands in the early twentieth century, before the two economies drifted apart, are corroborative (see Table 6.2). They suggest that output per worker in what would become the "Catholic" Irish Free State was slightly higher than in the "Protestant" six northern counties in 1912, and significantly so in the mid 1920s. This advantage can hardly have stemmed from a greater endowment of physical capital.[2] The land–labor ratio, it is true, was higher in the South, particularly when the quality of land is corrected for. In Table 6.2, where the correction applied is based on the poor law valuation, land productivity was higher in the North in both 1912 and 1925–1926. A back-of-the-envelope estimate of total factor productivity, applying 0.6 and 0.4 as the factor shares of labor and land to the data in Table 6.2, implies that it was marginally lower (by 3.7 percent) in the 26 counties at the earlier date and marginally higher (by 10.8 percent) at the later date.[3]

Table 6.2 Output and productivity in 1912 and 1925–1926

		26 Counties	6 Counties	All Ireland
A.	1912			
	Livestock (£m.)	37.2	8.0	45.2
	Crops (£m.)	10.1	4.8	14.9
	Total (£m.)	47.3	12.8	60.1
	Labor force (1,000)	765	212	977
	Output per worker (£)	62	60	60
	Land (*) (m.)	10.67	2.52	13.19
	Q/Land	4.4	5.1	4.6
B.	1925–1926			
	Livestock (£m.)	48.4	11.8	60.2
	Crops (£m.)	11.1	3.2	14.3
	Total (£m.)	59.6	15.0	74.5
	Labor force (1,000)	648	199	847
	Output per worker (£)	92	75	88
	Land (*) (m.)	10.67	2.52	13.19
	Q/Land	5.6	6.0	5.7

Source: Ó Gráda 1991: 444; Crotty 1966: 303.

Note:
(*) Land quality proxied by Poor Law Valuation.

Thereafter the South fell behind and the two agricultures went their separate ways. But policy shifts in Ireland and the United Kingdom were to blame for this, not some ingrained difference between farmers in the two Irelands. Between the early 1930s and the late 1940s policy in the Irish Free State benefited tillage at the expense of grass, and the agricultural policies of the United Kingdom deprived Irish producers of the easy access they had to the British market for centuries. The productivity of southern farmers, deprived of the higher British prices available to their northern counterparts and shunted off their comparative advantage, fell behind. From the 1970s on, however, the Common Agricultural Policy of the European Union placed the two agricultures on a level playing field once more. As a result they have become more similar again in terms of output mix, and southern agriculture has made up the ground it lost after independence (Ó Gráda 1991, 1997: ch. 5).

The new owners and the land market

The Great Irish Famine was the straw that broke the back of hundreds of already heavily indebted landed proprietors (Eiríksson and Ó Gráda 1996). It prompted in 1849 the creation of the Incumbered Estates Court, which freed up the Irish market in land by forcing bankrupt landlords to sell off part or all of their properties. The prolific Dublin lawyer-economist William Neilson Hancock (1820–1888) noted a significant drop in the cost of borrowing on the security of land in the wake of the court's creation, and attributed this to the reduced cost of securing transfer (Hancock 1851). For a time the market in Irish land was a very active one, and the ensuing transfers from careless, old-style Castle Rackrent landlords to a newer more grasping kind was much commented on.

Once the Incumbered Estates Court had done its work of purging bankrupt proprietors, the market in land became quiet once again for some decades. What of the post-Land War period? Hard, continuous data on the extent of the market for land in Ireland over the past century or so are lacking. However, a survey carried out in the late 1970s showed that on average only about 0.5 percent of all farmland passed through the market each year, and figures released by the Central Statistics Office suggest a similar proportion in the 1990s. Does this mean that the market for land is "thin"?

Here Denmark and the United Kingdom offer useful points of comparison. Danish data suggest that over the past century or so an average of about 5 percent of Danish farms and Danish land was bought and sold annually. Some of the sales might be inter-generational – in 1895–1909 28.5 percent of sales involved *familiesalg* (sale within the family); in 1918–1922 13 percent – but the bulk always represented *frie Salg* (free sale). The percentages, hardly surprisingly, were subject to wide fluctuation. At the turn of the century the proportion on the market was 3 to 4 percent, but in the depressed early 1930s it reached 8 percent.[4]

Continuous data on land sales of 5 hectares or above in England are available since 1946/1947. The number of transactions peaked at 10,259 in 1959/1960 and troughed at 2,720 in 1991/1992. The peak in terms of area sold was 399,029 hectares in 1948/1949 and the trough was 82,475 hectares in 1991/1992. These latter numbers represent 3.6 and 0.7 percent of all farmland. Between 1946/1947 and 1996/1997 the aggregate area sold averaged at just over 200,000 hectares, or slightly less than 2 percent of all farmland.

Such data are too partial for definitive comparisons, but in both Denmark and the UK the proportions dwarf the Irish level. Why has the market for land in Ireland been thinner? Hancock was one of several observers of Irish agriculture to wonder "why is the loan capital of Ireland not lent more freely to the farmers of Ireland?" (Hancock 1851). His answer was the difficulty and expense of recovering debt. Part of the answer is an ethos that did not consider land a commodity; when farmers defaulted the banks were not supposed to foreclose. This can only have increased the reluctance of banks to advance large sums to farmers on the security of their holdings.

One of the ironies of Irish land reform is that the new owners, because they were unwilling to let go of their land in order to repay debt, did not bring ownership to its logical conclusion. A submission from the Agricultural Credit Corporation to the 1934–1938 Banking Commission stated that the trouble associated with selling the land of an indebted farmer without his consent "militates against the extension of credit to the farming community". The Commission, echoing the sentiments of an earlier inquiry in 1926, called for legislation making foreclosure faster and more effective (Banking Commission 1938: para. 413).

Yet the problem of farm credit persisted. A few years later a scheme to provide farmers with soft loans, proposed by Senators John C. Counihan and Joseph Johnston, and supported by Deputy James Dillon, attracted considerable attention (*PDSÉ* 1939). The scheme prompted a scathing memo from the fearsome secretary of the Department of Finance, J.J. McElligott, who likened it to "the assignats of the French revolution." In McElligott's eyes, granting all farmers annuities which they could use as security against bank loans, was:

> no more new than the ideas of Major Douglas and others in the currency sphere which are ancient heresies furbished up and advanced as the fruit of independent thinking by their modern exponents.

Minister of Agriculture James Ryan was no less skeptical, convinced that most schemes relating to credit for farmers were "propaganda" and that easy credit would be "the ruination of farmers." McElligott sought to put the issue to sleep by organizing a special conference involving the two senators and representatives of the various government departments and the banking system. The redoubtable Sir John Keane, ex-senator and governor of the Bank of Ireland, raised the old bogey of irrecoverable loans:

> We find that problem in the Banks frequently and we cannot force a sale on account of the boycott. It would be much better if there was a free sale and not have this social boycott thereby enabling bona fide people to buy the land and work it to full production.

Robert Barton, chairman of the Agricultural Credit Company, also believed that the fault lay with the farmers themselves, regretting that land as a security had "a nuisance value," and was therefore a poor basis for credit. Against Counihan's lame objection that allowing the land of defaulters to be sold to "speculators" was bad "from a national point of view," Barton replied that farms had passed into the hands of people not short of capital and better than the previous occupiers. McElligott's final words to the second session of this unusual conference were that "we must have in mind a question of cardinal importance that whoever is going to advance credit must be repaid."[5]

The sense that farmers were starved of capital persisted. A 1960 memorandum from the Department of Agriculture noted that "for largely historical reasons land as such is practically untouched as a basis for credit in Ireland. This situation is a serious deterrent to the sound extension of long-term credit in Ireland."[6] Even today controversies about farmers' resistance against creditors occasionally make the headlines in Ireland (e.g. the high-profile eviction of the Graham brothers in Donegal in 1997 at the behest of National Irish Bank). Yet the disproportionate share of agriculture in the loans and advances of the associated banks suggests that land is now nearer to being a commodity than it used to be.

Cooperation and creameries

> The Irish are rightly annoyed at always having Denmark held up to them as a good example.
>
> (Barbara L. Solow 1971: 151n.)

The sense that "Irishness" or "Catholicism" somehow inhibited Irish agricultural progress was part of conservative pro-landlord rhetoric. Even Sir Horace Plunkett, liberal Unionist politician and inspirational founder of the Irish agricultural cooperative movement, was not immune. In *Ireland in the New Century* he complained about "the extravagant church building in a country so backward as Ireland" and the "anomalous" numbers of clergy, and berated the negative impact of Roman Catholicism's "reliance . . . on authority, its repression of individuality, and its complete shifting of . . .

the moral centre of gravity to a future existence" on material progress. Given Ireland's low level of education, Plunkett believed that such a combination was bound to produce fatalism and resignation among the rural masses. Inevitably, his bigotry gave offence (Plunkett 1904: 101–102, 108, 166–167; Keating [King] 1984: 342–346; West 1986; Kennedy 1996: 103–104).[7]

In the eyes of Plunkett and his Irish Agricultural Organisation Society (IAOS), such fatalism helps explain Ireland's failure to become "a second Denmark," a failure reflected in its relative lack of enthusiasm for agricultural cooperation. In late-nineteenth-century Denmark creameries and cooperation were almost synonymous. In Ireland not only did the diffusion of the new milk-separating technology lag behind Denmark, the cooperative mode of production was also much less to the fore. While nationalist Irish farmers – so the story goes – concentrated on battling and outwitting their landlords, their Danish rivals (who had no landlords to distract them) forged ahead by concentrating on the more mundane activity of increasing both output and productivity. This Hiberno-Danish rivalry spawned an extensive comparative literature in Ireland (e.g. Johnston 1931; Beddy 1943; Crotty 1966).

The two cartoons (6.1 and 6.2) reflect the enduring conviction that Irish milk and butter producers were needlessly and foolishly sacrificing output and markets to their Danish competitors. The cruder of the two cartoons (6.1), published in the IAOS organ, *The Irish Homestead* (December 12, 1896), draws an analogy between the ancient battle of Clontarf, where an army led by a coalition of Irish chieftains defeated the Danes and their local allies, and the ongoing "war" between dairy farmers, which the Irish were losing due to their failure to innovate and cooperate. The second, from the short-lived *Leprecaun* (June 1910), accuses the Irish dairy farmer of being lazier than his Danish rival. But although the Ireland–Denmark comparison has an obvious appeal, it is not the easiest or the most appropriate. Clearly the diffusion of creameries was slower and less complete in Ireland than in Denmark (Ó Gráda 1977). There are two distinct aspects to this. First, there was the lag in adopting the new dairying technology. Second, in Ireland proprietary firms, often belonging to merchants with long experience in the butter trade, were quicker to employ the new technology than cooperatives.

Supporters of the rural cooperative movement put this down to the inadequacy of the cooperative response in Ireland. They argue that whereas in Denmark farmers cooperated with alacrity, in Ireland the cooperative movement was a top-down operation, promoted by the gentry and greeted with skepticism at first by (mainly nationalist) dairy farmers. The slow start of the cooperative sector could equally, however, be seen as evidence of the adaptability and dynamism of the proprietary sector. Unfortunately, the proprietaries are less well documented than the IAOS's cooperatives.

Local histories of the cooperative movement list several proprietary creameries and indeed imply a vibrant proprietary sector in the 1880s and 1890s,
nonetheless (see in particular Jenkins 2000: 17–34; O'Shea 2001: 10–11).
It also bears noting that several of the early cooperatives had begun life as
proprietaries. The relative strength of the proprietary sector in Ireland is
a reminder that models of creamery diffusion that focus only on the cooperative mode are mis-specified.[8]

Apart from this institutional aspect, the different endowments and market
constraints facing Danish and Irish butter producers mattered. The resource
endowments of the two agricultures were different and are difficult to
control for. Complementarities between different forms of agricultural production complicated matters. Milk production constrained pig production,
and the choice of livestock breed dictated by the live cattle market
constrained milk production. Reliance on grass influenced the seasonality
of dairying output (on which more below). And, although in most respects

THE NEW DANISH INVASION OF IRELAND.

Cartoon 6.1 The new Danish invasion of Ireland
Source: *The Irish Homestead*, December 12, 1896.

Another Danish Invasion.

ERIN (to Irish Farmer taking his winter nap)—"Wake up, man, and drive these invaders from your door! If it was the British Government you would be holding meetings of protest all over the country. I suppose you are waiting for Home Rule to come. If you wait for that day you won't be troubled to make much butter."

Cartoon 6.2 Another Danish invasion
Source: *Leprecaun*, June 1910.

the trade between Ireland, Great Britain, and Denmark was free, the British embargo on live cattle imports from Denmark in 1892 tilted the choice of Danish producers towards more dairying and less fat cattle. This means that the much faster growth in Danish butter production in the 1890s and 1900s was in part a constrained response. Between 1875/1879 and 1910/1914 dairying's share in Danish agricultural output rose from 24 to 37 percent, while its share fell back marginally in Ireland, from about 21 to 18 percent. The sharp rise in the price of store cattle relative to butter in these years in Ireland doubtless had something to do with this (Aage Hansen 1984: 225; Turner 1996: 116, 266–267).

In an earlier study of cooperative dairying in Ireland Ó Gráda (1977) sought to explain the regional variation in the spread of cooperative creameries in terms of cow densities and the demand for milk for human consumption. To the extent that cow density in turn depended on creamery diffusion, my ordinary least squares estimation will have produced biased results. Concentrating on the situation on the eve of the First World War, by which time diffusion had three decades in which to proceed as far as it could, minimized the bias.[9] Surprisingly, perhaps, three explanatory variables – the milch-cow density, the number of cows, and population – accounted for over one-half of the variation across counties in cooperative density. Thus the spatial spread of cooperative creameries in Ireland on the eve of the Great War predicted by a very simple model "made sense."

Recently Kevin O'Rourke has revived this dormant subject, paying particular attention to whether Irish "culture" helps explain why Irish farmers failed to match their Danish rivals in terms of cooperation and innovation diffusion (O'Rourke 2001). O'Rourke's provocative study offers an opportunity to review some of the issues raised in the controversy about agricultural cooperation in Ireland. In this study culture is encapsulated by "education, uncertain property rights, and social capital." However, instead of comparing Ireland and Denmark directly, O'Rourke exploits the variation in the diffusion of cooperative creameries across Irish counties for explanations of under-performance. In other words his focus is on whether "variables identified as important for innovation and growth by cross-country regressions" also help explain the range of experience *within* Ireland.

Our interest here is in O'Rourke's three main proxies for "culture." These are (a) the percentage of the population that was illiterate (*ILLIT*), (b) the percentage professing the Catholic religion (*RCSHARE*), and (c) a variable representing harmony between landlord and tenant (*AGREE*). In the wake of the Irish land legislation of 1881 tenants were entitled to apply to a special court for a "fair" rent settlement that would last 15 years. Alternatively, they could register an agreed out-of-court settlement with their landlords. *AGREE* is defined as the percentage of tenants in a county opting for bilateral agreements. By implication the more "Danish" counties in Ireland were those with fewer Catholics and/or fewer illiterates, and those with more harmonious tenurial relations. O'Rourke estimates a model of diffusion which incorporates both the "economic" variables described earlier and these three "cultural" variables. He then uses the estimated coefficients on the "cultural" variables to simulate Danish conditions by setting *ILLIT* and *RCSHARE* equal to zero and *AGREE* equal to one. The new "non-economic variables" account for a further 10 percent or so of the variation in cooperative creameries. But are *ILLIT*, *RCSHARE*, and *AGREE* truly "non-economic variables?" Let us consider them in turn.

The literature on the diffusion of technology certainly tells us that regions with high levels of illiteracy are slower to adopt new technologies such as the centrifugal separator, be it in cooperative or proprietary guise. It is also true that the extent of illiteracy is sometimes taken as a proxy for "culture" (e.g. Foreman-Peck and Lains 2000). But literacy also costs money and time. That is why in the past, in Ireland as elsewhere, the children of the poor were less likely to attend school in the first place, and more likely to leave at a young age. One of the most robust findings of the anthropometric history literature is that in the eighteenth and nineteenth centuries literate convicts and soldiers were appreciably taller than their illiterate colleagues. In pre-famine Ireland literacy added about over 2 centimeters to height; in the 1880s it was still adding half a centimeter (e.g. Ó Gráda 1994; Mokyr and Ó Gráda 1996). The most plausible explanation for these differences is that those parents who could afford to send their children to school could also afford to feed and clothe them well and provide them with the available medical care. It is hardly surprising, then, that there was a strong correlation across Irish regions between illiteracy and excess mortality during the Irish Famine (Ó Gráda 1999: 30–33). In post-famine Ireland too literacy lagged where poverty was most intense. In Ireland a century ago the variable *ILLIT* measured a resource constraint, not a cultural option. If their history and poverty made late-nineteenth-century Irish farmers as a group less literate than their Danish peers, then their adoption of an unfamiliar process innovation was bound to be more hesitant.

Second, O'Rourke interprets *AGREE*, the percentage of tenants opting for out-of-court rent settlements, as a proxy for landlord–tenant relations. Not being able to agree on an out-of-court settlement meant, in the spirit of Barbara Solow's classic work, "the diversion of effort away from productive farming into rent-seeking; or a lack of social cohesion." This is only partly true, for several reasons (see Ó Gráda 1993: 172–174):

First, those tenants who litigated instead of agreeing on a rent reduction won, on average, bigger rent reductions. Given the relatively small costs involved, litigation paid.

Second, the more-or-less fixed legal costs associated with litigation must have made it not worthwhile for many small farmers. It is probably more than mere coincidence that small farms were more common in the north of Ireland where tenants were more likely to settle. In counties Cork and Kerry in the southwest, for example, the proportions of holdings under 15 acres in 1900 were 23 and 27 percent; in Cavan and Monaghan in the north (both strong dairying counties) they were 44 and 56 percent.

Third, tenants who were in arrears with their rent in the 1880s and 1890s were in a particularly poor position to argue, and so their landlord could force them into an out-of-court settlement. To the extent that this was a factor, then *AGREE* was less about "social cohesion" or "social capital" than about landlords being able to blackmail tenants into accepting low rent reductions.

Fourth, it is true that some tenants who settled out of court did so because their rents were low to begin with. But this could be taken as meaning that if more landlords had been reasonable, more tenants would have "agreed."

For all these reasons, *AGREE* is also more about "economic" than "cultural" considerations. To simulate "Danish conditions" in Ireland by setting *AGREE* = 1 and *RCSHARE* = 0 simply stacks the odds against the Irish farmer.

Finally, O'Rourke employs the Catholic population share (*RCSHARE*) as a proxy for "other sociological and political attributes in a divided society." As noted, Plunkett and his supporters implicitly or explicitly blamed aspects of Irish Catholic–nationalist culture for the laggard diffusion of Irish cooperative creameries. Whether this was because Catholics were less trustworthy,[10] or because they were lazier, or more prone to violence, or less rational, or less able to exercise self-control (as evidenced in their big families), or some combination of the above, is immaterial. O'Rourke proxies "Irishness" or "Irish culture" by the percentage of the population that was Roman Catholic. He hypothesizes that the more Catholic a county, the weaker the embrace of cooperation.

But, again, in the context of creameries and cooperation this variable is arguably a better proxy for poverty than for culture. Why? Because in Ireland non-Catholics owned a disproportionate share of the bigger and better farms. This may be clearly seen from Table 6.3, which describes the situation in the Irish Free State in 1926. Only 7.2 percent of all farmers were non-Catholic (they would have been mainly members of the Church of Ireland) but they owned 27.5 percent of the land. Areas with lots of Protestant farms also presumably had higher stocking rates, were less remotely located, and were more likely therefore to be in a position to benefit from the new technology. Indeed, for these reasons *RCSHARE* seems a better proxy for farm capital and land endowment than farm acreage alone.

An alternative, or complementary, interpretation of the tension between "Irishness" and cooperation, not considered by O'Rourke, is that there was a struggle for power and influence between the Catholic clergy, on the one hand, and the leadership of the cooperative movement, on the other. Plunkett, son of Lord Dunsany, regarded the IAOS as an embodiment of *noblesse oblige*, and indeed his "first two associates in the New Movement"

Table 6.3 Non-Catholic farmers as a percentage of the total, 1926

Farm size (acres)	Ireland	Leinster	Munster	Connacht	Ulster (*)
1–5	2.4	3.9	1.9	0.8	3.4
5–10	2.9	3.9	1.5	0.7	7.3
10–15	3.9	3.9	1.5	1.0	11.4
15–30	5.5	5.0	1.7	1.4	19.1
30–50	7.8	7.5	2.4	3.6	30.4
50–100	10.2	11.9	3.8	8.5	42.6
100–200	15.4	20.4	7.6	15.4	48.9
200+	27.5	38.0	16.4	23.1	38.4
Total	7.2	9.9	3.6	2.5	19.6

Source: 1926 Irish Free State census of population.

Note:
(*) Cavan, Donegal, Monaghan.

were Lord Monteagle, a Limerick landlord, and R.A. Anderson, sub-agent to the Cork proprietor, Lord Castletown. In the years that followed, Plunkett and his circle reserved a disproportionate number of the top positions in the movement for landed grandees. In the early years, both Monteagle and Col. Nugent Talbot Everard, a Meath landlord, served brief terms as IAOS president in Plunkett's absence. At the outset (1894–1895) 7 members of the IAOS executive committee were landed proprietors. In 1900 10 of the 22 men serving on the IAOS committee were landlords, and 15 years later the ratio was still 9 to 25. Several others were gentleman farmers. The attitude of such people towards the ordinary farmers and the Catholic clergy (mostly of farming stock) was not devoid of *de haut en bas* condescension (Plunkett 1904: 184; Anderson 1937: 1, 264–284; Keating [King] 1984: 107–108; Daly 2002: 7–8). *Their* gloss on things – and they were voluble propagandists – should not be taken as the last word. Local histories of individual cooperatives contain their own biases, but their more benign impression of the movement at grass-roots level and of the role of clergy in it offers a useful corrective to the version championed by Plunkett and his coterie.

Those who ran the IAOS may have left the clergy and, indeed, Nationalist Ireland, under-represented in the leadership, yet at grass-roots level priests were heavily involved in creating and supporting cooperative creameries. Local histories, of which there are many, are quite clear on clerical support and enthusiasm. Thus a recent history of Monaghan creamery describes how it set up in 1900 following a large meeting in the town hall, "attended by local clergy of all denominations and a very representative band of farmers" (Dunne 1983: 1). The prime movers behind the setting up of the Ardagh (Co. Limerick) coop were Edward W. O'Brien and Father Bob Ambrose C.C. One was a unionist landlord, the other the son of a small farmer (Hough 1997: 1–3). A recent history of Callan cooperative records: "One cannot recapture the excitement and expectation at the Town Hall in Callan on 26 March, 1899, where the parish priest, Very Rev. Canon Howley, presided at a thronged meeting" (McDonnell 1999: 88). In Emly, Co. Tipperary, the local parish priest was behind the efforts to organize a farmer buy-out of the local proprietary creamery, and priests fulfilled the roles of chairmen and secretaries throughout the area (Jenkins 2000: 43; for further examples see Murtagh 1986; Smith 1998). Given that the catchment area of the early creameries was about the same as that of an average parish, the church offered an excellent spatial template within which to organize. The contrast between priestly leadership at grass-roots level and their under-representation at executive level is stark. Carla King has noted that only 6 of the 69 men who served on the IAOS committee before 1914 were priests (Plunkett 1904: 92n.; Keating [King] 1984: 109).

Two further points. First, the claim that the Catholic Irish were poor in Putnamite social capital is difficult to square with the rise of highly innovative mass participation organizations such as the Gaelic Athletic Association and the Gaelic League in this very period. Many of Ireland's local history and archaeological societies also date their beginnings from this period. Indeed it may well be that the 1880–1914 period produced more "joiners" than any other era in Irish history, before or since. Finally, the productivity results in Tables 6.1 and 6.2 should be recalled here. They imply (a) that agriculture as a whole performed well before the 1920s, and (b) that farmers in the "Catholic" Irish Free State increased productivity more than their colleagues in the "Protestant" Northern Ireland between 1912 and 1926. These results seem hard to square with weakness in a sector as important as dairying, or with "Catholicity" acting as a brake on southern farmers.

Only further research will tell whether related aspects of Ireland's performance – the lower quality of its butter, its failure to produce a proper marketing strategy for dairy products, its failure to develop an associated cheese-making industry, the knock-on impact of seasonality in dairying on the pigs and bacon sector – strengthen the case for Irish under-performance.

Winter dairying

> Irish dairying was "outdoor" dairying because of cost considerations, not out of perverseness.
>
> (Barbara L. Solow 1971: 151n.)

Since time immemorial Irish dairy farmers have relied mainly on grass as feed for their cows. This strategy has dictated spring calving and a marked seasonality in the supply of milk. Farmers have shunned the alternative of "winter dairying," i.e. spacing the births of calves and lactation throughout the year through the stall-feeding of cows during the winter months. Winter dairying would have entailed both higher milk output and a more regular supply of butter to wholesalers and retailers in Great Britain. More milk in turn would have entailed more creameries and therefore, perhaps, more cooperation. The alternative would have been costlier, though in mitigation lower seasonality would presumably have increased the price commanded by Irish butter of any given quality in British wholesale and retail outlets. Cartoon 6.1 implies that part of the Irish dairy farmer's problem with winter dairying was sheer laziness.

The seasonality of Irish milk supplies has not changed much over time. Figures 6.1 and 6.2 compare the monthly shares of butter supplies to the Cork Market in 1875 and 1885, and the seasonality of milk supplies in 1934, 1950, 1975, and 1998 (see also Jenkins 2000: 8). While the pattern is broadly similar in all years, the supply of butter in the late nineteenth century was proportionately less early in the year, and greater in the autumn,

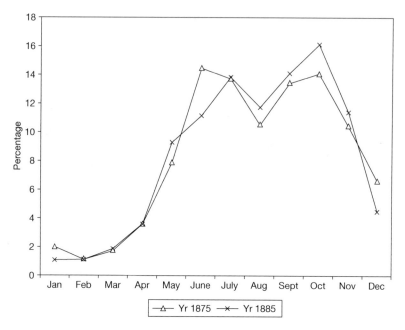

Figure 6.1 Monthly supply to Cork Butter Market, 1875 and 1885
Source: Calculated from market reports in the *Irish Farmers' Gazette*.

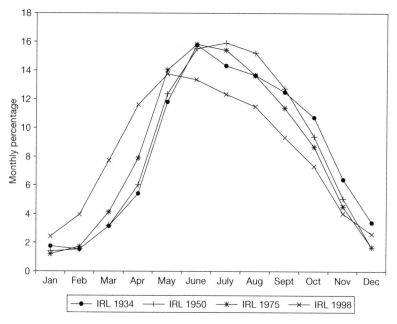

Figure 6.2 Milk supply to creameries, 1934–1998
Source: Central Statistics Office, Dublin.

than the supply of milk in the twentieth. Note too that there was some tendency for the seasonality to intensify up to 1950; since then it has lessened slightly. But the main implication is that winter dairying never really caught on in Ireland.

In an era of profound change and dynamism in nearly all other aspects of Irish agriculture, this persistence of seasonality suggests that earlier criticisms of farmers for not switching were misplaced. The reason is not far to seek: Ireland's temperate climate and extended grass-growing season allow its cattle to roam its pastures at relatively low cost for eight or nine months of the year. Denmark's climate, though mild compared to that of landlocked regions of western Europe, is harsh relative to Ireland's (Jensen 1937: 62–72; Freeman 1969: 44–52). Comparing mean monthly temperatures in Ireland and Denmark highlights the former's advantage in this respect (Figure 6.3). The annual averages are not too different (9.6°C in Dublin, 8.2°C in Copenhagen), but in Denmark the monthly variation, represented by the coefficient of variation, is much greater (0.82 versus 0.40). The example of New Zealand, with its equally temperate and rainy climate, and very long grass-growing season, clinches the case.[11] There the mean temperature was a bit higher than Ireland's (11.9°C) but the coefficient of variation was about the same. The seasonality of Ireland's milk supply was and is very much like New Zealand's turned upside down (Figure 6.4). Nobody has ever accused New Zealand farmers of the laziness, fractiousness, or Catholicity imputed to Irish farmers. Ireland's comparative advantage in grass is the most plausible explanation of both the sharp seasonality in its milk supply and the sluggish performance of its dairying sector.

Though exhortations to practice winter dairying persisted for decades, convincing empirical evidence in its favor has been lacking. Nor was there ever a time when even a minority of progressive farmers made the switch and grew rich as a result. Trials in the 1900s by the Irish Department of Agriculture were inconclusive. In its 1906–1907 annual report the IAOS conceded that winter dairying would require a milk price of 5½d per gallon, at a time when farmers were being paid only 3½d per gallon for their milk (IAOS 1908: 7). In the early 1920s Joseph Hanly's popular textbook supported winter dairying in principle, but conceded that the case for it had not yet been convincingly made. The claims and counterclaims would continue, with Joseph Johnston issuing "a plea for winter dairying," and Raymond Crotty insisting that trends in the relative costs of beef and butter and the higher cost of non-feed inputs in Ireland argued against the winter dairying option (Hanly 1924: 409–418; Johnston 1931; Crotty 1966: 72–77; Solow 1971: 151n.). But the very persistence of seasonality and the example of New Zealand indicate that the resistance of Irish farmers to winter dairying was quite sensible. To paraphrase John Maynard Keynes, they presumably knew more about the economics of farming that its proponents did.

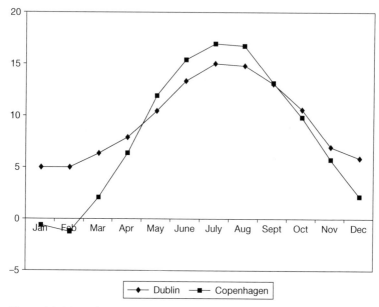

Figure 6.3 Mean daytime temperature in Dublin and Copenhagen (Celsius)

Source: Central Statistics Office, Dublin, and http://ph70.rz.uni-karlsruhe.de/~bh28/klima/tkopenha.html.

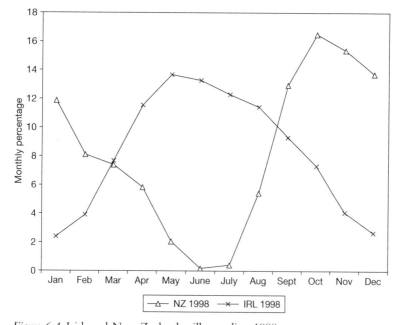

Figure 6.4 Irish and New Zealand milk supplies, 1998

Source: Central Statistics Office, Dublin, and New Zealand Ministry of Agriculture and Forestry.

Conclusion

The settlement of the Irish land question in the 1900s involved the transfer of land ownership from ten thousand or so landed proprietors, mainly Protestant and Unionist in politics, to half a million or so mainly Catholic and Nationalist landholders. The landlords were compensated out of public funds, while the former tenants undertook to pay their share to the British Treasury in the form of land annuities. In due course, the new landowners would contribute much to the conservative ethos and political leadership of independent Ireland. The settlement abolished one kind of inequality, but left another largely untouched. The highly unequal size distribution of farms meant that a minority of "strong" farmers were the main winners of the Land War. It would be left to the new state to deal with the structural problem of unviable and impoverished holdings, particularly in the west of Ireland.

Irish anti-landlord rhetoric, much like abolitionist rhetoric in the antebellum United States, held that what it opposed was both unjust and inefficient. The pro-landlord response, in turn, echoed that of the southern slave-owners and their allies: Irish farmers were unfit to manage Ireland's land endowment alone. This pro-landlord line was an agrarian version of the Unionist premise that Ireland was incapable of competent self-government. Horace Plunkett was a moderate Unionist of landlord stock, and his critique of Catholic Ireland was influenced by such thinking. His sense that Irish farmers were "failing" in their struggle against their Danish rivals reflected a belief that the Catholic Irish required guidance and prompting from their superiors.

Since the 1970s several historians have effectively debunked a neo-abolitionist historiographical tradition that highlighted the greed and venality of the Irish landlord class (Solow 1971; Vaughan 1994). Turning that tradition on its head, these historians implied that the demise of the landlords hurt Irish agriculture. This chapter takes a different tack, suggesting that even "good" landlords were economically dispensable. Our review of farm output estimates suggested that the revolution in land tenure cost little or nothing in terms of overall productivity foregone. Our reappraisal of the Horace Plunkett view that Irish farmers were unduly unenthusiastic about creameries, cooperation, and winter dairying found that there were good reasons for their lack of enthusiasm.

Notes

* Support from the Business Research Programme, University College, Dublin expedited the research. My thanks to Niall Ó Ciosáin for useful comments.

1 Much of W.E. Vaughan's *magnum opus* (Vaughan 1994), built on research carried out in the early 1970s, is very corroborative of Solow. My own estimates of total factor productivity change in 1854–1876 and 1876–1908 seemed to run counter

to the implication of "a turning point (for the worse) in the fortunes of Irish agriculture around the 1870s" (1993: 153).

2 The difference in terms of buildings was trivial but, at least *c.*1910, northern farmers had more machinery at their disposal (Ó Gráda 1991: 444–446).

3 Land's rather generous factor share biases the outcome in the six counties' favor.

4 My thanks to Ingrid Henriksen for these data.

5 National Archives of Ireland: Department of An Taoiseach, S12830.

6 National Archives of Ireland: Department of An Taoiseach, S15465(B).

7 For an effective rebuttal of the claim that the Catholic Church retarded Irish economic growth in the nineteenth century see Kennedy (1996: ch. 4).

8 It also bears remembering that in certain parts of Denmark proprietary creameries still accounted for a significant share of the total milk supply in the 1900s. In North Jutland they took 23.6 percent in 1909, and in Lolland-Falster they took 22.4 percent. See Bjorn (1982: 174).

9 Already by 1907 the IAOS was claiming that saturation point had been reached: "the available dairying ground in Ireland is pretty well occupied by co-operative and proprietary concerns" (IOAS 1908: 5). A few years earlier dozens of prospective cooperatives, mostly in marginal locations, were dissolved, never having proceeded beyond the planning stage (IAOS 1905).

10 A recent contribution by a well-known Irish journalist resurrects the stereotypes of "the honest, dutiful, upright Prod and the wily, shifty, untrustworthy Tague." See O'Toole (1999).

11 For this reason, New Zealand offers a better comparative yardstick for Irish farmers than Denmark.

Bibliography

Aage H.S. (1984) *Økonomisk vaekst i Danmark 1720–1914*, Copenhagen: Økonomisk Institut.

Anderson, R.A. (1937) *With Horace Plunkett in Ireland*, London: Macmillan.

Banking Commission (1938) *Commission of Inquiry into Banking, Currency and Credit: Reports*, Dublin: Stationery Office.

Beddy, J.P. (1943) "A comparison of the Principal Economic Features of Eire and Denmark," *Journal of the Statistical and Social Inquiry Society of Ireland*, 27: 189–220.

Bjorn, C. (1982) "Dansk mejeribrug 1882–1914," in C. Bjorn (ed.) *Dansk mejeribrug 1882–2000*, Odense: de danske Mejeriers Faellesorganisation.

Boyle, G. (1992) Contribution to National Economic and Social Council, *Impact of Reform of the Common Agricultural Policy*, Dublin: NESC.

Crotty, R.D. (1966) *Irish Agricultural Production*, Cork: Cork University Press.

Daly, M.E. (2002) *The First Department: A History of the Department of Agriculture*, Dublin: Institute of Public Administration.

Dunne, G. (1983) *Town of Monaghan Co-op: The First Eighty Years*, Monaghan: R. & S.

Eiríksson, A. and Ó Gráda, C. (1996) "Bankrupt Landlords and the Irish Famine," UCD Centre for Economic Research Working Paper 96/10.

Foreman-Peck, J. and Lains, P. (2000) "European Economic Development: The Core and the Periphery, 1870–1910," in S. Pamuk and J.G. Williamson (eds) *The Mediterranean Response to Globalisation before 1950*, London: Routledge.

Freeman, T.W. (1969) *Ireland: A General and Regional Geography*, 4th edn, London: Methuen.

Hancock, W.N. (1851) *Is There Really a Want of Capital in Ireland?*, Dublin: Dealy, Briars & Walker.

Hanly, J. (1924) *Mixed Farming: A Practical Text Book of Irish Agriculture*, 2nd edn, Dublin: Dealy, Briars, & Walker.

Hough, J. (1997) *Ireland's Co-operative Heartland: Ardagh C.D.S. – A History 1891–1974*, Limerick: Treaty Press.

IAOS (1905) *Report for 1903–4*, Dublin: IAOS.

IAOS (1908) *Report for 1906–7*, Dublin: IAOS.

Jenkins, W. (1995) "The Origin and Development of the Creamery System in South Tipperary," unpublished MA dissertation, National University of Ireland.

—— (2000) *Tipp Co-op: Origins and Development of Tipperary Co-operative Creamery*, Dublin: Geography Publications.

Jensen, E. (1937) *Danish Agriculture: Its Economic Development*, Copenhagen: J.H. Schultz Verlag.

Johnston, J. (1931) "A Plea for Winter Dairying," *Journal of the Statistical and Social Inquiry Society of Ireland*, 17: 33–44.

Keating [King], C.R. (1984) "Sir Horace Plunkett and Rural Reform 1889–1914," unpublished Ph.D. dissertation, National University of Ireland.

Kennedy, L. (1996) *Colonialism, Religion and Nationalism in Ireland*, Belfast: Institute of Irish Studies.

McDonnell, N. (1999) *Callan Co-operative Agricultural and Dairy Society Ltd. 1899–1999*, Kilkenny: Callan Co-operative Agricultural and Dairy Society.

Mokyr, J. and Ó Gráda, C. (1996) "Heights and Living Standards in the United Kingdom 1815–1860," *Explorations in Economic History*, 33: 141–68.

Murtagh, M. (1986) *Proud Heritage: The Story of Imokilly Co-op*, Dublin: Belbulben.

Ó Gráda, C. (1977) "The Beginnings of the Irish Creamery System," *Economic History Review*, 25: 284–305.

—— (1991) "Irish Agriculture North and South since 1900," in B. Campbell and M. Overton (eds) *Land, Labour and Livestock: Historical Studies in European Agricultural Productivity*, Manchester: Manchester University Press.

—— (1993) *Ireland Before and After the Great Famine*, 2nd edn, Manchester: Manchester University Press.

—— (1994) *Ireland: A New Economic History 1780–1939*, Oxford: Oxford University Press.

—— (1997) *A Rocky Road: The Irish Economy since the 1920s*, Manchester: Manchester University Press.

—— (1999) *Black '47 and Beyond: The Great Irish Famine in History, Economy, and Memory*, Princeton, NJ: Princeton University Press.

O'Rourke, K. (2001) "Culture, Politics and Innovation: Evidence from the Creameries," Centre for Economic Policy Research Working Paper 3235.

O'Shea, M. (2001) *One Hundred Years of Piltown Co-operative and its Branches*, Piltown: Piltown Cooperative Society.

O'Toole, F. (1999) "DIRT Inquiry Illuminates a Sectarian Stereotype," *Irish Times*, October 15.

PDSÉ (*Parliamentary Debates Seanad Éireann*) (1939) Vol. 22 (June 7), paragraphs 1708–1764.

Plunkett, H. (1904) *Ireland in the New Century*, London: John Murray.

Smith, R. (1998) *The Centenary Co-operative Creamery Society, Ltd.: A Century of Endeavour, 1898–1998*, Dublin: Mount Cross.

Solar, P.M. (1998) "The Pitfalls of Estimating Irish Agricultural Output for Post-Famine Ireland," *Irish Economic and Social History*, 25: 152–156.

Solow, B.L. (1971) *The Land Question and the Irish Economy*, Cambridge, MA: Harvard University Press.

Turner, M. (1996) *After the Famine: Irish Agricultural Production 1850–1914*, Cambridge: Cambridge University Press.

—— (2000) "Agricultural Output, Income and Productivity," in E.J.T. Collins (ed.) *The Agrarian History of England and Wales 1850–1914*, Vol. 7(1), Cambridge: Cambridge University Press.

Vaughan, W.E. (1994) *Landlords and Tenants in Mid-Victorian Ireland*, Oxford: Oxford University Press.

West, T. (1986) *Sir Horace Plunkett: Co-operation and Politics, an Irish Biography*, Gerards Cross: Colin Smythe.

7 Land disputes and ethno-politics

Northwestern Anatolia, 1877–1912

Yücel Terzibaşoğlu

Introduction

The second half of the nineteenth century witnessed large-scale population movements in the Balkans and Anatolia as a direct result of Russian–Ottoman wars fought out on battlefields in a vast stretch of land from the Crimea to the present-day suburbs of Istanbul. Throughout the century these wars led to dramatic land losses for the Ottoman Empire, which left most of its provinces in the Balkans first to the Russians and then to the several newly established nation-states in the region. Withdrawing Ottoman armies were often accompanied by long lines of refugee columns, mostly peasants who had lost their lands and were displaced either because of direct military action, political design, civil strife, or some combination of these. Thus, by the first decades of the twentieth century, the Ottoman Empire was reduced to its Anatolian and Arab provinces, with a total of more than 5 million of its Balkan inhabitants – predominantly Muslims – taking refuge in the remaining lands of the contracting empire (Quataert 1997: 793). The loss, within a very short time period, of some of the core provinces of the Empire had been devastating economically and politically, catastrophic socially, and traumatic for the Ottoman rulers, with dramatic long-term consequences. Russian and Bulgarian armies at the gates of Istanbul no doubt rang the death knell for the Empire as such. Hundreds of thousands of refugees in the streets of Istanbul were constant reminders of the losses both for the displaced and dispossessed refugees themselves and for the rulers.

Although the scale and extent of the population movements in the aftermath of the 1877–1878 Ottoman–Russian War were new, and thus acquired aspects which were unprecedented, the methods of population transfer and expulsion were in no way unfamiliar for the multi-ethnic empires in the region. The chapter will first outline the "toolbox" that the empires had before the age of nationalism in the form of policies aimed at nomadic tribes to encourage a sedentary life style, and the transfer and transplantation of population groups for colonization or resettlement. In fact, in the period prior to the advent of nation-states in the Balkans, the population policies of the Ottoman and Russian empires had developed in such a way that they turned into "demographic warfare" (Pinson 1970). The focus will then turn to Anatolia, and the pressure that the refugee influx placed on the available amount of land will be discussed in relation to the processes which were already under way there, namely the erosion of customary rights on land and the transformation of rights to use the land or to collect revenue from it into rights based on the title to land. The latter was in itself a highly contentious process as witnessed in the myriad land conflicts in Anatolia at this time. How immigration changed the nature of these conflicts forms one of the central themes of the chapter. This will be discussed in terms of the impact of immigration on land use and distribution, and also on the inter-communal relations in the Empire. How land came to be associated with the creation of an Ottoman homeland at the turn of the twentieth century, and was related to issues of nationality and sovereignty, forms the final section.

The geographical focus will be on northwestern Anatolia, the region to the south of the Dardanelles, namely the coastline and the interior of the Bay of Edremit on the Aegean coast facing the island of Mitylene. This area roughly corresponded to the Ottoman province of Karesi. Western Anatolia, and especially the region to the south of the Sea of Marmara, saw one of the largest concentrations of refugee settlement prior to but especially after the Russian–Ottoman War of 1877–1878. Although there were not many refugee settlements on the coastline, the coast from the town of Edremit to the north and south to Burhaniye and Ayvalık saw an unusual number of land disputes, not all related to refugee settlement.[1] Moreover, at the heart of this region was the port-town of Ayvalık, which had an unusual amount of local autonomy granted to its almost entirely Greek population, together with a high degree of self-government and special tax privileges (Terzibaşoğlu 2001). It is precisely these unusual features which rendered the region important as it contained within a small area the nature of the refugee problem: high refugee presence in the surrounding countryside, scarcity of settlement land, a history of previous land conflicts, and an unusual concentration of Christian population resident in a town with which the Ottoman administration was not at ease. The impact of immigration on the use and distribution of land was therefore more prominent and immediate in this region.

Rural mobility and population movements

Ottoman Anatolia retained a certain degree of rural mobility well into the nineteenth century, in spite of strict controls over the movement of the population of the Empire. Rural mobility was primarily due to the periodic movement of nomadic tribes in the countryside. But it was also due to the transference between the lives and economic activities of nomads and peasants. For the administrative officials concerned with registering and recording the population in the land and tax surveys, settled peasantry could

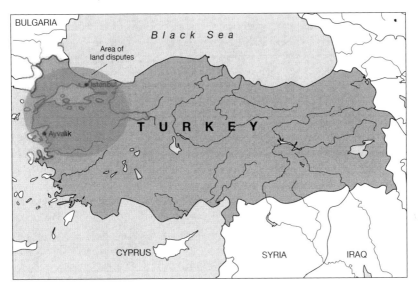

Map 7.1 Anatolia, 1913

Source: http://www.lib.utexas.edu/maps/middleeast_and_asia/turkey_nw_2002.jpg
Courtesy of The General Libraries, The University of Texas at Austin.

not be clearly separated and differentiated from the nomads. Peasants were also migrating between their villages, and summer and winter pastures, and could easily switch between agriculture and animal husbandry as rainfall provided most of the irrigation needs of the cultivators throughout Anatolia (Faroqhi 1984: 269). The land surveys frequently recorded that peasants in certain areas were "like nomads" or that the peasants in a certain area "turned nomad" (Çelik 2000: 84–85). Because of strict legal limitations on geographic and other types of mobility, these are poorly documented. But the involvement of tribal groups in seasonal agriculture (semi-nomadic tribes in southern Anatolia were growing cotton as early as the sixteenth century) in addition to animal husbandry, also rendered them closer to the more settled cultivators. Such movements of both cultivators and herdsmen between the mountains and the plain resulted in a persistent semi-nomadic existence in the countryside.

Forming the backbone of the conquering Ottoman armies in the fifteenth and sixteenth centuries, the nomadic Turcoman tribes gradually settled in the Ottoman Balkan provinces. Initially some of the groups surged on to the newly conquered lands for new pastures which were getting harder to find in Anatolia as the nomadic population of western Anatolia increased with the arrival of new groups from the eastern parts of the peninsula and from northern Syria. In addition to voluntary migration, Ottoman rulers actively encouraged and forced migration and settlement in the newly conquered territories in the Balkans (and thus "enlivened," in Ottoman parlance, otherwise vacant land). The groups which moved into the Balkans voluntarily or involuntarily were settled in villages formed around religious orders or *zaviyes* (Barkan 1980). The settlers brought in and settled in such *vakıf* (pious endowment) villages included cultivators as well as artisans and skilled workers, and were exempted from normal taxation, at least for a certain period of time. These *vakıf* villages were generally established at marshlands or abandoned places, and the settlers were expected to reclaim land for cultivation. Sixteenth-century tax surveys demonstrate a clear pattern whereby such settlement was orderly and regulated (Emecen 2001). Groups of nomadic shepherds who were thus removed from the rest of the tribal group were expected to turn to cultivation. It was a gradual process whereby tribal connections were weakened and nomads turned into settled peasants. This practice of moving populations from densely populated areas to areas where land was abundant was therefore one of the early population practices of the Ottoman administration. The outright expulsion or deportation of populations for settlement or resettlement in a new area was generally arranged with the double aims of relieving population pressure in the sender communities and of repopulating the receiving, usually newly conquered, lands. Not all settlers were nomadic animal breeders. The settlement of the newly conquered island of Cyprus is a case in point (Faroqhi 1984: 282–283). The Ottoman administration of the late sixteenth century instructed local *kadıs* in Anatolia to choose migrants from among those less integrated into their hometowns or villages. Apart from outlaws and similar marginal people, this meant that landless men, those involved in long-term land disputes and relatively recent immigrants, were singled out for deportation. Nomadic tribes who had been involved in land disputes were no doubt the prime target for such deportations. Inducements in the form of tax concessions were usually granted to the settlers for a prescribed period.

Security was another important consideration in the forced movement of populations. Nomadic groups were being settled at specified locations around mountain passes, river crossings, and along main trading routes, to provide security against brigand attacks and for the upkeep of bridges and roads, or for rendering certain specialized services. These villages, generally referred to as *derbend* villages, assumed an added importance at times when internal security in the countryside deteriorated. The officials were aware that the social distance between those who manned a *derbend* village and those who manned the groups of outlaws roaming the countryside was not very great, as one turned into the other very easily. Yet the setting up of such specialized villages was a frequent way of settling nomads, and was resorted to until the end of the eighteenth century (Orhonlu 1990: 105–115). In such settlement schemes a land survey had to be conducted prior to settlement to guarantee that there were no other claims on the designated land, and enough land for pastures had to be reserved for the settling nomads. Some of the very processes that led to insecurity in the countryside and flight of the peasantry in the first place also resulted in the failure of nomadic settlement in this period: the burden of, usually, extra-legal taxation imposed by the local officials and/or the notables and the very lack of security frequently turned settlers into nomads again.

During the course of the nineteenth century most of the nomadic and semi-nomadic tribes of the Anatolian countryside became sedentary. Overall, the extent and reach of the settlement policies as well as their content and effectiveness indicated the determination and the reach of the Ottoman central administration. It was at this time that administrative restrictions on the movement of the nomadic tribes forced the herdsmen to settle mostly in their winter pastures. Attempts at the power and authority of the tribal chiefs over the nomadic population eroded the latter's power base among the nomadic population and their authority with the local officials. Nomadic households were distributed among existing villages and settlements were designed with a view to weaken tribal allegiances. Of more significance, however, was the fact that the settlement schemes were now centrally organized and orchestrated under the initiative of the specially appointed powerful governors in provinces where nomadic settlement was more pressing. The settlement of the tribes and the eradication of the nomadic way of life was a matter of urgency for the Ottoman bureaucracy, which considered nomadism as a remnant of the past, an "uncivilized" burden to be rid of.[2] The prolonged and endless deliberations during the century, between Istanbul and the provinces, on the final settlement of the tribes attested to the determination of the central administration in this issue. It was also one manifestation of the transformation in the nature of landed property and taxation throughout the Empire. In the course of the nineteenth century, property rights on land were being redefined and enforced in such a way as to render rights to land more individual and exclusive; units of tax assessment and collection were being shifted from communities (whether tribe, town quarter, village, or religious community) to individuals. From the perspective of the nomadic organization it was a deadly blow for communal understandings and solidarities, for time-honored customary rights, and for the nomadic way of life in general. The claims and demands put forth by the opposing parties in land conflicts at this time in Anatolia underline the different understandings of landed property and the conflicting notions of rights related to land.[3]

Privatization of commons

The legal transformation culminating in the Land Code of 1858 and the ensuing legislation and land registration throughout the Empire was instrumental in altering the nature and definition of property on land (İslamoğlu 2000; Mundy 2000). Property was no longer defined in relation to the revenues derived from land but in relation to the title to land. This meant the end of multiplicity of claims on a single plot of land and the exclusion of many overlapping rights such as rights to passage, poaching, and grazing on a single plot, a transformation from multiple overlapping rights to individual rights. In parallel, the communal rights the nomads and the settled peasantry had on pastures, forests, and village commons, as well as the ill-defined proprietorship rights of the *vakıf* administrations on landed property were all in a process of erosion to the benefit of individual title and use, a transformation from communal to individual rights. This dual transformation therefore represented a transition from a plurality of rights on land to the uniform categories defined in the Land Code.[4] The majority of the conflicts that this transformation engendered centered around the rights of *tasarruf* (use). At issue was the very definition of the rights of *tasarruf*. Indeed the meaning of the term in the course of the century changed from denoting use rights on land to a bundle of rights defined around ownership of land. As far as the nomads were concerned, this meant that, unlike in previous centuries, the primary concern of the nomadic groups were no longer only arbitrary tax demands of the local officials or the conscription demands of the central state but, more pressingly, exclusion from their routes of seasonal migration and pastures.

Disputes on borders – whether of pastures or of routes of passage – were very common and a major bone of contention. Such disputes generally resulted from the nature of the landscape and pattern of land use. This tension was inherent in the coexistence of nomadic and sedentary modes of life. In general, determination of the exact borders of a *çiftlik* (farm) or pasture or any odd plot of land was marred by many problems. At the turn of the twentieth century, in conflict after conflict, it proved impossible or nearly impossible to determine the exact boundaries of a piece of land. The borders designated in an old *tapu* (title deed) or *hududname* (border plan) rarely coincided with the claimed boundaries in a conflict. In the absence of modern land surveying techniques this is perhaps to be expected. But the real significance of this problem lies in the fact that it actually shows, first, how the cultivators were continuously changing the landscape (opening up marshes and woods); and, second, and more importantly, how the cultivators and the nomads extended the boundaries of fields and pastures, or occupied lands in the hope and expectation that with long enough undisturbed cultivation they would actually be able to claim *tasarruf* for these lands.[5] One of the reasons this was made possible was that a considerable number of large landholders were absentee landlords residing in towns. The widespread practice of land boundary extensions was mostly induced by population pressure resulting from the immigration of refugees and settlement of nomadic groups (Terzibaşoğlu 2002).[6]

In claiming established rights on disputed land, two legal categories, both enshrined in the existing land law, were extensively used by nomads and peasants when confronted with the exclusionary *tasarruf* claims of the land owners: prescriptive rights (*hakk-ı karar*) and customary rights. The use of the rhetoric of customary rights is not new and had been assimilated in many *kanunname*s (provincial land laws) of the past but was also given place in the Land Code. Both of these categories referred to local knowledge and memory. For a right to be customary, there should exist no living person who could remember what rights there had been before (status quo ante). This implies a period of 40–50 years. Similarly, to prove *hakk-ı karar* and thus achieve *tasarruf* on a piece of land, a cultivator had to prove uncontested use (*tasarruf*) and cultivation of a particular plot of land for a period of at least ten years. The proof of both of these rested on a local inquiry, involving local witnesses, local commissions, village councils, and administrative councils of different degrees. In other words, by employing these categories the conflict was brought into the field of oral tradition and local power relations at the expense of the more centralized agencies such as the courts and *Şura-yı Devlet* (state council). This was where local custom played a defining role. It is worth stressing that this is not local custom as opposed to law but local custom as enshrined in law. Therefore peasant cultivators and nomads would always try to settle a conflict with reference to local witnesses or village councils, thereby giving primacy to local memory and custom, as opposed to the big landholders who would demand the appointment of external expert witnesses, provincial or higher courts, and commissions, and thereby pulling the conflict to the arena of more formal legal procedure (Terzibaşoğlu 2002). In this, customary rights were increasingly being sidelined in the face of land registration and the increasing primacy of title to land as proven by official title deeds. The primacy of official title deeds in the settlement of land disputes before the new *nizamiye* courts meant that not only was the legal language available to nomads being rendered futile, but, more importantly, the customary rights themselves were in the process of being criminalized.[7] At this stage one more language became available to oppose this process and it was mostly brought by the refugees from the Balkans. The next section deals with the way it developed and its implications.

Refugees and population pressure in the nineteenth century

In the middle of the nineteenth century, at a time when the settlement of nomads was finally taking root, immigration from the Balkans towards Anatolia gained pace in the wake of the endless wars with the Russians. This would contribute to the mobility in the Anatolian countryside in a radical fashion and had far more unstable results. It is estimated that between 1783 and 1913 more than 5 million refugees arrived in the Ottoman Empire. Some of these were already Ottoman subjects, retreating from the lost territories but 3.8 million were from Russia. Mostly after 1878, about 2 million Circassians and 1.8 million Tatars settled in Ottoman lands (Quataert 1997: 793). Western Anatolia was one of the regions most affected by this massive influx of refugees. About one-fifth of this total, or 1 million people, arrived within a period of just 20 years after the 1877–1878 Ottoman–Russian War. Even then these official figures were most probably undercounts, as there were many who simply escaped the official count by settling near refugees who had arrived earlier and settled in towns and villages in the Anatolian countryside. The fact that provincial statistics do not in some cases coincide with the overall figures given in more general statistics attests to this fact. Overall, the Ottoman population increased from 19.8 million in 1875 to 24.5 million in 1885 and to 27.2 million in 1895, a population increase of about 40 percent in 20 years (Karpat 1985). This increase was due chiefly to immigration and most importantly to the ever contracting land mass of the Empire. There were two significant consequences: first, the proportion of Muslims to Christians increased considerably, and second, the available land had to be used more intensively with the increase in the population density. This indeed led to increased agricultural production and output in Anatolia.

The scale of the immigration to Anatolia during the nineteenth century was immense; the extent of the geography and the numbers involved were unprecedented. More importantly, the ways in which it had happened had an indelible bearing on the future population policies in the region to be followed by the prospective regional nation-states. With hindsight one can see in the nineteenth century population movements the precursors to the population exchanges in the Balkans before and after World War I. In fact a formal migration agreement was signed between the Ottoman and Russian governments just after 1856 (Karpat 1985: 67). In 1860 there were diplomatic negotiations between the two governments to provide for an orderly transfer of populations. A study of the earlier phase of the migrations of the Tatars, Circassians, and Bulgarians concluded that the Ottoman and Russian governments in fact had been carrying out population policies since the latter part of the eighteenth century, which amounted to a de facto exchange of populations with the tacit approval of the two governments (Pinson 1970: 1). There were no official agreements spelling out these population transfers. The official peace treaties usually were silent on the population issue. In a few cases a unidirectional movement of populations was mentioned, but no areas of settlement were indicated except where there were some restrictions on where the refugees should not be settled, and, most importantly, much of the emigration took place through illegal use of force or pressure with the government seeking the emigration wishing to conceal its intentions. But a comparison of the sites involved manifests a close relationship between the two population movements and an exchange of settlement locations.

The Russian government policies of deliberate shifting of the population balance in the Black Sea area started in the course of the eighteenth century when, while various Christian communities (Russian, Cossack, Bulgarian, Armenian, and Greek) were encouraged to migrate to the region, Muslim Crimean Tatars and Circassians came under intensifying pressure to leave the Russian territories. In 1783, for example, 70,000 Russian peasants were settled in Crimea following the Russian annexation of the peninsula, in the immediate aftermath of which 80,000 Crimean Tatars left (Eren 1966: 32). In fact some of the early migrations had followed a similar pattern and were in effect based on mutual agreement of the Ottoman and Russian governments. With or without a formal agreement the mutuality of the population movements is clear. In 1812, for instance, Tatars were forced to leave the Bucak area for Ottoman territories in exchange for Bulgarian settlers, who, it was hoped, would entice further Bulgarian communities to leave Ottoman lands and settle in Russia. Similar policies were underway in the Caucasus where in 1829, when the Russian army retreated from eastern Anatolia, a large group of Armenians variously estimated to be between 60,000 and 90,000 followed the Russian army in retreat fearing reprisals by the returning Ottoman army. Cossacks were brought to the Caucasus at different times to settle along the Ottoman–Russian border for maintaining security along the frontier. Further to the south, the support of the British and Russian empires for the Greek uprising in Morea (Peloponnese) led to proposals in 1826 for the forced expulsion of the Muslims in Morea and the Aegean islands to Anatolia and the Balkans after the sale of their properties. Although this proposal was rejected, Russia managed to force the Ottomans, in the same year, to expel Muslims from Serbia. The treaty of 1826 foresaw that Serbians would be granted total autonomy in Serbia, taking over all the property belonging to Muslims who were to leave Serbia, as well as Walachia and Moldavia. And in 1830, when the Ottomans conceded the establishment of a Greek state in Morea, it had to engage in negotiations in Istanbul in the same year with Russia, Britain, and France for an orderly procedure for the evacuation of Muslims from Morea within a six-month period (Eren 1966: 35–37). In addition to the open warfare between the two empires which continued all through the century, a "demographic warfare" had thus long been underway. The Ottomans counteracted Russian policy by settling the Tatars and Circassians along the shifting frontiers in the Balkans.

An important aspect of the Russian policy towards Crimean Tatars consisted of policies aimed at dispossessing the Tatars from their lands in Crimea. The land commissions set up by the Russian government in Crimea had been instrumental in land dispossession. Set up with the avowed aim of settling land disputes, the rulings of the commissions had mostly favored the local non-Tatar gentry against the Tatars who failed in most instances to provide written proof of land ownership. Land registration practices of the 1830s had also the effect of transferring more land from the Tatar peasantry and nobility to the non-Tatar landholders. Sale of land in anticipation of dispossession had further diminished the land in Tatar possession (Pinson 1970: 25–43). It must be noted that although colonization and resettlement was a major motive for these dispossession policies, at the same time they were aimed at privatizing communally held land by the Tatars.

In this respect, the workings of the land commissions, and the registration practices of the Russian government, bear parallels to Ottoman land policies in the same period.

The importance of the impact of the migration into Anatolia from Caucasia and Crimea in the formulation of Turkish nationalism has been underlined (Arai 1992). But also important are the effects of such migratory movements on the material and social life in the countryside, and, for the purposes of the present argument, on the pattern of land use and distribution as well as on local inter-communal relations. The focus on one region in western Anatolia thereby gives an opportunity to zero in on the local inter-communal relations and their ramifications for the property relations on land. The tensions that were unleashed in the Anatolian countryside with the arrival of refugees no doubt resulted in conflicts with the local Christian population, who were seen by the refugees as the next of kin of those Christians who had taken their lands back in the Balkans. There were also, however, numerous instances of rising tensions between the local *Muslim* population and the newly arriving *Muslim* Circassians as well as the Cretan refugees in western Anatolia and elsewhere. Most of the time, these conflicts were sparked by issues surrounding refugee settlement.

Settlement and land conflicts

There were two, often contradictory, objectives in refugee settlement throughout the century. The first objective was dictated by the urgent need to repopulate an area as a defense line against the enemy. During the gradual retreat from Crimea and northern Bulgarian lands, the Ottoman army was concerned that the vast unpopulated plains that were now forming the border were hard to defend against further Russian attacks. While doing this, local officials had to closely watch the population ratios in these lands. Muslim refugees were to be introduced so that after settlement local Christian populations were not the majority in any single area (İpek 1994: 199–207). Otherwise it was feared that the Russians would use this as an excuse for annexation based on their claim as the Protector of the Orthodox in the Ottoman Empire.[8] This aspect of the settlement policy was the political–military objective. The second objective of refugee settlement, together with nomadic settlement, was, for the Ottoman officialdom, part of a grand project of modernization – a civilizing mission.[9] The project of settlement provided an opportunity for the administration to lay the designs of a modern Ottoman society. The concern for finding and applying "scientific" methods of setting up villages and towns, the preoccupation of bringing the nomads into the "circle of civilization," of increasing production, and breaking group solidarities, were all part of this project. In the Balkan settlements of the mid century, the political–military objective overrode the civilizing objective in the heat of the war, when defense lines had to be quickly established. Hence there was no time or money for setting up model villages or for breaking up group solidarities. In contrast, in later settlements in Anatolia, the Ottoman administration would fight hard to break communal group bonds when settling refugees.

Increasingly, at this same time, in the last decades of the nineteenth century, Muslim immigration and settlement were expected to remake Anatolia as a more homogeneous territory, a homeland, for the Muslim subjects of the Empire. The retreat from the Balkans was to be offset by restrengthening Anatolia with a Muslim population against the many national states that had developed out of the former Christian communities of the Empire and had torn apart the empire's lands in the Balkans. The flow of refugees into Anatolia offered a chance to do just that. For this the ethnic/religious composition of the lands on which the new refugees were to be settled had to be closely monitored. There are indications in the settlement schemes that if finding empty land for settlement was a major concern, equally important was the ethnic/religious composition in the area of settlement. In the second half of the nineteenth century, the presence of Christians in a certain area made it unsuitable for settlement in the eyes of the local officials as settlement of refugees in the area was feared to result in serious inter-communal frictions. The displaced and dispossessed refugees, in many cases compelled to leave their homes by force, felt they had been treated unjustly and were now looking to the Ottoman state to correct that. The feelings of injustice were magnified when, as in a considerable number of cases, the lands distributed to them were insufficient or uncultivable. For such reasons, the sender countries usually did not want newly displaced refugees to be settled along the new borders, given the fear that they could cross the border and carry out revenge attacks in their former lands against the local population. Toward the end of the century, and especially in the wake of the Balkan wars, however, there was a sharp change of policy and the refugee groups were deliberately settled near or in Christian villages. This turn of events was to lend credibility to the refugee claims that the Sultan had granted Christian lands to them.

Economically, the Ottoman administration had high expectations from settlement schemes. The presumed vast stretches of uncultivated empty land in Anatolia would be put to cultivation, and agricultural production would increase. Through the course of the nineteenth century, and especially toward the end, overall agricultural production did indeed increase in Anatolia. But this increase was to a large extent due to reclamation of land by the drying up of malarial marshlands and by the opening up of forests, as well as settlement in lands held by the treasury, including the Sultanic *vakıf* lands. The turning of pastures into fields was hotly contested by the nomads as they had some legally acknowledged claims on such grazing grounds. Indeed, central and local land officials of the Empire soon recognized that the lands which were thought to have been empty, and therefore assumed to have been free of any use rights, were not in fact empty at all. Some of them were uncultivated but there were legal claims on these lands.

Some of these legal claims were based on title deeds held by absentee land owners, others were based on accumulated use rights by the surrounding peasantry, who by the mere fact of having been using the land without contestation for ten years, gained ownership rights on the land. These prescriptive or constituted rights were to a large extent not recorded in the local land registers, and were at the basis of the many land conflicts triggered by refugee settlement (Terzibaşoğlu, 2002).

It was when a land dispute erupted that the refugees were heard to voice their claims and make their dissatisfaction heard. Refugee claims to land were usually worded in an ethnic/religious vocabulary, especially if the opposing party in the conflict was Christian. Yet it is worth underlining that the parties to land conflicts did not always belong to different religious groups. There were many conflicts between the Muslim refugees and Muslim inhabitants of Anatolia, be they nomads, peasants, or landholders. In such cases refugees were quite vocal about their claims to land and the local population equally vocal about their complaints. In order to understand the conditions under which claims were coached in an ethnically/religiously oppositional language, and to see the significance that that language assumed, this chapter will emphasize such conflicts. Otherwise, the tensions that refugee settlement created among the Muslim population of Anatolia had also been dramatic and still live on in local memory.

Equally important, of course, was how these ethnically/religiously inspired claims were perceived and received by those for whom they were intended. In the late 1870s the local population around the town of Ayvalık was alarmed at the lack of security in the countryside. They seemed to be especially worried about the Circassian refugees "who were running free in the countryside, robbing people," and who, they claimed, most of the time were acting under the implicit protection of the local authorities.[10] The foreign consuls were reporting that Christian farmers and merchants were being robbed on the roads and then murdered. The insecurity was such that the laborers were prevented from going to work in the fields for fear of their lives, crops were being neglected, and the farmers were in trouble. One merchant, Romanidhis, recounted that at an hour's distance from the town of Marmara to where he had headed for business, he met on the road eight mounted Circassians "armed to the teeth," who after taking all his belongings and horse, "rode away in a slow pace as if nothing had happened." The merchants were complaining about the "atmosphere of terror created by 'this plague called Circassians'," which the local authorities were either too weak to prevent or, they claimed, "had orders from the central state to be lenient toward." Allegedly the Circassians were spreading the word that they had been sent by the government to take possession of the property held by the Christians who were to be driven out of the country. The Circassian refugees, however, were not only attacking Christians but were a source of general trouble in the Anatolian countryside. There were equally common reports about the refugee attacks on nomads and disturbances in towns of western Anatolia, where the local Muslim population wrote repeated petitions to Istanbul. It was reported that the refugees were leaving their villages and settlements and regrouping in the countryside in large numbers.

If land scarcity underlined many of the land conflicts that at this time threatened general security in the Anatolian countryside, then what was its nature, and how was it dealt with? With refugee influx the central and local officials were at pains to locate empty lands anywhere in Anatolia. Scarcity of land for settlement had many manifestations. Refugees were compelled to open up marshes and forests to add land to the meager or infertile lands distributed to them, which in most cases were not enough for self-sufficiency. Settlement in or around forests was not a preferred choice by the administration and official settlement was not allowed in such areas. In practice we do not know how much of this was observed by the refugee groups who settled on their own initiative. Indeed, a report sent from Karesi to the Porte in 1885 complained that nearly all the forests in Karesi were destroyed because of refugee settlement in that region (İpek 1994: 217).[11] Use of forest land and poaching by the refugees were leading to clashes with those nomadic groups who claimed to have established use rights on forests (Saydam 1997: 190). Opening up of marshland was also very common. In one such incident 300 migrant families – more than 1,000 people in all – of Balkan and Circassian descent who were settled in the villages of the districts of Erdek and Bandırma to the south of the Marmara Sea, finding that the land allotted to them was not enough to provide for their subsistence, drained marshland near Lake Manyas in 1892. A total of 2,179 *dönüm*s of land was reclaimed by 1 group and distributed among 565 persons.[12] Now hearing that this land might be distributed to new migrants from the Balkans even more recently arrived than them, in fear of losing it, they petitioned Istanbul asking that the title to these lands be given them gratis since they had opened up the unhealthy marshland and made it cultivable in the first place.[13]

Despite the initial optimistic expectations of the Ottoman bureaucracy, who thought that there were vast empty stretches of land waiting to be cultivated by the incoming refugees, the surveys made on location by the local officials were painting a different picture. They were finding that the supposedly empty stretches of land might have been uncultivated but these lands were either registered to an absentee landlord, or had legally established claims on them by the nomads or the peasantry. The northwestern Anatolian provinces of Hüdavendigar and Biga, as well as Aydın to the south, were typical. These were among the provinces which attracted most of the refugees in towns and fertile valleys along the coasts of the Marmara and Aegean Seas. By 1891 a total of 150,000 refugees were registered in Hüdavendigar, some of whom had set up some more than 261 new villages and quarters in the districts and towns of the province. The majority of these villages and quarters were set up by Balkan refugees and the rest by

Circassians and Tatars. The 363,000 *dönüms* of empty land found in the province in 1878 must have reached its limits by 1882, when Süleyman Paşa, the head of the refugee commission of the province, "found" in the same year additional empty land in the district of Mihaliç suitable for the settlement of about 1,000 more Circassian refugees. It was considered that the town of Gemlik on the eastern tip of the Marmara Sea was also suitable for settlement as the Muslim population of the town had been declining. In 1882 it was seen that there were only eight or ten Muslim households left in the town, and thereupon 150 refugee households were planned to be settled there. Some refugees were settled in the *çiftliks* located in the Bursa plain and İznik as sharecroppers or farm laborers (İpek 1994: 187–197). Some settlements were moved to other locations as these were usually marshy areas. Many conflicts arose within the province due to settlement on lands under the *tasarruf* of local people. Christians in the district of Mihaliç petitioned the Porte, complaining of attacks by the Circassians. In one village in the district of Kirmastı, peasants and Circassians were embroiled in a land dispute involving clashes between the two communities in 1879. The peasants burned down the huts built for the Circassians claiming that the huts were built on fields belonging to them. In Bursa a group of Balkan refugees and the people of the village of Samanlı were involved in clashes because of land, as a result of which one person was killed and many wounded. It was understood that the refugees were not settled there by the instructions of the commission but by their own account and on the lands belonging to the peasants. In Manyas, Circassian refugees reportedly confiscated about 12,000 *dönüms* of land and pasture belonging to the peasants in the surrounding area. In order to prevent further confrontations and trouble the government had to buy land from the peasants and allow the Circassians to remain there.

Similarly, in Biga, along the Dardanelles, local officials reportedly purchased land under the *tasarruf* of the local population which was not at the time being cultivated, and distributed it to the refugees. In 1884, about 3,000 refugees were settled on such land in the area. Still land in the province was not enough and Circassians and Balkan settlers in six villages started attacking the lands held by the local population. There were special complaints from the Circassians who were apparently attacking local villages not only for land but for food and goods. In fact such complaints go back to the 1860s. In 1865 the local population of Biga undertook to pay the expenses of soldiers to be sent to the region to stop refugee attacks (Saydam 1997: 192). One estimate was that in the 1880s the newcomers were holding 20,000 *dönüms* of land confiscated by force from the local population. Such confiscation was carried out through gunfights, involving killing and wounding. To stop the insecurity in the area, refugee settlement in the province was banned in 1886, and 160,000 *kuruş* were sent to the local officials to enable them to buy land from the local population to settle the disputes. Since even this did not put a stop to the land disputes, a special commission was set up with members from the Şura-yı Devlet, the refugee settlement inspector of the Hüdavendigar province, *naib* (judge) and *defter-i hakani* (land registration) officials, and army personnel. The commission was to investigate the source of the conflicts and work as a settlement court. The commission had reportedly failed its objectives (İpek 1994: 198).

According to the aggregate figures and maps of empty lands throughout the Empire as compiled from the provincial reports by the central administration, there were about 360,000 *dönüm*s (out of a total of 1,600,000 *dönüm*s in Anatolia) of land available for refugee settlement in the province of Hüdavendigar in 1878 (İpek 1994: 163–167). In Aydın there were only 78,500 *dönüm*s. For the province of Diyarbakır, for example, there were no available lands and it was stated that although there were large empty lands within the province these were not suitable for settlement due to climatic and security reasons. For the Tekfurdağı sub-province of Edirne, although 6,000 *dönüm*s of available land was shown, a side note stated that this land was being cultivated by Greek peasants and refugee settlement was therefore risky. In the end most of the refugees were being sent to the provinces of Edirne, Aydın, Hüdavendigar, Ankara, and Kastamonu. In 1892, 24 years later, another general register of empty lands showed increases in the total amounts of available land both at the general and province levels as compared with the previous register. However, a closer inspection reveals another picture. According to this later register, in Hüdavendigar there were 390,000 *dönüm*s of empty land (out of a total of about 2 Trillion *dönüm*s for all of Anatolia). However, it was noted that 278,000 *dönüm*s of this was "found" by Ferik Muzaffer Paşa along the railway line (he reportedly also "found" another 660,000 *dönüm*s of land in the Ankara province again along the railway line). For Aydın a similar 135,000 *dönüm*s apparently were also discovered. Exactly how these empty lands were discovered, we do not know. Ignoring this "found" land, we see that there was a drastic decline in the amount of available land for settlement from 1878 to 1892, a decline of 70 percent. In 1892, 155,000 *dönüm*s of empty land was shown for Aydın, double the amount in 1878, but the increase was the result of 135,000 *dönüm*s "found" within the sub-province of Aydın in 1892. Likewise ignoring this large amount of land, nearly 80,000 *dönüm*s of land available in Aydın province in 1878 declined to 20,000 by 1892, a reduction of 75 percent.

In spite of the local variation of land availability through time, land for refugee settlement was limited from the beginning. Indeed reports from western and central Anatolia had complained much earlier that the amount of empty land had filled up with the settlements since 1855 and that there were no longer any empty lands (İpek 1994: 162). In 1864, for instance, the governor of the sub-province of Amasya was complaining that the lands first thought to have been empty and thus to be distributed to the refugees were afterwards claimed by their owners (Saydam 1997: 140). When empty lands filled up, *vakıf* lands, pastures, and unused lands reserved for the army were opened for settlement. Village commons and pastures came under close scrutiny by the Ottoman administration and any pasture or part of it that was not held by official deeds was immediately taken from the peasants and given to the refugees. With a decision of the Council of Ministers of August 11, 1886, any land which remained uncultivated for no justifiable reason for a period of 3 years was to be confiscated for refugee settlement on the basis of article 68 of the Land Code of 1858. The Council, however, had soon to review its decision since there were many lands in Anatolia which were left temporarily empty as they belonged to soldiers fighting the endless wars on the Russian front who thus had to leave their lands empty for more than the prescribed time. Also some of the seemingly empty land belonged to poor peasants who lacked the seeds or the agricultural implements for cultivation. Therefore the application of the 3-year rule was very difficult under the circumstances. The Council could only suggest that Sultanic lands in Rumeli and Anatolia, which had been rented out for periods of 15 years or more, should be turned into refugee settlements; and more land reclamation projects should be carried out to turn woods and marshy lands to cultivation. A project was even considered to drain all of Lake Manyas to the north of the province of Hüdavendigar and reclaim a land of about 100,000 *dönüms* (İpek 1994: 215–217).

The way *vakıf* lands came under closer scrutiny by the central administration and the transformation of them through time into forms of private ownership are also indicative of the pressure on land. Thus, for example, in one incident in 1913, following the unleashing of a conflict about the sale of 6,500 *dönüms* of land adjacent to the town of Ayvalık, it became imperative to determine the legal status of the land as it was claimed both by one Ayvaliot to be under his *tasarruf* since 1865, and by the Evkaf Ministry to be *vakıf* land.[14] The local land registry officials confirmed that, according to the local registers, the land was state land. On its part the Evkaf Ministry failed to provide documents proving the borders and the amount of the land it claimed to be *vakıf*, and its date and nature of endowment; even the original *vakfiyye* could not be located. What the dispute between the local land officials, backed by parts of the central administration (Interior and Land Registration Ministries), and the Evkaf Ministry highlighted was a pressing concern of the Ayvalık land registration office: the local land officials were complaining that although there were plenty of empty lands in the area for the settlement of the refugees, because of the intervention of the *evkaf* administration the land registration administration could not appropriate these empty lands. The fact that the issue of the settlement of the refugees comes up in a seemingly sterile dispute on the legal status of a piece of land is indicative of the extent and urgency of the settlement issue for the local officials. The local land office suggested that the matter should be resolved through reference to the certified copies of the registers at the Land Registration Ministry as the *evkaf* administration was unable to produce any relevant documentation to prove its case. What this suggestion implied was that in effect the local officials were taking the land out of the control of the *evkaf* and placing it under their own control, i.e. turning it de facto into state land.[15]

When the local officials found empty land they were not always very careful as to whose name the land was registered in, especially if the land seemed to belong to an absentee land owner. In one conflict unleashed after the settlement of a group of refugees in İzmit in 1911, one Miralay Mehmed Ali Bey sent a petition to the Interior Ministry complaining that the two *çiftliks* under his *tasarruf* on the strength of title deeds, which had been considered by the local administration to be empty, were distributed to the refugees and villages were established on them.[16] Mehmed Ali Bey was resident in Istanbul and it appeared that as an absentee land owner he did not work the land in any way and therefore the land was seen as empty. His lack of direct involvement with the land was also apparent in the fact that he did not want the land to be returned to him and the refugees to be evicted, but demanded that the government either pay him the money for the land or grant him an equivalent plot of land elsewhere, according to the law.

A land survey showed that many fields were opened within the borders of the farms by the local peasantry, but also by the newly settled refugees, who were then registered under the persons who had opened the fields. Indeed rights constituted on land by the local peasantry due to long enough usage were a major source of conflict. For instance, the Baltacı *çiftlik* in Yalova, south of the Sea of Marmara, which belonged to the Treasury, had been transferred to the Finance Ministry in 1911 with a view to the settlement of the Daghestan refugees in this dense refugee settlement region.[17] The Council of State ruled that part of the lands of the *çiftlik* should be distributed to the refugees and to the local peasants in need of land, observing a balance perhaps with the aim of preventing any potential disputes in the area. The Interior Ministry informed the Council that there were major problems with the implementation of its order. The difficulty arose from the fierce opposition of the peasants to the distribution of any lands to the refugees. The peasants claimed that they had a pasture within the borders of the *çiftlik*, which they had been using from time immemorial, and that they themselves were in need of the land in the first place.

Consequences of refugee settlement

Part of the idea of creating an Ottoman homeland in Anatolia involved the mixing of different population groups, and eroding the power and authority of communal leaders. This entailed disarming the Circassian refugees, disbursing them throughout the countryside in small groups, and co-opting or subduing tribal chiefs and notables who wielded power and influence over the refugee populations in different ways. When doing this the geographical distribution of the non-Muslim population was also taken into account. For creating a homeland involved both breaking different ethnic and group solidarities while settling the refugees, and at the same time, mixing up different ethnic groups and dispersing them on the designated geography of the homeland. At a time when exclusive Turkish nationalism had not yet been formulated, the homeland was mostly defined first as an Ottoman land and gradually as a Muslim Ottoman land, within which the different communities of the Empire were to dissolve. Areas where Christian communities were to be found in large numbers were chosen among settlement sites. Greek villages or larger settlements were therefore among such settlement sites for refugees as far as settlement was possible without creating conflict among the different groups. It was for this reason that the local and central land officials kept a close eye on population statistics when making decisions about the location of refugee settlement. For example, refugees were settled along the Dardanelles out of a consideration for achieving a balance between the Greek and Muslim villages along this strategic location. Several settlements around Istanbul were established for securing a Muslim majority in the capital. Settlements around the town of Gemlik on the eastern side of the Sea of Marmara were the result of similar considerations (İpek 1994: 158). During the Balkan wars the government did not want the refugees to cross into Anatolia but settle around Edirne because: "although the Muslims in this area make up the majority of the population, they decline with every other war, while the Greek population, although second in population, increases each passing day." Moreover, should the "Muslim population in this area increase with these measures, then the required soldiers could be recruited from this area without so much need to resort to the Anatolian population."[18] It was partly these concerns that led to refugee settlement in western Anatolia despite the fact that the region could not absorb any more new refugees as empty lands had been filled up and opening up new lands became much more expensive.

There were examples of settlements near or in Greek villages around Dikili and along the Edremit Bay (Halaçoğlu 1995: 116), and the consequent complaints by the Greeks of Ayvalık and Bergama about the "false accusations and interventions encouraged by the Muslim immigrants" in those areas and about the local officials who did not believe and act on their complaints.[19] As a result of these complaints, however, some of such settlements did not take root and in some instances refugees had to leave the settlement with the implicit approval of the local officials who were afraid of the security consequences. In one incident in February 1910, for example, it was reported that a group of refugees from the Balkans who had been settled in one village in Dikili could not get accustomed to the environment in this location and subsequently moved to Dikili town.[20] As a result no Muslim was left in the village, whose entire population was Greek. The provincial authorities requested permission from the Interior Ministry without causing the intervention of the military, to leave the village to the non-Muslim population resident there, and to build an entirely new quarter for the Rumeli refugees in the centre of Dikili town. Permission was subsequently granted by the Council of State. It should be noted here how the local administrative officials took the liberty, in an internal correspondence to the Interior Ministry, to imply the consequences of an intervention of the military authorities in the case of Rumeli refugees leaving their allotted houses and land in a Greek village. The political–military objectives of settlement in Anatolia after all did not seem be successful in all instances, here with the complicity of the local administration.

Issues relating to land thus became irreversibly connected with notions of sovereignty, nationality, and Muslim dominance, in fact with the very foundations of the Empire as it was in the 1910s. On September 23, 1911 the Interior Ministry sent a communiqué to all the provinces of the Empire informing them of the draft law on the use and transmission of immovable property. The new law required by the new developments was intended to increase the value of land in the country.[21] Attached to the draft law was an unsigned report apparently intended only for the Interior Ministry officials and not for general distribution. It is worth quoting in length from the report as it brings forth what was behind the seemingly undeclared and at times contradictory polices regarding land issues, and how the notion of land was connected with issues of ethnic/religious dominance:

> At a time when many precedents are conceded for the spreading of the objective of forming states based on the principle of nationality, and when there are many obvious indications of stoking up the objectives of separatism and independence in some places, the issues of the sale of land and land in general, as proposed in this draft law, attain an urgent importance.

The writer of the internal memo then underlined the significance of outside intervention in the Empire toward the attainment of these objectives. Outlining the general land situation in the new Balkan countries, he formulated proposals based on these observations. The summary information he gave on the development of the landholding system in the Balkans from the time of the Ottoman conquest and on the present land situation is entirely based on a reading of the land relations in terms of the religious Muslim–Christian divide. The reality at the moment, he argued, was that "Muslims are selling their lands, small or big, everywhere, and the majority of these lands are being purchased mostly by Christians who form a minority of the general population." Specifically he gave an account of the Muslim land owners in Bulgaria, who were gradually being forced by the Bulgarian government and through the actions of the nationalist militia there to sell or leave their lands. The Bulgarian government was reserving a certain amount of funds each year in its budget to be extended to Christians who wanted to buy Muslim land. Muslim landlords were kept under observation and whenever they had a default on their previous loans their lands were immediately sold off to Christians. In other instances large land owners were being threatened and sometimes killed to appropriate their lands at nominal prices. According to the author of the report, the success of the Bulgarians, Greeks, and Serbians in land issues was due to

> the distribution of the land acquired according to capacity and need; the administration of the issues relating to land by cadres who were cognizant that ownership of land is the basis of the transformation from a captive to a sovereign nation; the availability of cheap credit facilities for land transactions; and the carrying out of these measures with courage and perseverance.

Accordingly, the measures the Ottoman government should take to prevent Muslims selling land to Christians (presumably in the Ottoman Empire) were:

> To explain in plain language to all the Muslims the danger and damage that disposing of land will cause them. This advice, however, should not be made in a manner to create animosity among the Muslims against the Christians, otherwise it could be counter-productive. The question of land should be delegated to capable cadres who understand how critical it is for the Muslims to remain in ownership of the land if they are to remain the ruling *millet* [community]. For this, loans with low interest should be extended to Muslims for the purchase of land.

The author informed the intended reader that "the land issue" as he formulated it was bound with – what he called – "the population issue," which would be the subject of another report to be prepared by him. There is no indication in the file by whom this report was prepared or to what degree it influenced policy. The question of sovereignty and nationality, and how these were in turn related to the land issues in general, was manifested in two incidents in northwestern Anatolia taking place at about the same time. These two incidents, the boycott of Greek trade which evolved eventually into sanctions against Greek landlords, and an urban plot which became the subject of a controversy bringing the Muslim and Greek communities against each other in a small coastal town, are indicative of the spread at a popular level of many of the divisions and considerations discussed in the report.

    The boycott in western Anatolia against the trade and goods of Greek merchants, subjects of the Hellenic kingdom, who were based in Anatolia, which started on August 16, 1909 and lasted for about two years, is revealing of the prevailing tensions, and how easily it turned into an issue of landed property. It started in Izmir, the main port-town of western Anatolia, as a reaction to the political situation in Crete and the reported pressures exerted on the Muslim population of the island. No doubt, the Cretan refugees of old and new who were widely settled in the coastal towns and interior of the region had an important role in the initiative and within the committees. The British Consul in Izmir reported on August 18, 1909 that "the prevailing idea among the Turks is to make things so uncomfortable for the Hellenes that the latter may be compelled to leave the country in the same way in which they emigrated from Roumania some 3 years ago."[22] A boycott committee was formed in the summer of 1909, with many sub-committees in the interior towns. Purportedly it was aimed against commercial boats, products, shops, and employees working with Hellenic businesses. The committee's manifesto was careful to point out that the Ottoman Greek subjects were entirely different from the Hellenes, were to be kept out of any boycott, and were to be treated with utmost friendliness. Recounting a private conversation with the leaders of the boycott, the Consul wrote: "They declare that it is no longer possible for them to live side by side with the Hellenes who they say have for a long time been poisoning the minds of the *rayah*s [Ottoman Greeks] against the Turks." The governor of the province admitted that he was unable to stop it in spite of government orders during the boycott but the Consul believed that the local police in Izmir were collaborating with the boycotters.

Large amounts of the olive produce had been reportedly damaged in the olive-growing area of the Edremit Bay because of the boycott. According to the report of the governor of the district, the boycott was especially severe in the Ayvalık area, where it was extended in October 1910 against the entire Ayvalık town as the inhabitants were suspected of helping the Hellenic subjects.[23] The Greek notables of Ayvalık complained to the authorities that they were not being allowed to go near their olive groves in the vicinity of the town, which had been leased from the inhabitants of Emrudabad on down payment. The local governor accepted that a boycott was declared against the entire Ayvalık population (Ottoman subjects) as they had not participated in the boycott against the Hellenic subjects declared with the national feelings of the Ottoman subjects. The governor of Burhaniye was sent to the location for investigation. He brought together the members of the local boycott committee and the representatives of Ayvalık town and, consequently, an agreement to lift the boycott was reached only after the Ayvaliots agreed to declare a boycott on Greek goods and undertook not to accept any boats carrying the Greek flag into the harbor. The consular agent of the Hellenic Kingdom in Ayvalık sent a protest note to the Ottoman Foreign Ministry declaring the actions of the Ayvaliots "an act of rebellion" against Greece.[24]

The boycott soon turned against farms, fields, and orchards under Hellenic control. In January 1911, one of the large land owners around Ayvalık, Trikopis, could not collect his olive harvest as he found it impossible to recruit employees.[25] The tax collectors of the area were also concerned that with the spoilage of the produce they would not be able to recover the taxes from the olive produce. By June of the same year the Trikopis farms were still uncultivated and this was the fourth consecutive year the fields were left empty. The concern was that according to the land law, lands and fields left vacant for a period of three years gave the government the power to confiscate and sell them by auction to those who would be able to work them.[26] To prevent such an outcome the land owner rented out at least part of his farm to Charles Wilkinson, a British merchant, in July 1911, with the probable intention of ending the boycott.[27] The boycott committee, however, was quick to issue a public notice against the new tenant, pointing out that the tenant being British did not change the fact that it was still an Hellenic-owned property. During the boycott, Trikopis also sold that part of his olive groves adjacent to Emrudabad to one of the people who was behind the boycott, Mahmud Efendizade İsmail Efendi from Emrudabad. Whether this was a bribe to buy off the boycotters, we do not know.[28] The boycott came finally to an end in November 1911, the feared confiscation and resale did not take place, and work on the farms restarted.

As well as showing how a commercial boycott soon turned into a land blockade, the incident in Ayvalık highlighted the ease with which some Greek merchants and landholders were able to change nationality quickly. In Izmir there were instances where some Greek merchants acquired Austrian or Russian nationalities with the sole intention of evading the boycott. The Ottoman authorities were also concerned about the way the Hellenic government made use of an ambiguity in Hellenic law, which interpreted the word "Hellene" to be inclusive of Ottoman Greeks, and thus claimed jurisdiction over them.[29] Nationality, of course, defined who was an Ottoman subject and, hence, who was to going to partake in the "homeland" and to hold land. At a popular level, the deterioration of inter-communal relations was a manifestation of the problems inherent in the definition of Ottomanness. Part of the official anxiety on the issue was due to the increasing frequency of reference to land in inter-communal disputes.

One land dispute in Burhaniye, at about the same time the boycott on Greek goods was underway, involving the Greek and Muslim communities of the town, is illustrative of the tension over the meaning ascribed to land by different communities. The conflict revolved around 1 plot of land which was a little more than 100 square meters in surface area.[30] Over this small plot of land issues such as whether this was Muslim or Christian land, what this meant for the inter-communal relations in the Empire, and whether there existed a relationship between the refugees and such a land contestation, were all fought over. The fact that it did not stay as a local issue, and was reported to the Interior Ministry and the Şeyhülislam (the highest religious authority in the Empire) in Istanbul attests to the fact that there was more in this 100 square meters than an ordinary urban piece of land. The event seems to have started in April 1910 as a conflict between the Greek community of the town and the local *vakıf* administration, when the Greeks were seen enclosing the plot with a wall to be included in the sacred fountain lying next to it. However, "it was known that a small mosque stood on that location" and a wooden fence had been built around it about eight years previously to protect the borders, the local municipal authority claimed. On the application of the *vakıf* administration, the municipality issued orders to stop the construction of the wall. However, before the order could be implemented the Greeks "hurriedly" completed a gate in the wall and placed a cross on top of it, which prevented the officers taking any action in fear of insulting a sacred object. On the application of the Greek ecclesiastical council of the town, the case was brought before the *şeriyye* court, which ruled that the plot be returned to original use and gave instructions to that effect. In the meantime the administrative council of the town, including both Muslim and Christian members, agreed that, pending the order of the court, neither the Christians should restart building the wall and hence offend the Muslims, nor the Muslims should attempt to destroy the gate and offend the Christians.

The Greek ecclesiastical council blamed a group of influential persons in the town who "wanted to hold the Greek community hostage and to plant seeds of separation between the different communities" for putting forth false allegations that the sacred shrine they had been using for 40 years with title deeds was a Muslim *vakıf*. The council also made a connection between the dispute at hand and the actions of the Circassian refugees in the town. Allegedly four Circassians had by force closed down Greek taverns in the town and while doing this wounded two Greeks. The governor of the town, however, rejected out of hand that the issue had anything to do with the plot of land, claiming that it was only an ordinary criminal incident. While reporting the case to the Ministry, he was also very insistent on the point that the incident involving the Greeks and the Circassians was not an inter-communal conflict and it should not be interpreted as an "animosity between the Christians and Muslims. The mere mentioning of the incident in those terms might lend credit to it, and for that reason it is not appropriate to talk in those terms." The governor even convened the religious leaders and notables of the town and made them sign a declaration to the effect that there was no inter-communal friction and that "no relationship should be established with this ordinary criminal incident and the dispute on the plot of land." But this declaration did not seem to have solved the inter-communal problems at the town. At the end of the month the ecclesiastical council of Burhaniye, in the name of the Christian community of the town, sent letters to the Karesi representative at the Ottoman parliament and to the Interior Ministry informing them of new incidents of closing Greek taverns and more wounding. They wrote: "The local government tells us that these are ordinary criminal incidents. They remain ordinary only because of the patience and holding back of the Christians."

In the meantime the investigation conducted by the court showed that the title deeds presented by the Greeks pertained to a house and a warehouse, whereas the official documents presented by the *vakıf* administration showed the place to be a small mosque and a school. A commission was set up from the members of the local *vakıf* administration, *şeriyye* court, title deed office, municipality, and the Greek community elders to determine whether the documents at hand in fact corresponded to the disputed plot. However, the judge of Burhaniye and the Greek community opposed the make-up of the commission and the regional governor decided to send the provincial land registration officer to establish the correspondence between the land and two sets of documents. The officer found that the plot in fact belonged to the mosque and the school. The provincial administrative council, however, was still hesitant in certifying the decision and decided to ask the opinion of the Şeyhülislam in Istanbul. By doing so a local decision was avoided and reference was made to the central authorities as the arbiter of the dispute. For what was at stake was communal harmony and, by implication, national integration. The inter-communal aspect of the Burhaniye incident far outweighed its property-dispute aspect. Indeed the case is emblematic of the change in the nature of land conflicts in the 1910s. A land conflict was now not only about property as such, but was more of a "national" issue. At issue was still who owned property, but the ethnic and religious identity of the title holder had become a criterion for the determination of the rightful owner. The name written on the title deed had become as important as the title deed itself.

Concluding remarks

The flow of people into Anatolia, which intensified especially after the war of 1877–1878, contributed to a rapid and unforeseen increase in the population of the Anatolian provinces, and increased the population density of the remaining lands of the Empire. The consequent pressure for finding land to settle the refugees in this period culminated in the proliferation and intensification of land conflicts in parts of Anatolia where the incoming refugees had more than doubled the population density. Roughly coinciding with a period when ownership rights on land were becoming more exclusionary, and when various kinds of commons were under a process of privatization, such land conflicts created tensions all through the Anatolian countryside, which at times turned into bloody confrontations between the existing landholders and the refugees.

Yet the real qualitative impact of immigration to Anatolia was not the mere spreading of land conflicts as such. We know that various conflicts on land were settled by the courts mostly in favor of those who held title to the land. And, moreover, the refugees were not the only ones embroiled in long-lasting disputes with title-holders. The nomadic Turcoman tribes of the Anatolian countryside had for some time been fighting a losing battle for their customary rights to pastures and routes of passage, and peasants were fighting for their communal rights on commons and forests. The turnabout that was triggered by refugee settlement was to provide a vocabulary for translating the terms of a land conflict into one of ethnic and religious animosity. In an atmosphere of worsening inter-communal relations within the remaining territories of the Empire, it rapidly led to the framing of questions about land in terms of its relation to the ethnic and religious make-up of the title-holder. This change dominated and undermined, in several ways, the nature of the contestation regarding the process of privatization of land rights. The increasing reference to land in inter-communal conflicts meant that the contestation of the privatization process was channeled to the arena of ethnic politics, to the realm of nationalism.

In other words, the forces unleashed with the refugees' influx led rapidly to the politicization of land issues, with political considerations dominating the distribution and redistribution of land at the turn of the twentieth century. The policies of population mixing for the sake of creating an Ottoman homeland and the close interest in the ethnic make-up of the population inhabiting that homeland meant that land, or rather the ownership of it, was inextricably linked, for the Ottoman state, with sovereignty and nationality. "It was critical for the Muslims to remain in ownership of the land if they were to remain the ruling *millet*," as the unsigned report declared. The "success" of the Bulgarians, Greeks, and Serbians in acquiring the ownership of land on the basis of the nationality principle needed to be emulated. The end result of this change was to rapidly render the many communities of the Empire into minorities of the new nation-states that were to be established in Anatolia in 1923, and earlier in the Balkans. The building of national states and economies in this part of the world was accompanied at the time with subsequent displacement and dispossession of many communities of the former multi-ethnic empires. The aim here was to provide some context and circumstance for this displacement and dispossession by focusing on the relationship between land and population movements in the second half of the nineteenth century. At that time, the success of the nationalist projects in the Balkans and the mass waves of immigration turned the eyes of the Ottomans on Anatolia as an eventual homeland for a redefined and reconstituted Muslim Ottoman populace. It was during the long decade of war (starting with the Balkan Wars of 1912–1914, followed by World War I, and the Turkish War of Independence of 1919–1923) that Turkish nationalism would emerge from the ashes of the Empire.

Notes

1 The British Consul General in Izmir thought that the land troubles around Ayvalık, Burhaniye, and Edremit in the 1890s made the region deserving of the name "the black spot of western Asia Minor" (PRO (Public Record Office, London), FO 195/1899).
2 In one sedentarization scheme in the island of Mitylene in 1911 the Interior Ministry explained the objective of the scheme thus: "[. . .] the existence and continuation of the old ways of nomadism in a developed island such as Mitylene

cannot be approved. Settlement will bring the tribes into the circle of civilization, contribute to the development of the country and prevent the destruction of the forests" (BOA (Prime Ministry, Ottoman Archives, Istanbul) DH.ID 11/2).

3 For the account of a long-lasting conflict between one Greek land owner, nomads, and Balkan refugees in the area, which examines these different understandings, see Terzibaşoğlu (2001).

4 For accounts of the different interpretations of the Land Code, see Mundy (1994: 59–61) and Quataert (1997: 856–861).

5 Article 78 of the Land Code of 1858 states: "If a person has possessed arazi-i emiriye and mevkufe (state and endowment lands) for ten years without disturbance his prescriptive right (hakk-ı karar) becomes proved, and whether he has a title-deed or not [. . .], a new title-deed should be given to him gratis [. . .]" (from Ongley 1892).

6 For a fruitful conceptualization of the relationship between population and patterns of land use and tenure see Boserup (1965).

7 For criminalization of custom in eighteenth-century Britain see Thompson (1975) and Linebaugh (2003).

8 The Russian Empire assumed this role with the Küçük Kaynarca Treaty of 1774. See Davison (1990: 29–37).

9 For parallels with the modernization of rural France in the same period see Weber (1976).

10 PRO, FO 195/1161 and 1239.

11 In 1909, refugees were still settling, on their own initiative, in forests in Karesi and were setting up villages (BOA, DH.MUI 18–1/30 and DH.HMŞ 27/6).

12 1 *dönüm* equalled about 920 square meters.

13 BOA, İrade, Defter-i Hakani, No. 4.

14 BOA, DH.ID 135–1/23; 213/2; and 213/5.

15 Characteristically, the conflict was multi-faceted. It also involved the question of whether the land in question was within the boundaries of the town or not, which was directly related again to the legal status of the land. Moreover the claim of the Ayvaliot on the land seemed to be altogether sidelined and the sale by him of the land to two Ayvaliots was not allowed.

16 BOA, DH.ID 135–2/6.

17 BOA, DH.ID 135–2/61.

18 From a letter sent from the War to the Interior Ministry in 1913 (Halaçoğlu 1995: 116).

19 BOA, DH.H 67/32.

20 BOA, DH.MUI 69–2/29.

21 BOA, DH.ID 135–1/3.

22 PRO, FO 195/2331 and 2360.

23 BOA, DH.SYS 22/1–10.

24 BOA, DH.SYS 22/1–10.

25 BOA, DH.SYS 22/2–5.

26 BOA, DH.SYS 22/1–32.

27 PRO, FO 195/2374 and 2383.

28 BOA, DH.SYS 22/2–5.

29 BOA, DH.SYS 112–7B/7–60.

30 BOA, DH.ID 45/1.

Bibliography

Arai, M. (1992) *Turkish Nationalism in the Young Turk Era*, Leiden: E.J. Brill.

Barkan, Ö.L. (1980) *Türkiye'de Toprak Meselesi* [Land Issue in Turkey], Istanbul: Gözlem Yayınları.

Boserup, E. (1965) *The Conditions of Agricultural Growth: The Economics of Agrarian Change Under Population Pressure*, London: George Allen & Unwin.

Çelik, Ş. (2000) "XVI. yüzyılda İçel Yörükleri Hakkında Bazı Değerlendirmeler" [Some Considerations on the İçel Yörük of the Sixteenth Century], in Anadolu'da ve Rumeli'de Yörük ve Türkmenler Sempozyumu Bildirileri [Proceedings of the Symposium on the Yörük and Turcoman of Anatolia and Rumeli], Ankara: Yörük Türkmen Vakfı Yayınları.

Davison, R.H. (1990) *Essays in Ottoman and Turkish History, 1774–1923: The Impact of the West*, London: Saqi Books.

Emecen, F.M. (2001) *İlk Osmanlılar ve Batı Anadolu Beylikler Dünyası* [The First Ottomans and the Principalities of Western Anatolia], Istanbul: Kitabevi.

Eren, A.C. (1966) *Türkiye'de Göç ve Göçmen Meseleleri* (Migration and Migration Issues in Turkey), Istanbul: Nurgök Matbaası.

Faroqhi, S. (1984) *Towns and Townsmen of Ottoman Anatolia: Trade, Crafts and Food Production in an Urban Setting, 1520–1650*, Cambridge: Cambridge University Press.

Halaçoğlu, A. (1995) *Balkan Harbi Sırasında Rumeli'den Türk Göçleri, 1912–1913* [Turkish Migration from the Balkans during the Balkan Wars, 1912–1913], Ankara, TTK.

İpek, N. (1994) *Rumeli'den Anadolu'ya Türk Göçleri* [Turkish Migration from the Balkans to Anatolia], Ankara: TTK.

İslamoğlu, H. (2000) "Property as a Contested Domain: A Reevaluation of the Ottoman Land Code of 1858," in R. Owen (ed.) *New Perspectives on Property and Land in the Middle East*, Cambridge, MA: Harvard Middle Eastern Monographs.

Karpat, K. (1985) *Ottoman Population, Demographic and Social Characteristics*, Madison, WI: University of Wisconsin Press.

Linebaugh, P. (2003) *The London Hanged, Crime and Civil Society in the Eighteenth Century*, London: Verso.

Mundy, M. (1994) "Village Land and Individual Title: Musha' and Ottoman Land Registration in the 'Ajlun District'," in E.L. Rogan and T. Tell (eds) *Village, Steppe and State: The Social Origins of Modern Jordan*, London: British Academic Press.

—— (2000) "Village Authority and the Legal Order of Property (the Southern Hawran, 1876–1922)," in R. Owen (ed.) *New Perspectives on Property and Land in the Middle East*, Cambridge, MA: Harvard Middle Eastern Monographs.

Ongley, F. (1892) *The Ottoman Land Code*, London: William Clowes & Sons.

Orhonlu, C. (1987) *Osmanlı İmparatorluğunda Aşiretlerin İskanı* [Sedentarization of Tribes in the Ottoman Empire], Istanbul: Eren.

—— (1990) *Osmanlı İmparatorluğunda Derbend Teşkilatı* [Derbend Organization in the Ottoman Empire], Istanbul: Eren.

Pinson, M. (1970) "Demographic Warfare: An Aspect of Ottoman and Russian Policy, 1854–1866," unpublished Ph.D. thesis, Harvard University.

Prime Ministry, Ottoman Archives (BOA), Istanbul, various files.

Public Record Office (PRO), London, various files.

Quataert, D. (1997) "The Age of Reforms, 1812–1914," in H. İnalcık and D. Quataert (eds) *An Economic and Social History of the Ottoman Empire*, Cambridge: Cambridge University Press.

Saydam, A. (1997) *Kırım ve Kafkas Göçleri 1856–1876* [Crimean and Caucausian Migrations, 1856–1876], Ankara: TTK.

Terzibaşoğlu, Y. (2001) "Landlords, Refugees and Nomads: Struggles for Land Around Late-Nineteenth-Century Ayvalık," *New Perspectives on Turkey*, 24: 51–82.

—— (2002) "Struggles over Land and Population Movements in North-Western Anatolia, 1877–1914," paper presented at the International Colloquium on Rural Mobility in the Ottoman Empire, Centre français de culture et de coopération, Cairo, April 28–May 1.

Thompson, E.P. (1975) *Whigs and Hunters: The Origins of the Black Act*, New York: Pantheon Books.

Weber, E. (1976) *Peasants into Frenchmen: The Modernization of Rural France, 1870–1914*, Stanford, CA: Stanford University Press.

Part IV

Indigenous peoples, colonial settlers, and migrating laborers

Ethnic rivalries and rights to land, past and present

8 Explaining divergence in property rights

Fiji and Hawai'i in the nineteenth century*

Sumner J. La Croix

This chapter compares the history of land rights in two Pacific island groups, Hawai'i and Fiji, which shared relatively similar cultures and common historical experiences during the nineteenth century: both had Polynesian cultures;[1] relatively late contact with Europeans; development of a written language in the early nineteenth century; settlement by Christian missionaries; resource booms in the early nineteenth century followed by a sugar boom in the late nineteenth century; and eventual annexation by a major world power. Given these parallels, it is not surprising that private property rights in land emerged in both societies during the nineteenth century.

During the 1860s and early 1870s in Fiji, native chiefs sold urban lands to foreigners to settle outstanding debts and rural lands to foreigners to start plantations. Following several decades of fighting among native Fijian groups, the British annexed Fiji in 1874 at the request of ruling Fijian chiefs. The first colonial governor of Fiji, Arthur Gordon, banned the sale of native land to foreigners, while allowing foreigners to set up sugar plantations on land obtained via long-term leases. The governor also banned Fijians from working as laborers on the new plantations, thereby requiring plantation owners to use immigrant labor. The plantation owners responded by bringing over 60,000 indentured laborers to Fiji between 1879 and 1916, when the last indentured laborers arrived in Fiji.

In Hawai'i, the native Hawaiian king and his government reformed the traditional land tenure system in the mid 1840s. The Great *Mahele* (Division) established fee-simple rights and allocated lands to the government, king, chiefs, and commoners. In 1850, the law was changed to enable foreigners to purchase land. During the 1850s and 1860s, the government sold much of its land to foreigners and native Hawaiians, and foreigners purchased, absorbed, and leased additional lands from chiefs and commoners to start sugar plantations. After a boom during the US Civil War and a bust at its conclusion, the sugar industry flourished after Hawai'i negotiated a reciprocity treaty in 1876 with the United States, allowing Hawaiian sugar to enter the United States duty-free. Between 1876 and 1898, when the

United States annexed Hawai'i, over 120,000 indentured workers came to Hawai'i from Asia and Europe to work on sugar plantations.

The patterns of landholding have diverged in each society due to the different paths followed by each society with respect to foreign ownership of land. In 1850, the native Hawaiian government passed legislation *allowing* foreigners to purchase land, while in 1878, the British colonial governor of Fiji unilaterally *restricted* sales of land to foreigners. The consequences for native landholdings have been enormous. At the start of the twenty-first century, most land in Fiji is still controlled by native Fijians, while native Hawaiians have lost or sold much of their land. Why, then, did the patterns of land rights and land holdings diverge after beginning on a common path?

The chapter proceeds by examining the evolution of property rights in both countries; it then pays particular attention to how restrictions on foreign alienation were removed in Hawai'i and became entrenched in Fiji. Various hypotheses for the divergence in alienation restrictions are explored. First, the interests of a colonial governor interested in consolidating authority over warring factions are contrasted with the interests of a weak king in a country with a rapidly declining population facing foreign threats. Second, the optimal responses of colonial and native governments to foreigners seeking to use native assets to start agricultural ventures are developed and compared.

Evolution of property rights to land in Hawai'i

Economists who have studied transitions in property rights to land have often portrayed them as efficient responses to changing economic and demographic factors.[2] Population pressure has frequently been regarded as a major force behind the transformation in property rights. Population pressure usually brings an appreciation of land rents and a decline in real wages and therefore provides the incentives to define property rights in land more precisely. David Feeny's (1988) study of the development of property rights in land in Thailand, Burma, India, and the Philippines concluded that "the growth of population [and the increase in the terms of trade] were indeed associated with a rise in real land prices" and that land scarcity induced changes in the institutions governing its use.

In Hawai'i, however, private property emerged during the 1840s and 1850s after a 75-year period of severe population *decline*.[3] Hawai'i's rapid transition from a closed to an open economy removed the close association between land rents and population density. In an open economy, land rents are linked to movements in the terms of trade as well as to changes in population (Feeny 1988: 273–282).

The Hawai'i case presents an opportunity to explore three other economic factors that enhance the advantages of private property over collective arrangements. First, an economy's comparative advantage may turn away from goods that can be efficiently produced under traditional property rights. Second, the timing of the property rights transition in Hawai'i may have been influenced by considerations of public finance. Changes in population and the terms of trade affected the income earned by members of various social groups as well as the king and his government. These effects prompted the king and his government to promote establishment of private property rights to allow net government revenue collections to increase. Third, establishment of property titles and more delineated rights in land increased the collateral available to support foreign and domestic loans and may have been desired by the king to bolster his access to resources during periods of crisis and opportunity.

The pre-contact economy and population decline

The Hawaiian Islands are a chain of 132 islands, shoals, and reefs extending over 1,523 miles in the northeast Pacific Ocean. Eight islands – Hawai'i, Maui, O'ahu, Kaua'i, Moloka'i, Lāna'i, Ni'ihau, and Kaho'olawe – possess 99 percent of the land area (6,435 square miles) and are noted for their volcanic landforms, unique flora and fauna, and diverse climates. The Islands were uninhabited until sometime before AD 400 and 500 when Polynesian voyagers sailing double-hulled canoes arrived from the Marquesas Islands (Kirch 1985: 68). Since the settlers had no written language and virtually no contact with the western world until 1778, our knowledge of Hawai'i's pre-history comes primarily from archaeological investigations and oral legends. A relatively egalitarian society and subsistence economy were coupled with high population growth rates until about 1100, when continued population growth led to a major expansion of the areas of settlement and cultivation. Perhaps under pressures of increasing resource scarcity, a new, more hierarchical social structure emerged, characterized by chiefs (*ali'i*), priests (*kahuna*), and subservient commoners (*maka'āinana*). In the two centuries prior to western contact, there is considerable evidence that ruling chiefs (*ali'i nui*) competed to extend their lands by conquest and that this led to cycles of expansion and retrenchment.

Captain James Cook's ships reached Hawai'i in 1778, thereby ending a long period of isolation for the Islands. Captain James King observed in 1779 that Hawaiians were generally "above the middle size" of Europeans, a rough indicator that Hawaiians generally had a diet superior to eighteenth-century Europeans. At contact, Hawaiian social and political institutions were similar to those found in other Polynesian societies. Hawaiians were sharply divided into three main social classes: *ali'i* (chiefs), *maka'āinana* (commoners), and *kahuna* (priests). Oral legends tell us that the Islands were usually divided into six to eight small kingdoms consisting of an island or part of an island, each governed by an *ali'i nui* (ruling chief). The *ali'i nui* had extensive rights to all lands and material goods and the ability to confiscate or redistribute material wealth at any time. Redistribution usually occurred only when a new ruling chief took office or when lands were conquered or lost. The *ali'i nui* gave temporary land grants to *ali'i* who, in turn, gave temporary land grants to *konohiki* (managers), who then "contracted" with *maka'āinana*, the great majority of the populace, to work the lands.

The Hawaiian society and economy has its roots in extended families (*'ohana*) working cooperatively on an *ahupua'a*, a land unit running from the mountains to the sea. Numerous tropical root, tuber, and tree crops were cultivated. Taro, a wetland crop, was cultivated primarily in windward areas, while sweet potatoes and yams, both dryland crops, were cultivated in drier leeward areas. The *maka'āinana* apparently lived well above subsistence levels, with extensive time available for cultural activities, sports, and games. There were unquestionably periods of hardship, but these times tended to be associated with drought or other causes of poor harvest.

Contact with the western world interacted with ongoing demographic and political trends to rapidly change the society of pre-contact Hawai'i. Among other things, contact led to the formation of the nation-state in 1795, while access to western markets increased the benefits of a cartel among the chiefs. Access to western military technology lowered the costs to the chiefs of maintaining a political coalition, with one of the chiefs, Kamehameha I, dominating the others. The king maintained the cartel by allocating several *ahupua'a* on different islands to each of his chiefs, thereby making it more difficult for a particular chief to acquire a strong base of support on a single island. Kamehameha also prevented accumulation of power by rivals by requiring other powerful chiefs to join his court on O'ahu and to travel with him to other Hawaiian Islands. After unification, the chiefs' cartel made it feasible to enforce higher labor taxes, thereby pushing the commoners closer to subsistence.

Exposure to western diseases and reduced living standards after contact led to a massive decline in the native population of Hawai'i. Population estimates at the time of contact vary (see Table 8.1) from 225,000 to 795,000. Bushnell's (1993) estimate (300,000) is based on a critical survey of the earlier literature. Regardless of the initial estimates, the population declines were massive. A substantial portion of the decline between 1778

Table 8.1 Population of Hawai'i, 1778–1865

Year	Population	Source
1778	225,000	Schmitt
1778	795,343	Stannard
1778	300,000	Bushnell
1805	264,160	Youngson
1823	142,050	Census
1832	130,313	Census
1836	108,579	Census
1849	80,641	Census

Sources: Schmitt (1968: 42) and Stannard (1989: 56).

and 1831 can be attributed to a series of epidemics beginning after contact. Another factor that contributed significantly to the population decline was the decrease in the crude birth rate to below 30 per 1,000 and perhaps to as low as 15 per 1,000. The first accurate census conducted in the Islands revealed a population of 80,641 in 1849. The native population reached its nadir in 1900 when the US census revealed only 37,656 full or part Hawaiians.

Changing land tenure, 1795–1855

Abraham Fornander (1969: 300) related that "[i]t had been the custom since the days of Keawenui-a-Umi on the death of a Moi (King) and the accession of a new one, to redivide and distribute the land of the island between the chiefs and favorites of the new monarch." Following this ancient practice, Kamehameha I (who united all but one of Hawai'i's small polities in 1795) redistributed land rights to chiefs in his army after conquering islands governed by rival chiefs.[4] Yet during Kamehameha's subsequent long reign (1795–1819), "the leading families of chiefs enjoyed a greater degree of permanence and security in the possession of their lands than had been previously known" (Alexander 1890: 108). This conclusion is based on the observation that Kamehameha I implicitly recognized hereditary rights to property and did not arbitrarily redistribute land.

The second major change in the land tenure system came in 1819 with the death of Kamehameha I and the transition to the rule of Kamehameha II. Instead of redistributing land to form a viable coalition of chiefs to support his rule, the new king chose to solidify his support among the existing coalition of chiefs by relaxing his control over the chiefs' sandalwood trades with foreign merchants (La Croix and Roumasset 1984: 164). By ignoring one of the major options open to a new king, the prerogative of redistributing land was weakened for future rulers. This de facto security of tenure in the land was reinforced in 1825, when Kamehameha II succumbed to measles while visiting London. Neither the regent, Kaahumanu, nor the young king, Kamehameha III, redistributed property during their reigns.[5]

In 1845 a proposal to convert customary rights in land into private property rights came from Hawai'i's Interior Minister, Dr Gerrit Judd; he called for a law permitting the sale of land "as freehold property forever" to Hawaiian subjects (Kuykendall 1938: 278). Later that year the Hawai'i legislature passed a law establishing a board of commissioners which would award title to various tracts of land. A valid claimant would receive a "Land Commission Award," which could be exchanged for a title upon payment to the government of one-third of the value of the unimproved land. After several meetings of the king's Privy Council in December 1847, the council adopted a set of rules to facilitate the land division (Chinen 1958: 16–17; Kuykendall 1938: ch. 15).

On January 27, 1848, "245 landlords came forward to arrange their lands and divide with the King" (Kuykendall 1938: 288). By March 7, 1848, the "Great Division" or "Great *Mahele*" was completed. The next day the king divided his lands into government lands and "Crown lands," the latter and smaller portion to be his private lands. The process of division between the king and his landlords ended in the summer of 1850. "Many of the chiefs surrendered to the government portions of their land, which were accepted by the privy council as full commutation of the government's interest, and fee simple titles were accordingly given to those chiefs for the lands which remained to them" (Kuykendall 1938: 289).

> The Privy Council resolutions of December 21, 1849, specified procedures for tenants to claim land shares. These resolutions provided for fee simple titles free of commutation, [to] be granted to all native tenants for the lands occupied and improved by them, but not including houselots in Honolulu, Lahaina and Hilo. . . . The resolutions further provided that some government land on each island should be set aside to be sold in fee simple in lots of from one to fifty acres to such natives as were not otherwise furnished with sufficient lands at a minimum price of 50 cents per acre.[6]

The housing lots carried a commutation fee of one-fourth their un-improved value. In 1855 the completed division of lands was as follows: Crown lands, 984,000 acres; chiefs' lands, 1,619,000 acres; government lands, 1,495,000 acres; *kuleanas*, which were the land grants to commoners, 28,600 acres. The *Mahele* principles provided for commoners to receive one-third of the lands they occupied and cultivated, yet their final allocation was only a very small proportion of the total arable land.

In 1847 the legislature passed an act allowing foreigners to keep lands which they possessed; they could, however, only sell their lands to native subjects. New lands could not be acquired. Kuykendall argues that the boom in the demand for Hawai'i's agricultural products between 1848 and 1850 prompted a reconsideration of earlier positions regarding foreign ownership. The editors of the *Polynesian*, the major weekly newspaper, supported plans to allow foreign acquisition and conveyance of land to attract foreign capital and enterprise to agriculture. Legislation allowing foreigners to hold and convey land was rejected in 1848 but approved in 1850.[7]

Evolution of land rights: traditional and economic explanations

The traditional explanations offered by Hawai'i's historians identified the major forces behind the evolution of land rights, but we argue that two economic forces were also important determinants of the transition in land rights: (1) the effect of an open economy on factor and product prices; and

(2) the effect of population decline on factor prices, public finance, and social organization.

Pressure by the British, French, and American consuls to institute fee-simple titles for foreigners' building lots and farms caused numerous unpleasant episodes for the king.[8] Conflicts with British Consul Richard Charlton led to a provisional cession of the Islands to Great Britain on February 25, 1841. While the king's sovereignty was restored on July 31, 1841, the episode surely left an indelible impression on the king and chiefs.

The nontrivial probability of an unfriendly annexation in the 1840s undoubtedly increased the king's desire to secure his land holdings. If Hawai'i were annexed by a foreign power, the new authorities would have appropriated "public" lands, and the king would have lost his main source of income – land rent. This explanation is credible because the probability of annexation by a foreign power was significant when private property was established in the 1840s.

Foreigners also pushed for alienable property rights on economic development grounds. Some missionaries who responded to R.C. Wyllie's (1848) questions on the subject concluded that an influx of foreign capital could not be expected until transferable ownership rights were secured. Other missionaries responding to Wyllie's survey believed that establishment of private property rights in land was one way of motivating Hawaiians to work (Wyllie 1848: 7–13).

While these explanations all have some relevance, most of them concentrate on outside cultural and political influences and fail to examine the broad array of economic and demographic forces transforming Hawai'i's economy that also played a significant role in the evolution of a system of private land rights. Between 1778 and 1857 structural change in Hawai'i's economy was driven by two forces: changes in the terms of trade and persistent population decline. Both forces affected factor and product prices which, in turn, induced institutional change. Unfortunately, in Hawai'i, there are no factor price time series data for the mid nineteenth century, so our analysis is indirect, arguing that changes in factor endowments and the terms of trade would produce predictable changes in factor prices and, thus, institutional change.

The change from autarky to trade after 1778 induced major changes in Hawai'i's economy. The observations of contemporary observers made clear that living standards of commoners fell from the early 1790s until the sandalwood trade effectively ended in the late 1820s (La Croix and Roumasset 1984: 161–164). The decline in living standards was unusual as the change from autarky to trade, the expansion of a labor-intensive sector of the economy (sandalwood harvesting), and the decline in population were all forces that normally should have produced higher living standards. The change in population and comparative advantage points to the conclusion that throughout the 1830s and early 1840s the income of the king and the chiefs fell, while the lot of the commoner improved. Without sufficient skills and capital to begin new enterprises and with epidemics periodically affecting all native Hawaiians, the chiefs began to consider new commercial ventures that would increase their incomes.

The first major attempt to grow sugar commercially in Hawai'i was by the American mercantile firm of Ladd & Company in 1835. While this venture cannot be judged a success as it lasted only until 1844, it stimulated interest in sugar production. Numerous small sugar mills were established by missionaries and chiefs between 1835 and 1840. Sugar grown by commoners on chiefs' lands was milled on shares by these establishments. Population increases in Oregon and California created potentially large markets for commercial agricultural products, thereby enhancing the comparative advantage of exporting sugar.

While the Hawaiian government and the missionaries were adamantly against foreign ownership throughout the 1830s and 1840s, vigorous discussion took place over the necessity of stimulating the interest of the common people toward commercial agriculture. Considerable capital investment was required to mill and manufacture sugar. Changes in the methods of milling and manufacture came rapidly in the early nineteenth century, and J.H. Galloway (1989: 135) stated that the new technology "created larger mills and factories than the industry had known before and they demanded a more extensive hinterland of cane-pieces." Without alienable land, however, it could be difficult for a chief or commoner to assemble enough land to enable the new mills to operate near capacity. Commoners, who had traditional use rights in the lands they occupied, could not be compensated for the loss of these rights, as they were inalienable. Moreover, chiefs who did not have a comparative advantage in producing sugar or organizing sugar milling and manufacture could not capitalize their rights in the land. Given the declining income of chiefs during this period, the opportunity to move their lands into more valuable uses gave additional impetus to the movement to define alienable land rights. Even without such rights 11 mills for the manufacture of sugar had been established by 1846 (Kuykendall 1938: 315–316).

The declining demand for agricultural products reversed in the late 1840s due to the sudden appearance of a market for agricultural products in California during the 1849–1851 gold rush (Morgan 1948: 154–158). After 1851, as California's demand for Hawai'i's agricultural exports fell, there is some evidence that land rents resumed their downward path. Letters written by prominent residents of Hawai'i to Joel Turrill, US consul in Hawaii from 1846 to 1850, repeatedly indicated that land prices continued falling through 1858 (Turrill 1957).

Economic changes in the early 1800s tended to undermine the traditional Hawaiian social structure. First, agriculture was in decline due to a smaller population and increased competition for labor from the whaling services sector. These forces point to a decline in rental income for the king and chiefs and an increase in the real incomes of commoners. Second, prospects for commercial sugar production became evident as the population of the North American west coast increased. Land use rights in Hawai'i were, however, not structured to facilitate large-scale sugar production.

Establishment of the rule of law in urban areas and the rise of constitutional government reduced the power of the chiefs over the common people. Tenants who were dissatisfied with their role in the traditional economy migrated to urban areas. Moreover, rising tenant compensation, prompted by increased competition for labor from urban areas, reduced land rents earned by chiefs. Thus the decline in the chiefs' power was accompanied by a decline in their income.

The decline in land rents also reduced government revenues. Taxes collected by the king were directly tied to the number of commoners working in agriculture, as agricultural workers were obligated to work in the king's fields. With the increased competition from the whaling services sector for labor and a declining total population, it was in the interest of the chiefs to adjust the traditional obligations and taxes paid by tenants. In addition, since government is a labor-intensive enterprise, higher wages would increase expenditures just as revenues were falling.

The adjustments in traditional tenant obligations reduced rents available to the chiefs and taxes paid by the chiefs to the government. In 1842 revenue collected to finance the king's and the government's expenditures amounted to only $41,000. To increase government revenues, the legislature approved an *ad valorem* duty of 3 percent on all imports, effective at the beginning of 1843. Tax revenue increased to $50,000 in 1843, while government expenditures increased to $80,000. Although a bond issue was floated to cover the shortfall, a debt of this magnitude could not be regularly financed by the government unless it wished to compromise its independence from foreign powers. Other taxes were subsequently imposed. A tax on whaling activities was collected by arresting sailors from whaling ships for no apparent reason and then releasing them upon payment of a fine. The tariff was raised from 3 to 5 percent in 1845 and in 1855 some imported articles had duties of 10 and 15 percent imposed on them, with heavier charges imposed on wines and spirits. Chattel taxes on horses, mares, cattle, dogs, and cats were imposed in 1846.

The Great *Mahele* potentially provided two new sources of revenue to the Hawaiian government. First, the capitalization of the right to receive land rents enabled the government to sell a large proportion of its land allocation during and after the Great *Mahele*. An 1881 private compilation of government land sales (also known as "royal patent grants") and the 1858 Report of the Minister of the Interior provide data on land sales. The 1881 survey indicates that 654,622 acres or 44 percent of the original 1,495,000 acres awarded to the government were sold between 1841 and 1886. The bulk of the sales activity occurred between 1846 and 1861 when the government sold 470,782 acres, approximately 31 percent of its total holdings.

Table 8.2 Government revenue and land sale revenue, Hawai'i, 1846–1857

Year	Government revenue	Acres sold	Land sale revenue	Land Commission net revenue	Revenue from land sales as a percentage of government revenue
1846	75,000	861	576		0.77
1847	127,000	2,300	4,799		3.78
1848	155,000	917	2,407		1.55
1849	166,000	7,131	17,853		10.75
1850	194,000	26,578	36,690		18.91
1851	284,000	20,149	27,772		9.78
1852	278,934	31,989	32,645	-3,232	10.54
1853	326,620	12,001	13,962	523	4.43
1854	323,393	23,227	30,090	-214	9.24
1855	419,228	27,819	21,773	3,454	6.02
1856	319,521	20,009	15,981		5.00
1857	319,521	8,960	11,816		3.70

Sources: Government revenue data are taken from *The Report of the Minister of Finance*, various years, 1847–1860. The remainder of the data is taken from *The Report of the Minister of the Interior*, various years, 1847–1860.

Notes:
Government revenue for 1852 was calculated by adding one-fourth of the revenue from the March 1851–March 1852 revenue to the reported data for the period March to December 1852.
All revenue data are in US dollars.

The 1858 interior minister's report contains annual data on acreage sold and revenue received from sales on each island (Table 8.2). A comparison of land sales revenue with total government revenues indicates that a significant proportion of government revenues during this period was derived from land sales.

In Hawai'i, the fiscal crisis was partially caused by a fall in land rents stemming from a declining population. The fiscal crisis coincided, however, with economic changes that rendered alienable property rights in land more attractive. The Hawaiian rulers were able to sell land to commoners partly because commoners could resell the land to foreigners in the face of new prospects for commercial agriculture. The revenue from land sales and tax revenue from an expanding agricultural economy enabled the government to finance its increased expenditures without resorting to the instruments of mercantilism. The Hawai'i case thus provides an interesting example wherein the short-term revenue-seeking interests of the monarch had a positive effect on private investment and economic growth.

Evolution of property rights to land in Fiji

Fiji is an island group located in the tropical South Pacific, stretching over 1,000 kilometers. It consists of 300 islands, of which 95 are inhabited. There are two major islands, Vanua Levu and Viti Levu, and two scattered groups of outlying islands. Most islands have two primary climatic areas: a wet tropical windward side and a dry leeward with sparser vegetation. Colonized some 3,500 years ago from Melanesia, Fiji was invaded from Tonga and Samoa at around AD 1000. Unsurprisingly, the Fijian culture combines influences from Polynesia and Melanesia, with Polynesian influences more dominant in the eastern areas where Tongans maintained a quasi-permanent presence. Fiji did not have a written language until the first decade of the nineteenth century, so our knowledge of Fijian society stems primarily from archaeological investigations and oral legends.

At the beginning of the nineteenth century, Fiji was composed of numerous competing chiefdoms, each composed of groups of *yavusa*. Described as "something between a tribe and a clan," a *yavusa* consists of the descendants of the sons of the founder (*vu*).[9] Each brother's family constitutes a *mataqali*, a branch of the *yavusa*. Warfare among various groups meant that *yavusa* disappeared, merged, and engorged regularly. The results of conquest were often partially offset by gifts of food and highly ranked women. Root crops, tree crops, and fish provided a large portion of the diet. Fijian society depended heavily upon rank, which was traced through the male lineage. Elaborate ceremonies characterized many social occasions. An important ceremony was the *solevu*; villages exchanged gifts of produce and shark teeth, with those villages providing the most expensive gifts gaining the most in prestige.[10]

Ruling chiefs (*turaga*) were associated with the power and fertility of gods – as long as they were not too old, were not murdered by competitors, or their group failed to prosper. Commoners were reluctant to be in the presence of high chiefs, and human sacrifice was often associated with ceremonial occasions. Tribes were frequently linked by marriage and the need for mutual defense. Population growth usually led families to settle new lands, bringing them into conflict with villages and other tribes. Constant warfare led to population migration and resettlement. As in Hawai'i, chiefdoms expanded, shrank, and sometimes disappeared. When extensive contact with western adventurers and traders began in the early nineteenth century, hundreds, if not thousands, of warring factions were present.

Land tenure circa 1800

Land tenure institutions varied across *yavusa* and by island, thus the following account is by necessity somewhat stylized. Land tenure generally depended on the use to which the land was dedicated. Builders of homes generally gained rights to home sites (*yavu*), and those sites could be passed onto descendants when they decided to build a new home upon the death of the original occupant. Rights to the forest area (*veikau*) were vested in the chief, who would delegate rights to cultivation and would collect the first fruits as rents (*sevu*). If tribute were not paid to the chief, the tenant could be evicted. Rights to cultivated areas (*qele*) were generally held by extended families (*mataqali*) who would extend tribute via *sevu* or labor services to the chief and tribe. *Mataqali* would often specialize in particular tasks, serving as priests, warriors, craftsmen, and fishermen.

Mataqali who did not fulfill their duties could be expelled from their lands and the community, migrating to other areas and joining other communities. Villages would often seek the help of other villages in opening new fields; villages receiving help would provide a feast (*oco*), and reciprocal obligations to other villages were created. Communal preparation of a field or building of a house was, however, usually followed by exclusive rights by a *mataqali* to its use. As in Hawai'i, chiefs could be overthrown by the community if they engaged in capricious exactions. Land could be inherited or granted via gifts. France (1969: 17) noted that land grants depended not just on service or ceremonial occasions but also depended on "the relationship between the parties and the amount of land available." The nature and the duration of the rights granted also varied across time, place, and circumstances. Rights of landholders relative to chiefs were less strong in the eastern chiefdoms.

Contact and war

Western contact with Fiji began with Abel Tasman in 1643 but regular visits did not begin until the early nineteenth century. A major consequence of western contact was the spread of disease; the first well-documented epidemic is the spread of dysentery by castaways from an American schooner in 1800. Most of the population decline probably occurred close to mid century (Table 8.3). In the mid 1840s, the population was estimated to be roughly 300,000; just ten years later, very rough estimates showed a one-third decline to about 200,000 people.[11] Over the next 24 years, the population declined by almost 30 percent to 140,500. A measles epidemic in 1875 led to a further sharp loss, yielding a population at the 1881 census of only 114,748 people. The decline continued through the 1921 census; it counted just 84,475 native Fijians, a decline of approximately 72 percent since the mid 1840s.

More frequent western contact with Fiji at the turn of the nineteenth century was coupled with the discovery of sandalwood on a small area of the west coast of Vanua Levu in 1801. Ship crews did the harvesting at the beginning of the trade, but as it progressed chiefs would send out parties to harvest the wood. Rapid harvesting and small initial stocks led to the virtual exhaustion of the sandalwood stock by 1814, when the last major sandalwood voyage sailed. Sandalwood was often purchased with firearms, and some westerners settled in Fiji to maintain the firearms and to provide advice on their use. Villagers began to live in fortified towns with walls of timber and rock with cannon defenses. Some historians argue that the introduction of western armaments led to increased levels of fighting but others

Table 8.3 Native population of Fiji, 1844–1921

Year	Population
1844	300,000
1850	200,000
1874	140,500
1881	114,748
1891	105,800
1921	84,475

Sources: Corney *et al.* (1896) and Kirkendall (1998: table 3.3).

Note:
The 1881, 1891, and 1921 numbers are from the Census of Native Population. Earlier numbers are estimates from Corney *et al.* (1896).

are dubious, noting that intense rivalries were present prior to the introduction of firearms.

The sandalwood boom was quickly followed by a second resource boom in *bêche de mer* – sea cucumbers, a seafood highly valued in China. The first *bêche de mer* voyage sailed in 1822, and unlike sandalwood – which was restricted in supply – *bêche de mer* was present in abundant quantities in Fiji's coastal reefs. This led to 15 intense years of trade between 1830 and 1845. Traders and chiefs used Fijian labor to harvest and to dry the sea cucumbers in smokehouses.

The *bêche de mer* trade was accompanied by the founding of a permanent European settlement at Levuka on the outlying island of Ovalu and by the arrival of Christian missionaries. The London Missionary Society began to convert Fijians to Christianity in the 1830s. The arrival of the missionaries began to change the demands by westerners for land. Early traders had received temporary grants of land to build homes, and these tracts reverted back to the chiefs when the traders left. France (1969: 34) observed that early traders who had taken Fijian women as wives had been allotted land according to Fijian custom. Missionaries who arrived with wives and a family were the first to receive lands without explicit ties to Fijian families. They obtained grants of land just outside the village in order to build homes. Fencing off these lots, the missionaries treated them as lands in which they had exclusive private rights.

Western weapons fueled already intense conflicts between Fijian chiefs. Chiefdoms began to depend more on raw power than kinship ties, and the conflicts of the 1840s and 1850s resulted in a consolidation of power among fewer chiefs. By 1860, three major chiefdoms spread across the islands had become particularly influential: Bau – a small island off the southeast coast of Viti Levu; Cakaudrove – located in Vanua Levu; and Lakeba – an island in the Lau group nearest to Tonga. Three dominant figures competed: Cakabou, chief of Bau; Tui Cakau, chief of Cakaudrove; and Ma'afu, a

Tongan chief. The confederation of Bau was particularly important during the 1840s and 1850s. At several junctions, Chief Cakabou proclaimed himself Tui Viti, or king of Fiji. A critical victory in 1855 solidified his claims over Western Fiji. A similar consolidation occurred in Eastern Fiji, but in this case it was achieved by the Tongan chief, Ma'afu. By intervening selectively in Fijian warfare, he attained broad influence over Eastern Fiji by the end of the 1850s.

Debts, cotton, and deeds of cession

Western settlers arrived in Fiji during the early 1860s intent on starting cotton plantations to take advantage of the high prices resulting from the American Civil War. The number of permanent western residents increased from approximately 50 in 1860 to 1,500–2,000 at annexation. The planters' demands for land, labor, and law and order changed Fiji's political economy. Planters began to purchase lands from Fijians purporting to own the land. The lands being sold were often outside of the control of the seller; when the planter would move to occupy the land, the occupants would refuse to vacate and actively resist occupation.[12] Plantation owners also pressed ethnic Fijians into labor service and began to bring ethnic Melanesians to Fiji as indentured labor. Cotton production on farms operated by western settlers increased rapidly over the course of the decade (Table 8.4), stimulated by the high prices induced by the American Civil War and its aftermath. The collapse of cotton prices in the early 1870s – with the revival of American production – led to crisis in the industry and Fiji's political economy. Many cotton plantations were abandoned, and survivors searched for new crops, realizing they had few long-term prospects if the lower cotton prices persisted.

Plantation agriculture had been established during a period when there was ongoing conflict among Fijian chiefs. Conflicts over land ownership were frequent, and European settlers often turned to native authorities to bolster their claims. Strengthening central authority was one goal, and this led to the suggestion from some European residents that native chiefs form a confederation or, in the words of the British Consul Smythe, "a native government aided by the counsels of respectable Europeans" (as quoted in Derrick 1968: 158). The Confederacy of 1865 was generally intended to bring an end to the simmering war between Cakobau and Ma'afu. Under the leadership of Cakobau, the Confederacy was, however, only marginally effective in establishing law and order across the islands, and white settlers often organized temporarily to take revenge against thefts or murders. The Confederacy collapsed in 1867 after an attempt by Ma'afu to become president. A new government was formed in 1869, but lacking vital support from Levuka interests and the major foreign powers, it struggled to be effective.

Problems with maintaining law and order led to disputes with foreigners and entanglements over land rights. A prominent case involved the American

Table 8.4 Revenue from cotton production in Fiji, 1863–1870

Year	Revenue (£)
1863	400
1864	3,000
1865	9,200
1866	19,800
1867	34,004
1868	30,975
1869	45,000
1870	92,700

Source: *Consular Commercial Report*, various years.

consul, John Williams, who had originally claimed $5,000 "for trade goods allegedly stolen when his Nukulau compound took fire during the Fourth of July celebrations in 1849" (Scarr 1984: 27). Augmented by other American claims, the damages had grown to $43,000 at the time of Williams's death in 1860. Cakobau's difficulty in paying the claims led to a visit by an American warships in 1867, and a pledge by Cakobau – backed by 3 islands serving as collateral – to pay the loan in 4 annual installments. The US consul at Melbourne formed the Polynesian Company to facilitate resolution of the dispute and to gain Fijian land cheaply; the Company offered to pay the claim in return for a pledge of 200,000 acres, and the claim was paid in 1870. After annexation, the Company complained to the British colonial government that the promised lands had not been delivered.

The rapid increase in the number of European settlers between 1867 and 1871, the dissatisfaction of many of these settlers with their own disruptive behavior, a desire for more control of over Fijian affairs, and growing annexation sentiment prompted European settlers to attempt to form a government in 1870. The collapse of cotton prices and discord among settlers scuttled proposed arrangements. The vacuum was filled by Cakobau who became king in a new government formed on June 5, 1871. The new government reserved a powerful role for the king, who had control over the appointment of ministers. A legislative assembly was provided for, with a Privy Council consisting of chiefs and a lower house elected by Europeans. The Assembly enacted a new constitution, modeled after the 1864 Hawai'i Constitution, in August 1871. Unpopular poll taxes were enacted on both natives and Europeans.

Most of Chief Cakobau's ministerial appointments were European settlers, and they dominated the government. Its land policies facilitated settler acquisition of land and its labor policies were intended to increase the supply of Fijian labor to the plantations.[13] The government regularly offered to sell convicts and people from conquered tribes to the planters. Despite these pro-planter policies, the new government failed to receive recognition from the British consul, and Europeans settlers were dissatisfied over the government's failure to establish law and order. They alleged an increasing number of attacks by Fijians against white settlers and were disturbed at the extent of native Fijian involvement in the government. Many native Fijians also opposed the government; their opposition was in part due to the government's land and labor policies, which generated losses for numerous Fijians. The strongest opposition came from areas where white settlers had taken lands close to mountain villages, where central authority was weak or non-existent. Rising European opposition against the government[14] and schemes to promote annexation by British officials was held off until March 19, 1874, when the Privy Council offered Fiji to London. After a round of negotiations in September 1874, Fiji became a British colony on October 10, 1874. Annexation was followed just a few months later by a measles epidemic that killed more than 30,000 Fijians and left the society weakened during a crucial transition period to imperial rule.

Land rights in the British colony, 1874–1880

Article 4 of the Deed of Cession specified:

> That the absolute proprietorship of all lands not shown to be now alienated so as to have become the *bona fide* property of Europeans or other foreigners, or not now in the actual use or occupation of some Chief or tribe, or not actually required for the probable future support and maintenance of some Chief or tribe, shall be, and is hereby declared to be, vested in Her said Majesty, her heirs and successors.

The Colonial Office provided the first British Governor of Fiji, Sir Arthur Gordon, with specific instructions concerning the implementation of this article.[15] Colonial Secretary Carnarvon directed Gordon to establish a system of land tenure "with the view of disturbing as little as possible existing tenures."[16] Alienation of Fijian lands was prohibited in 1875 until the native land tenure system could be sorted out. These efforts began with Gordon asking the Council of Chiefs to elucidate the traditional system of land tenures. The chiefs responded by outlining procedures for land division that allocated lands by rank, position, and current occupation of the land; some chiefs advocated that the land be divided "so that each individual would have his own allotment" (as quoted in Ward 1995: 215).[17] The government rejected individual allocation, but further inquiry did not yield consensus among the chiefs for several reasons: Fijian customs varied according to time and place; they had been disturbed by the constant warfare of the prior 50 years; and there had been extensive use of shifting cultivation techniques and, therefore, only temporary occupation of much agricultural land (Ward 1995: 198–209). Moreover, the social group which "owned" land varied across regions. In sum, confusion reigned concerning which social units were typically awarded land rights and with respect to the extent and duration of the rights (France 1969: 112).

In December 1879 the Council of Chiefs declared that "the true and real ownership of land with us is vested in the *mataqali* alone, nor is it possible or lawful for any *mataqali* to alienate its land" (France 1969: 113). These principles would later be enunciated in a public speech in April 1880 by the eminent anthropologist, Lorimer Fison, an affirmation that would be repeatedly invoked to justify their use.[18] These principles were embodied, with some modifications, in the Native Lands Ordinance of 1880; they specified the *mataqali* as the social unit to which title would be assigned; allowed *mataqali* holdings to be converted to individual holdings; mandated a commission to sort out claims; prohibited sales to non-Fijians; and severely limited the extent of lands which would become Crown lands.

The Deed of Cession also affirmed the claims of Europeans to some lands and mandated that conflicting claims be sorted out. A Land Claims Commission began its work in 1875 and validated only about half of the 854,000 acres claimed by Europeans. Many claims were denied because the Commission found that the native Fijian seller did not possess rights over those lands. The Commission also determined that Fijian land had been frequently alienated, even prior to the arrival of Europeans. France observed that faced with "the conflict between the principles of land tenure accepted as traditional and the practices that were brought to its notice, the Commission's normal practice was quietly to ignore the application of the principles and to judge each case empirically as it came before them" (France 1969: 122). The land claims validated by the Land Claims Commission would become "the core of the present freehold land in Fiji" (Ward 1995: 213).[19]

With the growth of the sugar industry in Fiji after Cession, Europeans anticipated that Fijians would be more likely to work on their plantations. Instead Governor Gordon tightly restricted the employment of Fijians as plantation workers (Scarr 1984: 140).[20] Most Fijians continued to farm their lands within the context of the traditional Fijian governance institutions. Fijians retained significant control of their own governance via the Fijian Administration, led by the annual Council of Chiefs. Fijian custom became embodied in the formal law via the Native Regulations of 1877. In 1880, a Native Lands Commission began the work of documenting Fijian owner ship of land, placing boundaries in writing, and compiling a Register of Native Lands. Fijian resistance made the entire process ineffective during initial attempts to implement it in the 1880s.

One major change introduced by the colonial government was the replacement of the head tax by an in-kind tax on agricultural production.[21] Government agents purchased Fijian agricultural products and ostensibly competed to bid up product prices. The rationale behind this scheme was that the higher prices would stimulate further progress in Fijian agriculture and that tax proceeds could be used to finance public goods critical to economic development in the native Fijian sector.

The government's restrictions on the use of Fijian workers led to the importation of more than 60,000 indentured workers between 1879 and 1916. Working on the newly established sugar plantations, they allowed the new sugar industry to grow rapidly. Fiji's sugar exports increased at a 4.6 percent annual rate between 1883 and 1913 (Knapman 1987). Plantation owners worked the Indian labor intensively; work conditions for indentured labor were regulated by penal regulations as in Hawai'i. Dissent by workers was suppressed, and complaints by groups of more than five workers were illegal. Importation of ethnic Indians ended in 1916, and indentured servitude came to an end in 1920.

Hawai'i and Fiji: divergent paths, similar circumstances?

Hawai'i

In Hawai'i, why did a weak native government – with numerous foreign officials – establish private property rights and titles in land and then allow alienation to foreigners? With respect to the first question, La Croix and Roumasset (1990) argued that the Great *Mahele* accomplished two key purposes for the government. First, the establishment of private property rights in land facilitated capital-intensive investments on those lands – a key to their future value. Second, the revenue from land sales enabled the government to provide basic services, pay its debts, and, consequently, to remain in power even before the large-scale establishment of sugar plantations during the early 1860s. In an era in which western powers were rapidly annexing Pacific islands, this was a considerable achievement.

Does allowing land alienation to foreigners augment the answer to the question or does it have its own rationale? First, land prices – and, therefore, proceeds from land sales by the government and *ali'i* – should theoretically have been higher due to the addition of wealthy buyers to the land market. This would increase the government's ability to pay debts and provide critical services. Note that this result does not require a well-functioning land market or well-informed buyers and sellers – conditions which Kame'eleihiwa (1992) correctly argued were routinely violated in Hawai'i during the second half of the nineteenth century. Moreover, generating more revenue and thereby allowing the government to survive is only efficient if the alternative government is arguably better than the existing government – a problematic endeavor for the Hawai'i government of the 1850s and 1860s.

Second, the Hawai'i government would theoretically have greater access to foreign funds at a lower interest rate if collateral in the form of land could back its loans. This could only be accomplished if foreigners were allowed to own land; otherwise they would not be able to collect the collateral. However, sales and mortgages of Crown lands by Kamehameha III and Kamehameha IV brought forth legislation in 1864 prohibiting both activities. The legislation also provided for the Crown lands to be governed by a Board of Commissioners, a body that ensured that foreign interests would be represented in decisions to allocate these lands.

Third, fee-simple ownership of land could theoretically have allowed certain capital-intensive investments to proceed that would be difficult to undertake on leased land. If large injections of foreign capital were required to build capital-intensive irrigation systems, such investment might not be forthcoming if the land embodying the irrigation system could not be repossessed.[22] Fiji's sugar industry in the late nineteenth century stands, however, as testament to the ability of sugar enterprises to thrive on leased lands.[23] Moreover, sugar plantations in Hawai'i also thrived on leased private lands; leased lands from non-profit foundations; and leased government lands.[24] In sum, efficiency-based explanations for allowing alienation of land to foreigners can be constructed, but are not wholly convincing in the Hawai'i context or supported by strong evidence.

Alienation of Hawai'i land to foreigners may also have come about because it enhanced the interests of foreigners at the expense of Hawaiians. First, Kame'eleihiwa (1992: 298–310) found that foreigners with high positions in the Hawai'i government purchased or were awarded lands of significant size and value. Their prominent positions in the government may have enabled them to extract lower prices from sellers and to gain propri-etary information on the productivity and potential of various lands. Foreigner speculation in land was not immediately successful, as land prices fell throughout the 1850s (Turrill 1957).

Second, alienation of Hawai'i land to foreigners came with the cost of possible intervention by foreign governments in the event of disputes over ownership, taxation, and land use.[25] Even if intervention never actually occurred, its threat would serve to circumscribe actions taken by the Hawai'i government. Of course, actual intervention would have served to decrease the independence of Hawai'i's government by a larger degree and would have been favored by those groups and individuals favoring eventual annexation to a foreign power.

La Croix and Grandy (1997) argued that land alienation to foreigners interacted with the 1876 trade reciprocity treaty with the United States to produce threats to Hawai'i's independence.[26] The reciprocity treaty pro-vided duty-free access for Hawai'i sugar to the US market and duty-free access for US manufactured goods to the Hawai'i market. Sugar's duty-free access to the US market fueled a rapid expansion of Hawai'i's sugar industries and investment in sugar-specific capital. When the United States threatened not to renew the reciprocity treaty in 1882 unless it was granted rights to Pearl Harbor, foreigners receiving rents from the land via their sugar plantations had dual incentives to lobby the government to give in to the US demands: (1) to maintain market access, and (2) to increase the security of their investment in land by increasing US influence in Hawai'i. By contrast, domestic land owners leasing land to foreigners would have more mixed incentives; they would want to maintain market access but would be worried that increasing US influence in Hawai'i would decrease the security of their land rights.

In sum, there is some evidence regarding the efficiency rationale, some evidence for the annexation rationale, and more substantial evidence for the foreign insider rationale. Transfer of Hawai'i lands to foreigners facilitated expansion of the sugar industry between 1850 and 1914, but most of the gains went to immigrant workers and foreign-born plantation owners rather than Hawaiian owners of land or Hawaiian workers. It is not surprising that Hawaiians were dissatisfied with an "efficient" outcome in which most of the gains were absorbed by the king, the government, some *ali'i*, and missionary insiders at the expense of some *ali'i* and Hawaiian commoners (*maka'āinana*), a group which saw many of its traditional rights extinguished in the *Mahele*.

The finding that both efficiency and interest group considerations had a role in the *Mahele* is not unusual. Efficiency is represented as an increase in social surplus and this does not imply Pareto optimality; in fact, some interest groups must gain if social surplus increases from a policy change and if the new policy is to be implemented within the political system. Levmore (2002: S433) argues that interest group and efficiency explanations are difficult to distinguish in practice and that we should learn to live with the ambiguity. If, however, we assume that maintaining independence was a valued social good, then land sales to foreigners permitting the Hawai'i government of the 1850s and 1860s to survive could be viewed as efficiency-enhancing policies.[27] From this point of view, it is the reciprocity treaty of 1876 that begins to look more problematic, given the problematic investment in sugar industry-specific capital that it generated.

Fiji

The British colonial government's restrictions on land alienation and on labor contracts can be analyzed as a reaction to the conditions that led to British annexation and as a forward-looking measure intended to maximize the profits of British interests. As argued above, British annexation was prompted by several factors, with declining conditions of law and order in the presence of British settlers taking a prominent role.

Once the British began their rule, the pattern of colonialism in Fiji proved to be similar to patterns seen in other British possessions in the nineteenth century: the pacification of the countryside, the spread of plantation agriculture, and the introduction of foreign indentured labor. Some factors differed. Instead of natives being confined to small, crowded reservations and being forced to work the land by the pressures of population growth, Fijians retained between 80 and 90 percent of their lands; continued their traditional system of governance in native communities; and were not allowed to work as laborers on plantations. Colonial authorities justified these measures as necessary to achieve their twin goals of encouraging the preservation as well as the further development of the native Fijian economy. The result was the creation of economic and political institutions conducive to a dual economy, in which the traditional sector was explicitly isolated from the enclave plantation sector.

Why would such explicit dualism be encouraged in Fiji? Why, for example, was it necessary not only to prevent free alienation of native lands but also to prevent free alienation of Fijian labor? Suppose we begin from a profit-maximizing perspective in which the British colonial government serves as the imperfect agent of British capital and British settlers who desire to maximize their profits. The government then chooses among available political and legal institutions to facilitate profit maximization by the group of planters. One might expect that a free market in land would facilitate the assembly of parcels of land for plantations; or perhaps that traditional land uses would be restricted so as to reduce the value of land in alternative uses and, therefore, its market value. Or one might expect that labor market institutions would be structured to restrict Fijian opportunities in the traditional agricultural sector, thereby forcing them to work on plantations at low wages – an arrangement favored by the British in other colonies. Instead, land alienation was prohibited and labor market institutions were structured to prevent Fijians from working on the plantations.

These results may, however, be consistent with the colonial government's role as an agent for British interests if we take into account other constraints that influenced its choice of institutions. Four major constraints are identified. First, when the British government annexed Fiji in 1874, Fijians outnumbered white settlers by a factor of roughly 100 to 1. Second, the London government expected that the British colonial government in Fiji would require only minimal subsidies from London, particularly given Fiji's relatively minor role in British commercial and political strategies. Third, the colonial government recognized that alienation of Fijian lands had been a prime source of the tension between Fijians and European settlers in the 10–15 years preceding annexation. Fourth, the Anti-Slavery Society and the Aborgines Protection Society regularly provided information about the labor situation in Fiji to members of parliament, the press, and the religious establishment. These groups regularly lobbied to prevent formulation of colonial policies that would lead to further Fijian population declines or have an adverse economic impact on native Fijians.

The four constraints tied the colonial government's hands in several different ways. The first constraint essentially meant that the colonial government could not adopt policies that generated broad opposition among Fijians. Given the numerical superiority of Fijians, widespread opposition would have forced the government to commit additional resources to maintaining law and order. But how would the additional expenditures have been financed? London was opposed to extensive subsidies for Fiji. Only a small establishment loan had been offered at the founding of the colony, and the colonial government had used its proceeds to pay off previously incurred debts. Alternatively, the colonial government could levy new or higher taxes, but such measures might serve to heighten the level of opposition among doubly oppressed Fijians (high taxes and oppressive policies) and laissez-faire European planters opposed to a larger and more intrusive government.

Constraint three points to the difficulty of a free land alienation policy at the time of annexation, as it recognizes that land rights in Fiji were not defined carefully enough in 1874 to allow the transfer of a well-defined bundle of land rights to a foreign (or even domestic) purchaser. There was no central registry of land rights; it was unclear whether land rights were vested in individuals, the *mataqali*, or the *yavusa* – with the definition of such terms widely contested within Fijian society. In addition, the simmering warfare of the previous 50 years had resulted in numerous land confiscations, with new boundaries and ownership rights often in doubt. As noted above, there was no agreement among Fijians as to the nature of traditional land rights or even as to prevailing rights in lands in 1874. In this highly uncertain environment, Fijians had incentives to offer property to foreigners over which they had highly uncertain claims. Consummation of such sales over the preceding 10–15 years had generated opposition from other Fijians with claims over these lands and led to tensions between foreigners and Fijians. Such tensions would be incompatible with a colonial government committed to minimal expenditures and with limited abilities to enforce highly unpopular policies.

Finally, the fourth constraint is particularly important, as it implies that policy decisions in Fiji could not be insulated from broader political forces in Great Britain. One could interpret this constraint as meaning that the policies of the colonial government were required to be compatible with improvements in the income of native Fijians. Restrictions on land alienation could be rationalized along these lines in a number of ways. Expansion of plantations would lead to increased rent payments to Fijians leasing their lands to plantations; leased plantation lands could be available to Fijians for future use if population expanded significantly; poorly negotiated rental contracts would be limited in their duration; and additional lands would be available for traditional Fijian agriculture, as restrictions on land alienation would limit the size of the plantation sector.

Restrictions on labor alienation could be rationalized as protecting the Fijians from exploitative labor practices in the face of declining Fijian populations and limited ability by the colonial government to enforce detailed labor regulations on plantations; as creating a more captive labor force for Fijian chiefs – a group which the colonial government relied upon for support; and as a measure maintaining the support of public interest groups influencing public opinion in London.

Two other potentially plausible reasons for restrictions on land alienation should also be mentioned. First, restrictions on foreign land sales could also prevent a coalition of Fijian groups from accumulating liquid wealth in order to buy weapons for use in a rebellion against the colonial authorities. Second, the non-alienation policy covering native lands restricted the use of land as collateral against foreign and domestic debts. Such a policy would limit the ability of new interest groups to gain influence in Fiji. A colonial government content with the existing interest group constellation might favor such a policy as it would allow officials to reduce uncertainty concerning future rent extractions.

In sum, a politically constructed dual economy would limit the size of the new modern export sector, but would also serve to increase the likelihood that native groups would gain under the new regime. This would ameliorate opposition to the new colonial government; reduce the government's expenditures on establishing and maintaining law and order; and increase the likelihood that the government would be able to maintain support for its policies in London. While the efficiency consequences of these policies are debatable, they surely enhanced the position of the colonial government.

Conclusion

Trade-offs characterized the different choices of the Fiji and Hawai'i governments with respect to alienation of property to foreigners. The British colonial government made deals with native groups to maximize their position with respect to the London government and to minimize foreign disruptions to their positions. By contrast, the Hawai'i government was willing to reduce its support among native Hawaiians in order to accumulate enough annual revenue to survive. The policies in each country may or may not have been efficiency enhancing, but they are clearly examples of policies designed to transfer income, perhaps with minimum deadweight losses, to powerful interest groups (Becker 1983).

Notes

* Thanks to Ann Carlos, Alan Dye, and participants in the session on Ethno-Nationality, Property Rights in Land and Territorial Sovereignty in Historical Perspective at the XIII World Congress of the International Economic History Association, July 2002 for their helpful comments on an earlier version of this chapter

1 Fiji has a meld of Polynesian and Melanesian cultures.
2 See, for example, the articles in the special issue, "The Evolution of Property Rights," *Journal of Legal Studies*, 31, June 2002.
3 This section draws heavily from the discussion in La Croix and Roumasset (1984, 1990) and Roumasset and La Croix (1988).
4 Samuel Kamakau (1961, 175) and John Ii (1959: 13–14, 20, 26, 69–70), two contemporary Hawaiian observers, tell us who got what in many cases.
5 See, however, the argument propounded by Kame'eleihiwa (1992) that the Great *Mahele* was a substitute for a traditional redistribution of lands.

6 Kuykendall (1938: 291).

7 See the discussion in Kuykendall (1938: 294–298).

8 Earlier disputes between the Hawaiian government and foreign governments had resulted in foreign warships visiting the Islands to influence the course of negotiations. Two American warships arrived in 1826 to press for the repayment of debts incurred by the chiefs in the course of sandalwood trading. Ships returned later in the year and in 1829 to remind the chiefs of their unpaid obligations. Questions about the treatment of native Catholics, French priests, and foreign consuls produced a succession of visits by American, French, and British ships during the 1830s.

9 *Yavusa* could include other unrelated individuals incorporated into the group for economic, political, or social reasons.

10 Johnsen (1986) analyzed a similar ritual among the Kwakiutl Indians. He argued that the potlatch was an efficient institution that maximized the wealth of participating villages.

11 See Kirkendall (1998) for an overview of the decline in Fiji's population.

12 Derrick (1968: 185) noted the variation in land sale practices across locations: "On Vanua Levu, land sales were the assumed perogative of the high chiefs and few dared question them; in Lau they were forbidden altogether. On Viti Levu, on the other hand, the absence of adequate control rendered disputes with the natives inevitable."

13 Between 1864 and 1874, Fijian plantations imported labor from Polynesia and Melanesia. The "blackbirding" trade generated forcible conscription of workers; spread disease across the Pacific; yielded poorly enforced labor contracts; and produced high death rates among laborers.

14 In 1872 a group of British settlers organized a secret society, the Ku Klux Klan, modeled after the infamous US group. They vowed to pay no taxes to the new government, to ignore its decision, and to engage in armed resistance against it. There was substantial cooperation of the British consul March with the Ku Klux Klan until the fall of the Fijian government in 1874.

15 See Legge (1958) for a more detailed account of the evolution of Fijian land policy.

16 *Correspondence Respecting the Colony of Fiji*, C. 1337 of 1875.

17 Ma'afu had already introduced individual holding to Lau where he had divided land according to the new Tongan model (Ward 1995: 215).

18 Fison did not investigate the state of Fijian land tenure in the 1870s. Instead, he searched for an "uncorrupted" version of land tenure, i.e. land tenure from an era prior to its corruption by chiefs. Fison argued for joint ownership of the land by chiefs and commoners, thereby vitiating the right of chiefs to alienate the land.

19 Alienation to non-Fijians was also permitted from 1905 to 1908, and the total freehold acreage expanded accordingly.

20 During his earlier terms as governor of Trinidad (1866–1870) and Mauritius (1870–1874), Gordon had actively protected the rights of immigrant Indian workers.

21 Tax rates varied by district.

22 It would also be important to know whether the irrigation waters could be diverted to other plantations.

23 A careful study of the irrigation systems installed on leased lands in Fiji in the late nineteenth century would help to test this hypothesis.

24 While sugar cultivation thrived on leased land in Fiji, it is possible that the cost of cultivation would have been even lower on land owned by the plantations.

25 See Osorio (2002: 57–58) on the difficulties stemming from marriages between foreigners and Hawaiians.

26 See Osorio (2002: 193–249) for a discussion emphasizing the interaction between reciprocity and native Hawaiian politics.
27 One could, however, argue that land sales to Hawaiians could have generated sufficient revenue to ensure survival.

Bibliography

Alexander, W.D. (1890) "A Brief History of Land Titles in the Hawaiian Kingdom," in T.G. Thrum (ed.) *Hawaiian Annual for 1891*, Honolulu: Black & Auld, Printers.

Becker, G.S. (1983) "A Theory of Competition Among Pressure Groups for Political Influence," *Quarterly Journal of Economics*, 48: 371–400.

Beechert, E.D. (1985) *Working in Hawaii: A Labor History*, Honolulu: University of Hawai'i Press.

Britton, H. (1870) *Fiji in 1870, Being the Letters of "The Argus" Special Correspondent with a Complete Map and Gazeteer of the Fijian Archipelago*, Melbourne: Samuel Mullen.

Bushnell, A.F. (1993) "The 'Horror' Reconsidered: An Evaluation of the Historical Evidence for Population Decline in Hawai'i, 1778–1803," *Pacific Studies*, 16: 115–161.

Chinen, J.J. (1958) *The Great Mahele: Hawai'i's Land Division of 1848*, Honolulu: University of Hawai'i Press.

Consular Commercial Report, various years.

Correspondence Respecting the Colony of Fiji (1875) C. 1337.

Corney, B.J., Stewart, J. and Thomson, B.H. (1896) *Report of the Commission Appointed to Enquire into the Decrease of the Native Population, with Appendices*, Suva: E.J. March Government Printer.

Davenport, W. (1969) "The 'Hawaiian Cultural Revolution': Some Political and Economic Considerations," *American Anthropologist*, 71: 1–20.

Daws, G. (1968) *Shoal of Time*, New York: Macmillan.

Derrick, R.A. (1968) *A History of Fiji*, Vol. 1, Suva: The Government Press.

Feeny, D. (1982) *The Political Economy of Productivity: Thai Agricultural Development, 1880–1975*, Vancouver and London: University of British Columbia Press.

—— (1988) "The Development of Property Rights in Land: A Comparative Study," in R.H. Bates (ed.) *Toward a Political Economy of Development*, Berkeley, CA: University of California Press.

Fison, L. (1881) *Land Tenure in Fiji*, London: Harrison.

Fornander, A. (1969) *An Account of the Polynesian Race: Its Origins and Migrations*, 2 vols, Rutland, VT: C.G. Tuttle & Co.

France, P. (1969) *The Charter of the Land: Custom and Colonization in Fiji*, Melbourne: Oxford University Press.

Galloway, J.H. (1989) *The Sugar Cane Industry: An Historical Geography from its Origins to 1914*, New York: Cambridge University Press.

Gillion, K.L. (1962) *Fiji's Indian Migrants: A History to the End of Indenture in 1920*, Melbourne: Oxford University Press.

Heasth, I. (1974) "Toward a Reassessment of Gordon in Fiji," *Journal of Pacific History*, 9: 81–92.

Ii, J.P. (1959) *Fragments of Hawaiian History*, D.B. Barrere, (ed.), Honolulu: Bishop Museum Press.

Johnsen, D.B. (1986) "The Formation and Protection of Property Rights Among the Southern Kwakiutl Indians," *Journal of Legal Studies*, 15: 41–67.

Journal of Legal Studies (2002) "The Evolution of Property Rights," special issue 31, June.

Kamakau, S.M. (1961) *Ruling Chiefs of Hawai'i*, Honolulu: Kamehameha Schools Press.

Kame'eleihiwa, L. (1992) *Native Land and Foreign Desires: Pehea Lā E Pono Ai?*, Honolulu: Bishop Museum Press.

Kamikamica, J.N. (1987) "Fiji: Making Native Land Productive," in R. Crocombe (ed.) *Land Tenure in the Pacific*, Suva: University of South Pacific.

Kirch, P.V. (1985) *Feathered Gods and Fishhooks: An Introduction to Hawaiian Archaeology and Prehistory*, Honolulu: University of Hawai'i Press.

Kirkendall, M.A. (1998) *Demographic Change on Matuku Island, Fiji in Response to Infectious Diseases Introduced at European Contact*, unpublished doctoral dissertation, University of Hawai'i.

Knapman, B. (1987) *Fiji's Economic History, 1874–1939: Studies of Capitalist Colonial Development*, Pacific Research Monograph, Canberra: National Centre for Development Studies, Research School of Pacific Studies, Australian National University.

Kuykendall, R.S. (1938) *The Hawaiian Kingdom, 1778–1854: Foundation and Transformation*, Vol. I, Honolulu: University of Hawai'i Press.

La Croix, S.J. and Grandy, C. (1997) "The Political Instability of Reciprocal Trade and the Overthrow of the Hawaiian Kingdom," *Journal of Economic History*, 50: 161–189.

—— and Roumasset, J. (1984) "An Economic Theory of Political Change in Pre-Missionary Hawai'i," *Explorations in Economic History*, 21: 151–168.

—— and —— (1990) "The Evolution of Private Property in Nineteenth-Century Hawaii," *Journal of Economic History*, 50: 829–852.

Legge, J.D. (1958) *Britain in Fiji, 1858–1880*, London: Macmillan.

Levmore, S. (2002) "Two Stories About the Evolution of Property Rights," *Journal of Legal Studies*, 31: S421–451.

Malo, D. (1971) *Hawaiian Antiquities*, trans. N.B. Emerson, Honolulu: Bishop Museum Press.

Meek, C.K. (1946) *Land Law and Custom in the Colonies*, London: Oxford University Press.

Morgan, T. (1948) *Hawaii, A Century of Economic Change: 1778–1876*, Cambridge, MA: Harvard University Press.

Osorio, J.K.K. (2002) *Dismembering Lāhui: A History of the Hawaiian Nation to 1887*, Honolulu: University of Hawai'i Press

Polynesia Company, Melbourne (1887) *Copy of Despatch to the Right Honorable Earl of Carnarvon, Secretary of State for the Colonies, from the Polynesia Company: Being Remonstrance Against the Unlawful Withholding of the Company's Land at Fiji by His Excellency the Governor, Sir Arthur Gordon*, Melbourne: W.H. Williams.

Report of Commodore Goodenough and Mr. Consul Layard on the Offer of the Cession of the Fiji Islands to the British Crown, 1874.

Report of the Minister of Finance, Hawai'i, 1847–1860.

Report of the Minister of the Interior, Hawai'i, 1847–1860.

Roumasset, J. and La Croix, S.J. (1988) [2nd edn, 1993] "The Coevolution of Property Rights and the State: An Illustration from Nineteenth-Century Hawaii," in V. Ostrom, H. Picht, and D. Feeny (eds) *Rethinking Institutional Analysis and Development*, San Francisco, CA: Institute for Contemporary Studies Press.

Sahlins, M. (1972) *Stone Age Economics*, Chicago, IL: Aldine-Atherton.

Scarr, D. (1984) *Fiji: A Short History*, Sydney: George Allen & Unwin.

Schmitt, R.C. (1968) *Demographic Statistics of Hawaii: 1778–1965*, Honolulu: University of Hawai'i Press.

—— (1971) "New Estimates of the Pre-Censal Population of Hawaii," *Journal of the Polynesian Society*, 80: 237–243.

Stannard, D.E. (1989) *Before the Horror: The Population of Hawai'i on the Eve of Western Contact*, Honolulu: Social Science Research Institute.

Turrill, J. (1957) "The Turrill Collection, 1845–1860," *Hawaiian Historical Society Report, No. 66*, Honolulu: Hawaiian Historical Society.

Ward, R.G. (1969) "Land Use and Land Alienation in Fiji to 1885," *Journal of Pacific History*, 4: 3–25.

—— (1995) "Land, Law, and Custom: Diverging Realities in Fiji," in R.G. Ward and E. Kingdon (eds) *Land, Custom and Practice in the South Pacific*, New York: Cambridge University Press.

Wyllie, R.C. (1848) *Answers to Questions Proposed by R.C. Wyllie*, Honolulu.

9 Equals in markets?

Land property rights and ethnicity in Fiji and Sri Lanka

V. Nithi Nithiyanandam and
Rukmani Gounder

Prelude

An intriguing issue in development economics in recent times has been the impasse faced by several developing economies whereby they are, despite the fulfillments of most, if not all, of the traditional prerequisites for growth, locked into a "slow-growth steady state." But, it is now increasingly recognized that the cardinal missing link has actually been the absence of a favorable politico-institutional milieu.[1] Fiji and Sri Lanka could easily be cited as typical examples reflecting such a dilemma. They have both, in their efforts toward development, moved with times and adopted policies governed by suitable growth strategies, which have been in vogue and internationally recognized.[2] Yet, their economies are largely stagnant, posing serious challenges to policy makers. The fundamental reason for their failure lies not in the pursued policies but more in their inability to marry these policies with compatible sociopolitical management for desirable outcomes. Ethnic conflicts are at the core of such institutional mismanagement, affecting the political as well as economic spheres.

The ethnic conflict in each of the two countries has its own history. In both instances, the common contributory factor has, however, been western colonialism and the manner in which it set about expanding its economic scope. Production of primary commodities constituted the main interest and resulted in the development of sugarcane plantations in Fiji, and coffee followed by tea and rubber in Sri Lanka. The colonial investors were, in the process, also looking to employ cheap labor drawing mainly from the vast human reservoir of India. Consequently, at the end of western colonialism, the socioeconomic structure of the two countries was turned into one characterized by primary production with heavy reliance on Indian immigrant labor. But, despite the presence of these common elements, the nature of colonial contribution toward the rise of an ethnic conflict in each case differed widely with respective uniqueness.

First and foremost, the Sri Lankan conflict has a longer record involving more complex issues than the Fijian example. It is true that Sri Lanka has, compared to Fiji, a prolonged colonial experience.[3] But, it is not simply due to the length of the colonial history alone. In Fiji, the root cause of the conflict has been the labor migration initiated at the stroke of the colonial rule, which brought into the islands peoples belonging to different ethnicity hailing mainly from India. Although Sri Lanka too was subjected to the same experience, it was on a much smaller scale. In Fiji, with the acceleration of the sugar plantations, the immigrant dwellers grew ultimately into almost half of the total population of the country. Whereas, in Sri Lanka, the newly migrant Indian labor during the entire coffee and tea era (stretching roughly to a century during the period 1835–1930), could not ultimately add more than about 7 percent to the total population.[4] Consequently, the British colonialism did not, unlike in Fiji, directly contribute, in the form of a population transfer, to the country's conflict.

The introduction of immigrant Indian plantation labor to Sri Lanka did, nevertheless, exacerbate the ethnic problem, especially in the later stages. It happened in two ways. On the one hand, when the Indians were transplanted in the heart of the Sinhala dominated areas, it immediately created an ethnic imbalance eroding into majority status of the Sinhalese. The situation was made worse when this particular Kandyan (Sinhalese) host society was more conservative and tradition-bound than the rest of the Sinhalese nation in the island.[5] It did not therefore possess the necessary mindset to view these unfortunate and poverty-stricken, yet "uninvited guests" with compassion or sympathy. On the contrary, they were always treated as "aliens" forming an inherent part of the colonial invaders threatening the economic well-being as well as the cultural environment of the region. The immigrants were all drawn, in contrast to Fiji, from a singular ethnic stock, namely the Tamils of South India, who could remotely be linked to the indigenous Tamils in Sri Lanka.[6] The latter, though, for a considerable length of time did not regard their Indian counterparts as equals, while the Sinhalese from the beginning tended to exaggerate the few and distant similarities between both groups and identified them together as a common risk against Sinhalese progress, if not its very existence. The tendency became more marked with the escalation of the ethnic conflict. It was overstretched to an extent that native Tamils too had no alternative but to ultimately accept this rather manipulative routine as a challenge and absorb the Indian Tamils as another sub- or regional grouping of the community adding to the unified strength of the Tamils in Sri Lanka.[7] It is, however, ironic that, at the peak of the ethnic conflict, the Sinhala majority governments having initiated and promoted an "imagined" unity at the beginning, chose to indulge in political maneuvering to discourage an actual union occurring between the two.[8]

A comparison of the colonial experience of Fiji and Sri Lanka in terms of the ethnic conflict clearly demonstrates that the British economic objectives, while having a more direct influence on Fiji, had only an indirect impact on Sri Lanka and the outcomes were rather disguised. In Fiji, the colonial rulers had been directly instrumental in bringing one of the parties to the conflict, namely the Indo-Fijians. Thus, the conflict became a confrontation between the "natives" and the "immigrants." But in Sri Lanka, both parties to the conflict had been indigenous to the island.[9] Although British entrepreneurs brought, as in Fiji, a different community to the island to service the plantations as labor, it had only a marginal effect on the conflict. This immediately raises the issue of what was the actual basis of the conflict in Sri Lanka. Any attempt to answer this question would inevitably involve matters beyond direct colonial interests. Yet, it cannot be denied that western colonial ambitions highly influenced the evolution of the conflict.

The difference in the nature of origin of the ethnic conflict in the two countries is also indicative of the respective contribution of land property rights to the conflict. It could be mentioned at the outset that, in Sri Lanka, private land ownership did not figure as the source of the conflict. While the Tamils were predominantly domiciled in the northern and eastern parts, the Sinhalese occupied the rest of the island. Land property rights, nevertheless, became one of the key issues in the subsequent stages of the conflict. There was an attempt to usurp the traditional rights of the Tamils and transfer them to the Sinhalese. Yet, it remained a component of a package of other issues contributing to the problem. This chapter will shed some light on the overall problem by tracing the evolution of the ethnic strife very briefly and then examine the relative importance of the land question. But, on the other hand, in Fiji, when the entire conflict more or less rests on the issue of property rights, the existing (land) tenure arrangements at the dawn of colonialism need to be discussed. It will, then be possible to fully reveal the transformation brought about in property rights by British colonial intrusion.

Colonization and land issues in Fiji

The traditional Fijian society of pre-colonial times was organized on the basis of "communes," with each commune under the governance of a powerful local chief. A system of *kerekere*, meaning customary borrowing reciprocated in the future, was practiced. Land remained the mode of subsistence production of the entire population helping direct consumption. Thus, private property ownership was not only non-existent, but also was institutionally discouraged. Economic stratification was altogether absent and the collective owners of land were directly involved in the production and consumption processes. The institutional arrangement of *kerekere* addressed the issue of any inequality that could arise in the distribution of resources.

But, even before Fiji was ceded to Britain in 1874, numerous changes, both fundamental and irreversible, were already imminent. The causative factor behind these had been the continuous flow of traders, missionaries, and planters into Fijian territories. Large tracts of land were brought under the plantation system of cultivation utilizing native labor. The land alienation commenced around 1840 and operated as an ongoing process until Fiji was officially declared a crown colony of Britain in 1874 (Ward 1965). Of the total land acreage of 4.5 million in Fiji, it is estimated that the Whites owned about 1.5 million (Prasad and Tisdell 1996).

When colonization became a reality, the structural base for capitalistic development was set in place with its tantalizing effects on both the economy and society. Fiji was poised to become a part of the world economy with cross-border trade and money transactions. An export-oriented plantation system, while leading towards a permanent alienation of land from natives to foreigners, also converted land into a marketable commodity. Private ownership in property was introduced and instituted. The situation was very similar in labor, where a labor market was slowly beginning to surface.[10] However, among the factors of production land availability, as in many other colonies, was essentially a major concern of colonial investors that pertained to capital and labor. At the beginning, "the chief anxiety with regard to Fiji was finance."[11] Penetration of capital was indispensable for the establishment of a national productive system and making the country a viable export economy. Nonetheless, the shortage of large-scale capital and scarcity of cheap labor were interrelated problems. The planters could not attract capital into the economy without ensuring sufficient supplies of labor. A primary limitation on labor was the Native Policy, which restricted the availability of Fijian labor. Consequently, the sugar plantations had to, from the beginning, rely on outside labor originating mainly from other Pacific islands like Vanuatu and Solomon Islands, which proved futile.

With the establishment of colonial rule, providing sufficient relief to the problem of labor was a major priority for Britain. Yet, it was not by any means a daunting task. It had, by then, already accumulated adequate experience in satisfactorily resolving the issue. Sri Lanka itself served as a model in this respect, strengthened further by the circumstances in other British colonies like Malaysia, Trinidad, and Mauritius. Thus, the system of indentured labor was now repeated in Fiji. In 1879, Governor Gordon initiated the Indian Indenture System, under which the newly arrived could commence work, mainly in the sugar plantations. Thereafter, there was a steady growth of the Indian population.

It is necessary at this juncture to pinpoint a prime difference between Sri Lanka and Fiji in the manner the Indians entrenched themselves in the socioeconomic as well as sociopolitical fabric of their country of residence. In Sri Lanka, they were coming into a country where the local population had already gained enough exposure to the western political, economic, and cultural ethos and was well into the progressive loop based on modernization. A feudal way of life and management of resources was almost extinct. The Sinhalese and the Tamils had been reasonably active in politics and economics and were fast growing in stature, making their presence rapidly felt in every sphere of life, especially through the formation of an elite in their midst. An added factor which made this possible was the increasing literacy rates facilitated by the religious organizations, both indigenous and Christian.

When the Indian Tamils were indentured as plantation labor in Sri Lanka, they had very little opportunity to break into the rest of the economy and find a foothold immediately, or even gradually. They were more or less condemned to be in their original status of entry. Even when they managed to secure some alternate employment it was at unskilled lower-paid levels, mainly in the urban sector already controlled by the elite investors. The attitude of the local population too had not by any means, as already mentioned, been helpful in this regard. It was more hostile than cordial. The alien element was always emphasized and there is sufficient evidence to show that the locals were determined to thwart any attempt by the Indians to carve out a niche for themselves in the normal Sri Lankan way of living.[12] The zenith of this was achieved in the immediate post-independence period, when the entire community of Indian plantation workers was disenfranchised and made politically inactive.[13] It had thus been a "frozen" absorption without any allowance for collateral progress. It is not an exaggeration to say that, even today, the standard of living of the estate workers is among the poorest in the country.[14] Under these circumstances, it is a foregone conclusion that this community would be devoid of any private possession of lands, except perhaps tiny plots lying in the immediate vicinity of its coolie lines.

In Fiji, on the other hand, the Indian entry almost accompanied western colonialism and thus, along with the British, encountered a feudal society. Consequently, when the colonial pattern of modernization transpired, the new settlers could spread into various spheres of the economy and, without much hindrance, firmly establish a place for themselves. It is true that their experience at the beginning did not in any way differ from that of the Sri Lankan plantation workers. They went through the usual hardship of indentured labor and put up with a very low wage and life in coolie lines. At the termination of the indenture system in 1916, the Indian community participated in economic activities within other sectors. They could thus become, unlike in Sri Lanka, partners in development. Education played a central role in the life of the Indo-Fijians and they were soon in a position to make substantial contributions in both public and private enterprises. In agriculture, their role was important, entailing equal identification with other communities.

An economic categorization of the Indo-Fijian society in the post-1916 period shows that about 80 percent of the settlers had, in fact, been descendants of farmers. They came primarily to occupy the agriculture sector. Another 3 to 6 percent of the Indians found entry as free settlers when free settlement was sustained even after the abolition of the indenture system. They were mainly Gujaratis forming the trading community in the country engaged in business – the retail trade in particular (Ali 1973). The Indo-Fijian community constitutes, along with the Europeans and Chinese, the professional segment of the nation. In sum, Fiji, at the time of its independence, had transformed into a truly plural society of which the Indians formed an important component. Others in the fabric comprised, apart from the indigenous Fijians, Rotumans,[15] Europeans, Chinese, part-Europeans, and other Pacific islanders.

A predominant feature of this plurality had, however, been the evolution of compartmentalization, which ultimately permeated the entire socioeconomic system in Fiji. It is not a phenomenon observed simply in social terms with each group having its own language, religion, and culture besides, perhaps, work ethics. The ethnic divide extended into the realms of economics, reflected clearly in the structural participation of the Fijian population including the labor market. There existed an apparent ethno-based labor specialization. Indo-Fijians, Europeans, and Chinese dominated the productive and distributive sectors of the economy. The indigenous Fijians mainly joined the civil service and the private sector. A few were also seen in joint ventures, especially with the Europeans, in the business sector. The Indo-Fijians had also been proactive in providing professional services and expert skills both in the public and private sectors. It is true that a structural division of this nature embodied, on the one hand, the creative spirit in Fiji's community. But, on the other, it also gave rise to comparison and competition within the Fijian society (Premdas 1995). Although the groups lived within the same political system, "national integration" was totally lacking. It could only be described as "meeting at the market-place" syndrome. The contours of communal conflicts along political, economic, and socio-cultural lines were, during the colonial era itself, becoming increasingly evident. They were poised to extend into independent Fiji, manifesting as competition for political power. Attempts towards manipulation of the system according to the strength and influence of each group were only a matter of time. The ultimate casualty of the entire exercise had, no doubt, been the progress and development of the country.

Against a socioeconomic background described above, if land had, in terms of property rights, been considered equal to other assets or factors of production, then, it would have also been subject to the same social influence manifesting emphatically in its distribution. Land ownership too was certainly guided by social norms. But it did not in any way conform to the plural nature of the evolving social milieu already discussed. Social roots of land ownership and distribution went much deeper. They emanated entirely from the indigenous Fijian social system and did not, in the least, anticipate the changes during colonialism. They had not therefore made any allowance for the incoming social onslaught in the form of a plural structure, leave alone the Indian dominance. It would not thus be an exaggeration to say that the situation was seemingly critical. The Fijian land tenure in its original state was not compatible at all with the modernization traits the country was conceiving under western colonialism. Some changes were therefore imminent.

The dilemma faced by the colonial rulers was to devise a system, whereby land would be freely forthcoming for productive usage by investors other than the indigenous Fijians, but, simultaneously, it should also be seen as one safeguarding the existing rights of the latter group. In other words, a compromise framework suitable for both the indigenous and immigrants had to be designed. A system of releasing land under long-term leases provided the answer for this problem at that time.

An initial step in this direction was that the Fijians were, under the Deed of Session, allowed to possess any non-alienated land. The first leasing commenced in 1915 and lands were granted for 21 years with the possibility of an extension of another 9 years (Prasad and Tisdell 1996: 37). In 1940, the Native Land Trust Board (NLTB) was created whereby the land tenure system under the colonial government was institutionalized (France 1969). Nevertheless, the government also took further care to protect indigenous rights. Under the Fijian Affairs Ordinance of 1945, special status was accorded to the Fijians in matters of land ownership and other customary obligations. The legislation prevents any amendments to leasing being effected without the concurrence of the indigenous Fijians, the Great Council of Chiefs in particular.[16] In addition, there is a series of other acts entrenched with the explicit objective of protecting the collective land rights of the Fijians. Mention could be made of the Native Land Trust Act, the Fijian Development Fund Act, the Rotuma Act, the Rotuma Lands Act, the Banaban Land Act, and the Banaban Settlement Act.

The structure of land property rights at the time of Fiji's independence did not ring any alarm bells. Even when drafting the Constitution, it was never an issue, and displacing non-Fijian ethnic communities least occupied the minds of its framers. Elster's contention that the constitution of a country forms a key component of its economic performance and should promote stability, accountability, and credibility seems to have been well heeded (Elster 1994). Although the 1970 Constitution, promulgated with independence, did contain an ethno-based electoral classification, the source of authority was "the people of Fiji." The Constitution was clearly based on the lines of democracy with the provision of seats equally allocated between the Fijians and the Indians in proportion to their respective share in the total population.[17] Yet, it cannot be claimed that the 1970 Constitution served to imbue a common perspective cutting across the socioeconomic plurality and promote communal harmony. There was still "the perception of inter communal competition rather than inter communal cooperation" and the potential danger of "a legacy of cultural politics and the deployment of traditionalism as a means to a political end was always present" (Lawson 1996). The nation experienced, as a sequel, a military coup in 1987 following the formation of a coalition government between Labor and National Federation headed by Bavadra in April of that year.

Nevertheless, the prevailing dormancy of the 1970s had its favorable effects on both the distribution of land ownership and land utilization. In the immediate post-independence period, while the state owned 10 percent of the land, Native Land comprised 83 percent. The balance of 7 percent was freehold land. The classification makes it abundantly clear that leasing Native Land was an economic priority. Leasing arrangements consisted of two regulatory pieces of legislation. The Agriculture and Landlord Tenancy Agreement (ALTA) created the terms and conditions for leases, whereas the Native Land Act set the institutional framework for native land usage. The latter determined the rightful and hereditary property of native owners. The ALTA legislation of 1976, while laying down leasing terms and conditions, did not focus on the issue of economic security in land tenure. The terms remained at 30-year lease and conditions covering rent fixing, compensation, and related land usage remained unchanged. But with the intervention of the military coup in 1987 and cultural politics mixed with traditionalism becoming the dominant feature of Fiji's politics, the whole complexion of the land issue was threatened with change. When existing leases began to expire in the mid 1990s, a critically explosive situation was, if not politically, at least economically, looming ahead. In other words, land ownership was poised to become a core issue of the impending ethnic conflict.

Roots of the Sri Lankan conflict

In Sri Lanka, western colonialism did not, as earlier indicated, sow the seeds of the conflict. Yet, it did prepare the fertile grounds for the germination of the seeds already sown and, then, once the plant had surfaced, helped towards its flourishing growth.

Before the dawn of colonialism in the island of Ceylon (as it was known until 1972), it was already the home of two major ethnic groups, which were "nations" in their own right. When western colonial rule engulfed these nations and decided to bring them both under a single entity corresponding to the geographical boundaries of the island, it was inevitable that confrontation would develop sooner or later culminating in an ethnic conflict. The contribution of colonialism to the conflict was, therefore (unlike in Fiji), in the form of its efforts to marry two entirely different "nations," based simply on the reason that they were both within the same island. The obvious outcome was an attempt to convert the island itself into a suitable framework for a "nation-state." Once a wrong foundation was laid, it was never going to be easy to build a strong structure – in this case, the formation of a "nation-state." But, when it was made worse by gross sociopolitical mismanagement, both during and especially after the colonial rule, it is hardly surprising that the conflict led ultimately to the entire structure being endangered with a complete collapse. If there is anything to be learnt from the Sri Lankan experience, it is that geographical contiguity alone, irrespective of its (small) size and (administrative) convenience, cannot form the basis of a viable, leave alone a strong sovereign state.

When the nation-state conversion was effected in 1833, the Sinhalese could secure for themselves a "majority" status vis-à-vis the Tamils, which grew in importance with increased emphasis on a Westminster-style parliamentary form of government. At the stroke of independence in 1948, numerical strength became the determining factor of sociopolitical decisions, thus always rendering the Sinhalese a clear advantage. But the Sinhalese, instead of utilizing the advantage of pride as a "nation," acquired, on the other hand, a predatory character and unleashed the power of the majority with highly detrimental effects on the Tamils. In fact, the Sinhalese behavioral pattern soon reached colonial dimensions.

The Sinhalese expansionism had, compared to that of the western powers, a more lethal effect on the Tamils. The primary objective of the westerners, including Britain, had been to either procure local commodities for overseas trade or enlist more resources to expand their production possibilities in their own countries. They never competed in Sri Lanka, unlike in the Indian subcontinent,[18] with the locals for production or market power. In the context of the Tamils, even the curtailed colonial intentions were less applicable. Each colonial power had spared the Tamilian regions and Tamils were thus by and large left alone. But the Sinhalese agenda, on the other hand, had an altogether different make-up. Competition became the catchword and it spread into almost every sphere of Tamilian life. Thus, conflict between the two communities became distinctively inevitable.

Land issues

Once the Sinhalese behavior is deemed to be colonial, it is a foregone conclusion that land issues would figure prominently and form an inherent component of its comprehensive as well as swift execution. For there is no colonialism without land desires. But, when the colonizing power was in the garb of a "nation-state," already enjoying sovereignty over the territory of another nation, the effort immediately acquires not only a lenient passage but also a non-combatant posture.

A prior, perhaps conceptual, question would naturally arise: why should a state think, in the first instance, of colonizing a land over which it already possesses sovereign authority? But the said sovereignty had been derived from western colonial manipulations, which offered the Sinhalese nation a "majority" status and, thus, control over the Tamil nation. The latter had by now become a "minority." Although this manner of power acquisition could easily pass as "democratic" under the British Westminster system, facilitated further, in the Sri Lankan case, by the contiguity of an island structure, there is no denial that the acquired sovereignty was not "natural," but bestowed from above. When the Sinhalese nation was fully conscious that part of the derived sovereignty actually belonged to the Tamils, its options were clear. There arose an urgent necessity for the claims to be territorially justified through the settlement of its own people. Subsequent experience relating to land offers ample testimony that the Sinhalese thinking had, in fact, been guided by this notion. When direct confrontation was ruled out as grossly unnecessary, a more subtle strategy had to be devised. In this context, the neglect of lands unsuitable for primary production lying within the predominantly Tamilian regions of the Dry Zone of Sri Lanka by consecutive western colonial governments, culminating in a lethargic performance in the production of food crops, provided the viable option. An accompanying feature of the neglect of the Dry Zone had been the complete collapse of the irrigation systems operating from pre-colonial times.

But, during western colonial rule itself, there was increased awareness that the Dry Zone should be developed for enhancing the food supply of the country. Obviously, the reclamation of the Dry Zone was a task that could not be accomplished without institutional support from the state.[19] Yet, it was the articulation of government involvement which made the Dry Zone development a more than useful instrument for other purposes. Discussions regarding the formulation of a suitable state policy of Dry Zone development were initiated as early as 1914 and, ironically, the term "colonization" had been coined with clear objectives of settling peasant farmers in these areas. By 1931, with the inauguration of the Donoughmore Constitution (which inducted the concept of territorial representation and established Sinhalese "majority" power), "a fixed policy of accelerating aided peasant colonization" had been put together (Farmer 1957: 141). The final phase of the policy evolution was achieved in 1939, consolidating on the experience hitherto gained. The ultimate outcome after the penultimate stage was, in fact, described as a "New Policy." An important tenet of the policy evolution had been the increasing role assigned to state sector agencies in the settlement process. It came to fruition when the "New Policy" explicitly suggested that "the Government should hand over to the colonist a ready-made farm, complete with house" (Farmer 1957: 151, 210).

A policy approach of this nature, notwithstanding its merits and demerits, offered the ideal breeding ground for political intervention. There had indeed been allegations from the very beginning that politics influenced the management of the Dry Zone colonization schemes. But, with the escalation of ethnic politics, the whole complexion of political interference had been subjected to a formidable change, reducing any form of previous meddling to miniscule levels. It did not take long for the government to realize that the Dry Zone colonization schemes could serve as a convenient medium for the territorial translation of Sinhalese "majority" ambitions. Don Stephen Senanayake, the first Prime Minister of independent Ceylon, had a clear vision of the strategy and pursued an aggressive policy of Sinhalese settlement in the island's Dry Zone, which has to this day been sustained. The degree of implementation had, however, varied over time, depending very much on the prevailing ground (political) conditions determined by the ongoing ethnic strife.

It is not the intention of this chapter to go into a detailed analysis of the Dry Zone settlement process, quantifying its impact on the Tamils, which is well documented.[20] Nevertheless, it is necessary to highlight the overall implications for the Tamils, as a nation.

At the outset, two aspects concerning the Tamils, both relating to factor utilization, need mention. On the one hand, land colonization was one of the few areas where state interest was extended to incorporate resources within the Tamilian regions. But that too did not work to the benefit of the nation and, on the contrary, proved highly detrimental to not only its socioeconomic prospect, but also nationhood itself. On the other, Tamilian socioeconomic behavior was immensely favorable for Sinhalese settlement activity in the Dry Zone. As government apathy coupled with demographic pressure made the Tamils look for alternate economic opportunities outside their already densely populated areas, peninsular Jaffna in particular, they not only turned to the service sector, but also made it subject to individualism and internal competition rather than complying with any sociological exigency. When they accepted public service employment in their large numbers in the Sinhalese South, it did not lead to any social migration of Tamils. It was simply a matter of Tamil individuals, mostly breadwinners, finding a job opportunity in a new area. The society remained intact in its original places of domicile. The Tamils did not show much inclination to spread to the rest of the land area within their own regions either for settlement or farming activity. Their farming interest too remained within the individual loop similar to that of the service sector. It is true that it was a harsh option, especially without the institutional support which later became available to Sinhalese settlers. Yet, if the economic challenge had been viewed with a sense of social awareness, a socially organized Tamil Dry Zone migration would not have been altogether impossible. Later on, when the economic emergency had, at the peak of the ethnic conflict, turned into a crisis, a social response from the Tamils toward Dry Zone land development was forthcoming. But the Sinhalese "majority" attitude toward territory had, at this stage, become further calcified and the government was not willing at all to give in to Tamilian aspirations. It went to the extent of using force to evict Tamils from their newly settled areas.

The initial lethargy of the Tamils in land-related activity within their own regions had thus cost them dearly, allowing more or less a vacant possession to the Sinhalese. When the latter, with state-level backing in the required proportions, implanted themselves, unlike the Tamils, as a socio-cultural group, they became, no doubt, difficult to dislodge. It was, at the same time, relatively easy to drive away the few individual Tamil families and take full control of the land. Manogaran estimated that, between 1946 and 1971, a quarter of the island's population, consisting entirely of Sinhalese, was moved from the Wet Zone to the Dry Zone (Manogaran 1994: 85). This led to the creation of new electoral districts with a Sinhalese majority population within the former Tamilian regions. These electorates, while raising Sinhala representation in the country's legislative assembly, proved also to be major strides toward fulfilling the ambitions of territorial sovereignty over the whole island.

The Dry Zone colonization camouflage could, despite being so cleverly and diligently executed by Sinhalese majority governments, neither justify nor conceal its obvious colonial character. It amounted to no less than a "land conquest" experienced under western colonialism and, in fact, its worse kind. There was a major difference between the western colonial action and Sinhalese maneuvers. Under western colonialism land was first seized before it was put into any form of usage. But, with Sinhalese colonialism, "development" preceded the "conquest" or, to be more precise, both proceeded simultaneously, resembling a "hand and glove" operation. Conquest was taking place inconspicuously through the settlement of people identified with the conqueror, but alien to the indigenous. The end result was, as far as the Tamils were concerned, disastrous, because it turned out to be far more serious than what they experienced under western colonialism. The European interest in Sri Lanka belonged to the "non-settler" category, in contrast to "settler" objectives like those present in countries like Canada, Australia, South Africa, or former Rhodesia.[21] None of the western powers transferred its allegiance to the island on a full scale or acquired a personal stake by bringing in its own people to live permanently. Their interests were primarily based on business, and, in many respects, formed "an extension of those of the metropolitan country, and [were] limited both in their range and time horizon" (de Silva 1982: 54). But Sinhalese activity on the traditional Tamil homelands within the Dry Zone came, on the other hand, very close to western colonialism in the "settler" colonies. It had a clear settlement agenda and the settlers sought to engage in socioeconomic development entirely repudiating the indigenous interests.

It would be pertinent to emphasize here that literature on colonial activity tends to identify the term "colony" more with captured territories inhabited by a population of the conquering power. Engels mentioned, for example, that "colonies proper" were those occupied by a European population, as distinguished from those inhabited by a native population.[22] Clarence observed that the term "colony" does not apply to territories dominated by non-settler investors.[23] Furnivall, too, expressed more or less the same view in his authoritative study on Netherlands India. According to him, the "non-settler" type was colonized by capital rather than with men, implying that the term "colony" would be more appropriate to describe the latter than the former (Furnivall 1944: 102). It is therefore clear that, by the same token, the emerging definition of a "colony" is equally applicable to the intrusion of the Sinhalese into the Tamilian regions of Sri Lanka's Dry Zone and the whole gamut of their activity has been none other than "colonialism" of the worst kind. The fact that the "oppressor" and the "oppressed" were both of Asian origin and the scale of the operation was relatively small (taking place within an island), should not hide its actual historical standing. It has, however, been made feasible by a larger western colonialism of the "non-settler" type providing the necessary biting (sovereign) power to the majority Sinhalese within the island.

From a Tamilian perspective, large tracts of land falling within the former Tamilian sovereign territory were now converted into areas of Sinhalese domination. The action was justified on the flimsy excuse that the land was vacant and unoccupied and that there was a more urgent need to enhance the food capacity of the island country. The fact that the land so used could easily form marginal tracts reserved for future use by the Tamil nation was altogether ignored. But, more importantly, the operation could not be justified in economic terms either. Cost-benefit analyses done on many of the settlement schemes revealed that the costs were much higher than the actual benefits and that they were, as part of the food development drive, not a viable option. In 1970, the committee probing the cost-benefit on the Gal Oya Scheme (considered to be one of the major and multi-purpose settlement schemes), for example, concluded that dis-counted costs exceeded the benefits by a staggering Rs277 million. The committee estimated that, during the period 1949–1966, the scheme consumed a total of Rs910 million (Ponnambalam 1981: 22). It is not there-fore surprising that Elliot adjudged the Dry Zone colonization schemes as exaggerated efforts towards solving the country's food problem (Elliot 1975: 64). Wijetunga (1974) a Sinhalese scholar, not only also formed the same view, but, in addition, emphasized the political connotations behind the schemes.

In political terms, too, the schemes were proving more and more costly. One of the major concerns of European settlers when they forcibly occu-pied foreign territory was their own security (de Silva 1982: 67). The Sinhalese were spared of this risk for a very long time mainly due to two reasons. Firstly, they had the full backing of the government, which was, unlike the western powers, close at hand to meet any challenge coming from the Tamils. At the beginning, the government support was covert leaving the initiative to the settlers themselves. In fact, the first anti-Tamil riot in 1958 broke out in the Tamil majority province where Sinhalese peasants had been settled under the Gal Oya Scheme (Manogaran 1999).[24] The other reason why the Sinhalese had a smooth sailing was the passive attitude of the Tamils discussed earlier. But, when the Tamils woke up to reality and grasped the gravity of the situation somewhere around the 1970s, land colonization became a contentious issue and triggered many violent incidents.

The Sinhalese governments were, nevertheless, prepared for such an eventuality and the state involvement was steadily growing into an overt operation unleashing the predatory character of a true colonial force. The manifestation was starkly visible in the two important areas: land and security.

In terms of land seizure, Sinhalese colonization of Tamilian districts was, until the 1980s, largely confined to marginal regions, where there was a mixed population of Tamils and Muslims. But, by the 1980s, it commenced targeting exclusively Tamil areas in the east and northeastern portions (Batticaloa and Mullaitivu Districts) of the island. Once again, a major irrigation settlement scheme, namely the Mahaweli Programme, provided the required cover. The Manal Aru (later named as Weli-Oya in Sinhalese) Project[25] in the Mullaitivu District had the added objective of breaking the hitherto existing linkage between the Tamil areas of Northern and Eastern Provinces.[26] But, now, since the Tamils too were fully conscious of Sinhalese motives and resisting settlement operations, security became a paramount concern. The government was, however, prepared to come out in the open and protect the settlers. A good excuse for the government in this respect was the Tamil youth militancy coupled with violence gradually gaining ground in Sri Lankan politics. It could not, however, conceal the government intentions of furnishing direct and ready security to the Sinhalese. The Janakapura settlement inaugurated under the Manal Aru Project in 1985 was, for example, accompanied by the adjacent opening of an army camp for security purposes. The settlement itself was named after Janaka Perera, the army commander who led the forces into the area. Manogaran neatly captures the emerging scenario in the following terms:

> The violence has been confined to those . . . districts where the Tamil-speaking people are in the majority and where Sinhalese settlements were recently established or expected to be established in the near future. Most of the incidents involving brutal killings of civilians and destruction to personal property in the 1980s were confined to these Tamil-majority . . . divisions. *More than 100 army camps were established in these . . . Tamil-majority divisions by Sri Lankan security forces* after the anti-Tamil riots of 1983.[27]

It is clear that land has always been at the core of the Sri Lankan ethnic conflict. Besides other issues, it has always been the major driving force of the Sinhalese behavior, a facet that did not escape the attention of even foreign scholars. Mick Moore observed, for example, that "land policy, and the ideologies which support it, have in general focused much more on the control of land than on the cultivation of or use of land" (1985: 45). It had thus given an apparent colonial focus to the entire ethnic issue, magnifying it more than a simple conflict between two ethnic groups.

Policy implications

The foregoing account of the origins of the ethnic conflict in Fiji and Sri Lanka, and the manner in which land property rights figured in it, make the policy implications in the two countries entirely different. In Fiji, it is mostly a question of deciding on private rights by embracing the nature and duration of the claim on land, whereas in Sri Lanka, the disposition is of a much higher order, falling within the realms of nationhood and rights and privileges going along with it. While Fiji is concerned with individual rights to enhance one's earning capacity, in Sri Lanka, national sovereignty over land is the fundamental issue.

Yet, despite these differences, there are, ironically, some similarities in the policy approach governing the resolution of the two problems. There seems to be some common recognition that property rights are tied to the ethnic rights enjoyed by respective communities. When ethnic rights and liberties are satisfactorily determined, land problems too could, it is reckoned, easily be solved. There is also a general understanding that the country's Constitution should form the key instrument through which the role of each community in the national context would be ascertained. Both Fiji and Sri Lanka have, from the time of their independence, experimented with three separate Constitutions each.[28] A major concern of these documents has been to demarcate the sociopolitical status of the various communities within their island states. Although the declared objective has been to improve on the existing situation, in reality, actual conditions in both countries have, after the promulgation of the new Constitutions, deteriorated further. The majority domination and minority discontent have simultaneously increased. It is a truism that the Constitutions were nowhere near disentangling the basic issues. It is necessary to consider, before concluding this chapter, the policy implications of such efforts in each country.

Equals in markets: reason before identity in Fiji

The integrity of human beings to solve a dispute amicably is important to avoid adverse effects on the nation and its people. Learning from the experience of pre-colonial times and moving the economy toward a market-oriented system of earning should also make people aware of the advantages of creating a compatible social environment. Conflicts in the form of confrontation, threats, personalized politics, and long-standing prejudices between races, bringing ethnicity as a root cause, are all conditions that could defeat this objective with long-term implications for the future.

National reconciliation to build a society based on goodwill and compromise needs to be translated from mere rhetoric into action. Such words of wisdom also plainly apply to how markets and societies work, any lack of political, economic, and social values in a society's respective functions being seen as "reason before identity."

The sense of social identity has a significant impact on human behavior. But the question of social identity and its overpowering influence has to be posed as "where identities emerge by choice or passive recognition and how much reasoning can enter into the development of identity" (Sen 1999: 6). Rawls (1971) posits in his *Theory of Justice* that the framework of fairness for a group of people involves arriving at rules and guiding principles of social organization that pay particular attention to everyone's interests, concerns, and liberties. Applying this to the market economy and tracing the forceful assumption of Adam Smith's self-interest and human motivation suggest the prevalence and the important social role of such values as sympathy, generosity, public spirit, and other affiliate concerns do matter.

The economic functions of production and distribution and social norms contribute to the success of a market-based economy where productivity and discipline are greatly influenced by work ethics. Important to the "culture of the Fijian way of life" is the question of the glory of capitalism that everyone wants to share. Yet, moral quality of good business behavior is just as important. The unconstrained greed and/or moral success in societal behavior, or defense of particular customs and traditions, split up the nation whose citizens are not within normative reach of each other. Capitalism based on ethnic identity and economic affirmative actions came into conflict with economic liberalization policies of the globalization process in Fiji. Liberalization ultimately threatens state policies that seek to grant ethnically based preferences (Ratuva 2000).

The main drawback has been the absence of an inclusive political system, which could involve all communities in the country into unified action. The 1990 Constitution, for example, adopted a racially prescriptive stance, to the point that it caused an international outcry (EIU 1998). During the early 1990s, it is true that Fiji was making an effort toward pursuing a market-friendly strategy through various policy reforms. But, for the effective development of the necessary incentive regime, which needs to be tailored within such policies, (social) institutions need to be assigned a central role as the public sector is still a key player. The existing political atmosphere has, however, been far from conducive to ideal results. Prasad assesses the prime shortcoming in the following terms:

> The perception among the Fijian institutions is that Fijian aspirations can be enhanced in isolation from others' rights and against established norms and values of civil society, and that economic progress can be achieved without the certainty of property rights and equality of political rights based on sound democratic principles and good governance.[29]

A review of the 1990 Constitution, initiated in 1995, served as a good indication that favorable sociopolitical conditions were, in fact, lacking and had to be created.

The impact of institutional fallacy on economic prospects mainly operated through property rights. Land property rights in Fiji have unfortunately become, not simply institutional, but a key racial issue with grave economic consequences. The repercussions are visible both in the national economic performance and in the ethnic-wise contribution to gross domestic product.

Turning first to the ethnic-wise contribution, the Indo-Fijian community has been adversely affected by lack of secure land property rights. When a majority of them are engaged in sugarcane cultivation, there has been a significant disparity between their income and the income of those employed in the commercial and trading sectors. Income from cane farming has, as with other agricultural crops, been subjected to year-to-year fluctuations depending mainly on crop yields. Cost of production has been relatively high. Land has usually been under lease and, apart from the regular rent, additional payment of goodwill and other dues are also periodically demanded. Then there are the costs of fertilizer and processing. When allowance is made for defraying costs, the ultimate revenue does not compare favorably with what is earned in the commercial sector. It is posited that, since 1977, the difference between the incomes of an average Fijian and Indo-Fijian has risen by only 4 percentage points. Nevertheless, the income distribution variance between the two ethnic groups (i.e Fijians and Indo-Fijians) was substantially higher than that which prevailed across these groups.[30] This is besides the variability in income within the Indo-Fijian community, which has been the highest for any ethnic grouping in Fiji (Ahlburg 1995).

In the context of overall growth, the uncertainty in state policy on the renewal of land leases has affected productivity and development in the sugar and tourism sectors. There is, however, some room for optimism when the state is a partner with the private sector. According to Chand, the foreign companies in these joint ventures,

> particularly many large international hotel chains that operate in Fiji, do so in concert with the chiefs of the land-owning *mataqali*. These organizational arrangements exist as mechanisms to reduce uncertainty of property rights to resources. The outcome is once again at a cost to economic efficiency and the level of aggregate output.[31]

Another venture, which suffered due to weak and insecure property rights, has been the garment industry. Although preferential trading access through contracts with advanced countries provided some relief, there are several other areas where the industry has been on a losing trend. Operations like unsatisfactory offshore management, failure to reinvest profits, and the absence of linkages with domestic investors have deprived Fiji of long-term infrastructure investment and local capacity building. Insecurity of tenure has also led to exploitation and misuse of resources for personal gains and subverting political processes.

In the sugar industry, the non-renewal of land leases and land issues have contributed toward a decline in sugar production. Of the leases which expired between 1997 and 1999, only 26 percent have been renewed under the existing terms. Changes were suggested by the NLTB based on a two-part rental system: market rent plus a percentage of the production. But this "would be equivalent to double-dipping and could be regarded as repressive" (Lal *et al.* 2001). Nevertheless, the interim government of 2001 also suggested the two-part rental system with a rolling of 5, 10, 15, 20, or 30-year leases plus renewal halfway through the lease period. Furthermore, this is in addition to the goodwill payment to be made to the land owners, and to the NLTB for considering lease renewal under a new lease consideration fee that was previously called goodwill.[32] The opportunity cost of staying on the farm seems higher than the net return expected for most families, particularly for those with uncertainty of lease renewal, higher rental prices, and imperfectly specified property rights, as well as those farmers who experience violence.[33]

Lack of land property rights, where there were cultural differences mainly inferred by leaders for political and economic purposes, would lead to horizontal inequalities. Increasing anxiety has also, for example, been expressed in the land claims compensation of Fiji's hydroelectric dam, closure of a primary school and a health care centre, and mismanagement of funds by the Ministry of Agriculture after the May 2000 coup.[34] The displacement of people from the land due to cultural differences and the resentment position accentuated by leaders for institutional reasons have become sources of conflict in agrarian societies. In such a context where the government is dominated by one group the policies to correct inequalities may be thwarted. "Although the government acknowledged the severity of land problems, it continued to announce new deadlines and promises only to break them regularly" (Kurer 2001b: 304).

A common allegation is that the Fijians (the land owners) received a smaller proportion compared to the Indo-Fijian farmers. The available literature is, however, able to sufficiently explain the inequality of payment under the NLTB. Ward points out, for example, that tenancy of traditional landholdings and authority over groups' land provides the economic basis of the chiefly status, and that "30% of the land rents finds their way into chiefly coffers" (Ward 1995: 221). In 1998, NLTB distributed F$18,726,453, of which F$5.6 million was allocated to the chiefs (NLTB 1998). Another relevant factor is that, under the traditional Fijian practices, accountability for funds received is something of a non-entity.

The present state in Fiji indicates a lack of institutional structures and opportunities for cooperative problem solving, especially when societies are sharply divided on ethnic lines. The poorer sections in the capital market would face barriers in the form of a lack of income-earning capacity, which, in turn, would reduce a society's potential for productive investment, innovation, and human resource development. The political milieu in Fiji does not, under these circumstances, point towards a government motivated by considerations of improving its political support base and implementing redistributive reforms. The different communities in Fiji have contributed to increasing productivity and enhancing credibility of commitments. Thus, creating a social environment more conducive to property rights is vital. When the poor have more stakes in the asset base, the accountability of the various institutions for checking abuse of power at all levels is indispensable. Here, it is possible to cite the NLTB and other land-owning units of different levels: head of *vanua*, head of *yavusa*, head of *mataqali*, and members of *mataqali*. If ethnicity and social conflicts could be dismissed, not only would a range of hardship for all the communities disappear, but they would also involve themselves in the production process providing security for all. The government too could work, in consultation with all parties, towards a potentially favorable condition for better performance of the economy.

Impending "break-up": a challenge for Sri Lanka

It is, now, over a decade since the eminent political scientist Jeyaratnam Wilson titled the book he authored in 1988 as *The Break-Up of Sri Lanka* and wrote in its preface:

> My considered view is that Ceylon has already split into two entities. At present this is a state of mind; for it to become a territorial reality is a question of time. Patchwork compromises . . . are passing phenomena. The fact of the matter is that under various guises the Sinhalese elites have refused to share power with the principal ethnic minority, the Tamils.[35]

While it is true that, for all official purposes, Sri Lanka still remains intact, it is equally well known that, in reality, there are, true to Wilson's prophecy, two states exercising sovereign power over different territories within the island. Adrian Wijemanne, the Sinhalese historian, succinctly captures the condition in the following terms:

> The immediate question that arises from this situation is whether the Sri Lankan state in its original form encompassing the entire land mass of the island of Sri Lanka is still in existence. The answer must be in the negative for a substantial, recognizable and defined area of the island

is now under the control and occupation of another power, namely, the LTTE. The present Sri Lankan state exists and functions only within its area of control on the island – it has shrunk in size and reach and jurisdiction.[36]

He asserts that further proof is the presence of two contending armies and navies within the island's borders.

It has, on the whole, been an inevitable outcome of the dismal failure of Sri Lankan governments both in political and military terms. During the interim between Wilson's prediction and the present day, the government security forces were unable to militarily defeat the LTTE, fighting for an independent Tamil sovereign state. Neither did governments take any concrete or meaningful steps toward solving the problem and preventing an imminent collapse.

The Sinhalese and their governments are, however, fortunate that there is still room for some optimism and that they could, at least nominally, claim jurisdiction over the entire island. International political developments have, no doubt, been to their advantage. Lately, as a sequel to the Norwegian initiative, a cease-fire between the Sinhalese and Tamil warring parties was declared in February 2002 and a Memorandum of Understanding is currently in force with a view to safeguarding the truce. Moreover, a series of formal negotiations are also being held in a number of neutral locations.

Under these circumstances, policy implications in the Sri Lankan problem, unlike that of Fiji, are relatively less complicated and straightforward. Basically, the Sri Lankan conflict is a confrontation between two nations for land. The ethnic war is, in other words, a war for terrain. Land represents, in the end, the ideal resource base for economic power. But there has been a fundamental change in the historical relationship between land and economic power. There was a time when territorial domination and control over resources therein was the key to economic predominance. It is under these conditions that colonialism was pursued by western nations and, obviously, political power had to precede economic power. But, under the ongoing globalization process, economic domination is no longer tied to land. Capital accumulation, the basic prerequisite for modern-day growth, is possible only through economic integration in contrast to political integration of the past.

In this changing global context, the colonial character of the ethnic war in Sri Lanka is therefore anachronistic. It would be in the best interests of the Sinhalese nation to give up on its aggressive policy of land control and recognize the Tamilian will for nationhood and territorial sovereignty within their own regions. The Sinhalese government could, then, seek an economic integration, which would be beneficial for both Sinhalese and Tamil nations and ensure overall progress.

Moreover, on the other hand, the global political order too is gradually changing toward political disintegration. The birth of new nation-states based on ethnic lines is becoming an increasing reality. Meadwell, writing on the international order and the future of world politics, recognizes that:

> Those forces gathered together as "globalization" sometimes are argued to be the causes of a forthcoming watershed in world politics. Transnational dynamics . . . weaken the capacities and competences of states, both from within and from without. When these states contain stateless nations, these forces lower the opportunity costs of new state formation.[37]

He not only further posits that "State-making via unification is unlikely to be as important as it has been in the past," but also strongly argues that, in the event of a nation being stateless and members of such a nation actively seeking their own state, "accommodation" should be discouraged. Because arguments for accommodation, according to him, "including political accommodation (via consociational or federal arrangements, for example) . . . actually underestimate the importance of nationalism" (Meadwell 1999: 264–265).

The emerging scenario makes it immensely clear that a fundamental political rethink from Sinhalese quarters is paramount to salvage the situation. It is a truism that Sinhala chauvinism coupled with (Buddhist) religious nationalism is a major stumbling block. But, unless these forces wake up to reality or the ruling governments find ways and means of overwhelming their opposition, the de facto existence of a two-state Sri Lanka would continue indefinitely and mutate gradually towards a *de jure* situation.

Conclusion

The foregoing analysis traced how the democratic political structures of Fiji and Sri Lanka, inherited from the very fountain of parliamentary democracy, have slowly but steadily moved along a course of disintegration, signalling all the way a political degeneration. Besides the presence of other factors, land occupied a place of singular importance. Yet, the nature of its contribution in the two countries has been subject to a wide disparity.

In Fiji, the land problem is basically one of seeking property rights for the Indo-Fijians so that they could be equal players in the market. But, at the same time, they were fully aware that the tenure right was with the indigenous Fijians. The Indo-Fijian ethnic group was thus making only an economic claim without a political underpinning. When the gradual economic domination of the Indo-Fijians led to their acquiring political power, the Fijians became determined to oust them both from the political as well as economic arena. The worst casualty of this strategy has, however, been the Fijian economy, bringing misery to all concerned.

The Sri Lankan ethnic issue is, on the other hand, a conflict over territorial sovereign rights. Thus, the causes for the discord also run much deeper and are embedded in the history of the Sinhalese and Tamil nations. Although Tamil tenure rights have been violated in the Dry Zone colonization schemes, the hidden agenda has always been establishing Sinhalese sovereign right, which the Tamils have opposed. Even the current stance of peaceful negotiations does not seem to have affected the land policy of the Sri Lankan government, because there have been continued allegations from Tamil quarters that "colonization" efforts continue unabated.

The long duration of hostilities culminating in an ethnic war has, like Fiji, had its adverse consequences on the Sri Lankan economy. But Tamils, due to the continued persecution of Sinhalese governments, have suffered most. This has, in fact, been one of the major contributory factors to the outward migration of the Tamils.

Despite the complex issues involved in the conflict of the two countries, the chapter proposed that the policy options are relatively explicit and clear. But the real tragedy of Fiji and Sri Lanka has been that they have both been experimenting with policies which have attempted to treat the symptoms at the fringes without addressing the core issues.

Notes

1 For example, see Olson (1996) for an discussion of why some nations are rich and others poor.
2 For Fiji's experience, see Gounder (2002) and for Sri Lanka's, V. Nithiyanandam (2000).
3 Sri Lanka's colonial subjugation commenced in 1505, when the Portuguese captured the Western and Southern regions of the island and then the Northern Jaffna Kingdom in 1619. In 1658, the Dutch succeeded in ousting the Portuguese and taking control of the same areas. In 1796, it was the turn of the British to extend the western colonial hold on the island. They were, in their bid, able to overrun the remaining central region, paving the way not only for a unified island-wide administration, but also for the opening of plantations, which came to ultimately dominate the basic character of the island economy. The colonial experience of Fiji had, on the other hand, been relatively very short. It became a colony under the British Empire in October 1874 and remained so until its independence in October 1970. Fiji's colonial confrontation lasted, therefore, unlike Sri Lanka's, less than a century and had also singularly been under British influence. In contrast, Sri Lanka, after its multifaceted colonial domination of over four centuries, attained its independence in 1948. However, this study, in terms of Sri Lanka, will, for obvious reasons, entirely focus on the British colonial period.
4 But, despite this lower percentage, it is pertinent to note that at the time of independence, the Indian Tamil population constituted almost the same or sometimes even marginally exceeded the proportion of local Tamils. In the 1946 Census (the last conducted before Sri Lanka's independence in 1948), for example, while the Ceylon Tamil proportion was 11 percent, the share of the Indian Tamils was 11.7 percent. See also Department of Census and Statistics (1951: 113).

5 This has mainly been due to the belated exposure of the central Kandyan regions to western colonialism. When the rest of the Sinhala nation was under western colonial rule from 1505, the Kandyan Kingdom preserved its independence until the British captured it in 1815.

6 It should, however, be emphasized that the differences between the Sri Lankan and Indian Tamils were, at least at the time of the induction of the latter, very distinct and conspicuous. The indigenous Tamils displayed a superior quality of life with an obviously higher standard of living. Even the similarity in language and religion had been very thin and non-comparable. The Tamil language was spoken with differing accents and the Hindu religious worship and practices too were far apart. The geographical distance and the absence of a "Jinnah corridor" between the areas of Indian settlement and traditional homelands of local Tamils also prevented any form of easy interaction and more or less froze the separation.

7 S.J.V. Chelvanayakam had been in the forefront of this promotion toward unity and coined the new terminology "hill-country Tamils," giving up on the designation "Indian" and underlining the regional focus. See Wilson and Chelvanayakam (1994: 7, 50).

8 Later developments, however, signify that the Indian Tamils on their own are inclined to gravitate toward the native Tamil leadership. When a cease-fire was declared between the government security forces and Tamil militants in February 2002, some of the Indian Tamil political leaders volunteered to meet the Tamil militant leader Prabhakaran and solicited his support and assistance in protecting the rights of their people.

9 There is, however, an ongoing debate between the Sinhalese and Tamils on the issue of original settlement in the island. It is an area within historical and archaeological studies and lies outside the scope of this chapter. The nature of the debate itself suggests that it has only remote relevance to the current conflict, and both the ethnic communities have been present in the island from very ancient times. It could therefore be easily surmised that, for our purposes, both are indigenous to the island. For a concise account of the nature of the debate and issues involved, see Manogaran (2000).

10 For details, see Narayan (1984).

11 Extract of a letter from Herbert to Governor Gordon. Cited in Narayan (1984: 34).

12 The Sinhalese animosity was, as Nawaz Dawood points out, misdirected. It had picked on the hapless Indians, instead of the real enemy – the British imperialism. See Dawood (1980: 140).

13 For an elaborate account of this episode, see Shastri (1999: 65–86).

14 Backwardness of Indian Tamil population is well documented. The limited advance in the field of education has been examined by Little (1999). See BBC News/South Asia, "Hardships of Sri Lanka's Indian Tamils" (http://news.bbc.co. uk//low/english/world/south_asia/newsid_903000/903606.stm, August 30, 2000).

15 Rotuma is an island about 300 miles north of Fiji. The British annexed it in 1879 and administered it as a dependency of the colony of Fiji. After Fijian independence, Rotuma became a part of Fiji.

16 See also Powles (1996: 73–75).

17 The Fijians and Indo-Fijians held 22 seats each with another 8 allocated to other ethnic communities. See Government of Fiji (1970).

18 In the Indian subcontinent, Britain competed with the local entrepreneurs for production and markets, especially in the cotton textiles and iron and coal industries, leading to a high level of hostility and bitterness between the two parties.

19 For a comprehensive study of the Dry Zone in terms of agrarian development, see Farmer (1957).

20 The contribution of Manogaran (1994) in this context has been highly illuminating. For two of his noteworthy studies, see Manogaran (1994: 84–125; 1999: 151–159). For a case study on the Gal Oya Scheme, in one of the pioneering settlement projects, see Thangavelu, who presents interesting viewpoints on the project: "Sinhalese Have Cause to Celebrate the Golden Jubilee of Gal Oya Colonization Scheme" (http://www.tamilcanadian.com/eelam/analysis/coloni. html, June 10, 1999).

21 For a comprehensive analysis of the dichotomy between "settler" and "non-settler" colonial activity, see de Silva (1982: 51–72).

22 Engels to Kautsky, September 12, 1882, *Marx and Engels Selected Correspondence* (1943: 359; quoted from de Silva (1982: 53)).

23 L.B. Clarence, "One Hundred Years of British Rule in Ceylon," *Proceedings of the Royal Colonial Institute*, 27: 1895–1896; quoted from de Silva (1982: 53).

24 Manogaran (1994: 85).

25 It was also referred to as the Yan Oya Project, because water from the Mahaweli Ganga, the longest river in the island, was to be channeled via the Yan Oya into the Manal Aru valley to augment its supply of water.

26 Colonization in the Eastern Batticaloa District came under the Maduru Oya Project. When preliminary measures were undertaken in the early 1980s, many Tamils were evicted from the villages to make way for Sinhalese peasant settlers.

27 Manogaran (1994: 116; emphasis added).

28 It is interesting that both countries not only experimented with the same number of constitutions, but the interval between the documents has also been roughly the same. Sri Lanka began with the 1948 Soulbury Constitution and floated, after a little over two decades, the Republican Constitution in 1972, before substituting it within five years with another in 1977. Fiji's Constitution at independence in 1970 was replaced after two decades of its existence (with an interim gap of the coup in 1987) by a new one in 1990, only to be substituted after seven years in 1997 by a new document.

29 Prasad (1997: 7–8).

30 UNDP and Government of Fiji (1997). See also Ahlburg (1995).

31 Chand (2001: 106).

32 For a dichotomy of fee estimates based on Class I, II, and III land, see Lal *et al.* (2001).

33 Kurer concludes that "neglecting long-term effects will arise from cultural factors coupled with an inefficient system of land management" (2001a: 315).

34 www.fijilive.com/news.php3.01/v.htm, October 1, 2001.

35 See Wilson (1988: v).

36 Wijemanne (2002) explores this issue extensively in his work.

37 Meadwell (1999: 266).

Bibliography

Ahlburg, D.A. (1995) *Income Distribution and Poverty in Fiji*, Suva: UNDP.

Ali, A. (1973) "The Indians of Fiji," *Economic and Political Weekly*, 7 (36), September 8.

BBC News/South Asia (2000) "Hardships of Sri Lanka's Indian Tamils," http://news. bbc.co.uk//low/english/world/south_asia/newsid_903000/903606.stm, August 30.

Chand, S. (2001) "Lessons for Development from Pacific Island Countries," *Pacific Economic Bulletin*, 16: 95–108.

Dawood, N. (1980) *Tea and Poverty: Plantations and the Political Economy of Sri Lanka*, Hong Kong: Urban-Rural Mission, Christian Conference of Asia.

Department of Census and Statistics (1951) *Census of Ceylon 1946, Vol. I*, Colombo: Ceylon Government Press.

de Silva, S.B.D. (1982) *The Political Economy of Underdevelopment*, London: Routledge & Kegan Paul.

EIU (Economist Intelligence Unit) (1998) *Country Profiles: Pacific Islands*, London: EIU.

Elliot, C. (1975) *Patterns of Poverty in the Third World*, New York: Praeger.

Elster, J. (1994) "The Impact of Constitutions on Economic Performance," in M. Bruno and B. Pleskovic (eds) *Proceedings of the World Bank Annual Conference on Development Economics*, Washington, DC: The World Bank.

Farmer, B.H. (1957) *Pioneer Peasant Colonization in Ceylon: A Study in Asian Agrarian Problems*, London: Oxford University Press.

France, P. (1969) *The Charter of the Land: Customs and Colonisation in Fiji*, Melbourne: Oxford University Press.

Furnivall, J.S. (1944) *Netherlands India*, Cambridge: Cambridge University Press.

Gounder, R. (2002) "Democracy, Economic Freedom, Fiscal Policy and Growth: Findings and Reflection for Fiji," *Contemporary Economic Policy*, 20: 234–245.

Government of Fiji (1970) *Constitution of Fiji 1970*, Suva: Government of Fiji.

Kurer, O. (2001a) "Land Tenure and Sugar Production in Fiji: Property Rights and Economic Performance," *Pacific Economic Bulletin*, 16: 94–105.

—— (2001b) "Land Politics in Fiji: Of Failed Land Reforms and Coups," *Journal of Pacific History*, 36: 299–315.

Lal, P., Lim-Applegate, H., and Reddy, M. (2001) "The Land Tenure Dilemma in Fiji: Can Fijian Landowners and Indo-Fijian tenants Have Their Cake and Eat it Too?," *Pacific Economic Bulletin*, 16: 106–119.

Lawson, S. (1996) *Traditional Versus Democracy in the South Pacific*, Cambridge: Cambridge University Press.

Little, A.W. (1999) *Laboring to Learn: Towards a Political Economy of Plantations, People and Education in Sri Lanka*, London: Macmillan.

Manogaran, C. (1994) "Colonization as Politics: Political Use of Space in Sri Lanka's Ethnic Conflict," in C. Manogaran and B. Pfaffenberger (eds) *The Sri Lankan Tamils: Ethnicity and Identity*, Boulder, CO: Westview Press.

—— (ed.) (1999) "Settlements and Forced Evictions of Tamils in the Northern and Eastern Provinces," in Academic Society of Tamil Students, *International Conference on Tamil Nationhood and the Search for Peace in Sri Lanka*, Ottawa: Carleton University and the University of Ottawa.

—— (2000) *Untold Story of Ancient Tamils in Sri Lanka*, Chennai: Kumaran Publishers.

Meadwell, H. (1999) "Stateless Nations and the Emerging International Order," in T.V. Paul and J.A. Hall (eds) *International Order and the Future of World Politics*, Cambridge: Cambridge University Press.

Moore, M. (1985) *The State and Peasant Politics in Sri Lanka*, Cambridge: Cambridge University Press.

Narayan, J. (1984) *The Political Economy of Fiji*, Suva: South Pacific Review Press.

Native Land Trust Board (1998) *ALTA Task Force Final Report, Vol. 1: The Survey, Findings and Recommendations*, Suva: Parliament of Fiji, Parliamentary Paper No. 4.

Nithiyanandam, V. (2000) "Ethnic Politics and Third World Development: Some Lessons from Sri Lanka's Experience," *Third World Quarterly*, 21: 283–311.

Olson M. Jr (1996) "Big Bills Left on the Sidewalk: Why Some Nations are Rich and Others Poor?," *Journal of Economic Perspectives*, 12: 3–24.

Ponnambalam, S. (1981) *Dependent Capitalism in Crisis: The Sri Lankan Economy, 1948–1980*, London: Zed Press.

Powles, G.C. (1996) "Constitutional Reforms in Fiji," *Pacific Economic Bulletin*, 11: 73–75.

Prasad, B.C. (1997) "Property Rights, Governance and Economic Development," in G. Chand and V. Naidu (eds) *Fiji: Coups, Crises, and Reconciliation, 1987–1997*, Suva: Fiji Institute of Applied Studies.

—— and Tisdell, C.A. (1996) "Getting Property Rights 'Right': Land Tenure in Fiji," *Pacific Economic Bulletin*, 11: 31–46.

Premdas, R. (1995) *Ethnic Conflict and Development: The Case of Fiji*, Aldershot: Avebury.

Ratuva, S. (2000) "Addressing Inequality? Economic Affirmative Action and Communal Capitalism in Post-coup Fiji," in A. Haroon Akram-Lodhi (ed.) *Confronting Fiji Futures*, Canberra: Asia-Pacific Press.

Rawls, J. (1971) *Theory of Justice*, New York: Oxford University Press.

Shastri, A. (1999) "Estate Tamils, the Ceylon Citizenship Act of 1948 and Sri Lankan Politics," *Contemporary South Asia*, 8: 65–86.

Sen, A. (1999) *Reason Before Identity*, Oxford: Oxford University Press.

Thangavelu, V. (1999) "Sinhalese Have Cause to Celebrate the Golden Jubilee of Gal Oya Colonization Scheme," http://www.tamilcanadian.com/eelam/analysis/coloni.html, June 10.

UNDP (United Nations Development Programme) and Government of Fiji (1997) *Fiji Poverty Report*, Suva: UNDP and Government of Fiji.

Ward, R.G. (1965) *Land Use and Population in Fiji*, London: Her Majesty's Stationery Office.

—— (1995) "Land, Law and Customs: Diverging Realities in Fiji," in R.G. Ward and E. Kingdom (eds) *Land Custom and Practice in the South Pacific*, Cambridge: Cambridge University Press.

Wijemanne, A. (2002) "The Core Issue," *Circle Digest*, May 21.

Wijetunga, W.M.K. (1974) *Sri Lanka in Transition*, Colombo: Wesley Press.

Wilson, J.A. (1988) *The Break-Up of Sri Lanka*, London: C. Hurst & Co.

—— and Chelvanayakam, S.J.V. (1994) *The Crisis of Sri Lankan Tamil Nationalism, 1947–1977*, London: C. Hurst & Co.

10 Indigenous accumulation and the question of land

The Kimberley region of Western Australia in the second half of the twentieth century*

Tony Smith

Introduction and background

> The granting of land to former hunter-gatherers in the United States, Canada and Australia during the 1970s raises several questions, not least why capitalist nation states should recognise or deliberately create non-capitalist forms of land holding. Australia is especially significant.
>
> (Peterson 1985: 85)

In Australian Aboriginal affairs the period popularly known as "self-determination," or what I have termed "indigenous trusteeship," began in the late 1960s and early 1970s, coinciding with the end of the post-World War II long boom. This period – especially in the Kimberley, an extensive and remote district situated in the far north of Western Australia (see Map 10.1) – was ushered in by the growing failure of both segregationary and integrationary policies as directed by state trusteeship. The policy of state trusteeship had seen, since the time of federation in 1901, the state as the principal instrument and facilitator of development and involved, among other things, sequestering indigenes on pastoral stations and reserves.[1] This approach was devised for facilitating the provision of much required Aboriginal labor to the pastoral industry, as well as to assist in maintaining social order.

The inability of these policies to deal with changing economic conditions – at the close of the global long boom in the late 1960s and early 1970s – was graphically illustrated by rates of rapidly increasing unemployment and the subsequent mass migration of regional indigenous populations to towns and centers across the Kimberley. This chapter will argue that, as a consequence, new policies were instituted, including most notably the introduction of land rights.[2]

The established liberal orthodox[3] or conventional view, however, points to a number of factors which combined to "create a favorable climate for

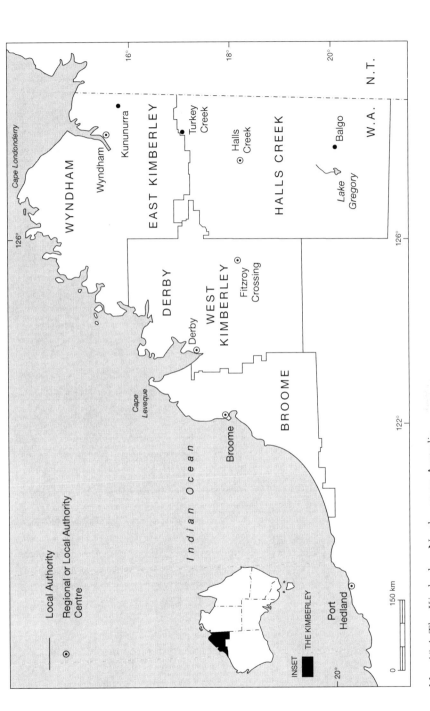

Map 10.1 The Kimberley, Northwestern Australia

Source: *Western Australia, Pastoral Edition North Sheet*, Department of Lands and Surveys, Perth (1: 2,000,000).

changes in [government] policy" during the early 1970s. The anthropologist Nicolas Peterson argues that these factors for change included the increasing "international attention paid to Australia because of its colonial role in Papua New Guinea, the embarrassment of the White Australia policy at a time when links with Asia were being built and the influence of black activists such as the Black Power movement" (Peterson 1985: 94). According to this view, the new policy agenda was implemented because the Western Australian and Commonwealth governments had been the essential cause for the "peripheralization of such fourth world people by perpetuating an unequal distribution of resources," especially land, and was "now seeking a more complete incorporation of such people on any one of a number of grounds, such as equity, elimination of political problems or expansion of the labor force" (Peterson 1985: 85). Manning Clark, the eminent Australian historian, has suggested that the Labor government (1972–1975) led by Gough Whitlam introduced Aboriginal land rights and social reform on the basis that it was "not just because their case was beyond argument but because all Australians were diminished so long as Aborigines were denied their rightful place" (Clark 1986: 241). Moreover, many of the supporters of this policy, according to Rosemary Neill, embraced the "belief that winning back ancestral lands can by itself rehabilitate communities fragmented by the brutalities of history, welfarism and an everyday culture of substance abuse" (Neill 2002: 25).

The orthodox view, however, has largely ignored or chosen not to consider the impact that material issues such as growing unemployment had on the maintenance of social order. And the rapid increase in unemployment, more than anything else during the early 1970s, as will be shown, was determining changes in Federal and State government policy, not just in Australia but elsewhere (see for example the situation in the United States and Canada throughout this period).[4] The advent of large numbers of unemployed gathering on the outskirts of towns, and the corresponding social dislocation and poverty, explains to a large degree the Western Australian and Federal governments' attempts – previously achieved by the policy of state trusteeship – to retain people in regional and remote areas by, among other things, ceding large tracts of land to Aboriginal controlled corporations and organizations.

In the Kimberley, in an effort to deal with the consequences of a growing relative surplus population – of which indigenes were a significant part – the Commonwealth and State governments, in consultation with an emerging Aboriginal leadership, began to formulate the new policy direction of indigenous trusteeship. By the early 1970s it was possible to conclude that: "The emphasis was now more on community development and on acknowledgment that some aspects of aboriginality might have merit" (Jennet 1988: 229). In 1971 the Commonwealth government's Council of Aboriginal Affairs argued that, "increasing emphasis must be given to measures to promote the greater economic independence of Aboriginal Australians" on "their land," particularly in the "north and centre as communities, and to strengthen their capacities to manage their own affairs."[5] Further, the Western Australian and Commonwealth governments would no longer direct trusteeship themselves but ostensibly passed the responsibility of trusteeship to local indigenous groups – such as "community leaders" or "traditional elders"[6] – in an endeavor to maintain order and contain the effects of unemployment.

Utilizing empirical data (most never before accessed) – collected from, among other sources, the State Records Office, National Archives, and Hansard – this chapter investigates the policy of state trusteeship that was instituted during the period prior to the late 1960s, which, *inter alia*, supplied indigenous labor to white commercial operations, as well as effectively obstructing Aboriginal access to land and business opportunities. State trusteeship will be contrasted with the policy of indigenous trusteeship that began to emerge in the late 1960s and early 1970s. The principal architect of, and advisor to, the policy of indigenous trusteeship – a policy that was highly conducive to indigenous commercial activities – was an emerging Aboriginal leadership. The economic space created by these policies, especially those designed to soak up unemployment, provided an indigenous business class – at this stage, predominantly small business operators – with many commercial opportunities. In short, Aboriginals were now to be the instruments of their own development. It will be argued here that the shift toward a new policy of "indigenous trusteeship" was important in several ways in underpinning the expansion of indigenous business. This is the sense in which the chapter will explore the evolution of Aboriginal business development out of a realignment in government Aboriginal development policy.

The idea of development, which arose at the genesis of capitalism, assumed as its most important goal the "amelioration of the social crisis" that had accompanied capitalist industrialization. Industrialization, including that which occurred in rural Australia,[7] substantially involved the rapid transfer of people from disparate regions to areas of industrial production (Cowen and Shenton, 1996: 116). "Progress," or unmitigated development, is comprised of both destructive (negative) and constructive (positive) components, which occur simultaneously as immanent process. According to the positivists, who first identified this process in the early nineteenth century, "Progress" could only be maintained by way of "intentional constructive activity" of development. For the positivists, "industrial production and organisation" was accepted as the historically given component of the motion toward an "organic positive or natural stage of society in Europe" (Cowen and Shenton 1996: 116). And, as Michael Cowen and Bob Shenton have shown, the "making of tradition" (as artifice) as part of the modern idea of development, embodied an expectation that for development to occur necessarily requires compensation for the destruction, or negative aspect, caused by "how development happens" (Cowen 1998: 2).[8]

In the period after World War II – and in light of the destructive implications of immanent (or spontaneous) development that had become obvious during the Great Depression – in a move to retain productive potential and to shore up social cohesion and order, the implementation by governments (guided by advisors such as J.M. Keynes)[9] of a welfare or social security system, and overseen by their agents or trustees, was viewed as an integral part of "progressive" development policy. The provision of government-sponsored welfare, such as unemployment benefits, has been one method, albeit artificial, of providing the second best alternative to the effort of work.

The well-known Aboriginal leader and political activist, Noel Pearson, relates this situation as it occurred in Australia. Pearson has argued that, beginning in the late 1960s and early 1970s, the collapse of the once dominant regional pastoral industries employing large numbers of indigenous labor witnessed the introduction of across-the-board welfare:

> Welfare schemes for Aboriginal people have been slightly modified and extended to accommodate our circumstances, but our passive welfare provisioning is fundamentally similar to the schemes that support marginalized groups among non-Aboriginal Australians. Because of our history of dispossession, our remoteness from economic growth centres and our current inability to compete on the labour market we qualify, almost to a woman and to a man, as recipients of passive welfare.
>
> (Pearson 2000: 14)

The aim of government policy, especially in the late twentieth century, in order to ameliorate the negative, has been to reassert, or reinvent, the "value of community," particularly when confronted by the destructive element that manifests itself, for example, in high rates of unemployment, poverty, and social dislocation. "This purpose has been so well assimilated in the course of social action that the value of community has come to be seen as a natural quality of being human" (Cowen and Shenton 1996: 56). As the function of development became the means to repair the negative tendencies of capitalism through the reconstruction of social order: "[t]o develop then, was to ameliorate the social misery which arose out of the immanent process of capitalist growth" (Cowen and Shenton 1996: 56).[10]

In regions such as the Kimberley, the "administrative changes" involved in the policy move to indigenous trusteeship directly corresponded with a period of great social upheaval for Aboriginal people (Bolton 1981: 168). In 1967 Kim Beazley senior, later Federal Minister for Education in the Whitlam Labor government (1972–1975), explicitly recognized the terms of the shift in Aboriginal conditions and the "new" parameters for government policy, when he argued:

The Aboriginal population at present is an underprivileged, underfed, underpaid, untrained labour force, increasing in numbers and not closely considered. While we enthuse about the development of our natural resources we make no real effort to draw this force into the process of development. We are allowing social dynamite to accumulate.[11]

From the late 1960s, the global economy, and the Western Australian economy in particular, encountered crises that were reflective of the coming to an end of the global post-war long boom. One result of the end of the long boom was that export prices for many Australian primary commodities, including beef, were significantly less buoyant than in the two decades preceding the 1970s. In the late 1960s and early 1970s, pastoralists were especially hard hit, and this had its greatest impact on the Kimberley, where the majority of Aborigines were employed in the pastoral industry (Bolton 1981: 168).

State trusteeship, pre-1968

In the Kimberley region of Western Australia, prior to the late 1960s, Federal and State governments actively restricted indigenous capital's access to land, labor, and capital markets. These restrictions were mainly instigated to protect white pastoralism and other commercial ventures, as well as part of an overarching policy of state trusteeship, whereby church missions and pastoral stations were part of an arrangement to order rural Aboriginals. Before European contact in the Kimberley, Aboriginal social relations were dynamic and involved concepts of land ownership, and wide-scale trading and production. The arrival of pastoralism, which in the Kimberley began in the 1880s, witnessed both the impoverishment of the indigenous population and the checking by local colonial power of the possibility of indigenous primary accumulation. The Western Australian explorer, Edward John Eyre, considered that "the manner in which . . . [the original owners'] lands had been appropriated for the benefit of white settlers was thoroughly iniquitous" (Hiatt 1996: 18).

From the commencement of the Kimberley pastoral industry – which quickly became the mainstay of the regional economy and by far its largest employer – substantial tracts of the most productive land were given over to white pastoralists and farmers. As an indication of the extent to which the pastoral industry had developed, by the end of the nineteenth century, sheep numbers in the West Kimberley had reached 232,000, while the cattle herd throughout the whole of the Kimberley was estimated at 205,000 head (*Kimberley Region Plan* 1987: 65).

State governments of all political persuasions during the period 1897–1969, through various means, assisted in providing much needed labor to these white enterprises by way of, among other things: subsidizing the cost of maintaining indigenous labor on station properties, church missions and reserves; restricting the movement of indigenous people; and providing training and education. As the Secretary of the Pastoralists Association argued in 1927:

> The Aboriginal is a valuable adjunct to the pastoral industry, and without him . . . it would be impossible to carry on under conditions as they exist. . . . Frankly until their Profit and Loss Accounts warrant it, pastoralists think there should be no cash payment to or on behalf of aboriginals employed by them.[12]

Indeed, low-cost indigenous labor – either paid in truck or at wages well below award rates – is what maintained pastoral station profit margins up until the late 1960s.

Policies to do with Aboriginal affairs instituted by Western Australian governments, in the period before the late 1960s, can best be summarized as "state trusteeship," and involved a complex mixture of "integration" and "segregation." Government officials and others directed these policies. Crucial aspects of this policy included enlisting agencies such as the Church, who believed they possessed the understanding of what was required to make development constructive (trusteeship). As the Reverend Jobst, of the Kimberley Vicariate, made clear:

> We owe our Aborigines the services we have extended to them since 1890, such as education both academic and technical, religious and social, housing and general improvement of their standard of living. Our missionaries have been and have acted as *trustees* [my emphasis] of the Aborigines, and when both the Government and Church authorities are satisfied that the Aboriginal people can manage their own affairs, have their own teachers, doctors, lawyers and religious ministers, then we will gladly hand over management and ownership to them. In my opinion these people have a long way to go.[13]

These policies were put in place for the intention of developing those who remained underdeveloped – in this case impoverished indigenous Western Australians. In other words, the implementation of these policies saw the state (and its agents) as the principle instrument of development.

Significantly, during the course of state trusteeship, especially in the Kimberley, State government administrations, by giving wholesale support to white-owned businesses, effectively and purposefully stifled indigenous commercial activities. There is much evidence of budding indigenous enterprise throughout this period. However, aspirant indigenous capital was not yet sufficiently organized – either politically or economically – to be able to successfully compete with more established sectors of capital, particularly those with strong links to government, and any advance was quickly checked.

Indigenous enterprise during the period of state trusteeship: one step forward two steps back

In Australia, according to Ian Palmer, demands for the control and owner-ship of land by Aboriginal persons, albeit largely unsuccessful, can be traced back at "least as far as the 1930s" if not further (Palmer 1988: 1). In 1928, it was reported in *The West Australian* newspaper that a number of Western Australian Aboriginals, some of whom were farmers, came together to form a short-lived political pressure group in order to lobby the State Labor government and its Premier (Philip Collier) for, among other things, citizen-ship rights, including the right to own property. These initiatives were vehemently opposed by the agricultural industry and – with much assist-ance from their political representatives – these demands by indigenous agitators were quickly silenced.[14]

Don McLeod,[15] Aboriginal activist and company director, maintains that in the early 1940s the Northern Development and Mining Corporation was the first privately owned Aboriginal Company registered in Western Australia, and most likely Australia (McLeod 1984: 100). The company was initially involved in mining in the northwest, and a report noted that the company had become viable and felt that it "will become a permanent establishment." The report goes on to suggest that to a "large extent, com-plete success is dependent upon the success of its mining operations, the sole source of finance for all activities. At the present time the chief mineral being mined is columbite, valued up to £3,000 per ton. If the demand continues the project is an assured success" (McLeod 1984: 100). Later, during the early 1950s, the Northern Development and Mining Company commenced pastoral operations by purchasing four station properties. These properties included: Riverdale Station (£10,000), Yandeyarra Station (£9,000), Meentheena Station (£5,000), and Glen Ern Station (for an undisclosed sum) (McLeod 1984: 104).

In spite of, or more correctly because of, the successful commercial enter-prises undertaken by the Northern Development and Mining Company, there were deliberate and effective acts of sabotage. Sustained government action, often utilizing draconian means,[16] on behalf of vested interests, ulti-mately forced the Company to scale down operations dramatically.

As an indication of the concern shown by white business interests toward McLeod and similar indigenous operations, the Secretary of the Pastoralists and Graziers Association wrote to the Minister for Native Welfare, E.H. Lewis, and stated:

> The Yalgoo District Committee of this Association has notified the Executive of the presence of Mr. D. McLeod in the Yalgoo area. The Association is deeply concerned at his presence there as it is only too mindful of his activities . . . and its effects both on the native and pastoral industry. . . . No doubt your Department is watching the activities

closely. The Association wishes to assure you of its assistance should it be needed.[17]

According to McLeod, during the period between the 1940s and early 1960s, "the authorities were bent on wrecking any [indigenous] project" (1984: 105). Furthermore, "The destruction of our companies was accomplished quite deliberately by a morally corrupt state" (McLeod 1984: 122).

In the mid 1950s, assets of the Northern Mining and Development Company, including the mining and pastoral operations, were broken up and sold to corporations including Bell Brothers – a large Western Australian company (McLeod 1984: 104).[18] State intervention as experienced by indigenous enterprises, throughout the period of state trusteeship, shows that indigenous businesses were not sufficiently organized – either politically or economically – to adequately combat other commercial interests. Indigenous enterprises held little state power at both State and Federal levels and remained severely restricted in their commercial activities.

Another incident reflective of this situation was a letter sent by the District Officer to the Commissioner of Native Welfare, dated May 13, 1954. The District Officer outlined a complaint received from the Fitzroy Crossing storeowner, Mr Fallan, regarding the establishment of a store on the nearby mission, which was in direct competition with his business:

> Mr. Fallan [a white store owner] . . . was adamant on the point that Mr. P. Walker [indigenous proprietor] sold goods in a quantity that affected his trading. . . . As Mr. Walker is absent . . . the matter has been left in abeyance until such time as I [the District Officer] am able to interview him in respect to Mr. Fallan's allegations.[19]

Presumably, the complaint was made in the knowledge that the Department of Native Welfare would act on the "allegations" and close the offending store.[20]

As a consequence of the privileged position extended to white commercial interests, there was generated a great deal of anger within sections of the indigenous population. As one Commissioner of Native Affairs reported: "There is evidence . . . of a growing resentment and bitterness between white and hybrid populations that is bordering upon class hatred." What is more, according to the Commissioner, "it cannot be considered racial since the hybrids are descendants of Caucasian stock" (Native Affairs 1949: 6).

In 1958 recognition was made by the Special Committee investigating Aboriginal matters in Western Australia that there should be some consideration for those indigenous people who had been deprived of their land and were being constrained in their commercial activities: "The fact [is] that the aborigine has suffered such extreme disabilities and injustices in the past that common humanity demands that he be given some appropriate recompense. One factor alone (and there are many others) may justify special assistance – the confiscation of his land without due compensation" (*Report of the Special Committee* 1958: 9).

It was argued by the Special Committee that in some areas, such as the Kimberley, there existed a stratum of indigenous people, who, the Committee believed, had the ability and desire to operate small businesses and should be assisted: "The deserving native warrants special financial and other assistance, and there is now ample legislative provision under the Native Welfare Act to cover such projects, provided the necessary funds are made available." It was also noted that: "The committee is of the opinion that these surveys should not be confined to farming only, but should extend to pastoral, mining, fishing, market gardening and any other likely industries." Accordingly, "It may be possible to operate small commercial concerns cooperatively, but no desire to combine in such a way has been evidenced by the part-aboriginal who lives in localities where such experiments could be tried" (*Report of the Special Committee* 1958: 26).

In other words, Aboriginal business people at this time had yet to reach a scale where the benefits of organizing collectively were recognized. Yet the individualist stance taken by these business people also suggests a keen understanding of the debilitating effects on commercial operations of having to provide welfare to friends and relatives. Indeed, as the Special Committee specifically noted, a "number of men who would have been suitable leaders in such enterprises, informed the committee that, while they would welcome financial assistance to undertake certain commercial activities, they preferred this to be on an individual rather than a collective basis" (*Report of the Special Committee* 1958: 26). Needless to say, the recommendation by the Committee for government support of indigenous "commercial concerns," either in the provision of land or finance, was left in abeyance.

Ernie Mitchell, Chairman of Directors of the indigenous corporation known as the Pindan Group, published a pamphlet in the early 1960s calling for a government license to allow his organization to export iron ore from Mt Goldsworthy (a rich and massive source of iron ore) in the northwest of Western Australia. According to Mitchell: "The granting of an export licence to us, the only successful self-contained Aboriginal group in Australia, would go a long way towards silencing the many critics of Australia's policy towards the original Australians."[21] Furthermore:

We do not ask for an export licence on terms different from those that would be applied to other persons or groups. We do ask that the following facts be considered:

(a) We are lifetime residents of the district.
(b) We have the mining skills, and the workforce necessary to handle the project.

(c) We are familiar with the problems that may arise, and have experience of solving such problems in recent years. We have been
basically responsible for producing many thousands of tons of
valuable minerals.

(d) We can make arrangements equivalent to those of any other sound
business concern, and we have a pool of labour, resident in the district, and accustomed to working in the climactic and other arduous
conditions of the Mt Goldsworthy area.

(e) We are aware, as all Australians should be, that our country's policy
in New Guinea towards the natives, and in Australia towards us,
has been vigorously attacked in the councils of the United Nations
Organisation. . . . We feel to grant us, the Aboriginal people of the
Pindan Group, an iron ore export licence, would go a long way
towards convincing such critics of our Government's sincerity
and goodwill towards us, and would be a major contribution to
the realization of our plans to raise our standards to the level of our
white fellow Australians by enterprise and hard work. We do not
seek charity.[22]

In 1962, despite the pleas of the Pindan Company, Goldsworthy Mining
Ltd (a BHP-controlled company) was granted a lease to mine ore at Mt
Goldsworthy (Crowley and de Garis 1970: 98).[23] It was not until the 1970s
and 1980s, and the advent of land rights legislation and later the High Court
Mabo decision (overturning the legal concept of *terra nullius*),[24] that indigenous corporations – this time represented by well-organized political
structures, such as the Kimberley Land Council – would enter into part-
nerships and other arrangements with mining companies and receive
royalties and associated economic benefits from commercial operations
conducted on "their land." Insofar as the scale of indigenous business activities is concerned, there is a distinct contrast between the period covering
the pre-1940s–1960s (state trusteeship), and the multiplex business operations that arose in the 1970s and 1980s (indigenous trusteeship).

To a significant degree, the burgeoning labor scarcity during the 1950s
and 1960s explains the State and Federal governments' continuing engage-
ment in the reproduction of indigenous labor for commercial operations in
the Kimberley. This action was undertaken on behalf of not only those
established and well-organized commercial associations that had historically
cultivated strong and effective political connections and representation, but
also the emerging mining and industrial concerns.

The Department of Native Welfare, "a very effective labour exchange," 1960–1969[25]

There is marked over-employment in this district, and the Field Officer is in
the happy position of having more jobs available than natives to fill them –

this results in a firm policy of guiding the workers to the stations that provide the best conditions and amenities.

(Native Welfare 1962: 34)

In Western Australia, between 1960 and 1968, due to a growing labor shortage, indigenous labor was required in increasing numbers. This was especially the case in agricultural and pastoral regions such as the Kimberley. For example, the Department of Native Welfare could report that in the Kimberley district of Broome:

> Wages and general conditions of employment show a gradual improvement. The average minimum wage being paid is in the vicinity of £6 per week with the more skilled worker demanding and receiving the basic wage or better . . . at the present time the native is more favorably regarded as an employee than for many years past.
>
> (Native Welfare 1962: 34)

According to the Department, the "traditional industries" of the Kimberley were in the early 1960s still providing the "greatest employment opportunities for native laborers." Throughout this time, the vast majority of indigenous labor was "employed on cattle and sheep stations but running a clear second at this stage," more than at any time before, was the "employment of natives in towns. So great [was] the demand from this quarter that the stations [began to] lose more and more each year" (Native Welfare 1960: 35).

During the 1960s, as a consequence of severe labor shortages and the continuing drift into towns, indigenous labor was still forcibly sequestered on pastoral stations and missions. In 1961 the Western Australian Police Commissioner, J.M. O'Brien, responding to complaints from the Pastoralists' Association about Aboriginal people leaving their designated place of work, pointed out:

> My District Inspector at Broome reports that vagrancy laws are applied to natives at various times in Northern towns, by police throughout the district, with the consent of and by arrangement with the local Native Welfare Officer. Discretion is naturally exercised in applying this law in Northern areas.[26]

This was done in order to return itinerant "natives" to their pastoral or mission settlements.

From the early 1960s, development in the Kimberley was occurring at such a rapid pace that the Commissioner of Native Welfare could make this bold assertion:

> There is no doubt that natives will always fit the pattern of economic life in the remote area and the new skills imparted and old skills

improved natives will never want for employment here. Wages are always improving and must continue to improve due now mainly to the shortage of labour but also the vastly more educated and semi-skilled natives entering employment.

(Native Welfare 1960: 35)

In 1966, labor shortages in the Kimberley reached such a level that some farmers at Kununurra "went to the extent of importing native labour from outside the State" (Native Welfare 1966: 10). This predicament, according to the Department, did not affect the "local employment situation in any way and the position for the future appears very promising." The Department also assumed that, in the "event of the pastoral award coming into force, a vast unemployment situation is not anticipated as it is felt that many employment avenues outside the pastoral industry will be open to native workers" (Native Welfare 1966: 10). The Department's optimism about future employment potential was, of course, premised on the continuation of the global long boom, and the ongoing pro-development policies of the State and Federal governments.

By the late 1960s however, global forces that had sustained the post-1945 long boom were already abating, and for the Kimberley region the decline would lead to a very dramatic transformation in economic conditions, especially those experienced by indigenes. The Kimberley pastoral industry, hitherto the largest employer of indigenous labor, was to be particularly affected.

End of an era: the Kimberley pastoral industry, 1968–1975

with poor economic conditions and heavy domestic supplies of beef in the mid 1970s many of the major importing countries imposed quantitative limitations on their beef imports. Major beef exporting countries such as Australia, were hard hit.

(CBCS 1980: 344)

The dramatic reduction in Aboriginal pastoral employment beginning in the late 1960s was driven to a large degree by changes in the long-term structure of the pastoral industry, with increases in capitalization and expansion of corporate entities,[27] coupled with decreasing rates of viability and profitability. In other words, the ongoing process of the concentration of ownership was expedited by the deteriorating economic situation. The Commonwealth Bureau of Census and Statistics depicted the industry, as it existed in the late 1960s and early to mid 1970s, as being "associated with low beef prices, poor seasonal conditions and producer liquidity pressure" (CBCS 1980: 344).

The Kimberley Pastoral Industry Inquiry, chaired by Brian Jennings and set up by the Western Australian Burke Labor government to investigate the

Table 10.1 Lease numbers and business number changes between 1963 and 1983

Year	No. of leases	No. of station businesses	Total area (million ha.)
1963	342	123	22.25
1979	101	68	22.77
1983	93	63	22.04

Source: Jennings (1983: 35).

viability of the industry, described the immediate aftermath of the global long boom period, beginning in the early 1970s, as the time when the "apparently relatively stable economic climate," that had existed in the Kimberley during the 1950s and 1960s, came to a close. And, by the early 1970s, the "full effect of the beef slump" had become obvious (Jennings 1983: 18). The decline in beef prices – culminating in 1974 when beef reached its lowest price in over two decades – was attributed to worldwide overproduction, especially in Europe. "As a result prices collapsed on world export markets and the slump in Australia's beef industry was severe."[28] Importantly, "Beef from cattle slaughtered at Wyndham, Broome and Derby in the Kimberley Division [was] principally for export" (CBCS 1977: 377–378).[29]

The Pastoral Industry Inquiry also recognized that a major transformation of the industry was occurring which included the growing concentration of the ownership of pastoral leases and businesses in the hands of what it termed "absentee-owners" (see Table 10.1).[30] The Inquiry also noted the increasing ownership of pastoral enterprises by Aboriginal "owner-operators" (Jennings 1983: 18).

In 1968 compulsory award wages were introduced into the pastoral industry – previously Aboriginal pastoral workers had been paid at rates below those paid to white workers.[31] Combined with the global economic slump, the exodus of rural labor, and the worsening unemployment situation can be immediately attributed to the introduction of these award wages:

> A major topic of conjecture and concern has been the introduction into the industry of the application of the Federal Pastoral Award to the employment of natives on station properties and its effects on rural communities. It was felt in many quarters that this would be responsible for the movement of large numbers of natives from the stations into towns and, indeed, it appeared that this was so during the first three months after the application of the Award in December 1968.[32]

The decision to introduce the Pastoral Award meant that station owners could justifiably evict their Aboriginal tenants on the grounds that it was too expensive to pay wages to all inhabitants. In effect, the Award enabled pastoralists to significantly reduce their costs in increasingly difficult macroeconomic conditions. As one Kimberley station owner commented: "The stores . . . used to comprise about 4 tons of flour, 2 tons of sugar, several tons of tinned goods, a couple of bales of blankets for the wet season, and much clothing. . . . Now the order could be much smaller and a lot of money saved" (Schubert 1992: 88).[33] Thereafter, rather than assume the burden of indirect wages themselves in an unfavorable economic climate, pastoralists successfully transferred the costs of maintaining a surplus population to the public sector, namely the Commonwealth, even though this would mean payment of award wages to some Aboriginals (Hartwig 1978: 136). According to one account, "It was no accident" that the Federal parliamentary leader of the Country Party, Jack McEwen, "himself took the initiative in formulating the new policy," in an effort to reduce labor costs to an absolute minimum on pastoral stations and farms (Hartwig 1978: 136).

Station owners, battling falling commodity prices and decreasing rates of profit, from the late 1960s, were driven even more emphatically to restructure production. Now with the aid of technology, such as aerial mustering and the use of motorbikes, pastoral stations need only employ contractors during busy times. As the Western Australian Minister for Native Welfare, E.M. Lewis, pointed out: "I understand that generally pastoralists are applying the award rates to Aboriginal employees. It is possible that the cattle industry will become a purely seasonal source of employment and there could be a recession when the next wet arrives."[34] In 1969 the results of a report undertaken by the Commonwealth Department of Labour and National Service found that in Halls Creek:

> There is an Aboriginal population of approximately 400 of which 130 are under the age of 15 years (during the wet season this builds up to over 600). A number of these were retrenched from neighbouring stations. It appears that the present policy of the pastoralists in the area is to reduce the numbers permanently employed and to engage contractors for mustering and yard building.[35]

As Dr H.C. Coombs – senior government advisor, economist, and bureaucrat – observed:

> The accommodation reached between Aboriginals and the pastoralists was shattered by declining viability and structural change in the pastoral industry, coinciding with legislative change requiring the compulsory payment of award wages. . . . Again, Aborigines were forced to build up *new communities* [my emphasis] and had to adjust to life as dependents of government, given the lack of other sources.
>
> (Coombs 1989: 1–2)[36]

Table 10.2 highlights the decline in pastoral and agricultural employment for Aboriginal workers in the Kimberley region between the years 1969 and 1972 – a decrease of 43 percent.

Table 10.2 Kimberley division: agricultural and pastoral
            Aboriginal employment

District	1969(a)	1972(b)
Wyndham	175	103
Halls Creek	327	281
Derby	468	164
Broome	97	61
Total	1,067	609

Sources: (a) Aboriginal employment for agricultural and
pastoral workers as at 30 June 1969 (Native Welfare 1969:
42); (b) Aboriginal employment for agricultural and pastoral
workers as at 30 June 1972 (Native Welfare 1972: 41).

The passing of the "golden age" of full employment

> It is a reasonable hypothesis that the population is going to increase in numbers
> at the [Kimberley] towns … without the ability of the towns to absorb the
> population in the normal economic stream.[37]

In the late 1960s the "golden age" of full employment and rising living
standards for the working population residing in the Kimberley, and especially indigenous labor, came to a close when the global phenomenon of
the post-war long boom began to wind down. Unemployment, poverty
and social dislocation became a fact of life for many Aboriginal people:

> It is suspected that the cumulative effect of the introduction of the
> Pastoral Industry Award and the general rural recession is adversely
> affecting employment of Aborigines in these areas [the Kimberley].
> Unless adequate data collating schemes are established serious situations
> could develop unexpectedly.[38]

Contiguous with the collapse in rural employment was accelerated migration of indigenous labor to urban centers. These centers, according to the
Department, were "providing more opportunity for employment in industrial and other activities" (Native Welfare 1969: 13). The Department
envisaged that – in response to the economic difficulties now confronting
the Kimberley pastoral industry – the shift to a more seasonal pattern of
employment would increase. It was also predicted by the Department that
one major consequence of the economic downturn would be the "impetus
given to mustering by contract"; in other words, pastoral contractors would
now perform the bulk of the work historically done by a labor force
resident – with their families – on individual pastoral properties (Native
Welfare 1969: 13).

During the late 1960s and early 1970s, the "combination of thousands
of people leaving the stations, missions closing, universal availability of social

security payments, no alcohol restrictions, all in a few short years, was shattering" (Yu 1994: 25).[39] In February 1969, a "thorough" census of people in Fitzroy Crossing alone found "133 displaced persons as a direct or indirect result of implications of the Pastoral Award."[40] Furthermore, the population of Halls Creek, Wyndham and Derby had "almost doubled over night." Turkey Creek was "suddenly transformed into a refugee camp of more than 300 people" (Yu 1994: 25).[41]

Indicative of the concern shown by the Federal government, in regard to increasing unemployment in the Kimberley, was a letter written by the Minister-in-Charge of Aboriginal Affairs, W.C. Wentworth, on February 5, 1969. Wentworth wrote to E.M. Lewis, the Western Australian Minister for Native Welfare, and stated:

> I have been told that, *whether or not as the result of recent wages decisions* [my emphasis] there is likely to be some unemployment among Aboriginals in the pastoral industry in the northern part of Western Australia, and that they and their families may lose accommodation on pastoral properties. In particular, I am told that some twenty families, about 120 persons in all, have been sent off Christmas Creek by Mr. Emmanuel. . . . If it is desired to develop any property (especially property in reserves) for the benefit of Aboriginals consideration should be given to providing the necessary funds. . . . I can assure you that the Commonwealth realises the difficulties which are not confined to one State, and indeed which exist within the Commonwealth's own territories. We will continue to co-operate with you in your endeavours to overcome your problems in Western Australia. Please do not hesitate to let me know any way in which you think we can help.[42]

It was calculated by the Department that in 1968 only 26.8 percent of the male Aboriginal work force was engaged in the agricultural industry, as compared with 30.7 percent 5 years previously. Further, by 1969, across Western Australia, rural employment accounted for only 20.4 percent (a reduction of over 10 percent in only 6 years), while there was a corresponding increase in the overall percentage of Aboriginal industrial workers – from 23.8 percent in 1968 to 29 percent in 1969 (Native Welfare 1969: 13). The Commissioner inquired as to whether this "drift from the casual and seasonal employment of the rural areas to centres where regular unskilled and semi-skilled work is available will continue" (Native Welfare 1969: 13). The ongoing labor migration, the Department believed, signaled a "growing dissatisfaction with the seasonal type of work at present available for Aboriginals in rural areas, with its consequent depressed family economy" (Native Welfare 1969: 13).

By 1970, the Commissioner had largely acknowledged that the "more seasonal form of employment and the development of contract mustering . . . appears now to be the future pattern of employment in this industry."

Moreover, the "immediate effects of this change have been the rapid urban-isation of many women and children in towns, while their menfolk move from job to job" (Native Welfare 1970: 13).

The Department explained the continuing deterioration in rural sector indigenous unemployment, throughout Western Australia during the early 1970s, by citing the effects of the global economic slump, which was further exacerbated by drought conditions:

> The decreasing influence of agriculture as a major source of employ-ment for Aboriginals was heightened during the year by the widespread drought. . . . In the last report it was observed that from providing employment for 30.7% of the male Aboriginal workforce, five years earlier, rural industry had dropped to only 20.4% in 1969. This trend has continued to the point where agricultural, farming and related workers constitute only 13.4% of the male Aboriginal workforce. . . . While admittedly inconclusive, these figures are not inconsistent with population movements from areas predominantly rural to those with a secondary industry bias.
>
> (Native Welfare 1970: 13)

In 1971 the indigenous exodus from rural to urban locations throughout Western Australia accelerated, and the subsequent repercussions became even more obvious and critical. "The continued agricultural recession has meant a severe reduction in employment opportunities in country areas and this has had a particularly bad effect on Aboriginal country populations and increased the overall movement towards the city in a search for more stable employment" (Native Welfare 1971: 7). In the Kimberley, in particular, the migration (which began at the end of 1968) was still in progress and, as the Commissioner confirmed, "many families have moved from station properties to the nearest towns, overcrowding reserves and [are] placing a strain on available accommodation. The results of these upheavals in long established socio-economic patterns are manifested in ways which are distressing" (Native Welfare 1971: 7).

Throughout this period, "it was . . . reported in the local newspaper[s] that there were signs of unrest and dissatisfaction among aboriginals."[43] The Pastoralists and Graziers Association was also well aware of the consequences of an environment of social discontent. In a *West Australian* newspaper article entitled "Graziers Commend Welfare Action," the (absentee owner) E.H. Lee-Steere – later Lord Mayor of Perth – was reported as saying:

> The government was showing an appreciation of the problems that had arisen with the introduction of the Pastoral Industry Award for aborig-inal workers, Mr. E.H. Lee-Steere, the president of the Pastoralists and Graziers Association said. . . . The Association was concerned about the drift of aboriginals into towns when they could not be employed under

the award on stations. Mr. Lee-Steere said the specifically prepared native compound at Fitzroy Crossing was a good start on the State Government's part. It was hoped that Native Welfare Minister Lewis's plan for vocational training in the North West was brought into effect as soon as possible.[44]

Symptomatic of the spiraling indigenous unemployment that occurred was the related rapid growth in crime and social unrest. The dramatic rise in crime is emphasized by the substantial increase in the numbers of Aboriginal convictions, especially those cases involving "offences against property." Between 1965 and 1969, across the whole of Western Australia, convictions for "offences against property" increased from 825 to 2,129 (CBCS 1971: 259).[45]

To give an indication of the rate of increase in the number of criminal offences committed in the Kimberley, in 1961 the Commissioner of Native Welfare reported that in the Broome region, "no serious cases of crime occurred in the native community . . . whilst no figures are yet to hand, it is felt sure that the number of court cases of natives during 1960/61 was less than the previous year" (Native Welfare 1961: 59). For the Halls Creek area it was recorded that "the native population" was "remarkably law-abiding," and, what is more, "during the year [1961] there has not been one native case before the Court of theft or interfering with property" (Native Welfare 1961: 60).[46]

Emerging government responses for dealing with indigenous unemployment and disorder

> [T]he advancement of Aboriginals should be considered . . . in their taking up avenues of self-employment or business undertakings. These developments should be fostered wherever possible. . . . [A]ttention [was drawn] to the value of the continuing development of individual business and corporate enterprises conducted by Aborigines and affirmed that the further development of such projects would be encouraged. – Federal Minister for Territories, C.E. Barnes, 1967.[47]

In the late 1960s, in the context of this turbulent period in regional Australia, both the Federal and State governments tacitly abandoned the "assimilation policy." By then it was becoming clear – in the growing rates of unemployment, crime, poverty, and social dislocation – that the policy of state trusteeship was not just "inhumane" (Turner 1997: 5), but, more significantly, completely ineffective in terms of achieving its desired aims of dealing with a growing relative surplus population. State trusteeship's policy objectives, especially in the Kimberley, had been structured in the context of prosperous pastoral and rural industries, and thus it was rapid change that the old policy was incapable of mediating.

In 1901 the constitution under which the Australian States federated gave no legislative power to the Commonwealth government insofar as Aboriginal welfare or the allocation of land were concerned, except in places such as the Northern Territory. The government of Western Australia throughout this time was solely responsible for Aboriginal affairs (Native Welfare 1967: 7). However, after 1967, following the successful passing of the referendum that gave the Federal government power to legislate on Aboriginal affairs,[48] a new "sense of purpose" pervaded Federal initiatives on Aboriginal affairs. These new initiatives were guided by advisors including the likes of Dr H.C. Coombs and W.E.H. Stanner and cabinet ministers from both major parties, such as W.C. Wentworth and Gordon Bryant (Bolton 1981: 167). As Coalition Prime Minister, Harold Holt, marking the beginning of the Federal government's shift away from its former policy of "assimilation," pointed out: "To attain our goal, patience, persistence and understanding are essential. What we are doing will not mean that Aboriginals, as citizens, will lose their identity, their pride of race and their culture."[49]

An important aspect of the evolving policy of indigenous trusteeship invoked notions of community and ethnicity. The Western Australian Acting Commissioner of Native Welfare argued:

> retention or rediscovery of "identity" is essential if a person is to adjust in any society. . . . Socio-economic advancement of Aboriginals requires community effort to be successful. Sending them to gaol . . . is a negative approach, the positive one being to deal with the root causes of maladjustment found in the areas of health, education, and the social, home and economic aspects.[50]

In addition, the need to grant some type of tenure in land was explained by the Gibb Report (1970) if the "lot of Aborigines was to be ameliorated" (Peterson, 1985: 95). In the early 1970s, the implementation of land rights and the provision of land, on the strength of the Gibb Report and others, by the Federal Coalition government were planned. The recommendations of the Gibb Report regarding the situation of Aboriginals in pastoral areas argued that the only way government could "improve their situation" was to "carve out 'living areas' (i.e. areas from a few sq. hectares to a few sq. kilometres) so that they had tenure" (Peterson 1985: 95) and, in the process, as part of the formative policy of indigenous trusteeship, transfer capital resources to indigenous people. A concomitant procedure was the push for the legal incorporation of regional "Aboriginal communities" in order that they could receive government grants as well as other benefits (Peterson 1985: 95).[51]

Legislation was enacted to create the Aboriginal Lands Trust. In 1972 the Aboriginal Lands Trust began operations and at its inaugural meeting it was announced: "The object of the Trust is to exercise control, on behalf of the Aboriginal community, over those lands for which it has assumed responsibility. As at 30 June 1973, this amounted to 23,965,610 acres." In Western Australia, the total amount of designated Aboriginal land at the time was 47 million acres. And, "[t]he remaining Aboriginal reserves will be transferred to the Trust as soon as the necessary formalities can be completed" (Aboriginal Affairs Planning Authority 1973: 10). Significantly, "Membership of the Trust is [and was] restricted to persons of Aboriginal descent" (Aboriginal Lands Trust 1978: 23). An important part of the Aboriginal Lands Trust operations was the promotion of indigenous commercial activities of which land was a vital ingredient. According to the Trust's 1973 *Annual report*:

> The economic utilisation of these great areas is governed by many factors. . . . In the Kimberleys many reserves are in remote locations . . . many mission reserves have been partially developed to allow some economic flow-on to their immediate communities. To date, these have been limited largely to pastoral type enterprises. Cohesive Aboriginal groups are now forming and coming to the forefront for the purpose of developing economically a number of reserves.
>
> (Aboriginal Lands Trust 1973: 15)

On June 30, 1972 the Western Australian Aboriginal Affairs Planning Authority came into existence to perform those functions that could not be delivered by existing government departments. Importantly, for indigenous business interests and others, these functions included "formal consultation with Aborigines, economic development of Aboriginal reserves, support of Aboriginal culture, and planning and advisory services" (Bolton 1981: 167). That same year, following a trial period that began in 1969, the Western Australian Aboriginal Advisory Council – "consisting entirely of delegates from seven regional consultative communities" – was given specific legal status (Bolton 1981: 167). Action was undertaken to make the Advisory Council an "effective sounding board for Aboriginal opinion, for the pooling of information, the airing of grievances, and the exchange of ideas" (Bolton 1981: 168).

The Western Australian Commissioner of Native Welfare could inform: "Consultation between Aboriginals and the Government continued during the year through the regional Consultative Committees and the State-wide Advisory Council for Aboriginals." Further, "It is proposed that, in the future, the Council will be an all Aboriginal body of twelve persons and that departmental officers will only be present in consultative capacity" (Native Welfare 1971: 19). The Commissioner reiterated the Department's commitment to the policy that can be described as indigenous trusteeship when he said that, "it is an indisputable fact that, for the first time, there is genuine consultation between Aboriginals and the government and the hard facts of economic and political reality are being absorbed by an emerging [Aboriginal] leadership." In addition, "All Superintendents report that, at a regional level, the methods of handling matters of local concern have been immeasurably assisted by the understanding and advice of the Consultative Committee" (Native Welfare 1971: 19).

Increased funding by both the Federal and State governments of "self managing Aboriginal organisations" underpinned the overall policy objective – that was now indigenous trusteeship. Reflective of this situation, on November 23, 1972 (at the first meeting of the Aboriginal Lands Trust), was the Western Australian Minister for Community Welfare, W.F. Willesee's, statement that:

> [the] formation of the Trust was the most important step taken in Western Australia for Aboriginal development planning and [he also] touched upon the necessity for Aborigines to involve themselves in the political arena *and in the field of leadership* [my emphasis] in both professional and public vocations. Mr. Willesee continued, stating that legislation had provided for the care of individuals regardless of racial origin and that the Trust was responsible for Aboriginal ethnic groups – *to help them, to protect them and to provide opportunities* [my emphasis] – through the land for which the Trust is to become responsible.[52]

On the Federal level, once the former policy of "assimilation" had been completely dismantled, the Whitlam government consolidated the policy, which affirmed "that aboriginal citizens have a right to effective choice about the degree to which, and the pace at which, they come to identify themselves with society" (Turner 1997: 6). The aim was to move away from programs that were "designed and executed by white administrators and based on their judgments of the needs of the situation" (Turner 1997: 6). According to Charles Perkins, later to be the head of the Federal Department of Aboriginal Affairs,[53] the "main single emphasis of the political resurgence during the 1970s was the push for Aboriginal and Islander self-management and self-determination" (Perkins 1988: 238). Both the Federal government and Perkins agreed that, "Aboriginal leaders best understood the cultural and social needs of their people" and as a result found themselves "to be directly involved in decision making and program and service delivery." These initiatives "naturally" and purposefully "encouraged the formation of new community and other service-based organisations" (Perkins 1988: 238).

> There is no doubt that the growth of [community] organisations interesting themselves in Aboriginal affairs is a phenomenon which is still very much on the increase and is a significant factor in a progressive Aboriginal involvement in local affairs.
>
> (Native Welfare 1971: 19)

Beginning in the 1970s, the concept of "community" became a central element in the administration of indigenous people in the Kimberley. It was the vehicle by which self-determination came to operate, particularly in dealing with the issue of the maintenance of social order. In 1972 the Department of Native Welfare pointed out that: "Particular attention has been given to the study of techniques and skill based on *community development principles established in other parts of the world* [my emphasis]. It has been interesting to note the change in emphasis in the conduct of programs for social development among Aboriginals from one that centered on the individual to one that places Aboriginals in a group or community context" (Native Welfare 1972: 15).

Community councils were intended and devised to be the vehicle of self-determination as part of the policy of indigenous trusteeship. In an unpublished 1968 Commonwealth Report, the Interdepartmental Committee, investigating Aboriginal policy, flagged the intention of the Federal government's future support for "community" and "self-help organisations." The Report argued that:

> The types of Aboriginal self-help organisations, which it is desired to encourage, are proprietary companies, co-operatives, savings and loan groups, social welfare associations etc.
>
> (a) It is envisaged that these organisations should register with appropriate State Authorities (e.g. registrars of Co-operatives) and with the Office of Aboriginal Affairs. It is intended that Special Liaison Officers be appointed to work, preferably in association with State and other authorities, to train Aboriginal groups to form and conduct such organisations.
>
> (b) It is hoped that in time the elected officers of these organisations might constitute a source of whence consultants and possibly Aboriginal Council members could be drawn.[54]

The institution of community associations, "with membership presided over by an elected council, itself convened by an elected chairman," was a process designed as an instrument capable of dealing with matters of social control and replacing the existing systems which were failing, "such as the Euro-legal, administrative and political apparatuses" (Sullivan 1996: 31). As one illustration of the emphasis now placed on "community elders and councilors" for the responsibility of imposing order, it was recorded in the minutes of an Aboriginal Lands Trust meeting, that Ernie Bridge – Aboriginal businessman, politician and member of the Trust[55] – had stated, "for some time now councilors from various Aboriginal reserves have undertaken the task of maintaining discipline amongst their own people. . . . In order for this system, which has proved successful, to continue, Mr. Bridge suggested that perhaps a set of uniforms be provided."[56]

In 1972 the draft of the proposed Mirima Council Constitution so revealed the status now conferred on "traditional community" and "councilors or elders" when it stated:

Objects: (a)   to reproduce the values and authority of the Aboriginal way of life . . .

         (b)   to encourage and develop self-help projects such as:
              (i)   Market gardens
              (ii)   Orchards
              (iii)   Farming domestic animals
              (iv)   Business enterprises . . .

Members: (a)   Members shall be persons of Aboriginal descent who wish to promote the objectives of the Council . . .

Officers: (a)   The officers of the Council shall be a president and five other elected members who will be recognised as the executive committee by the Council (known as the Elders).[57]

The formation of increasing numbers of "Aboriginal self-help community groups" in remote and regional areas of the Kimberley each undertaking activities on their "own behalf," was according to the Department of Native Welfare, one of the most "significant developments of recent times." The Department noted, "recent undertaking of activities on their [Aboriginals] own behalf is of great importance, and is an indication of self-confidence and group identity" (Native Welfare 1972: 15). In 1972 it was reported that at Wyndham, "a small body of Aboriginal women formed the Aboriginal Progress Movement, under the leadership of Mrs. Thelma Birch" (Native Welfare 1972: 21). Another organization, which formed at Wyndham at the same time, was the Oombulgurri Association:

[The Association] was brought about by two families attempting to re-establish themselves by developing market gardens, one at the Old Forrest River Mission and the other at Oondaguri (20 miles from Wyndham on the west side of the Cambridge Gulf). These efforts have led to an exploration into the development of a pallet making factory. (Native Welfare 1972: 21)

In the East Kimberley, the Warmun center at Turkey Creek was established in the early 1970s for those Aboriginal people expelled by pastoral stations. Warmun was set up to cater for the exodus of people forced to leave Texas Downs, Alice Downs, Mabel Downs, Violet Valley, Bow River, Nicholson, Turner, and possibly other pastoral stations. Prior to the establishment of the Warmun center, Turkey Creek was a small police and telegraph station on the Wyndham road. The Department of Aboriginal

Affairs began to "fund houses, a power station, bores for drinking water and the Catholic Education Office set up a school" and placed "community leaders" in charge of the overall operation (Sullivan 1996: 23). In other words, land was obtained and a "community" was created in line with the policy of indigenous trusteeship. This, therefore, was the "future for Aboriginals in the Kimberleys – new fully serviced townships [or villages] from which the population would seek employment on surrounding stations, in craft industries, community enterprises and in domestic duties" (Sullivan 1996: 23).

Not surprisingly, some "forms of analysis suggest it [the maintenance of social order] proceeds by the calculated distortion of the principle of self-determination with the sinister intention of subjugating Aboriginals as firmly as in the past" (Sullivan 1996: 43) – that is, reminiscent of the segregationary period. As Rosemary Neill points out, "Many of these 'communities' are really synthetic remnants of government reserves and church-run missions in which different clans were brought together in an artificial way, usually on . . . land that no one else wanted. . . . Yet the word 'community' is often apportioned in public debate as if it is an indigenous value in itself: as if it captures the essence of Aboriginal identity" (Neill 2002: 74).

Indicative of this situation is correspondence between the Department's Supervising Anthropologist and the Derby field anthropologist in 1973, which reports: "I have taken the liberty of drawing administration's attention to your more general comments on the issue of "isolationism" . . . which appear to be among the risk elements in the present . . . policy."[58] In many ways it could be argued that self-determination was operating as the new means of fixing indigenes to isolated and regional areas for the purpose of halting – or at least slowing – urbanization and unemployment. As Peterson has pointed out:

> what the rhetoric of unique and specific religious links to land of Aboriginal entitlement and of natural justice has obscured is the fact that in essence land rights [and in Western Australia land purchases] are a welfare measure and not the act of compensatory justice they appear to be.
>
> (Peterson 1985: 97)

The farm gate opens: accumulation opportunities available to indigenous business operators in the early 1970s

> The emergence of Aboriginals who provide an articulate voice for their peoples' aspirations is a new phenomenon, which has characterised the last few years. Their presence on television and radio is no longer a novelty; they are very much a part of the media's daily material and their views sought and published. Once an inarticulate and ignored segment of society, they are steadily becoming a political force.
>
> (Native Welfare 1972: 9)

The period from the mid 1960s to the 1970s witnessed the emergence of a "new group of Aboriginal leaders." They were, according to Charles Perkins, mostly "mixed-race people" and many "were well qualified educationally." Throughout this period, these emerging "leaders" were viewed as "radicals operating in the image of the black rights campaigners" who were active in the United States at the time (Perkins 1988: 237).[59]

Aboriginal leaders became the chief architects in determining the government's self-determination policies and subsequent change in state forms. This was achieved through, among other things, their participation in "functionally based Aboriginal organisations." These organizations "ranged from a mixture of independently funded operations, to quasi-government organisations which had independent administrations but received funding from . . . the federal government" (Perkins 1988: 237).

During the 1970s this "new Aboriginal leadership" generally formed into two groups. One group was associated with "socio-economic matters such as health, education, training, employment, legal aid and housing." The other concerned itself essentially with the acquisition of land (Perkins 1988: 237). Some members of this "new Aboriginal leadership" can be considered "straddlers" (Cowen and MacWilliam 1996: 16),[60] within the context of an indigenous business class. Many of these individuals, especially the well educated, combined employment in the newly formed black bureaucracy with private business activities.

Beginning in the late 1960s and early 1970s, Commonwealth and State government agencies began to provide finance for the benefit of Aboriginal enterprises. The Commonwealth Capital Fund for Aboriginal Business Enterprises[61] became a principal source of finance for Aboriginal business ventures:

> Our aim is to restore Aboriginal initiatives and independence in both the social and economic sense. Indeed, I do not believe that it is possible to achieve either of these two objectives in isolation. Social independence cannot be effectively exercised unless it is built upon a secure economic foundation. . . . We aim to make Aborigines self supporting in the economic sense. . . . One of the most significant of the Commonwealth projects has been the establishment of the Capital Fund under Aboriginal Enterprises (Assistance Act) 1968. The Fund has nominal capital of $5 million. . . . The guiding concept of the Fund is to provide capital and technical help for individual Aboriginals and groups of Aboriginals who wish to undertake productive enterprises.[62]

The Commonwealth's Capital Fund was initiated by H.C. Coombs and was devised to expressly alleviate burgeoning rural unemployment and poverty. For Coombs, Aborigines were not to become a "dependent, landless proletariat with no other options" (Coombs 1993: 3).[63]

With changes in indigenous accumulation occurring in the early 1970s, especially those opportunities arising out of the government's policy response to the social condition of Aboriginals, the stratum of Aboriginal leaders who either held or were seeking land – such as pastoral stations and former reserves – was now able to access financial assistance for economic activities and enterprise development on "their land," and elsewhere. As indigenous economic ventures began to enjoy increasing access to government financial support, commercial opportunities began to proliferate.

As just mentioned, the Commonwealth Office of Aboriginal Affairs administered the Commonwealth Capital Fund for Aboriginal Enterprises, which, when operational, was specifically instituted:

(i)   to take up equity shares in a co-operative, or limited liability company with predominantly Aboriginal shareholders;

(ii)   to make a loan to an individual, co-operative, or corporate enterprise predominantly Aboriginal owned;

(iii) to provide a guarantee for a loan made to such an enterprise by a bank approved by the Minister and the Treasurer;

(iv) to make a deposit with an approved bank as a backing for a loan made by that bank to such an enterprise.

. . . It will be noticed that there is no provision for assistance to *an organisation which merely employs Aborigines; the enterprise itself must be predominantly Aboriginal owned* [my emphasis] or have a preponderance of Aboriginal shareholders.[64]

Once the Capital Fund became operational in Western Australia, the Department of Native Welfare recorded: "The Aboriginal Enterprise (Assistance) Act, 1968, which established the Commonwealth Capital Fund . . . generated interest and resulted in many enquiries being submitted. To date [June 30, 1970] three projects in the State have been approved with a total of twenty-two applications . . . still current" (Native Welfare 1970: 15).

In 1971 the Department reported that: "A growing interest has been invoked in self employed, enterprise projects" and this interest was reflected in the number of enquiries and applications (submitted for consideration) to the Commonwealth Capital Fund (Native Welfare 1971: 12). A number of "community enterprises" also submitted requests for assistance in preparing applications.

In 1972 further assistance to commercial activities was made available through the Capital Fund. "Impetus to community activities and enterprises . . . can now be accelerated following the Prime Minister's [William McMahon] policy statement of January 26 1972." The policy announcement "established an additional source of funds to assist Aboriginal communities with grants, in addition to loans, which [were] made through the Capital Fund" (Native Welfare 1972: 17).

It was recorded by the Department of Native Welfare in 1972 that "Aboriginal groups and communities" taking "advantage of the funds available through this Act," that is the Aboriginal Enterprises (Assistance Act), 1968, were on the increase. Commercial activities financed by the Capital Fund at this time included, among others, "small garden projects, such as those at Fitzroy Crossing and Kununurra and the Ieramugadu Gardening Service at Roebourne to the more ambitious projects such as the Esperance Carrying and Pastoral Company." Assistance in providing the necessary managerial skills was "provided through a network of interested local residents and Departmental officers" (Native Welfare 1972: 17).

Although the McMahon (Coalition) government had foreshadowed indigenous land purchases, it was the Whitlam (Labor) government that began the policy of large-scale land acquisitions on behalf of "Aboriginal groups." In 1974, the Royal Commissioner, Mr Justice A.E. Woodward, at one time counsel for the Yirrkala of Gove, investigated land rights for Aboriginals in the Northern Territory. In its final report, the Woodward Royal Commission argued the necessity of granting land to Northern Territory Aboriginals.[65] To this end, the Commonwealth government enacted the Aboriginal Land Fund Act, 1974. This Act provided for the establishment of the Aboriginal Land Fund Commission (ALFC), which was to purchase land on behalf of indigenous people throughout all parts of Australia, including the Kimberley (Aboriginal Lands Trust 1975: 25). The ALFC formally began operations in May 1975 and comprised a majority of Aboriginals as its commissioners, consisting of a chair and four members. Ernie Bridge, Kimberley businessman, politician, and a foundation member of the Aboriginal Lands Trust, was an inaugural member (Aboriginal Lands Trust 1975: 25). The Commission set certain conditions and priorities for the purchase of land, which included the following:

(i)   Land to which the applicants had a proven traditional claim and which would apparently offer them some economic advantage.

(ii)   Land to which a traditional claim could be established, on the assumption that when those involved in the claim began to live on the land an economic base would develop.

(iii) Land purchased primarily on the basis of economic need. Purchases included large pastoral properties [especially in the Kimberley].

(Young 1988a: 3)

The essential function of the Commission, particularly in relation to Western Australian land acquisition, as outlined by an Aboriginal Lands Trust *Annual Report*, was:

[to] make grants of money to an Aboriginal Corporation to enable it to acquire an interest in land for the purpose of enabling the members

of that corporation to occupy that land and to an Aboriginal land trust to enable it to acquire an interest in land for the purpose of enabling Aboriginals to occupy that land. The effect of this legislation is that the [Aboriginal Lands] Trust in seeking funds from the Federal government for land or fixed assets now approaches the Aboriginal Land Fund Commission and not the Department of Aboriginal Affairs as in the past.

(Aboriginal Lands Trust 1975: 25)

Throughout the period of the late 1960s and early 1970s the implementation of the policy of indigenous trusteeship, and especially the establishment of organizations such as the ALFC, regularly attracted stringent criticism. Often the most vocal opposition came from those with commercial interests such as white pastoralists. As a result, the transition to the policy of indigenous trusteeship throughout this period was not without its obstructions, difficulties, and ideological battles.

Ian Palmer, in his study of the ALFC, describes the existence of the underlying enmity between the Federal Department of the Interior and the Office of Aboriginal Affairs, during the period of Federal Coalition government in the early 1970s. The hostility between these two departments was emblematic of wider issues and involved "more than an administrative split for it entailed an ideological division as well." This "split" had occurred due to the fact that a Country Party minister usually headed the Department of the Interior (Palmer 1988: 15). And for this reason, the "relative dominance of pastoral capital interests [was] represented at the federal level through" the Department of the Interior (Palmer 1988: 23). According to Palmer, although the Department had partial responsibility for Aboriginal affairs, its general "philosophy appears merely to have represented [white] pastoral interests" (Palmer 1988: 15). Not surprisingly, the "reorganisation by Labor of the administration of Aboriginal affairs," in its term of government (1972–1975), "did not stop attempts by pastoral interests to contain the DAA's practice of purchasing pastoral properties." Vigorous opposition to the policy of indigenous trusteeship by these "interests was expressed in Parliament and through the media," in particular: "A two-pronged ideological attack on the purchasing of pastoral properties for Aborigines surfaced during 1973 and 1974" (Palmer 1988: 31).[66]

Immediately after the 1972 federal election, but prior to the establishment of the Aboriginal Land Fund Commission, two purchases were made – that of Pantijan Station in the West Kimberley, for people living on the Mowanjum Mission near Derby; and that of Willowra, on the eastern edge of the Tanami Desert in the Northern Territory. Both purchases were presented as satisfying the "social needs of aboriginal groups claiming strong traditional attachment to the land" (Young 1988a: 3). According to a Department report:

The Mowanjum Mission is located 6 miles from Derby on the Derby/Fitzroy Crossing road ... the mission occupies an area of 170,000 acres on which natives have run cattle for the past 15 years. At the present time it is half freehold and half lease, and will be free standing in the next ten years. Recently the community acquired another station known as Pantijan Downs and registered it as the Pantijan Cattle Company Pty Ltd. Pantijan Downs is located 200 miles north of Derby. The Mowanjum Community is comprised of three tribal groups. ... Eight elders control the community. ... The industries they hope to develop are pigs, poultry, cattle and fishing.[67]

Between 1972 and 1977, the Federal government purchased a number of cattle stations in the Kimberley – including Pantijan – on behalf of "Aboriginal communities." The purchase of Noonkanbah, Billiluna, and Lake Gregory Stations and their transfer to "Aboriginal ownership" allowed "Aboriginals to attain ownership of their lands and to run associated economic enterprises" (Ross and Drakakis-Smith 1983: 330). Noonkanbah, Billiluna, and Lake Gregory Stations were considered extremely viable pastoral stations and equivalent to the "best of other non-Aboriginal stations" (Jennings 1983: 165):

> From the financial records of four stations, including the two considered to have above-average potential as cattle stations (Billiluna/Lake Gregory and Noonkanbah), the survey team qualified the impact of Government support for these Aboriginal stations. Records were available for fifteen financial years (3 stations with 4 sets of accounts covering the period 1979/80 and 1 station with 1 set of accounts for the period 1979/80 to 1981/82). During this period, surplus income over and above operating costs [profit] was generated in eight periods, with government support. If Government support was excluded, then cattle trading activity generated surplus income in only 3 out of 15 financial years. ... At Billiluna/Lake Gregory, the turn off of heavy-weight bullocks showed a high degree of cattle control despite the lack of mustering facilities.
>
> (Jennings 1983: 169)

In addition, in the Kimberley and elsewhere, sizable areas of land, many plots being former Aboriginal reserves, were leased to Aboriginal enterprises. In 1972, for example, the Commonwealth advanced a grant and loan to the Mugarinya Group Pty Ltd on the proviso that the Aboriginal Lands Trust made Reserves 31427 and 31428 available to Mr P. Coffin. Coffin was, at the time, Managing Director of the Mugarinya Group, as well as a foundation member of the Aboriginal Lands Trust.[68]

The tensions within

Two important questions arise in response to the issue of Aboriginal business as trustees for state development policy. First, whether this emerging business class is willing to or capable of remaining trustees of state development policy for absorbing surplus labor. A second question relates to whether the level of conflict that was apparent between white-owned pastoral stations and their Aboriginal occupants and workers has reemerged with the maturing of Aboriginal ownership and the program of indigenous trusteeship. In many cases, as Bill Arthur points out, people living within station "communities" do not always support the Aboriginal management in their "attempts to operate the stations commercially" (Arthur 1994: 31). There have also been reports of disputes over such issues as, "whether the community should be allowed to take cattle for its own consumption without paying the station; and whether sections of station land should be made available for new communities and outstations" (Arthur 1994: 31).

Ernie Bridge, an Aboriginal businessman, who was an owner of several pastoral properties at the time, argued (in an Aboriginal Lands Trust meeting) against an application for a land excision because

> such an area would develop into a reserve situation and the behaviour would get out of hand. [Bridge] felt that the inhabitants would be restricted by the Station and be subject to staunch scrutiny. The establishment of such an area would not be in the best interests of the Station and . . . [he] felt a sense of proportion must be maintained. Precedents would be set and then it would be difficult to determine where excisions start and finish.[69]

Ironically, but not surprisingly, these are the same sorts of disputes that Aboriginal workers had in the past with the non-Aboriginal owners. This dissent emphasizes the major difference of opinion that exists between the management and the occupants, and relates to the reasons why these pastoral enterprises were established. In other words, is a pastoral station a welfare or commercial resource? (Arthur 1994: 31). To maintain a viable commercial operation (just as their white counterparts), the Aboriginal management must generate a profit and continue to accumulate, and therefore cannot allow revenue to be "disbursed to relatives and friends, all of whom, according to Aboriginal custom [allegedly], have a perfect right to ask for their share" (Young 1988b: 110).

Conclusion

In the late 1960s and early 1970s, in areas such as the Kimberley region of Western Australia, mass unemployment occurred due mainly to a combination of the ending of the post-war global long boom, the consequences of growing capitalization and concentration of ownership in the pastoral industry, as well as the increased cost of labor due to the granting of the pastoral award. The effects of the end of the long boom on rural industries employing Aboriginal labor, such as the pastoral industry, included cost inflation against the background of the emergence of overproduction in many international commodity markets.

To ensure even short-term viability pastoral stations required a rapid restructuring in production methods and techniques. One immediate effect of this restructuring was the expulsion of Aboriginal labor from pastoral stations, and the emergence of surplus Aboriginal labor in rural towns, with attendant social problems. Without obvious new industries to absorb this displaced labor, the Western Australian and Federal governments were confronted with the prospect of significant and potentially long-term social problems should the drift to rural towns and then cities not be arrested. The Federal and State governments' existing development policy, what I have called state trusteeship, was clearly incapable of dealing with these changed circumstances. Any alternative policy regime thus had to both halt the drift of labor from the countryside, and gradually reabsorb those unem-ployed Aboriginals that had already been displaced, and do so in a economic environment with no obvious industries to attach such a policy to.

The aim of the new policy of indigenous trusteeship, a policy devised by government in conjunction with an emerging Aboriginal leadership, was to give the indigenous leadership the responsibility of directing trustee-ship. In part, these policies were an attempt to ameliorate the worsening social conditions for many indigenes in rural and remote areas. In the process, the new government policies provided an indigenous business class – which had hitherto been actively stymied by the state – with assistance, such as the provision of land, finance, and labor. While initially the importance of Aboriginal-run enterprises was seen more in their employment potential (and thus their "social" role was emphasized along with a recognition of the need for ongoing state assistance), the government subvention allowed for the expansion of indigenous commercial activities on "their land," first in pastoralism and later in agriculture and other sectors of the economy.

By the 1980s, Aboriginal enterprises had emerged not only as significant employers in the Kimberley; many were now highly profitable across a range of commercial activities. And in 2002, for example, a Kimberley Develop-ment Commission report found that "Kimberley Aboriginal business interests [now include] tourism, pastoral stations covering 68,000 sq km, a 75,000-head cattle herd, 28 major retail businesses and 2 investment houses with substantial asset portfolios," among others.[70]

Notes

* This chapter is a summary of some research findings for my Ph.D. thesis. I wish to thank Michael Rafferty, Scott MacWilliam, and Howard Willis for their helpful

suggestions and comments in the writing of this chapter. Thanks are also due to the *Australian Economic History Review*, for the permission to quote extensively from my article "Indigenous Accumulation in the Kimberley During the Early Years of 'Self-Determination': 1968–1975," *Australian Economic History Review*, 42(1) (March 2002), on which this chapter draws.

1 It is worth noting that at the 1966 census the Aboriginal population of the Kimberley comprised 5,905 persons – the white population constituted 1,739 – out of a total population of 7,644 (or about 77 percent), whereas across Western Australia the Aboriginal population constituted approximately 2.2 percent of the total population (CBCS 1971: 137, 140).

2 There is no claim here that "economic" factors were the only reason for the shift in government policy. Changes in state policy were expressions of a complex range of forces. Indeed the reader is asked to consider the role of Aboriginal self-assertion both politically and socially, as well as shifts in the wider social context of Aboriginal development policy. Moreover, it is part of the argument here that the changing social context (including social issues from rural displacement) is critical for an understanding of the changing policy regime. But inasmuch as "economic" issues have tended to be neglected in research and debate, it is the aim of this particular article to bring them into focus once again.

3 I use the term "liberal" in the broad sense of how thinkers such as John Stuart Mill, John Maynard Keynes, John Rawls, or H.C. Coombs would understand the term, similar in many respects to the tenets of social democracy and in opposition to classical liberalism.

4 It is instructive for any investigation of the history of Australian Aboriginal affairs to also view the historical evolution of Indian policy in the United States and Canada. As Stuart McGill and Gregory Crough point out: "The broad similarity with Australian policy is striking" (McGill and Crough 1986: 13). In comparing indigenous policy in Australia and the United States, Rosemary Neill highlights the case of the United States where "self determination for Native Americans has long had bipartisan political support. In fact it was Richard Nixon who in 1970 announced a national policy of self-determination for Native American tribes. At the center of that policy was a commitment by Washington to encourage self-government" (Neill 2002: 45).

5 Cited in Parliamentary Debates, Hansard No. 24, Senate, December 24, 1971. Second Reading States Grants (Aboriginal Advancement) Bill. Senator Greenwood (Victoria – Attorney General).

6 As Scott MacWilliam points out, "while trusteeship smacks of 'European paternalism', stewardship of non-human material, particularly land, can take its place in the search for sustainable development. However, when it is social order that is threatened, stewardship must take another form." "Tribal elders," for example, "underpinned by the national state become trustees, the authority with the capacity to restore order, whether of a democratic or despotic disposition" (MacWilliam 1997: 97).

7 As J. Eyer correctly points out, for the Australian Aboriginal example, "many of the changes to the health profile of Aborigines during this period [introduction of capitalist agriculture] mirrored those of large sections of the European peasantry who in the eighteenth and nineteenth centuries had been transformed by capitalism into a surplus population enduring both malnutrition and stress-related diseases" (Eyer, cited in Saggers and Gray 1991: 384).

8 In other words, one "common sense of development" is the recognition that the immanent process of capitalist development destroys, *inter alia*, the "social value of community" (Cowen and Shenton 1996: 56).

9 In Australia, it is interesting to note that H.C. Coombs (central banker and government bureaucrat) was an early disciple of J.M. Keynes. See p. 250 and note 36 below.

10 As a major exponent of positivist thought, John Stuart Mill, "a liberal philosopher with an international reputation," summed up the ameliorative role of positivism by stating: "poverty in any sense implying suffering, may be completely extinguished by the wisdom of society . . . even the most intractable enemies . . . may be reduced" (Seaman 1968: 9).

11 Commonwealth of Australia, Parliamentary Debates, House of Representatives, September 7, 1967.

12 Memo, The Secretary, Pastoralists Association of North and Central Australia, June 1, 1927.

13 Letter to the Director of the Office of Aboriginal Affairs, Canberra, from Vicariate of the Kimberleys, Most Reverend J. Jobst, Broome Western Australia, re Beagle Bay and La Grange Mission, September 10, 1970.

14 *West Australian* newspaper article cited in Bolton (1981: 142).

15 Don McLeod was a director of Northern Development and Mining. McLeod was also a one-time member of the Australian Communist Party and was convinced that indigenous controlled enterprises would lead to Aboriginal "self-sufficiency." It is worth noting that the Comintern and V.I. Lenin in the 1920s acknowledged and supported the worth of indigenous entrepreneurial activity, as it was believed that this was one effective way to combat and eventually overcome colonial power. See Cowen and MacWilliam (1996: especially 23–80). When undertaking research on Don McLeod, the author requested access to file *1957/2239, Donald McLeod activities in connection . . .* from the National Archives in Canberra, to which I was informed "our records indicate that it may have been destroyed." Letter from Carolyn Connor, National Archives, to Tony Smith, July 12, 2001.

16 The Yandeyarra lease was forfeited because the operation had not "complied with the stocking conditions." In short, a technicality was invoked as a means of stripping the Northern Mining and Development Company of the lease (McLeod 1984: 101). However, as the *Report of The Pastoral Leases Committee* makes obvious, it was usually the case that the stocking conditions "cannot be complied with without overstocking and degradation of the country. Conditions in pastoral areas vary so much that it is impossible to lay down rigid general provisions regarding either maximum or minimum stocking rate" (*Report of The Pastoral Leases Committee* 1963: 93). Further, "In some instances properties were purchased by Eastern States interests [and others] who . . . considerably over-estimated the carrying capacities" (*Report of The Pastoral Leases Committee* 1963: 18).

17 Letter to E.H. Lewis, Minister for Native Welfare, from the Secretary of the Pastoralists and Graziers Association of Western Australia, April 29, 1963.

18 Meentheena Station purchased by Northern Mining and Development for £5,000, was sold to Bell Brothers for £2,500. (Bell Brothers itself was later taken over by Robert Holmes a Court, whose wife Janet Holmes a Court inherited the estate on her husband's death. Janet Holmes a Court is now considered one of the largest landholders particularly of pastoral stations in Western Australia.)

19 Letter to the Commissioner of Native Affairs, from District Officer (J. Beharrel), re Fitzroy Crossing Native Reserve, May 13, 1954.

20 In Fitzroy Crossing since the late 1980s Leedal Investment Co. Pty Ltd, partly owned and operated by the Aboriginal Resource Agency Marra WorraWorra, now operates most if not all the commercial enterprises in the town.

21 "An Opportunity for Statesmanship," Pamphlet written by Ernie Mitchell, Chairman of Directors, Pindan Pty Ltd, Port Hedland, Western Australia. Date unknown.

22 Mitchell argues further:

> of all the contenders for the Mt Goldsworthy iron ore export licence who
> can make out a better case than we can make? Let us profit from the mineral
> resources of our tribal territories. Mt Goldsworthy has for countless centuries
> been a prominent feature of our secret ceremonial life, and has a special place
> in our culture. All our best hunting grounds have been taken over by grazing
> interests without any compensation to our People, and now is the opportu-
> nity for some measure of Justice to be done to us. Let us, the Black
> Australians, stand level with our white fellow Australians. No kind word, no
> hand-out, nothing at all could weigh with world opinion as would the
> granting to us of the opportunity to attain the standards we seek.

23 It is significant that a multinational company such as BHP, with much access to
political power at the Federal and State level, was granted the licence to mine
ore at Mt Goldsworthy at the expense of both local white and black capital. Lang
Hancock (a local mining rentier) was also denied the right to mine ore at various
locations throughout the State, although, unlike Pindan, he received substantial
mining royalties from iron ore discoveries in the Pilbara region of Western
Australia. As a consequence of this denial, Hancock reportedly financed
Democratic Labour Party candidates at the 1971 State election on the basis that
he had good reason to "resent both Labor and Liberal ministers with whom he
had been at loggerheads over the granting of mining leases" (Black 1981: 469).

24 The convenient but erroneous judgment by the local colonial administration,
pastoralists, and others that there was no concept of land ownership (commonly
known in Australia as *terra nullius*) held by sections of the indigenous population
before European contact perfectly justified the appropriation of Aboriginal land
for the establishment of pastoral and agricultural operations. The Australian High
Court in the 1992 *Mabo* judgment finally overturned the idea of *terra nullius*.

25 "The District Office functions as a very effective Labour Exchange and in future
it is intended to keep an accurate record of jobs found" (Native Welfare 1962:
33).

26 J.M. O'Brien (Commissioner of Police), letter to the Secretary, Western Australian
Pastoralists' Association, Perth, November 23, 1961.

27 Even in 1966 absentee owners controlled more than 70 percent of Kimberley
cattle stations; the 4 major absentee groups included Vestey's, Hookers, Peel
River, and Naughtons (*The West Australian*, May 25, 1966).

28 According to the Inquiry, about 75 percent of the meat from northern export
abattoirs went to the North American market as hamburger mince. The balance
of export production was spread between nine other major offshore markets
(Jennings 1983: 54). In other words, Kimberley beef prices were, in the 1970s
and later, very dependent on offshore markets.

29 In 1976 the "Kimberley Statistical Division carried 741,358 head of cattle for meat
production, or 29.8 per cent of the State total" (CBCS 1977: 377–378).

30 Corporate entities in the pastoral industry, during the difficult economic times
post-1968, took advantage of their larger economies of scale and their corresponding ability to further reduce costs to protect their profit margins.

31 In late 1968 the introduction of the Cattle Industry Pastoral Award was implemented, which guaranteed equal wages for Aboriginal pastoral labor in the
livestock industry. Hitherto Aboriginal labor had been paid at lower rates than
white labor. The Department reported that:

> [in] September 1967 a varying order to the Pastoral Industry Award 1965
> was handed down by the Commonwealth Conciliation and Arbitration

Commission, a major provision being for the employment of Aborigines under award conditions. To assist in the readjustment of the industry in Western Australia, a "phasing in" period of 15 months was written into the award making it operative in other than the South West Land Division, in respect of . . . Aborigines, from 1st December 1968.

(Native Welfare 1968: 13)

32 Letter to the Commissioner of Native Welfare, from K.T. Johnson, Super-intendent Northern Division, Department of Native Welfare, June 27, 1969.

33 Schubert was at the time of the award decision a proprietor of Louisa Downs Station in the East Kimberley.

34 Letter to Minister-in-Charge of Aboriginal Affairs, W.C. Wentworth, from Minister for Native Welfare, E.H.M. Lewis, September 3, 1969.

35 Report on visit to Aboriginal communities, Missions, and Pastoral Stations in northern part of Port Hedland DEO area. P.J. Bright (Clerk) Aboriginal employ-ment, September 23, 1969. The report undertaken by the Department of Labour and Service was carried out after the need for such a survey was recommended by the *Report of the Interdepartmental Committee* in its 1968 Cabinet Submission. The *Report* recommended:

> that the Department of Labour and National Service, in consultation with the Council and Office of Aboriginal Affairs where appropriate,
>
> (a) estimate the size and composition of the Aboriginal workforce and popu-lation of working age and its future growth;
> (b) survey employment opportunities for Aboriginals and methods of increasing opportunities;
> (c) investigate methods of providing incentives and employment training for Aboriginals; with a view to
> (d) providing incentives and training for employment;
> (e) increasing employment opportunities, including migratory, seasonal and contract employment opportunities;
> (f) placing Aboriginals in employment in urban and country areas.

36 Coombs was a well-known banker and economist with a special interest in Aboriginal affairs. He was personal advisor to seven Australian Prime Ministers, and both sides of the political spectrum accepted his counsel.

37 Department of Native Welfare. Memo to Commissioner of Native Welfare, from K.I. Morgan, Superintendent, North West Division, re Projects-Economic Surveys, April 10, 1970.

38 Economic Project Reports, Native Welfare Department, North West Division. Memo from Superintendent Economic Development, to Deputy Commissioner Native Welfare, May 10, 1971.

39 Missions closed included the United Aborigines Missions: Sunday Island, Fitzroy Crossing, Mowanjum, and Forrest River. The Catholic missions collapsed during this period as well.

40 Letter to Commissioner of Native Welfare, from K.T. Johnson, Superintendent Northern Division, June 27, 1969.

41 By 1975, the population of Fitzroy Crossing had "swelled to over 2,000" (Yu 1994: 26).

42 Letter to E.M. Lewis, Minister for Native Welfare, from Minister-in-Charge of Aboriginal Affairs, W.C. Wentworth, February 5, 1969.

43 Letter to Commissioner of Native Welfare, from K.T. Johnson, Superintendent Northern Division, June 27, 1969.

44 "Graziers commend welfare action," *West Australian*, March 5, 1969.

45 According to the 1966 census, 32.02 percent of the Western Australian Aboriginal population lived in the Kimberley (CBCS 1971: 140).

46 The Commissioner's concluding remark on the section dealing with indigenous crime for the Kimberley region, in the 1961 *Annual Report*, was that "the ratio of offences to population is roughly the same as for whites and would be lower except for discriminatory legislation against natives" (Native Welfare 1961: 60).

47 Ministerial Statement, C.E. Barnes (McPherson – Minister for Territories), Parliamentary Debates, House of Representatives, September 7, 1967.

48 The key proposal of the referendum, as the bi-partisan "yes" case put it, was to alter the constitution so as to "make it possible for the Commonwealth Parliament to make special laws for the people of the Aboriginal race, wherever they may live, if the Parliament considers it necessary" (Jaensch 1992: 90).

49 Speech by Mr Harold Holt, Prime Minister, "Commonwealth of Australia," Parliamentary Debates, House of Representatives, September 7, 1967.

50 Letter from Acting Commissioner of Native Welfare to Minister for Native Welfare, January 13, 1970.

51 See note 55.

52 Aboriginal Lands Trust, Inaugural Meeting, November 23, 1972. Members present: J.L. Davis – Central Region, Chairman; S. Canning – Eastern Region; A. Barunga – Northern Region; E. Bridge – Northeastern Region; H. Calgaret – Southern Region; P. Coffin – Northwestern Region; K.I. Morgan – Acting Secretary; R. Hayward – Clerk Lands and Reserves, Aboriginal Affairs Planning Authority.

53 It is an interesting point that Perkins in the 1980s campaigned vigorously against Asian immigration (cited in Bolton 1993: 287).

54 Unpublished Confidential Report of the Interdepartmental Committee, Cabinet Submission No. 92, 1968. Appendix "I," "Encouragement of Newly-Emerging Forms of Aboriginal society."

55 Ernie Bridge is perhaps the leading representative of the emerging Aboriginal business class, as it expanded in the Kimberley. Bridge was "grandson on his father's side of a pioneering overlander and on his mother's side of a senior man of the local Aboriginal clan in the Halls Creek district" (Bolton 1981: 17). Bridge has owned many businesses, including the Kimberley pastoral stations Koongie Park Station and Elvire, a butcher's shop, general store, picture garden, MacRobertson Miller Airline agency, and a contract mustering operation, and was also for a time Halls Creek Shire President.

56 Minutes of Aboriginal Lands Trust Meeting, December 11–13, 1974.

57 Interim Report on Mirima Council and Kununurra Garden Project. S.F. Davey, Employment Officer, Wyndham, April 18, 1972.

58 Letter to anthropologist (Derby), from Supervising Anthropologist, re Freddie Johnstone Land Claim, February 20, 1973.

59 In the 1968 Report of the Interdepartmental Committee's Cabinet Submission No. 92, investigating Commonwealth Aboriginal policy, it was stated:

> Hesitation in formulating a [new] policy could have quite serious repercussions for us, both internally and internationally. Communists are devoting great efforts to capturing Aboriginal organizations, and unless we have an alternative to offer, they are likely to succeed. They plan both to develop an "American Negro injustice" image and to focus the hatred of Asian peoples upon Australia.

60 Cowen and MacWilliam describe straddlers as "putative social agents for the trusteeship of development, such as state officials and the "technocrats," [who]

also own private property and seek to extend the basis of property" (Cowen and MacWilliam 1996: 16).

61 Commonwealth Capital Fund for Aboriginal Enterprises, *First Annual Report for the Year 1968–1969*, Parliamentary Paper No. 14, 1969.
62 States Grants (Aboriginal Advance Bill) Senate, September 19, 1969.
63 It is worth noting that Coombs was an early disciple of the economist J.M. Keynes.
64 Letter to Superintendent of Native Welfare, Northern Division, from F.E. Gare, Commissioner of Native Welfare, April 15, 1969.
65 Woodward recommended the "creation of land trusts holding reserves in inalienable land communal freehold, backed by community-based land councils and by a government fund for the repurchases of traditional lands. Entry for mining, tourism and other purposes would be subject to the consent of the local community" (Bolton 1993: 235–236).
66 Palmer cites the example of the Federal Country Party parliamentarian, Stephen Calder, who stated in 1973: "The Government is spending millions of dollars on the purchase of cattle stations and at present the Aboriginals are threatening the pioneers who own another one" (Palmer 1988: 32).
67 The Mowanjum Mission – via Derby. Department Report.
68 Minutes of inaugural meeting of Aboriginal Lands Trust, November 23–24, 1972.
69 Minutes of Aboriginal Lands Trust, 2nd meeting, March 8–9, 1973.
70 "The Aboriginal component of the Kimberley economy" Report cited in *The Australian*, January 15, 2002. The Minister for the Kimberley, Tom Stephens, said, at the release of the report, that, "Aboriginal people owned and controlled an important and increasing share of regional business activity across a range of sectors."

Bibliography

Aboriginal Affairs Planning Authority, WA (1973) *Annual Report*, Perth.
Aboriginal Lands Trust, WA (1972–1978) *Annual Reports*, Perth.
—— (1972–1981) Minutes of Meetings, Perth.
Arthur, B. (1994) "Cultural Autonomy, Economic Equity and Self-Determination within Nation States: Australian Aboriginals in Remote Regions," *Australian Aboriginal Studies*, 2: 28–37.
Australian, The (2002).
Black, D. (1981) "Liberals Triumphant," in C.T. Stannage (ed.) *A New History of Western Australia*, Nedlands: University of Western Australia.
Bolton, G. (1981) "Black and White after 1897," in C.T. Stannage (ed.) *A New History of Western Australia*, Nedlands: University of Western Australia.
—— (1993) *The Oxford History of Australia: The Middle Way 1942–1988*, Melbourne: Oxford University Press.
Clark, M. (1986) *A Short History of Australia*, Ringwood: Penguin.
Commonwealth Bureau of Census and Statistics (CBCS) (1971, 1977) *Western Australian Year Book*, and (1980) *Year Book, Australia*, Perth.
Commonwealth Department of Aboriginal Affairs (1972–1975) Correspondence.
Commonwealth of Australia (1967–1975) *Parliamentary Debates*, Canberra.
Coombs, H.C. (1989) "The Ideology of Development," in H.C. Coombs, H. McCann, H. Ross, and N.M. Williams (eds) *Land of Promises: Aborigines and Development in the East Kimberley*, Canberra: CRES Australian National University.
—— (1993) *Issues in Dispute, Aborigines Working for Autonomy*, Darwin: Northern Australian Research Unit.

Cowen, M. (1998) "Trust in development," *IDS working paper*, 10, Helsinki: Institute of Development Studies, University of Helsinki.

—— and MacWilliam, S. (1996) *Indigenous Capital in Kenya*, Helsinki: Institute of Development Studies, University of Helsinki.

—— and Shenton, R. (1996) *Doctrines of Development*, London: Routledge.

Crowley, F.K. and de Garis, B.K. (1970) *A Short History of Western Australia*, Melbourne: Macmillan.

Department of Land Administration (1999) *Lessee Contacts Report*, July.

Eyre, E.J. (1845) *Journals of Expeditions of Discovery into Central Australia*, London: Boone.

Foulkes-Taylor, D. (n.d.) *Roe, Phillips*, Perth: publisher unknown.

Hartwig, M. (1978) "Capitalism and Aborigines: The Theory of Internal Colonialism and its Rivals," in E.L. Wheelright and K. Buckley (eds) *Essays in the Political Economy of Australian Capitalism*, Volume 3, Sydney: ANZ Book Company.

Heppel, M. (ed.) (1979) *A Black Reality*, Canberra: Australian Institute of Aboriginal Studies.

Hiatt, L.R. (1996) *Arguments about Aborigines*, Cambridge: Cambridge University Press.

Jaensch, D. (1992) *The Politics of Australia*, South Melbourne: Macmillan.

Jennet, C. (1988) "Australian Aborigines: Politics, the Law and Aborigines," in J. Jupp (ed.) *The Australian People: An Encyclopaedia of the Nation, Its People and Their Origins*, North Ryde: Angus & Robertson.

Jennings, P. (Chair) (1983) *Kimberley Pastoral Industry Inquiry*, Perth: Department of Regional Development and the North West.

Kelly, S.M. (1980) *Proud Heritage*, Perth: Artlook.

Kimberley Land Council (1998) *Conference Report: The Kimberley, Our Place Our Future*, Derby.

Kimberley Region Plan (1987) *Study Report: A Strategy for Growth and Conservation*, Broom: Department of Regional Development and the North West and the Department of Planning and Urban Development.

Kolig, E. (1981) *The Silent Revolution: The Effects of Modernization on Australian Aboriginal Religion*, Philadelphia, PA: Institute of the Study of Human Issues.

McGill, S. and Crough, G.J. (1986) *Indigenous Resource Rights and Mining Companies in North America and Australia*, Canberra: AGP.

McLeod, D. (1984) *How the West Was Lost: The Native Question in the Development of Western Australia*, Port Hedland: self-published.

MacWilliam, S. (1997) "Liberalism and the End of Development: Partington against Coombs and Hasluck," *Island*, 70: 89–100.

Native Affairs, WA Commissioner of (1949) *Annual Report*, Perth.

Native Welfare, WA Commissioner of (1954–1972) *Annual Reports*, Perth.

——, WA Commissioner of (1967–1972) Correspondence, Perth.

Neill, R. (2002) *White Out*, Crows Nest: Allen & Unwin.

Palmer, I. (1988) *Buying Back the Land*, Canberra: Aboriginal Studies Press.

Pearson, N. (2000) *Our Right*, Cairns: Noel Pearson & Associates.

Perkins, C. (1988) "Australian Aborigines: Politics, the Law and Aborigines," in J. Jupp (ed.) *The Australian People: An Encyclopaedia of the Nation, Its People and Their Origins*, North Ryde: Angus & Robertson.

Peterson, N. (1985) "Capitalism, Culture and Land Rights: Aborigines and the State in the Northern Territory," *Social Analysis*, 18: 85–101.

Report of the Pastoral Leases Committee (1963) Perth.

Report of the Pastoral Leases Committee (1963) Perth.

Report of the Special Committee on Native Matters (1958) Perth.

Ross, H. and Drakakis-Smith, D. (1983) "Socio-Spatial Aspects of Australian Aboriginal Underdevelopment: Empirical Evidence from the East Kimberley," *Geoforum*, 14: 235–332.

Rowse, T. (2000) *Obliged to be Difficult*, Cambridge: Cambridge University Press.

Saggers, S. and Gray, D. (1991) "Policy and Practice in Aboriginal Health," in J. Reid and P. Trompf (eds) *The Health of Aboriginal Australia*, Marrickville: Harcourt Brace Jovanovich Group.

Schubert, L.A. (1992) *Kimberley Dreaming*, Mandurah: Words Work Express.

Seaman, R. (1968) *The Liberals and the Welfare State*, London: Cox & Wyman.

Sullivan, P. (1996) *All Free Man Now*, Canberra: Australian Institute of Aboriginal and Torres Strait Islander Studies.

Sykes, B. and Bonner, N.T. (1975) *On Trial: Black Power in Australia*, Victoria: Heinemann Educational Australia.

Turner, P. (1997) "Public Policy in Indigenous Affairs," *Australian Journal of Public Administration*, 56: 3–11.

Weekend Australian, The (2001).

West Australian, The (1966, 1969, 1986).

Western Australian Government (1995) *Western Australian Native Title Progress Report*, No. 2, Perth.

Young, E. (1988a) *Aboriginal Cattle Stations in the East Kimberley: Communities or Enterprises*, Canberra: Australian National University.

—— (1988b) "Aboriginals and Land in Northern Australian Development," *Australian Geographer*, 19: 105–116.

Yu, P. (1994) "The Kimberley: From Welfare Colonialism to Self-Determination," *Race and Class*, 35: 21–33.

11 Sub-Saharan Africa

Land rights and ethno–national consciousness in historically land–abundant economies

Gareth Austin

A Sub-Saharan perspective brings two basic elements to the comparative discussion of the historical interrelations between "ethno-national" consciousness and rights in land. One is that most of the region, for most of its history, has been land-abundant in the economic sense that at any given time the expansion of output was constrained by a lack of effective demand, or of labor and capital, but not of cultivable land. There are qualifications to this generalization, as we shall see. But both the fact of land abundance, and its rapid dwindling during most of the twentieth century, have had major implications for African histories of territorial sovereignty and landed property, state formation, and ethnicity. The other basic element is Africa's reputation, externally and to some extent internally, as the part of the world where states are weakest and ethnicity strongest (meaning by "ethnicity" the sense of collective identity as defined by common descent, origin, or heritage – real or alleged). Land abundance itself has made it harder to establish effective monopolies of power over given territories.

This chapter is organized into five main sections. The first explores the nature of, and qualifications to, land surpluses, and traces their implications for property rights. The second identifies the sources of progressive diminution of land surpluses, mainly in the twentieth century, and considers the consequences for land tenure systems. The third discusses the experiences, especially the difficulties, of state construction within the region, and the implications for notions of territory. The fourth outlines the complex historiography of ethnicity in Africa. The fifth section comments on the interactions of factor ratios, ethnicity and nation-building in relation to territory and property in land.

Land abundance and its implications for property rights

Sub-Saharan Africa has long been one of the more lightly populated regions of the world. This applies both to those parts heavily afflicted by external slave trades, and to those more fortunate (Hopkins 1973; Iliffe 1995). More directly pertinent is that descriptions of African farming, for example during the last two centuries before the European partition of the continent, mostly indicate that agricultural output was unconstrained by the availability of land. In some cases this was proximately due, at least in part, to a prior demand constraint. The British traveler Mungo Park, who journeyed from the River Gambia to the Niger in 1795–1796, commented that "the Mandingoes . . . not having many opportunities of turning to advantage the superfluous produce of their labour . . . are content with cultivating as much ground only as is necessary for their own support." They used the time not required for subsistence cultivation for fishing, hunting and "manufacturing cotton cloth" (Park 1983: 215). Very commonly, though, there was also a pair of labor supply constraints. One was seasonal: crop output was restricted by the amount that could be planted during the rains. This regular bottle-neck was especially tight in savanna areas, which naturally have shorter rains than the forest zones (Tosh 1980). The other was general: labor scarcity shackled the production possibility frontier, whether at the level of the individual, the household or the state (cf. Hopkins 1973).[1]

Because of the abundance of land in relation to population, a basic dynamic of African history was that of applying labor to natural resources, to extract iron ore or gold or a range of naturally occurring forest products, but also to clear and settle. This very long-term expansion of settlement, extending the areas devoted to cultivation (in eastern Africa especially, often combined with herding), is evoked in Iliffe's remark that Africans "are the frontiersmen of mankind" (Iliffe 1995: 1). With the use of large animals prevented by endemic sleeping sickness and other diseases, in the forests and in much of the savannas, tilling the soil remained overwhelmingly dependent on human muscle applied to simple tools.

Thus while land is literally the fundamental factor of production, in most of African history it has not been the most important economically. It is true that in pre-colonial societies land often had religious significance, as for instance the colonial ethnographer R.S. Rattray emphasized in the case of the Asante, in what is now Ghana (e.g. Rattray 1929: 360–361). A distinction should be made between respect for the earth itself, expressing people's awareness that they depended upon it, and deference to the spirits of the ancestors who had made farms upon it. Asantes demonstrated the former by honoring their earth goddess by abstaining from farming one day a week; the latter, by taking care to propitiate the spirits of those hard-working predecessors with appropriate drinks in the event that they were obliged to alienate the usufruct of it (Rattray 1929: 342–343, 358, 360–361). This combination of a sense of an ontological dependence upon the earth with an economic pragmatism about using it can perhaps most realistically be seen not as an expression of a physical scarcity of land but rather a reflec-tion of the fundamental demographic, economic, cultural, indeed existential process of African pre-colonial history, namely the application of labor to wrench land from the realm of nature and convert it to cultivation and habitation.[2] Such beliefs did not prevent the development of markets in land – or at east in land-use rights – when and where cultivable land became scarce (see, e.g., Hill 1963; Hopkins 1973: 39; Austin forthcoming). Unless and until that happened, boundaries between land owners (which in the Asante case were the local chiefdoms) tended to be defined only loosely (e.g. Austin forthcoming).

Meanwhile, as Hopkins put it in 1973, and in contrast to pre-industrial western Europeans, "Africans measured wealth and power in men rather than in acres; those who exercised authority were man-owners rather than landowners" (Hopkins 1973: 26). This observation might now be amplified to specify the importance of control over women, both in polygamous households and in a demand for female slaves which often appears to have exceeded that for male slaves (e.g. Robertson and Klein 1983). In pastoral economies, wealth was counted also in cattle (e.g. Etherington 2001: 86). The extraction of surplus from the direct producers, whether by household heads, local chiefs, or heads of state, was rarely achieved by control of land rights. The largest and most enduring exception was Abyssinia, where peasants paid the ruling class, if not exactly land rent, then a tribute that was essentially in return for tenure of the soil (Crummey 1980). But Abyssinia was an exception which "proves" rather than falsifies the rule that land abundance was associated with an absence of landlordism. For much of it was comparatively densely populated, and had already a long history of – by Sub-Saharan standards – relatively intense cultivation, based on a light plow (McCann 1999). On the other side of the continent the only significant parallel is a partial one. The rulers of the jihadist Sokoto Caliphate (1804–1903), located primarily in what is now northwest and north-central Nigeria, which became the largest state of its era in West Africa, imposed a land tax on free peasants (owners of slave plantations were generally exempt). The rates varied with location, being highest near towns, which provided the markets in which the farmers could sell their grain – for the tax had to paid in cash, in the form of cowries (Lovejoy and Hogendorn 1993: 162–172). Even in the Sokoto Caliphate land seems to have been economically scarce only in the vicinity of major towns. In Abyssinia peasants were legally free and enjoyed considerable autonomy from their lords, as was expressed in the saying "Man is free, and land the tributary" (Crummey 1980: 130). In contrast, in the Sokoto Caliphate as in most parts of Sub-Saharan Africa at the time, the main institutions for appropriating economic rents involved property rights over people rather than land: various forms of slavery and, in many societies, also debt bondage and/or labor service (*corvée*).[3]

The sense that African labor was of more economic value than African land was shared by outsiders, in that – with the partial exception of the Portuguese – the demands for African slaves by North Africans, Asians, and above all Europeans long predated attempts at colonization of sizeable areas of the continent.[4] Again, in the early colonial era, when European regimes legislated in favor of white settlers, what they sought to engineer was as much a supply of cheap labor (the availability of labor at below its reservation price[5] in this labor-scarce environment) as a supply of land. Thus the archetype of such legislation, the South African Natives Land Act of 1913, not only reserved land for Europeans but prohibited African tenancy on European-owned lands. The implication was that African participation in the market should be in the market for labor, not for produce.[6] The results of such legislation put intense pressure on African labor supplies, while the lands provided often exceeded the capacity of the settlers to farm them. In Kenya settlers encouraged African squatters on their lands (in return for labor) until the 1940s (Bates 1989), while in Northern Rhodesia (now Zambia) much land reserved for European settlers by the colonial administration went unclaimed by them (Vail 1977). As Bates has commented, what European settlers in Kenya wanted was not a "White Highlands" but a highlands with high land values. As long as inputs of African labor were the key to achieving that, the settlers encouraged and (helped by the indirect coercion of the colonial state) cajoled Africans to reside on their estates. When market and technological change made it possible for the settlers to earn much higher incomes by switching to a capital-intensive form of dairy farming in the 1940s, the now superfluous laborers were expelled in favor of machinery (Bates 1989).

Given the widespread abundance of land in an economic sense until recently, it is not surprising that access to land was relatively easy and cheap in most pre-colonial societies, and in some cases remained so well into, and even beyond, the twentieth century. The details of pre-colonial land tenure systems varied enormously, but perhaps the most general pattern was for citizens or subjects of the local polity, however centralized or otherwise that was, to be allocated land for their use virtually free; and for even outsiders to be given use rights at only nominal expense, providing they symbolically acknowledged that the ownership of the land remained in the original hands (e.g. Austin forthcoming). Herders required the use of pastoral resources beyond those over which any particular group had ownership; but they seem to have permitted each other access on reciprocal terms (e.g. Spear and Waller 1993). But such systems increasingly came under pressure to change, particularly during and since the colonial period.

Finally in this section, we need to enter a significant qualification to the general picture of land abundance, especially before the twentieth century: land was not homogenous. Areas containing accessible minerals, or economically valuable forest products, were fought for and, if possible, secured against outsiders. In *c.*1860 Msiri, a Sumbwa-Nyamwezi warlord-trader from western Tanzania, created his own state occupying the copper-rich area of what is now Katanga (or Shaba) in eastern Congo. The Asante state had already secured a near-monopoly of kola-nut trees and of gold deposits within the local region (Lovejoy 1978: 14–17). The natural resource rents the Asantes secured helped to pay for the large numbers of slaves they imported, partly to expand output of kola nuts and gold (Austin forthcoming). In these cases, territory mattered for economic purposes.

The dwindling of land surpluses and the development of markets in land rights

Clearly, land abundance is a condition liable to erosion from increased demand for land. Local demographic crises, as numbers of people and/or their cattle stretched local supplies of water, cultivable land, or pasturage, were far from being a twentieth-century innovation. They tended to be dealt with by onward movement: by migration and re-settlement (e.g. Johnson 1981; Kopytoff 1987). Another form of adaptation was by adjusting occupations, as in the Rift Valley when, faced with more arid conditions in the eighteenth and nineteenth centuries, the various groups who raised both cattle and crops specialized, many Maasai concentrating on the former while others focused on the latter (Spear and Waller 1993). As a response to such pressure on resources, whether exogenous or not, the systematic use of force seems to have been unusual – perhaps because it was costly and often unnecessary (cf. Lonsdale 1981: 175). But competition for increasingly scarce pasturage seems to have been an element among the complex origins of the formation and aggressive expansion of the Zulu kingdom in the 1820s and 1830s, precipitating the establishment of a series of other new or reformed states in southeastern Africa (Guy 1980; Gump 1989).[7]

For most of Africa, it was not until the twentieth century that land abundance came under sustained and widespread challenge. In the settler economies (mostly in East and southern Africa) and in the plantation colonies (mainly in central Africa) land was made artificially scarce for the indigenous population where land was appropriated by the state and reserved for European owners. In the "peasant" colonies (including most of West Africa and much of East Africa) the area under cultivation was massively increased by the widespread adoption of export agriculture (e.g. Weiskel 1988). Across the continent population climbed steadily from the ending of the 1918 world influenza pandemic until the onset of large-scale mortality from the HIV AIDS epidemic in the 1990s. By that final decade of the century land was still abundant, in the economic sense, in much of equatorial Africa and in the Sudan, and in localities in many other areas. Rapid urbanization, especially after 1945, acted as a brake on the general growth of rural population, and in some areas farmers invested in land quality, apparently enough to sustain and even increase returns to labor despite the growing labor:land ratio (Tiffen *et al.* 1994; see also Fairhead and Leach 1996; Maddox 2002). These qualifications are important, but the broad trend was for the dissipation, and in many areas the elimination, of land abundance. Perhaps the most extreme cases of population pressure on cultivable land, with commonly less than a hectare per household, occurred in the last quarter of the twentieth century in the forested (or formerly forested) hills of Rwanda, Burundi, and parts of Kenya. In a local study within Rwanda, for instance, André and Platteau found that the average size of household holdings was 0.46 of a hectare in 1988, and still falling (André and Platteau 1998).

Where and when land became scarce, its implicit economic value tended to be reflected quite quickly in the emergence of markets, for the use rights or for the land itself (e.g. Hopkins 1973). This began to happen before colonial rule, for example in southern Ghana in the mid nineteenth century, where Krobo farmers, expanding their production of oil palm for the market, bought land from Akyem chiefs and elders (Johnson 1964, 1965). Where pastoralists had previously considered land as indeed a "territory" available for communal or reciprocal ownership by a lot of individuals and groups, the tendency in the twentieth century, as pasturage became scarce, was for portions of it to be claimed as the exclusive property of particular groups (Spear and Waller 1993).

Faced with diminishing land surpluses for Africans, both in settler colonies and elsewhere, colonial officials debated what to do. Some argued for the introduction of compulsory land registration and related measures designed to facilitate a free land market (Phillips 1989). This was indeed not dissimilar to the policy followed by the British immediately after they acquired their first foothold in what became Nigeria, by the annexation of Lagos in 1861 (Hopkins 1980). But, on the whole, the colonial regimes of the twentieth century in Africa were less enthusiastic about promoting or accommodating social change. Freehold land tenure was generally reserved for urban areas and for settler farms. Colonial administrations frequently discouraged the alienation of land, both between individuals and households within the same ethnic group and, especially, between members of different ethnic groups. It was realized that every piece of land had an "owner"; colonial officials preferred that that owner, or owners, had to be from what they considered to be the group that had traditionally owned the land in question. Thus in the Rift Valley people had to assert Kikuyu or Maasai identity and claim land – or rather, territory – accordingly (Spear and Waller 1993). Again, in what is now Ghana the colonial government actively defended Asante ownership of Asante lands, bringing pressure to bear on chiefs to ensure that they did not sell or mortgage land to outsiders, even culturally close neighbors such as their fellow Akan-speakers (Austin forthcoming).

Yet it is easy to over-state the social conservatism of colonial policy. In the forest zone of Ghana, where the farmers rapidly adopted cocoa during the early colonial period, the colonial administration ultimately never introduced compulsory land titling (despite internal controversy). But they did insist that farmers' investments be protected, refusing to allow land-owning chiefs to evict strangers who had planted cocoa trees on the land, for example. Without such basic security of tenure – of the farm, though not of the land beneath, which was often litigated over – it is hard to imagine that Ghana would have experienced not one, but two massive cocoa booms: the first of which (*c.*1890–1916) made the colony the world's largest exporter of cocoa beans (by 1910–1911), while the second more than doubled the country's cocoa output during the era of decolonization and early independence (1950s–1965) (Austin forthcoming).

Independent governments were not necessarily more relaxed about land markets. In Rwanda, for instance, land sales were prohibited. Yet they occurred (André and Platteau 1998). More generally, the main twentieth-century tendency was for the rules of tenure that existed at the time of colonization to be reinterpreted and modified, with much argument, the overall effect being to facilitate individual land ownership. On the Kikuyu Reserve, for example, far from the growing density of population leading to a democracy of poverty, in the 1930s–1950s some farmers became fairly prosperous peasants, growing wattle for sale before the colonial government finally removed restrictions which had prevented all but a few from growing the more lucrative cash crops, coffee and tea. Young men who had left the Reserve to live and work on European farms and returned in the 1940s found that the customary rules – or their interpretation – had been changed during their absence; elders had redefined the range of kin by whom land could be inherited much more narrowly. Thus the more prosperous peasants and their close kin accumulated; others not so. This division was reflected in the social composition of the Mau Mau ("Land and People") revolt of the mid 1950s: landless former squatters provided many recruits for the rebels, while peasant household heads with property to lose tended to oppose them.[8]

Overall, tenurial regimes tended to shift to reflect the rising economic value of land (Feder and Noronha 1987; for a critique of this perspective, see Platteau 1996); but the changes were nuanced and often informal, often made by African elders, rather than imposed by governments – who were usually reluctant to recognize them anyway.

State formation and territory

The first generation of post-colonial historians of Africa emphasized that state formation has a long and, in some cases, imposing history south of the Sahara (e.g. Omer-Cooper 1966; Vansina 1966; Wilks 1975). This makes it the more remarkable that, as late as 1650, or indeed by the time of the European "Scramble for Africa," large swathes of forest and savanna (not just desert) were in no sense politically centralized, while the scale of central-ization in much of the rest was fairly local. City-states and independent chiefdoms numbering their subjects in thousands or at most tens of thou-sands almost certainly accounted for more of the Sub-Saharan population than did the larger polities (Lonsdale 1981: 139, 172). Statelets and state-less societies were still common by the time of the European Scramble for

Africa, 1879–*c.*1903. On the whole, though, in the late pre-colonial era, state dissolutions were outweighed by new bouts of state formation, notably in West Africa from the late seventeenth to the early nineteenth century and, most dramatically, in southern Africa in the early and mid nineteenth century. Over the long term, by comparison with Europe, North Africa, and much of Asia, the impulse for political centralization south of the Sahara was operative but much more resistible.

The abundance of land was a major source of this resistance, by making it harder for rulers or would-be rulers to control populations (Kopytoff 1987). Distance made it easier to evade or defy taxation or conscription demands. Without scarce land, states could not trade land rights for revenue payments, i.e. exact "feudal" rents. In principle, despite its physical abundance, states could have made land institutionally scarce. But there was a chicken and egg problem: to appropriate land from the population in the first place required coercive and administrative resources which states would have been able to acquire only if they could extract land revenue already. It was easier, and perhaps unavoidable, for most pre-colonial states to settle for other sources of revenue, such as trade tolls. Above all, pre-colonial states sought subjects, whether slaves or otherwise (captives being frequently resettled in the interior, as by the kingdom of Asante and the Sokoto Caliphate),[9] or cattle. The material base of the Zulu monarchy, as Shaka constructed it, was royal control over the labor power of men in the warrior grade, who were used both for fighting and herding; while the kingdom has been described recently as "a perpetual cattle-raiding machine" (Etherington 2001: 86).

Despite these alternative sources of wealth, rulers' acceptance (with certain exceptions) of the absence of land rents or agricultural taxes in turn meant accepting the continuation of severe resource constraints for the polities concerned. The fact that pre-colonial state revenues were rarely founded on control of cultivable land was reflected in the way in which power was projected from the center: not evenly over contiguous territory, but along networks in which towns were the nodes (Mabogunje and Richards 1985: 6–14). Unlike their European counterparts, most African states were not compelled by pressure on space to fight (literally) to press their frontiers to the utmost extent (Herbst 2000).

The colonial annexations modified rather than transformed this situation. At the Congress of Berlin in 1884–1885 the colonial powers recognized each other's sovereignty over their respective territories. But, as Herbst has commented, this agreement made it unnecessary for the colonial administrations to project power effectively throughout their territories. The same pattern was repeated shortly after independence, when the members of the newly formed Organisation of African Unity likewise guaranteed, in effect, that they would respect each other's borders even when there was no effective authority behind them (Herbst 2000). Like their African predecessors – and in contrast to pre-colonial and colonial India – the colonial rulers of

Africa did not generally extract revenue directly from agriculture. Rather, they taxed people (poll tax) and/or trade (customs duties). During World War II British administrations in West Africa found that the surpluses of statutory export monopolies offered revenues beyond the imaginings of previous regimes, colonial and pre-colonial. Most post-colonial regimes based their finances on revenues from exports of agricultural products or minerals. Yet even with agriculture so important to public finance, the revenue was extracted during the marketing phase rather than directly from production or land use (e.g. World Bank 1981).

In this context, it is not surprising that pre-colonial kingdoms appear to have regarded their territories, as such, as less important than their populations or, in some cases, than their herds; and that their rulers, like village elders in the same period, generally welcomed immigrants with rights of access to cultivable land within those territories. Here, however, colonial and post-colonial borders, and the notion of the sovereign territory that the borders defined in international law, eventually began to make a difference. In particular, they gave a political focus to the demands of indigenous residents and their politicians for mass evictions of foreigners, where and when the latter came to be seen as unwelcome competition for local resources. Examples are the mass expulsion of aliens, many of them Nigerians, from Ghana in 1969; and the mass expulsion of Ghanaians from Nigeria in 1983.

Ethnicity and nationalism south of the Sahara

In discussions of Africa ethnic and national identities are often seen as pulling in opposite directions. In journalistic discussions of the post-colonial period, especially from outside the region, the ethnic is often seen as all too powerful, immovably rooted in indigenous culture and experience; the national as a fragile foreign graft. A brief consideration of the scholarly debate, while not abolishing the distinction between the two, will underline the historicity of both, and point to some overlapping features.

There is a firm consensus in the scholarly literature that ethnicity, in principle and specifically in Africa, is not "primordial," in the sense of being an original and permanent feature of African societies. Rather, scholars overwhelmingly see it as a social and historical phenomenon, therefore subject to change. Over time some ethnic identities decline and even disappear, others are created and reinforced. Hardin has commented that "nothing that must first be socially learned can be primordial" (Hardin 1995: 37). Indeed, since the 1970s historians and anthropologists of Africa have tended emphatically to reject the notion of ethnicity as "primordial." Led by some influential writing of that era, scholars insisted that "tribes" were "invented," often only quite recently, and some writers specified that ethnicity was "instrumental."[10] To take two of the largest ethnic identities in contemporary Africa, it seems that only a small proportion of the ancestors of those who would today define themselves as Yoruba or Zulu (in what is now Nigeria and South Africa respectively) would have applied the term to themselves in 1800.[11] Other ethnonyms may have been comparably widely accepted then as now, but with the critical difference that the identities were much more fluid. Iliffe commented of pre-colonial Tanganyika (mainland Tanzania) that "social groups had remained so amorphous that to write of them is to oversimplify them" (Iliffe 1979: 318). Meanwhile in what are now the Kikuyu areas of Kenya, "Immigrants became Kikuyu"; such assimilation became much more difficult during and after colonial rule (Lonsdale 1992; quotation at 346). It was widely the case in the nineteenth century that being an immigrant in an African society was not a permanent status to those prepared to respect the local authorities, learn the local language, and adopt the local customs. In Cameroon, according to Bayart, the "contemporary ethnic groups, far from being the links between the postcolonial Cameroonian State . . . and its historical background, are often of recent creation, and do not seem to have existed for much longer than the State itself" (1993: 47).

A variety of causes stimulated the emergence of a strong or stronger sense of common identity in such cases. In the case of the Asantes (Ghana) and Zulus, it is clear that pre-colonial state formation and conflicts with other pre-colonial states, as well as pride in histories of resistance to the colonizers, were vital. In other cases, such as Yoruba, the translation of the Christian Bible into the vernacular, by Protestant missionaries, served to provide for the first time a standard, written version of the language concerned (Asiwaju and Law 1985: 413). The main theme in the critical literature on the creation or hardening of tribal identities, however, is that colonial policies, and African responses to them, were most commonly responsible. Because colonial administrations sought to maintain order and control, and to do so at minimum expense to metropolitan taxpayers, they ruled where possible through African chiefs (especially in the British and Belgian colonies, less so in the French), whether the chieftaincies already existed or were created by the colonial government. European officials usually considered chiefs to be the leaders of defined, coherent ethnic groups. Thus it was cheaper, and more convenient, for colonial administrations – and indeed, for European employers and missionaries – to treat Africans as socially organized into "tribes." Some Africans had little alternative but to behave as if this was the case, as when claiming land on the basis of "tribe" rather than risking losing access to it completely, for example in the Maasai/Kikuyu borderlands in the Rift Valley of East Africa (Spear and Waller 1993). Further, some African dynasties and other elites took opportunistic advantage of the colonial obsession with tribe, embracing it for their own purposes – notably the Tutsi ruling dynasty in Rwanda (Newbury 1988; Prunier 1995).

The instrumentalist dimension of this literature is the contention that ethnic claims are motivated by an expectation of collective gain: both under colonial regimes (as above), and in post-colonial electoral or military politics

(Bates 1983). In 1981 Lonsdale argued that "ethnicity is best seen as a form of constituency of access to state power" (1981: 170). In this context, far from being a predecessor of the state, tribes were tools by which the members of the governed organized themselves to pursue their interests within the state; and means by which the governors could seek to divide and rule, to arrange coalitions of support, or – especially in the case of colonies – bring order to incipient land markets.

This revisionist literature has itself come in for revision in the last few years.[12] It has been recognized that, while many ethnic identities were indeed colonial, or at least colonial-era, inventions, others were genuinely pre-colonial, some of them pre-nineteenth century. Atkinson (1999) has made this point strongly for the case of the Acholi of Uganda. In Rwanda, colonial intervention was notoriously exacerbated and hardened ethnic divisions (for a summary see, for example, Prunier 1995). Yet even in Rwanda, there was something to exacerbate; ethnic conflict there has much longer historical roots (Vansina 2001; Webster 2003).

Yet much remains of the original revisionist case. Among collective identities in pre-colonial societies, ethnicity was only one of a number, and in many cases not the most salient: "subject" and "townsman" being two of the most important (Ranger 1999). Again, while many ethnic identities were not exactly "invented," there is a very strong scholarly consensus that they were socially constructed, albeit often over a long period. Moreover, when an ethnic (or national) identity exists, the historically important issue is what is done with it. As Lonsdale put it, "Tribes . . . themselves do nothing. They are mobilized by groups of like-interested people who can persuade a latent or potential community to think and act like one in their support" (Lonsdale 1981: 201).

Most importantly, once an ethnic identity existed, it frequently became reinforced through the experience of competition, and even conflict, with members of other ethnic groups. What economic historians call "path dependence" is a very salient fact in the post-colonial history of African ethnicity. Lemarchand remarked that the 1972 genocide of Hutu in Burundi and the 1994 genocide of Tutsi in Rwanda, "Far from canceling each other," appear to have resulted in "an unbridgeable moral distance between Hutu and Tutsi" (Lemarchand 1996: xii). In such extreme cases a process of mutual "othering" and a cycle of mutual hurt, it seems, can result in senses of ethnic loyalty and division so strong as to at least loosen any relationship with instrumentality and to be almost as impervious to short-term change as if they were primordial after all.

National consciousness is often considered to have turned out to be a mirage in post-colonial Africa, once the struggle for independence from colonial rule had been won. As of *c*.1980, after two decades of frequent military coups and plenty of evidence of ethnic competition within Africa's "new nations," Somalia was commonly described as the only genuine nation state south of the Sahara (albeit, Lesotho and Swaziland could have challenged that).[13] Twenty years further on, popular and some academic assessments are even more downbeat: Somalia is now frequently cited as the archetypal "failed state" (e.g. Herbst 2000: 255–258), in which the effective collective identities are those of the clans. While "nation-building" has often disappointed, however, it is easy to overlook the effects on national consciousness, not so much of flags and struggling national airlines, but of state education, international football competition, and, in some cases, even originally "artificial" international frontiers. What became the Ghana–Togo border, defined by agreement between colonial powers, divided the Ewe-speaking people. Yet, as Nugent has shown, the Ewe unification movement, increasingly vocal during the colonial period, faded away after independence. The people on both sides of the border have adapted to it, helped to shape its impact on their daily lives, and seemingly accepted it. Nugent comments that in this case – and he suggests that it is not unique in twentieth-century Africa – "territorial identification has proved more powerful than ethnicity in the long run" (Nugent 2002: quotation at 274).

Interactions of the changing factor ratios with ethnic consciousness and nation building

The emergence of land shortages led to a tendency for rights of access to land to be reinterpreted more narrowly. Kikuyu squatters (labor-tenants) on settler farms in the White Highlands of Kenya, expelled as we have seen when European farmers adopted labour-saving methods of dairy farming in the 1940s, returned to their home areas in Central Province to find that household heads – whose predecessors had generally welcomed all hands – now denied them access to land, on the grounds that their family links were insufficiently close (Bates 1989). In western Ghana, Boni noted the "emergence of the permanent 'stranger'," as land-holding chiefs and their communities now insisted that immigrants remain as rent-paying strangers, rather than being recruited as additional subjects of the chief, paying only token fees for land (Boni 1999).

The combination of this general, long-term tendency with recent cases of civil war and even genocide, has raised the question of whether the latter horrors should be seen as responses, in part, to land shortage. It is necessary to balance two sets of observations. On one hand, neo-Malthusian accounts of Africa's civil wars of the 1990s and since have been much too readily offered in many cases, and in that of Sierra Leone, for example, have been convincingly rejected by specialist research (Richards 1996). Again, when considering ethnicity in contemporary Africa it is crucial to make the elementary distinction between ethnic diversity and ethnic "fragmentation": the former does not automatically result in the latter.[14] Moreover, as the cases of Rwanda and Burundi show, the worst fragmentation may be in the least ethnically diverse states. Again, the 1990s conflicts were not reducible to inter-ethnic rivalry. This is particularly true of Sierra Leone and Liberia, but even in Rwanda the victims of the 1994 massacres included Hutu political opponents of the perpetrators, as well as Tutsis (Prunier 1995; Ellis 1998; Zack-Williams 1999).

Yet ethnic conflicts have occurred, and in those cases where – unlike in Sierra Leone and Liberia – pressure on land had become extreme, it cannot be excluded as an element contributing to polarization of ethnic relations. A thought-provoking finding, albeit from a small sample, was provided by André and Platteau's study of an administrative district in Rwanda. They found that all but 1 of the 28 murdered in the area during the 1994 massacres were actually non-Tutsi (there had anyway been only 1 Tutsi inhabitant). The other deaths seem to have been related to local disputes, often over the division of land. There is thus some evidence of opportunistic killings motivated by land shortage. While that land shortage alone would not have led to genocide, the fact that tensions over land could provide lethal motivation even outside the Hutu–Tutsi conflict is consistent with the view that it contributed to the build-up and scale of the inter-ethnic violence that occurred on a massive scale elsewhere in the country (André and Platteau 1998). Overall, it seems fair to say that land has been a major contributory element in turning ethnic diversity into inter-ethnic violence where ethnicity is associated with territorial claims. Rwanda is an extreme example, in both the level of population pressure on land and in the scale of ethnic violence. Nigeria is a more representative one for the region, as land becomes scarce in what was formerly a land-abundant economy (Egwu 1998).

Conclusions

The general pre-colonial picture, to which there were exceptions in space and time, was one of land being relatively abundant in economic terms, such that it rarely commanded a market price. Correspondingly, use rights for purposes of cultivation or pasturage were usually relatively easy to obtain, though lands bearing commercially valuable natural resources were targets for warlords or expansionist states. Territory per se was less important for states than was possession of population, of subjects.

The twentieth century, above all, saw a major shift towards land scarcity. This trend was geographically uneven and was incomplete even before it began partly to be reversed by AIDS-related deaths in the 1990s, especially in southern and eastern Africa. Where the tendency toward land shortage operated it created pressures and incentives for more exclusive definitions of property rights in land, and toward the exclusion rather than assimilation of newcomers. Colonial administrations tended to resist the emergence of land markets, while trying to stabilize land ownership and control in the hands of the groups currently occupying them. This policy was one of a range of colonial and post-colonial changes that made ethnic identities much more salient than they had been before.

On the whole, the trend toward a strengthening of individual property rights in land continued throughout the century, despite the contrary efforts of colonial and some post-colonial regimes. In this sense, the "evolutionary" (induced innovation) theory of land rights is vindicated in this case, but through informal more than formal measures; reinterpretations of custom from below, and, at least until the era of Structural Adjustment, with very few impositions of compulsory land registration from above. If the growing economic value of land induced an economically "rational" response in the form of a shift toward easier and more frequent buying and selling of land, and greater individual control over its disposal through sale or inheritance, it also stimulated greater ethnic consciousness in the context of competition for land.

Just as land could be sold but rarely was in many pre-colonial settings, so ethnic identities were often not the most important for the occupants of those settings. By and during the later twentieth century, again with variations and exceptions, the general pattern was that land was increasingly a commodity and ethnicity increasingly salient among the various social forms of collective identity.

Notes

1 The notions of pre-colonial land abundance and labor scarcity, though valid at a general level, need significant revision, however (Austin forthcoming: ch. 4).

2 For examples of this process from opposite sides of the continent, Kikuyu (Kenya) and Asante (Ghana), see Lonsdale (1992: 333–342) and McCaskie (1983: 28) respectively.

3 Slave holding seems to have become considerably more common during and in the decades following the ending of the Atlantic slave trade. For the various forms of property in persons see Lovejoy (1983), Lovejoy and Falola (2003), and, for a detailed case-study, Austin (forthcoming).

4 For overviews of the history of the external (and internal) slave trades, see Lovejoy (1983) and Manning (1990).

5 Reservation price of labor: the lowest rate of remuneration for which someone would be willing to work for someone else.

6 This proposition stands up well from the controversy over the "rise and fall of the Southern African peasantry," put forward by G. Arrighi, C. Bundy, and others in the 1970s (see, especially, Arrighi 1970; Palmer and Parsons 1977), and subjected to revisionist critique by, most notably, Mosley (1983). It should be said that the ban on tenancy in South Africa was not implemented everywhere, for a telling reason. In some areas poor white farmers, reliant on African sharecroppers to provide not only labor but also the plow team, were able to evade the 1913 law, finally evicting their tenants when the coming of affordable mechanization enabled them to do so, in the 1940s. For a vivid case see Van Onselen (1990).

7 There has been intense controversy about the origins of the Zulu kingdom and its repercussions. Here I can only point readers to Cobbing (1988) and Eldredge (1992); and, for further discussion, to Hamilton (1995) and Etherington (2001).

8 The literature on the Mau Mau is enormous. A pertinent summary and analysis for present purposes is Bates (1989).

9 Wilks (1975: 83–85); Lovejoy (1978); Austin (forthcoming).
10 The most influential contributions were perhaps those of Iliffe (1979) and Ranger (e.g. 1983). See, further, Vail (1989).
11 The Zulu case being particularly complicated. See Etherington (2001: 86–87) and, on the Yoruba, Asiwaju and Law (1985: 413–414).
12 For a masterly survey see Spear (2003).
13 As Lonsdale noted (1981: 154–155).
14 The anthropologist Pauline Peters drew attention to this fallacy (Peters 1998; see, further, Lonsdale 2002), which is a basic problem with recent econometric explorations of such issues (Easterly and Levine 1997; Collier 1998).

Bibliography

André, C. and Platteau, J.-P. (1998) "Land Relations under Unbearable Stress: Rwanda Caught in the Malthusian Trap," *Journal of Economic Behavior and Organization*, 34: 1–47.
Arhin, K. (1967) "The Financing of Ashanti Expansion (1700–1820)," *Africa*, 37: 283–291.
Arrighi, G. (1970), "Labour Supplies in Historical Perspective: A Study of the Proletarianization of the African Peasantry in Rhodesia," *Journal of Development Studies*, 6: 197–234 (reprinted in G. Arrighi and J. Saul (1973) *Essays on the Political Economy of Africa*).
Asiwaju, A.I. and Law, R. (1985) "From the Volta to the Niger, c.1600–1800," in J.F.A. Ajayi and M. Crowder (eds) *History of West Africa*, Vol. I, 3rd edn, Harlow: Longman: 412–464.
Atkinson, R.R. (1999) "The (Re)constructing of Ethnicity in Africa: Extending the Chronology, Conceptualisation and Discourse," in P. Yeros (ed.) *Ethnicity and Nationalism in Africa: Constructivist Reflections and Contemporary Politics*, London: Macmillan.
Austin, G. (forthcoming) *Labour, Land and Capital in Ghana: From Slavery to Free Labour in Asante, 1807–1956*, Rochester, NY: University of Rochester Press.
Bates, R.H. (1983) "Modernization, Ethnic Competition, and the Rationality of Politics in Contemporary Africa," in D. Rothchild and V.A. Olorunsola (eds) *State Versus Ethnic Claims: African Policy Dilemmas*, Boulder, CO: Westview.
—— (1989) "The Demand for Revolution: The Agrarian Origins of Mau Mau," in R.H. Bates, *Beyond the Miracle of the Market: The Political Economy of Agrarian Development in Kenya*, Cambridge: Cambridge University Press.
Bayart, J.-F. (1993) [French original, 1989] *The State in Africa: The Politics of the Belly*, trans. M. Harper, C. and E. Harrison, London: Longman.
Boni, S. (1999) "Hierarchy in Twentieth-Century Sefwi (Ghana)," D.Phil. dissertation, University of Oxford.
Cobbing, J. (1988) "The Mfecane as Alibi," *Journal of African History*, 29: 487–519.
Collier, P. (1998), "The Political Economy of Ethnicity," *Annual World Bank Conference on Development Economics*, Washington, DC: World Bank: 387–399.
Crummey, D. (1980) "Abyssinian Feudalism," *Past and Present*, 89: 115–138.
Easterly, W. and Levine, R. (1997) "Africa's Growth Tragedy: Policies and Ethnic Divisions," *Quarterly Journal of Economics*, 112: 1203–1250.
Egwu, S. (1998) *Structural Adjustment, Agrarian Change and Rural Ethnicity in Africa*, Uppsala: Nordiska Afrikainstitutet.

Eldredge, E. (1992) "Sources of Conflict in Southern Africa, ca. 1800–30: The 'Mfecane' Reconsidered," *Journal of African History*, 33: 1–36 (reprinted in Hamilton (1995)).

Ellis, S. (1998) "Liberia's Warlord Emergency," in C. Clapham (ed.) *African Guerillas*, Oxford: James Currey.

Etherington, N. (2001) *The Great Treks: The Transformation of Southern Africa, 1815–1854*, Harlow: Longman.

Fairhead, J. and Leach, M. (1996) *Misreading the African Landscape: Society and Ecology in a Forest-Savanna Mosaic*, Cambridge: Cambridge University Press.

Feder, G. and Noronha, R. (1987) "Land Rights Systems and Agricultural Development in Sub-Saharan Africa," *World Bank Research Observer*, 2: 143–169.

Gump, J. (1989) "Ecological Change and Pre-Shakan State Formation," *African Economic History*, 18: 57–71.

Guy, J. (1980) "Ecological Factors in the Rise of Shaka and the Zulu Kingdom," in S. Marks and A. Atmore (eds) *Economy and Society in Pre-Industrial South Africa*, London: Longman.

Hamilton, C. (1995) (ed.) *The Mfecane Aftermath: Reconstructive Debates in Southern African History*, Johannesburg: Witwatersrand University Press.

Hardin, R. (1995) "Self-Interest, Group Identity," in A. Breton *et al.* (eds) *Nationalism and Rationality*, Cambridge: Cambridge University Press.

Herbst, J. (2000) *States and Power in Africa*, Princeton, NJ: Princeton University Press.

Hill, P. (1963) *The Migrant Cocoa-Farmers of Southern Ghana*, Cambridge: Cambridge University Press. (2nd edition 1997, with introduction by G. Austin: Hamburg: LIT; and Oxford: James Currey.)

Hopkins, A.G. (1973) *An Economic History of West Africa*, London: Longman.

—— (1980) "Property Rights and Empire Building: Britain's Annexation of Lagos, 1861," *Journal of Economic History*, 40: 777–798.

Iliffe, J. (1979) *A Modern History of Tanganyika*, Cambridge: Cambridge University Press.

—— (1995) *Africans: The History of a Continent*, Cambridge: Cambridge University Press.

Johnson, M. (1964) "Migrant's Progress," Part I, *Bulletin of the Ghana Geographical Association*, 9: 4–27.

—— (1965) "Migrant's Progress," Part II, *Bulletin of the Ghana Geographical Association*, 10: 13–40.

—— (1981) "Elephants for Want of Towns," in C. Fyfe and D. MacMaster (eds) *African Historical Demography II*, Edinburgh: University of Edinburgh.

Kopytoff, I. (1987) "The Internal African Frontier: The Making of African Political Culture," in I. Kopytoff (ed.) *The African Frontier: The Reproduction of Traditional African Societies*, Bloomington, IN: Indiana University Press.

Lemarchand, R. (1996) *Burundi: Ethnic Conflict and Genocide*, Cambridge: Cambridge University Press.

Lonsdale, J. (1981) "States and Social Processes in Africa: A Historiographical Survey," *African Studies Review*, 24: 139–225.

—— (1992) "The Moral Economy of Mau Mau: Wealth, Poverty and Civic Virtue in Kikuyu Political Thought," in B. Berman and J. Lonsdale, *Unhappy Valley: Conflict in Kenya and Africa*, Book II, London: James Currey.

—— (2002) "Globalization, Ethnicity and Democracy: A View From 'the Hopeless Continent'," in A.G. Hopkins (ed.) *Globalization in World History*, London: Pimlico.

Lovejoy, P. (1978) "Plantations in the Economy of the Sokoto Caliphate," *Journal of African History*, 19: 341–368.

—— (1983) *Transformations in Slavery: A History of Slavery in Africa*, Cambridge: Cambridge University Press.

—— and Falola, T. (eds) (2003) *Pawnship, Slavery, and Colonialism in Africa*, Trenton, NJ: Africa World Press.

—— and Hogendorn, J. (1993) *Slow Death for Slavery: The Course of Abolition in Northern Nigeria, 1897–1936*, Cambridge: Cambridge University Press.

Mabogunje, A.L. and Richards, P. (1985) "Land and People: Models of Spatial and Ecological Processes in West African History," in J.F.A. Ajayi and M. Crowder, (eds) *History of West Africa*, Vol. I, 3rd edn, Harlow: Longman.

McCann, J.C. (1999) "A Tale of Two Forests: Narratives of Deforestation in Ethiopia, 1840–1996," in J.C. McCann, *Green Land, Brown Land, Black Land: An Environmental History of Africa, 1800–1990*, Portsmouth, NH: Heinemann.

McCaskie, T.C. (1983) "Accumulation, Wealth and Belief in Asante History: I. To the Close of the Nineteenth Century," *Africa*, 53: 23–44.

Maddox, G. (2002) "'Degradation Narratives' and 'Population Time Bombs': Myths and Realities about African Environments," in S. Dovers, R. Edgecombe and B. Guest (eds) *South Africa's Environmental History: Cases and Comparisons*, Cape Town: David Philip.

Manning, P. (1990) *Slavery and African Life: Occidental, Oriental, and African Slave Trades*, Cambridge: Cambridge University Press.

Mosley, P. (1983) *The Settler Economies: Kenya and Southern Rhodesia 1900–1953*, Cambridge: Cambridge University Press.

Newbury, C. (1988) *The Cohesion of Oppression: Clientship and Ethnicity in Rwanda, 1860–1960*, New York: Columbia University Press.

Nugent, P. (2002) *Smugglers, Secessionists and Loyal Citizens on the Ghana–Togo Border*, Oxford: James Currey.

Omer-Cooper, J.D. (1966) *The Zulu Aftermath*, London: Longmans.

Palmer, R. and Parsons, N. (eds) (1977) *The Roots of Rural Poverty in Central and Southern Africa*, London: Heinemann.

Park, M. (1983) [1st edn 1799] *Travels into the Interior of Africa*, London: Eland.

Peters, P. (1998) "Comment" (on Collier 1998), *Annual World Bank Conference on Development Economics,* Washington, DC: World Bank: 400–440.

Phillips, A. (1989) *The Engima of Colonialism: British Policy in West Africa*, London: James Currey.

Platteau, J.-P. (1996) "The Evolutionary Theory of Land Rights as Applied to Sub-Saharan Africa: A Critical Assessment," *Development and Change*, 27: 29–86.

Prunier, G. (1995) *The Rwanda Crisis: History of a Genocide 1959–1994*, London: Hurst.

Ranger, T. (1983) "The Invention of Tradition in Colonial Africa," in E.J. Hobsbawm and T. Ranger (eds) *The Invention of Tradition*, Cambridge: Cambridge University Press.

—— (1999), "Concluding Comments," in P. Yeros (ed.) *Ethnicity and Nationalism in Africa: Constructivist Reflections and Contemporary Politics*, London: Macmillan.

Rattray, R.S. (1929) *Ashanti Law and Constitution*, Oxford: Oxford University Press.

Richards, P. (1996) *Fighting for the Rain Forest: War, Youth and Resources in Sierra Leone*, London: International African Institute and James Currey.

Robertson, C.C. and Klein, M.A. (1983) "Women's Importance in African Slave Systems," in C.C. Robertson and M.A. Klein (eds) *Women and Slavery in Africa*, Madison, WI: University of Wisconsin Press.

Spear, T. (2003) "Neo-Traditionalism and the Limits of Invention in British Colonial Africa," *Journal of African History*, 44: 3–28.

—— and Waller, R. (eds) (1993) *Being Maasai*, London: James Currey.

Tiffen, M., Mortimore, M., and Gichuki, F. (1994) *More People, Less Erosion: Environmental Recovery in Kenya*, Chichester: John Wiley.

Tosh, J. (1980) "The Cash-Crop Revolution in Tropical Agriculture: An Agricultural Reappraisal," *African Affairs*, 79: 79–94.

Vail, L. (1977) "Ecology and History: The Example of Eastern Zambia," *Journal of Southern African Studies*, 3: 129–155.

—— (ed.) (1989) *The Creation of Tribalism in Southern Africa*, London: James Currey.

Van Onselen (1990) "Race and Class in the South African Countryside: Cultural Osmosis and Social Relations in the Sharecropping Economy of Transvaal," *American Historical Review*, 95: 99–123.

Vansina, J. (1966) *Kingdoms of the Savanna: A History of Central African States Until European Occupation*, Madison, WI: University of Wisconsin Press.

—— (2001) *Le Rwanda ancien: Le royaume nyiginya*, Paris: Karthala.

Webster, J.B. (2003), "The Dark Shadow of Rwabugiri," in T. Falola (ed.) *Ghana in Africa and the World: Essays in Honor of Adu Boahen*, Trenton, NJ: Africa World Press.

Weiskel, T. (1988) "Toward an Archaeology of Colonialism: Elements in the Ecological Transformation of the Ivory Coast," in D. Worster (ed.) *The Ends of the Earth*, Cambridge: Cambridge University Press.

Wilks, I. (1975) *Asante in the Nineteenth Century: The Structure and Evolution of a Political Order*, Cambridge: Cambridge University Press.

World Bank (1981) *Accelerated Development in Sub-Saharan Africa: An Agenda for Action*, Washington, DC: World Bank.

Zack-Williams, A. (1999) "Sierra Leone: The Political Economy of Civil War, 1991–98," *Third World Quarterly*, 20: 143–162.

12 Ethnic competition and claims to land in South Africa

The Kat River valley, Eastern Cape

Robert Ross

One of the first democratically passed acts in South African history, brought into law by the 1994 Parliament of the Republic, was the Restitution of Land Rights Act (South Africa, Act 22, 1994). Its purpose was to redress one of the most hated activities of the apartheid regime and its predecessors, namely the confiscation of land and the forced removal of its inhabitants because they happened to be of the wrong "racial" group, according to the classification which the government had imposed. Where possible, the land was to be returned to those who had been dispossessed, or their heirs. Where this was not possible, some other form of compensation, monetary or in terms of alternative land, was to be provided.[1] Certain conditions were imposed on the land claims, of which the most important is that the dispossession had to take place after the enactment of the Land Act of 1913, which for much of the country formed the basis of the racial segregation of at least the countryside. This meant that in principle no claims could be entertained which resulted from the original colonial conquest of South Africa, which had in principle been completed before the Land Act came into operation.

As can be imagined, the number of claims which were put into the Land Claims Commission was vast – 68,878 in total – the issues were complicated and the progress slow, even though the Court was prepared to accept a lesser degree of proof than would have been necessary in any other Court action. Individual claims have to be demonstrated to have been historically plausible, not legally proven. The cases, indeed, have provided many South African historians with welcome subventions to their income, as consultant researchers. As of December 31, 2002, 36,279, or about 53 percent, of the cases had been decided, and the Commission courts seem likely to churn on for many years to come, incidentally providing future historians with a fascinating, if somewhat indigestible, mass of source material (*Business Day* February 3, 2003).

In this chapter, I wish to discuss the issues involved in land compensation and competition, not in its totality, but rather with relation to one particular locality, the upper Kat River valley, which is the locus of my current research (see Map 12.1). It is not claimed that the Kat River valley

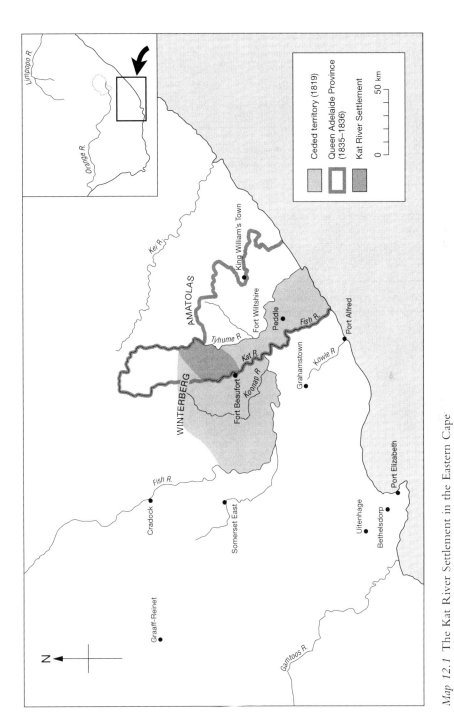

Map 12.1 The Kat River Settlement in the Eastern Cape

Source: Adapted from Bergh and Visagie (1985).

is typical of South African developments in any way except for its complexity. Nevertheless, the very complexities, which require a return to the early nineteenth century if they are to be understood, do provide a metonym for the processes of land alienation and ethnic competition which have been so central to the South African past, and indeed to its present. Thus the unraveling of this complexity can illustrate the ways in which ethnicity and land have become intertwined, or in other words how *Blut* (blood) can justify claims to *Boden* (soil).

Of course, neither *Blut* nor *Boden* are immutable, or immediately obvious categories. Ethnicity, we have learned to appreciate, is something to be imagined (Anderson 1983), to be invented (Hobsbawm and Ranger 1983; Ranger, 1993), or in some way or other constructed. Equally, within Africa, certainly within southern Africa, we are used to realizing that the making of ethnicities was often as much the work of Europeans as of Africans, even though, obviously, Africans had to accept and work with the ethnicities so created (Vail 1989). Certainly, on the Eastern Frontier of the Cape Colony, or the Western Frontier of Xhosaland (Ross 2003: 117), the distinction between Xhosa and Khoi was heavily accentuated by the Europeans, particularly the English. It did not emerge from nothing, however. Even though, as will be shown below, individuals could on occasion move between the statuses of Khoi and Xhosa, the distinction between the two ways of life was much older. Khoi and Xhosa languages, material cultures, economic systems, and political institutions had been coexisting as separate entities for at least a millennium before the Europeans arrived, even though the latter attempted, eventually with considerable success, to freeze the two communities from each other (Harinck 1969; Ross 1980). And in general it is easy to exaggerate the degree to which the "traditional" institutions of Africa, thus including ethnicity, were indeed recent, and certainly colonial, inventions (Spear 2003).

Land might seem to be a less constructed category. In one sense it is. Land and landscape are not invented by humans, but are in some sense out there, created by erosion and deposition, and by the actions of animals and plants. But in three respects, at least, land is a human construction. First, almost everywhere, humans are the most intrusive of the animals, plants, and natural forces which shape the landscape. Second, the division of land among people is not merely a human activity, but more importantly it is by no means universal to all human societies. In South Africa, it was known, in broad terms, who controlled particular pieces of territory, but the precise delineation and demarcation of specific parcels of real estate was in a major part the creation of the colonial conquest. In the Kat River, as elsewhere, the land surveyor was an agent of colonial capitalism as crucial as the soldier, the merchant, or the farmer. (Crais 2002: 72–79) Third, of course, such meaning as has been given to land can only be given to it by men and women.

The setting

The Upper Kat River valley is a basin of about a thousand square kilometers, with a floor at about 600 meters above sea level virtually completely surrounded by mountains which rise to over 2,000 meters. There is one exit for the river, through a narrow *poort* to the south, and a couple of easy passes to the east and southeast into the broad Tyume valley. It is situated in what is now the Eastern Cape Province of South Africa, just to the north of the town of Fort Beaufort. With around 500 cm a year, its average rainfall is fairly high, at least for the region,[2] but is rather irregular. It is, however, well watered by the various streams which flow down from the wooded mountain slopes and which have, over the millennia, cut the valley into a mosaic of fertile bottom land, which can be irrigated, at the moment primarily by means of pumps put into the streams, and aloe-covered hillsides, which provide rough grazing. The mountainsides around the valley were once covered with indigenous forest, and a surprising amount has survived, though now interspaced with exotic plantations, largely of conifers.

Since the provincial reorganization in 1994, the Kat River valley has been more or less in the center of the Eastern Cape Province. More importantly, it has historically been right on the most important frontier in the country, which is in the first instance an ecological one – that between those areas of the country where crops could be grown on the basis of summer rainfall and those where they could not. In the former, over the last couple of millennia, fairly densely settled agro-pastoralist societies developed, whose members spoke one of the various Bantu languages and were subject to chiefly rule. In the latter, such an organization was impossible. Population densities were much lower. The inhabitants were almost exclusively pastoralist, or hunter-gatherers, and spoke one of the Khoisan languages. This was at least the case until the arrival of the European colonists, who were able to import crops from the Mediterranean region which could flourish in the winter rain areas of the Western Cape. With their technological advantages, the Europeans were able to subdue the Khoisan of the Cape Colony in the century or so after the foundation of the Colony in 1652. By the early nineteenth century they had extended their dominance to the boundaries of the summer rain zone to the east. At this stage, the colonists came into conflict with the most southwesterly of the Bantu-speaking chiefdoms, those of the Xhosa.

Before the beginning of the nineteenth century, so far as can be reconstructed, the Kat River valley was used by both Xhosa and Khoikhoi herders for summer grazing (Peires 1981: 8–9), but neither seem to have settled there permanently. According to Khoi three decades later, the land was "in possession of a tribe of Hottentots called Heintemas" [whoever they may have been], and was not thought of as part of Xhosaland (Elbourne 2002: 265). Hendrik Joseph remembered having come into the valley as a boy, probably in the last decade of the eighteenth century, perhaps even earlier, to hunt for hippopotami, and finding only Gona Khoi living there (*South African Commercial Advertiser* September 3, 1834). And if it was still worthwhile hunting hippo in the valley, there cannot even have been very many of them.

Maqoma

By the end of the eighteenth century, the invading colonists had more or less subdued the various Khoisan groups as far east as the boundary with Xhosa. While a number were able to find refuge at the various mission stations, which were founded from around 1800 on, and a number of more or less independent villages survived, the great majority were reduced to the status of laborer on the white farms, generally in a status scarcely to be distinguished from that of slavery. The Servants' Revolt of 1799–1803, in which the Eastern Cape Khoikhoi attempted vainly to better their condition, represented the final outburst of protest against the loss of independence (Newton-King and Malherbe 1981; Newton-King 1999).

The Servants' Revolt took place during what is known in Cape history as the First British Occupation, which lasted from 1795 to 1803. Three years later, the British were back, in what proved to be the definitive incorporation of the Cape into the British Empire. One of the consequences of this was that, in theory at least, the might of the British Army could be employed on the Eastern Frontier of the Cape Colony, thus definitively shifting the balance of force between colonists and the Xhosa, which had been more or less equal up till then, in favor of the former. First in 1812 and then in 1819–1820, the British fought wars against at least some of the western Xhosa, which ended in decisive victories for the Cape Colony, even though, at least in the latter case, the British were only saved from a serious defeat in the Battle of Grahamstown by the timely arrival of a group of Khoi elephant hunters under the leadership of Captain Boezak (Maclennan 1986; Peires 1989).

The war of 1819–1820, Nxele's war as it is often known, was not a clear contest between black and white – none of the wars in South African history ever were. In this case, the British became involved in a power struggle between two of the Xhosa rulers, Ngqika and his uncle Ndlambe. Their intervention enabled Ngqika to become by far the most important figure among the western Xhosa, those known, after the common ancestor of the two main protagonists, as the Rharhabe. Indeed, Ngqika saw himself as just as much aiding the British against their Xhosa opponents as being aided in his own contest with his uncle. All the same, the British extracted a price. A wide swathe of territory, between the Fish and the Keiskamma Rivers was declared "Neutral," and was to be held as an empty buffer zone between the Xhosa and the Colony. This included, at its northern end, the Upper Kat River valley (Bergh and Visagie 1985).

For Ngqika, and his sons, this hit hard. Whereas Ngqika lived all his life in the Tyume valley, just across the mountains to the east, his sons were increasingly moving into the Kat River basin. The most notable of these was Maqoma, Ngqika's eldest son, though not his heir. Maqoma, who had been born in 1798, was the most impressive Xhosa of his generation, perhaps together with his half-brother Tyali. By the early 1820s he wanted to assert his independence from his father. As head of Ngqika's "right-hand house," he had every right to do this.[3] As a result he moved into the valley, first below the *poort*, near where the town of Fort Beaufort was to be established, and then, after 1820, in the north of the upper basin, establishing a great place, as a chiefly capital is called, in the hills above Balfour, where the Glasgow Missionary Society was to establish a station. This Maqoma did, the unilateral proclamation of the Neutral territory by the British notwithstanding. In early 1821, the first of Maqoma's followers were settling in the valley, and by the end of that year Maqoma himself had established a "great place" up against the mountains (*Report* 1836: 404; Stapleton 1994: 40–41).

There can be little doubt that Maqoma's move into the Kat River valley constituted the first more or less permanent settlement in the area, although he had been preceded by a number of those Xhosa who had come under the influence of European missionaries. The most notable of these Xhosa was Ntsikana, in many ways the founder of Xhosa Christianity, who lived, died, and was buried in a small valley near what is now Hertzog, where his grave has become an object of pilgimage (Hodgson 1980). The descendants of the Khoikhoi now living there claim that their ancestors gave Maqoma permission to go there.[4] This is a claim in terms of the convoluted ethnic politics, which now characterizes much of the Eastern Cape, and is particularly salient as Maqoma's descendants still have a degree of political power around Seymour, which was to become the magistracy of the valley. It is obviously a claim made in the light of subsequent history, which will be explored further in this chapter, but it is also evident that the Khoi would have been powerless to have prevented him at the time, and furthermore there is no shred of contemporary evidence that they did so. In any event, it is difficult to see who would have been empowered to make such a decision, and equally improbable that concepts of land ownership were sufficiently developed to have made such a transaction plausible. What does seem to have been the case is that Gonaqua Khoi who had lived in the valley and others who had come under the influence of a short-lived London Missionary Society mission near the *poort* of the valley came to acknowledge Maqoma's suzerainty (Kirk 1973: 412).

During his stay in the Kat River, Maqoma assembled a substantial following. By 1828 there were at least 33 homesteads under his leadership, entailing a population in the thousands (Stapleton 1994: 56). He was also becoming rich in stock, and in 1823 there were at least 7,000 head of cattle in his cattle kraals (*Correspondence* 1837: 5; Stapleton 1994: 44). These of course are minimum estimates, well under the true figure, while the self-interested comment of the colonial Field-Cornet that Maqoma had some 16,000 subjects was almost certainly an exaggeration (Stapleton 1994: 43). At any event, it is clear that in the few years after his arrival in 1821 Maqoma had been able to build up a chieftainship of considerable proportions, by the standards of Xhosaland at the time. It was seen as a threat, both by the whites and by his father Ngqika, who did what he could to prevent his own followers crossing the mountains to settle with his son. The politics of Xhosaland were brutal. Apparently, Ngqika had homestead heads who were threatening to move to Maqoma smelt out for witchcraft and burnt to death (Stapleton 1994,: 42).

The Europeans did not resort to witchcraft accusations, or at least they did so within their own idioms. The attack on Maqoma was for being a stock rustler. For some years there was a running contest between his followers and the European-descended farmers of the Baviaans River district, to the west across the mountains. It was a contest in which a number of Xhosa, but no Europeans, were killed, and which in 1823 led to the temporary confiscation of virtually all Maqoma's cattle. Maqoma, too, was attempting to transform his fighting force into mounted gunmen, as Moshoeshoe was to do in Lesotho a couple of decades later with greater success. Acquiring sufficient horses and guns was not easy, because the British attempted to prevent the Xhosa from coming into the possession of firearms and the horses largely had to be stolen (Stapleton 1994: 46–48). In any event, the presence of an armed and growing Xhosa chiefdom in the highlands of the Kat River was considered to be a great threat to the European farms to its west. And among those farmers was Andries Stockenstrom, once magistrate of the border district of Graaff-Reinet and now Commissioner-General for the Eastern Cape, who owned land at what was later to become the village of Bedford.

In 1829, largely at the instigation of Stockenstrom, Maqoma was expelled from the valley by British forces. The excuse which was used was that he had attacked the Thembu, to the north across the mountains, in a major raid for cattle. Maqoma claimed that he had intervened in an internal Thembu dispute at the invitation of one of the parties, the chief Bowana, and indeed he offered to return the cattle he had taken. Nevertheless, the British were adamant that the Xhosa should be removed from the Neutral Zone. An expedition of the Cape Mounted Rifles during the early days of May 1829 drove Maqoma and his followers out of the headwaters of the Kat and burnt their crops, which were still standing in the fields. The Xhosa who were thus forced out had to flee across into the Tyume valley, where they were reabsorbed into the chiefdom of Maqoma's father, Ngqika.

The Kat River Settlement

With the valley now cleared of its Xhosa inhabitants, it was now given over by the British to Khoikhoi settlers. Although he later denied it (*Report* 1854:

1–2), there can be no doubt that the idea of doing this was in Stockenstrom's mind before he instigated the attack on Maqoma. As early as 1821, a suggestion had been made, by Thomas Pringle, who was one of Stockenstrom's associates, that Khoi should be placed within the Neutral territory (Macmillan 1963: 83). In 1828, well before Maqoma's raids on the Thembu, Stockenstrom himself had suggested that the Neutral territory, renamed the Ceded territory, should be occupied by British subjects as soon as possible (Stockenstrom 1887: I 302, II 350–351). Maqoma's conflicts with the Thembu merely gave the British the opportunity for a policy which they had already conceived.

The move to settle the Kat River valley with Khoi was in part the reaction to the "emancipation" of the Khoikhoi, as a result of Ordinance 50 of 1828. By this measure, all civil disabilities on the basis of race (though not of course in consequence of slavery) were abolished within the Cape Colony, and its provisions were later extended throughout the British Empire (outside of India) (Ross 1989). This entailed, specifically in South Africa, that the Khoisan, who had been subject to particular discrimination going back at least to 1809 – and indeed under Dutch rule theretofore – were now able to own land and were not subject to random arrest while on the road (Elbourne 2002: 233–258). However, it was acknowledged that such a measure was going to be useless unless some land was opened to Khoikhoi occupation. Since the great majority of potentially fertile land was already in European hands, this could only be done in an area newly annexed to the Colony, and the Kat River valley was by far the largest such tract of country.

There was, of course, another motive. Khoikhoi units had fought well on the colonial side in the war of 1820 against the Xhosa. If the Kat River valley were settled with sufficient Khoikhoi, then they might form a bulwark against future Xhosa attacks, and thus preserve the rich white farms to the east, for instance in the Koonap valley – and specifically of course Stockenstrom's own farm – from further destruction. This would entail a settlement pattern distinct from the extensive land use generally maintained within the Colony. It was reckoned that Khoikhoi would be the only possible takers for such land, particularly as the attempt to concentrate smallholdings of British immigrants further to the south had by this stage largely broken up. In general, the amount of land required to maintain a European family in the state to which they wished to become accustomed was such that Europeans settlement could never act as a sufficient defense against the Xhosa. The Khoikhoi, in contrast, who had nothing before, would be content with grants of land in the order of 10 hectares each, with commonage, which could be made productive by the establishment of an extensive irrigation system (Stockenstrom 1887: II 350–351; Winer and Ross 2000).[5] Only the Commandant of the District, Christian Groepe, a so-called Bastard, received a larger portion of land, in recognition of his services, namely the farm known as Tamboekies Vlei, about 1,800 hectares in extent.

These plans were put into operation. In the course of 1829, Khoikhoi families from across the Eastern Cape began moving into the valley and establishing themselves as small farmers. By 1833, there were 2,185, and within a decade or so, the Khoi population of the valley was in the order of 6,000.[6] They came from all over the Eastern Cape, but three (by no means exclusive) groups were the most prominent, namely those who had served as soldiers in the Cape Mounted Rifles, those who had lived on one of the mission stations, particularly of the London Missionary Society and the Moravian Brotherhood, and now hoped to expand their landholdings, and those, known as Bastards,[7] of mixed white and Khoi parentage, who had lived on white farms but could never hope to be fully accepted into white society, or inherit land. These were all, nonetheless, considered to be Khoi by the colonial authorities, who laid down that the Kat River Settlement was to be exclusively for Khoi.

During the 20 years following its foundation, the Settlement flourished, at least intermittently. There were years of good harvest, though of course also years of drought and relative penury. The Khoi were becoming a relatively prosperous peasantry, or at least would have been were it not for the repeated destruction of their property and housing and the loss of virtually all their stock in the wars with the Xhosa. In both Hintza's war (1834–1836) and in the War of the Axe (1846–1847), the Settlement fulfilled its function as protector of the farms to the west, at least in part, but at terrible cost to itself. Ninety percent of the adult men fought alongside the British (Le Cordeur and Saunders 1981: 89). The women and children were herded together in what were in effect South Africa's – and thus the world's – first concentration camps, where they suffered grievously from hunger and infectious diseases.[8] In the wake of both the wars, the farms had to be built up from nothing, and in places the destruction was so great that only the presence of fruit trees showed that, only a couple of years before, the land had been under the plough (*Correspondence* 1837: 339).[9] But the resilience of the Kat River Settlers was such that, on both occasions, the agricultural land was taken back into use, with success. Now that they had acquired land, they had developed a very considerable pride in it, and were beginning, metaphorically as well as literally, to put down roots in it (*South African Commercial Advertiser* September 3, 1834).

The Kat River Settlement was set up as ethnically exclusive. This produced at least two complexes of problems. The first was the question of who was, and who was not, Khoi. Most of the Kat River Settlers, except for those known as Bastards, were of Gona (also known as Gonaqua) descent. The Gona were the easternmost of the Khoikhoi tribes, and as such had the longest contact with the Xhosa (Harinck 1969; Ross 1980). Many of them were bilingual in Xhosa and Khoi (although by the second quarter of the nineteenth century the Khoi language in the Cape was dying out, to be replaced by Dutch, or proto-Afrikaans). There was much intermarriage. Maqoma himself, for instance, had Khoi forebears, via his mother

Nothontho (Stapleton 1994: 21). A number of the Kat River Settlers had lived under Xhosa chiefs, while still maintaining a Gona identity – or at least being prepared to put on that cloak when it suited them – before coming to settle in the Kat River (Stockenstrom 1887: II 419), and others, notably Andries Stoffels, one of the most prominent of the Settlers, had spent periods of their youth in Xhosaland (Elbourne 1995: 88). There were even those, such as the Nouka (or Noeka) family, who had been home-stead heads under Maqoma during his sojourn in the valley, but who remained there after 1829 (Kirk 1973: 412). Others had kin among the Xhosa, in William Brass's case a brother with whom he committed a robbery in 1837. It was thus largely a matter of personal, and political, choice, or at least a consequence of the accidents of biography, whether a man (or woman) "was" a Xhosa or a Khoi, and even more so whether the self-proclaimed Gona received land in the Settlement at its foundation or whether he lived in the Settlement as a client of some man who had.

The British were unable to understand this uncertainty, this fluidity. They themselves had a fiercely ethnic consciousness, certainly in the colonial situation of South Africa, and were unable to comprehend those whose national loyalties were more subject to change. If the Gona were "Hottentots," then they might be in the Kat River; if they were "Kaffers," then they were there illegally and should be expelled. Increasingly, British spokesmen came to believe that the latter was the case. As early as 1825, a Wesleyan missionary wrote that the Gona "have long been completely blended and intermixed with all the tribes in Cafferland, and can no longer be recog-nised as a distinct race" (Theal 1897–1905: XIX 458). Certainly military men were unnecessarily uncertain as to the Gona loyalty toward the British during the 1835 war (*Correspondence* 1837: 84–86). Captain Armstrong, British Army commander in the valley, explained his problem with the Gona as follows:

> The Gonahs are a race between a Caffer and a Hottentot. At one time the Caffer took a number of Hottentot into their service; they compelled the Hottentot women to live with them. The children are Gonahs, entertaining partly a Caffer and partly a Hottentot feeling.
>
> (*Correspondence* 1837: 84–86)

As British settlers' antipathy towards the Kat River people increased, such sentiments became more important as a motor of policy.

The second problem concerned those non-Khoi whose position within the taxonomy was not in doubt but who nevertheless found their way into the Kat River. There were two main groups of these. First, from time to time, Mfengu,[10] who had been granted land near Fort Beaufort to the south of the Settlement, came to establish themselves across the border in the valleys of the Gonzana and Mancazana Rivers, tributaries of the Kat.[11] Rather more came to live in the well-watered, though non-irrigable, northwest of the valley, in the field-cornetcy of Buxton, where they ran cattle and cultivated maize, sorghum, and pumpkins on the commonage, effectively living as herdsmen and labor tenants for the Khoi of the area.

Second, in the Blinkwater valley and the adjacent *kloofs* to the west of the settlement, up against the Kroome mountains, groups of Xhosa came to establish themselves, largely out of the control of the chiefs. The most prominent of these was Hermanus Matroos, otherwise known as Ngxukumeshe. He was the son of an escaped slave and a Xhosa woman, who had been adopted into the Xhosa Jwara clan and remained a Xhosa "in his habits, his customs and his notions." As he had, in his youth, worked on a white farm, he was able to act as interpreter between Ngqika and the colonists, but later fell out with the Xhosa ruler, fought on the side of the Colony in Hintza's war and the War of the Axe and was granted the right to live in the Blinkwater, since it was thought too dangerous for him to reside with the Xhosa. He was able to acquire a substantial following, of around 48 families, Xhosa, Gona, Thembu, and Mfengu, in 1842,[12] and was eventually able to rebuild his relations with the Xhosa proper, marrying one of Maqoma's own dependents.[13] There were others who began to congregate in the region, often indeed from the ranks of those who had fought against the Colony (*Proceedings* 1852: 90–95).

In the course of 1850, the colonial authorities launched a major attack on the various groups which they considered did not have the right to remain within the confines of the Kat River Settlement. During the winter of that year, in a week of rain, wind, and even snow, a party of the Xhosa police in colonial service, led by Captain David Davies, proceeded through the western part of the Settlement eliminating the homesteads of those they described as Xhosa "squatters." Their first targets were the Xhosa in Fullers Hoek and the other *kloofs* on the western boundary of the Kat River Settlement. Some of these were relatively independent, or at least the subjects of Xhosa chiefs, including Bhotomane. One of the leaders, one Mali, was known to have fought against the Colony during the War of the Axe. Others claimed to be followers of Hermanus, but were living outside the restricted area which had been allowed to him. Davies and his party then moved on to Buxton, where they found more squatters than in any other place, among the followers of Field-Cornet Andries Botha. Here again, many huts were burned, to make the total for operation more than 300. The men, women, and children were then shepherded off to Fort Hare, together with their goats and cattle. In total, 145 men, 350 women, and an unknown number of children were driven off the land, together with nearly 2,500 head of cattle and nearly 1,400 goats (Freeman 1851: 176–179).

It is nowhere made clear how Davies and the rest of police force decided who were squatters who should be expelled. The boundary between Xhosa and Khoi was always vague, especially when Gona were involved. Botha himself was identified by the Xhosa police to Davies as "a Ghona Kaffir"

(Freeman 1851: 178), but a man with the office of Field-Cornet, a regularly granted *erf* and a rectangular wattle and daub house could not be considered a squatter.[14] My guess is that those whose homes were destroyed had made the mistake of maintaining a round, beehive-style, isiXhosa hut. According to Botha, many were among his friends, and perhaps his kin, who had come to the Settlement from Xhosaland in 1829. Those of this group who had settled in Balfour had received *erven* immediately, and some of those who had gone to Philipton had later got land, largely in the Lower Blinkwater. However, very few of those who had gone to Buxton, a more pastoral region where irrigated agriculture had failed, had been granted title to land, and many had in the meantime grown up to maturity:

> they have always been expecting to get *erfs*, according to promise, but it was not done, and as they were among the friends, and no complaints, we did not urge their leaving; thus they have remained among their friends until now. They were ready for any duty, paid regularly the taxes as long as we paid, went on patrols against the [Xhosa], and fought two wars.
>
> (Freeman 1851: 183)

Indeed, according to a list drawn up by the Reads, out of 36 Gona "burnt out" at Wilberforce and Buxton, 29 had been in the Settlement for 20 years, that is from its foundation, 5 since the 1835 war, 1 (whose name would suggest that he had relatives among the others) for 3 years and for 1 no period was given. There were also 10 Mfengu families who had come to Settlement in the wake of Hintza's war and 6 who had been policemen and were afraid to reside among the other Xhosa who had entered the Colony in 1842, in part because they had fought with the Colony in the War of the Axe.[15] There were also those who worked as servants for the Kat River Settlers, including at least 1 case in which the year-long labor contract had been registered with T.H. Bowker (who had recently been appointed as magistrate of the Settlement) only 4 months before the laborer in question, Mahe, had his hut burnt.[16] The repulsion which Botha, as the leader of the Buxton and Wilberforce community, felt at what had happened is totally understandable, and, though it is not expressed in the historical record, that of the younger inhabitants of the area was as great, if not greater. The fact that the inquiry into this affair brought down a reprimand on Bowker's head, and his replacement as magistrate of the Settlement did little to mollify them (Du Toit 1954: 50).

This campaign exacerbated the growing animosity between the Kat River people and the colonial government, particularly since many of those who were attacked by Davies and his Xhosa police were the clients, and often the relatives, of legally established Settlers. There can be no doubt that the events of July 1850 contributed materially to the decision, first, of Hermanus Matroos to throw in his lot with the Xhosa at the beginning of the war which broke out in the subsequent December, which led to his death in the streets of Fort Beaufort, and, second, of many of the Kat River Khoi to take up arms in rebellion against the Colony. This is not the place to discuss the course of the rebellion, which occurred in the context of the longest and bloodiest war in southern Africa during the nineteenth century – if the South African war of 1899–1902 is excepted, probably the longest and bloodiest in the colonial conquest of the continent, outside the Maghreb. For these purposes, it is enough to say that approximately one third of the valley's Khoi inhabitants went into rebellion, and that the war led to the total physical destruction of the housing and agricultural infrastructure of the Settlement, largely at the hands of British forces, to enormous hardship for those who remained loyal and, effectively, to the victory of those who had long been the Settlement's opponents, the conservative British settlers of the Eastern Cape.

Reconstruction and the end of ethnic exclusiveness

By the middle of 1853, the rebellion had been crushed, although there remained a considerable number of rebel men in the mountains of the Transkei. The reconstruction of the valley had to be commenced. This marked the beginning of the process whereby the landholding within the valley shifted from being exclusively Khoi to being predominantly white.

In the first instance, this was a matter of colonial policy. A Commission set up by Government in the aftermath of the rebellion stated that such lands as were vacant, for whatever reason, should be granted to white men, "in order to break up this exclusively Hottentot settlement" (*Report* 1854: 3–4). It was evidently thought that the rebellion had been caused in part by the concentration of Khoikhoi together in a single location, and by the opportunities which this gave for the development of political ideas which were not in accord with the ruling ideology of the Cape Colony. Even prior to the rebellion, somewhat speciously, it was considered that the presence of European enterprise would act as a leaven to raise up Khoi initiative and provide a stimulus to economic progress,[17] as if the repeated destruction of the Settlement were not reason enough for the poverty of its inhabitants, and the taming of the landscape and the construction of the most extensive irrigation system in the Cape not evidence of Khoi diligence, when the rewards were evident.

The possibility for the distribution of land after the rebellion was given by the confiscation of the property of those who were rebels. In total there were 509 *erven*, as they were called, in the Kat River. Of these, 236 belonged to those considered "loyal," 26 to men whose loyalty was doubtful, five to men who had surrendered under the promise of a free pardon, and 159 to those proved to have been rebels and who had been either convicted of high treason or were still among those in the mountains, while 83 of the original owners had abandoned their *erven*, many since the war of 1835

(*General Report* 1858: 52). It was thus decided that the 242 parcels of land in the latter two categories, thus just under half the land ownership of the valley, was to be distributed among white men. The dilution was thus enormous.

In the years that followed, it was discovered that there was a problem with this regulation. According to the Roman-Dutch law in force in the Colony, it was illegal to confiscate land, even for high treason. This had been overlooked by the legal officers of the Cape in the original formulation, presumably because they were themselves all Britons, and thus not schooled in the details of Roman-Dutch law, which was indeed by this stage obsolete in the Netherlands. The Government was thus in the embarrassed position of having to return to convicted rebels the land from which they had been dispossessed. A Commission was therefore instigated with the formal task of returning land, or at least providing compensation, to the illegally deprived Khoi. This it did with bad grace, not least because the very first applicant for the return of land was Andries Botha, the most prominent of those who had been convicted of treason, in what was in effect South Africa's first political trial.[18] The Commission then attempted to find other grounds for maintaining the dispossession, effectively by saying that many of those who had land had not complied with the original conditions of grant that the land should be enclosed, brought into cultivation and that a substantial house be built on the property. Often a house had been built, but had been destroyed in the war, which was not considered sufficient for the continued possession. In total, 134 claims were entered for repossession. Of these, 13 claimants, including Andries Botha and the London Missionary Society, were confirmed in the possession of their property, five were considered "special cases" and seem to have received compensation, while another eight applicants were granted monetary compensation for what they had lost. Thus in total about 45 percent of the land, both the *erven* and the rights to commonage, within the Kat River valley, now known as Seymour district, passed from Khoi to white ownership in the course of the 1850s (*General Report* 1858: 14–33). The rebellion had thus led, directly, to the ending or exclusive Khoi control over the valley's land and, indirectly, to the widespread dispossession of the Khoi.

While by no means all the whites who acquired farms in the Kat River valley were successful, a number were able to monopolize considerable tracts of land. This was not problematic while those who had managed to hang onto their own *erven* still had use of the great swathes of commonage around the irrigated valleys. There were a number of complaints, notably about the extent to which the white farmers who came to occupy positions on the management boards of the various villages granted themselves privileges to the use of the commonage which they refused to the "colored" landowners (*Report* 1903: 64). At the same time there was long pressure from the local white notables on those "colored" land owners. This culminated in the *Boedel Erven* Act of 1905, passed at the instigation of the MP for the area, who was also one of its crooked lawyers. This Act, passed after a major commission, set out in principle to remedy what was seen as an abuse. It had regularly come about that *erven* which were inherited by the (multiple) heirs of the original grantee were not in fact divided up, but remained as part of his unpartitioned legacy (*Boedel*). The possibility for overcrowding on the undivided lots was great, but does not seem to have caused many complaints. Nevertheless, the Act was passed requiring the legal transfer of these lands to the individual heirs, with all the costs of survey and title which this involved. The result was that, while before the Act there were 89 *Boedel erven* in the district, a few years later the district's lawyers, who acted as small-town lawyers are stereotypically supposed to do, held bonds for 87 pieces of land there (*Report* 1903; Peires 1987: 75). Some of these would have been for land which had not been *Boedel erven*, and in other cases it is probable that the lawyers held bonds only for sections of the original *erven*. All the same, the effects are clear, and primarily the result of the lawyers' fraudulent actions.

The second provision of the *Boedel Erven* Act was that the great commonages could be divided into freehold properties, provided that the owners of two-thirds of the *erven* agreed. To the descendants of the Khoi land owners, therefore, the Act is known as the *snywet* (cutting law). The result was a South African equivalent of the English enclosure movement, and the results, as in much of England, were to the disadvantage of the small property owner who could no longer run his or her cattle and sheep on the commonage, and to the advantage of the rich. The cadastral map of the district began to take on its modern pattern, with many individual farms (though by South African standards not particularly large), and also the small *erven*, of a few acres of the original, irrigated grants. The largest single block of land, the farm of Tamboekies Vlei, had been granted to Commandant Groepe in the early nineteenth century and left to his numerous descendants. They have retained this right and many still live there. For the rest, by the middle of the twentieth century, what was now known as Seymour district had thus become something of a typical part of rural white South Africa, specializing in the production of tobacco and citrus fruit, and surrounded by a large area of state forest reserve in the mountains. The dominant group, however, had become the whites, both Afrikaners and, in the majority, English speakers.

As elsewhere in South Africa, to describe a district as made up of white farms is a statement about ownership, not about occupation (Jeeves and Crush 1997). The laborers on the farms were in general Xhosa, and the families who came to live in Seymour district came to consider the area as their home, perhaps not in the sense that their umbilical cords were buried there – the definition of "home" for the Xhosa, who need not necessarily have ever lived there, or even visited with any great regularity – but certainly as places where several generations had made their livelihood and where they had developed a degree of proprietary, if informal, interest. How far those who came to live on the farms of the district were the descendants of those Xhosa or Mfengu who had been in the Settlement before 1850 is something which I do not know, and I am not sure that the people in question do either. It is, however, clear that a substantial proportion of those in the valley now see themselves as Jingqi, that is as the subjects of the line of chiefs founded by Maqoma.

The Ciskei and the new South Africa

Seymour district might have been an increasingly "white" farming district, and have been designated as such, but it was nevertheless still in the region of South Africa known as the Border and just across the low hills from the Tyume valley which was part of the Xhosa heartland, and still held in communal tenure. Indeed there was a block of African land which reached the Kat River at the south of the valley, near the *poort*, and which was occupied by Mfengu, largely associated with the old Wesleyan mission station and boarding school of Healdtown, where many of the Eastern Cape elite, including Nelson Mandela, had been educated. This made the area vulnerable to the extension of Bantustan land rights in the 1980s. Thus, on January 1, 1983 the valley was transferred to the Ciskei, whereafter it became known as Mpofu district.

The proposals for the transfer caused considerable resistance among the hundred or so families of settler descendants who had remained in the valley. Aided in particular by Jeff Peires, then a historian and political activist in Grahamstown, a series of petitions was sent to the relevant minister, at one stage F.W. de Klerk, who denied ever having received them. In the course of the campaigns, Peires recorded the remarkable lament of Piet Draghoender, one of the last "colored" land owners in Bergman's Hoek in the north of the valley (Peires 1987, 1988). This is a great piece of oral poetry in which Draghoender, looking out over the great valley running south from the Katberg mountains towards the town of Seymour, explains how the land, which was sown with mealies, beans, peas, and potatoes, had been made free by the blood of those who had fought for it, his father and grandfather, and his sons in World War II. But to no avail. Draghoender was sent off the land, and went to live on a plot of a relative near King William's Town.[19]

The extension of the Ciskei entailed yet another twist in the ethnic claims to the valley. The Ciskei was formed to create a "homeland" for at least some of the Xhosa-speakers in South Africa, and came to be dominated by the Rharhabe Xhosa, including the followers of the descendants of Maqoma. Indeed, Lent Maqoma, who was recognized, illegitimately, as the head of the Jingqi, which his great-great-grandfather had founded, played a role of some significance in the politics of the Ciskei, and other claimants to the Jingqi chiefdomship lived in the valley (Stapleton 1994: 35–37; Anon 1989). There was thus an attempt to incorporate – some would claim to reincorporate – the valley into Xhosaland proper. What this entailed was the purchase of the land from the white farmers who had come to dominate the valley, and the expropriation, with minimal compensation, of those of the descendants of the Khoi who still owned small parcels of land there.

The farms were attractive to the Ciskeian notables because they were held in freehold, and were thus the only part of the new Ciskei where there was no communal tenure. The President of the putatively independent new country, Lennox Sebe, could thus acquire his own farm, as a true South African should. He himself claimed Lorraine, probably the finest farm in the valley, near the confluence of the Kat and the Mancazana Rivers. Various others of his immediate entourage also became the owners of substantial properties, many of which soon degenerated substantially as agricultural enterprises. But that, of course, was a small price to be paid for the gratification of the desires of the apartheid regime's important clients.

Not all was a total disaster, however. There is a small number of Xhosa farmers in the valley who have gained title to their land via the Ciskei but who are nevertheless transforming their enterprises into flourishing concerns, and thereby incurring the jealousy both of the other Xhosa and of the Khoi. There are rather more of those who had been farm laborers under the white regime who have taken over the land their erstwhile employers vacated, and are often making a reasonable attempt to maintain the productivity, for instance of the citrus orchards (Nel *et al.* 1997; Nel and Hill 2000; Personal observation 2000, 2002). One set of farms has been transformed into the Mpofu game reserve, which seems to be flourishing in its way. There have also been a lot of families who have moved into the district to find some sort of land, and to escape from the overcrowded squalor of the rest of what was the Ciskei. But these people, together with those who have failed to find the capital, or the interest, to maintain their lands, have only contributed to the impression of degeneration which much of the valley now exudes.

With the political changes in South Africa during the mid 1990s, the conflicts entered a new, and as yet unresolved, phase. The Ciskei as a political entity disappeared, to general relief.[20] For a while, at least, it did not seem to have been replaced by any new organ of local government. Those who had held power locally before 1994 seem to have been able to maintain their position, and their power and income derived from the protection rackets they were able to run. Nevertheless, the total reorganization of South Africa's local government, which came into force in 2002, has led to the incorporation of Mpofu district into the much larger Amatole regional authority, based on Fort Beaufort. Some degree of local government seems to have been reestablished, and non-governmental aid organizations are finding their way back into the valley. In this sense, there are signs of hope, although the difficulties of ruling what is South Africa's second poorest province mean that the tasks facing the new administration are exceedingly heavy.

Many of the problems faced in the district, of course, derive from the uncertainty of land tenure. The Land Claims Commission has received a multiplicity of often conflicting claims for the farms in the valley, as individuals claim land on the basis of the rights they held before 1983, including the rights they lost to the crooked lawyers in the early twentieth century, on the basis of long residence, for instance from ex-farm laborers, and on the basis of occupancy. As yet the Commission has not come up with any rulings. Not only do some very complicated matters have to be worked out, but also, as might be expected given the valley's history, extremely sensitive political decisions have to be made. Divisions are still clear. Some are expressed in ethnic terms, particularly between the Khoi descendants, whose political consciousness as such is increasing, and the Xhosa. Others relate to the recent history of the region, as some of those who had acquired land under the Ciskei feel themselves to be disadvantaged, even though they are often the ones with the drive and the capital to make the valley once again productive. But there were many of the old Ciskeians who are hanging onto land without attempting to work it, and they are often thought to be the ones with the political connections which influence the commissioners' decisions. It is difficult to see how these divisions can be easily resolved. However, without such resolution, any possibility for the resuscitation of the agriculture of the valley seems impossible. Without this, though, the prosperity of what was once a prosperous, if racially unjust, farming region is going to remain far lower than its potential.

Conclusion

What, then, does this all mean? First, the Kat River Settlement, and its successors, had a peculiar history, many of whose features were not replicated elsewhere in South Africa, or abroad. The details of the interweaving of ethnic identities and claims to land were very specific, deriving as they did from the use by the invading colonialists of an ethnically defined intermediate group, the Khoi, who were later dropped, but who always remained a cut above the Xhosa in the colonial and apartheid hierarchy. Only in the 1990s was the old order broken, but the process of reordering, or disordering, has not yet been accomplished.

Second, the symbolism of land, and of particular parcels of land, varied greatly between the various peoples competing for it. Maqoma and his followers, in the early nineteenth century, continually struggled to regain the land from which they had been expelled, and this sentiment has been maintained, at least up till the transfer of Mpofu district to the Ciskei. Ntsikana's grave has become the symbol for this. The Khoi saw the land first as the only place where they could settle, and further as land for which they had fought – the "land which had been swept by blood," that of the ancestors, as Piet Draghoender described it. There are also particular sites of great importance for them, notably the churches of Philipton and Hertzog and, for the descendants of Commandant Groepe, the farm of Tamboekies Vlei which is held in trust by all of them. On the other hand, to Europeans and to the Ciskeian notables after 1982, what mattered was having a farm, and thus being able to behave as a member of the South African landed class, not the specific plot on which this farm may have been located.

Third, though, and finally, for all the specificity of conflicts over land in the Kat River valley, and over the valley as a whole, their contorted history is symptomatic of, indeed emblematic of, much of South African history, in at least two senses. The first is the omnipresence, through time, of conflict and competition between groups variously described as ethnic or racial; the second is that those groups themselves are at the very least fuzzy around the edges, and it is never quite certain to which any given individual belongs. Much of the effort of colonization was an attempt to fix those boundaries, in the interests of order and in reflection of the colonists' views of society, but it never succeeded totally. Therein has lain part of the dynamic, and also often part of the tragedy, of South Africa's history.

Notes

1 The reasons why it might not be possible to return the land were of course various, including the difficulty and cost of buying out the current owner, for whatever reason. It would, to give one example, not have been feasible to destroy the Mercedes-Benz factory in East London, the city's most prominent employer, to compensate those who had been driven out of the West Bank location on which it stands.

2 Seymour, in the center of the valley, receives on average around 534 cm per year (*Climate of South Africa* 1950).

3 By Xhosa law, the heir of a chief is the son of his "great wife," whom he marries after he accedes to the chieftainship, whose bridewealth is paid by the tribe as a whole and who, in principle, is a princess of a neighboring chiefdom. Thus Ngqika's heir was to be Sandile, who was more than 20 years younger than Maqoma, and the son of Ngqika's great wife Suthu, a member of the Thembu royal family.

4 Interview with Hymie Groepe, Lower Blinkwater, July 2000.

5 See also D. Campbell, Detailed Report of the Progress and Present State of the Settlement at the Head of the Kat River, District of Albany, Cape Archives Depot (hereafter CA) CO 2742.

6 D. Campbell, Detailed Report of the Progress and Present State of the Settlement at the Head of the Kat River, District of Albany, CA CO 2742; W. Atherton to J. Montagu, July 30, 1846, CA CO 2333, gives a population for the valley as 5,287, which is almost certainly an underestimate.

7 "Bastard" in Dutch means half-caste as well as, perhaps before, it means illegitimate.

8 A. Armstrong to D. Campbell, April 7, 1835, CA LG 49; A. Armstrong to G. Jarvis, May 1, 1835, CA LG 297; G. Jarvis to Sir B. D'Urban, June 13, 1835, CA CO 2756; J. Clark to Foreign Secretary, London Missionary Society (hereafter LMS), September 30, 1835, LMS papers, Council for World Mission Archives, School of Oriental and African Studies, London, South African Correspondence (henceforth LMS-SA) 14/4/E; J. Read to W. Tidman, June 4, 1845, LMS-SA 22/2/A; J. Read to W. Tidman, August 31, 1846, LMS-SA 22/2/A; J. Read to Directors, March 23, 1847, LMS-SA 23/1/C.

9 See also J. Read to Secretary, LMS, December 1, 1847, LMS-SA 23/3/B.
10 Mfengu were people of Nguni extraction who had come into the Cape Colony in the aftermath of the 1835 war. Many of them were recent immigrants to Xhosaland from Natal, who were considered to have been treated harshly by the Xhosa chiefs; others were perhaps longer-term subjects of the Xhosa chiefs. They can perhaps best be described as Africans who had chosen the colonial side in the long conflict between the Europeans and the Xhosa (Webster 1991a, 1991b; Moyer 1976).
11 See in particular N.J. Borcherds to M. West, February 10, 1842, CA LG 592, and other letters in this file.
12 N.J. Borcherds to H. Hudson, July 30, 1842, CA 1/FBF 6/1/1/3.
13 A. Armstrong to H. Hudson, August 15, 1837, CA 1/FBF 6/1/1/1.
14 Notebook of the Kat River Commission of Enquiry, 1858, CA 1/UIT 14/37, case 1.
15 This list is to be found in LMS-SA 25/4/B.
16 Contract between Louis Hendrik and Mahe, before T.H. Bowker, Resident Magistrate of Stockenstrom, February 8, 1850, in LMS-SA 26/4/C.
17 T.H. Bowker to J. Montagu, September 28, 1848, CA CO 2849.
18 Botha was found guilty, somewhat dubiously given the evidence supplied, and sentenced to death. However, the sentence was commuted, because of his long and distinguished service in the colonial forces in the previous wars, and he was quietly released within a couple of years (*Trial* 1852).
19 It is only fair to say that there are still a few "colored" families in Bergman's Hoek, who somehow had ridden out the period of Ciskeian occupation and live on their *erven*, in relative poverty.
20 Perhaps not entirely in people's experience, as the capital of the new Province of the Eastern Cape was located in Bisho, the Ciskei's old capital – something had to be done with the buildings – and "Bisho" is still used as a metonym for the provincial administration.

Bibliography

Anderson, B. (1983) *Imagined Communities: Reflections on the Origin and Spread of Nationalism*, London: Verso.
Anon [J.B. Peires] (1989) "Ethnicity and Pseudo-Ethnicity in the Ciskei," in L. Vail (ed.) *The Creation of Tribalism in Southern Africa*, London, Berkeley, and Los Angeles, CA: James Currey & University of California Press.
Bergh, J.S. and Visagie, J.C. (1985) *The Eastern Cape Frontier Zone, 1660–1980: A Cartographic Guide for Historical Research*, Durban: Butterworth.
Business Day (2003) "Restitution Process Gathers Pace," February, 3.
Climate of South Africa (1950) *Climate of South Africa Part 2: Rainfall Statistics*, Pretoria and Cape Town: Government Printer.
Correspondence (1837) *Correspondence Relative to the Caffre War at the Cape of Good Hope*, British Parliamentary Paper 503.
Crais, C.C. (2002) *The Politics of Evil: Magic, State Power and the Political Imagination of South Africa*, Cambridge: Cambridge University Press.
Du Toit, A.E. (1954) "The Cape Frontier: A Study of Native Policy with Special Reference to the Years 1847–1866," *Archives Year Book for South African History*, 17.
Elbourne, J.E. (1995) "Early Khoisan Uses of Mission Christianity," in H. Bredekamp and R. Ross (eds) *Missions and Christianity in South African History*, Johannesburg: Witwatersrand University Press.

—— (2002) *Blood Ground: Colonialism, Missions, and the Contest for Christianity in the Cape Colony and Britain, 1799–1853*, Montreal: McGill-Queens University Press.

Freeman, J.J. (1851) *A Tour in South Africa: With Notices of Natal, Mauritius, Madagascar, Ceylon, Egypt, and Palestine*, London: Snow.

General Report (1858) *General Report of the Commission Appointed by His Excellency the Governor to Inquire into Claims for Compensation for the Loss of Erven in the Kat River Settlement*, Cape Parliamentary Paper G 18.

Harinck, G. (1969) "Interaction between Xhosa and Khoi: Emphasis on the Period 1620–1750," in L.M. Thompson (ed.) *African Societies in Southern Africa*, London: Heinemann.

Hobsbawm, E.J. and Ranger, T.O. (eds) (1983) *The Invention of Tradition*, Cambridge: Cambridge University Press.

Hodgson, J. (1980) *Ntsikana's Great Hymn: A Xhosa Expression of Christianity in the Early Nineteenth Century Eastern Cape*, Cape Town: Communications of the Centre for African Studies, University of Cape Town, no. 4.

Jeeves, A.H. and Crush, J. (eds) (1997) *White Farms, Black Labor: The State and Agrarian Change in Southern Africa, 1910–1950*, Portsmouth, Pietermaritzburg, and Oxford: Heinemann, University of Natal Press and James Currey.

Kirk, T. (1973) "Progress and Decline in the Kat River Settlement, 1829–1854," *Journal of African History*, 14: 411–428.

Le Cordeur, B. and Saunders, C.C. (eds) (1981) *The War of the Axe, 1847: Correspondence between the Governor of the Cape Colony, Sir Henry Pottinger, and the Commander of the British Forces at the Cape, Sir George Berkeley, and Others*, Johannesburg: Brenthurst.

Lester, A. (2001) *Imperial Networks: Creating Identities in Nineteenth-Century South Africa and Britain*, London and New York: Routledge.

Maclennan, B. (1986) *A Proper Degree of Terror: John Graham and the Cape's Eastern Frontier*, Johannesburg: Ravan.

MacMillan, W.M. (1963) [originally published 1929] *Bantu, Boer and Briton: The Making of the South African Native Problem*, Oxford: Oxford University Press.

Moyer, R.A. (1976) "A History of the Mfengu of the Eastern Cape, 1815–1865," unpublished Ph.D. thesis, University of London.

Nel, E.L. and Hill, T.R. (2000) *An Evaluation of Community-Driven Economic Development, Land Tenure and Sustainable Environmental Development in the Kat River Valley*, Pretoria: Human Sciences Research Council.

——, Hill, T.R., and Binns, T. (1997) "Development from Below in the 'New' South Africa: The Case of Hertzog, Eastern Cape," *Geographical Journal*, 163: 57–64.

Newton-King, S. (1999) *Masters and Servants on the Cape Eastern Frontier, 1760–1803*, Cambridge: Cambridge University Press.

—— and Malherbe, V.C. (1981) *The Khoi Rebellion in the Eastern Cape, 1799–1803*, Cape Town: Communications of the Centre for African Studies, University of Cape Town, no 5.

Peires, J.B. (1981) *The House of Phalo: A History of the Xhosa People in the Days of Their Independence*, Johannesburg: Ravan.

—— (1987) "The Legend of Fenner-Solomon," in B. Bozzoli (ed.) *Class, Community and Conflict: South African Perspectives*, Johannesburg: Ravan.

—— (1988) "Piet Draghoender's Lament," *Social Dynamics*, 14: 6–15.

—— (1989) "The British and the Cape, 1814–1834," in R. Elphick and H.B. Giliomee (eds) *The Shaping of South African Society, 1652–1840*, 2nd edition, Cape Town: Maskew Miller Longmans.

Proceedings (1852) *Proceedings of and Evidence given before the Committee of the Legislative Council respecting the proposed Ordinance "to prevent the practice of settling or squatting on Government lands,"* Cape Town: Saul Solomon.

Ranger, T.O. (1993) "The Invention of Tradition Revisited: The Case of Colonial Africa," in T.O. Ranger and O. Vaughan (eds) *Legitimacy and the State in Twentieth-Century Africa: Essays in Honour of A.H.M. Kirk-Greene*, Houndsmill: Macmillan in Association with St Anthony's College Oxford.

Read, J. (1852) *The Kat River Settlement in 1851: Described in a Series of Letters Publ. in the South African Commercial Advertiser*, Cape Town: A.S. Robertson.

Report (1836) *Report from the Select Committee on Aborigines*, British Parliamentary Paper 538.

Report (1854) *Report of the Commissioners Appointed for Investigating into the Causes of the Kat River Rebellion*, Cape Parliamentary Paper.

Report (1903) *Report of the Departmental Commission appointed to Inquire into Boedel Erven, Encroachments on Commonage and other Matters, Division of Stockenstrom*, Cape Parliamentary Paper G 7.

Ross, R. (1980) "Ethnic Identity, Demographic Crises and Xhosa-Khoikhoi Inter-action," *History in Africa*, 7: 259–271.

—— (1983) *Cape of Torments: Slavery and Resistance in South Africa*, London: Routledge.

—— (1989) "James Cropper, John Philip and the Researches in South Africa," in H. Macmillan and S. Marks (eds) *Africa and Empire: W.M. Macmillan, Historian and Social Critic*, London: Temple Smith for the Institute of Commonwealth Studies.

—— (1999) *Status and Respectability in the Cape Colony, 1750–1870: A Tragedy of Manners*, Cambridge: Cambridge University Press.

—— (2003) "Ambiguities of Resistance and Collaboration on the Eastern Cape Frontier: The Kat River Settlement 1829–1856," in J. Abbink, M. De Bruijn, and K. Van Walraven (eds) *Rethinking Resistance: Reflections on Revolt and Violence in African History*, Leiden: Brill.

South African Commercial Advertiser (1834) September 3.

Spear, T. (2003) "Neo-Traditionalism and the Limits of Invention in British Colonial Africa," *Journal of African History*, 44: 3–28.

Stapleton, T.J. (1993) "The Memory of Maqoma: An Assessment of Jingqi Oral Tradition in Ciskei and Transkei," *History in Africa*, 20: 321–335.

—— (1994) *Maqoma: Xhosa Resistance to Colonial Advance 1798–1873*, Johannesburg: Jonathan Ball.

Stockenstrom, A. (1887) *The Autobiography of the Late Sir Andries Stockenstrom Bart.*, C.W. Hutton (ed.) 2 vols, Cape Town: Juta.

Theal, G. McC. (1897–1905) *Records of the Cape Colony*, 36 volumes, London: Clowes.

Trial of Andries Botha, Field Cornet of the Upper Blinkwater in the Kat River Settlement for High Treason (1852), Cape Town: Saul Solomon.

Vail, L. (ed.) (1989) *The Creation of Tribalism in Southern Africa*, London, Berkeley and Los Angeles: James Currey and University of California Press.

Webster, A. (1991a) "Land Expropriation and Labour Extraction under Cape Colonial Rule: The War of 1835 and the 'Emancipation' of the Fingo," MA thesis, Rhodes University.

316   *Robert Ross*

—— (1991b) "Unmasking the Fingo: The War of 1835 Reconsidered," in C. Hamilton (ed.) *The Mfecane Aftermath: Reconstructive Debates in Southern African History*, Johannesburg and Pietermarizburg: Witwatersrand University Press and University of Natal Press.

Winer, M. and Ross, R. (2000) "Kat River Settlement Historical Archaeology Project: Report on July 2000 Reconnaissance Trip," unpublished report to South African Heritage Resource Agency, Cape Town.

Part V

Natural resources and the livelihood of native populations

Economy and environment in tradition and modernity

13 Survival through generosity

Property rights and hunting practices of Native Americans in the subarctic region*

Ann M. Carlos and Frank D. Lewis

Introduction

Property rights were central to the harvesting of beaver and other resources by Native Americans; indeed their system of property rights may have been the key to the long-term prospects of Natives, even their very survival. At the heart of the rules governing the use of resources was what has been termed the "Good Samaritan" constraint or the Ethic of Generosity. Those in need had the right to get help from others. For example, Indians, by right, could hunt for game in territories assigned by custom to other tribes or families. But the Good Samaritan constraint distinguished between those resources that provided for basic needs and those used for exchange; accordingly, it did not extend to beaver or other animals whose pelts were destined for the fur trade; rather, the constraint applied only to animals needed for survival. Given that property rights were apparently weaker on game than on beaver, it would seem that the over-harvesting of game should have been a more serious problem; yet the historical accounts and the work of Carlos and Lewis (1993) suggest the opposite. Game remained plentiful, at least until the nineteenth century, while beaver stocks were depleted.

The impact of Europeans on aboriginal populations is another major theme of the historical literature on Native Americans. Estimates for the early years are necessarily rough, but all point to a similar scenario – dramatically falling Indian populations followed by slow recovery. Even as late as 1900, the North American Indian population is estimated to have been only 550,000, although over the next 70 years it rose to 1.1 million (Ubelaker 1988). The estimates for Native population at the time of contact are much less defined, ranging from Ubelaker's 1988 estimate of 1.9 million to Dobyn's 1983 estimate of 18 million (Ubelaker 1992: 171). A consensus view would put the pre-contact figure at between 6 and 12 million. In explaining the precipitous decline in population, the emphasis has been placed quite rightly on disease, most importantly influenza, measles, and smallpox; but by focusing almost exclusively on this aspect, historians may have underplayed another significant element in Native American demography. For hunter-gatherer societies, especially those in colder climates, meat from large game was central to survival. Native American populations, in the subarctic region particularly, were sensitive to the stock of large game and to the effort that was devoted to hunting, effort that may have been diverted to the fur trade. Krech (1999: 85) has noted that, in addition to European diseases, the contribution to mortality of malnutrition or inadequate diet should be considered. To address these issues, this chapter will explore the relation between the stock of game, hunting effort, and Indian population, where the point of departure will be a predator–prey model of the type often applied in biology.

Rules of property, especially when they involve open access issues, are often identified with resources rather than final output. The distinction may be important in explaining the conservation of large game animals by Native Americans. In the standard common property model, once a resource is exploited, the output becomes private property; and it is the transfer of the property right that can provide an incentive to overuse the resource. The Good Samaritan rule in Native American culture removed, or at least weakened, property rights to final output, because Indians, who were in need, had the right to the food and supplies of those who were better off. As Leacock put it: "a man finding himself in need of food on another's land may kill the [animal]" (McManus 1972: 49). This right, common to aboriginals throughout much of the Americas, provided insurance in a society where reliance on large ungulates meant that food and other animal products could be highly variable.

The Good Samaritan ethic may have served yet another purpose. The issue of territoriality has long concerned anthropologists; and, more recently, Morantz (1986) documents a notion of trespass held by the eastern James Bay Cree, and Charles Bishop (1986) cites instances where Native groups demanded "gifts" or tolls to secure passage through their territory. At the same time, the right to hunt game could extend beyond the family territory, even to areas that were controlled by members of different tribal groups. Widespread access to game, while approximating conditions of pure common property, also promoted a common interest among Indians, living over an extended region, to preserve the animals, which ranged over a large area as well. It is, of course, well known that sole ownership of a resource often leads to a preferred outcome. In the context of aboriginal hunting in the region of Hudson Bay, this result can be illustrated using a two-agent model, where moving to joint ownership helps preserve the animal stock by promoting a lower, and closer-to-optimal, level of harvesting effort.

In this chapter we begin by reviewing the results of our earlier work (Carlos and Lewis 1993, 1999, 2001), which deals with the reaction of the Indians to the policies of the European traders, most importantly the Hudson's Bay Company, and how Indian reaction affected the beaver stocks. We then discuss some of the historical literature on the harvesting of game and the exploitation of other resources not directly associated with the fur trade. We try to make sense of the different patterns of resource use, particularly in regard to large game and beaver, by making use of a simple harvesting model, where the degree of access to the resource turns out to be a crucial element in determining the size of the animal population and the level of harvesting effort. Finally, we speculate on how effort levels in hunting and trading may have affected not only the stock of resources, but ultimately the Native American population.

Property rights, conflict, and depletion

The beaver was the cornerstone of the Canadian fur trade. Although many types of furs were sold by the Indians, beaver was by far the most important in terms of both number of pelts traded and value. Yet our estimates of beaver populations derived in Carlos and Lewis (1993) show that in much of the region served by the Hudson's Bay Company, the underlying stocks had diminished significantly by the 1750s. The Company's trading hinterland is shown in Map 13.1. The York Factory hinterland was by far the largest both in area and in number of beaver, and the region served by Fort Albany and Moose Factory was second in importance. The Fort Churchill hinterland was a large area, but supported far fewer beaver due to its inferior

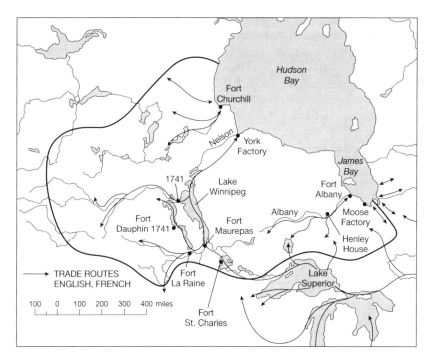

Map 13.1 Hudson's Bay Company hinterlands
Source: Ray (1987: plate 60).

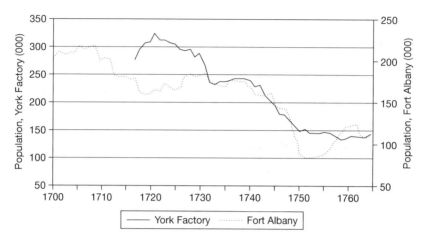

Figure 13.1 Simulated beaver populations: York Factory and Fort Albany, 1700–1763

Source: Carlos and Lewis (1993).

habitat. The simulated beaver populations in the areas served by York Factory and Fort Albany, as derived in Carlos and Lewis (1993), are described in Figure 13.1.[1] In both hinterlands, the beaver population dropped well below the levels consistent with maximum sustained harvesting, which in the York Factory hinterland was, according to the Carlos and Lewis simulations, 231,000, and in the Fort Albany hinterland, 172,000. By contrast, the beaver stocks in the Fort Churchill region did not experience serious depletion.

The decline in population in the York Factory and Fort Albany areas began about 1740 and appears to have been related to the prices Native traders were receiving at the posts. At Fort Albany the prices started increasing in the early 1730s and at York Factory in the late 1730s (see Figure 13.2).[2] It was after several years of higher prices that we see the (simulated) beaver populations falling. Carlos and Lewis (1993, 1999) argued that higher fur prices induced greater harvesting effort on the part of Indians, and it was the increased effort that led to depletion. Why the Hudson's Bay Company chose to raise fur prices as it did involved a form of property right, but in this case a property right of the Company. In the late 1720s the price of beaver pelts in Europe began to increase, a response to the rising demand for beaver hats. Where the Hudson's Bay Company was a monopsonist in the trade, with an implicit property right to the beaver stock, it maintained low fur prices at the trading posts. This policy discouraged overharvesting by the Indians. In the Fort Albany and later the York Factory hinterlands, however, French traders actively competed with the Hudson's Bay Company. At these posts, the Company responded by raising prices. The Fort Churchill post was too isolated to face French competition,

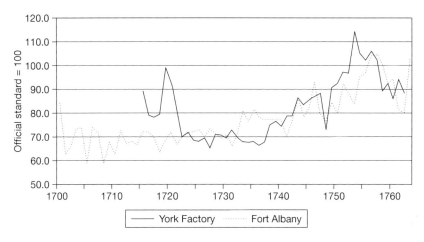

Figure 13.2 Fur prices at Fort Albany and York Factory
Source: Carlos and Lewis (1993).

and there the Company held prices down, a policy that helped maintain the beaver stocks.

Throughout the region, Native property rights to the beaver stocks were similar; what differed apparently was the nature of the market that Indian traders faced. As in most regions of North America, it was Native Americans who did the hunting; and they were, therefore, directly responsible for depleting the beaver resource base upon which the welfare of their communities rested. In fact the geographical expansion of the trade has long been attributed by historians to overexploitation by Natives, who forced the trade further west, as areas in the east were no longer ecologically sustaining. Our beaver population estimates lend support to these assertions and are in keeping with the work of ethnohistorians, who have become increasingly concerned with why Indians depleted the beaver and other fur-bearing animals.[3]

Conservation often requires that an agent curtail their exploitation of the resource, but there must be a belief that the resource will be available to that same agent in the future. In understanding why the beaver was depleted or, alternatively, why in some regions at least beaver populations were driven to levels below the biological optimum, it is important to consider the nature of the resource, the market for the product of the resource, and the structure of property rights. Common pool resources share two key characteristics, which make them highly vulnerable to over-exploitation. The first characteristic is an inability by potential exploiters to control access. This problem has been at the center of the decline of many ocean fisheries, and has contributed to the extinction or near extinction of migratory animals, especially those that cross community borders. The second characteristic, termed subtractability (Feeny *et al.* 1990), requires that what one person takes is not available to another. As long as the resource is available in such abundance that exploitation by one party does not affect the return to anyone else, common access to the resource is not a problem. But where the supply of the resource is limited, a potential for overexploitation will exist.

Because of the problems associated with common property and subtractability, Harold Demsetz (1967) argued that the commercial fur trade gave Indians an incentive to move to a more clearly specified structure of property rights. The new market for beaver increased the current value of each animal and the value of the beaver stock in the future, but Natives had the incentive to restrict hunting only if they had rights to those animals. Despite some statements to the contrary, there appear to have been no social or cultural reasons preventing Native Americans from establishing such property rights. Demsetz points out that the Montagnais in Labrador did, in fact, respond to changes in resource values by introducing land tenure arrangements. And, quoting fur trader Joseph Chadwick, William Cronon describes how in the eighteenth century Maine Indians divided their land into inheritable family hunting territories: "their hunting ground and streams were all parcelled out to certain families" (Cronon 1983: 105).

Important to the debate on property rights in the fur trade is the work of Frank Speck, who based his judgments to a large extent on personal observations, during the early twentieth century, of Indian practice in areas south and east of James Bay (see Map 13.1). In the introduction to a book of his papers, Edward Rogers summarizes Speck's views:

> from time immemorial each family owned a specific tract of land that was clearly demarcated. From this territory, the family members could extract whatever resources they needed or desired. No one else might do so. Trespass was forbidden, and it was punished supernaturally when it occurred.
>
> (Rogers 1985: x, xi)

Much of the debate has centered on whether the rules of trespass were limited to the fur trade. Bishop (1970), in his study of the Ojibwa, pointed out that, although travelers were required to provide gifts to pass through a territory, it was understood such gifts were required only if trapping would take place, and elsewhere he concluded that "territorial rule applied only to the right to trade and to obtain exchange goods, and not to the right to exploit subsistence necessities" (Bishop 1974: 49). Morantz (1986: 71) agrees that the notion of territoriality applied only to animals intended for the trade.

It appears, therefore, that by distinguishing between animals used for food and those destined for the fur trade, Native Americans were able to adapt their property rights structures to help preserve threatened resources, which makes the question of Indian depletion of the beaver puzzling. John McManus (1972) may have part of the answer. He has argued that the Good Samaritan rule attenuated the ability of a tribe to establish private property and also reduced the incentive to save. Edward Umfreville writing on the state of the Hudson's Bay Company in the eighteenth century, described Indians in a way that provides one of the first and perhaps best accounts of the arrangement:

> We find them kind, courteous, and benevolent to each other, relieving the wants and necessities of their distressed brethren with the greatest good nature, either by counsel, food or clothing. The good effects of this excellent disposition are frequently experienced by themselves; for, as in their mode of life no one knows how soon it may be his own fate to be reduced to the verge of extremity, he secures for himself a return of kindness, should he experience that vicissitude.
>
> (Umfreville 1954: 19)

Thus, the Good Samaritan policy was a useful, perhaps vital element of Native American economic life; but at the same time it led to "the Indians' relative indifference to property accumulation" (Cronon 1983: 62). The weak inclination to save may have extended to the preservation of the beaver stocks, which would have involved a form of capital accumulation.

The policy of implementing a system of property rights to fur-bearing animals was further complicated by the tribal and European rivalries that became a feature of the fur trade. In the St Lawrence and Great Lakes basin, for example, warfare, "originally conducted primarily for reasons of prestige, revenge, and religion, gradually changed in purpose and increased in intensity after European contact" (Harris 1987: plate 35). The conflict among Native hunters reduced the incentive to preserve the animal stocks, as Richard White points out:

> Virtually all Indians granted the right of hungry people to take game, including beaver, where they found it, but the furs became the property of those who had the primary hunting rights to the land. These rights the Iroquois claimed by conquest, but the Algonkians regarded Iroquois as uninvited and unwelcome guests rather than conquerors. As a result, both groups murdered each other with alarming frequency and recklessly overhunted beaver and other fur bearers in the contested area. Young beaver, which the French reported had earlier been routinely spared, now flooded the market. Apparently, Indian hunters acted on the theory that their rivals would take any animals that they left.
>
> (White 1991: 150–151)

Conflict, often involving the Iroquois, led to the break-up and dispersion of many tribes. In the mid seventeenth century, the Iroquois confederacy scattered first the Huron tribes, then the Petun, the Nipissing and the Neutrals. Fearing the Iroquois, many other tribes fled west and north into Algonquin and Nipissing territory. In the late 1660s, the French burned a number of Mohawk villages and forced a peace on the Iroquois confederacy; but by the 1680s war had broken out again, as the Iroquois, Mohawk, and Mohicans were aided by the English (Harris 1987: plate 38). Although a formal peace was again imposed, the dispersal of tribes continued. In 1700, for example, the resumption of hostilities by the Dakotas caused much of the Native population to move toward the lower Great Lakes, changing once again the pattern of contact between English and French traders. This pattern of conflict through the Great Lakes region continued through the 1720s and 1730s. For the next 15 years there was calm, but then English and French traders became involved in the Seven Years War, usually referred to in the American theater as the French and Indian Wars. Once again the interior was in turmoil with its attendant migration of Indian tribes. The Treaty of Paris restored peace in 1763, brought the cession of New France to Britain, and ended a significant French military presence in North America.

Thus, the 100 years prior to 1763 saw the forced and voluntary migration of Indian tribes in the St Lawrence, Great Lakes, and Hudson Bay basins. These migrations, moreover, were not into vacant lands but rather into regions occupied by groups already involved with the fur trade. The result was not only a mixing of cultures and languages, and sometimes further conflict, but also an environment in which property rights to the stock of fur-bearing animals was blurred or non-existent. It was in this climate that depletion of the beaver took place, for even though it would have been in the Indians' interest to conserve, no one tribe had the security of tenure necessary to make this the optimal strategy. Conservation on the part of any tribe, as White (1991) points out, likely meant reducing current consumption and enhancing the future consumption of a rival.

A final factor possibly contributing to the depletion of the beaver stocks was the nature of the European goods that the Indians were receiving in trade. As noted above, the increase in the price of furs at the post appears to have been related to the decline in beaver stocks, and we argued in Carlos and Lewis (1993, 1999) that indeed it was higher prices that led to increased harvesting by Natives. Yet much of the historical literature claims that higher prices reduced Indian effort. Conrad Heidenreich and Arthur Ray (1976: 19) give what is perhaps the most succinct statement of the generally accepted view: "The Indians brought only enough furs to the fort to obtain these [European] goods. By giving him increasingly favorable terms of trade, the trader often obtained fewer furs because the Indians could bring fewer pelts to obtain the same goods." Citing Ray, Shepard Krech (1999: 184) makes a similar point in *The Ecological Indian*: "even when traders signaled a greater demand for furs in the prices (in goods) they were willing to pay, Indians did not respond by increasing the supply. Instead they brought the same number or sometimes less."[4]

In Carlos and Lewis (2001) we argue that the nature of the trade goods made the backward-bending labor supply curve, implied by this view of Indian behavior, implausible. Table 13.1 describes the trade at York Factory over the period 1716–1770. Values are given in *made beaver* (MB), which was the unit of account used at all Hudson's Bay Company trading posts. Many of the items, which are listed in the table as *producer goods*, were used to help the Indians acquire food and other products necessary for subsistence; but there was an even greater range of what we term *luxury goods*. Tobacco and alcohol were important components, but the group included a wide variety of luxuries, among them cloth of various kinds, beads, jewelry, and vermilion. In non-Native societies luxuries tend to have high price and income elasticities of demand, implying that as the price of these goods falls and incomes rise total expenditure on these goods goes up. Trading patterns at Hudson's Bay Company posts indicate that Indians were responding to price and income in much the same way as non-Natives (Carlos and Lewis 2001). Figure 13.3 describes changes in how Indians allocated their income as the price of furs increased. Over the period 1740–1760, as fur prices at the post were rising, the share of Native expenditure on producer goods fell from about 60 percent to 40 percent, while expenditures on luxuries increased accordingly. Since purchases of producer goods likely increased in response to the higher fur prices (and could hardly have fallen), the declining produce goods share implies much greater purchases of luxuries, which would have required greater labor input by Indians to the trade. It was the greater labor input that ultimately caused the depletion.

The depletion of beaver stocks, at least in the York Factory and Fort Albany regions of the Hudson Bay lowlands came about as result of the confluence of a number of factors. First were the influences that limited property rights to beaver, despite the presence of defined hunting territories. These factors included the ongoing conflict between tribes, the migration of some of these groups, and the Good Samaritan rule or Ethic of Generosity, which affected the notion of property ownership and may seriously have affected the incentive to accumulate. Second was the change in the market for furs in Europe and the resulting increase in French competition. While European fur prices were low, the Hudson's Bay Company paid correspondingly low prices to the Indians. Low prices discouraged harvesting and thus protected the beaver stock. Once fur prices in Europe increased, the Hudson's Bay Company responded by raising prices at the posts. However, beaver stocks might still have been protected had Indian labor supply been perfectly inelastic, or even backward-bending, as much of the historical literature suggests. But because so much of the trade involved luxury items, Natives responded as would modern consumers, by greatly increasing their purchases. This reponse implied an increase in their level of harvesting and trading effort, supporting an elastic supply of labor.

Table 13.1 Goods received at York Factory, 1716–1770 (made beaver (MB))

	MB/Unit[a]	1716	1720	1725	1730	1735	1740	1745	1750	1755	1760	1765	1770
Producer goods													
Files	1		190	240	329	214	308	484	166	243	360	261	327
Fishhooks	0.071				11				30		26	9	
Flints	0.083	150	304	460	256	185	192	276	294	92	208	66	155
Guns	14	3,770	1,820	3,906	4,410	1,876	3,500	2,730	1,106	1,638	2,380	1,288	1,876
Gun worms	0.25	38	56	60	70	22	85	61	23	38	23	31	15
Hatchets	1	712	1,500	763	854	657	762	853	341	508	897	732	662
Ice chizzles	1	547	224	813	846	407	472	549	396	196	253	242	169
Knives	0.25	688	622	1,121	843	684	828	649	275	356	586	532	485
Mocotaggans	0.5	46	68	22	4						4		
Net lines	1	23	49	185	245	200	218	221	80	158	169	174	163
Powder horns	1	138	126	229	440	59	181	178	71	17	66	79	117
Powder (lb)	1	3,048	2,057	4,050	4,796	2,661	3,360	3,282	1,703	1,689	4,080	1,326	2,114
Scrapers	0.5	89	90	113	150	108	108	144	26	26	18	8	11
Shot (lb)	0.25	1,423	840	1,812	2,356	1,284	1,847	1,281	605	761	578	782	976
Twine (skein)	1	51	22	57	139	57	114	90	45	62	66	18	26
Guns[b]		8,566	5,204	10,517	12,327	6,086	9,165	7,808	3,801	4,234	7,334	3,572	5,253
Other		2,155	2,765	3,314	3,421	2,327	2,810	2,990	1,359	1,549	2,378	1,976	1,843
Total		*10,721*	*7,968*	*13,831*	*15,748*	*8,413*	*11,974*	*10,798*	*5,160*	*5,783*	*9,712*	*5,548*	*7,096*
Household goods													
Awls	0.125	126	115	169	167	120	105	67	25	58	53	32	13
Blankets	7	280	581	791	1,659	749	1,323	1,729	791	938	1,064	259	756
Fire steels	0.25	124	160	94	164	106	94	150	31	39		26	
Kettles	1.5	808	214	1,360	1,482	1,162	1,018	910	853	343	876	581	615
Total		*1,338*	*1,069*	*2,414*	*3,472*	*2,137*	*2,540*	*2,856*	*1,700*	*1,378*	*1,993*	*898*	*1,384*
Tobacco and alcohol													
Brandy (gal)	4		499	727	1,568	1,248	1,514	2,391	1,554	2,190	2,296	1,461	1,847
Rundlets	1			44	216	267	350	554	337	493	445	451	734

Table 13.1 Continued

	MB/Unit	1716	1720	1725	1730	1735	1740	1745	1750	1755	1760	1765	1770
Tobacco (lb)	2	2,369	2,704	4,077	4,679	3,944	4,543	5,991	2,625	3,674	4,234	3,408	4,036
Tobacco boxes	1	41	1	167	156	177	162	193	54	194	92	42	56
Tobacco tongs	0.5	8	19	36	75	2						1	
Water, strong (gal)	4			60		94	132	167	102	300	196	40	99
Alcohol[c]		0	499	831	1,784	1,609	1,996	3,112	1,993	2,983	2,937	1,952	2,680
Tobacco[d]		2,418	2,724	4,280	4,910	4,123	4,705	6,184	2,679	3,868	4,326	3,451	4,092
Total		*2,418*	*3,223*	*5,111*	*6,694*	*5,732*	*6,701*	*9,296*	*4,672*	*6,851*	*7,262*	*5,403*	*6,772*
Other luxuries													
Baize (yd)	1.5	33	42	3			11				16		
Bayonets	1	173		121	303	214	150	190	106	188	452	500	488
Beads (lb)	2	629	513	514	337	386	318	196	134	322	565	272	412
Buttons	0.25		2	15	9	7	10	23	2	9	13	1	5
Cloth (yd)	3.5	593	1,869	2,856	2,984	1,677	3,454	3,053	1,510	2,507	2,572	1,845	3,002
Combs	1	135	157	390	445	269	346	328	150	158	213	190	258
Duffel (yd)	2	6	184	38	155	32	14	70	80	67	104	114	138
Egg boxes	0.333		82	8	32	36	47	43	28	29	17	21	22
Flannel (yd)	1.5	24	24			9	29	28	76	31	50	27	212
Gartering (yd)	0.667	24	36	95	264	238	244	104	58	167		117	166
Glasses burning	0.5			4	3	4	16	18	9	13	12		
Handkerchiefs	1.5				56	18	18			26			4
Hats	4	99		136	40	152	140	296	64	52		80	4
Hawkbells (pair)	0.083		39	75	78	40	42	17	5	10	28	38	31
Lace (yd)	0.667						123	27				133	
Looking glasses	1	88	87	126	132	141	108	168	59	61	82	98	116
Needles	0.083	8	46	41	40	42	34	33	2	20	85	25	33
Pistols	7			7	98	147	182	77		28	21	49	7
Rings (3 kinds)	0.12–0.33		22	37	67	91	106	108	29	121	73	54	96
Sashes	1.5				66	48	72	48	5	23	2		16
Scissors	0.5	26	7	23	3	25	28	6	18	16	18	10	10

Table 13.1 Continued

	MB/Unit	1716	1720	1725	1730	1735	1740	1745	1750	1755	1760	1765	1770
Shirts	2.5	4	21	72	142	244	226	156	82	76	30	66	190
Shoes (pair)	3					3			4				12
Spoons	0.5			1	2		12				12	2	
Stockings	2.5	8	15	36	60	80	64	28		2	11	24	26
Sword blades	1	2	5	4	4		5	6	4	1	15	10	8
Thimbles, thread			48	3	2	10	53	65	11	22	2	1	3
Trunks	4					46	148	68	152	20	160	56	88
Vermilion (lb)	16	196	400	447	571	338	296	232	118	124	50	280	288
Worsted (yd)[e]	0.5–0.67					24	59	140		2	2	138	
Miscellaneous[f]				28	26		64	50	32	10	40	12	20
Total		*2,048*	*3,599*	*5,079*	*5,919*	*4,321*	*6,418*	*5,577*	*2,737*	*4,142*	*4,641*	*4,164*	*5,654*
Producer goods		10,721	7,968	13,831	15,748	8,413	11,974	10,798	5,160	5,783	9,712	5,548	7,096
Household goods		1,338	1,069	2,414	3,472	2,137	2,540	2,856	1,700	1,378	1,993	898	1,384
Alcohol & tobacco		2,418	3,223	5,111	6,694	5,732	6,701	9,296	4,672	6,851	7,262	5,403	6,772
Other luxuries		2,048	3,599	5,079	5,919	4,321	6,418	5,577	2,737	4,142	4,641	4,164	5,654
Grand total		*16,524*	*15,858*	*26,435*	*31,834*	*20,603*	*27,633*	*28,527*	*14,269*	*18,153*	*23,609*	*16,013*	*20,905*
Shares (%)													
Producer goods		64.9	50.2	52.3	49.5	40.8	43.3	37.9	36.2	31.9	41.1	34.6	33.9
Household goods		8.1	6.7	9.1	10.9	10.4	9.2	10.0	11.9	7.6	8.4	5.6	6.6
Alcohol & tobacco		14.6	20.3	19.3	21.0	27.8	24.2	32.6	32.7	37.7	30.8	33.7	32.4
Other luxuries		12.4	22.7	19.2	18.6	21.0	23.2	19.5	19.2	22.8	19.7	26.0	27.0

Source: Carlos and Lewis (2001).

Notes:

a Made beaver (MB) per unit.
b Guns – flints, guns, gun worms, powder horns, powder, shot.
c Alcohol – brandy, rundlets (barrels), strong water.
d Tobacco – tobacco, tobacco boxes, tobacco tongs.
e Worsted binding and worsted knit.
f Brass collars, earrings, feathers, medals, pumps, razors.

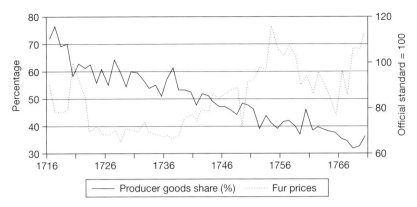

Figure 13.3 Fur prices and the share of producer goods in Native expenditure: York Factory, 1716–1770

Source: Carlos and Lewis (2001).

Comparing property rights to beaver and game

The literature on Native American economic behavior suggests a clear distinction between the property rights to inputs that were a direct source of food and other subsistence goods, and inputs more associated with the luxuries obtained through trade with the Europeans. Resources such as game were essentially common property. For even though Native groups, often to the level of the family unit, had well-defined hunting territories, the rights to these territories were severely curtailed. Outsiders were prohibited from trapping animals specifically for the fur trade, but they were permitted onto the territory to hunt for food. Thus, beaver and other non-migratory fur-bearing animals were, nominally, private property resources, whereas large game was common property. For the reasons outlined in the previous section, beaver were depleted in many areas despite the property right, yet there is little indication that there was a serious shortage of game until the nineteenth century.

The Indians in the trading hinterlands of Hudson Bay had, and continue to have, a diet consisting mainly of meat and fish. During the eighteenth century, the meat component included beaver and waterfowl, but by far the larger part of meat consumption was provided by large game; mainly caribou, moose, and bison. There are references in the literature to the importance of beaver in the Native diet, but an analysis of the returns from York Factory indicates that even in this highly productive beaver region, beaver flesh could have accounted for no more than a small part of meat and fish consumption, perhaps 5 percent.[5] Rather, big game ungulates, which were plentiful, supplied much of the Native food requirement.

Why large game remained plentiful long after the introduction of guns and other producer goods is a question for which there are several possible explanations. It may have been that game was so abundant that even the improved hunting technology had little effect on the stock; but this hypothesis implies that something other than a resource constraint was limiting the Native population.[6] Alternatively, it has been suggested that guns, although widely used, did not greatly improve the Indians' ability to hunt the animals. Finally, there remains the possibility that Indians both before and after European contact were hunting in a way that promoted conservation, or at least prevented severe depletion. Bishop (1986: 54) among others is skeptical of such deliberate attempts by Indians to control the animal stocks: "given a lack of understanding of biomass systematics, [Natives] could have not known that their hunting strategies were either reducing or increasing the overall game population." Adrian Tanner (1979: 44), on the other hand, argues that the Mastassini hunters in the region of James Bay learned the nature habits of the animal species in the region and were sensitive to population changes. Their hunting strategy included avoiding areas where the stocks appeared to be threatened.

It remains an open question whether Indians preserved the game in the region of Hudson Bay through deliberate calculation, or whether the moose and caribou remained numerous despite unrestrained hunting. Nevertheless, for the purpose of the analysis here, Native Americans will be assumed to follow a non-depletion strategy, which, although difficult to verify as conscious policy, appeared to maintain the stocks of large game. The model illustrates that, by treating game as a resource that was commonly and widely owned, Native hunters could harvest at closer to optimal levels.

The model begins with a standard fisheries-type natural growth function:

(1) $X^* = aX - bX^2$

where X is the biomass, * indicates the rate of change of a variable, and a, b are positive constants.[7] The harvest function is assumed to take a simple form also common in fisheries models:

(2) $H = EX$

where H is the harvest and E the level of harvesting effort. A more realistic harvesting function for game would likely assume that the elasticities of the harvest with respect to both E and X are less than one.[8] Suppose that each hunter, i, has a utility function of the form:

(3) $u_i = (h_i - s)^\alpha e_i^{-\beta}, \; \alpha, \beta > 0$

where h is the harvest, e is effort, and s is subsistence consumption. Note that utility is positively related to output above subsistence and negatively related to effort. In the pure common property case, each hunter maximizes utility, where the biomass is taken as given. The first order conditions imply:

(4) $h_i^{cp} = \beta s/\beta - \alpha$

where h_i^{cp} is the common property solution.[9] Assuming the same preferences for each hunter, the total harvest is:

(5) $H^{cp} = \beta S/\beta - \alpha$

where S represents the subsistence requirements of the entire population.
To the extent that consumption beyond subsistence had little effect on
utility, parameter α would be small and the harvest would approximate
the subsistence requirements of the population. Setting H^{cp} equal to X^* in
equation (1) gives the equilibrium population of game in the open access
case:

(6) $X^{eq} = \left(a + \sqrt{(a^2 - 4b(\beta S/(\beta - \alpha)))} \right)/2b$

The equilibrium biomass depends on the parameters of the natural growth
function as given in equation (1), the parameters of the Natives' utility function, and the total subsistence requirements, S, of the Native population.
If, over time, the Native population approached its maximum, that population would necessarily correspond to the maximum-sustained-yield level
of the stock of game. The solutions are:

(7) $X^0 = a/2b$, $H^0 = a^2/4b$, and $E^0 = a/2$

where superscript 0 indicates the solution at the biological optimum of the
stock of game.[10]

Next consider the case of two groups of hunters, each with a well-defined
hunting territory, but assume each group wants to maximize their own
population. This would imply the objective of a maximum harvest on a
sustained basis, but each group must now take account of the fact that the
other group is harvesting from the same common pool. Even if hunting
territories were well defined, there would have been variation, perhaps
substantial variation, in the share of the herd located in each of the territories, but here it assumed that animal population density is the same in
both territories. The harvest by each group is given by:

(8) $H_i = E_i X$

where $i = 1, 2$. Since each group harvests on a sustainable basis, the amount
they harvest depends on the level of effort of the other. The maximum
harvest for group 1, under these assumption can be written as:

(9) $H_1^s = aX - bX^2 - H_2$

where E_1^s is the sustainable harvest of group 1 for a given harvest by group 2. Maximizing equation (9) with respect to X, holding the effort level of the other group, E_2, constant, it follows from equations (8) and (9) that the effort level consistent with a maximum sustainable harvest is:[11]

(10) $E_1 = a/2 - E_2/2$

The Cournot-Nash equilibrium for the stock of game, the harvest, and the level of effort is given by:

(11) $X^{CN} = a/3b$, $H^{CN} = (H_1^s + H_2^s) = 2a^2/9b$,

and $E^{CN} = (E_1 + E_2) = 2a/3$

Equations (7) and (11) highlight why common access to game across Native groups may have been a better arrangement than one with well-defined and exclusive hunting territories. In the Cournot-Nash scenario, each group maximizes their own population subject to the actions of the other group. This behavior ultimately leads to a lower total Native population than if both groups had treated the resource as implying a common interest. Under the assumed specifications, the game population is one-third below the level that results with a common approach, the harvest (and human population) is one-ninth lower, and the total level of effort is one-third greater. Effort per hunter is 50 percent greater under Cournot-Nash.[12] These results are based on simple and perhaps unrealistic functional forms; nevertheless they suggest the advantages of the system that characterized Native game hunting, rather than one where territories were regarded as exclusive.

Estimates of the Native American population

The property rights of Native Americans over large game may have been a key to their survival, but conjectures, assumptions, and assertions surround the debate as to how successful they were in supporting a population prior to European contact. Current estimates for North America, or that area "north of the urban civilizations of central Mexico" (Ubelaker 1988: 170) range from a low of 1,900,000 argued by Ubelaker to 18 million as suggested by Dobyns (1983). A consensus view would put the figure between 6 and 12 million. The range of estimates reflects a difference in methodology. Given the lack of written documentation on Native American groups before contact, the extant evidence on which to base a population assessment is limited. All current estimates are backward projections using information from later periods. To obtain population benchmarks, researchers have used archaeological evidence, ethnographic sources, census materials, and diaries and letters from traders and others, who had early contact with the Natives. They have worked backward from these benchmarks to generate pre-contact populations.

The earliest accepted figures were developed by J. Mooney in 1910, who estimated the population of North America to be 1,148,000 (see Ubelaker 1992: 171). Mooney derived population group by group using the most extant numbers and then extrapolated to earlier periods. Assumptions about the timing and mortality impact of the epidemics that affected Native peoples turn out to be critical. Mooney and later researchers have regarded epidemics as largely a post-contact phenomenon. As a result, the numbers they generate for the pre-contact years are based on measures of population in the early post-contact phase combined with estimated mortality associated with these first recorded epidemics.

Basing his work on Spanish/American death registers, Dobyns (1983) challenged the view that the impact of epidemics was restricted to the post-contact phase. He argued that in various parts of the continent, since disease vectors could move ahead of physical contact, the mortality from European disease could and did predate actual contact between Native groups and Europeans. Moreover, because of the virgin nature of the environment, these pre-contact epidemics could generate mortality rates as high as 90 to 95 percent. Thus, the populations, which were estimated by Europeans at contact, might already have been significantly affected by European diseases. Dobyns first estimated a pre-contact population of 9.8 million, but he subsequently adjusted this figure arguing that his original mortality estimates were too low, and projected a pre-contact population for North America of 18 million (Dobyns 1983).

The range of estimates depends critically on when the pandemic levels of mortality affected Native groups. In Dobyns's world, the epidemics affected all groups early on and with the same level of intensity. If, however, disease vectors affected groups differentially and at different times, the implied pre-contact population would be lower. If one believes that the disease impact post-dates actual physical contact with Europeans, we move to the world of Mooney and Ubelaker, who estimate much lower pre-contact populations. Krech notes that:

> to decide on a sensible number, does not mean trivializing the extent of disease nor the extent of biological change introduced by Europeans. But to agree with the highest estimates assumes that diseases arrived early, spread widely and were invariably fatal; that populations did not recover between epidemics; and that diseases can actually be identified.
> (Krech 1999: 85)

Krech argues that, in addition to European diseases, the contribution to mortality of malnutrition or inadequate diet needs to be considered.

In order to narrow the range of estimates, researchers have looked to other evidence, in particular the information provided by archeology and also by immunology. Ramenofsky (1987) uses archeological evidence from the Lower Mississippi Valley, central New York State and the Middle Missouri region near the South and North Dakota border to test the "Dobyns hypothesis." She tries to determine whether there is evidence of a dramatic shift in population and social structure in the sixteenth century, which was the earliest period when European disease could have affected Native Americans, but before there was an actual European presence in the region. Ramenofsky (1987: 89) finds that in the Lower Mississippi Valley "aboriginal collapse did not begin with sustained French presence in the valley, but rather with the De Soto *entrada* more than 150 years earlier. . . . Furthermore, since the loss predates sustained European presence, infectious disease is causal." Although the evidence for central New York State is not as clear cut, Ramenofsky finds that the Iroquois tribes were significantly smaller in the eighteenth century than they had been 100 years earlier. But, given the early contact in this region, she argues that European trade goods and infectious diseases likely reached the Native groups at the same time. By contrast, the decline in population in the Middle Missouri region appears to have predated the arrival of Europeans.

The archeological evidence from the various sites supports a large decline in population after the arrival of Europeans in the Americas but before a sustained presence of Europeans in many regions. It would have been possible for war to have caused these changes; but, using the work of other epidemiologists, Ramenofsky argues that, in fact, disease was the source of the decline. Osteological and bioarcheological work, for example for the Northern Plains, also suggests disease rather than war was the cause (Owsley 1992). Smallpox was particularly deadly, with mortality rates of 90 percent and higher in pandemic situations. Smallpox could last many years in a dry form and still be transmitted. As a result, Ramenofsky (1987: 162) infers that, because mortality was so high, pre-contact populations were large, possibly on the order of 12 million. In addition to the timing and severity of the epidemics, another unresolved issue is the failure of impacted Native populations to rebound. The following section represents a preliminary attempt to explore the dynamics of a Native population affected by disease, a resource base founded on large game, and the new trade opportunities that came with European contact.

The Native population and the resource base: a predator–prey approach

A predator–prey model

There is an extensive literature which leaves little doubt that in many, perhaps all regions, European disease devastated the Native population; but the slow recovery of these populations is also deserving of attention. A few simple calculations illustrate the dimensions of the issue. In the more northerly part of the continent the Native populations appear to have been less affected than those further to the south. It is plausible that disease reduced the population by no more than 50 percent during the early years of contact, which in the hinterland of Hudson Bay would have been the late seventeenth century. Allowing for a modest recovery rate of 1.5 percent per year, the population could have been expected to have returned to its pre-contact level in less than 50 years or certainly by the mid nineteenth century. Yet, even in the early twentieth century, estimates put Native populations still well below their pre-contact levels.[13]

Many factors could account for the slow recovery, but here the focus is on the stock of large game and the opportunities that were opened up to Indians by the fur trade. It is argued that Native harvesting of beaver and other animals destined for the fur trade reduced the rate of exploitation of the large game, and the resulting decline in meat output ultimately affected the Native population. In the region of Hudson Bay, the evidence is that Native Americans subsisted primarily, if not exclusively, on the flesh of large ungulates, most importantly moose or caribou. It is not clear what constrained the Native population both before and after European contact, but if the supply of meat was a factor, and certainly an adequate supply was essential for survival, then the Native population was determined by the balance between the biomass of large game and Native food requirements.

This predator–prey relationship has been widely studied in biology and the main insights may have application here.[14] The model, in its simplest form, includes a population of prey that follows a path determined by the natural growth of that population, the number of predators exploiting it, and the effectiveness or effort of those predators:

(12) $X^* = X(a - bX - eP)$

where X is the population of prey, in this case large game, and P is the population of predators, interpreted here as humans. This relation embodies both the characteristics of the standard Lotka-Volterra relation and the harvest relation used in fisheries models. The next equation describes the change in the population of predators. Here, it is assumed that unless the harvest of prey is sufficient, the predator population will decline; but large enough harvests will lead to population growth:

(13) $P^* = P(-c + deX)$

where c is the rate of decline of the predator population when no prey are harvested and d is a parameter that defines the equilibrium harvest (i.e. the harvest consistent with a constant predator population). More realistically, one can include an upper bound to the growth rate of the predator population, but it would have little effect on the interpretation of the model. Note that eX represents the per capita harvest of prey. Equations (12) and (13) imply the following equilibrium prey and predator populations:

(14) $X^{eq} = c/de$, and

(15) $P^{eq} = [1/e][a - bc/de]$

Of interest is not just the equilibrium levels, but also the adjustment path. After all, much of the literature, quite rightly, is concerned with the effect of shocks, notably disease shocks, on Native populations. Here, the advent of a European trade will be considered as well. The pattern of population movements is described by a phase diagram, where the lines labeled $X^* = 0$ and $P^* = 0$ imply constant animal and human populations, respectively (see Figure 13.4).[15] If, for example, the initial stock of game is above the equilibrium, X^{eq}, as shown in Figure 13.4, the human population will grow, which will cause the stock of game to fall. This decline in turn will ultimately put an end to human population growth. Different adjustment paths are possible but the one described, a gradual approach to equilibrium, seems the most appropriate.[16]

Figure 13.5 illustrates the combined effect of a population shock and decline in hunting effort, *e*. Although the introduction of guns and other European producer goods improved the productivity of time spent in subsistence production, here it is assumed that the gain is more than offset by the diversion of time to the fur trade. The decline in effort increases the

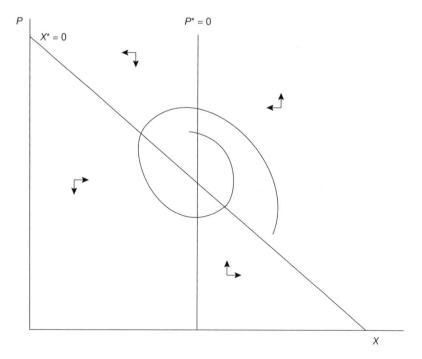

Figure 13.4 Native population and large game

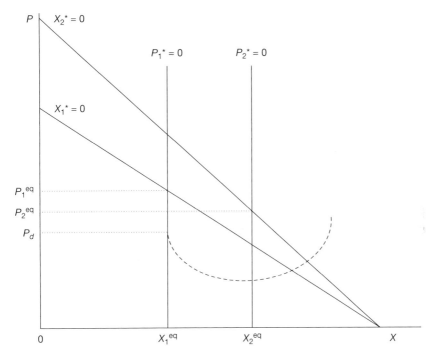

Figure 13.5 Native population and game: adjustments to shocks

equilibrium animal population (i.e. the population where the human population is constant), but the effect on the equilibrium human population is
ambiguous. If, however, we consider a scenario where the human population, prior to contact, was at the maximum sustainable by nature, then
the equilibrium human population is reduced. Note that, whatever the new
equilibrium, the human population, even after the negative shock, will
continue to decline for a period because of the reduced hunting effort. It
is only after the animal population has increased to the new equilibrium
that the human population will begin to recover.

Native and animal populations: some simulations

Applying the predator–prey model, illustrative simulations of the Native
population will be presented using estimates drawn from the northerly part
of the Hudson Bay hinterland, including areas further to the west. In much
of the subarctic region, caribou and moose were the large game on which
Natives relied. There were, of course, other food sources, but given the
need for a high-fat diet, large game was an important if not vital source of
nutrition. Estimates of the caribou population in the region are in the
"several millions." Parker (1972) reports that a family of five, who relied

exclusively on caribou meat, would be consuming 150 caribou per year. Most Native families, especially those further south, would have been less reliant on this food source.

The growth function for caribou, consistent with equation (12) is suggested by other evidence reported by Parker (1972). He found that, in the region of Kaminuriak, about 9 percent of the population were calves who had survived through the first year. Allowing for mortality of older animals, it seems plausible to assume a maximum growth rate (*a* in equation (12)) of 0.05. The population estimates of the previous section suggest a Native population in the region numbering in the several thousand. Here it is assumed that 5,000 were reliant to some degree on the caribou, but rather than the consumption requirements reported by Parker, the simulations assume annual consumption at equilibrium of 10 caribou per person. If 5,000 represented the maximum human population that the region could support on a sustained basis, the implied caribou population at that level is 2 million. Equation (12) can thus be written as:

$$(16) \quad X^* = X(0.05 - 0.0000125X - eP)$$

where *X* and *P* are in thousands. The value of *e* that gives rise to a human population of 5,000 is 0.005. The maximum rate of decline of the human population, *c*, is assumed to be 10 percent; and given that 2 million is assumed to represent an equilibrium, the implied value of *d* is .01. Thus

$$(17) \quad P^* = P(-0.1 + 0.01\,eX)$$

There are 4 simulations reported. In the first 2, the human population is reduced by a disease shock, in 1 case to 4,000 and in the other to 2,500 (see Figures 13.6 and 13.7). Population is then allowed to recover at a rate determined by equations (16) and (17). The result is a gradual approach to equilibrium where the original population of 5,000 is reached in 40 years and 54 years, respectively.[17] The next 2 simulations allow for the possibility that the fur trade caused a diversion of effort from hunting large game (see Figures 13.8 and 13.9). In these simulations, *e* is assumed to be 0.004 rather than 0.005. This change, which reduces the equilibrium human population to 4,688 and raises the equilibrium stock of game to 2.5 million, implies much slower recovery of the human population from the disease shock. As noted above, because lower hunting effort implies a higher equilibrium caribou population, the human population declines despite the loss due to disease, and continues to do so until the caribou population increases enough to offset the fall in (per capita) hunting effort. Rather than recovering in about 40 to 50 years, full recovery of the human population now takes roughly 90 years.

The demographic history of North American Indians, after European contact, has been based largely on the periodic epidemics that ravaged the population. The role of the food supply, especially that part of the food

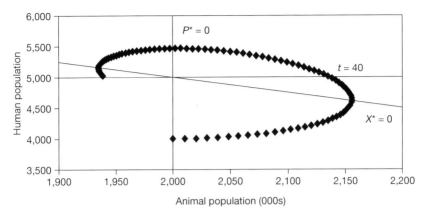

Figure 13.6 Animal and human populations: $P_0 = 4,000$; $e = 0.005$

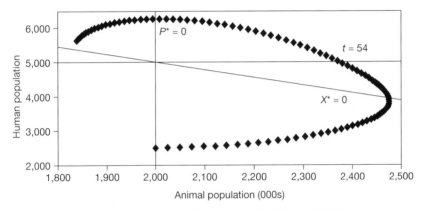

Figure 13.7 Animal and human populations: $P_0 = 2,500$; $e = 0.005$

supply derived from hunting large game animals, while not completely ignored, has been kept in the background. The model and illustrative simulations of this section are intended to raise questions about the existing interpretation. The results suggest that, in keeping with research on other populations, nutrition may have played an important role. Moreover, to the extent that trade with the Europeans affected the behavior of Native Americans, causing them to shift their effort from obtaining food to acquiring new goods, it may be that European trade, in addition to European diseases, accounted for the demographic failure that persisted through to the twentieth century.

Concluding remarks

There is little evidence that large game was depleted during the eighteenth century, and although the evidence for beaver and other animals involved

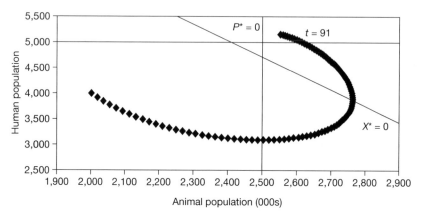

Figure 13.8 Animal and human populations: $P_0 = 4,000$; $e = 0.004$

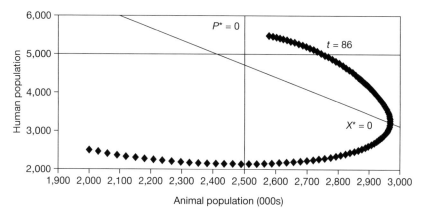

Figure 13.9 Animal and human populations: $P_0 = 2,500$; $e = 0.004$

in the fur trade is not fully conclusive, there is substantial anecdotal evidence that, in the eastern regions, stocks of beaver had seriously declined. In addition, Carlos and Lewis (1993) simulate depletion in much of the Hudson Bay hinterland. These outcomes were despite property rights to fur-bearing animals, especially beaver, that were apparently stronger than those on game animals. Here, we have argued that this apparently perverse outcome was related to the nature of the output that was produced. Beaver pelts allowed Indians to move beyond subsistence and acquire goods that were luxury in nature. Moreover, these goods had little externality component as did food, where an objective was survival of the entire group. The cloth, tobacco, alcohol, and other goods that Natives acquired through trade benefited only the households receiving these goods. In such a case, a property right to beaver could only be effective if it was defined at the individual or household level. Speck and others report that in lands to the southeast of Hudson Bay, family hunting territories were common; although in the more westerly regions property rights to beaver might not have been so well defined.

Despite the apparent property right to beaver, there were features of Native culture that may have inhibited conservation. The Ethic of Generosity, that was part of Indian practice, appeared to have reduced the incentive to save in all forms, including in the form of the beaver stocks. Also important was the fluctuating nature of the hunting territories. Beaver are non-migratory but the Indians who hunted them could not be sure that a given territory would be held for a long period. Tribes and smaller tribal groups were changing their hunting and trapping grounds throughout much of the eighteenth century, partly in response to the shifting game and partly as a result of conflict. These changes further reduced the incentive to conserve. Carlos and Lewis's estimates of the labor supply response of Indians to higher fur prices suggests that, despite conventions on the harvesting of beaver, Natives treated them much as common property. This behavior led to a much greater conservation role for the Hudson's Bay Company. In some cases the Company responded by putting in place rules that encouraged Indians to preserve the beaver, and it adjusted prices at the trading posts to control the harvesting effort of the Indians.

This policy of the Hudson's Bay Company to conserve beaver was maintained as long as the Company had a property right to the animals through its monopsony of the trade in the region. But once the property right was lost, as it was once French traders from the east entered its trading hinterlands, the property right and hence the incentive to conserve were sharply curtailed. In Carlos and Lewis (1999) we show that, with the entry of French traders into the Hudson's Bay Company trading hinterland, the Company began reacting differently to the price of furs in Europe. Higher prices in Europe now led to much higher prices at the posts. These high post prices, combined with the lack of individual property rights to beaver, led to serious reductions in the animal stocks. Indeed the timing of the loss of the Company's exclusive position, which occurred during the late 1730s in the York Factory region, the rise in fur prices at the posts, which took place at the same time, and the fall in beaver populations, which began shortly thereafter and continued through the early 1750s, all point to a scenario where property rights and depletion were closely connected.

The apparent success of Natives in preserving large game in the Hudson Bay lowlands may also have been related to property rights, as well as to the nature of the resource. Large game provided food and skins, goods that provided subsistence. Once their needs were met, there was little incentive on the part of individual family units to greatly increase the harvest. On the other hand, there was a strong incentive on the part of all Indians in the region to ensure that large game was preserved. An advantage of not extending property rights in hunting territories to game is that it promoted a common interest among all Indians in the region to preserve the resource. The result, according to the model presented on pp. 331–334, was a closer to optimal game population, a somewhat larger harvest, and a much reduced level of hunting effort than would have been the case if the various groups had competed for the animals.

In the final part of the chapter, the fur trade is related to literature on Native American populations. It appears not only that the population was reduced sharply by epidemics, but recovery was slow as well. A predator–prey model is proposed and applied to a stylized description of the hunting of large game in the subarctic. The results suggest that a diversion of effort from hunting game to the fur trade may have been a cause of persistently low Native American populations.

Notes

* Versions of this chapter were presented at the Western Economic Association Meetings (San Francisco) and the Canadian Economic Association Meetings (Ottawa). Support from the Social Sciences and Humanities Research Council of Canada is gratefully acknowledged.

1 Fort Albany and Moose Factory were assumed to serve the same area, which we call the Fort Albany hinterland.
2 For each post, Figure 13.2 reports a price index, where the *Official standard* is based on the prices listed by the Company for furs and European goods. Note that, until the latter part of the period, Indian traders were receiving less than these listed prices. For an account of Hudson's Bay Company pricing policy see Ray and Freeman (1978) and Carlos and Lewis (2001).
3 Martin (1978), who dismissed economic factors as having been important to depletion, has generated considerable debate, much of it revolving around the terms of his analysis (see Krech 1981).
4 Ray had argued that:

> One of the inherent weaknesses in the fur-trading system . . . related to the fact that . . . they [Indian traders] did not react in the same manner as did the Europeans. . . . With demand levels relatively fixed, a drop in the effective price for goods meant that the Indians could bring in fewer furs to obtain what they wanted. Their potential free time was thereby increased and they could spend it at the posts drinking and smoking.
>
> (Ray 1974: 68)

5 See an appendix to this chapter, available on request.
6 In many areas the aboriginal population was devastated by European diseases; but, in the northern part of the continent, epidemics seemed to have been less of a factor.
7 In the case of large game, particularly, there would be a point below which the population would be on an extinction path, even in the absence of harvesting, in which case the growth function might be represented by $X^* = a(X - X_m) - b(X - X_m)^2$, where X_m is that minimum population.
8 In Carlos and Lewis (1993: 486), which applied a harvest function for beaver, the elasticities with respect to effort and population were put at 0.67 and 0.5, respectively.

9 The Lagrangian function is:

$$L = (h_i - s)^\alpha \, e_i^{-\beta} + \lambda(e_i X - h_i).$$

10 Note that the biomass at maximum sustained yield is given by $a/2b$. Substituting this value as E^{eq} in equation (6) and applying equations (2) and (5) with α equal to 0 gives the results.

11 Equation (9) is derived from

$$E_1 X = aX - bX^2 - E_2 X; \text{ and } dH_1/dX = a - 2bX - E_2 = 0.$$

12 In general, where there are n competing groups, the equilibrium game population is

$a/(n + 1)b$ and the equilibrum harvest is $na^2/(n + 1)^2 b$.

13 For population estimates of subarctic tribal groups see Helm (1981).
14 See, for example, Hofbrauer and Sigmund (1988: 40–52).
15 Note that, if the animal population is X^{eq}, the human population will be constant.
16 The alternatives are an extinction path and a direct path to equilibrium, but cycles are the more typical predator–prey outcome.
17 In deriving these simulations, the human population is assumed to grow at a maximum annual rate of 1.5 percent.

Bibliography

Bishop, C.A. (1970) "The Emergence of Hunting Territories Among the Northern Ojibwa," *Ethnology*, 9: 1–15.

—— (1974) *The Northern Ojibwa and the Fur Trade: An Historical and Ecological Study*, Toronto: Holt, Rinehart & Winston.

—— (1986) "Territoriality Among the Northeastern Algonquians," *Anthropologica, New Series*, 28: 37–63.

Carlos, A.M. and Lewis, F.D. (1993) "Indians, the Beaver and the Bay: The Economics of Depletion in the Lands of the Hudson's Bay Company 1700–1763." *Journal of Economic History*, 53: 465–494.

—— and —— (1999) "Property Rights, Competition and Depletion in the Eighteenth-Century Canadian Fur Trade: The Role of the European Market," *Canadian Journal of Economics*, 32: 705–728.

—— and —— (2001) "Trade, Consumption, and the Native Economy: Lessons from York Factory, Hudson Bay," *Journal of Economic History*, 61: 1037–1064.

Cronon, W. (1983) *Changes in the Land: Indians, Colonists, and the Ecology of New England*, New York: Hill & Wang.

Demsetz, H. (1967) "Toward a Theory of Property Rights," *American Economic Review, Papers and Proceedings*, 57: 347–359.

Dobyns, H.F. (1983) *Their Number Become Thinned: Native American Population Dynamics in Eastern North America*, Knoxville, TN: University of Tennessee Press.

Feeny, D., Berkes, F., McCay, B., and Acheson, J.M. (1990) "The Tragedy of the Commons: Twenty-Two Years Later," *Human Ecology*, 18: 1–19.

Harris, R.C. (ed.) (1987) *Historical Atlas of Canada, Volume 1*, Toronto: University of Toronto Press.

Heidenreich, C.E. and Ray, A.J. (1976) *The Early Fur Trade: A Study in Cultural Interaction*, Toronto: McClelland & Stewart.

Helm, J. (ed.) (1981) *Handbook of North American Indians, Volume 6, Subarctic*. Washington, DC: Smithsonian Institution Press.

Hofbrauer, J. and Sigmund, K. (1988) *The Theory of Evolution and Dynamical Systems: Mathematical Aspects of Selection*, New York: Cambridge University Press.

Krech III, S. (ed.) (1981) *Indians, Animals, and the Fur Trade: A Critique of 'Keepers of the Game'*, Athens, GA: University of Georgia Press.

—— (1999) *The Ecological Indian: Myth and History*, New York: Norton.

McManus, J. (1972) "An Economic Analysis of Indian Behavior in the North American Fur Trade," *Journal of Economic History*, 32: 36–53.

Martin, C. (1978) *Keepers of the Game: Indian–Animal Relationships and the Fur Trade*, Berkeley, CA: University of California Press.

Morantz, T. (1986) "Historical Perspectives on Family Hunting Territories in Eastern James Bay," *Anthropologica, New Series*, 28: 64–91.

Owsley, D.W. (1992) "Demography of Prehistoric and Early Historic Northern Plains Populations," in J.W. Verano and D.H. Ubelaker (eds) *Disease and Demography in the Americas*, Washington, DC: Smithsonian Institution Press.

Parker, G.R. (1972) *Biology of the Kaminuriak Population of Barren Ground Caribou*, Canadian Wildlife Service, Report No. 20, Ottawa: Environment Canada.

Ramenofsky, A.F. (1987) *Vectors of Death: The Archaeology of European Contact*, Albuquerque, NM: University of New Mexico Press.

Ray, A.J. (1974) *Indians in the Fur Trade: Their Role as Hunters, Trappers and Middlemen in the Lands Southwest of Hudson Bay 1660–1870*, Toronto: University of Toronto Press.

—— (1980) "Indians as Consumers in the Eighteenth Century," in C.M. Judd and A.J. Ray (eds) *Old Trails and New Directions: Papers of the Third North American Fur Trade Conference*, Toronto: University of Toronto Press.

—— (1987) "Bayside Trade, 1720–1780," in R.C. Harris (ed.) *Historical Atlas of Canada* Volume 1, Toronto: University of Toronto Press: plate 60.

—— and Freeman, D. (1978) *"Give Us Good Measure": An Economic Analysis of Relations between the Indians and the Hudson's Bay Company before 1963*, Toronto: University of Toronto Press.

Rogers, E.S. (1983) "Cultural Adaptations: The Northern Ojibwa of the Boreal Forest, 1670–1980," in A.T. Steegman (ed.) *Boreal Forest Adaptations: The Northern Algonkians*, New York: Plenum Press.

—— (ed.) (1985) *A Northern Algonquian Source Book, Papers by Frank G. Speck*, New York: Garland Publishing.

Tanner, A. (1979) *Bringing Animals Home: Religious Ideology and Mode of Production of the Mistassini Cree Hunters*, Social and Economics Studies, No. 23, St John's, Newfoundland: Institute of Social and Economic Research, Memorial University of Newfoundland.

Ubelaker, D.H. (1988) "North American Indian Population Size, A.D. 1500–1985," *American Journal of Physical Anthropology*, 77: 289–294.

—— (1992) "North American Indian Population Size: Changing Perspectives," in J.W. Verano and D.H. Ubelaker (eds) *Disease and Demography in the Americas*, Washington, DC: Smithsonian Institution Press.

Umfreville, E. (1954) *The Present State of Hudson Bay*, W.S. Wallace (ed.), Toronto: Ryerson Press.

White, R. (1991) *The Middle Ground: Indians, Empires and Republics in the Great Lakes Region, 1650–1815*, New York: Cambridge University Press.

14 Owners, intruders, and intermediaries

The claim for lands within the Mbyá-Guaraní community (Valley of Cuñapirú, Misiones, Argentina)

María Rosa Martínez, Marta Alicia Crivos, and Laura Teves

The *Paranaense* forest is the area inhabited by the Mbyá. The Mbyá-Guaraní ethnic groups have been characterized by their broad mobility since pre-Hispanic times. Nowadays they face more restrictions on moving, but, even so, small groups of people migrate from one place to another within the present territories of Paraguay, Brazil, and Argentina, developing traditional life strategies. The subsistence activities of these communities are basically carried out in the *monte*. This ecosystem, characterized by a rich biodiversity, has allowed them to develop their economic activities over time: hunting, fishing, harvesting, and clearing and burning agriculture. The colonization of this region has modified the area, affecting its characteristics, as well as the aboriginal lifestyle. Timber industry and plantations of tea, *yerba mate*, tobacco, and tung have spread out over these territories, taking the lands where the Mbyá ethnic groups had settled.[1]

The material provided by the ethnographic studies carried out in two communities of Mbyá-Guaraní – Kaaguy Poty and Yvy Pytá – since 1996, allows us to examine the meaning natives assign to the land.[2] In the interviews with male youngsters and adults, they show their concern for the recognition and possession of the lands where some communities have been established. These lands belong to *Universidad Nacional de La Plata* and are located in a multipurpose reservation area.[3]

Past and present of the Mbyá

The lifestyle and, especially, the economy of the Mbyá-Guaraní, have been modified over time as a result of the interactions with other American ethnic groups and with Europeans during the long process of conquest and colonization. The same phenomena have affected most aboriginal groups throughout the Americas. References to the Mbyá in historical documents cover a period of three centuries, but their ethnic specificity remained

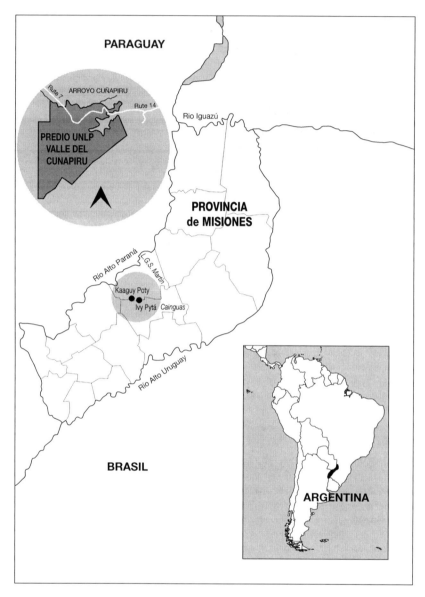

Map 14.1 Province of Misiones, Argentina, and the area belonging to UNLP

Source: Provincia de Misiones. República Argentina y zonas limítrofes con Paraguay y Brasil.
Mosaico Landsat V-Tm (Bandas 4, 5, 3)
Gobierno de la Provincia de Misiones
Ministerio de Ecología y Recursos Naturales Renovables.
Dirección de Cómputos y Procesamiento de Imágenes Satelitales
Path/Row: 223/78, 223/79, 224/78, 224/79
Escenas Octubre de 1996

invisible. The reason is that the Guaraní communities were not included in work systems such as *encomiendas* (Garlet 1997).[4] Historical literature, particularly ethnographic studies, refer to Mbyá's ancestors as Kay'gua, Kaingua, and Caingua. These terms mean "those of the forest" or "those of the *monte*" (*montaraces*). Other groups that were not placed in missions can also be referred to by these terms.

Regarding their place of origin, they call it Yvy Mbyte or center of the earth or of the world, locating it in Paraguay. Dobrizhoffer (1784) is one of the most accurate chroniclers. His writings are considered a starting point for the delimitation of land as his descriptions and map suggest a territorial division in correspondence with the different denominations of each ethnic group. In every case, these names make reference to the characteristics of the flora, fauna, and geographical features of the place where they settle.

Later research, such as that carried out by Ambrosetti (1893, 1895), Müller (1989), and Cadogan (1960, 1971) do not contradict these considerations, although they establish different boundaries. The Mbyá's entry into Argentinian territory can be traced back to the mid nineteenth century. The analysis of both historical and ethnographic sources shows an uninterrupted change since then in the Mbyá's productive activities as well as in their socio-political organization. Their settlements, once characterized by a high concentration of individuals grouped around leaders with political and religious tasks, gradually turned into settlements of lower population density, with kinship relations and a looser political authority. These changes in the socio-political organization are associated with modifications observed in their subsistence activities, such as the reduction in the lots assigned for cultivation and the smaller variety of species grown.

With respect to the Mbyá living in Paraguay, Cadogan (1960: 133) states: "Today, agriculture is an activity of second order of importance in their economy. However, Jesuit chronicles show that the Mbyá were originally excellent farmers." This author quotes Charlevoix who, in his well-known *History of Paraguay* (original edition, 1756), studied the group of 400 families that escaped after they were taken to Santa María (Misiones). He says that when he found them "they were well-established in a region where they harvested plenty of grains and legumes; food which this nation prefers to any other kind." Even after the bloody wars against the Spaniards, and later on against their descendants, the Paraguayans, the Mbyá were still good farmers.

Nowadays, the Mbyá recognize hunting, fishing, and horticulture on a large scale, as having been their main activities in the past. A lesser importance of agricultural activities in the present day is justified by many reasons: the destruction of the woodlands, the increasing recruitment of youngsters and adults as the labor force in the harvests of *yerba mate* and tobacco that take place within units called *colonias* (Chase-Sardi, 1989: 41; Pochettino *et al.* 2002: 697), and the emergence of new economic alternatives, such as handicraft trade.[5]

Since pre- and post-Hispanic times, the Mbyá-Guaraní ethnic groups have been characterized by their great mobility, even if restrictions have gradually been increased. Their settlements are located in parts of Paraguay, Argentina, Brazil, and, more recently, Uruguay.

The *Paranaense* forest is the area currently inhabited by the Mbyá in Argentina. They move around in small groups among their villages, which are either located in the periphery of towns and cities, or near the *monte*. According to the data provided by the *Dirección Provincial de Asuntos Guaraníes*,[6] in 1995 there were 50 communities, with an overall population of 3,700 individuals.

Today, the economy of these communities is fundamentally based on horticulture, primarily on clearing and burning, combined with hunting, fishing, vegetable harvesting, honey gathering from the *monte*, and, increasingly, on the production and trade of handicrafts. Men – youngsters and adults – are hired as temporary labor for the harvests of tobacco and *yerba mate*. On these occasions, one often sees young couples with their little children leaving for different places in the province in order to find this kind of job.

Life in these communities is influenced by activities carried out in the space usually referred to as *monte*. In Mbyá language, this environment is denominated as *kaaguy* (forest) or as *kaaguy e te* (true *monte*) (Cadogan 1992). *Monte* alludes both to the space containing economic resources and to a particular lifestyle which depends on the existence of that space.

The colonization of the forest in the province of Misiones is based on different kinds of economic activities – i.e. industrial-type cultivation and the exploitation of timber-yielding forest species (Schiavoni 1998) – and has gradually reduced and modified the features of this habitat, affecting the territory and culture of the native communities. These economic activities were promoted by national policies of immigration, which granted lands to central European immigrants – *colonos* – who, through the system of concessions, settled in much of the territory inhabited by the Mbyá.

Our approach

Ethnographic research, given its current character, enables us to gain access to the record of the different voices which – in a given period of time – express, argue, and set the basis for action concerning a number of issues.

Across cultures, land ownership has certainly had (and continues to have) different implications. In this respect, we agree with Miguel Angel Bartolomé (2000: 25) that:

> in spite of all its personal contradictions and contextual limiting factors, the ethnographic enterprise is feasible as well as necessary. Theories go by, but ethnographic studies remain. Even though their authors can be

the subject of methodological criticisms, the fact of trying to see the world with the eyes of the other makes ethnography useful. Their works not only attempt to understand other cultures, but also provide historical documents of dynamic and changing realities.

With regard to this, our ethnographic approach shows the pragmatic use of discourse – at times convincing or at times contradictory or ad hoc. This discourse is sometimes based on traditions or else adjusted to the rhetoric of national and international organizations devoted to the defense of aboriginal people's rights.

Verbal arts – eloquence and verbal skills – are key aspects associated with leadership among the Mbyá. Orality among the Guaraní contributes to a dramatic act which implies a performance. Political oratory reinforces traditional values and practices. Speakers' flexibility allows them to introduce innovations in their speeches, developing new strategies to respond to a changing medium and the pressures imposed by the national society. These skilled speakers put their knowledge of social norms and ethical values into practice (Hirsch 1996).

The analysis of the discursive corpus obtained in two communities of Mbyá-Guaraní (Valley of Cuñapirú, province of Misiones, Argentina) allows us to trace back the process of occupation of Misiones' forest. This ethnographic record is helpful in exploring the relationship between these groups and the natural environment in different enclaves chosen for their settlement over time.[7] The methodology of oral history in the context of recent studies of ethnography is suggested as a means to gain access to the Mbyá life strategies in their natural environment, from a present-day narrative toward a reconstructed past and a projected future.

References to the economic strategies applied in the past are presented in the account of informants as "fragmented memories," which constitute not only indicators of a "real past – keys to collective and personal identity – but also a form of the past still active in the present" (Thompson 1993). These strategies are better understood when they are interpreted as a justification for different means of occupation and demands over the territory.

The material that has been collected since 1996 in 2 communities of approximately 300 people – Kaaguy Poty and Yvy Pytá – enables us to understand the meaning aborigines assign to their relationship with the land. The statements about the characteristics and transformations of the natural environment in which the community lives emphasize the symbolic and pragmatic components of the notion of *monte*. The individual and social stories show a common factor: the importance assigned to the *monte* as a crucial space for making decisions concerning settlement and projects for the future.

For the Mbyá's economic strategies, the *monte* is an essential place. It is an environment that includes everything related to the natural world, and it has to guarantee the supply of resources for their subsistence (Crivos and

Martínez 2000).[8] To this effect, the *monte* appears as a non-homogeneous environment, with spaces that are connected with human intervention in the forest – *trillos* (i.e., paths resulting from man and animal displacement), particular vegetation groupings (canebrakes, feeding sources of the animals that men hunt), and streams and springs (fishing and water supplying places) where, in times not long ago, there used to be plenty of fish (Pochettino *et al.* 2002).[9]

The members of the Mbyá communities recognize the distinctive characteristics of the *monte* by categorizing these spaces. Thus, they assign them names and features which are related to the development of different activities.[10] References to the value of the *monte* in the present day are based on a close, long-standing, relationship between the Mbyá and their natural environment. In these references, the *monte*, which appears as the scene of Mbyá living in the past, presents the attributes of an idealized and lost world. This is recreated in the present by the accounts of the elderly.[11]

The *monte* is a sacred space for the Mbyá. It is, like human beings, a creation of the gods. Horticulture, hunting, and harvesting are activities to be carried out observing a set of prohibitions established by their religion.[12] The *monte* is an unpolluted space, where the interaction between its dangerous and sacred characteristics gives support to a balanced exploitation strategy. In this narrative, there is an overlapping of mythical and secular arguments that explain the present lifestyle and guarantee a harmonic project of nature utilization. To this respect, the Mbyá perspective of the world is related to current ecological perspectives in which conservation of bio-diversity is presented as an ideal goal. This ideal is embodied in the agreement signed by the *Universidad Nacional de La Plata* (UNLP) and the *Ministerio de Ecología y Recursos Naturales Renovables*[13] of the Province of Misiones. This agreement was signed on November 18, 1999 and created a multipurpose reservation located on the lands donated to the University in 1991 by their former owners, the company *Celulosa Argentina*. These lands have a surface area of 6,035 hectares, and are located in the departments of General San Martín and Cainguás. Both communities have settled on these lands.

The University's opinion about how the *monte* should be preserved becomes apparent in scientific projects aiming at "minimizing the degradation of natural resources attending to the environmental and socio-cultural problems of the region." Emphasis is put on the value of rational components – the sustainable use of biological diversity – corresponding to ancestral life strategies of Mbyá aborigines. However, the increasing sedentary character of the present groups (in contrast with the nomadic behavior of their ancestors) leads to an excessive exploitation of the natural resources. This, along with the presence of people searching for exotic animals and vegetation species much coveted in the market, is perceived as a threat to the sustainable development project carried out by UNLP.

On the other hand, from the Mbyá point of view, the UNLP has come to represent the actions of *juruá* (i.e., white men), which are focused on a utilitarian perspective, and are deprived of the symbolic and ethical components that guide the interaction of the Mbyá with their natural environment.

There are good reasons to back both perspectives. This is the scenario in which we have to place the Mbyá's present claim for lands. However, considering the nature of both protagonists – the UNLP is not a western institution and the Mbyá are not just occupants of the premises – it is possible to reach an agreement between scientific principles and Mbyá beliefs with respect to the ideal of conservation of the natural environment.

The *monte*: the land of the Mbyá

The accounts show direct allusions, paraphrases, and contradictions regarding the interest Mbyá communities have in the possession of the lands. But these accounts take place in a certain context. The interviews of members of both communities were made by ethnographers from the UNLP. This was the context in which they expressed their claims – either explicitly or implicitly – to the "owner" of the lands they currently occupy. Other owners – i.e., timber businesses and *colonos* – to whom successive claims were presented in the past, are evoked in an account articulating the deep temporal settlement of the Mbyá in that place, the need of the *monte* as a space to develop their economic activities, and their concern that future generations should be allowed to stay in the territory where their lifestyle can be preserved.

Several agents interrupt this projected scenario concerning the *monte*, putting at risk the Mbyá project of life. All of them share a characteristic: to be *juruá*, i.e., white men. Thus, businessmen, *colonos*, UNLP, ENDEPA,[14] the *Dirección de Asuntos Guaraníes*, and furtive poachers invade and impose their own limits to a space formerly indispensable to the existence of the Mbyá.[15]

At the present, the university project of a reservation produces distrust/rejection among the leaders of the aboriginal people. They perceive that their existence is threatened and that their condition is reduced to that of objects of scientific interest. The intervention of institutions such as ENDEPA and other organizations devoted to the defense of the aboriginal people's rights has deepened the gap between the academic ideal of conservation and sustainable development and the ideal of complete return of the lands to their authentic owners. Even though the proposal from the UNLP includes the aboriginal communities as significant actors, the claim made by the aboriginal people regarding the ownership of the lands constitutes a precondition to any participation in joint projects. In this scenario, different actors take on different roles. For example, the UNLP, as the current legal owner of the lands, is represented by a number of agents – officers and scientists – who take on the role of intermediaries in the claims made by the Mbyá, the real owners. ENDEPA, in turn, performs this role through its legal representation of the Mbyá communities, as well as through the role of facilitator of trips to cities and institutions where the aboriginal people present their claims. The intruders – i.e., furtive poachers and *colonos* advancing on the premises – constitute a menace to the environment of the multipurpose reservation.

However, such roles are not fixed: poachers and settlers become intermediaries between the Mbyá and the world of the white people in some of their economic transactions. We, as ethnographers from the UNLP, become intruders when inquiring by means of observation and interviews about their lifestyle. Hence, depending on the context, the same actors alternate the roles of owners, intruders, and intermediaries, forming the social scenario in which the Mbyá make claims for the lands.

Notes

1 Tung is a tree of Chinese origin bearing seeds that yield oil, which is used for industrial purposes.
2 The ethnographic material included in this chapter is derived from interviews carried out by the authors and other members of their research team with male adults living in both communities. The interviews took place between 1996 and 2001. We use the initials of those interviewed so as not to disclose their identities. The complete record of these interviews is in our laboratory, and is available upon request.
3 The university's name in English is The National University of La Plata. UNLP is its acronym in Spanish.
4 Aborigine villages and their inhabitants granted for use by Spanish colonists by royal decree.
5 The term *colonia* refers to an agricultural unit, usually small in acreage, given to the families of European immigrants, who arrived in Argentina after the second half of the nineteenth century. Today these lands are exploited by their descendants who are called *colonos*.
6 Provincial Department of Guaraní Affairs.
7 Enclave is a territory included in another territory, which has different political, administrative, and geographical characteristics.
8 "We don't have the property title . . . that's why we can't definitively get the land back. That's why we are worried, we want to be in the records, we follow the line, we do not plant much but we walk a lot, we have to walk in the *monte*, we don't occupy much land but we need it to look for resources, this is our idea."

> Answer (A): We'll go for a walk into the virgin *monte*, we'll see the *monte*'s pig, kure kaaguy, there are koachi (coati), wild boar (kochi), that's the same as kure kaaguy. There are two types, tateto (taytetu) and wild boar (tatetu) wild boar is kochi . . .
> Question (Q): And which kinds of plants are there in the *monte*?
> A: For the kochi there is the pindó yvyrapepe that is called alecrin, and the pitanga and the guavira are food for the kochi.
> Q: And for the people?

A: For us the guavira, pitanga, guaporovyty, apoty guapytã. We bring this coconut from the *monte* . . . it is in the virgin *monte*.

Q: And which other plants are there?

A: Only these ones. We use the guapytã and the cogollo from the pindó. We bring it from there . . . and the worm rises from where the cogollo is pulled out, the big worm. I don't know if you saw, I don't know if they showed you, the pindó is checked with the ax. There's the big worm.

(Oral record passage (fragment) from
a prior chief of Kaaguy Poty 2000)

9 A: In the *monte* it grows more beautiful, the takua rembo in the capuera is not so beautiful, the takuapi yes, if you are going to make a rozado you can use it already after three years, because it sprouts fast in the kokuere.

Q: And in the *monte* comes takuapi.

A: In the *monte*, where there the stream shore is, where the stream goes, just around, not in the high *monte*.

Q: And is the stream in the *monte*?

A: Yes. . . . further away there's a little stream Pepa, that's kaaguy karapé, because it's like a bañado, it accumulates water there. . . .

(Oral record passage (fragment) from
a prior chief of Kaaguy Poty 2000)

10 A: Yes, it may be a beautiful place, like a landscape, beautiful landscape. Sometimes we find a beautiful place and we are very happy. This *monte*, very thick, it seems it was already used, it is virgin *monte*, you can walk just like that.

Q: How is this thing with plenty of takua rembo called?

A: Kaaguy karapé.

Q: And where is the takua rembo?

A: Kaaguy vai.

Q: What does it mean?

A: Ugly place, it's ugly where the takua rembo is because you cannot see downwards, jai vai, we said to the children, go to the *monte* but do not enter into the ugly *monte*, and we said something else to the childen, after the rain when the sun comes the snake comes out to the trail and you have to be careful.

(Oral record passage (fragment) from
a prior chief of Kaaguy Poty 2000)

11 "Nowadays we have some more work to do. Before, our grandparents lived in a different way, calm, no one bothered them, they were in the *monte*, disease didn't reach there. It's nice but it's changing now, it's not like before, we change a little, it's not good, it's not better than before" (Oral record passage (fragment) from a prior chief of Yvy Pytá, LG 1996).

12 "The cemeteries are in the *monte*. It has always been like this, because we natives cannot have it next to our house, it has to be a little further away. In the *monte* is a good place . . . the spirits . . . it has to be the Pai, he is the one who must know, he knows where" (Oral record passage (fragment) from a prior chief of Yvy Pytá, LG 1996).

A: Here in the *monte* there are many dangers. . . . Because something may happen anytime, anything may happen, some things are dangerous so sometimes I feel that I cannot get up. It was like this with our grand-parents, now everything has changed for us but some of us continue as before.

Q: And what happens in the *monte*, what dangers are there?

A: There's the danger of snakes and some tigers but there aren't so many. It's not dangerous with the many animals because sometimes you cut yourself or you fall, you can hurt yourself in any way.

Q: And you . . . you only go hunting?

A: Yes. For example, I go alone. Sometimes someone from the other houses comes as well, and then yes . . . we are two or three. Maybe we go to *melar* and then a bunch of us go . . . four, five. . . . Sometimes I go to *melar* and sometimes I go alone, because if there's not much out there it's not worth it for so many of us to go.

For example if I go to the *monte*, I do not make stops in the *monte*. I go walking, I turn and come back. . . . I do not take anything with me but the hope to hunt and I take a machete and that's it. Sometimes, if I feel hungry I cut pindó and eat.

(Oral record passage (fragment) from a native of Kaaguy Poty 1996).

13   Ministry of Ecology and Renewable Natural Resources.
14   National Pastoral Action Team for Aboriginal People.
15   It's not to destroy the *monte*, as the *colonos*, the companies that take everything, knock down everything and plant pine, eucalyptus, . . . it's not for that that we want

(Oral record passage (fragment) from a prior chief of Kaaguy Poty 1998).

There was much more planting being done than nowadays. People went more to the *monte*, *palmito*, took honey, people walked more into the *monte*. Now they do not want to go into the *monte*. They know that you go, you get lost and they do not want to go anymore. They go to work to the colony, they do some work there

(Oral record passage (fragment) from a native of Kaaguy Poty 1996).

Yes, we were already here, but we did not have a general chief, there was a chief in each community, who gives orders in his community, there was no General Chief, that's why we cannot get our land definitively back. That's why we are worried, we want to be in the records, we follow the line, we do not plant much but we walk a lot, we have to walk in the *monte*, we don't occupy much land but we need it to look for resources. This is our idea. ENDEPA did not work well with the paisanos, that's why she didn't do the paperwork for the land with Celulosa (Paper Company). After Celulosa gave the land to the University we were told they had handed it over. We didn't know about it, and then Celulosa told the nun – why didn't the paisanos do the paperwork for the land, we were going to hand everything over to the paisanos, because we do not want the land anymore, Celulosa Argentina said, right then we knew the land was not Celulosa's, because we were saying it was their property, then we knew it was the University's property, that everything was handed over, even the community with the paisanos, and afterwards the people of Posadas told us, we went to the Provincial Department of Guaraní Affairs to see what was going on. They told us that the land we are occupying now belongs to the University, but there are no records of the presence of our community in that land, they told us, so the University didn't know the paisanos existed. Then we had to do some other paperwork, finding out things, until we found out that it's true that Celulosa donated the land to the University, because we asked to build the house, but we didn't want to build it without permission of the landlord. Then the lawyers of Santa Fe investigated. They got the order to make the house, that's why the Organization Juan Perón was to build the house but afterwards we do not know if the land will be for us because yesterday we heard the comment that they'll not give the land to the paisanos, that the landowner will throw all of us paisanos out of Tierra Colorada and Cúña Piru

 (Oral record passage (fragment) from a prior chief of Kaaguy Poty 2000).

Bibliography

Ambrosetti, J.B. (1893) "Segundo Viaje a Misiones por el Alto Paraná e Iguazú," in *Boletín del Instituto Geográfico Argentino*, Tomo XV, Buenos Aires, Argentina.

Ambrosetti, J.B. (1895) "Viaje a las Misiones Argentinas y Brasileras por el Alto Uruguay," in *Revista del Museo de La Plata*, I, Parte Descriptiva, 1892, Tomo III, IV y V, La Plata, Argentina.

Bartolomé, M.A. (2000) En defensa de la etnografía. El papel contemporáneo de la investigación intercultural, in Actas CAAS 2000, Mar del Plata, Argentina.

Cadogan, L. (1960) "En torno a la aculturación de los Mbya-Guaraní del Guairá," in *América Indígena*, Vol. XX, no. 2, México.

—— (1971) *Ywyra ñe'ery. Fluye del árbol la palabra*, Textos en guaraní y español, CEADUC-CEPAG, Asunción, Paraguay.

—— (1992) *Diccionario Mbyá Guaraní − Castellano*, Biblioteca Paraguaya de Antropología, Vol. XVII, CEADUC-CEPAG, Asunción, Paraguay.

Crivos, M. and Martínez, M.R. (2000) "Historias culturales − historias naturales. Movilidad y paisaje en la narrativa Mbyá-Guaraní," in *Proceedings XI Conference International Oral History*, Tomo 3, Istanbul, Turkey.

Chase-Sardi, M. (1989) "El Tekoha. Su organización social y los efectos negativos de la deforestación entre los Mbyá-Guaraní," in *Suplemento Antropológico*, Vol. XXIV, no. 2, Asunción, Paraguay.

Dobrizhoffer, M. (1967) [1784] *Historia de los Abipones*, Volumen I y II, Facultad de Humanidades, Universidad Nacional del Nordeste, Santa Fe, Argentina.

Garlet, I.J. (1997) *Mobilidade Mbyá: Historia e Significado*, Tesis de Maestria, Pontificia Universidade Católica do Rio Grande do Sul, Ms. Brasil.

Hirsch, S. and Alberico, A. (1996) "El don de la Palabra. Un acercamiento al arte verbal de los Guaraníes de Bolivia y Argentina," *Anthropos*, 91: 125–137.

Müller, F. (s.v.d) (1989) *Etnografía de los Guaraní del Alto Paraná*, CAEA, Buenos Aires, Argentina.

Pochettino, M.L., Martínez, M.R. and Crivos M. (2002) "The Domestication of Landscape among Two Mbyá-Guaraní Communities of the Province of Misiones, Argentina," in R. Stepp, F. Wyndham, and R. Zarger, (eds) *Ethnobiology and Biocultural Diversity*, Athens, GA: University of Georgia Press.

Schiavoni, G. (1998) *Colonos y Ocupantes. Parentesco, reciprocidad y diferenciación social en la frontera agraria de Misiones*, Editorial Universitaria, Universidad Nacional de Misiones, Posadas Argentina.

Thompson, P. (1993) "La transmisión entre generaciones," in D. Bertaux, and P. Thompson (eds) *Between Generations: Family Models, Myths and Memories: International Yearbook of Oral History and Life Stories*, Vol. 2, Oxford: Oxford University Press.

15 Establishing territorial sovereignty in Finland

The environmental consequences of ethno-nationalization of resource management in Inari

Jukka Nyyssönen

Introduction and theoretical framework

The case of Inari offers an opportunity to study the environmental consequences of the establishment of Finnish territorial sovereignty in a unique land ownership and ethnic setting. The establishment of Finnish territorial sovereignty, or "colonization" (the term will be discussed later on in this chapter), meant, among other things, establishing new property rights and land régime structures in the lands formerly owned by the *siidas*, or lapp-villages.[1] In the present situation, the land in Inari is owned almost exclusively by the state: in 1975, 93.7 percent of the land was state-owned (*Lapin metsätalous* 1975: 19–21). Land is managed by the Forest Government of Finland (*Metsähallitus*) and its local representative, the District of Inari. As a state property régime, the Forest Government has the right to regulate use of and access to land in Inari. The Forest Government's authority, however, is not "full ownership." The other régime utilizing the same land in the Finnish Lapland is the Reindeer Herders' Association (*Paliskuntain yhdistys*). At a local level, reindeer herding is managed by the association's subordinate herding cooperatives (*paliskunnat*), which resemble common property régimes. However, this is only a resemblance, since a régime's claim to land is not one of private property for a group of co-owners. Cooperatives have rights to use the land, and they lease small areas from the Forest Government for herding infrastructure.

The ethnic constellation is complex. A minority in Inari, the Sami reindeer herders are a majority in the herding cooperatives of Inari. Finns also have the right to practice reindeer herding. In addition, there are Sami loggers on the payroll of the Forest Government. As is often the case with land ownership, the pattern of ownership is complex and natural resources are multi-functional. There are several layers of administrative control relating to land use. The entitlement rule applicable here is a rule of liability: reindeer herders have the right to use the property, but they are required to compensate the land owner (Hahn 2000: 22, 25, 28, 88). This is accomplished by means of pasture fees.

Ethno-national process, or the establishment of territorial sovereignty, took on a unique face in Finland. Even Sami researchers admit that the "colonization" that occurred in Finland was not the harshest in global context (Seurujärvi-Kari 1994: 175–176). Although there was an establishment of state-owned lands, there was no exclusion of "others" on an ethnic basis from the land markets. However, there did occur the formation of an ethno-nationally affected land régime, the Forest Government. It became an organization responsible for the economic utilization of the natural resources and regulation of access to leaseholds and estates in Inari. The industrial land usage, as well as the land markets, were dominated by the ethno-national majority. Reindeer herding survived as an important and sometimes even major means of living. The case can be studied more fruitfully from the institutional point of view than from the point of view of private land markets, since they are only of marginal significance in the vast state-owned lands of Inari.

I shall study the process of establishing the territorial sovereignty in Inari and its environmental consequences. What was the nature of the process? One of colonization? Ethno-national? Or one of integration? Were there administrative hindrances to the Sami in land markets? The results of "colonization" have been viewed not only as economic, but also as ecological exploitation (Sklair 2000: 341). Was the economic outcome of territorial sovereignty, the introduction of forestry, ecologically depriving? This question is addressed in the first, empirical, part of the study. The second part of the study concentrates on the reasons for the success or failure of the régimes. The environmental consequences are studied by looking into the sustainability of the land régimes, the District of Inari, and the herding cooperatives. Did the régimes succeed in maintaining the ecological basis of the livelihoods: has there been deforestation or overgrazing? Was the "colonization" state intervention and the introduced régime constellation successful, or a root cause for diminishing resources? The performance of the régimes is studied by means of the analytical model provided by ecological economics studies in resource management sustainability. The aim is to study the success of the régimes in concrete terms, rather than at a purely notional level, through the analysis of the property rights régime constellation in Inari. Although I shall concentrate on the ecological viewpoint, I shall also make brief references to social legitimacy. I am leaving aside the question of economic sustainability: the periods during which forestry in the district of Inari made a profit were, in fact, quite exceptional. The District viewed its task as more social in nature: it was a job provider more than an employer, and resources were not utilized for long periods of time.

Since the process of establishing territorial sovereignty was essentially one of introducing holders of property rights in Inari, the land régimes are studied as property rights régimes. These régimes are studied by a new branch of economics, ecological economics. In classical economics, the prevailing object of study was economic efficiency; in ecological economics, economic efficiency is subsumed to become part of a larger problem of sustainability in the performance of a régime. The success of a régime is judged by its ability to combine a maximum flow of generated income, maintenance of its stock of assets (economic sustainability), and maintenance of the integrity of its social and cultural systems as well as the security of equity (social sustainability) and the stability of its biological and physical systems, at the same time as utilizing them economically (environmental sustainability). The environment's sustainability is kept at a satisfactory level by maintaining the ecosystem's dynamic ability to adapt to change, rather than by trying to conserve an ideal state of nature. Cultural sustainability can also be studied. In order to achieve sustainable performance, the tasks of a property rights régime must be well delineated and congruent with its environmental and social context. It needs to have the power to monitor its own area, as well as the tools to enforce processes of adaptation. It must be capable of adjusting to both the ecological processes of change in the environment and the boundaries of governance. In order to function properly, the régime must have social, ecological, and political legitimacy (Bromley 1991: 1–3, 22; Hanna *et al.* 1995: 17–18, 22; Hanna and Munasinghe 1995: 4–5; Hahn 2000: 5, 7).

Broadly speaking, since the collapse of the state-owned planned economy systems, private ownership has once again been viewed favorably in the field of economics, as well as in national economic thinking. The argument for poor efficiency in publicly owned enterprises states that a company or régime with a clearly defined right of profit will perform better than those whose rights are diffused or uncertain. The "consensus" has been blurred in many respects (Siedl 1980: 135–138; Hartley and Ott 1993: 1–8). There is an extensive body of literature that concentrates on denying the assumed "tragedy of commons," a situation in which natural resources with open access are plundered in the absence of any real sense of responsibility. Garrett Hardin, who introduced the idea in 1968, saw private ownership as a necessity in order to sustain environmental resources (Hardin 1968: 1244–1245, 1248). In response, there is a growing new consensus about the advantages of common property régimes. Recommending the decentralization of resource management has become something of a slogan in the study of resource management in the Third World and areas inhabited by indigenous peoples. A third strand of thought in studies currently being undertaken examines the growing evidence that the sustenance of environmental resources is not dependent on the particular structure of the ownership. The management of the resource can fail or succeed regardless of whether it is privately or commonly owned (Pradhan and Parks 1995: 168–177; Bjørklund 1999: passim).

Traditionally, "property rights" are viewed as a necessary condition for efficient market operation. According to Daniel Bromley (1991), "property rights" are widely misunderstood. There is even greater disparity in the use and given meanings for the terms "commons" and "common property." Bromley sees "the tragedy of commons" merely as a political weapon. Common property resources do not exist as a unified entity. Bromley states that there are natural resources, which are governed as common, state, or private property. In addition, there are open access resources (*res nullius*), to which no one claims recognized property rights (Bromley 1991: 1–2). Bromley's conceptualization offers the possibility of seeing into the sustainability of the management of the "colonized" resources. The neo-institutional way of seeing property rights as social relations (Granér 2002: 10–11) opens up possibilities for studying the processes of establishing power and hierarchies, as well as discussing processes of exclusion, adaptation, integration, resistance, and questions of legitimacy.

In this chapter, "property" is defined as a benefit (or income) stream, and, accordingly, "property rights" are defined as a claim to a benefit stream that is recognized by the state and protected by the assignment of duty to others, who may somehow interfere with the benefit stream. Property is a social relation that defines a property holder with respect to something of value, a triadic social relation involving (1) a benefit stream, (2) rights holders, and (3) duty bearers. A property rights régime is a structure of rights and duties that characterizes the relationship between individuals with respect to a particular environmental resource. Property rights régimes have the authority to decide what is scarce, i.e. possibly worth protecting, and what is valuable, and therefore certainly worth protecting (Bromley 1991: 1–3; Hahn 2000: 21). In this chapter environmental sustainability involves securing the ecological basis of the recurrence of a natural resource, whilst utilizing it economically. "Sami" refers to the reindeer herding Sami of Inari, unless otherwise stated.

Short settlement history of Inari

The whole area of Finland was populated by the Sami until the Middle Ages, when the *siidas* south of Lapland were broken up due to resettlement pressure. The Lapp-mark was established in 1543 and reinforced at the beginning of the seventeenth century.[2] The Lapland border prohibited Finnish and Swedish settlement and granted the rights of hunting and fishing to the Sami. Inari was originally populated by the Aanaar Sami (sämmilaš on Inari Sami, or anáráš on Northern Sami, now 900 in population) whose subsistence was based mainly on fishing. The Aanaar Sami encountered a growing number of reindeer Sami, or northern Sami from Norway. The closure of the national borders with Norway meant that the reindeer herding northern Sami (Davvi Sápmelaš) became the majority group in Inari. The third Sami group, the Skolt Sami (sä'mmlaž,

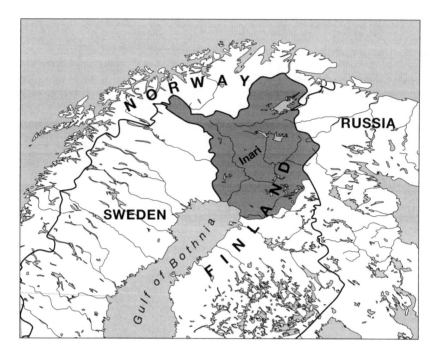

Map 15.1 The rural District of Inari

approximately 500 in population), settled in the eastern parts of Inari in the 1950s due to a loss of Petsamo to the Soviet Union in 1944. In addition, with Finnish settlement and modernization impulses, the Sami have been strongly assimilated into the Finnish modes of production and ways of life. The Aanaar Sami have been most strongly assimilated, with three folk groups settling in their areas. However, all three Sami groups have been ethnically mobilized (V.-P. Lehtola 1997b: 64, 67).

The history of Finnish settlement begins in the seventeenth century. Settlement was encouraged at that time by means of legislation and tax relief. The Finnish settlement continued spontaneously and escalated due to wars and famines in the eighteenth century. As a consequence, the Finnish settlers seized the fishing-sites and there was a subsistence crisis for the *siidas*. The settlers reached Inari in 1758. In the nineteenth century, settlement was encouraged again by a set of proclamations from the Czar of Russia. The Finnish population exceeded that of Sami in Inari by the 1920s. The post-World War II rebuilding era with its work opportunities meant another wave of Finnish settlement in Inari. The draw of the north was completed in the 1960s, when the logging in Inari and the water power projects in the Kola Peninsula of the Soviet Union brought along Finnish workers, some of whom stayed in the area. From this point onward, Inari suffered from migration and a decrease in population, which is a familiar feature in the peripheries of post-agrarian and industrial Finland. The population of Inari today is 7,268, of which Sami constitute approximately 2,200. Inari is the largest rural district in Finland. The area is 17,321 square kilometers (Kitti 1988: 111, 114–115; Korpijaakko 1989: 538–556, 579–584; V.-P. Lehtola 1997b: 23, 26–27, 30–32, 36–37).

Colonization: establishment of territorial sovereignty or territorial expansion?

The formation of the property rights system in Inari

The relevance of speaking about "colonization" comes from the Sami way of seeing the process. The group identity of indigenous people, which the Sami adopted from the global indigenous peoples' movement in the 1970s, implied colonial conquest. The Sami refer to settlement history as the time in which the indigenous land and other customary usage rights were forgotten and the state deprived the Sami of land. *Sápmi*, the Sami-land, and the *siida* system began to disintegrate (Seurujärvi-Kari 1994: 172, 175–176).[3] The notion should not be denied solely on basis of dividing the sea between the colonizer and the colonized, which would make the process one of mere territorial expansion. There was an occupation of land, an effort to cultivate it, and settlement of the lands of ethnic others (Ferro 1997: 1–2, 9).

The *siida* system traditionally consisted of autonomous territorial areas over which each village claimed a right of usage. These areas, with more or less strictly controlled borders, were owned by the *siida*. Subsistence was based on a circulatory system consisting of fishing, hunting, and gathering. The *siida* system entered a phase of deep change in the sixteenth and seventeenth centuries because of the influence of the crown and resettlement, as well as internal changes to the Sami livelihood. Nomadic, extensive, and, in some cases, expansive reindeer herding begin to dominate the Sami subsistence from approximately the 1650s onwards. The annual circulatory system also changed: summers were spent in the coastal areas by the Arctic Ocean and winters in the forests and lichen-pastures. Consequently the area of the *siida* expanded. Although the crown tightened its grip on the areas owned by the Sami, Sami land ownership was recognized by the state in the 1750s. There was a sophisticated resource management and judicial system in existence before the arrival of the Finnish settlers, who increasingly settled in the Lapp-marks. Nomadic reindeer herding persisted longer in northern Lapland, but the southern Sami settled in permanent dwellings, and their subsistence was based on agriculture. In the process, the Sami language vanished from the southern *siidas*, resulting in a major cultural change. The closure of the state borders (in 1852 between Norway and Finland, and in 1889 between Sweden and Finland) meant an end to the circulatory system. Expansive reindeer herding was practiced in Finland and in Inari in the remaining winter pastures. Thus the crown, and later the modern state, found itself in a situation that was not based on *res nullius* with regard to property rights and livelihood. The settlers did not meet a tragedy of commons situation either: access to pastureland was regulated throughout this whole period and the stocks were kept apart from each other. Pasture circulation became based on a balance of labor, reindeer, and pastures. In practice, the herder regulated the size of the stock according to the quality of pasturelands and the availability of a labor force (Bjørklund and Brantenberg 1981: 32–37; Korpijaakko 1989: 538–556, 579–584; Paine 1994: 14–17, 103–104; V.-P. Lehtola 1997b: 23, 26–27, 30–32, 36–37; Bjørklund 1999: 20–21; Hahn 2000: 92).

The motivation behind the Finnish settlement was economic: the economic possibilities unfolding in Lapland were numerous. The early phase of settlement in the eighteenth century was backed by physiocratic thinking, which promoted agricultural expansion in Lapland. This was in most cases unsuccessful due to climatic reasons. The nomadic Sami were viewed as uncivilized in relation to the peasants. During the eighteenth century this notion began to appear as hierarchical: the Sami were undeveloped people in a natural state. This notion prevailed long into the twentieth century, for example in the sciences (V.-P. Lehtola 1997a: 50–51). The process was colonial in this sense: there was a need to both cultivate the land and to civilize the "primitive" people living there.

Along with their traditional means of living, a new Sami strategy emerged: establishing a fixed settlement. The land right situation in Inari began to change in the 1830s, when the Aanaar Sami began to convert their fishing areas into estates and established fixed settlements in the crown lands. Once the estate was established, the Sami could better claim their fishing rights than they previously could have by appealing to customary rights. Alongside the first phase of settlement of the Aanaar Sami, which reached a peak in 1850s, there was the introduction of stock raising, which constituted in many cases an end to the wandering way of life typical to the Aanaar Sami. Another resettlement phase began after the proclamation from the Czar in 1877 regarding the establishment of the "Crown Forest lease-holds." From the year 1876 onwards, the Forest Government began to lease land. The leaseholds were granted to Aanaar Sami, and in growing numbers also to the reindeer Sami, moving from Norway to Inari. Renting a lease-hold was in many cases the only affordable option for the Sami without access to reindeer herding. Leasehold granted access, for example, to fuel wood. In the "Great Partition," which began in Inari in 1925, all the lease-holds could be claimed as independent estates. The Great Partition aimed to simplify the parceling of the estates in the whole of Finland. During the whole period there were no ethnic-based measures of exclusion in land lease policy. On the cultural level, however, the fixed settlement meant, in some cases, integration of the Sami into Finnish culture and language. This was amplified by the growing Finnish settlement in Inari from the 1870s onwards (Nahkiaisoja 2003a: 168–173, 2003b: 218–224, 226; Nahkiaisoja and V.-P. Lehtola 2003: 293). The "ethno-national" process in Inari was integrative, not one of exclusion. The Sami intention was not to integrate, but merely to secure the basis of their subsistence, while maintaining a way of life based on many different sources of income.

On the state level, integration was motivated by economic reasons – the possibilities opened by the sea-way to the Arctic Ocean by the annexation of Petsamo in 1920 raised high hopes of economic prosperity for Lapland. The annexation brought the economic, administrative, and cultural integration of Lapland into the newly independent state of Finland. The "mildness" of the Finnish "colonization" is highlighted by the simultaneous region-building process that occurred in Lapland. Central authority was challenged on conceptual and symbolic levels (with the term *Lappi*, Lapland), as well as in identity and economic territory building. However, Lapland was brought into the Finnish system of regions. The integration of Lapland was regional, symbolic, and political, as well as economic, administrative, and cultural. The integration began to crack the trans- and multi-national regionalism, which was the characteristic way of regional organization in the Arctic area of northern countries. The settler culture saw itself as, and was presented as, higher than the Sami culture. Also, social Darwinist thinking prevailed in Finnish sciences at the time. The notion was one of "lower" and "weaker" Sami. The greatest obstacles for the Sami were the openly racist views held by some of the Finnish officials (V.-P. Lehtola 1997a: 33–35, 55–58, 61).

The Great Partition resulted in 306 independent estates being established by the year 1943. The process was supported by strong agrarian spirit from the municipality. The Forest Government was criticized for its land policy: the estates were too small for profitable agriculture and the people were forced to seek work. The land policy not favoring agriculture was partly a result of systematic prioritization of forestry. In the long run, the policy was successful, since the agricultural project had no real chance of success in subarctic Inari. Also, the Forest Government wanted to establish only viable estates (V.-P. Lehtola 2003: 360, 387).

After World War II, Inari, which was almost completely burned by the retreating Germans, entered a new phase of resettlement history. Most of the people returning from evacuation started to rebuild their estates supported by loans from the state. The only option for those moving to be settled in Inari was to lease or buy an estate from the Forest Government. This meant the firmer establishment of the fixed settlements, which is most evident in the case of the Skolt Sami settled in Inari. Their former way of life based on winter and summer villages was "fixed" into permanent dwellings. The Forest Government was criticized again for its strict estate policy. On a cultural level, Inari and the Sami of Inari were deeply integrated into the Finnish culture and way of life. The process was not ethno-national, but inclusive and integrative, and it was adopted by the Sami more or less willingly. The ethno-national process was most obvious in the continuous stream of Finnish population into Inari: the employment opportunities provided by the water power projects and forestry brought wandering working men to Inari, of whom most did not settle in Inari permanently. Inari modernized, and the ethnic majority of Finns increased. The Sami were forced to seek employment, if they did not have reindeer. However, reindeer herding was one of the first means of living to recover from the war. The land rights situation did not change after this time. The Forest Government concentrated on its top priority, forestry in the state-owned lands (V.-P. Lehtola 2003: 378–387).

The post-war state-run settlement marked the beginning of a new phase in the settlement history of Inari, one of social settlement and the provision of estates for the reindeer herders. The project was motivated by welfare politics. The idea, for example, of parceling out "reindeer estates" in the late 1960s was intended to provide possibilities for livelihood. The results have varied, and, in spite of the projects, there has been a migration from Inari.

Establishing the land régimes and ethno-nationalizing the resource management

If the settlement history of Inari does not fulfill the requirements of ethno-nationality, let alone of a colonial process of exclusion, the management of means of living does. The traditional Sami resource management system was reorganized and regulated from the Finnish side, and a new land régime system was established in Inari. Hence the case is most fruitful when studied from an institutional point of view.

The modern state entered Inari and the administrative integration began by the end of the nineteenth century, when the Finnish local government system was introduced into the Sami areas. The forests of Inari were taken under the control of the Forest Government in 1866. The main tasks of the officials were to control fuel wood use and to check brush fires. Timber trade in the 1800s was of marginal significance and sporadic. State ownership of land was established by means of the Forest Law (1886). Land outside the established estates, which had formerly been owned by the *siidas*, was designated *res nullius*, and was thereafter regarded as state property. The ideological and scientific argument behind the establishment of the state ownership of land was a social Darwinist one: the nomadic Sami culture was stagnant and they had no concept of property rights relating to land. In addition, property rights institutions seemed feasible only for more advanced (i.e. majority) cultures. The Forest Law was based on ideas of ownership that followed the agricultural model, and it guaranteed the right for people with no estate to seek land to establish a leasehold on state-owned land. Another motivation for this law was to protect the northernmost forests of Finland from extensive fuel-wood harvesting and over-use. Reindeer herding was viewed as a harmful means of living. In Inari this resulted in the prohibition of access to pasturelands that had been "conquered" by agriculture (T. Lehtola 1998: 191–192; Hahn 2000: 96; V.-P. Lehtola 2000a: 30, 33, 38, 40, 45; Nahkiaisoja 2003a: 182–183, 2003b: 266–267).

The Forest Government took over the Sami area as a state property regime and was the state body responsible for the control of state-owned land. It claimed by definition the right to determine regulations and had a say in the practice of reindeer herding in Inari. Fees were established for access to state property (Bromley 1991: 23, 25–26; Hanna *et al.* 1995: 17–18, 29; V.-P. Lehtola 1997b: 42).

The reindeer herders were regulated in 1901. Access to herding and herding itself were regulated, sanctioned, and territorialized in a new way. In 1916, the Senate of Finland granted the herders, Sami and Finnish alike, a license to herd in State forests. At the same time, a quota was set for the maximum number of reindeer (Nahkiaisoja 2003b: 232, 234). Reindeer herding management was based on a principle of reindeer herding cooper-atives. The management system in Finland took account of the Finnish settlers' interests and forms of herding, unlike the systems in Sweden and Norway. The distribution of the areas was not based on any kin or *siida* system. The model was adopted from the Finnish local government system, with a chairman and self-governing bodies, which were responsible to the state. The Reindeer Herders' Association was established in 1926 as a national governing body for herders. Although the laws did not support the interests of nomadic reindeer herding, but instead juxtaposed it against a hostile agricultural system, the Sami strategy was to adjust to the system and integrate itself within it (V.-P. Lehtola 1997b: 42). The Sami herders joined the governing bodies at both a local and a regional/national level. But, the Sami are said to be under-represented in the national body when compared with Finnish reindeer herders.

The introduction of the reindeer herding cooperative system created the possibility for expansion of the stocks. The reindeer were gathered in public round-ups for separation and marking. The shift from a semi-nomadic form of herding to cooperational herding meant access to larger pastures, since there was no need to keep the stocks separated. At first, the introduction of a cooperative system meant a crisis for the Sami herders (Nahkiaisoja and V.-P. Lehtola 2003: 302).

According to Stuart Corbridge, the formation of colonial rule is marked by four key points or activities. First is the establishment of territories and territorial boundaries which had not existed before. Second is the estab-lishment of political order and the administrative hierarchy to run it where the ultimate basis is force. Third, colonialism brings with it a series of ties that bind a colony into the wider networks of trade and production that define the colonial world economy. And finally, colonialism brings with it a foreign culture of rule and a foreign language to practice it. In the case of Sami Lapp-marks all the points apply, but the second and third with qualifying comments: the nature of the process was not violent, but spontaneous. Coercion and violence were not needed due to integrative intention on both sides, and the disputes were settled in courts. Whether the emerging economic ties were a product of "colonial" intervention and a consequence of intensified utilization of the natural resources is beyond doubt. But was the emerging economic system built after the colonial model? Many would argue yes, but the process is also one of feedback and industrialization of the peripheries: there was an allocation of industrial and welfare resources to the old Lapp-marks that was greeted with pleasure. New territorial boundaries, new political order and hierarchy, new economic ties, and foreign dominating culture and language were introduced by establishing the territorial sovereignty of the state of Finland. One must also bear in mind that the Sami were not excluded from any of the "colonial activities," which is the most important exception from the colonialist models (Corbridge 1995: 176).

Although it entails the conversion of land into national territory, territorialization is not a one-time change resulting in a static end state, but is instead a dynamic process (Kaiser 2002: 231). The outcomes of the Finnish process differ from those of economic imperialism: the structural transformations were profound in Inari, but they did not totally exclude the old modes of production. The Finnish territorial expansion did not bring about deindustrialization and non-food-producing agricultural specialization. The process resulted in a periphery Nordic post-industrial welfare state with modernized, semi-nomadic primary production and services and a revitalized modernized indigenous economy and culture. The land of the Sami is still "colonized," and new links to the world economy create possibilities as well as ties to the post-decolonization, economically run "imperialism without colonization," or globalization (Ferro 1997: 17, 19–20).

Finally, the Sami strategies of accommodation and integration blocked total integration in the late nineteenth and early twentieth centuries. More crucially, the Sami and the settler cultures accommodated each other and the populations mixed. In central Lapland this usually meant adopting the Finnish culture, but in northern Lapland, and in Inari, this usually meant adopting the Sami culture. Adopting many sources of income was a necessity for the settling Finns because of limitations on agriculture. In addition, Sami culture and identity were regional, village-based, and remote. While the remoteness and the unique regional organization protected the Sami from assimilation, the division into localized communities hindered the rise of ethnic consciousness and unity even among the Sami intellectuals (V.-P. Lehtola 1997a: 41, 53).

In conclusion, one must be careful when labeling the process as colonial. The process was one of establishing territorial sovereignty within recognized national borders with more or less willing cultural, economic, and administrative integration of the indigenous people whose property rights were overthrown in the process. The mutually integrative system separates the process from the colonial and ethno-national. However, there are features that give some legitimacy to talk about colonization: the integration was carried out under Finnish initiative, and the process resulted in a Finnish model in the fields of administration and resource and land management. Also, the raw materials, as we will see, were transported out of Inari in a true colonial manner.

Economic integration: the phases of forestry in Inari

The establishment of territorial sovereignty in Inari did not mean agricultural colonization. On the economic and ecological levels the most important consequence of the process was the introduction of efficient forestry, which meant more or less continuous exploitation of natural resources. Only reindeer herding has been a more continuous means of living in post-war Inari. In this section I shall look at the history of forestry in the established property rights situation in Inari. How did the land régime perform? How was the conquered land used? Was the intensifying forestry socially and environmentally sustainable, or not? Did deforestation occur?

Due to a combination of natural resources and geographical factors, reindeer herding was the main source of subsistence in Inari at the beginning of the twentieth century. Reindeer herding was also the first attempt to adapt an organized livelihood to the subarctic environment. The main natural resources Inari had to offer were reindeer pastureland and timber. The forests of southern Inari are the northernmost pine forests in Finland. The regeneration period is long, the growing season short, and the stock of timber large. The timberline ecosystem consists of few species and is thus vulnerable to damage. Cattle were raised and corn was grown occasionally, but with low-yield and mostly unsuccessful crops. The infrastructure was incomplete and the road network nearly non-existent. Hence industry, aside from a few sawmill entrepreneurs later on, was of little significance. Given the pre-modern state of the distribution of livelihood, the introduction of forestry and public services in general was one of the strongest factors in the push toward modernization in Inari (Kollstrøm *et al.* 1996: 88; Nyyssönen 2000: 22–24). Consequently, unlike the situation in southernmost Lapland, the threat of diminishing pasturelands came from forestry, not from agriculture.

The inter-war period was the first phase of forestry in Inari. Cuttings were spread over large areas because only wood of timber quality was logged. The 1930s were marked by the blossoming of the rural district of Petsamo (an area to the east of Inari) and opportunities presented by expanding commerce and transportation facilities. This involved the modernization of infrastructure in southern parts of Inari, but the actual

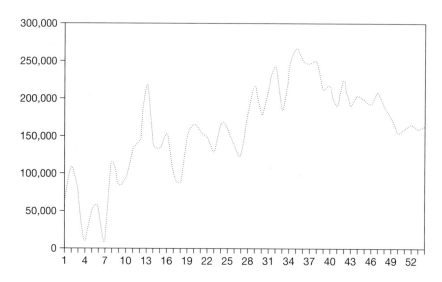

Figure 15.1 The amount of timber logged in the District of Inari, in cubic meters, 1946–1999

Source: Nyyssönen (2000: 307–308).

economic results were weak: Inari was a gateway to the Arctic Ocean and remained a provider of raw materials. The cuttings provided employment at that time for both Finnish settlers and the Sami. There are no signs of Sami resistance, although this may be due to a lack of sources. During World War II, the Forest Government was occupied with providing wood for the German troops situated in the Lapland. The war meant the introduction of a monetary economy. Due to the loss of Petsamo, the only log-floating route via Paatsjoki was removed, which brought a halt to the timber trade with Norway. The post-war period, during which the Sami area was rebuilt in a Finnish style, was a time of accelerated modernization and a diminished sense of Sami ethnicity. However, the full force of Finnish modernization was inhibited by two factors: an economic shortage and consequent delay in the resettlement program, and a recovery of reindeer herding, in spite of the aforementioned shortage. Forestry (see Figure 15.1) experienced a short-lived upswing in resettlement cuttings, but after the resettlement was finished, a longer recession followed (V.-P. Lehtola 1997b: 52–53; Veijola 1998: 83–84; Nyyssönen 2000: 22–39).

During the 1950s there was a weak, and therefore unsuccessful, effort to launch forestry in Inari. The effort was unsuccessful because of weaknesses in infrastructure, such as the road network (which remained insufficient for another couple of decades), long distances to the manufacturing plants in southern Lapland, and weak profitability. Although the effort was supported at the presidential level (President Urho Kekkonen was a keen supporter of the industrialization of the peripheries of Finland), in industrial circles, and at a local as well as Sami level, the breakthrough of forestry was not achieved at this time. Between 1952 and 1958 cuttings increased steadily, but not in the way that Forest Government officials wanted: timber was not mobilized on a large scale and the means of forestry were unsatisfactorily light, both in terms of the machinery used and results achieved. The unemployment of forest workers was a problem throughout the 1950s (Veijola 1998: 83; Nyyssönen 2000: 51–67).

During the late 1950s, the first large-scale timber trade occurred when wood from Inari was exported to central Europe and southern Lapland. This upswing, based on the manufacture of railway sleepers, was short-lived. The cuttings were spread over large areas, but were made mainly near the few roads that existed. According to the Sami press, the legitimacy of the cuttings was perceived to be high at this time. Forestry was welcomed, and the Forest Government was encouraged to intensify cuttings in northern Lapland. The rare openings of the timber trade with Norway were welcomed, and road construction works were seen as a problem only in the sense that there was not any in progress in Inari. Even though the Sami criticized the allocation of profits from the usage of natural resources (Veijola 1998: 84; Nyyssönen 2000: 68–73, 236–240), economic modernization was not a problem as such. The emphasis on profit allocation indicates that economic modernization was also perceived as a feasible strategy for the Sami. This further enhanced the perceived legitimacy of the cuttings, and perhaps even the property rights situation.

Economic inefficiency but social efficiency, boosted by a perception of great legitimacy, marked the performance of the Forest Government. It was regarded as a potential employer and a source of modernization by many parts of the Sami community. The Forest Government employed a small number of Sami workers. Environmental sustainability was evident only in the areas outside the cutting zones that were preserved, or used exclusively as pasturelands. Environmental sustainability was achieved "incidentally." It was not on the Forest Government's agenda, but infrastructural inadequacies prevented the Forest Government from fulfilling its silvicultural plans, which at this time were extremely harsh and, when applied, mostly unsuccessful. The reason for these failures was that a means of efficient forestry suitable for southern forests was introduced into the subarctic forests of Inari. The ecological damage sustained was not widespread (Nyyssönen 2000: 128–132). The success of the economic as well as ecological "colonization" was far from perfect, given the difficulties in mobilizing the natural resources.

The period from the beginning of the 1960s to the present day has been marked by consistent cuttings (though on a periodic basis), a somewhat fluctuating amount of timber being logged, and the consequent periodic unemployment of the loggers. The geographical distribution of the cuttings has expanded as a result, concentrating mainly in the southeastern parts of

Inari. The final breakthrough of efficient forestry occurred in Inari in the mid 1970s, once the 1968 completion of the paper mill in Kemijärvi began to influence the timber trade. The amount of timber being logged increased, whereas forestry methods were scaled down. In spite of this, the first voices of resistance were heard from the reindeer herding community. From 1972 onwards, demands for local democracy were met by negotiations over the location of the cuttings. However, interest groups other than Forest Government officials had no real power in the planning of cuttings until the 1990s (Nyyssönen 2000: 229–231, 282). Economic sustainability improved during this time, as the timber trade became more continuous. Social sustainability also improved since the recession in the primary industry and changes in the structure of Finnish agriculture (which was directly connected to forestry through agrarian forest ownership) hit northernmost Lapland later than the agrarian areas of southern Finland. This was due to the late introduction of forestry in Inari. However, the perceived legitimacy of the Forest Government by the Sami was beginning to crack.

The Forest Government was a significant employer in Inari, even up to the late 1970s. Equity in the allocation of input to the local economy was achieved by employing the Sami. Environmental sustainability began to appear on the agenda, but in an ambivalent, negative sense. This was due to the numerous conservation projects during this period. From the Forest Government's point of view, conservation restricted the area reserved for cuttings, which were considered to be ecologically sustainable. However, environmental sustainability was taken into consideration. For example, the mechanization of forestry was not completed, clear-cuttings were exceptional, and plowing was not practiced in its most extreme forms. Thus, by definition, forestry in Inari was not efficient. Deforestation was more evident in areas hit by brush fires. However, this applies only to the forests of Inari: the means of forestry were harsher and more harmful to reindeer herding in other parts of Lapland (Veijola 1998: 87–90; Nyyssönen 2000: 177–191; Jernsletten and Klokow 2002: 139–141).

The performance of the Forest Government has been evaluated in different ways and from different points of view. The environmentalists claim that even the lighter cuttings are not suitable for the subarctic forests of Inari where recurrence is easily damaged. The Sami emphasize the harm to reindeer herding. The interaction between lichen growth and cuttings is something of an open question, but the harmful effect of forestry upon winter pasturelands, the condition of which is crucial to the success of reindeer herding, has been largely acknowledged. Winter grazing is hindered both by freezing snow, due to a change in micro-climate at the cutting sites, and by cutting waste (Helle 1995: passim). Seen from the point of view of forestry officials, the picture is uncomplicated. In comparison with the unfortunate cuttings in southern Lapland in the 1950s that were carried out by means of the most efficient forestry methods, the cuttings in Inari stand out as a success in the history of forestry in Lapland. The forestry strategy in Finland and in Inari has been to secure the recurrence of the forests, thus securing the ecological and economic basis of timber industries. Cutting methods and silvicultural means have been adjusted to subarctic forests, so cases of deforestation are rare.[4] However, the beliefs of the forestry officials suffer from the lack of a larger perspective, i.e. beyond the sphere of forestry alone.

The perception of forestry

The early manifestations of Sami resistance to economic integration were expressed in the 1950s, during the first phase of Sami activism in Finland. The Sami activist front was not coherent, and the resistance was characterized by a lack of continuity. The early statements of resistance were aimed at the allocation of profits from the use of natural resources in the Sami heartlands. The issue was raised at the first Sami Congress in 1953, and it was held on the agenda of the Nordic Sami Council, which was established in 1956. These statements form an exception in what was, to a great extent, a modernization-friendly Sami ideological environment in the 1950s. There was a short period of criticism in the Sami press at the end of the 1950s, which pointed out the need to examine relations between forestry and reindeer herding. In one of the most radical expressions of the Sami rights movement of the 1950s, the *Saamelaisasiain komitean mietintö* (a report published by the Commission of the Sami Cause in 1952), forestry was viewed positively, as it created potential for Sami employment. The main issues for the Sami activists were reindeer herding, media politics, education, and language. During this period a common Sami ethnicity was built, which involved breaking away from the old, village-based identity. A more radical Sami ethnic movement emerged in the 1960s that viewed the first phase of the Sami activism as too sympathetic to Finnish modernization. Accordingly, the demands radicalized. Demands concerning the recognition of Sami ownership of the old Lapp-marks were voiced, but the main emphasis was placed on legal and cultural issues (Commission of the Sami Cause 1952: 44–45, 49, 55, 64–65; V.-P. Lehtola 1997b: 57–60, 62, 70, 2000b: 242–244; Hahn 2000: 114–5). Following Ian Brownlie's analysis of the evolution of group rights claims, Sami resistance evolved from calls for action to maintain the cultural and linguistic identity to land rights claims in the traditional territories. The claim of self-determination (Brownlie 1992: 37–40) was a later phenomenon on the Sami agenda.

The voices drawing attention to pastureland damages were absent in the 1950s, which may be an indication of the success of the Forest Government in maintaining environmental sustainability; although social sustainability was seen as a crisis, the actual pastureland situation was not. The absence of protests may indicate only that there was no environmental frame of reference on which to build a resistance. The environmental movement and environmental issues were just beginning to appear in the Finnish media from the late 1960s onwards (Myllyntaus 1991: 328). According to studies undertaken regarding the pasturelands during this period, the pastureland situation in Inari was good by comparison with the situation in southern parts of Lapland. However, the majority of studies undertaken were quite consistent in pointing out that the pasturelands were weakening in Inari as well (Nieminen 1987: 33–37).

The actual harm done to reindeer herding was observed and reported by the reindeer herders later, at the end of the 1970s, during the period of continuous cutting. Pastureland and forestry researchers came to almost identical conclusions concerning the harm to the lands and reindeer herding as a result of efficient forestry (Nyyssönen 2000: 263). This was the first time the property rights situation had been questioned from the point of view of environmental sustainability. Later, in the 1980s, the course of Sami resistance began to follow that of the Forest Government's cuttings – Inari entered an era of ongoing forest disputes, mobilizing both the environmentalists and the Sami. To this day, the Forest Government has emerged as a "winner": none of the cases taken to court were won by the Sami, and the cuttings, supported by a strong local minority employed by the Forest Government, were merely postponed or restricted in area. According to a large number of critics, the environmental sustainability of the Forest Government's performance was low. The involvement of the environmentalists created problems in maintaining economic sustainability during this period. In addition, social sustainability reached a crisis in the late 1980s. The cuttings in Kessi, in eastern Inari, were postponed due to a forest dispute in 1987–1988, and members of the Skolt Sami community of the village of Nellim were threatened with unemployment. For the Skolt Sami of the village of Nellim, forestry was an important source of extra income from the 1970s onwards. One must also bear in mind that the number of reindeer in Lapland was rising, reaching its peak in 1991 (Nyyssönen 1997: 114–120; 2000: 214). This last-mentioned factor reflects difficulties in applying property rights régime theories to conditions relating to a modernized indigenous people who have gained from the modernization and whose livelihood is more or less committed to growth. The multiplicity of interest groups also creates difficulties in planning resource allocation.

The Sami questioning of the property rights system has been motivated by both financial and, especially in the late 1980s, ideological factors: they have begun to question the whole pattern of power and allocation of benefit streams in the Sami areas of the Nordic Countries (Hahn 2000: 33). Although the Sami movement has a strong national variety, it is a part of the global indigenous peoples' movement, and of the larger international ethnic awakening and radicalization that motivated and provided modes of thought to the Sami resistance in Finland (V.-P. Lehtola 2000c: 194; Minde 2000: 27–37). The land right claims have become a major part of the Sami political discourse. Especially in the institutionalized Sami movement they have substituted for traditional Sami demands of protecting traditional means of living.

The performance of reindeer-herding management

The widely acknowledged notion that reindeer herding is the most sustainable means of livelihood in the Sami region is quite new. Traditional Sami resource management has been criticized as wasteful, especially when it came to the use of fuel-wood at the start of the twentieth century. Forest officials who feared the lowering of the timberline in northern Lapland expressed this criticism. Geographer Karl Nickul criticized the *siida* system of the Skolt Sami for its inability to control excessive deer hunting in the nineteenth century, although there were negotiations and feedback systems between the *siidas* (V.-P. Lehtola 2000a: 52).

Reindeer numbers fluctuated throughout the period of inquiry. The number of reindeer was affected by modernization itself: reindeer herding was capitalized and mechanized in this period, and the herders were tempted or, as they would argue, forced to increase their stocks because of increased costs. Even though there has been a shift from "ecological to economical" reindeer herding (Jomppanen and Näkkäläjärvi 2000: 86), the number of reindeer is still strongly affected by natural conditions. There have been many sudden declines in the number of reindeer due to, for example, snow conditions. The northern reindeer cooperatives, especially those of Inari, experienced a near-collapse in the number of reindeer between 1971 and 1980. This was due to a number of factors, most notably a dependency on just one source of nutrition (*Cladina stellaris*). The pasture researchers also stressed the role of pasture sustainability, which had reached its limits. This was partly because of a change in methods and focus on pasture research; a shift from looking at relations between different means of living and larger-scale, ecosystem-based research. In practice, the new focus highlighted the role of an excessive number of reindeer in pasture damage. The number of reindeer peaked at the beginning of the 1990s (see Figure 15.2), and the effects of over-grazing became more evident in Inari, where pasturelands had traditionally been in better shape compared to the situation elsewhere in the reindeer herding area of Finland. The pastureland damage and damage to young forests in Inari are the result of a multiplicity of factors. However, according to scientists, the most important factor is the excessive number of reindeer. The sulfur emissions from the smelting furnaces of Nikel, an externality from the Soviet Union/Russia, which cause short-term stress in the forests of eastern parts of Inari, are a lesser cause of damage. Forestry itself is the third factor. How decisive is it? (Kollstrøm *et al.* 1996: 86–89; Näkkäläjärvi 2000: 83; Nyyssönen 2000: 212, 215)

The Sami blame external influences. Cuttings hinder winter grazing. The rise of snow scooter hours and winter feeding, and a consequent rise in costs, are also due to cuttings and diminished pasturelands. According to Marja Sinikka Semenoja, in those cooperatives where the cuttings have been long-lasting and widely dispersed and the pastures diminished, the profit margins of the small reindeer owners have weakened. There has also

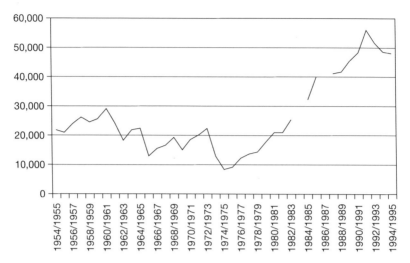

Figure 15.2 The number of reindeer in Inari, 1954–1995
Source: *Poromies* 1955–1996.

been a rise in the number of reindeer. Semenoja blames a rise in costs for this, as well as a profitability crisis in small-scale reindeer ownership, which forces a herder to increase his stock (Semenoja 1988: 38). This viewpoint may be one-sided since it neglects the internal factors. Semenoja does not refer to the fact that the rise in reindeer numbers in itself diminishes the area of pastureland available, as well as the dry substance amount of lichen, and worsens the over-grazing of pasturelands. The rise in reindeer numbers and the diminished pasturelands as a result of forestry are two sides of the same coin. All the same, the rising numbers of reindeer worsen the pasture-land situation in its own right, keeping the vicious circle moving ever faster.

The pastureland situation has also weakened in regions beyond the timberline, as well as in those regions outside the areas reserved for forestry or areas of conservation. This is evident, for example, in the rural district of Ohcejohka, Utsjoki, located north of Inari (Kollstrøm *et al.* 1996: 88; Nyyssönen 2000: 215). The Sami, the Forest Government, and the scientists studying the pasturelands have all acknowledged the worsening situation. The Sami, while stressing the continuity of their close relationship to nature and the harm caused by other livelihoods, admit that steps must be taken in order to improve the state of the pasturelands. One suggestion is to change the structure of ownership by creating pension arrangements that would secure the continuity of reindeer herding (Magga 2000: 168–169). Scientists have shown a greater readiness to stress the reindeer's role in complex interactions that cause damage to the pastureland and are keen to propose a reduction in the number of reindeer. In Inari, the encouragement of the growth of *Cladina stellaris*, a lichen that is the main source for nutrition for reindeer during the winter, will require both a reduction in the number of reindeer and more careful planning of the use of pasturelands, which have been damaged by the Forest Government's cuttings (Nieminen 2000: 166–167).

The performance of the régimes

The most difficult task facing a property rights régime is to sustain the stock of ecosystem assets while capturing the flow of the economic benefits thereof. In the case of Inari, where the ecosystem resilience is quite weak due to a long recurrence period, and in some cases also due to over-grazing, continuous wear and tear is evident.[5] I have outlined above the performance of the reindeer herding and forestry régimes with regard to environmental efficiency. It is evident that both régimes have to some extent failed. The failure to maintain the ecological basis of livelihood is more evident in the case of reindeer herding, since they did not manage to check the rise in reindeer numbers. Why was this? Why did the coexistence cease, and why were resources used unwisely? Does all the blame go to the intro-duced régime constellation or to the process of territorial sovereignty?

Traditionally, the main reason for problems in the pastureland situation has been said to be reindeer herding itself. Until the 1940s, reindeer herding was viewed as a harmful and obsolete livelihood. After a change in the ideo-logical environment, from the 1960s onwards, economic modernization, Finnish "colonization," and state intervention in reindeer-herding manage-ment and legislation were blamed. A lack of expertise and the hindrance of the Sami from managing the pasturelands would have resulted in the depri-vation of the resource and in a lowered, or non-existent, perception of the régime's legitimacy among reindeer herders (Bjørklund 1999: 23–27; Nyyssönen 2000: 193–199). The former notion is obsolete, not to mention politically incorrect, and the latter grasps only the structural change and presupposes colonial intervention. It is sympathetic to the Sami herders, but it oversimplifies the impulses and changes within the herding community after the establishment of and intervention by the property rights régime. Or, to be more precise, it perceives the changes only with regard to state intervention, implying that the Sami are mere passive reflectors adapting to the process.

Next I shall analyze the reasons for the failure of the régimes by looking at the régime constellation. This provides an opportunity to examine the management structure and power relations, as well as the performance under both régimes. The components of the model used in this analysis and the prerequisites of environmentally sustainable management are: (1) the tasks of the property rights régime must be well specified and congruent with its environmental and social context; (2) the régime needs to have the power to monitor its area, as well as the tools to enforce the adaptation processes; (3) the régime needs to be able to interact with the overall governing structure and share similar interests; (4) the régime must be capable of adjusting to both the ecosystem and the boundaries of governance; and (5) the régime's legitimacy needs to be accepted in social, ecological, and political terms.[6]

In the case of Finland, blaming the intervention of the state for the failure of the system is justified, but only to an extent. The management structure was established along the lines of the Finnish model. After the state intervention, the rationale used in resource management was based on academic silvicultural knowledge, and the management did not utilize the local knowledge of the pasturelands. There was an ethno-national intervention into planning and managing of means of living. The connection between the two means of livelihood and the management régimes was marked by a twisted power structure, where indigenous knowledge was considered to be outdated and worthless. There was no exchange of opinion and no opportunity for feedback – the complaints of the reindeer herders were met with silence or disparagement, even in the 1960s. The Forest Government has encountered great difficulty in establishing a transparent participatory process based on an equal say in land use. In the era before the forest disputes, there was no need to establish constructive conflict management. From the 1980s onwards, when the perceived legitimacy and social desirability of the property rights system collapsed in many parts of the Sami community, the lack of conflict management or possibilities for feedback contributed to a long series of dead-end disputes over land use. There was neither interaction nor any perception of legitimacy. An opportunity to utilize local, indigenous knowledge in resource management has been lost to this day (Hahn 2000: 72; Nyyssönen 2000: 229–231, 282).

During the entire post-war period, the absence of the will on the part of the Forest Government to make contact and initiate discussion on land use is highlighted by numerous disputes over the nature of conservation areas in the Sami heartlands. Here discussion was possible, because of a different hierarchy in the decision-making process. The Forest Government was not able to monopolize the negotiation process, as it did with negotiations about the cuttings. The process was led by the Ministry of Agriculture and Forestry and later by the Finnish Ministry of the Environment. The Sami stake in the conservation cases was taken into account; the Sami mostly promoted nature conservation, since it provided protection for reindeer herding from other forms of land use (Kollstrøm et al. 1996: 90; Nyyssönen 2000: 255–257).

The root of the imbalance of power was that the groups with a stake in the resource were defined from a Finnish point of view. The Sami point of view was not taken into account. This led to a problem of poorly defined boundaries: the two geographically inconsistent and overlapping property rights régimes made decisions that affected one another's ecosystem. The external pressure on the pasturelands, created by forestry, was made worse by the poor distribution of authority in the decision-making process (Hanna et al. 1995: 19–20).

In terms of its role as a property rights régime, the construction of reindeer-herding management was unsuccessful. In the first place, the° decision-making rules of the régime were not consistent with the pattern of ownership. Reindeer-herding management combines a cooperative system in decision making, but a system of private ownership in relation to the commodity produced, and the commodity is produced on state-owned land. This inconsistency is inefficient and leads to problems in decision making and authority (Hanna *et al.* 1995: 20). Second, reindeer-herding management has a double task, and its tasks are not well specified: it looks after the interests of the herders, but it also checks that the quotas set by the Ministry of Agriculture and Forestry are not exceeded. These tasks contradict one another in times of low profitability, which are frequent in reindeer herding in Finland. Third, and perhaps most crucially, the reindeer herders lack any means of excluding non-owners from their property, which renders their property rights only nominal, rather than having full common property rights. The régime's inability to check the private profit seeking of the herders and the excessive number of reindeer also implies a lack of internal authority on the part of the reindeer herders. However, this is a question that requires closer study. The adjustment of the boundaries of governance was also unsuccessful: it neglected the age-old *siida* system and forced the herders to use the same land as another, more powerful, property rights régime. The régime lacked the power to monitor and exert authority over other profit seekers. These are the institutional reasons for the depreciating adjustment of ecological boundaries.

One factor that persisted long after the establishment of the new régime constellation was the integrative strategy and the high legitimacy of the forestry and modernization projects among the Sami, which made the coexistence of the two livelihoods possible. The forestry project was welcomed and reindeer herding was mechanized. Since the collapse of the perception of legitimacy, Sami strategies regarding both livelihoods have changed. There has been an increase in adjustment and defensive strategies, which are evident, for example, in an increase in livestock and the launching of several lawsuits. The problem is that both strategies have proven to be unsuccessful: the former has led to overgrazing and a need to decrease the number of reindeer, and the latter has resulted in unfavorably decided lawsuits.

In the case of forestry, a long period of environmental sustainability, with its consequent legitimacy, was partly the unforeseen result of the lack of opportunity to make use of natural resources and the utilization of lighter means of forestry. Recently, both livelihoods have lost their perceived legitimacy, or at least their credibility in the eyes of the public. There is strong evidence that this is not only a matter of image and reciprocal propaganda in an era of globalized environmental disputes, which has reached the old forests of Lapland. The Sami herders have to some extent lost the goodwill they enjoyed from the environmental movement because of matters of systematic winter feeding and over-grazed pastures.

Analyzing the situation with the aforementioned model, the Forest Government failed on point one, since its tasks were not congruent. The Forest Government is responsible for both the cuttings and nature preservation in Inari. It has also an indirect say in matters relating to reindeer herding, for example in leasing land for reindeer round-ups. It also failed on point three, and *because of that*, on points four and five. The adjusting mechanisms, for example situating the cuttings away from winter pasturelands, were not utilized because of a lack of interaction. Consequently their perceived legitimacy collapsed. The reindeer-herding cooperative system failed in points one and two. The failure was built into their administrative composition and power structure. The régime, with its ill-defined tasks, lacked power. The power structures in the régime configuration prevented the herders from interacting with the Forest Government (interaction of this kind would have met the requirements of point three). The failures on points four and five go hand in hand: the lack of internal authority may be the reason for the failure in environmental efficiency, since the régime's own adjusting mechanisms, for example checking the quotas, have proven to be inefficient.[7] The lack of power might be a more decisive factor in the case of the reindeer-herding management. The cooperatives have no means of keeping other profit seekers off the pasturelands.

The legitimacy of the present property rights situation has been strongly questioned by many parts of the Sami community (Helander 2000: 179). The ongoing work to reconstruct the property rights situation in the Sami area of Lapland has some positive indications for the Sami, though the situation concerning land ownership is not clear. The Forest Government is still carrying on forestry in the remaining area reserved for economic use. The proposal concerning land ownership made by the Sami committee, led by the provincial governor of Lapland, Hannele Pokka, has not been accepted because of disagreements concerning the legitimacy of the Sami claim to collective land ownership. The rejected proposal would have provided a means for progress in régime constellation and resource management. The proposal was based on the shared management of land. The Northern Lapland District for Wilderness Management (formerly the District of Inari) would undergo some institutional changes, which have been frozen (as at November 2002). The new property rights régime would be called the District of the Sami home area, which would assume responsibility for directing the use of land. The new régime would still be linked constitutionally to the Forest Government, but it would be governed by a board consisting of the Sami, Skolt-Sami, other interested parties, for example the rural districts of the Sami heartlands, and inhabitants of Finnish extraction. The Sami would not have exclusive rights of resource management. The proposal is marked by a feature traditional to the Finnish way of handling the Sami question: the avoidance of conflict and extremism, and the desire for compromise. The aim has been to secure both the minority rights of the Sami and the equality of all interested parties (Tuulentie 2001: 267–268; Mulari 2002b: passim).

The new, rejected Finnish institutional arrangement does not rise to the challenge of an adaptive management pattern, using measures such as institutional flexibility, learning, and participation. (This would enable unnecessary institutional procedures to be checked by a continuous process of renegotiation.) The Finnish model utilizes only the principles of transparency and local participation (Röling and Jiggins 1998: 301–304). The process of redesigning the land ownership pattern has been relatively short, in a Nordic context, but a painful one for Finland. The search for compromises has been hindered by fear of a loss of assets, by quarreling based on misinformation, and by an increased sense of dichotomy between the local communities. History has been harnessed to renounce the legitimacy of the Sami collective land ownership claim.[8]

A renewal of the management constellation has been prolonged because of an unusual ethnic constellation in Inari, a result of which is that this case cannot be studied as a pure example of indigenous versus modern, western means of livelihood. There is no united (let alone pre-modern) Sami reindeer-herding front, which is resisting the plundering of its natural resources. The current situation is that the Forest Government has been more or less obliged to listen to demands and change the property rights system, but the reluctance of the herders to take firm action to improve the pastureland situation is still evident at times.

Conclusions

Even though the integrative features of the process of establishing territorial sovereignty makes the case of Finland not the most dramatic in terms of ethno-nationality, the case is relevant. Ethno-nationalization occurred there where it matters: in land and resource management. The exclusive mechanisms were not intentional, but as a result of the administration of ethno-nationalization there was a partial exclusion of the Sami from resource management and a juxtaposition of the traditional indigenous means of living with a more powerful and harmful form of land use. The unsuccessful agricultural expansion involved ethno-national and colonial features, and, in the first phase, traditional Sami means of living suffered from economic and administrative integration. The forestry project was not intentionally exclusive, or hostile to reindeer herding, but the interests of the herders were neglected for a long time.

In states that have incorporated the homelands of ethnic others, members of the dominant nation frequently come to perceive the territory of the entire state as their homeland (Kaiser 2002: 236–237). This applies also to Finland, which is in a global context a very homogenous state when it comes to the ethnic composition. Hence, when the Sami questioned the process of territorialization, their land claims on the Finnish side were met with some slight amazement. This is partly because the post-war minority policy of Finland is based on a democratic–liberal and pluralistic basis (Roessingh 1996: 229) and because of the marginality of the Sami question: the Sami land question has either not existed, or has been non-consciously neglected.

The case of Inari illustrates also the annulment of the ethno-national process. The Sami have substituted a variety of projects, alliance buildings, and loyalties for the integrative strategy of the national project. New ties are established on local, regional, ethnic, trans-national, international, and global levels. This does not mean that the state level should be viewed as outdated. The existing boundaries guide the protests and the politics to be executed on a national level.

When it comes to the ecological consequences of the process, the case of Inari is not a case of conservation-oriented traditional use substituted for by state-run over-use (Jodha 1995: 183). This interpretation covers only the structure of the property rights situation: it does not say enough about the implications of the situation and its actual environmental consequences. Nor is this a case of the party that holds the right of use of state-owned land undermining the basis of its own subsistence. Inari represents an instance of the recent failure of two property rights régimes. Or, to be more precise, this case illustrates the failure of the régimes, handicapped by an unsuccessful property rights régime constellation. There are three associated reasons for the over-use: the problems originating from the régime constellation (state intervention/external influences), the performance of individual régimes (inefficiency), and the Sami strategy for dealing with external influences.

Reindeer-herding management has been crippled by a lack of power to safeguard its resources from outside intervention. This is due to the overall régime constellation in Inari. The herding management also suffered from an internal inability to prevent the unwise use of resources. The internal reasons for this are to be found in the inefficiencies of decision-making and incongruent dual responsibilities. The Forest Government, the régime with both power and incongruent tasks, failed to sustain the public's perceived legitimacy of the forestry project. This is a problem in régime constellation, which was exacerbated by the reluctance for negotiation by the Forest Government, as well as a lack of conflict management. This has been partly responsible for prolonging the crisis. The collapse of the Forest Government's perceived legitimacy was partly due to the harm caused to the pasturelands. In other words, there were also weaknesses in the régime's performance.

Environmental sustainability reached a crisis at the turn of the 1970s and 1980s, with an increasing number of reindeer and continuous cuttings, both of which diminished the pasturelands. As discussed above, state intervention, the established management structure, and the ethno-nationalization of resource management form only part of the explanation for the problems both livelihoods have faced. However, they created the basis for forestry to dominate the pasturelands, and in so doing became the most harmful external influence on reindeer herding in Inari. The domination was not complete: for various economic, silvicultural, and geographical reasons, there are large areas not used for forestry. Some of these areas suffer from overgrazing. For this reason, it is not sufficient to explain the difficulties of reindeer herding as based upon external influences alone. Reindeer herding has suffered from serious problems of profitability that it has tried to solve by increasing the livestock. This Sami strategy has proven unwise: the pastures in some parts of Inari are exhausted and the extensive winter feeding is not always cost-efficient. This is a process that has been the hardest for the reindeer-herding management to revise, and where the failure of the régime has been most evident. The causes of this over-use are to be found in the interaction between three levels: externalities, Sami initiative (the unsuccessful response to the externality), and the dysfunction of the composition of the institution. The Sami tendency to blame forestry for its difficulties is partly a political strategy, partly a post-colonialist ideological slogan, partly a sign of genuine concern in the face of weakened pasturelands, and partly a legitimate concern about major disturbance in the winter pastures.

The ethno-political accusations of ecological deprivation due to colonization are more relevant in other parts of the Finnish Sami home areas, especially in the area of the herding cooperative of the Lappi in Sodankylä, where the water power projects destroyed pasturelands in the late 1960s. This area was one of the core areas for earlier Sami mobilization. Here the supporters of the common property régimes can muster a clear case of state-run over-use and colonialist plundering of the indigenous people. One must also bear in mind that there has been a decrease in the number of reindeer in Inari since 1991, which has been partly explained as an adjustment measure taken after the pastureland situation worsened (Jernsletten and Klokow 2002: 132–133). However, the reduction in the number of reindeer has been relatively modest.

Environmental sustainability, i.e. the recurrence of the resource, is not fully explained by the nature of land ownership. Nor is the environmental sustainability fully explained by management efficiency. Models are only models. One problem in applying property rights theories and management models, from the perspective of an environmental historian, is that the theories set an expectation of strict causality with regard to a complex ecological pattern concerning the recovery of the ecosystem. The recovery can be hindered by a lack of knowledge or by a scarcity of resources, but the recovery of the resource is also dependent on various ecological factors with complicated connections, not just on the property rights system applied. The theories also tend to view the environment as either a management object or an externality. Ecologically oriented historians might criticize the theorists' way of placing human beings outside nature as its mere managers. In environmental history, the environment is shifted to the center of focus, and indeed, by some historians, as a subject of history. The environment, or to be precise, nature, is not seen as a mere provider of livelihood, but also as the function of a tight-fisted provider of resources, which in turn places limits on human activity and requires humans to adjust, or even abandon, their plans (Myllyntaus 1999: 123–124).

In trying to find reasons for over-use and in consideration of policy suggestions, it is necessary to pay greater attention to ecological relations and consequences. A conflict management system, participation, information, and planning are all necessary, but in a modernized and growth-orientated environment indigenous knowledge is not an automatic solution to the problem of the exhaustion of resources. The demand for openness applies to both régimes: reindeer-herding management must also be made more transparent.

Notes

1   *Siida* is Northern Sami, and means a Lapp or reindeer village. It refers both to the area and the people living in the autonomous area of *siida*. As this is the most specific term relating to the governmental area, and covers both the livelihood and legal aspect of the area formation, I shall use the term in this chapter. It was the main feature in community organization in most of the Finnish Lapland until the end of the nineteenth century (Tanner 1929: 86–87).

2   Lapp-mark is a governmental term, meaning the area north of the Lapland border, where Finnish and Swedish settling was prohibited. The prohibition and the rights of hunting and fishing were given by Gustav Vasa in 1543, and they were strengthened again by Carl IX at the beginning of the seventeenth century. However, settlement was encouraged during the seventeenth century, in spite of the border, by means of legislation that offered settlers tax relief.

3   *Sápmi* is a political construction which means the area populated by Sami in three Nordic countries and in Russia. The claims of establishing *Sápmi* vary a great deal. The most radical Sami have a political goal of independent state, but voices demanding self-determination are more numerous.

4   When compared to forestry in the US, for example, Finnish forestry has been quite enlightened in its way of taking the entire ecosystem as a basis for its thinking. See for example Bakuzis (1971: 194); on the cuttings in Inari and their suitability, see Kylmälä (1973: 37, 71). Pauli Kylmälä is a forest professional who wrote a pamphlet criticizing the cuttings in southern Lapland for being too harsh and for their poor recurrence results. However, he acknowledged that the cuttings in Inari were suitable for the ecology of the forests. See also Nyyssönen (2000: 277–281).

5   The ecosystem resilience here means the measure of perturbation that can be absorbed before an ecosystem shifts into another state. Systems are complex and self-organizing, permeated by uncertainties and discontinuities, and have several possible equilibrium states. There is no single possible equilibrium state (Hanna *et al.* 1995: 21).

6   Hanna *et al.* (1995: 17–18). The model is somewhat outdated in its use of the ecosystem concept. This does not, in my view, diminish the usability of the model, if and when the stress is laid on nature's ability to recover and change.

7   In fact the quotas were adjusted upwards last time, in 1994 (*Poromies* 2, 1995).
8   See two recent statements on the matter: Kitti (2002); Mulari (2002a: passim).

Bibliography

Bakuzis, E. (1971) "Forestry Viewed in an Ecosystem Perspective," in G. van Dyne (ed.) *The Ecosystem Concept in Natural Resource Management*, second printing, New York: Academic Press.

Bjørklund, I. (1999) "Når ressursene blir allmenning – samisk ressursforvaltning mot det 21. århundre," in I. Bjørklund (ed.) *Norsk ressursforvaltning og samiske rettighets-forhold, Om statlig styring, allmenningens tragedie og lokale sedvaner i Sápmi*, Gyldendal: Ad Notam.

—— and Brantenberg, T. (1981) *Samisk reindrift – norske inngrep, Om Altaelva, reindrift og samisk kultur*, Tromsø: Universitetsforlaget AS.

Bromley, D. (1991) *Environment and Economy, Property Rights and Public Policy*, Padstow: Blackwell.

Brownlie, I. (1992) *Treaties and Indigenous Peoples: The Robb Lectures*, Brookfield: Oxford University Press.

Commission of the Sami Cause (1952) *Saamelaisasiain komitean mietintö*, 12.

Corbridge, S. (1995) "Colonialism, Post-Colonialism and the Political Geography of the Third World," in P. Taylor (ed.) *Political Geography of the Twentieth Century, A Global Analysis*, Chichester: John Wiley & Sons.

Ferro, M. (1997) *Colonization: A Global History*, Trowbridge: Routledge.

Granér, S. (2002) *Samhävd och rågång, Om egendomsrelationer, ägoskiften och marknadsintegration i en värmlandsk skogsbygd 1630–1750*, Göteborg: Ekonomisk-historisk institutionen, Handelshögskolan vid Göteborgs universitet.

Hahn, T. (2000) *Property Rights, Ethics and Conflict Resolution: Foundations of the Sami Economy in Sweden*, Uppsala: Acta Universitatis Agriculturae Sueciae Agraria 258.

Hanna, S. and Munasinghe, M. (1995) "An Introduction to Property Rights and Environment," in S. Hanna, and M. Munasinghe (eds) *Property Rights and the Environment, Social and Ecological Issues*, Washington, DC: The Beijer International Institute of Ecological Economics and World Bank.

——, Folke, K., and Mäler, K.-G. (1995) "Property Rights and Environmental Resources," in S. Hanna, and M. Munasignhe (eds) *Property Rights and the Environment, Social and Ecological Issues*, Washington, DC: The Beijer International Institute of Ecological Economics and World Bank.

Hardin, G. (1968) "The Tragedy of the Commons," *Science*, 162: 1244–1248.

Hartley, K. and Ott, A. (1993) "Introduction," in A. Ott, and K. Hartley (eds) *Privatization and Economic Efficiency: A Comparative Analysis of Developed and Developing Countries*, Ipswich: Edward Elgar Publishing.

Helander, E. (2000) "Saamelainen maailmankuva ja luontosuhde," in I. Seurujärvi-Kari (ed.) *Beaivvi Mánát, Saamelaisten juuret ja nykyaika*, Tietolipas 164, Vammala: SKS.

Helle, T. (1995) "Porolaidunnuksen vaikutus metsänrajametsien primaarisukkessioon," in T. Tasanen, M. Varmola, and M. Niemi (eds) *Metsänraja tutkimuksen kohteena, Tutkimuspäivä Ylläksellä 1994*, Jyväskylä: Metsäntutkimuslaitos.

Jernsletten, J.-L. and Klokow, K. (2002) *Sustainable Reindeer Husbandry*, Gjøvik: Centre for Saami Studies, University of Tromsø, Arctic Council.

Jodha, N. (1995) "Environmental Crisis and Unsustainability in Himalayas: Lessons from the Degredation Process," in S. Hanna, and M. Munasinghe (eds) *Property*

Rights in a Social and Ecological Context: Case Studies and Design Applications, Washington, DC: The Beijer International Institute of Ecological Economics and World Bank.

Jomppanen, T. and Näkkäläjärvi, K. (2000) "Poronhoitoon kohdistuvat paineet," in J. Pennanen, and K. Näkkäläjärvi (eds) *Siiddastallan, Siidoista kyliin, Luontosidonnainen saamelaiskulttuuri ja sen muuttuminen,* Jyväskylä: Pohjoinen.

Kaiser, R. (2002) "Homeland Making and the Territorialization of National Identity: Ethnonationalism in the Contemporary World," in D. Conversi (ed.) *Walker Connor and the Study of Nationalism,* Chippenham: Routledge.

Kitti, J. (1988) "Kessi – kenen maa," in T. Osala (ed.) *Pohjoinen erämaa Kessi-Vätsäri,* Vaasa: O. & G. Kustannus.

—— (2002) "Ketkä omistavat lapinkylien maat," *Helsingin Sanomat,* September 29.

Kollstrøm, R., Makarova, O., and Tynys, T. (1996) *Enare-Pasvik: Natur og folk i grenseland, Priroda i naselenue progranitshnoi oblasti, Inari-Paz, Inarijärvi-Paatsjoki, Yhteinen elävä erämaa,* Oslo: Svanhovd miljøsenter.

Korpijaakko, K. (1989) *Saamelaisten oikeusasemasta Ruotsi-Suomessa, Oikeushistoriallinen tutkimus Länsi-Pohjan Lapin maankäyttöoloista ja – oikeuksista ennen 1700-luvun puoliväliä,* Mänttä: Lakimiesliiton kustannus.

Kylmälä, P. (1973) *Avohakkuut,* Rovaniemi.

Lapin metsätalous (1975) Sarja A, No. 10, Rovaniemi: Lapin seutukaavaliitto.

Lehtola, T. (1998) *Kolmen kuninkaan maa, Inarin historia 1500-luvulta jälleenrakennusaikaan,* Jyväskylä: Kustannus-Puntsi.

Lehtola, V.-P. (1997a) *Rajamaan identiteetti, Lappilaisuuden rakentuminen 1920-ja 1930-luvun kirjallisuudessa,* Pieksämäki: SKS.

—— (1997b) *Saamelaiset – Historia, yhteiskunta, taide,* Jyväskylä: Kustannus-Puntsi.

—— (2000a) *Nickul, rauhan mies, rauhan kansa,* Jyväskylä: Kustannus-Puntsi.

—— (2000b) *Saamelaispolitiikan alkuvaiheet Suomessa,* Faravid 24, Pohjois-Suomen historiallisen yhdistyksen vuosikirja, Acta Societatis historiae Finlandiae Septentrionalia, Oulu: Oulun yliopiston historian laitos.

—— (2000c) "Kansain välit – monikulttuurisuus ja saamelaishistoria," in I. Seurujärvi-Kari (ed.) *Beaivvi Mánát, Saamelaisten juuret ja nykyaika,* Tietolipas 164, Vammala: SKS.

—— (2003) "Tuhon ja kasvun vuodet," in V.-P. Lehtola (ed.) *Inari Aanaar, Inarin historia jääkaudesta nykypäivään,* Oulu: Inarin kunta.

Magga, J. (2000) "Poronhoidon tulevaisuuden näkymiä," in I. Seurujärvi-Kari, (ed.) *Beaivvi Mánát, Saamelaisten juuret ja nykyaika,* Tietolipas 164, Vammala: SKS.

Minde, H. (2000) "Samesaken som ble en urfolkssak," *Ottar,* 4: 27–38.

Mulari R. (2002a) "Professorikaartin mustalla listalla," *Metsätalous-Forestry,* 1.

—— (2002b) "Valtio omistaa ja hallinnoi kunnes toisin todistetaan, Kiista Ylä-Lapin omistuksesta," *Metsätalous-Forestry,* 1.

Myllyntaus, T. (1991) "Suomalaisen ympäristöhistorian kehityslinjoja," *Historiallinen Aikakauskirja,* 4: 321–331.

—— (1999) "Environment in Understanding History," in T. Myllyntaus, and M. Saikku (ed.) *Encountering the Past in Nature: Essays in Environmental History,* Helsinki: Helsinki University Press.

Nahkiaisoja, T. (2003a) "Uudisasuttajien aika 1750–1876," in V.-P. Lehtola (ed.) *Inari Aanaar, Inarin historia jääkaudesta nykypäivään,* Oulu: Inarin kunta.

—— (2003b) "Inarilasyhteisön murroksen aika 1877–1920," in V.-P. Lehtola (ed.) *Inari Aanaar, Inarin historia jääkaudesta nykypäivään,* Oulu: Inarin kunta.

—— and Lehtola, V.-P. (2003) "Ivalon nousun aika 1920–1939," in V.-P. Lehtola (ed.) *Inari Aanaar, Inarin historia jääkaudesta nykypäivään*, Oulu: Inarin kunta.

Näkkäläjärvi, K. (2000) "Porotalouden tuotto maksimoituu 1990-luvulla," in J. Pennanen, and K. Näkkäläjärvi (eds) *Siiddastallan, Siidoista kyliin, Luontosidonnainen saamelaiskulttuuri ja sen muuttuminen*, Jyväskylä: Pohjoinen.

Nieminen, M. (1987) "Suomen porolaiduntutkimuksen historiaa," *Poromies*, 4: 166–167.

—— (2000) "Pilaako poro luontoa?," in I. Seurujärvi-Kari (ed.) *Beaivvi Mánát, Saamelaisten juuret ja nykyaika*, Tietolipas 164, Vammala: SKS.

Nyyssönen, J. (1997) "Luonnonkansa metsätalouden ikeessä? Saamelaiset ja tehometsätalous," in H. Roiko-Jokela (ed.) *Luonnon ehdoilla vai ihmisen arvoilla? Polemiikkia metsänsuojelusta 1850–1990*, Jyväskylä: Atena-Kustannus.

—— (2000) "Murtunut luja yhteisrintama, Inarin hoitoalue, saamelaiset ja metsäluonnon valloitus 1945–1982," unpublished Licentiate thesis, University of Jyväskylä.

Paine, R. (1994) *Herds of the Tundra: A Portrait of Saami Reindeer Pastoralism*, Washington, DC: Smithsonian Institution Press.

Poromies (1995) "Paliskuntain yhdistyksen vuosikertomus 1994.

Pradhan, A. and Parks, P. (1995) "Environmental and Socioeconomic Linkages of Deforestation and Forest Land Use Change in Nepal Himalaya," in S. Hanna, and M. Munasinghe (eds) *Property Rights in a Social and Ecological Context: Case Studies and Design Applications*, Washington, DC: The Beijer International Institute of Ecological Economics and World Bank.

Roessingh, M. (1996) *Ethnonationalism and Political Systems in Europe: A State of Tension*, Amsterdam: Amsterdam University Press.

Röling, N. and Jiggings, J. (1998) "The Ecological Knowledge System," in N. Röling, and M. Wagemakers (eds) *Facilitating Sustainable Agriculture: Participatory Learning and Adaptive Management in Times of Environmental Uncertainty*, Cambridge: Cambridge University Press.

Semenoja, M. (1988) "Ensimmäinen kirje," in M. Puikko, M. Semenoja, E.J. Tennilä, and P. Veijola, *Kirjeitä Kessistä* (ed. by editorial staff), s.p.: Like.

Seurujärvi-Kari, I. (1994) "Saamelaiset alkuperäiskansojen yhteisössä," in U.-M. Kulonen, J. Pentikäinen, and I. Seurujärvi-Kari (eds) *Johdatus saamentutkimukseen*, Tietolipas 131, Pieksämäki: SKS.

Siedl, C. (1980) "Poverty Measurement: A Survey," in D. Bös, M. Rose, and C. Siedl (eds) *Welfare and Efficiency in Public Economics*, Berlin: Springer Verlag.

Sklair, L. (2000) "Social Movements and Global Capitalism," in T.J. Roberts, and A. Hite (eds) *From Modernization to Globalization: Perspectives on Development and Social Change*, Padstow: Blackwell.

Tanner, V. (1929) *Antropogeografiska studier inom Petsamo-området, I. Skolt-lapparna*, Fennia 49, Helsinki: Societas Geographica Fenniae.

Tuulentie, S. (2001) *Meidän vähemmistömme, Valtaväestön retoriikat saamelaisten oikeuksista käydyissä keskusteluissa*, Helsinki: SKS.

Veijola, P. (1998) *Suomen metsänrajametsien käyttö ja suojelu*, Saarijärvi: The Finnish Forest Research Institute.

Index

Abdelal, Rawi: "Markets and meanings"
9, 10, 16, 111–27
Abramov, Shlomo Zalman 101–2
Abyssinia 278
Acholi 286
Adams, John Quincy 46
Adams, Robert 33–4
Aegean Sea 165
Africa, Sub-Saharan: agriculture 276–7,
280, 284; AIDS 280, 288; alienation
of land 281; average holding 281;
cattle 278, 283; chiefdoms 285;
Christianity 285; civil war 287; cocoa
281–2; coffee 282; competition for
pasture 280; conscription 283;
customs duties 284; dairy farming
279; debt bondage 278; dwindling
land surpluses 280–2; ethnicity
276–93; foreign ownership of land
284, 287; forest products 279; gender
278; genocide 286, 287; herders 279;
influenza 280; kola-nut trees 279,
280; labor service (corvée) 278; land
abundance 276–93; land markets
277–8, 280–2; land rights 276–93;
land titling 281; military coups 286;
minerals 277, 279, 280, 284;
missionaries 285; nationalism 284–8;
nation-building 287; oil palm 281;
population 277, 280–1; property
rights and land abundance 276–80;
religious significance of land 277;
'Scramble for Africa' 282–3; slavery
276, 278, 280, 283; specialists 280;
squatters 282, 287; state formation
282–4; taxation 284; tea 282;
technology 279; territory 281, 282–4;
trade tolls 283; tribes 285, 286;
urbanization 280; see also under
individual African nations
Akyem 281
Aland Islands 9
Alice Downs 259
Allen, Douglas W.: "Homesteading the
Property Rights" 39
Ambrose, Fr Bob 144
Ambrosetti, J. B.: "Segundo Viaje" 349;
"Viaje" 349
Anatolia 16; Amasya 167; Armenians
161; Aydin 165, 167; Bandirna 165;
Biga 165, 166; boycott of Greek
trade 172–4; Bulgarians 153, 160,
161, 162, 172, 177; Bursa plain 166;
Christians 160, 162, 163, 164, 166,
171, 172, 175; çiftlik 158, 166, 169;
Circassians 159, 160–1, 164, 165,
166, 169, 175; commons 157–9, 168;
Cossacks 161; cotton 155; Daghestan
refugees 169; derbend villages 156;
Diyarbakir 167; Edirne 167; Erdek
165; ethno-politics 153–80; evkaf 168,
169; Greeks 170, 172–4, 175, 176,
177; hakk-i karar 158, 159;
Hüdavendigar 165, 167, 168;
hududname 158; Izmit 169; Iznik
166; kadis 156; kanunnames 159;
Kirmasti 166; land disputes 153–80;
Mihalic 166; Muslims 153, 160, 161,
162, 163, 164, 165, 166, 170, 171,
172, 173, 174, 175, 177; niza-miye
courts 159; population movements
155–7, 162, 163; population pressure

159–62; refugee settlement 159–62, 162–9, 169–76; rural mobility 154–7; *seriyye* court 175, 176; Sura-yi Devlet 159, 167; *tapu* 158; *tasarruf* 158, 159, 166, 168, 169; Tekfurdagi 167; *vakif* villages 156, 158, 167, 168, 174, 175, 176; Yalova 169; *zaviyes* 156; *see also* Ottoman Empire

André C.: "Land relations under unbearable stress" 281, 288

Ankara 167

Anti-Slavery Society 203

Argentina (Cuñapirú, Misiones) 23, 347–57; Cainguás 352; Celulosa Argentina 352; deforestation 349; Dirección Provincial de Asuntos Guaraníes 350; ENDEPA 353–4; fishing 349, 350; General San Martín 352; handicrafts 350; horticulture 349, 350, 352; hunting 349, 350, 352; Ministerio de Ecológia, Misiones 352; *monte* 347, 349, 350, 351–2, 353–4; Spain 349; tea 347; timber 347; tobacco 347, 349, 350; tung 347; Universidad Nacional de La Plata 347, 352–3, 353–4; *yerba mate* 347, 349, 350; *see also* Mbyá-Guaraní

Armstrong, Captain 303

Arthur, Bill 266

Asante 277, 278, 279, 280, 281, 283, 285

Ash, Timothy Garten 116

Atack, Jeremy: "Northern Agriculture and the Westward Movement" 38

Atkinson, R. R.: "(Re)constructing of ethnicity in Africa" 286

Austin, Gareth: "Sub-Saharan Africa" 16, 276–93

Australia (Kimberley) 12–13, 236–75; Aboriginal Affairs Planning Authority 256; Aboriginal business leaders 260–6, 267; Aboriginal Enterprises (Assistance Act) (1968) 261, 262, 263; Aboriginal Land Fund Act (1974) 263; Aboriginal Land Fund Commission 263, 264; Aboriginal Lands Trust 255–6, 257, 258, 264, 265, 266; Aboriginal leaders 239, 260–6; Aboriginal population share 21; Aboriginal Progress Movement 259; Aboriginal wealth share 21; Aborigines Protection Society 203; beef slump 249; BHP 246; Catholic Education Office 260; colonial settlement 12; Commonwealth Capital Fund for Aboriginal Business Enterprises 261, 262; Commonwealth Department of Labour and National Service 250; Commonwealth Office of Aboriginal Affairs 262; Council of Aboriginal Affairs 238–9; Country Party 250, 264; crime and disorder 251–4, 254–60; Department of Aboriginal Affairs 259–60; Department of Native Welfare 246–8, 252–3, 255, 257, 258, 259, 260, 262, 263; deteriorating economy 248–51, 251–4; drought 253; Esperance Carrying and Pastoral Company 263; Federal Department of the Interior 264; Federal Pastoral Award 249–50, 251–4; federation (1901) 236; Gibb Report (1970) 255; Ieramugadu Gardening Service 263; indigenous trusteeship 236, 239, 240, 241–8, 254, 255; Interdepartmental Committee, investigating Aboriginal policy 258; Kimberley Development Commission 267; Kimberley Land Council 246; Kimberley Pastoral Industry Inquiry 248–9; Labor government (1972–5) 238; labor migration 251, 267; labor shortage 247, 248; Mabo judgment 13, 246; Mirima Council Constitutional 259; Native Welfare Act 245; Northern Development and Mining Corporation 243–4; Office of Aboriginal Affairs 264; Oombulgurri Association 259; pastoralism 236, 240, 248–51, 267; Pastoralists and Graziers Association 243, 253; Pastoralists' Association 242, 247; Pindan Group 245–6; plural voting 10; postwar boom 236, 241, 248, 266; segregation/integration 236, 242; Special Committee investigating Aboriginal matters (1958) 244–5; state

trusteeship (pre-1968) 241–8; *terra nullius* 12–13, 246; unemployment 236, 238, 239, 240, 248, 251–4, 254–60, 266, 267; White Australia policy 238
Austria 56
Ayvalik 154, 164, 168, 170, 173, 174

Bader, Yohanan 101–2
Balfour 299
Balfour Declaration (1917) 90
Balkans 16, 153, 155–6, 159, 160, 162, 163, 165, 166, 170, 170, 171, 177
Barnes, C. E. 254
Bar-Rav-Hai, David 103
Bartolomé, Miguel Angel 350–1
Barton, Robert 137
Bateman, Fred: "Northern Agriculture and the Westward Movement" 38
Bates, R. H.: "Demand for revolution" 279
Bavadra 217
Baviaans River 300
Bayart, J.-F.: *State in Africa* 285
Beazley, Kim 240–1
Becker, G. S.: *Economics of Discrimination* 22
Bedford 300
Begin, Menachem 101
Belarus 111, 116, 122
Bell Brothers 244
Ben-Gurion, David 100
Bergama 170
Bergman's Hoek 309
Berkeley, William 13
Berlin, Congress of (1884–5) 283
Bernhard, Ludwig: *Polenfrage* 78–9
Bhotomane 304
Billiluna Station 265
Birch, Thelma 259
Bishop, C. A.: "Emergence of Hunting Territories" 324; *Northern Ojibwa* 324; "Territoriality among the Northeastern Algonquians" 320, 332
Bismarck 58
Black Power 238
Blinkwater valley 304, 305

Blut and *Boden* 296
Bobelis, Kazys 119
Boezak, Captain 298
Boni, S.: "Hierarchy in twentieth-century Sefwi (Ghana)" 287
Botha, Andries 304–5, 307
Boudinot, Elias 50
Bow River 259
Bowana 300
Bowker, T. H. 305
Brass, William 303
Brazauskas, Algirdas 113, 114
Brazil 347, 350
Breton, Albert: "Economics of Nationalism" 20; "Nationalism Revisited" 20–2
Breton, Margot: "Nationalism Revisited" 20–2
Bridge, Ernie 258, 263, 266
Britain: Colonial Office 198; Empire 161; Fiji annexed (1874) 183, 198, 203, 212–13; Greece and 161; Irish trade 135, 140, 145; land sales 135–6; Law of Property Act (1925) 18; Palestine 87–106; plural voting 10; productivity 133; Seven Years War 326; South Africa 298, 306; War of 1812 37, 46
Brodnicki, von 58, 59
Bromberg 61, 62, 64
Bromley, Daniel: *Environment and Economy* 361
Broome 247, 249, 254
Brownlie, Ian: *Treaties and Indigenous Peoples* 373
Bryant, Gordon 255
Bucak 161
Buchanan, Allen: *Secession* 8–9, 10
Buchanan, President 42
Buddhism 230
Burhaniye 154, 173, 174, 175, 176
Burke 248–9
Burma 184
Burundi 281; ethnicity 287–8; genocide 286
Bushnell, A. F.: " 'Horror' Reconsidered" 186
Buxton 304, 305
Bydgoszcz, *see* Bromberg

Cadogan, León: "En torno a la aculturación" 349; *Ywyra ñe'ery* 349
Cakabau 195–6, 197
Cakaudrove 195
Cambridge Gulf 259
Cameroon 285
Canada 221; animal and human populations 322, 341, 342; fur trade 321–31, 331–3; game 331–4; homesteading 23; Kaminuriak 340; Labrador 324; Mastassini hunters 332; Native American hunting practices 319–46; Native American property rights 319–46; unemployment 238; *see also* Hudson's Bay Company
capitalism 225, 229, 239, 240, 267
Carlos, A. M. 2, 23, 318–46; "Indians, the Beaver, and the Bay" 319, 321, 322, 326, 342; "Property Rights" 322, 326, 343; "Survival through generosity" 23; "Trade, Consumption, and the Native Economy" 327
Carlson, Leonard A. 2, 14, 15, 17, 30–55; "'Squatterism'" 35, 41, 42; "Were there alternatives to disaster?" 14, 17, 22
Carnarvon, Colonial Secretary 198
Cass, Lewis 33
Castletown, Lord 144
Caucasus 161, 162
Chadwick, Joseph 324
Chand, S.: "Lessons for Development" 226
Charlevoix: *History of Paraguay* 349
Charlton, Richard 189
Cherokee Nation v. The State of Georgia (1831) 14, 46–8
Cherokee Phoenix, The 43, 50
China 195, 215
Christianity 183, 195, 214, 285; Africa 285; Fiji 183, 195; Hawai'i 183; Ireland 133, 137, 143, 144, 147, 149; Ottoman Empire 160, 162, 163, 164, 166, 171, 172, 175; South Africa 299
Christmas Creek 252
Clarence, L.B. 221
Clark, Manning: *Short History of Australia* 238

Clontarf, battle of 138
Coffin, P. 265
Cohen, Morris: "Property and Sovereignty" 7, 15, 18
Cold War: ends 113
Collier, Philip 243
Commonwealth of Independent States, *see* Russia: CIS
Communism 9, 16
concentration camps 302
Congo 279
Connor, W.: *Ethnonationalism* 22
Cook, Captain James 185
Coombs, H. C.: "Ideology of development" 250, 255; *Issues in Dispute* 261
Cooper, William: *American South* 41
Corbridge, Stuart: "Colonialism" 367–8
Counihan, John C. 136, 137
Cowen, Michael: *Doctrines of Development* 239–40
Crete 162, 172–3
Crimea 153, 161, 162
Crivos, Marta Alicia 2, 23, 347–56; "Owners, intruders, and intermediaries" 23
Cromwell, Oliver 131
Cronon, William: *Changes in the Land* 324, 325
Crotty, Raymond: *Irish Agricultural Production* 132, 147
Cuñapirú, *see* Argentina
Cyprus 156

Dardanelles 154, 166, 170
Davies, Captain David 304, 305
Davitt, Michael 132
de Klerk, F. W. 309
De Soto 336
Delbrück, Hans: *Polenfrage* 58, 59
Demsetz, Harold: "Toward a Theory of Property Rights" 324
Denmark 133, 135–6, 138, 142, 147, 149
Derby 249, 252, 264–5
Deutsche Mittelstandskasse 74
Development Economics 210
Diaspora 100
Dikili 170, 171
Dillon, James 136

Dobrizhoffer, Martin: *Historia de los Abripones* 349
Dobyns, H. F.: *Their Number Become Thinned* 319, 334, 335, 336
Douglas, Major 136
Draghoender, Piet 309, 311
Dunsany, Lord 143

ecological economics 360
Eddie, Scott M. 2, 10, 25, 56–86; "Ethno-nationality and property rights" 10, 18, 22, 23, 24, 89
Edgworth, Maria: *Castle Rackrent* 135
Edirne 170
Edremit 154, 170, 173
Efendizade Ismail Efendi, Mahmud 174
Elster, J.: "Impact of Constitutions" 216
Emmanuel, Mr 252
Emrudabad 173, 174
Enecerus 56
Engerman, Stanley L. 1–3, 7–28
Eron River 105
Eshkol, Levi 103
Estonia 111, 112, 117
European Union: CAP 135; EMU 116, 117; Lithuania 111, 114, 115, 116–17, 118, 119, 121, 122
Evans, Congressman 34–5
Everard, Col. Nugent Talbot 144
Everts, Charles 34
Ewe 287
Eyre, Edward John 241

Fallan, Mr 244
Fallen Timbers, battle of (1794) 36
Feeny, David: "Development of Property Rights in Land" 184
Fiji 183–209, 210–35; agriculture 193; Agriculture and Landlord Tenancy Agreement 217; Assembly 197; Banaban Land Act 216; Banaban Settlement Act 216; Bau 195; British annexation (1874) 183, 198, 203, 212–13; chiefdoms 193, 194, 195–6; Christianity 183, 195; colonization 212–17; communes 212; compartmentalization 215; Confederacy (1865) 196; constitution 197, 216, 224, 225–6; cotton 196,

197; Council of Chiefs 198, 199, 216; coup (1987) 216–17, (2000) 227; Deed of Cession 198, 199, 216; disease 194; ethnic conflict 212–17, 224; ethnicity 210–35; ethno-based labor specialization 215; Fijian Affairs Ordinance (1945) 216; Fijian Development Fund Act 216; fishing 193; foreign ownership of land 18, 23, 184; GDP 225; human sacrifice 193; independence 224; Indo-Fijians 212, 214–15, 216, 226, 227, 230; *kerekere* 212; Lakeba 195; Land Claims Commission 199; land leasing 216, 226–7; land market 15–16, 224–8; land property rights 210–35; Lau islands 195; migrant labor 15, 183, 200, 210, 211, 212, 214; Ministry of Agriculture 227; Native Land Act 217; Native Land Trust Act 216; Native Land Trust Board 216, 227, 228; Native Lands Commission (1880) 199; Native Lands Ordinance (1880) 199; Native Policy 213; Native Regulations (1877) 199; Ovalu 195; poll taxes 197; population 193, 194, 195, 202, 203; Privy Council 197, 198; property rights 183–209, 212–17; Register of Native Lands 199; Rotuma Act 216; Rotuma Lands Act 216; Rotumans 215; sandalwood 194–5; sea cucumbers 195; sugar 183, 199, 200, 201, 210, 211, 226–7; Vanua Levu 193, 194, 195; Viti Levu 193, 195
Finland (Inari) 25, 358–87; cattle 369; circulatory system 363–4; co-operatives 358, 359, 367, 375, 383; corn 369; economic integration 369–73; ethno-nationalization 358–88; ethno-nationalization 358–88; fishing 361, 362, 364; Forest Government 358–9, 364, 365, 366, 367, 371, 372, 373, 374, 376, 377, 378, 380, 381, 382; Forest Law (1886) 366; forestry 369–73, 373–4, 375–6, 377, 379, 381; German occupation 365; 'Great Partition' 364, 365; land regimes 366–9, 377–81;

Lapp-marks 361, 363, 368, 373;
leaseholds 364; logging 362, 366;
Ministry of Agriculture and Forestry
378, 379; Ministry of the
Environment 378; Nikel 375;
Northern District for Wilderness
Management 380; *paliskunnat* 358;
paper mills 372; pasture fees 359;
Petsamo 362, 365, 369, 370;
population 362–3; property rights
363–6; Reindeer Herders' Association
358, 367; reindeer herding 358, 361,
363, 364, 366, 367, 369, 372, 374,
375, 379, 381, 382, 384; resource
management 358–88; resource
management 358–88; settlement
history 361–3; *siidas* 358, 361, 362,
363, 366, 367, 375, 379; Sodankylä
383; water power projects 362, 383;
World War II 365, 370; *see also* Sami
Fish river 298
Fison, Lorimer 199
Fitzroy Crossing 244, 254, 263
Fornander, Abraham: *Account of the
Polynesian Race* 187
Forsyth, John 34
Fort Beaufort 297, 299, 303, 306, 310
Fort Hare 304
Fort Jackson, Treaty of (1814) 46
France 161, 325, 326, 327, 343
France, P.: *Charter of the Land* 194, 199
Freeman, J. J.: *Tour in South Africa* 305
Frelinghuysen, Charles 34
Fullers Hoek 304
Furnivall, J. S.: *Netherlands India* 221–2

Gaelic Athletic Association 145
Gaelic League 145
Galloway, J. H.: *Sugar Cane Industry* 190
Gambia, River 277
Gemlik 166, 170
Generosity ethic, *see* Good Samaritan
ethic
George, Henry 93, 132
Germany, *see* Poland, Prussian
Ghana 277, 281–2; border 287;
ethnicity 285; expulsions 284; foreign
ownership of land 287
Gladstone, W. E. 133, 134

Glasgow Missionary Society 299
Glen Ern Station 243
globalization 224, 229
Goldsworthy, Mt 245–6
Gonzana river 303
Good Samaritan ethic 319, 320, 325,
327, 343
Gorbachev, Mikhail 113
Gordon, Sir Arthur 183, 198, 199, 213
Gounder, Rukmani 2, 16, 210–35;
"Equals in markets?" 16
Gove 263
Graham brothers 137
Grahamstown 298, 309
Grandy, C.: "Political Instability of
Reciprocal Trade" 201
Great Depression 240
Great Lakes 325, 326
Greeks, *see* Anatolia
Greimas, Algirdas Julius 114–15
Groepe, Christian 301, 308, 312
Guri, Yisrael 103

Halls Creek 250, 252, 254
Hancock, William Neilson: *Is There
Really a Want of Capital in Ireland?*
135, 136
*Handbook of Landownership in the German
Empire* 81
Hanly, Joseph 147
Hardin, R.: "Self-interest, group
identity" 284
Harris, R. C.: *Historical Atlas of Canada*
325
Harrison, William Henry 36
Hawai'i 183–209; agriculture 186;
Board of Commissioners 201; census
(1900) 187; chiefdoms 185–6, 193,
194; Christianity 183; constitution
197; Crown lands 200, 201; diseases
186–7; extended families 186; fiscal
crisis 188, 192; foreign ownership 18,
23, 184, 202; 'freehold property
forever' 187; government revenue
192; Great *Mahele* (1848) 183, 188,
191, 200, 202; Kaho'olawe 185;
Kaua'i 185; labor regulations 200;
Lana'i 185; land market 15, 190, 192;
Maui 185; Moloka'i 185; Ni'ihau

185; O'ahu 185, 186; population 184, 186, 187, 189, 192; Privy Council 187, 188; property rights 183–209; Report of the Minister of the Interior (1858) 191–2; royal patent grants (1881) 191–2; sandalwood 189; sugar 183, 190, 191, 200, 201, 202; US annexation 184; US trade reciprocity treaty 201

Hawtrey, Ralph George: *Economic Aspects of Sovereignty* 8

Healdtown 309

Heidenreich, C. E.: *Early Fur Trade* 326

Henry VIII 11

Herbst, J.: *States and Power in Africa* 283

Hertzog 299, 311

Hilo 188

Holt, Harold 255

Honolulu 188

Hopewell, Treaty of (1791) 42–3

Hopkins, A. G.: *Economic History of West Africa* 278

Howley, Very Rev. Canon 144

Hudson Bay 23, 320, 326, 332, 337, 339, 342, 343

Hudson's Bay Company 319–46; alcohol 327; Fort Albany 321–2, 327; Fort Churchill 321–2; Moose Factory 321; prices 322–3, 326, 327, 343; tobacco 327; York Factory 321–2, 327, 331

Hutu 286, 288

Iliffe, J.: *Africans* 277; *Modern History of Tanganyika* 285

India 283; Indian Indenture System 213, 214; migrant labor 15, 210, 211, 214; population 184, 213; Tamils 211

Indian Springs, Treaty of (1825) 37, 41

Indians, North American, *see* Native Americans

Ireland 24, 131–52; Agricultural Credit Company 137; Agricultural Credit Corporation 136; Banking Commission (1934–8) 136; boycotts 132; British market 135, 140, 145; CAP 135; Catholic/Protestant 133, 137, 143, 144, 147, 149; Central Statistics Office 135; co-operatives 137–45; creameries 137–45; dairying 137–45, 145–8; and Denmark 133, 135–6, 138, 142, 147, 149; Department of Agriculture 137 147; education 138; Great Famine 132, 135, 142; Incumbered Estates Court 135; Irish Free State 134, 135, 143, 145; land market 135–7; Land War 11–12, 131–52; milk supply 146, 148; Nationalists/Unionists 131, 133, 137, 143, 144, 149; and New Zealand 148; night raids 132; Orange Order 133; productivity 131–5; Ulster 133, 134, 145

Irish Agricultural Organization Society 138, 143, 147

Irish Homestead, The 138, 139

Islam: Anatolia 153, 160, 161, 162, 163, 164, 165, 166, 170, 171, 172, 173, 174, 175, 177; Sri Lanka 223

Israel 87–110; Absentees' Property Law (1950) 96; Association for Civil Rights in Israel 105; Basic Law: Israel Lands (1960) 98, 99, 100, 101, 104; citizenship and nationality 104; Communist Party 100; covenant with Jewish Agency (1979) 105; covenant with JNF (1961) 97, 98; Declaration of Independence 96, 101; Defense Service Law 105; Development Authority 96–7, 98, 100, 105; ethno-nationality 87–110; formative years (1948–61) 95–104; Galilee 99; Gaza strip 88; General Zionist Party 101–2; Golan heights 88; Herut Party 101; High Court of Justice 104, 106; holocaust 87; Israel Lands Administration 98, 99, 102, 103, 104, 105; Israel Lands Authority Law 98; Israel Lands Law 98, 103, 105; Jewish land prior to establishment 89–95; Jewish National Fund Law (1953) 97; Katzir Cooperative Society 105; Katzir ruling 104–6; *kibbutzim* 94, 103; Land Development Administration 99; land regime 10, 87–110; Lands of Israel Legislation (1960) 97; Mapai Party 99, 103; Mizrahi Democratic Rainbow 104;

moshavim 94, 103; Moshavot 102;
parliament (Knesset) 96, 97, 98,
99–100, 103; population 88; Sinai
peninsula 88; state created (1948) 95;
Supreme Court 104; tax-deductible
donations 97; Transfer of Property
Law (1949) 100; war (1948) 11, 88,
95, 102, (1967) 11, 88; West Bank
88; World Zionist Organization-
Jewish Agency Status Law (1952) 97,
99–100
Istanbul 153, 157, 161, 165, 169, 174,
176
Izmir 172, 173, 174

Jackson, Andrew 31–2, 34, 41, 46, 47,
50
Jacobs, Alfred and Richter, Hans:
Grosshandelspreise 65
Jaffna 220
James Bay 324, 332
Japan 21, 133
Jarasiunas, Egidijus 119
Jasukaityte, Vidmante: "Ar atversime
pilies vartus?" 118
Jefferson, Thomas 38
Jennings, Brian: *Kimberley Pastoral
Industry Inquiry* 248–9, 265
Jerusalem 100
Jewish Agency 95, 105, 106
Jewish National Fund 88, 89, 90, 91,
92, 93, 94, 95, 96, 97, 98, 100,
101, 103, 104, 105; Land
Department 102; Memorandum
and Articles of Association 99,
105
Jewish National Home 88, 90, 99
Jewish National Institutions 97, 99, 100,
104, 105
Jobst, Reverend 242
Johnson, Harry: "Theoretical Model of
Economic Nationalism" 22
Johnston, Joseph 136, 147
Joseph, Hendrik 297–8
Judd, Dr Gerrit 187

Ka'adan, Adel and Iman 105
Kaaguy Poty 347–57
Kaahumanu 187

Kame'eleihiwa, L.: *Native Land and
Foreign Desires* 200, 201
Kamehameha I 186, 187
Kamehameha II 187
Kamehameha III 187, 200
Kamehameha IV 200
Kanazawa, Mark T.: "Possession Is Nine
Points of the Law" 39–40
Karbauskis, Ramunsa 121
Karesi 154, 165, 175
Kastamonu 167
Kat River valley, *see* South Africa
Katanga (Shaba) 279
Katberg mountains 309
Keane, Sir John 137
Keawenui-a-Umi 187
Keiskamma river 298
Kekkonen, Urho 370–1
Kemijärvi 372
Kenya 281, 285; dairy farming 287;
Mau Mau 282; squatters 279
Kessi 374
Keynes, John Maynard 147, 240
Kikuyu 282, 285, 287
Kimberley, *see* Australia
King William's Town 309
King, Captain James 185
King, Carla: *Sir Horace Plunkett* 144
Knox, Henry 35–6, 42–3
Koonap valley 301
Krech, Shepard: *Ecological Indian* 320,
326, 335
Kretzmer, D.: *Legal Status of the Arabs in
Israel* 98, 100
Krobo 281
Kroome mountains 304
Kubilius, Andrius 119
Kununurra 248, 263
Kuykendall, R. S.: *Hawaiian Kingdom*
188

La Croix, S. J. 2, 15, 18, 23, 183–209;
"Explaining divergence in property
rights" 15–16, 18, 23; "Political
Instability of Reciprocal Trade" 201;
"Private Property in Nineteenth-
century Hawaii" 200
Ladd & Company 190
Lagos 281

Lahaina 188
Lake Gregory Station 265
Landsbergis, Vytautas 112, 113, 122
Lapp-marks, *see* Finland
Latvia 111, 117
Leacock 320
League of Nations 87, 90
Lee-Steere, E. H. 253–4
Leprecaun, The 138, 140
Lesotho 286–7, 300
Levmore, S.: "Two Stories" 202
Levuka 195, 196
Lewis, E. M. 243–4, 250, 252, 254
Lewis, F. D. 2, 23, 318–46; "Agricultural Property and the 1948 Palestinian Refugees" 95; "Indians, the Beaver, and the Bay" 319, 321, 322, 326, 342; "Property Rights" 322, 326, 343; "Survival through generosity" 23; "Trade, Consumption, and the Native Economy" 327
Liberia 287–8
Lithuania 16, 111–27; Academy of Sciences 112; agricultural land 120–2; Center Union 115; Chamber of Agriculture 120, 121; Communist Party 112, 113, 115; Congress of People's Deputies 114; constitution 10, 117, 118; Constitutional Act on Nonalignment (1992) 116; elections (1989) 114, (1990) 114, (1992) 114, (1993) 114; EMU 116, 117; EU 111, 114, 115, 116, 117, 118, 119, 121, 122; Europe Agreement (1996) 115; Europe and Eurasia 116–17, 122; foreign ownership of land 112, 118, 119; Free Market Institute 121; GDP 117; geography 111; land market 111–28; LDDP 114, 115; Lithuanian Christian Democrat Party 115; Lithuanian Movement for Restructuring 112; Lithuanian Social Democratic Party 115; National Land Service 120; nationalism 111–28; NATO 111, 114, 116, 120, 122; non-agricultural land 117–19; OECD 120, 122; parliament (Seimas) 116,
118, 120, 121; political economy 112–16; property ownership 111–28; and Russia 113, 114, 116, 119; 'safety catches' 121–2; Sajudis/Homeland Union 111, 113, 114, 115; Soviet Union 113; Supreme Council 113
Livne, Eliezer 99–100
London Missionary Society 195, 299, 302, 307
Lonsdale, J.: "States and social processes in Africa" 286
Lorraine 310
Lotka-Volterra relation 337
Lukashenko, Mr 122
Lumpkin, Wilson 32

Ma'afu 195–6
Maasai 280, 281, 285
Mabel Downs 259
McElligott, J. J. 136, 137
McEwen, Jack 250
McIntosh, Chief William 37, 41
McLeod, Don: *How the West Was Lost* 243, 244
McMahon, William 262, 263
McManus, John: "Economic Analysis of Indian Behavior" 325
Maghreb 12, 306
Mahe 305
Maksvytis, Kazys 120
Malaysia 213
Mali 304
Malthus, T. R. 287
Mancazana river 303, 310
Mandela, Nelson 309
Mandingos 277
Manogaran, C.: "Colonization as Politics" 221, 223
Manyas, Lake 165, 166, 168
Maqoma 298–300, 301, 302–3, 304, 309, 311
Maqoma, Lent 309
Marmara, Sea of 154, 164, 165, 166, 169, 170
Marquesas Islands 185
Marshall, Chief Justice 14, 46–8
Martínez, María Rosa 2, 23, 347–56; "Owners, intruders, and intermediaries" 23

Matroos, Hermanus 304, 305–6
Mauritius 213
Mbyá-Guaraní 23, 347–57; ethnography
    350–3; history 347–50; land claims
    347–57; oratory 351
Meadwell, H.: "Stateless Nations"
    230
Meentheena Station 243
Mehmed Ali Bey, Miralay 169
Melanesia 193, 196
Melbourne 197
Metzer, Jacob 1–3, 7–28, 87–110;
    "Jewish land - Israel lands" 10, 18,
    22, 23, 24
Mexico 334
Mfengu 303–4
Miquel 64
Mitchell, Ernie 245–6
Mitylene 154
Moldavia 161
Monteagle, Lord 144
Mooney, J. 335
Moore, Mick: *State and Peasant Politics
    in Sri Lanka* 223–4
Morantz, T.: "Historical Perspectives"
    320, 324
Moravian Brotherhood 302
Morea 161
Moshoeshoe 300
Mowanjum Mission 264–5
Msiri 279
Mugarinya Group Pty Ltd 265
Müller, F.: *Etnografía* 349
Muslims, *see* Islam
Muzaffer Pasa, Ferik 167

nationalism 10, 18–22, 25; Africa
    284–8; Ireland 131, 133, 137, 143,
    144, 149; Jewish 89; Lithuania
    111–28; Ottoman Turkey 153, 162,
    170, 177; Prussian Poland 58; Sri
    Lanka 230
Native Americans: Algonquins 325, 326;
    American Civil War 51; Canadian 13,
    319–46; Cherokee 31–55; Chickasaws
    34, 36, 46; Choctaws 34, 36, 46, 51,
    52; Creek 36, 37, 41, 46, 50; Dakotas
    326; diseases 335–6; emigration routes
    49; First Nations (Canada) 14; Five

Civilized Tribes 33, 36, 46, 52;
    hunting practices 23, 319–46; Huron
    326; Iroquois 325–6, 336; James Bay
    Cree 320; land cessions 45, 47, 48;
    Maine 324; Mohawk 52, 326;
    Mohicans 326; Montagnais 324;
    Neutrals 326; Nipissing 326; Ojibwa
    324; Petun 326; population 21,
    334–6, 336–41; Powhatan 13;
    predator-prey model 336–41;
    property rights 319–46; reservations
    51–2; Seminole 36, 46; Seneca 52;
    USA 13–15, 17, 21, 31–55; wealth
    share 21
Ndlambe 298
Necowotance 13
Neill, Rosemary: *White Out* 238, 260
Nellim 374
New Echota, Treaty of (1835) 31
New Zealand 147
Ngqika 298–9, 300, 304
Ngxukumeshe, *see* Matroos, Hermanus
Nicholson 259
Nickul, Karl 375
Niger, River 277
Nigeria 281; ethnicity 285; expulsions
    284; land tax 278; population pressure
    288
Nipperdey, Thomas: *Deutsche Geschichte*
    79
Nithiyanandam, V. Nithi 2, 16, 210–35;
    "Equals in markets?" 16
Noonkanbah Station 265
North Atlantic Treaty Organization
    111, 114, 116, 120, 122
Northern Rhodesia (Zambia) 279
Norway 229, 361, 363, 367, 371
Nothontho 303
Nouka (Noeka) family 303
Nozick, R.: *Examined Life* 19
Ntsikana 299, 311
Nugent, P.: *Smugglers* 287
Nukulau 197
Nyyssönen, Jukka 2, 23, 25, 358–87;
    "Establishing territorial sovereignty"
    23, 25

O'Brien, Edward W. 144
O'Brien, J. M. 247

Ó Gráda, Cormac 2, 11, 18, 24, 131–52; "Beginnings of the Irish Creamery System" 140; "Irish agriculture" 11–12, 18, 24
Ohcejohka 376
Old Forrest River Mission 259
Oondaguri 259
open access resources, *see res nullius*
oral history 351
Organization for Economic Co-operation and Development 120, 122
Organization of African Unity 283
O'Rourke, Kevin: "Culture, Politics, and Innovation" 141, 142, 143
Ottoman Empire: Council of Ministers 168; Council of State 169, 171; Finance Ministry 169; Foreign Ministry 173; Interior Ministry 168, 169, 170, 171, 174, 175; Land Code (1858) 157, 158, 159, 168; land policies 162; Land Registration Ministry 168; migration agreement 160, 161; parliament 175; refugees 159, 163; Russian conflict 16, 153–4, 159, 160, 162,l 168; Seyhülislam 174, 176; Treasury 169; Turkish nationalism 162; Turkish War of Independence (1919–23) 177; *see also* Anatolia

Pagano, Ugo: "Can Economists Explain Nationalism?" 19–20, 22
Palestine 10–11; Arab refugees 95, 96, 97, 102; Arab revolt (1936) 87; Jewish immigration (1949–52) 95; land market 24; Mandate 11, 23, 24, 87, 88, 90, 94, 95, 96, 100; partition 87, 102; *see also* Israel *and* Zionism
Palestine Land Development Company 89, 90
Palmer, Ian: *Buying Back the Land* 243, 264
Pantijan Station 264–5
Papua New Guinea 238, 246
Paraguay 347, 349, 350
Paranaense forest 347, 350
Pareto optimality 202
Paris, Treaty of (1763) 326
Park, Mungo 277

Parker, G. R.: *Biology of the Kaminuriak* 339, 340
Parker, William: "Northern Agriculture and the Westward Movement" 38
Paulauskas, Arturas 120, 121
Pearl Harbor 201
Pearson, Noel: *Our Right* 240
Peires, J. B.: "Piet Draghoender's Lament" 309
Perdue, Theda and Green, Michael D.: *Cherokee Removal* 35–6, 42–3
Perera, Janaka 223
perestroika 112, 113
Perkins, Charles: "Australian Aborigines" 257, 261
Peterson, Nicholas: "Capitalism, culture and land rights" 236, 238, 260
Philippines 184
Philipton 305, 311
Platteau, J.-P.: "Land relations under unbearable stress" 281, 288
Pleckaitis, Vytautas 119
Plunkett, Sir Horace: *Ireland in the New Century* 137–8, 143, 144, 149
Pokka, Hannele 380
Poland, Prussian 10–11, 23, 24, 56–86; anti-Polish measures 76; *Befestigung* (consolidation) 74–6; ethno-nationality 56–86; First World War 76–80World War, First 76–80; land prices 62–70, 73, 81; peasant properties 71–4; property rights in land 56–86; *Regierungsbezirk* 62; *Rentengut* 57, 74; Royal Prussian Settlement Commission 10–11, 56, 58, 59, 60, 61, 62–70, 71–4, 74–6
Polynesia 183, 185, 193
Polynesian Company 197
Polynesian, The 188
Porte, the 165, 166
Portugal 278
Posen 59, 62, 64, 89
positivists 239
Poznan, *see* Posen
Poznania 59, 74
Prasad 225
predator-prey model 320, 336–41

Pringle, Thomas 301
progress 239
Prucha, Francis P. 50–3; "Andrew
    Jackson's Indian Policy" 31–2, 34, 41,
    52; *Great Father* 37
Prussia, *see* Poland, Prussian
Putnamites 144

Ramenofsky, A. F.: *Vectors of Death*
    336
Ransom, Roger: "Economics of the
    Civil War" 41–2
Rattray, R. S.: *Ashanti Law and
    Constitution* 277
Rawls, J.: *Theory of Justice* 225
Ray, A. J.: *Early Fur Trade* 326
Reads, the 305
Remini, Robert 50, 52–3; *Andrew
    Jackson* 32, 34; *Andrew Jackson and His
    Indian Wars* 32; "Jackson versus the
    Cherokee Nation" 32, 47–8
res nullius 361, 364, 366
Rhodesia 221
Ridge, John 50
Ridge, Major 50
Rift Valley 280, 281, 285
Riverdale Station 243
Robbins, Roy M.: *Our Landed Heritage*
    37, 39, 40
Roberts, Mark: "Squatterism" 35, 41,
    42
Roebourne 263
Romanidhis 164
Ross, John 50
Ross, Robert 2, 16, 25, 265, 294–316;
    "Ethnic competition" 16, 25
Roumasset, J.: "Private Property in
    Nineteenth-century Hawaii" 200
Rumeli 168, 171
Russia 111; CIS 111, 114, 116, 117,
    119; Europe 122; Greece and 161;
    land policies 162; migration
    agreement 160, 161; Ottoman
    conflict 16, 153–4, 159, 160, 162,
    168; Poland 56; "Protector of the
    Orthodox" 162; *see also* Soviet Union
Rwanda 281, 285, 286; ethnicity 287–8;
    genocide 286, 288
Ryan, James 136

St Lawrence basin 325
Samanli 166
Sami: Aanaar 361, 362, 364; activism
    373–4; ethnic consciousness 368,
    373–4; first congress (1953) 373; Inari
    358–84; Nordic Sami Council 373;
    Skolt 361–2, 365, 374, 375, 380
Samoa 193
Santa María 349
Schapira, Herman 89, 92
Scott, General 50
Sebe, Lennox 310
Semenoja, Marja Sinikka:
    "Emsimmäinen kirje" 375, 376
Senanayake, Don Stephen 219–20
Sequoyah 43
Serbia 161, 172, 177
Sering, Max 78
Seymour 299, 307, 308, 309
Shaka 283
Shenton, Robert: *Doctrines of
    Development* 239–40
Sierra Leone 287–8
slavery: Africa 276, 278, 280, 283; USA
    38, 40–2, 43, 50–1, 149
Smith, Adam 225
Smith, Tony 2, 9, 12, 25, 236–75
Smith, Anthony: "Indigenous
    accumulation" 12–13, 25; "National
    Construction of Social Space" 111
Smythe, Consul 196
Sneh, Moshe 100–1
Social Darwinism 365, 366
Sokoto Caliphate 278, 283
Solar, P. M.: "Pitfalls of estimating Irish
    agricultural output" 132
Solomon Islands 213
Solow, Barbara L.: *Land Question and the
    Irish Economy* 132, 137, 142, 145
Somalia 286–7
South Africa (Kat River) 16, 25, 221,
    294–316; Afrikaners 308; apartheid
    16, 294, 306; Bantustan land rights
    309; Bastards 301–2; *Blut* and *Boden*
    296; Boedel Erven Act (1905) 307–8;
    Boer War (1899–1902) 306; British
    conflict with Xhosa (1812) 298,
    (1819–20, Nxele's war) 298; Cape
    Colony 296, 297, 298, 301, 306;

Cape Mounted Rifles 300, 302; Christianity 299; Ciskei 309–11; concentration camps 302; Eastern Cape 297, 298, 299, 302; ethnic competition 294–316; First British Occupation (1795–1803) 298; geography 297; Gona (Gonaqua) Khoi 297, 299, 302, 303, 304, 305; Graaf-Reinet 300; Heintemas 297; Hintza's War (1834–6) 302, 304, 305; history 297–8; 'Hottentots' and 'Kaffirs' 303, 306; isiXhosa 305; Jingqi 309; Khoi 296, 299, 300, 302, 304, 306, 308, 310, 311; Khoikoi 297, 298, 299, 301, 302, 306; Khoisan 297, 298, 301; Land Act (1913) 294; land claims 294–316; Land Claims Commission 294, 311; land confiscation 294; Mfengu 304, 305, 309; Mpofu 309, 310, 311; Natives Land Act (1913) 279; Neutral (Ceded) Territory 298, 299, 301; 'New' 16, 309–11; Ordinance 50 (1828) 301; reconstruction 306–9; Restitution of Land Rights Act (1994) 294; Rharhabe Xhosa 298, 309; Servants' Revolt (1799–1803) 298; *snywet* 308; Thembu 300, 301, 304; Transkei 306; War of the Axe (1846–7) 302, 304, 305; World War II 309; Xhosa 296, 297, 299, 300, 301, 302, 303, 304, 305, 308, 309, 310, 311

Soviet Union: collapse of (1991) 16, 111, 114, 117; Communist Party 112, 113, 114; Kola Peninsula 362; Nikel 375; Petsamo 362, 365, 369, 370; *see also* Russia

Spain 37, 349

Speck, Frank 324, 343

Sri Lanka 16, 210–35; Batticaloa district 223; 'break-up' 228–30; coffee 210, 211; colonial experience 210–11, 217–24; constitution 219, 224; Dry Zone 219–24, 231; ethnicity 210–35; Gal Oya Scheme 222; independence (1948) 218, 224; Janakapura settlement 223; land property rights 210–35; LTTE 229; Mahaweli Programme 223; Manal Aru (Weli-Oya) Project 223; Memorandum of Understanding 229; migrant labor 210, 211, 212, 213, 214; Mullaitivu district 223; Muslims 223; name change (1972) 217; "New Policy" 219; parliament 218; rubber 210; Sinhalese-Tamil conflict 211, 212, 213, 214, 217–24, 228–30, 231; tea 210, 211; Wet Zone 221

Stanner, W. E. H. 255

Stockenstroem, Andries 300, 301

Stoffels, Andries 303

Sudan 280

Suleyman Pasa 166

Sumbwa-Nyamwezi 279

Swaziland 286–7

Sweden 361, 363, 367

Switzerland 9

Syria 155

Tamboekies Vlei 301, 308, 312

Tanami Desert 264

Tanganyika 285

Tanner, Adrian: *Bringing Animals Home* 332

Tanzania 279, 285

Tasman, Abel 194

Tatars 159, 160–1, 166

Tauras, A. P. 118–19

Tecumseh 36

Terrill, Thomas: *American South* 41

Terzibaşoğlu, Yücel 2, 18, 153–80; "Land disputes and ethno-politics" 16

Teves, Laura 2, 23, 347–56; "Owners, intruders, and intermediaries" 23

Texas Downs 259

Thailand 184

Theal, G. McC. 303

Tippecanoe, battle of (1811) 36

Togo 287

Tonga 193, 195, 196

Trikopis 173–4

Trinidad 213

Troup, George Michael 41

Tui Cakau 195–6

Turcoman tribes 155

Turkey Creek 252, 259

Turkey, *see* Anatolia *and* Ottoman
Empire
Turner, Michael 39; "Agricultural
output" 132–3
Turrill, Joel: "Turrill Collection" 190
Tutsi 285, 286, 288
Two-agent model 320
Tyali 299
Tyume valley 297, 299, 300, 309

Ubelaker, D. H.: "North American
Indian Population Size" 319, 334,
335
Uganda 286
Umfreville, Edward: *Present State of
Hudson Bay* 325
Union of Soviet Socialist Republics, *see*
Soviet Union
United Nations 246; Lithuania 118;
Palestine 87–8, 102
United States of America: allotments 51;
Census (1835) 44; Civil War 40, 51,
183, 196; cotton plantations 43;
Democrats 38; federal Indian policy
35–40; federal tariff (1828) 41;
federalism 38, 40–2; General
Preemption Law (1840) 39–40, 41;
Georgia and the Cherokee 42–6; gold
rush (1849–51) 190; Homestead Act
(1862) 39–40, 42; House of
Representatives 32–5; Indian
Removal Act (1830) 32–5, 46–53;
Japanese ownership in 21; Land Law
(1785) 37–8; land lottery 44–5, 46,
(Georgia, 1832) 50; Mississippi Valley
336; marrying to acquire land 51;
Mexico and 38; Missouri 336; New
York State 336; Northwest
Ordinance (1787) 37–8; population
190; Preemption Act (1830) 42;
productivity 133; property rights
restrictions 9; removal of Indians
from south-east 31–55; slavery 38,
40–2, 43, 50–1, 149; South Carolina
nullification ordinance 41, 48; Spain
and 37; squatters 38–9, 40, 50; states'
rights 40–2; Supreme Court 14–15,
41, 44, 48; third Anglo-Indian War
13; Trade and Intercourse Act (1790)
36; Treaty Party 50; unemployment
238; Virginia 13–15; War of 1812 37,
46; War of Independence 37, 43, 44;
Yazoo Land case 44
Uruguay 350

Vanuatu 213
Veselka, Julius 121
Vienna, Congress of (1815) 56
Violet Valley 259

Walachia 161
Walker, P. 244
Wallace, Anthony: *Long Bitter Trail* 33,
43, 52
Washington, George 42–3
Wayne, General 'Mad Anthony' 36
Weitz, Yoseph 102
Wentworth, W. C. 252, 255
West Australian, The 243, 253–4
White, Richard: *Middle Ground* 325,
326
Whitlam, Gough 238, 240, 257, 263
Wijemanne, Adrian 228–9
Wijetunga, W. M. K.: *Sri Lanka in
Transition* 222
Wilberforce 305
Wilkinson, Charles 174
Willesee, W. F. 257
William III 131
Williams, Colin: "National
Construction of Social Space" 111
Williams, John 197
Willowra 264
Wilson, Jeyaratnam: *Break-up of Sri
Lanka* 228, 229
Wilson, Woodrow 16
Wirsitz 64, 69, 70
Wishart, David M.: "Evidence of
Surplus Production" 44
Woodward, Mr Justice A. E. 263
Worceser v. Georgia (1832) 14, 46–8, 50
World War: First 16, 61, 74, 76, 80, 87,
89, 90, 132, 133, 134, 141, 160, 177;
Second 16, 240, 284
World Zionist Organization 87, 90, 95,
99, 100, 101; London Conference
(1920) 90–3; Palestine Bureau 89;
Status Law (1952) 97

Wyllie, R. C.: *Answers to Questions Proposed* 189
Wyndham 249, 252, 259
Wyrzysk, *see* Wirsitz
Wyzan, Michael: "Economies Show Solid Performance" 115–16

xenophobia 21; *see also* nationalism

Yalgoo 243
Yandeyarra Station 243
Yirrkala 263

Yoruba, 285
Yvy Mbyte 349
Yvy Pyta 347–57

Zionism 87–110; Fifth Congress (1901) 89; First Congress (1897) 89; Jewish land prior to Jewish State 89–95; 'Jewish people' defined 92; Sixth Congress (1903) 89; *see also* Israel; Palestine; World Zionist Organization
Zulus 280, 283, 285

Printed in the United States
by Baker & Taylor Publisher Services